Justice, Conflict and Wellbeing

Brian H. Bornstein • Richard L. Wiener
Editors

# Justice, Conflict and Wellbeing

## Multidisciplinary Perspectives

Springer

*Editors*
Brian H. Bornstein
Department of Psychology
University of Nebraska-Lincoln
Lincoln
Nebraska
USA

Richard L. Wiener
Department of Psychology
University of Nebraska-Lincoln
Lincoln
Nebraska
USA

ISBN 978-1-4939-0622-2 ISBN 978-1-4939-0623-9 (eBook)
DOI 10.1007/978-1-4939-0623-9
Springer Heidelberg New York Dordrecht London

Library of Congress Control Number: 2014943418



Printed on acid-free paper

Springer is part of Springer Science+Business Media (www.springer.com)

# Preface: Justice, Conflict and Wellbeing: An Introduction

The present book includes not one, or even two, but three enormous topics, each of which is broad and deep enough in its own right that it would be impossible to cover adequately in a single volume. Justice. Conflict. Wellbeing. What do these words mean, where do they intersect, and how do social science researchers investigate them? To borrow a phrase from Raymond Carver (1981), what do we talk about when we talk about justice, conflict and wellbeing? *Webster's College Dictionary* defines them (in part) as follows:

- Justice (n.): The quality of being just; righteousness, equitableness, or moral rightness.
- Conflict (n., though also v.): A fight, battle, or struggle, esp. a prolonged one; strife.
- Wellbeing (n., also well-being): A good or satisfactory condition of existence; a state characterized by health, happiness, and prosperity; welfare.

A Google search for "justice and conflict" yielded approximately 167,000,000 results, with entries covering blogs, books (e.g., Hampshire 2001; Kals and Maes 2012), research centers, policy statements, and so on. Searches combining the other terms are comparably large and diverse. It therefore seems obvious that when we talk about justice, conflict, and wellbeing, we're talking about a large amount of work that cuts across several social science disciplines.

These definitions make it clear that the three concepts are closely connected: Conflict often (but not always) impairs wellbeing, whereas justice often (but not always) enhances it; perceived injustice is a common source of conflict, at multiple levels; and calls for justice are a common response to conflict. Thus, the valence and causal connections among the concepts are complex. In addition, each construct has subtypes, such as distributive and procedural justice, individual and group conflict, and physical and psychological wellbeing. Moreover, each construct operates at multiple levels, ranging from individuals, through groups of varying size, to societies and nations. Consider conflict, for example. Two kids can get in a fight on the school playground (see Part VI); two neighborhood organizations might go to an arbitrator to settle a dispute over who has rights to a certain piece of property (see Part V); or nations go to war over disagreements about sovereignty and territory (see Part IV). For these same instances, we could ask whether the conflict itself is just, how to resolve it fairly, and in what ways, positively or negatively, the experience of conflict or its resolution affects the parties' wellbeing.

Justice, conflict, and wellbeing are large topics that occupy researchers from a variety of disciplines, as well as laypeople and policy makers. For example, the law seeks to further justice, establishes mechanisms to resolve conflict, and has the capacity both to enhance and to diminish the wellbeing of those who use the legal system. Psychology, in its various subdisciplines (e.g., social, clinical, cognitive, educational, developmental), seeks to understand the affective, behavioral, and cognitive underpinnings of justice, conflict, and wellbeing. Other disciplines, such as philosophy, political science, and sociology have long histories of studying these topics as well. Although there are established traditions of research on the topics in multiple disciplines, there is little cross-fertilization across disciplines. This situation is not particularly surprising, as the social sciences have been relatively slow to adopt interdisciplinarity (Christakis 2013). Though not surprising, it is unfortunate: Interdisciplinary scholarship yields better science, in terms of having a higher impact and being more innovative (American Academy of Arts and Sciences 2013; Wuchty, Jones, and Uzzi 2007; Yamamoto 2013). *Interdisciplinary research*, which "integrates information, data, techniques, tools, perspectives, concepts, and/or theories from two or more disciplines or bodies of specialized knowledge to advance fundamental understanding or to solve problems whose solutions are beyond the scope of a single discipline or area of research practice" (Committee on Facilitating Interdisciplinary Research 2004, p. 2), is harder to perform than *multidisciplinary research*, which simply involves multiple disciplines in juxtaposition. Nonetheless, the latter is often a precursor to the former (Atkinson and Crowe 2006; Chandramohan and Fallows 2009; Committee on Facilitating Interdisciplinary Research 2004). A major goal of the present volume is to establish a multidisciplinary social scientific foundation for the study of justice, conflict, and wellbeing, from which future interdisciplinary work can proceed.

To that end, the present volume brings together researchers from social, clinical, and educational psychology; law; and political science. The unifying theme is how injustice and conflict pose threats to wellbeing, at the micro (individual) and macro (groups and societies) levels. Multi- and interdisciplinary research are at the vanguard of science in the twenty-first century, and the present work applies multi- and interdisciplinary perspectives to the important real-world topics of justice, conflict, and wellbeing.

The remainder of this volume consists of six parts that sample from the numerous ways that justice, conflict, and wellbeing intersect. Part I contains two chapters on the theme of distributive justice, which deals with the fairness of outcomes, especially with respect to the distribution of resources. It is often contrasted with procedural justice, which focuses on the fairness of the processes used to determine those outcomes (Lind and Tyler 1988; Tyler 2005). Questions of distributive justice play a role in a wide swath of human endeavors, ranging from interpersonal interactions (e.g., how to apportion responsibilities and benefits for everyday tasks) to governmental policies (e.g., allocating foreign aid, welfare benefits, tax burdens, etc.; see, generally, Brams and Taylor 1996). Perceived injustice in "who gets what" is a common source of conflict, whether the conflict takes the form of a heated argument or a war; whereas a just distribution contributes to the recipient's sense of wellbeing. Chap. 1, by Brian Bornstein, Sarah Gervais, Hannah Dietrich, and Justin Escamilla, introduces different principles of distributive justice (e.g., proportionality, equality, need) and describes original research examining the effect of those principles, as well as interpersonal power, on resource allocation in experimental tasks. Their results indicate a strong norm toward egalitarianism. While not disputing the importance of equality in resource allocation, John Scott shows, in Chap. 2, that equality has a rich history–dating back at least to Aristotle–and has been interpreted differently by various thinkers over the years.

Just as an unjust allocation of some commodity can be a source of conflict, so too can treating people *like* a commodity—that is, treating them as objects, without human qualities. This occurs in many situations, as when we treat members of disadvantaged groups (e.g., racial or ethnic minorities) as less than human, or when individuals' sexualized body parts overshadow their individual identities. The two chapters in Part II address the topic of objectification, focusing especially on its negative consequences for objectified persons' wellbeing. Chap. 3, by Richard Wiener, Sarah Gervais, Ena Brnjic, and Gwenith Nuss uses objectification as a framework for understanding the causes and consequences of hostile environments, sometimes prohibited in law but sometimes simply in violation of public norms. The following chapter, by Lee Budesheim, takes a somewhat contrary approach, asking whether objectification is necessarily harmful, and whether it is avoidable. It also offers a critique of recent social psychological research on objectification.

According to the definition with which we began this chapter, wellbeing is "a state characterized by health, happiness, and prosperity." By definition, then, those who are ill—whether they suffer from a physical or mental illness—are lacking in wellbeing. Moreover, their illness can bring them into conflict with others, both other individuals and social institutions. Conversely, those same institutions, especially the legal system, have the power to implement and enforce procedures that can improve the wellbeing of those who need it most, an approach to law and policy known as *therapeutic jurisprudence* (TJ; Wexler and Winick 1991, 1996). Part III explores this issue by focusing on people with mental illness. Chaps. 5 (by William Spaulding, Elizabeth Cook, and Andrea Avila) and 6 (by Robert Schopp) apply therapeutic jurisprudence to persons with severe mental illness. Spaulding and colleagues show how TJ can contribute to the treatment and rehabilitation of persons with severe and disabling mental illness. The chapter by Schopp discusses how mental health courts and civil commitment can both enhance mentally ill persons' wellbeing and protect the public by reducing the risk that they will commit further crimes. Schopp's chapter also addresses the role of psychological experts in predicting whether individuals with mental illness are dangerous. In Chap. 7, David Wexler—one of the originators of the TJ movement—takes a slightly different tack, applying its principles to attorneys themselves, who may be in need of intervention to improve their own wellbeing because of the daily stress that characterizes their work lives. Wexler shows how work with individuals with psychosocial problems can be challenging, thereby threatening the wellbeing of professionals who work with mentally ill clients, in much the same way (though at a lower level) that living with and caring for mentally ill family members can have adverse health consequences (e.g., Baronet 1999).

The biggest scale on which conflict occurs, of course, is war. Even in a "just" war—laying aside the debate over whether such a thing genuinely exists—war undeniably exerts an enormous, and mostly negative, impact on the wellbeing of both soldiers and ordinary citizens. The two chapters in Part IV address this aspect of war by using the example of the International Criminal Tribunal for the Former Yugoslavia (ICTY). Chap. 8, by Patrice McMahon and Jennifer Miller, explores how the ICTY has affected the lives of individuals of various ethnicities and nationalities in the region affected by the Tribunal. Jelena Subotić, in Chap. 9, focuses on the ICTY itself, and asks whether it is feasible and just to hold a small number of individuals accountable for large-scale, political conflict.

Although the major institutional venue for resolving conflicts and obtaining justice is the legal system, many conflicts are resolved outside the courts, either because the courts are not the optimal mechanism for some types of dispute resolution, or because the dispute does not rise to the level of a legal infraction. The book's final two parts explore these situations of "private justice." Part V contains two chapters on alternative dispute resolution (ADR). Although ADR mechanisms are efficient in many respects, they raise some unique justice-related concerns of their own. For example, as Kristen Blankley describes in Chap. 10, the ethical rules (or lack thereof) imposed on arbitrators can both enhance and impede conflict resolution efforts. Moreover, by drawing judges away from traditional careers on the bench, ADR raises concerns about the quality of justice administered by public courts. Chap. 11, by Maureen Weston, examines this issue and some of the other costs associated with ADR.

The book ends with an examination of what many recall as their first experience with conflict, namely, childhood conflict with peers. Other than in the home, with siblings, where do such conflicts take place? In schools, on playgrounds (which can be part of schools or public), on sports fields, and anywhere else children might congregate. Part VI contains two chapters on childhood conflict. Chap. 12, by Catherine Bohn-Gettler and Anthony Pellegrini, raises the important premise that not all conflict is necessarily bad, as we all need to learn effective strategies for dealing with conflict, and schools can help accomplish this goal, especially by allowing time for recess and providing the structure needed for children to learn to negotiate conflicts with other children. Their chapter summarizes a wealth of research on the benefits of school recess and the implications for educational policy. Chap. 13, by Beth Doll and Susan Sarver, extends this argument by looking at the valuable social skills that children can acquire through experiencing and successfully resolving conflict with peers on the playground. Their chapter also examines the ways in which the features of recess and the playground environment can influence children's interactions with peers.

The impetus for this edited volume came from a conference on the same themes that were held at the University of Nebraska-Lincoln in November 2011. Many people's efforts are necessary to produce a successful conference (and book). We are especially grateful to the speakers/chapter authors for their active participation and thoughtful contributions; to the University of Nebraska-Lincoln for its financial and administrative support; to Allison Skinner for her assistance in organizing the conference; and to Sharon Panulla and Sylvana Ruggirello at Springer Publishing for their support in turning a successful conference into what we hope will be a successful book that will contribute to future research on justice, conflict, and wellbeing.

Brian H. Bornstein
Richard L. Wiener

## References

American Academy of Arts and Sciences. (2013). *ARISE II: Unleashing America's research and innovation enterprise*. Cambridge: American Academy of Arts and Sciences. http://www.amacad.org/arise2/.

Atkinson, J., & Crowe, M. (2006). *Interdisciplinary research: Diverse approaches in science, technology, health and society*. Chichester: Wiley.

Baronet, A. M. (1999). Factors associated with caregiver burden in mental illness: A critical review of the research literature. *Clinical Psychology Review, 19,* 819–841.

Brams, S. J., & Taylor, A. D. (1996). *Fair division: From cake-cutting to dispute resolution*. Cambridge: Cambridge University Press.

Carver, R. (1981). *What we talk about when we talk about love*. New York: Knopf.

Chandramohan, B., & Fallows, S. (2009). *Interdisciplinary learning and teaching in higher education: Theory and practice*. New York: Routledge.

Christakis, N. A. (2013, July 19). Let's shake up the social sciences. *New York Times*. http://www.nytimes.com/2013/07/21/opinion/sunday/lets-shake-up-the-social-sciences.html?emc=eta1&_r=1&.

Committee on Facilitating Interdisciplinary Research, National Academy of Sciences, National Academy of Engineering, Institute of Medicine. (2004). *Facilitating interdisciplinary research*. Washington, DC: National Academies Press. http://www.nap.edu/catalog.php?record_id=11153.

Hampshire, S. (2001). *Justice is conflict*. Princeton: Princeton University Press.

Kals, E., & Maes, J. (2012). *Justice and conflicts: Theoretical and empirical contributions*. New York: Springer.

Lind, E. A., & Tyler, T. R. (1988). *The social psychology of procedural justice*. New York: Springer.

Tyler, T. R. (2005). *Procedural justice* (Vol. 1–2). Burlington: Ashgate.

Wexler, D. B., & Winick, B. J. (1991). Therapeutic jurisprudence as a new approach to mental health law policy analysis and research. *University of Miami Law Review, 45,* 979–1004.

Wexler, D. B., & Winick, B. J. (1996). *Law in a therapeutic key: Developments in therapeutic jurisprudence*. Durham: Carolina Academic Press.

Wuchty, S., Jones, B. F., & Uzzi, B. (2007). The increasing dominance of teams in production of knowledge. *Science, 316,* 1036–1039.

Yamamoto, K. R. (2013). Time to play ball. *Science, 340,* 1375.

# Contents

# Contributors

**Andrea Avila** Department of Psychology, University of Nebraska-Lincoln, Lincoln, NE, USA

**Kristen M. Blankley** College of Law, University of Nebraska-Lincoln, Lincoln, NE, USA

**Catherine M. Bohn-Gettler** Education Department, College of Saint Benedict - Saint John's University, St. Joseph, MN, USA

**Brian H. Bornstein** Department of Psychology, University of Nebraska-Lincoln, Lincoln, NE, USA

**Ena Brnjic** Department of Psychology, University of Nebraska-Lincoln, Lincoln, NE, USA

**Thomas Lee Budesheim** Department of Psychology, Creighton University, Omaha, NE, USA

**Elizabeth Cook** Department of Psychology, University of Nebraska-Lincoln, Lincoln, NE, USA

**Hannah L. Dietrich** Center on Children, Families, and the Law, University of Nebraska-Lincoln, Lincoln, NE, USA

**Beth Doll** Department of Educational Psychology, University of Nebraska-Lincoln, Lincoln, NE, USA

**Justin Escamilla** Center for Research in Law and Justice, University of Illinois-Chicago, Chicago, IL, USA

**Sarah J. Gervais** Department of Psychology, University of Nebraska-Lincoln, Lincoln, NE, USA

**Patrice C. McMahon** Department of Political Science, University of Nebraska-Lincoln, Lincoln, NE, USA

**Jennifer L. Miller** School of Government and Public Policy, University of Arizona, Tucson, AZ, USA

**Gwenith Nuss** Department of Psychology, University of Nebraska-Lincoln, Lincoln, NE, USA

**Anthony D. Pellegrini** Department of Educational Psychology, University of Minnesota, Minneapolis, MN, USA

**Susan C. Sarver** Deptartment of Child, Youth and Family Studies, University of Nebraska-Lincoln, Lincoln, NE, USA

**Robert F. Schopp** College of Law, University of Nebraska-Lincoln, Lincoln, NE, USA

**John T. Scott** Department of Political Science, University of California-Davis, Davis, CA, USA

**William D. Spaulding** Department of Psychology, University of Nebraska-Lincoln, Lincoln, NE, USA

**Jelena Subotić** Department of Political Science, Georgia State University, Atlanta, USA

**Maureen A. Weston** School of Law, Pepperdine University, Malibu, CA, USA

**David B. Wexler** School of Law, University of Puerto Rico, San Juan, PR, USA and University of Arizona, Tucson, USA

**Richard L. Wiener** Department of Psychology, University of Nebraska-Lincoln, Lincoln, NE, USA

# Part I
# Distributive Justice

# Chapter 1
# All Else Being Equal: Overcoming the Egalitarian Norm

**Brian H. Bornstein, Sarah J. Gervais, Hannah L. Dietrich and Justin Escamilla**

"Is it fair?" has been a central question in philosophy and social science for hundreds, if not thousands, of years. A basic problem of all societies regards the allocation of goods to its members, and understanding distributive justice norms has normative, empirical, and prescriptive implications. Yet despite the long-standing interest in questions of distributive justice, empirical research on the topic is of relatively recent vintage (for review, see Deutsch 1985; Elster 1995, 2004; Frohlich and Oppenheimer 1992; Lerner and Lerner 1981; Skitka 2009; Skitka and Crosby 2003; Tyler et al. 1997).

Research on distributive justice suggests that individuals' behavior reflects reliance on a number of norms (e.g., equity, equality, need), pervasive social and contextual influences (e.g., preference for in-group over out-group members (Tajfel and Turner 1979); different "spheres of justice" (Walzer 1983)), and individual differences, such as attitudes and demographic characteristics. For example, men tend to be more concerned with abstract principles of justice, such as equity (i.e., outcomes proportional to inputs), whereas women are more oriented toward process than outcome (Gaeddert 2004; Sweeney and McFarlin 1997).

The allocation of resources to different individuals and groups has a tremendous impact on many aspects of social life, ranging from personal relations to public policy-making. For example, individuals allocate both tangible (e.g., money, various goods) and intangible (e.g., love, attention) resources to family members and others in their social circle (Foa and Foa 1974; Marshall et al. 2001; Montada 2003).

B. H. Bornstein (✉) · S. J. Gervais
Department of Psychology, University of Nebraska-Lincoln, Lincoln, NE 68588-0308, USA
Phone: +1402-472-3743
e-mail: bbornstein2@unl.edu

H. L. Dietrich
Center on Children, Families, and the Law, University of Nebraska-Lincoln,
206 S. 13th St., Suite 1000, Lincoln, NE 68588-0227, USA

J. Escamilla
Center for Research in Law and Justice, University of Illinois-Chicago,
921 W. van Buren St., Suite 230, Chicago, IL 60607, USA

B. H. Bornstein, R. L. Wiener (eds.), *Justice, Conflict and Wellbeing*,
DOI 10.1007/978-1-4939-0623-9_1, 

In work settings, employers distribute jobs (in hiring, promotions), wages, and so forth (Greenberg and Colquitt 2005). And within the public arena, notions of fairness inform governmental allocations of health care (e.g., Koch 2001); educational (e.g., Sabbagh et al. 2006) and environmental resources (e.g., Macias 2008); emergency relief (e.g., Scott and Bornstein 2009); tax burdens (Kinsey et al. 1991; Paul et al. 2006); foreign aid (Roper and Barria 2007); welfare benefits (Marmor et al. 1990); and other government policies and services (see generally Elster 1993; Kluegel et al. 1995; Tyler et al. 1997).

Thus, distributive justice research has significant implications for policy-makers who need to set and evaluate allocation policies. Lessons learned from the studies are applicable to other distributive schemes, in both the public and private sectors. Justice judgments have important consequences for people's thoughts, feelings, and behaviors, whether they are on the allocating or the receiving end (Fischer and Skitka 2006; Lerner and Lerner 1981; Lind and Tyler 1988; Skitka and Crosby 2003; Tyler 2006). The research is particularly timely in light of the heightened public discourse about resource allocation in both sectors in early twenty-first century America and elsewhere, such as debates over limited environmental resources, term limits for government officials, emergency relief, health-care reform, appropriate compensation for top business executives, government bailouts, and corporate downsizing.

In many, if not most instances of resource allocation, a power differential exists: parents divvy resources (ranging from dessert to their estate) to children, bosses allocate various goods (e.g., raises, workloads) to employees, and governments distribute resources (e.g., health care, tax burdens) to citizens. Being in a position to allocate resources confers power, and conversely, powerful people have more resources at their disposal than powerless people. Across essentially all distributive contexts, then, resource allocation is inextricably bound with questions of power—both the power afforded by the role of allocator or recipient and subjective feelings of power.

The chapter organization is as follows: First, we present a brief overview of distributive justice theory, followed by a review of relevant research on power. We then present two experiments that examine the effect of power and a number of situational, demographic, and personality variables on individuals' allocation behavior. The results indicate a strong norm of equality, which appears to trump other considerations, such as recipients' apparent need, merit, or similarity to the allocator. The final section discusses the findings' implications, such as whether this egalitarian norm can be overcome, and whether it is desirable to do so.

## Distributive Justice Theory: Standards for Resource Allocation

A basic problem of all societies regards the allocation of goods to its members: Should it be based on effort, need, or position? Is it fair for some to get more than others, and under what circumstances? Do perceptions of fairness differ depending on whether one is making the decision regarding resource allocation or one is the decision recipient?

In most societies, the government or political ideologies provide guidelines for allocating its resources. For example, in the USA , the government dictates who receives welfare aid, and how much benefit one receives is based on a list of qualifications. In this sense, the notion of *need* drives decisions about distribution. Communal norms and empathy may increase allocations on the basis of need. The political ideals of democracy and capitalism, however, propose another method of distribution—that hard work and persistence lead to success. This notion of distribution does not require need; it simply implies that anyone—regardless of gender, race, or socioeconomic status—deserves resources based on *merit* or the amount of *effort* produced. While this does not imply equal distribution, it does suggest equality in opportunity; people can earn their share of resources. On the other hand, other political ideologies, such as collectivism, as well as egalitarian beliefs, tend to dictate relatively equal distributions regardless of individuals' merit or need. Moreover, "equality" itself can mean different things in different circumstances (see the chapter by Scott, this volume).

*Distributive justice* refers to a set of norms for the allocation of resources—such as money, governmental aid, or various other resources—that rational individuals would see as legitimate or fair (see generally, Deutsch 1985; Frohlich and Oppenheimer 1992; Hegtvedt and Cook 2001; Miller 1999; Rawls 1971; Scott, this volume; Scott et al. 2001). It is often contrasted with *procedural justice*, which refers to the processes by which outcomes are determined, rather than the outcomes themselves (Lind and Tyler 1988). Distributive and procedural justice are independent constructs that have different antecedents and consequences (e.g., Skitka et al. 2003; Tyler 1994, 2006; Tyler et al. 1997), but they are interrelated. For example, procedural variables affect judgments about resource distribution as well as about procedural justice (Brockner et al. 2003; Ramamoorthy and Flood 2004), and outcome concerns influence judgments of procedural fairness (Heuer et al. 2007). Both constructs are important, with one often taking precedence over the other depending on the circumstances (Bornstein and Dietrich 2008; Bornstein and Poser 2007; Skitka et al. 2003; Tata 2000; Tyler 2006).

Experimental research on allocation behavior shows that it is multifaceted yet predictable, involving a reliance on many principles. The number and names of these principles vary, leading one commentator to observe that "new principles of justice seem to sprout like weeds in a garden" (Folger et al. 1995, p. 261); but most theories of distributive justice emphasize the distinct allocation principles mentioned above, namely, *need, merit, and equality* (Deutsch 1985; Folger et al. 1995; Miller 1999; Sabbagh 2002; Scott, this volume). *Need* implies that those who need more should receive more, while those who need less should receive less. *Merit* functions to distribute benefits proportional to contribution or effort (i.e., one can earn his or her benefits or goods by working harder or otherwise being more deserving). *Equality* is the idea that everyone should get the same amount.[1]

[1] Drawing on Aristotle, Scott (this volume) refers to this situation as absolute equality, as opposed to proportional equality, which is more akin to merit or equity.

These principles apply in a number of diverse contexts, such as interpersonal behavior, organizational/business settings, government programs, and dispute resolution. Allocators' sense of what is fair is "complex yet structured" (Scott et al. 2001, p. 764). Individuals rely on, and make trade-offs among, multiple justice principles simultaneously (Leventhal et al. 1980; Matania and Yaniv 2007; Michelbach et al. 2003; Mitchell et al. 1993; Ordóñez and Mellers 1993; Scott et al. 2001; Skitka and Tetlock 1992). Which principle is paramount at any given time varies depending on a number of individual, situational, and resource factors (e.g., Frohlich and Oppenheimer 1992; Michelbach et al. 2003; Mitchell et al. 1993; Sabbagh 2003; Sabbagh et al. 1994; Scott and Bornstein 2009; Scott et al. 2001; Skitka and Tetlock 1992), reflecting what Walzer (1983) refers to as "spheres of justice."

What factors does one consider when making resource allocation decisions? A variety of characteristics of the situation, allocator, and recipient can come into play. Not surprisingly, allocators tend to give greater rewards and less punishment to recipients who are similar to themselves (i.e., in-group members) than to those who are dissimilar (out-group members; e.g., Huo 2002; Kerr et al. 1995; Tam et al. 2007; McGregor et al. 1998; see generally Tajfel 1970). The strong tendency to engage in more charitable giving toward groups with which one identifies more strongly (e.g., Brown 1978; Carson 1990; Rimor and Tobin 1990) is further evidence of this in-group bias in resource allocation. Similarly, allocators—even young children—are more generous with friends than with familiar non-friends or strangers, especially when giving more to another means less for oneself (Moore 2009). In-group bias does have its limits, however; for example, Inness et al. (2004) found that men allocated less money to other men than to women under some conditions—specifically, when they were in a negative mood and believed that the recipient was less deserving than they were themselves.

Other recipient characteristics reflect allocators' reliance on distinct principles of justice. For example, many allocation programs explicitly consider recipients' need, as when welfare workers consider income and number of children in distributing food stamps and other forms of aid, or when health-care officials consider current health status when deciding who should receive an organ transplant. The principle of need is especially likely to take precedence over other principles when a particular resource is scarce, or when an emergency exists (Scott and Bornstein 2009; Skitka and Tetlock 1992).

Other allocation situations explicitly emphasize merit, as when a worker's raise depends on some measure of productivity (e.g., sales volume, billable hours). The reliance on merit as a principle for determining resource allocations is pervasive in a "meritocracy" like the USA (McCoy and Major 2007). Individuals are sensitive to the degree to which recipients' effort is responsible for the outcomes they receive (Scott et al. 2001).

Which distributive principles prevail also depends on the distribution context and type of resource being allocated (Elster 1993; Foa and Foa 1974; Johnson et al. 2007; Keysar et al. 2008; Matania and Yaniv 2007; Sabbagh 2003; Sabbagh et al. 2006; Walzer 1983). For example, Scott and Bornstein (2009) found that when making (hypothetical) resource allocations, participants relied more on the principle of merit than on need or equality when allocating money; but the principle of need was emphasized when the good was prescription medications. Justice judgments and behavior also vary as a function of whether one is distributing a good or a "bad," such as business costs (Gamliel and Peer 2006; Sabbagh and Schmidt 1998; van Dijk et al. 1999), and whether the allocation is public or private (Major and Adams 1983). When allocating goods (positive outcomes), people generally rely on nonegalitarian principles such as merit or need, whereas they are more likely to favor equality when allocating bads (negative outcomes; Gamliel and Peer 2006; Goodwin 1992; Kayser and Lamm 1980).[2] From these examples, it is evident that standards of justice in distribution are context dependent. We examine the distribution of both a good (money) and a bad (work time) in the current project.

The application of distributive justice principles is complicated further by individual characteristics of the one allocating goods and services. For example, conservatives are more likely to apply the principle of merit, compared to liberals, who tend to rely more on the principles of need and equality when allocating resources (Scott et al. 2001). Women tend to be more concerned with equality and need than men, who are more concerned with equity or merit (Gaeddert 2004; Johnson et al. 2007; Major and Adams 1983; Major et al. 1989; Marshall et al. 2001; Scott et al. 2001). Moreover, gender differences interact with the context or type of good being distributed. For example, men have a stronger preference than women for the norm of equity in the work domain, but not when it comes to relationships (Major et al. 1989). Sabbagh (2003) similarly found that gender differences in preferring equity varied across resources, generally being greater for particularistic resources (e.g., power, prestige) than for more convertible resources (e.g., money).

Michelbach et al. (2003) also found that racial minorities are influenced less than whites by information about recipients' merit, perhaps reflecting different values or underlying beliefs across racial groups (cf. Rasinski 1987). Perceptions of justice vary cross-culturally and cross-nationally as well (Fischer and Skitka 2006; Henrich et al. 2005; Miller and Bersoff 1992; Murphy-Berman and Berman 2002; Tyler et al. 1997). These ethnic and cultural differences suggest that it is important to assess aspects of individuals' beliefs that might bear on resource allocation (e.g., belief in a strong work ethic, individualism vs. collectivism, political orientation, etc.), an approach we take in the present research.

Finally, individuals' ideological beliefs about equity, egalitarianism, and other aspects of social exchange predict judgments of fairness and support for macro-level distribution programs, such as social welfare policies (see generally Feldman and Steenbergen 2001; Jost et al. 2009). Some of these beliefs also implicate notions of power, such as power–distance orientation, which reflects conceptions about the degree of power that authorities should have over subordinates (Hofstede 1980). These dispositional attitudes can moderate people's justice judgments. For

[2] Some instances of goods versus bads can be construed as a framing effect, as when the withholding of a desirable commodity (e.g., a raise) is construed as a negative outcome (i.e., a bad), or the withholding of an undesirable commodity (e.g., forced overtime) is construed as a positive outcome (i.e., a good; see Gamliel and Peer 2006; Kinsey et al. 1991).

example, the relationship between perceived distributive justice in the workplace and job satisfaction is stronger for employees low in power–distance orientation than for employees high in power–distance orientation (Lee et al. 2000).

More transitory individual differences matter as well. Negative moods can lead allocators to deviate from equitable distributions (Inness et al. 2004), while also making recipients less willing to accept unequal distributions (Harlé and Sanfey 2007). Thus, it is important to account for a number of individual differences—both stable dispositions and transitory mood states—in examining distributive justice.

*Methodological Considerations* Many studies examining principles of distributive justice use hypothetical situations to determine which justice principles individuals prefer in resource allocation (e.g., Frohlich and Oppenheimer 1992; Gamliel and Peer 2006; Mitchell et al. 1993; Scott and Bornstein 2009; Scott et al. 2001). In these studies, participants are given a scenario, and asked either to distribute a given good fairly or to evaluate different possible allocations. Other studies require participants to allocate actual goods with real consequences for the recipients (e.g., Brenner and Vriend 2006; Haselhuhn and Mellers 2005).[3] Both approaches have value, especially considering that many distributive outcomes of interest, such as those involving courts and government programs, can rarely if ever be studied experimentally. However, the psychological processes underlying real, consequential decisions and those underlying hypothetical, "what-if" decisions are often different (Bornstein and McCabe 2005; Hertwig and Ortmann 2001; Kühberger et al. 2002). For purposes of influencing public policy, as well as furthering scientific theory, it is therefore important to study real behaviors whenever feasible (Hertwig and Ortmann 2001; MacCoun 2005). The research described below does just that: We use distributive justice paradigms in which people allocate real resources, such as time and money.

Another way in which distributive justice research varies is in whether the allocator/decision-maker is also one of the recipients. That is, in some cases the allocator makes (or evaluates) an allocation between himself and one or more others, whereas in other cases, the allocator makes an allocation among two or more others, who may be familiar to the allocator or anonymous. Both of these situations have real-world parallels, as in a supervisor divvying up a workload between herself and a coworker, as opposed to dividing the same work between two subordinates. The psychological processes involved in decision-making tasks where the allocator has a stake have been investigated experimentally, as in two-player games like the Ultimatum Game (UG) and the prisoner's dilemma (Camerer 2003; Deutsch 1985; Schroeder et al. 2003; the UG is described in more detail below). In these situations, the allocator's self-interest necessarily competes with abstract notions

[3] Studies employing real monetary allocations are probably in the minority in psychology, but they are common in other fields, such as experimental economics (Camerer 2003; Hertwig and Ortmann 2001). On the other hand, a fair amount of psychological research does investigate the allocation of other resources, such as time-on-task (Chen et al. 2001) or helpfulness (Tesser and Smith 1980). The present research integrates these approaches by using multiple kinds of real-world allocation tasks.

of fairness, which, though interesting, creates an additional complicating factor. Because allocators' motivations inevitably differ in the two paradigms (i.e., be fair vs. be fair while also maximizing self gain), they may invoke different processes (Moore 2009). Thus, the present studies involve both situations, where the allocator is or is not also a recipient.

In summary, the principles that people follow in resource allocation are systematic, yet the process is complex because it is influenced by a variety of characteristics of the allocator, the recipient, and the situation. Distributive justice has been studied in a variety of contexts, for many types of resources, and with diverse research methodologies. The majority of resource allocations imply a power differential; the very act of controlling the distribution confers power on the allocator over the recipient. However, even within more or less powerful roles, people may subjectively experience different amounts of power. Furthermore, the power perspective on resource allocation in the context of distributive justice has not previously been studied explicitly.

## Power Theories

Power has long been considered a fundamental concept in social science (Russell 1938). Power has traditionally, and most frequently, been defined in social influence terms. Like others, we define social power as the ability to influence others in psychologically meaningful ways (Copeland 1994; French and Raven 1959) through the giving or withholding of rewards and punishments (Keltner et al. 2003; see also Gervais and Vescio 2007; Vescio et al. 2005). In this definition, psychologically meaningful influences include actions that affect the cognitions, emotions, and behaviors of another. Powerful people have more control over their own and others' outcomes than powerless people (Dovidio et al. 1988; Ellyson and Dovidio 1985; Fiske 1993; Thibaut and Kelley 1959). Dependence and power are also inversely related (Emerson 1964); those who depend on others for rewards and punishments are less powerful than those who do not. Classic and contemporary theories of power (Cartwright 1965; Emerson 1964; Fiske 1993; French and Raven 1959; Keltner et al. 2003; Thibaut and Kelley 1959) have been used to explain a host of psychological consequences (see Guinote and Vescio 2010 for review).

French and Raven (1959) described five types of power relationships: (1) *Legitimate* power is the influence associated with holding a position that confers authority and legitimates influence (e.g., the power bosses have over employees); (2) *Reward* power is the influence associated with the ability to give or withhold rewards (e.g., giving raises or promotions); (3) *Punishment* power is the influence associated with the ability to give or withhold punishments (e.g., firing an employee); (4) *Informational* power is the influence associated with having information desired by others (e.g., the power of physicians over patients); (5) *Referent* power is the influence associated with feelings of oneness and identification with others (e.g., the power of a charismatic leader over her followers). The allocator role primarily bestows legitimate, reward, punishment, and informational power over the recipient role. Allocators are often in positions that grant them legitimacy and authority, as well as the ability to influence others through distributing or withholding rewards, punishments, and information. Furthermore, powerless people often identify with powerful people. Thus, we refer to the power difference between allocators and recipients on the basis of any (or combinations) of these bases of power as *role power*.

However, even within allocator and recipient roles, people can experience different levels of *subjective power,* which represents the degree to which they perceive themselves as powerful in a given situation, independent of role power (Anderson and Berdahl 2002). For example, having power affords people the ability to act with less interference from others, whereas lacking power renders people subject to the rewards and punishments of others. The parent who is unable to stop a temper tantrum from his child has more social power than the child, due to his role, even though he may not subjectively experience himself as powerful in that situation. Conversely, people may feel subjective power even when they have relatively little role power (Fiske et al. 1996; see also Pratto et al. 2008; Saguy et al. 2008).

Importantly, most existing research has focused on instances where roles and subjective experiences of power match. This focus is warranted because people in positions of power also tend to feel relatively powerful, whereas people in positions of low power tend to feel relatively powerless (Anderson and Berdahl 2002). However, sometimes there is a mismatch between powerful positions and subjective experiences of power. For example, a parent might feel powerless over a screaming child, a boss might feel powerless after having her legitimacy questioned by an employee, or a President belonging to one party might feel powerless when battling a Congress controlled by the other party. In those situations, the powerful can feel relatively powerless, whereas the powerless can feel powerful, even though the powerful party objectively has more influence than the powerless party. And mismatches between role and subjective power can significantly alter the behaviors of allocators and recipients (e.g., Bugental et al. 1997; Lammers et al. 2008; Maner et al. 2007).

Many classic theories assume that power has a corruptive influence (e.g., Kipnis 1972), but contemporary theories suggest that powerful people act in both exploitative and benevolent ways, depending on the situation (e.g., Galinsky et al. 2003; Gervais et al. in press; Gervais and Vescio 2007; Guinote 2007a, b; Handgraaf et al. 2008; Schmid Mast et al. 2009; Vescio et al. 2005) and their individual dispositions (e.g., Chen et al. 2009, 2001; Schmid Mast et al. 2009; Vescio et al. 2006). According to situated power theories, powerful people are better able to act in situation-appropriate ways than powerless people because power is associated with the ability to focus on cues relevant to the situation and to ignore cues irrelevant to the situation (Guinote 2007a, b; see also Smith et al. 2008).

Galinsky et al. (2003), for example, found that powerful (vs. powerless) people were more likely to take risky action and help themselves to a greater proportion of resources in a common pool when the norms of the situation dictated such action. High-power people were also more likely than low-power people to remove an aversive stimulus (e.g., an annoying fan) from a work environment and give more resources to a common pool when communal norms were salient. Similarly, Vescio et al. (2005) found that powerful people only stereotyped their subordinates when stereotypes matched powerful people's primed beliefs about appropriate ways to influence their subordinates (see also Overbeck and Park 2001). Finally, Guinote (2008) demonstrated that powerful people respond to both social and work situations in line with what the situation affords more than powerless people. Extending this to justice, allocators with high subjective power should be more sensitive to and more likely to act in response to situational norms of distributive justice for resource allocation than allocators with low subjective power.

Elevations in power also enhance the likelihood that people will behave in line with their own desires (Chen et al. 2001). Increased power is associated with an abundance of resources (e.g., material assets) and few constraints (e.g., freedom from the punishments of others). Added resources and freedom from constraints result in situations where internal states and individual differences are likely to be expressed (Galinsky et al. 2008; Schmid Mast et al. 2009). Chen et al. (2001), for example, demonstrated that power enhanced people's dispositional tendencies to behave in egoistic or benevolent ways; when divvying up tasks between themselves and another, exchange-oriented powerful people were more likely to assign their partner tasks that would take more time (i.e., allocating a bad), whereas communal-oriented powerful people were more likely to assign their partner tasks that would take less time, compared to their powerless counterparts. Extending this to the current work, allocators primed with power should be more likely to allocate resources in ways that reflect their individual dispositions.

Despite the importance of this issue, the empirical research examining subjective experiences of power in the distributive justice and power literatures is lacking. Furthermore, most of the research that has examined the mismatch between role power and subjective power has focused on when powerful people make decisions that are beneficial to the self and detrimental to powerless people (e.g., Maner and Mead 2010; Van Vugt 2006). However, in many distributive justice situations, allocators make decisions that have little to no direct benefit to the self. As a result, there is a critical need to examine instances when role power and subjective power do not match for the distribution of goods to others.

Just as gender is central to questions of distributive justice, so does it figure in discussions of power. Women are less likely to be in powerful positions (e.g., business, military, or family leaders); and compared to men in the same role, women often feel themselves to be less powerful and in less control (Eagly and Karau 2002; see also Davies et al. 2005). Thus, it is very difficult, if not impossible, to consider questions of either justice or power without considering the role of gender. This project integrates theories of distributive justice and power as a framework for understanding the fairness of allocation behavior. It addresses the question of distribution fairness by studying multiple allocation contexts involving different resources, perceptions and behaviors of male and female allocators, and primes that heighten the salience of distributive justice norms, subjective power, and group membership.

## Integrating Power and Distributive Justice

Importantly, people who are in powerful positions (e.g., government officials, employers, professors) often decide how to allocate goods to other people. As exemplified by the different bases of power, powerful people often have access to rewards, punishments, and information. How might power holders make decisions about the appropriate allocation of these resources? According to theories on power, how and why powerful people allocate goods may depend on both situational norms and their individual beliefs about what constitutes fair resource allocation.

Although research on resource allocation has not manipulated power explicitly, relevant research has been done within the context of two-person games. For example, the UG is a well-studied social decision task that developed in experimental economics (Camerer 2003; Guth et al. 1982) but has since been employed as a social psychological research paradigm for studying fairness in social interactions (e.g., Blount 1995; Handgraaf et al. 2008; Harlé and Sanfey 2007; Larrick and Blount 1997; van Dijk and Vermunt 2000). The UG consists of two players who decide how to split a given sum of money. One player (the "proposer" or "allocator") makes an offer to the second player (the "recipient" or "responder") who can either accept or reject the offer. If the second player chooses to accept, both participants receive their share of the offer. If the second player rejects the offer, however, then neither player receives anything.

It is interesting to assess the UG from a power perspective. On the one hand, the allocator seems to have greater power, in that he/she decides how to split the pot, without any input from the recipient, and has a greater chance of winding up with more than 50 % of the total resources. On the other hand, the recipient controls whether both players get any money at all, which seems to confer greater power on the recipient, despite the fact that the recipient almost never receives more than 50 % of the resources (Camerer 2003). Previous research on the UG has not addressed questions of power, which are a focus of the present studies.

A related experimental paradigm is the Dictator Game (DG), which differs from the UG in that the responder does not have the option of rejecting the allocator's offer (Camerer 2003; van Dijk and Vermunt 2000). This means that the responder is totally powerless in the DG, which can lead to different behaviors in the two types of situations (van Dijk and Vermunt 2000; Handgraaf et al. 2008).

From a normative, rational perspective, it is in the best interest of the first player in an UG to offer as little money as possible, and the second player is best-off to accept any proposed offer, regardless of how little the offer is, because some money is better than none. Studies show, however, that allocators often offer substantial non-zero sums, with modal offers around 50 % of the pot; whereas responders reject "low" offers—commonly operationalized as approximately 25 % of the pot or less—about half the time (Camerer 2003; Guth et al. 1982). The rational behavior in the DG is, again, to offer very little money—and possibly none at all. Yet DG allocators offer significantly non-zero amounts, even more than they offer in an UG, where they have less power (Handgraaf et al. 2008).

These departures from rationality suggest strongly that these games activate notions of distributive justice, as well as strategic decision making (e.g., concern that too low an offer would be rejected; see Henrich et al. 2005; Kagel and Roth 1995), in both responders and allocators (Guth and Tietz 1990). Because of strategic and other (e.g., emotional) considerations, departures from rational choice theory can be justified (Hardy-Vallée and Thagard 2008).

Taken together, the distributive justice and power literatures suggest that how and why powerful and powerless people allocate goods and respond to allocations of goods depends on both situational norms and their individual beliefs about what constitutes fair resource allocation. The research on power and resource allocation is intriguing, but it is limited because it has not explored the principles of fairness relied upon by allocators varying in power. Power is unlikely to exert a blanket effect in terms of creating generous or stingy allocators, but rather, should exacerbate the tendency to behave in line with one's own beliefs about fairness and should make one more sensitive to situational cues and recipient characteristics.

The current research addresses several theoretical gaps within the power and distributive justice literatures. Although power research has included allocation tasks, these studies have not focused on which allocation principles people use when making decisions (e.g., Chen et al. 2001; Handgraaf et al. 2008). Similarly, although distributive justice research typically involves relatively powerful actors distributing some resource (e.g., money) to relatively powerless recipients, these studies have neither experimentally manipulated nor assessed power. Additionally, although social power is often inherent to roles (i.e., allocators have more power than recipients by definition), people may experience subjective power differently within these roles (Keltner et al. 2003; McClelland 1975, 1987; Ng 1980; van Dijke and Poppe 2006; Winter 1973, 1988).

The current set of experiments addresses these issues by investigating how power and principles of distributive justice influence resource distribution by allocators. The experiments examine allocation of two different resources: money (Experiment 1) and time on work assignments (Experiment 2). The experiments address individual differences by examining variables such as gender, political orientation, communal orientation, merit orientation, work ethic, egalitarianism, collectivism, and empathy.

## *Experiment 1: Power, Distributive Justice, and Group Membership in the Ultimatum Game*

In Experiment 1, we examined how people who had role power through their naturally occurring positions divvied up resources using variations of the UG. Specifically, participants took on the allocator role in the UG, the modified UG, or the DG. These different versions of a two-player paradigm vary the degree to which the allocator has power. With the original version of the UG, the allocator makes an offer, but the recipient ultimately decides whether to accept or reject the offer, and thus, the allocator is relatively low in power. With the modified version of the UG, the allocator always receives a proportion of his or her offer, even when the responder rejects the proposed offer (but receives more when the responder accepts); thus, the allocator has a moderate amount of power. Finally, with the DG, the allocator makes the offer and the recipient must accept the offer, and thus, the allocator is relatively high in power. Using variations of this game allowed us to examine how allocators distribute money (i.e., a good) when they have varying levels of power.

*Hypothesis 1* We hypothesized that participants playing the DG would offer less money compared to participants playing the modified UG and the UG. We reasoned that because participants playing the DG would feel more powerful (vs. the modified and original UGs), they would offer the recipient less money (but see also Handgraaf et al. 2008). We also hypothesized that participants playing the modified UG would offer less money compared to participants playing the UG. We reasoned that because participants playing the modified UG would feel more powerful than participants playing the UG, they would offer the recipient less money.

*Hypothesis 2* We also hypothesized that male allocators would offer less money than female allocators. This hypothesis stems from the notion that women often feel less subjectively powerful than men, even when they are in powerful roles (Eagly and Karau 2002). Additionally, the female gender roles require that women be more communally oriented and relationship focused (Eagly and Wood 1991), and focusing on the needs of others may lead to giving more resources to the recipient.

*Hypothesis 3* Finally, we also varied features of both the situation and the recipient to examine further whether allocators would distribute more money not only to themselves but also to people who are like themselves, that is, members of their in-group (vs. out-group). We reasoned that people with more power would be more generous in their offerings to fellow in-group members than out-group members (i.e., a power × recipient interaction). Social identity theory (Tajfel and Turner 1979) suggests that we tend to favor people who are members of our in-groups because we get a sense of self-esteem and belonging through in-group favoritism. These effects are particularly pronounced when people's mortality is salient because favoring in-groups is a means of reducing the threat associated with awareness of one's mortality (Jonas et al. 2002; see Burke et al. 2010 for review). Thus, we hypothesized that people would favor in-groups, offering them more money than out-groups, particularly when their mortality was salient.

## Method

*Participants and Design* Participants were 37 undergraduates who received up to $10 for their participation. Specifically, participants received the amount of money they allocated to themselves during two rounds of the UG, modified UG, or DG. Participants were randomly assigned to a 3 (game: ultimatum, modified ultimatum, or dictator) × 2 (mortality: salient or control) × 2 (group: in-group and out-group) mixed model design. Group was the within participants factor. We included gender as a factor as well.

*Procedure* After obtaining informed consent, participants learned that they would be playing a game in which one participant would be the allocator and the other participant would be the recipient. The allocator would play the game twice and would distribute $5 between him/herself and the recipient for each game. In the UG condition, participants learned that the allocator would make an initial offer to divvy up the $5 and the recipient could choose whether to accept or reject the offer. If the recipient accepted the offer, then the money would be divided according to the offer. If the recipient rejected the offer, then neither the allocator nor the recipient would get any money. The modified ultimatum condition was the same, except in this version, the allocator would always receive money, regardless of whether or not the responder accepted or rejected the proposed offer. If the responder accepted the proposed offer, both players would receive the amount proposed by the allocator. If, however, the responder rejected the offer, the allocator would still receive half ($\delta = 0.5$) of the amount he or she originally allocated to him- or herself in the original offer, but the responder would get no money. Finally, in the DG, participants learned that the allocator would distribute the $5 and the recipient was required to accept the offer. Next, participants were ostensibly assigned to the allocator position through a coin toss, but in actuality the toss was rigged and all participants were assigned to the allocator position.

Mortality salience (MS) was then manipulated. Participants were told they would be taking an assessment designed to understand the relationship between personality and feelings and attitudes about significant aspects of life. The standard MS manipulation (responding to two questions about death or dental pain; Greenberg et al. 1986) was used. Participants respond to either the death or dental pain variation of the following two statements: (1) "Please briefly describe the emotions that the thought of your own death (dental pain) arouses in you"; (2) "Type, as specifically as you can, what you think will happen to *you* as you (experience dental pain) physically die and once you are physically dead." Participants were given 3 min to write a response to each question, before advancing to the next part of the study.

Participants played the game twice: one time where the recipient was an in-group member, and the other time where the recipient was an out-group member. Order was counterbalanced. To manipulate in-group versus out-group membership, participants read an essay ostensibly written by the other participant that included pro-American (in-group) or anti-American (out-group) beliefs (Greenberg et al. 1992). Specifically, in the in-group condition, participants read:

> People in this country have a great amount of freedom. Here there is freedom to go to school, freedom to work in any job you want. In this country people can go to school and train for the job they want. Here anyone who works hard can make their own success. In other countries, most people live in poverty with no chance of escape. In this country, people have more opportunity for success than in any other and success does not depend on the group you belong to. While there are problems in any country, America truly is a great nation.

In the out-group condition, participants read:

> I believe the United States of America is the "land of opportunity" but this is only true for the rich. The system here is set up for the rich against the poor. All people care about here is money and trying to have more than other people. There is no sympathy for people. It's all one group putting down others and nobody cares about the poor. The people only let foreigners have jobs like picking fruit or washing dishes because no American would do it. Americans are spoiled and lazy and want everything handed to them. America is a cold country that is insensitive to the need and problems of its members. It thinks it's a great country, but it's not.

After each essay, participants answered a series of questions about the author of the essay: How much participants liked the author, how intelligent and knowledgeable they thought the author was, how much they agreed with the author's opinion of America, and how true the author's opinion of America was (Greenberg et al. 1992). The questions were all rated on a nine-point scale (1=*not at all,* 9=*totally*).

Following each round of the game, participants were asked to complete the manipulation checks. Participants were asked two questions about power: "Who had the power in the game?" (1=*allocator*, 9=*recipient*; reverse coded) and "How powerful do you feel in this game?" (1=*not at all*, 9=*very powerful*). Participants completed these judgments for both rounds of the game. Negatively worded items were reverse coded, and we computed a mean subjective power score ($\alpha = 0.89$), with higher numbers indicating more power. Additionally, participants were asked to indicate how similar they were to the recipient (1=*very dissimilar*, 5=*very similar*). This item was used to assess in-group versus out-group similarity.

Finally, participants completed a mood questionnaire (the Positive and Negative Affect Schedule, PANAS-X; Watson et al. 1988) and demographic survey. A positive mood score was calculated by taking the mean of *inspired, alert, excited, enthused,* and *determined* ($\alpha = 0.79$), with higher numbers indicating more positive emotion. A negative mood score was calculated by calculating the mean of *distress, scared, nervous, upset,* and *afraid* ($\alpha = 0.76$), with higher numbers indicating more negative emotion. The mood results were uninformative, so we do not discuss them further. Participants were then paid and thoroughly debriefed.

### Results and Discussion

*Power* An effect of game on power scores demonstrated that type of game affected power in the expected direction, $F(1, 35) = 11.87$, $p < 0.001$, $\eta_p^2 = 0.41$. Playing the DG was associated with the most power (M=7.68, SD=0.69), followed by the modified UG (M=6.44, SD=1.95), followed by the UG (M=4.75, SD=1.64). The differences between the DG and the UG ($p < 0.001$) and the modified UG and the UG ($p = 0.009$) were significant, whereas the difference between the DG and modified UG was marginally significant ($p = 0.065$). Thus, the manipulation of game effectively varied subjective power.

*Group* An effect of group on similarity scores demonstrated that group affected perceived similarity in the expected direction, $F(1, 35) = 9.42$, $p = 0.004$, $\eta_p^2 = 0.21$.

The in-group recipient (M=3.54, SD=1.10) was regarded as more similar to the allocator than the out-group recipient (M=2.81, SD=1.00).

*Recipient Offers* The mean recipient offer was slightly less than half (M=2.36, SD=1.15). However, almost half of participants (48.6%) made an equal distribution between the allocator and recipient ($2.50), although 5.4% offered nothing to the recipient; surprisingly, even more (8.1%) offered the entire $5 to the recipient.

To test our hypotheses, recipient offers were submitted to a 3 game (ultimatum, modified ultimatum, or dictator) × 2 gender (men or women) × 2 mortality (salient or control) × 2 recipient (in-group and out-group) mixed model analysis of variance (ANOVA). Recipient was the within participants factor. This analysis did not reveal a significant effect of game, $F(1, 35)=0.28$, $p=0.76$, $\eta_p^2=0.02$, which is inconsistent with Hypothesis 1. However, the means were somewhat in the hypothesized direction, with the DG ($M$=$2.13, $SE$=0.31) resulting in lower offers than the modified ultimatum ($M$=$2.41, $SE$=0.31) and ultimatum ($M$=$2.40, $SE$=0.27) games.

Consistent with Hypothesis 2, there was a significant effect of gender, $F(1, 35)=5.92$, $p<0.022$, $\eta_p^2=0.20$, with women ($M$=$2.72, $SE$=0.23) making higher offers than men ($M$=$1.90, $SE$=0.26). This is consistent with the notion that women generally feel less power and control than men and that women are more communally oriented and relationship focused than men. Thus, women make higher offers than men, regardless of role power. In fact, the mean offer female allocators made to recipients was more than half of the money.

Finally, there was a significant recipient × mortality salience interaction, $F(1, 35)=5.19$, $p<0.031$. When mortality was not salient, participants made (nonsignificantly) higher allocations to in-group recipients ($M$=$2.59, $SE$=0.29) than out-group recipients ($M$=$2.13, $SE$=0.30); whereas when mortality was salient, this pattern was reversed, with participants making (nonsignificantly) higher allocations to out-group recipients ($M$=$2.49, $SE$=0.27) than in-group recipients ($M$=$2.04, $SE$=0.26). Although this finding is inconsistent with Hypothesis 3, it is consistent with research suggesting that in-group favoritism can be reduced and sometimes reversed (resulting in out-group favoritism), depending on which identities are salient (Giannakakis and Fritsche 2011). For example, making superordinate identities salient can reduce, and sometimes even reverse, in-group bias (Giannakakis and Fritsche 2011). Applied to the present work, it is possible that reading an anti- and pro-American essay served to remind participants of the superordinate identity of being American, regardless of whether one holds pro- or anti-American beliefs.

## *Experiment 2: Power, Distributive Justice, and Merit in Work Allocation*

Rather than examining subjective power as it varies naturally across different kinds of tasks, as in Experiment 1, Experiment 2 manipulated allocators' subjective power, as well as the justice principle of merit, to investigate their influence on a different kind of allocation task (i.e., time at work). We manipulated power and merit by priming tasks, and we manipulated merit further by varying the deservingness of the allocation recipient. This allowed us to investigate merit as both a feature of the situation and a feature of the individual receiving the distribution. We also examined a different kind of resource, shifting from monetary allocation (a good) to the distribution of work and time in a shared-effort task (a bad).

*Hypothesis 1* Our first hypothesis addresses the effect on resource allocation of a match (or mismatch) between situational or dispositional goals and recipient features. In general, powerful (vs. powerless) participants should be more likely to adhere to a given principle of distributive justice when that principle is made salient by virtue of recipient characteristics, and when that same principle is consistent with either the allocator's disposition or situational cues. Specifically, when the norms of the situation call for taking recipients' merit into account and one of the recipients is more deserving, then powerful people will allocate more resources on the basis of merit than powerless people.

*Hypothesis 2* Because individuals vary in terms of their dispositional tendency to behave in need-based, merit-based, or equality-based ways, a number of individual difference variables should predict allocation behavior and recipient perceptions. We assessed a number of attitudes, beliefs, and response orientations that are likely to be correlated with dispositional distributive justice perspectives, such as empathy and communal orientation; work ethic and meritocracy beliefs, which should be especially relevant to merit; and egalitarianism and collectivism. Political orientation and gender, which are correlated with justice beliefs (e.g., Jost et al. 2009; Marshall et al. 2001; Scott et al. 2001), were included as well.

*Participants and Design* Participants were 103 undergraduates who received course credit. Participants were randomly assigned to one of eight conditions, resulting from a 2 (power: powerful vs. powerless) × 2 (situation merit: high vs. control) × 2 (recipient merit: high vs. low) between participants design. There were 10–15 participants per condition.

*Procedure* Participants were told that the session involved three separate studies, two completed individually and one in teams. Power was manipulated by asking participants to complete a scrambled sentence-priming task consisting of 16 items (Smith and Trope 2006). Five words for each item were listed and participants had to use four of the words to make a grammatically correct sentence. In the high-power condition, 8 of the 16 sets of words contained a word related to having power (i.e., *authority, captain, commands, controls, dominates, executive, influenced, privileged*). In the low-power condition, the same eight sets contained a word related to lacking power (i.e., *complied, janitor, obey, passive, servant, submits, subordinate, yield*).

Then participants were told that the second study concerned reading comprehension. *Situation merit* was primed by having participants complete an additional scrambled sentence task (McCoy and Major 2007). Participants unscrambled either sentences that endorsed meritocracy (e.g., effort positive prosperity leads to) or control sentences (e.g., by college goes quickly time).

After answering five reading comprehension questions about the sentences, participants were led to another room. Participants learned that the final study would examine resource distribution in teams; a rigged draw assigned all participants to the role of allocator. The experimenter informed the participant that the two other participants were still working on the reading comprehension task. To manipulate *recipient merit*, we gave participants information about why one of the fellow participants (the confederate) was late. In the low-merit condition, participants learned that one confederate arrived to the experiment 15 min late. In the high-merit condition, participants learned that one confederate completed both tasks on time, but that the computer crashed after the reading comprehension task, so the participant was completing the task again. In both conditions, no information was provided about the other fellow participant (in reality, there was no other participant, though participants were led to believe that there was one in another cubicle; we therefore refer to this person as the "ghost participant").

While the experimenter ostensibly checked on the other participants, the experimenter handed the participant a list of 11 fictitious tasks, each listed with a different amount of time required to complete it (listed in descending order, e.g., 7, 6, 5, 2, 2 and 1 min). The total time required to complete all of the exercises (38 min) was printed at the bottom of the list (see Chen et al. 2001 for a similar time allotment task). Participants were simply told to allocate the tasks between the other two participants. The procedure was timed so that approximately 25 min remained in the session; this way all participants made their choices with the same amount of time left in the session, and both recipients apparently still had time to complete the remaining tasks.

Once participants allocated the tasks, the experimenter instructed the participants to complete a final set of individual difference measures, including: the PANAS-X; the Protestant Work Ethic Scale (PWES, 11 items; Katz and Hass 1988); a Humanitarianism-Egalitarianism scale (HE, 10 items; Katz and Hass 1988); the Interpersonal Reactivity Index (IRI, 28 items; Davis 1980, 1983), a measure of empathy; a measure of communal exchange orientation (CXO, 23 items; Gervais et al. 2010; based on Clark et al. 1987); the Individualism/Collectivism Scale (IC, 16 items; Triandis and Gelfand 1998); and Belief in Individual Mobility (BIM, 4 items; Major et al. 2002), a measure of one's belief that individuals from all ethnic backgrounds have equal opportunity for advancement in the American system. All of the scales had acceptable reliability (see Table 1.1).

Participants rated the task's distributive and procedural fairness ("The assignment of tasks that I made was fair," "The procedure by which the tasks were assigned was fair"), using 5-point agree/disagree scales. They also indicated their political orientation on a scale ranging from 1 (*strong conservative*) to 5 (*strong liberal*). Finally, participants completed the remaining manipulation checks and were debriefed.

**Table 1.1** Scale reliability

| Scale | Reliability ($\alpha$) |
|---|---|
| PWES | 0.72 |
| IRI | 0.80 |
| BIM | 0.66 |
| IC | 0.74 |
| CXO | 0.64 |
| HE | 0.77 |

*PWES* protestant work ethic scale, *IRI* interpersonal reactivity index, *BIM* belief in mobility, *IC* individualism/collectivism, *CXO* communal exchange orientation, *HE* humanitarianism-egalitarianism

## Results and Discussion

*Manipulation Checks* Several questions assessed participants' attention to the recipient merit manipulation (e.g., the other person's computer crashing). Six participants missed one or more of these questions, so they were excluded from all subsequent analyses. Additional questions assessed the effectiveness of the power and merit primes (not all participants answered these questions). Two questions gauged participants' sense of power: "I feel powerful" and "I feel like I have control in this situation." Responses were highly correlated, $r=0.64$, $p<0.001$, so were summed to create a single measure of subjective power (higher numbers indicated more power). High-power participants (M=8.51, SD=2.59) reported feeling slightly more powerful than low-power participants (M=7.98, SD=3.00), but this difference was not statistically significant, $t(77)=0.85$, $p=0.40$.

Three questions measured participants' belief about merit in American society (e.g., "In our society, harder work leads to better outcomes"). Responses were intercorrelated, $rs=0.24-0.31$, $ps<0.05$, so they were summed to create a single measure of merit belief (higher numbers indicated a stronger belief). The merit beliefs of high- (M=14.32, SD=3.9) and low-situation merit participants (M=15.15, SD=2.43) did not differ, $t(77)=1.30$, $p=0.20$. Thus, the two manipulations designed to prime situational power and merit were relatively ineffective, despite their use in previous studies (McCoy and Major 2007; Smith and Trope 2006). Subsequent analyses collapsed across these variables.

*Work Allocation and Fairness Ratings* The principal dependent measures were the amount of work (in minutes) assigned to the confederate, and perceptions of distributive and procedural fairness. Recipient merit did not affect participants' work assignments, $t(95)=0.27$, $p=0.79$ (Ms=18.82 vs. 18.72 for high and low merit, respectively). Recipient merit also did not affect participants' perception of fairness for either the allocation outcome, $t(91)=1.49$, $p=0.14$ (Ms=1.71 vs. 1.93 for high and low merit, respectively), or the procedure, $t(82)=0.38$, $p=0.70$ (Ms=2.00 vs. 1.92 for high and low merit, respectively).

*Individual Differences* Allocation was not significantly correlated with any of the individual difference measures or political orientation, although the correlation between negative affect on the PANAS and allocation was marginally significant, $r=0.22$, $p=0.065$. The stronger participants' negative mood, the more time they assigned to the confederate. Some of the scales were correlated with one another. For example, the PWES was correlated with mobility belief ($r=0.40$, $p=0.001$) and political orientation ($r=-0.32$, $p=0.012$). The egalitarianism scale was correlated with empathy, $r=0.35$, $p=0.002$, as well as CXO, $r=-0.36$, $p=0.002$. Specifically, participants who were more empathetic, and less exchange oriented, had more egalitarian beliefs.

Men and women did not differ on the various individual difference measures. However, there was a nonsignificant trend for women to be somewhat more egalitarian (Ms = 3.75 vs. 3.47), $t(69)=1.37$, $p=0.175$. Women also had a higher belief in merit (Ms = 15.16 vs. 13.29), $t(76)=2.46$, $p=0.016$.

*Egalitarianism* Given the strong tendency of participants in Experiment 1 to make an equal allocation, we examined egalitarianism more closely. Overall, participants assigned as much work to the confederate ($M=18.79$, $SD=1.92$) as to the ghost participant ($M=19.17$, $SD=1.87$), $t(97)=1.02$, $p=0.31$. This result suggests a strong egalitarian norm. Supporting this tendency, although the number of minutes assigned to the confederate ranged from 13–23, the modal response (27.6%) was right at the midpoint (19). Moreover, 63.3% of participants assigned 18–20 min, and 86.8% of participants assigned 17–21 min. Thus, the data show a reluctance to deviate little, if any, from a strictly egalitarian apportionment.

## General Discussion

*Summary of Major Findings* The major finding from the present studies was that allocators evinced a strong egalitarian norm. In Experiment 1, nearly 50% of participants split the amount exactly in half; and in Experiment 2, over 60% made a practically equal apportionment (assigning 18–20 min). This is a higher rate of egalitarian behavior than demonstrated in previous research. For example, Scott and Bornstein (2009) identified only 9.5% of their participants as "strict egalitarians," which they defined as preferring an equal split of resources even when other considerations, such as merit and need, favored an unequal distribution. They found that egalitarianism was relied on more for some types of resources (e.g., food) than others (e.g., money, medicine), but the rate still did not exceed 20% in any of the conditions—much lower than the rate observed here. Moreover, Experiment 1 found a much higher rate of egalitarianism using money, one of the same goods used by Scott and Bornstein (2009), and on a "micro-level" allocation task, where Scott (this volume) would predict less egalitarianism than on a "macro-level" task. In addition, the high rate of egalitarianism observed here was for strict, or absolute, equality; the rate for relative equality, which borders on equity, would likely be even higher (see Scott, this volume).

There are two important distinctions between the present research and the Scott and Bornstein (2009) study. First, we used actual money, whereas Scott and Bornstein's participants made hypothetical decisions. Decision-making processes are often different depending on whether the decision has real anticipated consequences or merely hypothetical ones (Bornstein and McCabe 2005; Kühberger 2002). Egalitarianism might be stronger when allocation involves actual goods, as in the present studies, as opposed to studies involving hypothetical allocations or a mere expression of preferences. Allocating disparate amounts, even to unseen recipients, can be awkward and embarrassing; it is therefore easier in the abstract than in actuality. There is often a disjunction between what people say they would do in various social situations and what they actually do when placed in those situations (e.g., Wicker 1969; Milgram 1975; Mischel 1968; see also Baumeister et al. 2007).

Second, our allocators in Experiment 1 had a stake in the outcome (i.e., they were distributing money between themselves and another player), whereas Scott and Bornstein's participants were distributing goods between two other parties. Perhaps equality is more salient when there is self-interest because of motivations related to self-presentation, such as a desire not to appear selfish. Even if this is the case, however, it cannot explain the high rate of egalitarianism observed in Experiment 2, where allocators were not also recipients themselves.

In designing the present studies, we deliberately chose to examine allocation behavior for resources that could be characterized as both goods (money, in Experiment 1) and bads (work, in Experiment 2). Importantly, we observed a high rate of egalitarianism for both kinds of resources. Although egalitarian beliefs did not predict allocation behavior, they were correlated with empathy and communal/exchange orientation. Thus, egalitarianism might be part of a broader construct drawing on support for others, especially those in need; importantly, however, it is distinct from other attitudes toward the needy, such as humanitarianism (Feldman and Steenbergen 2001).

A secondary finding was that it proved difficult to prime either power or principles of justice. One possible explanation for the power finding is that an allocator role is associated with feeling powerful, regardless of situational primes. For example, in Experiment 2, participants had legitimate and punishment bases of power, regardless of the situational prime. They were placed into a legitimate high-power position as the allocator, and they had the ability to punish the recipients by assigning them tasks that took more time. When in this position, the situational power prime (reading powerful or powerless words) had very little influence on participants. However, it does appear that characteristics of the actual allocator position do have a meaningful impact on allocators' feelings of subjective power. Although everyone was assigned to an allocator role in Experiment 1, participants' subjective experience of power depended on the actual power bestowed by their allocator role, with participants reporting the most power in the DG, a moderate level of power in the modified UG, and the least power in the UG.

*Overcoming the Egalitarian Norm* In light of the present findings demonstrating a strong egalitarian norm, one might reasonably ask how it could be overcome. Before addressing possible strategies for overcoming the egalitarian norm, we first need to address whether, as a matter of public policy, it would be desirable to do so. Although it might seem desirable from a Western, capitalist perspective, ideals of distributive fairness vary widely across cultures, with some cultures considerably more egalitarian than others (e.g., Alwin et al. 1995; Miller and Bersoff 1992; Murphy-Berman and Berman 2002).

There are also differences in egalitarianism within societies (Feldman and Steenbergen 2001; Scott et al. 2001). And as the chapter by Scott (this volume) makes clear, the extent of egalitarian behavior varies as a function of the type of task and how equality is defined. Moreover, situational cues can prime people to be more egalitarian in certain circumstances (e.g., Biernat et al. 1996). For example, Butz et al. (2007) found that merely exposing participants to a picture of an American flag activated egalitarian concepts. If it is possible to make people feel more egalitarian, then it should also be possible to make them feel less egalitarian. Activating a competing justice principle, such as merit, should accomplish that; although the merit prime in Experiment 2 was ineffective, it seems reasonable that a stronger merit priming manipulation would also make people less egalitarian.

*Conclusions* When it comes to the allocation of resources, "Is it fair?" represents an important and seemingly simple question. According to distributive justice theory and research, however, the answer is multifaceted. Is the allocation based on merit, equality, need, or another principle? Is the resource a good (e.g., money, medication) or a bad (e.g., economic sanctions, time on a task)? Who is allocating and who is receiving the resource? Such situational factors as power, in-group versus out-group distinctions, mood, and threat play a role, whereas individual differences in meritocracy, egalitarianism, collectivism, or empathy are also important. Despite the complexity of determining whether the allocation of assets is fair, the findings from the present pair of studies suggest that people's actual allocation behavior can be quite straightforward. At least in the situations under investigation here, people's default allocation appears to be egalitarian—they tend to divvy up resources equally. This emerges whether they are distributing goods or bads and whether the allocations could serve self-interest or whether the recipient is particularly needy or meritorious. Thus, instead of asking "Is it fair?" researchers should perhaps be asking "When is it *not* fair?" Determining when and why people overcome the egalitarian norm in their allocation of resources is a critical direction for future research.

## References

Alwin, D.F., Gornev, G., & Khakhulina, L. (1995). Comparative referential structures, system legitimacy, and justice sentiments: An international comparison. In J. R. Kluegel, D. S. Mason, & B. Wegener (Eds.), *Social justice and political change* (pp. 109–130). New York: Aldine.

Anderson, C., & Berdahl, J. (2002). The experience of power: Examining the effects of power on approach and inhibition tendencies. *Journal of Personality and Social Psychology, 83,* 1362–1377.

Baumeister, R., Vohs, K., & Funder, D. (2007). Psychology as the science of self-reports and finger movements: Whatever happened to actual behavior? *Perspectives on Psychological Science, 2,* 396–403.

Biernat, M., Vescio, T. K., & Theno, S. A. (1996). Violating American values: A 'value congruence' approach to understanding outgroup attitudes. *Journal of Experimental Social Psychology, 32,* 387–410. doi:10.1006/jesp.1996.0018.

Blount, S. (1995). When social outcomes aren't fair: The effect of causal attributions on preferences. *Organizational Behavior and Human Decision Processes, 63,* 131–144.

Bornstein, B. H., & Dietrich, H. (2008). Fair procedures, yes. But we dare not lose sight of fair outcomes. *Court Review, 44,* 72–77.

Bornstein, B.H., & McCabe, S.G. (2005). Jurors of the absurd? The role of consequentiality in jury simulation research. *Florida State University Law Review, 32,* 443–467.

Bornstein, B. H., & Poser, S. (2007). Perceptions of procedural and distributive justice in the September 11th Victim Compensation Fund. *Cornell Journal of Law and Public Policy, 17,* 75–100.

Brenner, T., & Vriend, N.J. (2006). On the behavior of proposers in ultimatum games. *Journal of Economic Behavior & Organization, 61,* 617–631.

Brockner, J., Heuer, L., Magner, N., Folger, R., Umphress, E., van den Bos, K., Vermunt, R., Magner, M., & Siegel, P. (2003). High procedural fairness heightens the effect of outcome favorability on self-evaluation: An attributional analysis. *Organizational Behavior and Human Decision Processes, 91,* 51–68.

Brown, R. (1978). Divided we fall: An analysis of relations between sections of a factory workforce. In H. Tajfel (Ed.), *Differentiation between social groups*. London: Academic.

Bugental, D., Lyon, J. E., Krantz, J., & Cortez, V. (1997). Who's the boss? Differential accessibility of dominance ideation in parent-child relationships. *Journal of Personality and Social Psychology, 72,* 1297–1309. doi:10.1037/0022-3514.72.6.1297.

Burke, B. L., Martens, A., & Faucher, E. H. (2010). Two decades of terror management theory: A meta-analysis of mortality salience research. *Personality and Social Psychology Review, 14,* 155–195.

Butz, D. A., Plant, E. A., & Doerr, C. E. (2007). Liberty and justice for all? *Personality and Social Psychology Bulletin, 33,* 396–408.

Camerer, C. F. (2003). *Behavioral game theory: Experiments in strategic interaction*. New York: Russell Sage.

Carson, E. D. (1990). Pattern of giving in Black churches. In R. Wuthnow & V. A. Hodgkinson (Eds.), *Faith and philanthrophy in America*. San Francisco: Jossey-Bass.

Chen, S., Lee-Chai, A. Y., & Bargh, J. A. (2001). Relationship orientation as moderator of the effects of social power. *Journal of Personality and Social Psychology, 80,* 183–187.

Chen, S., Langer, C., & Mendoza-Denton, R. (2009). When dispositional and role power fit: Implications for self-expression and self-other congruence. *Journal of Personality and Social Psychology, 96,* 710–727.

Clark, M. S., Oullette, R., Powell, M. C., & Milberg, S. (1987). Recipient's mood, relationship type, and helping. *Journal of Personality and Social Psychology, 53,* 94–103. doi:10.1037/0022-3514.53.1.94.

Copeland, J. T. (1994). Prophecies of power: Motivational implications of social power for behavioral confirmation. *Journal of Personality and Social Psychology, 67,* 264–277.

Davies, P. G., Spencer, S. J., & Steele, C. M. (2005). Clearing the air: Identity safety moderates the effects of stereotype threat on women's leadership aspirations. *Journal of Personality and Social Psychology, 88,* 276–287.

Davis, M. H. (1980). A multidimensional approach to individual differences in empathy. *JSAS Catalog of Selected Documents in Psychology, 10,* 85.

Davis, M. H. (1983). Measuring individual differences in empathy: Evidence for a multidimensional approach. *Journal of Personality and Social Psychology, 44,* 113–126.
Deutsch, M. (1985). *Distributive justice*. New Haven: Yale University Press.
Dovidio, J., Ellyson, S., Keating, C., Heltman, K., & Brown, C. (1988). The relationship of social power to visual displays of dominance between men and women. *Journal of Personality and Social Psychology, 54,* 233–242.
Eagly, A. H., & Karau, S. J. (2002). Role congruity theory of prejudice toward female leaders. *Psychological Review, 109,* 573–598.
Eagly, A. H., & Wood, W. (1991). Explaining sex differences in social behavior: A meta-analytic perspective. *Personality and Social Psychology Bulletin, 17,* 306–315.
Ellyson, S. L., & Dovidio, J. F. (1985). *Power, dominance, and nonverbal behavior*. New York: Springer.
Elster, J. (1993). *Local justice: How institutions allocate scarce goods and necessary burdens*. New York: Russell Sage.
Elster, J. (1995). The empirical study of justice. In D. Miller & M. Walzer (Eds.), *Pluralism, justice, and equality* (pp. 81–98). Oxford: Oxford University Press.
Elster, J. (2004). *Closing the books: Transitional justice in historical perspective*. Cambridge: Cambridge University Press.
Emerson, R. (1964). Power-dependence relations: Two experiments. *Sociometry, 27,* 282–298.
Feldman, S., & Steenbergen, M. R. (2001). The humanitarian foundation of public support for social welfare. *American Journal of Political Science, 45,* 658–677.
Fischer, R., & Skitka, L. J. (2006). Justice: Social-psychological perspectives. In A. J. W. Taylor (Ed.), *Justice as a basic human need* (pp. 85–93). Hauppauge: Nova Scientific.
Fiske, S. T. (1993). Controlling other people: The impact of power on stereotyping. *American Psychologist, 48,* 621–628.
Fiske, S., Morling, B., & Stevens, L. (1996). Controlling self and others: A theory of anxiety, mental control, and social control. *Personality and Social Psychology Bulletin, 22,* 115–123.
Foa, U. G., & Foa, E. B. (1974). *Societal structures of the mind.* Springfield: Charles C. Thomas.
Folger, R., Sheppard, B. H., & Buttram, R. T. (1995). Equity, equality, and need: Three faces of social justice. In B. B. Bunker & J. Z. Rubin (Eds.), *Conflict, cooperation and justice* (pp. 261–289). San Francisco: Jossey-Bass.
French, J., & Raven, B. (1959). The bases of social power. In D. Cartwright (Ed.), *Studies in social power* (pp. 150–167). Ann Arbor: Institute for Social Research.
Frohlich, N. & Oppenheimer, J. A. (1992). *Choosing justice: An experimental approach to ethical theory*. Berkeley: University of California Press.
Gaeddert, W. P. (2004). Gender, justice, and social change. In M. A. Paludi (Ed.), *Praeger guide to the psychology of gender* (pp. 207–218). Westport: Praeger.
Galinsky, A. D., Gruenfeld, D. H., & Magee, J. C. (2003). From power to action. *Journal of Personality and Social Psychology, 85,* 453–466.
Galinsky, A., Magee, J., Gruenfeld, D., Whitson, J., & Liljenquist, K. (2008). Power reduces the press of the situation: Implications for creativity, conformity, and dissonance. *Journal of Personality and Social Psychology, 95,* 1450–1466. doi:10.1037/a0012633.
Gamliel, E., & Peer, E. (2006). Positive versus negative framing affects justice judgments. *Social Justice Research, 19,* 307–322.
Gervais, S. J., Guinote, A., Slabu, L., & Allen, J. (in press). Power increases situated creativity. *Social Influence*.
Gervais, S. J., Hillard, A. & Vescio, T. K. (2010). Confronting sexism: The role of relationship orientation and gender. *Sex Roles, 63,* 463–474.
Gervais, S. J., & Vescio, T. K. (2007). The origins and consequences of subtle sexism. In A. M. Columbus (Ed.), *Advances in psychology research* (pp. 137–166). Hauppauge: Nova Science.
Giannakakis, A. E., & Fritsche, I. (2011). Social identities, group norms, and threat: On the malleability of ingroup bias. *Personality and Social Psychology Bulletin, 37,* 82–93.
Goodwin, B. (1992). *Justice by lottery*. Chicago: University of Chicago Press.
Greenberg, J., & Colquitt, J. A. (2005). *Handbook of organizational justice*. Hillsdale: Erlbaum.

Greenberg, J., Pyszczynski, T., & Solomon, S. (1986). The causes and consequences of a need for self-esteem: A terror management theory. In R. F. Baumeister (Ed.), *Public self and private self* (pp. 189–212). New York: Springer.

Greenberg, J., Simon, L., Pyszczynski, T., Solomon, S., & Chatel, D. (1992). Terror management and tolerance: Does mortality salience always intensify negative reactions to others who threaten one's worldview? *Journal of Personality and Social Psychology, 63,* 212–220.

Guinote, A. (2007a). Power and goal pursuit. *Personality and Social Psychology Bulletin, 33,* 1076–1087.

Guinote, A. (2007b). Power affects basic cognition: Increase attentional inhibition and flexibility. *Journal of Experimental Social Psychology, 43,* 685–697.

Guinote, A. (2008). Power and affordances: When the situation has more power over powerful than over powerless individuals. *Journal of Personality and Social Psychology, 95,* 237–252.

Guinote, A., & Vescio, T. K. (2010). *The social psychology of power*. New York: Guilford.

Guth, W., Schmittberger, R., & Schwarze, B. (1982). An experimental analysis of ultimatum bargaining. *Journal of Economic Behavior and Organization, 3,* 367–388.

Guth, W., & Tietz, R. (1990). Ultimatum bargaining behavior: A survey and comparison of experimental results. *Journal of Economic Psychology, 11,* 417–449.

Handgraaf, M. J. J., Van Dijk, E., Vermunt, R.C., Wilke, H. A. M., & De Dreu, C. K. W. (2008). Less power or powerless? Egocentric empathy gaps and the irony of having little versus no power in social decision making. *Journal of Personality and Social Psychology, 95,* 1136–1149.

Hardy-Vallée, B., & Thagard, P. (2008). How to play the ultimatum game: An engineering approach to metanormativity. *Philosophical Psychology, 21,* 173–192.

Harlé, K. M., & Sanfey, A. G. (2007). Incidental sadness biases social economic decisions in the ultimatum game. *Emotion, 7,* 876–881.

Haselhuhn, M. P., & Mellers, B. A. (2005). Emotions and cooperation in economic games. *Cognitive Brain Research, 23,* 24–33.

Hegtvedt, K. A., & Cook, K. S. (2001). Distributive justice: Recent theoretical developments and applications. In J. Sanders & V. L. Hamilton (Eds.), *Handbook of justice research in law* (pp. 93–132). New York: Plenum.

Henrich, J., et al. (2005). "Economic man" in cross-cultural perspective: Behavioral experiments in 15 small-scale societies. *Behavioral and Brain Sciences, 28,* 795–855.

Hertwig, R., & Ortmann, A. (2001). Experimental practices in economics: A methodological challenge for psychologists? *Behavioral and Brain Sciences, 24,* 383–451.

Heuer, L., Penrod, S., & Kattan, A. (2007). The role of societal benefits and fairness concerns among decision makers and decision recipients. *Law and Human Behavior, 31,* 573–610.

Hofstede, G. H. (1980). *Culture's consequences: International differences in work-related attitudes*. Beverly Hills: Sage.

Huo, Y. J. (2002). Justice and the regulation of social relations: When and why do group members deny claims to social goods? *British Journal of Social Psychology, 41,* 535–562.

Inness, M., Desmarais, S., & Day, A. (2004). Gender, mood state, and justice preference: Do mood states moderate gender-based norms of justice? *British Journal of Social Psychology, 44,* 463–478.

Johnson, C., Hegtvedt, K. A., Brody, L. M., & Waldron, K. W. (2007). Feeling injustice, expressing injustice: How gender and context matter. *Advances in Group Processes, 24,* 149–186.

Jonas, E., Schimel, J., Greenberg, J., & Pyszczynski, T. (2002). The scrooge effect: Evidence that mortality salience increases prosocial attitudes and behavior. *Personality and Social Psychology Bulletin, 28,* 1342–1353.

Jost, J. T., Kay, A. C., & Thorisdottir, H. (2009). *Social and psychological bases of ideology and system justification*. Oxford: Oxford University Press.

Kagel, J. H., & Roth, A. E. (1995). *Handbook of experimental economics*. Princeton: Princeton University Press.

Katz, I., & Hass, R. G. (1988). Racial ambivalence and American value conflict: Correlational and priming studies of dual cognitive structures. *Journal of Personality and Social Psychology, 55,* 896–905.

Kayser, E., & Lamm, H. (1980). Input integration and input weighting in decisions on allocations of gains and losses. *European Journal of Social Psychology, 10,* 1–15.

Keltner, D., Gruenfeld, D. H., & Anderson, C. (2003). Power, approach, and inhibition. *Psychological Review, 110,* 265–284.

Kerr, N. L., Hymes, R. W., Anderson, A. B., & Weathers, J. E. (1995). Defendant-juror similarity and mock juror judgments. *Law and Human Behavior, 19,* 545–567.

Keysar, B., Converse, B. A., Wang, J., & Epley, N. (2008). Reciprocity is not give and take: Asymmetric reciprocity to positive and negative acts. *Psychological Science, 19,* 1280–1286.

Kinsey, K. A., Grasmick, H. G., & Smith, K. W. (1991). Framing justice: Taxpayer evaluations of personal tax burdens. *Law & Society Review, 25,* 845–873.

Kipnis, D. (1972). Does power corrupt? *Journal of Personality and Social Psychology, 24,* 33–41.

Kluegel, J., Mason, D. S., & Wegener, B. (1995). *Social justice and political change: Public opinion in capitalist and post-communist states.* New York: Aldine.

Koch, T. (2001). *Scarce goods: Justice, fairness, and organ transplantation.* Westport: Praeger.

Kühberger, A., Schulte-Mechlenbeck, M., & Perner, J. (2002). Framing decisions: Hypothetical and real. *Organizational Behavior and Human Decision Processes, 89,* 1162–1175.

Lammers, J., Galinsky, A. D., Gordijn, E. H., & Otten, S. (2008). Illegitimacy moderates the effects of power on approach. *Psychological Science, 19,* 558–564. doi:10.1111/j.1467-9280.2008.02123.x.

Larrick, R. P., & Blount, S. (1997). The claiming effect: Why players are more generous in social dilemmas than in ultimatum games. *Journal of Personality and Social Psychology, 72,* 810–825.

Lee, C., Pillutla, M., & Law, K. S. (2000). Power-distance, gender, and organizational justice. *Journal of Management, 26,* 685–704.

Lerner, M. J., & Lerner, S. C. (Eds.). (1981). *The justice motive in social behavior.* New York: Plenum.

Leventhal, G. S., Karuza, J., & Fry, W. R. (1980). Beyond fairness: A theory of allocation preferences. In G. Mikula (Ed.), *Justice and social interaction: Experimental and theoretical contributions from psychological research* (pp. 168–218). New York: Springer.

Lind, E. A., & Tyler, T. R. (1988). *The social psychology of procedural justice.* New York: Plenum.

MacCoun, R. J. (2005). Voice, control, and belonging: The double-edged sword of procedural justice. *Annual Review of Law and Social Science, 1,* 171–201.

Macias, T. (2008). Conflict over forest resources in northern New Mexico: Rethinking cultural activism as a strategy for environmental justice. *The Social Science Journal, 45,* 61–75.

Maner, J. K., Gailliot, M. T., Butz, D. A., & Peruche, B. (2007). Power, risk, and the status quo: Does power promote riskier or more conservative decision making? *Personality and Social Psychology Bulletin, 33,* 451–462. doi:10.1177/0146167206297405.

Major, B., & Adams, J. B. (1983). Role of gender, interpersonal orientation, and self-presentation in distributive-justice behavior. *Journal of Personality and Social Psychology, 45,* 598–608.

Major, B., Bylsma, W. H., & Cozzarelli, C. (1989). Gender differences in distributive justice preferences: The impact of domain. *Sex Roles, 7/8,* 487–497.

Major, B., Gramzow, R. H., McCoy, S., Levin, S., Schmader, T., & Sidanius, J. (2002). Perceiving personal discrimination: The role of group status and legitimizing ideology. *Journal of Personality and Social Psychology, 82,* 269–282.

Maner, J. K., & Mead, N. L. (2010). The essential tension between leadership and power: When leaders sacrifice group goals for the sake of self-interest. *Journal of Personality and Social Psychology, 99,* 482–497. doi:10.1037/a0018559.

Marmor, T. R., Machaw, J. L., & Harvey, P. L. (1990). *America's misunderstood welfare state.* New York: Basic Books.

Marshall, S., Adams, G. R., & Ryan, B. A. (2001). Distributive justice reasoning in families with adolescents. *Journal of Family Issues, 22,* 107–123.

Matania, E., & Yaniv, I. (2007). Resource priority, fairness, and equality-efficiency compromises. *Social Justice Research, 20,* 497–510.

McClelland, D. C. (1975). *Power: The inner experience*. New York: Irvington.

McClelland, D. C. (1987). *Human motivation*. Cambridge: Cambridge University Press.

McCoy, S. K., & Major, B. (2007). Priming meritocracy and the psychological justification of inequality. *Journal of Experimental Social Psychology, 43,* 341–351.

McGregor, H., Lieberman, J., Greenberg, J., Solomon, S., Arndt, J., Simon, L., & Pyszczynski, T. (1998). Terror management and aggression: Evidence that mortality salience motivates aggression against worldview threatening others. *Journal of Personality and Social Psychology, 74,* 590–605.

Michelbach, P., Scott, J., Matland, R. & Bornstein, B. (2003). Doing Rawls justice: An experimental study of distributive justice norms. *American Journal of Political Science, 47,* 523–539.

Milgram, S. (1975). *Obedience to authority*. New York: Harper & Row.

Miller, D. (1999). *Principles of social justice*. Cambridge: Harvard University Press.

Miller, J. G., & Bersoff, D. M. (1992). Culture and moral judgment: How are conflicts between justice and interpersonal responsibilities resolved? *Journal of Personality and Social Psychology, 62,* 541–554.

Mitchell, G., Tetlock, P. E., Mellers, B. A., & Ordóñez, L. D. (1993). Judgments of social justice: Compromises between equality and efficiency. *Journal of Personality and Social Psychology, 65,* 629–639.

Montada, L. (2003). Justice, equity, and fairness in human relations. In T. Millon & M. J. Lerner (Eds.), *Handbook of psychology: Personality and social psychology* (Vol. 5, pp. 532–568). Hoboken: Wiley.

Moore, C. (2009). Fairness in children's resource allocation depends on the recipient. *Psychological Science, 20,* 944–948.

Mischel, W. (1968). Personality and assessment. New York: Wiley.

Murphy-Berman, V., & Berman, J. J. (2002). Cross-cultural differences in perceptions of distributive justice: A comparison of Hong Kong and Indonesia. *Journal of Cross-Cultural Psychology, 33,* 157–170.

Ng, S. H. (1980). *The social psychology of power*. London: Academic.

Ordóñez, L., & Mellers, B. A. (1993). Trade-offs in fairness and preference judgments. In B. A. Mellers & J. Baron (Eds.), *Psychological perspectives on justice: Theory and applications* (pp. 138–154). Cambridge: Cambridge University Press.

Overbeck, J. R., & Park, B. (2001). When power does not corrupt: Superior individuation processes among powerful perceivers. *Journal of Personality and Social Psychology, 81,* 549–565.

Paul, E.F., Miller, F.D., & Paul, J. (2006). *Taxation, economic prosperity, and distributive justice*. Cambridge: Cambridge University Press.

Pratto, F., Pearson, A., Lee, I., & Saguy, T. (2008). Power dynamics in an experimental game. *Social Justice Research, 21,* 377–407.

Ramamoorthy, N., & Flood, P. C. (2004). Gender and employee attitudes: The role of organizational justice perceptions. *British Journal of Management, 15,* 247–258.

Rasinski, K.A. (1987). What's fair is fair-or is it? Value differences underlying public views about social justice. *Journal of Personality and Social Psychology, 53,* 201–211.

Rawls, J. (1971). *A theory of justice*. Cambridge: Belknap Press of Harvard University Press.

Rimor, M., & Tobin, G. A. (1990). Jewish giving patterns to Jewish and Non-Jewish philanthropy. In R. Wuthnow & V. A. Hodgkinson (Eds.), *Faith and philanthropy in America*. San Francisco: Jossey-Bass.

Roper, S. D., & Barria, L.A. (2007). Gatekeeping versus allocating in foreign assistance: Donor motivations and contributions to war crimes tribunals. *Journal of Conflict Resolution, 51,* 285–304.

Russell, B. (1938). *Power: A new social analysis*. London: Allen and Unwin.

Sabbagh, C. (2002). A taxonomy of normative and empirically oriented theories of distributive justice. *Social Justice Research, 14,* 237–265.

Sabbagh, C. (2003). Evaluating society's "spheres of justice": The Israeli case. *Social Psychology Quarterly, 66,* 254–271.
Sabbagh, C., Dar, Y., & Resh, N. (1994). The structure of social justice judgments: A facet approach. *Social Psychology Quarterly, 57,* 244–261.
Sabbagh, C., Resh, N., Mor, M., & van Huysse, P. (2006). Spheres of justice within schools: Reflections and evidence on the distribution of educational goods. *Social Psychology of Education, 9,* 97–118.
Sabbagh, C., & Schmidt, M. (1998). Exploring the structure of positive and negative justice judgments. *Social Justice Research, 11,* 381–396.
Saguy, T., Dovidio, J., & Pratto, F. (2008). Beyond contact: Intergroup contact in the context of power relations. *Personality and Social Psychology Bulletin, 34,* 432–445.
Schmid Mast, M., Jonas, K., & Hall, J. A. (2009). Give a person power and he or she will show interpersonal sensitivity: The phenomenon and its why and when. *Journal of Personality and Social Psychology, 97,* 835–850. doi:10.1037/a0016234.
Schroeder, D. A., Steel, J. E., Woodell, A. J., & Bembenek, A. F. (2003). Justice within social dilemmas. *Personality and Social Psychology Review, 7,* 374–387.
Scott, J. T., & Bornstein, B. H. (2009). What's fair in foul weather and fair? Distributive justice across different allocation contexts and goods. *Journal of Politics, 71,* 831–846.
Scott, J., Matland, R., Michelbaum, P., & Bornstein, B. (2001). Just deserts: An experimental approach to distributive justice. *American Journal of Political Science, 45,* 749–767.
Skitka, L. J. (2009). Exploring the "lost and found" of justice theory and research. *Social Justice Research, 22,* 98–116.
Skitka, L. J., & Crosby, F. J. (2003). Trends in the social psychological study of justice. *Personality and Social Psychology Review, 7,* 282–285.
Skitka, L. & Tetlock, P. (1992). Allocating scare resources: A contingency model of distributive justice. *Journal of Experimental Social Psychology, 28,* 1205–1223.
Skitka, L.J., Winquist, J., & Hutchinson, S. (2003). Are outcome fairness and outcome favorability distinguishable psychological constructs? A meta-analytic review. *Social Justice Research, 16,* 309–341.
Smith, P. K., Jostmann, N. B., Galinsky, A. D., & Van Dijk, W. W. (2008). Lacking power impairs executive functions. *Psychological Science, 19,* 441–447.
Smith, P. K., & Trope, Y. (2006). You focus on the forest when you're in charge of the trees: Power priming and abstract information processing. *Journal of Personality and Social Psychology, 90,* 578–596.
Sweeney, P. D., & McFarlin. D. B. (1997) Process and outcome: Gender differences in the assessment of justice. *Journal of Organizational Behavior, 18,* 83–98.
Tajfel, H. (1970). Experiments in intergroup discrimination. *Scientific American, 223,* 96–102.
Tajfel, H., & Turner, J. C. (1979). An integrative theory of intergroup conflict. In W. G. Austin & S. Worchel (Eds.), *The social psychology of intergroup relations* (pp. 33–47). Monterey: Brooks/Cole.
Tam, K.-P., Chiu, C.-Y., & Lau, I. Y.-M. (2007). Terror management among Chinese: Worldview defence and intergroup bias in resource allocation. *Asian Journal of Social Psychology, 10,* 93–102.
Tata, J. (2000). Influence of role and gender on the use of distributive versus procedural justice principles. *Journal of Psychology: Interdisciplinary and Applied, 134,* 261–268.
Tesser, A., & Smith, J. (1980). Some effects of friendship and task relevance on helping: You don't always help the one you like. *Journal of Experimental Social Psychology, 16,* 583–590.
Thibaut, J., & Kelley, H. (1959). *The social psychology of groups*. Oxford: Wiley.
Triandis, H. C. & Gelfand, M. J. (1998). Converging measurement of horizontal and vertical individualism and collectivism. *Journal of Personality and Social Psychology, 74,* 118–128.
Tyler, T. R. (1994). Psychological models of the justice motive: Antecedents of distributive and procedural justice. *Journal of Personality and Social Psychology, 67,* 850–863.
Tyler, T. R. (2006). *Why people obey the law*. Princeton: Princeton University Press. (Reissue; originally published in 1990).

Tyler, T. R., Boeckmann, R. J., Smith, H. J., & Huo, Y. J. (1997). *Social justice in a diverse society*. Boulder: Westview.
van Dijk, E., & Vermunt, R. (2000). Strategy and fairness in social decision making: Sometimes it pays to be powerless. *Journal of Experimental Social Psychology, 36,* 1–25.
van Dijk, E., Wilke, H., Wilke, M., & Metman, L. (1999). What information do we use in social dilemmas? Environmental uncertainty and the employment of coordination rules. *Journal of Experimental Social Psychology, 35,* 109–135.
van Dijke, M., & Poppe, M. (2006). Striving for personal power as a basis for social power dynamics. *European Journal of Social Psychology, 36,* 537–556.
Van Vugt, M. (2006). Evolutionary origins of leadership and followership. *Personality and Social Psychology Review, 10,* 354–371. doi:10.1207/s15327957pspr1004_5.
Vescio, T. K., Gervais, S. J., Heidenreich, S., & Snyder, M. (2006). The effects of prejudice level and social influence strategy on stereotypic responding to racial outgroups. *European Journal of Social Psychology, 36,* 435–450. (Special Issue on Power).
Vescio, T. K., Gervais, S. J., Snyder, M., & Hoover, A. (2005). Power and the creation of patronizing environments: The stereotype-based behaviors of the powerful and their effects on female performance in masculine domains. *Journal of Personality and Social Psychology, 88,* 658–672.
Walzer, M. (1983). *Spheres of justice: A defense of pluralism and equality*. New York: Basic Books.
Watson, D., Clark, L. A., & Tellegen, A. (1988). Development and validation of brief measures of positive and negative affect: The PANAS scale. *Journal of Personality and Social Psychology, 54,* 1063–1070. doi:10.1037/0022-3514.54.6.1063.
Wicker, A.W. (1969). Attitudes vs. actions: The relationship of verbal and overt behavioral responses to attitude objects. *Journal of Social Issues, 25,* 41–78.
Winter, D. G. (1973). *The power motive*. New York: Free Press.
Winter, D. G. (1988). The power motive in women and men. *Journal of Personality and Social Psychology, 54,* 510–519.

# Chapter 2
# Cutting Your Cake and Having It Too: Or, Is Equality a Distributive Justice Principle?

**John T. Scott**

Equality has almost universally been treated as a distributive justice or allocation principle in empirical studies of justice beliefs and behavior. Much of this empirical research has been influenced by Deutsch (1975, 1985), who argues that equality is one of the three principles of justice, along with equity and need. Researchers in this field have often also turned to the history of philosophy in order to confirm the pedigree of equality as a justice principle, going back at least as far as Aristotle and also drawing on more contemporary philosophers such as Rawls (1971), Miller (1999), and Dworkin (2000) to understand the role of equality in justice. Certainly, equality is a strong norm in contemporary democratic societies such as the USA where we imbibe the principle of the Declaration of Independence telling us, "We hold these truths to be self-evident, that all men are created equal…," and where social and economic justice movements appeal to the principle of equality when decrying the inequalities we see around us. Indeed, the norm of equality has been progressively expanded from arguments for equality of rights to equality of conditions (Dahl 1989). In short, equality remains the presumptive principle in nearly all modern theories of justice, as well as a central norm in debates over democracy, the social welfare state, and the distribution of income and other goods (Weale 1985).

But is equality actually a distributive justice principle? Or, less strongly, to what extent and under what conditions do individuals employ equality as a distributive justice principle? The goal of this chapter is to raise this question and, at minimum, to provide enough evidence to suggest that we should take the question seriously. In order to do so, I first reexamine some representative treatments of equality in the history of philosophy, specifically those by Aristotle, Hobbes, and Rawls. In doing so, I make two broad claims. First, I show that equality does not in fact play a central role in these political and moral theories, even theories such as Hobbes'

J. T. Scott (✉)
Department of Political Science, University of California-Davis,
683 Kerr Hall, Davis, CA 95616, USA
e-mail: jtscott@ucdavis.edu

B. H. Bornstein, R. L. Wiener (eds.), *Justice, Conflict and Wellbeing*,
DOI 10.1007/978-1-4939-0623-9_2, 

where equality is asserted to be fundamental. Second, I argue that the conversion of distributive justice claims into procedural justice claims, first seen in Hobbes but brought to its culmination in Rawls, has the effect of privileging equality not as a distributive justice principle, but as a privileged outcome that is the result of treating the allocation problem as a procedural one. Or to put the second claim in particular more pithily: In theory and practice, justice as equality means being able to cut your cake and have it too.

With this reexamination of the role of equality in the history of philosophy in mind, I then turn to a few representative empirical studies of justice behavior in order to raise questions about what is actually going on when we see individuals behave in a way that *seems* to accord with the theoretical expectation that they are treating equality as a distributive justice principle and to suggest that they may not *actually* be doing so. Finally, I conclude with some reflections on the implications of this examination for the empirical study of justice beliefs and behavior and suggest some potentially fruitful lines of further research.

## A Brief History of Equality

"Equality" seems at first to be a straightforward and simple concept, but upon examination it turns out to be devilishly complicated. The entry on "equality" in the *Stanford Encyclopedia of Philosophy* admits this complexity from the outset: "In its prescriptive usage, 'equality' is a loaded and 'highly contested' concept" (Gosepath 2011; quoting Dworkin 2000, p. 2). The article proceeds to disentangle the skein of equality, differentiating among formal equality, proportional equality, moral equality, and presumptive equality and then weaves these different strands through a survey of the role of equality of distribution. Working both within and against the highly influential framework of Rawls' *Theory of Justice* (1971; see Daniels 2003), numerous philosophers have tried to articulate precisely what we should equalize, whether equality of resources or "basic goods" (Rawls 1971; Dworkin 1981), equality of opportunity or access to advantage (Cohen 1989; Arneson 1990; Roemer 1998), moral capabilities (Williams 1973), or equality of capabilities more tangibly considered (Sen 1992; Nussbaum 1992, 2000). This complexity of "equality" has led some scholars either to worry about the confusion they believe reigns in people's minds over what they hold to be equal or to accept this confusion as complexity. For example, Hochshild (1981) concludes that Americans confusedly entertain different senses of the term simultaneously. In turn, Rae (1981) decides to speak in the plural rather than the singular, of "equalities" rather than "equality," whereas Sen (1992) begins his work on welfare economics by first asking "Equality of What?"

Part of this complexity, if not confusion, concerning equality is due to the polyvalent character of the word "equality" itself. This polyvalence can be seen clearly in the Greek term *isos,* which means both "fair" and "equal." As Aristotle writes in his examination of distributive justice: "If, then, the unjust is unequal [or: unfair], the just is equal [or: fair], which is in fact what is held to be the case by everyone, even without argument" (*Nicomachean Ethics* 5.3.1131a (2011, p. 95)).[1] I will turn to Aristotle's argument momentarily, but for now it suffices to note that "equality" can mean, at minimum, either absolute or numerical equality or proportional equality. That is, two things can be absolutely equal, as Smith and Jones receiving US$ 100 each in a given distribution, or proportionately equal, as Smith receiving US$ 200 and Jones receiving US$ 100 where Smith has for example done twice as much work as Jones or owns twice as many shares in a company. This dual meaning of *isos* is central to Aristotle's theory, but whereas he offers a certain order or solution to the problem that takes advantage of the two senses, ambiguity—intentional or unintentional—pervades both theoretical and empirical examinations of equality. This ambiguity is part of what lies behind Rae's (1981) "equalities" and Sen's (1992) "Equality of What?" It is likewise seen in the empirical literature, sometimes directly inspired by Aristotle (e.g., Mellers 1982), where the term "equality," meaning the principle that outcomes should be proportional to inputs (as reward proportionate to contribution), is used instead of the potential synonyms "desert" or "merit" (e.g., Adams 1965; Deutsch 1975, 1985; Messick and Cook 1983). Since the term "equity" can also mean "equality," the ambiguity of usage that stems in part from the polyvalent character of the term "equality" has perhaps needlessly, even if understandably, led to confusion.

A full analysis of the theoretical debate over the term "equality" is not my purpose here. Rather, the purpose of the present analysis is to question the role of "equality" as a distributive justice principle in both the history of philosophy and in empirical justice research, so I will restrict my analysis to "equality" as absolute or numerical equality: 1 = 1, 100 = 100, etc. Indeed, one result of this analysis will be to show how over the course of the history of philosophy the proportional sense of equality (or equity or desert) is quietly subsumed within the absolute sense of equality. By beginning with the absolute sense of the term, we will be in a position to witness this transformation.

## *Aristotle on Inequality*

The title of this section is not "Aristotle on Equality" for a simple reason: Aristotle in many respects begins from the assumption or observation of *inequality* rather than *equality* among human beings. In this regard, Aristotle might even be said to be representative of premodern thought in general. This characterization of Aristotle is too strong, and I will point out places where he is arguably more egalitarian than we might at first think, but it is not entirely misleading. Further, since Hobbes later characterizes his predecessor as privileging inequality, this characterization of Aristotle is useful for analyzing how Hobbes and other modern philosophers have transformed the relationship between equality and distributive justice, in large part in direct opposition to Aristotle.

[1] Subsequent references to Aristotle's *Nichomachean Ethics* will include only the standard referents to book, chapter, and Bekker page number.

The pervasiveness of inequality in Aristotle's philosophy is signaled from the outset of his *Politics*, where he outlines the various "partnerships" (*koinônia*) that make up the city or *polis*: man and woman, parent and child, and, most tellingly, master and slave. Aristotle articulates a central principle of his approach to human things when he explains with reference to master and slave that there is "naturally ruling and ruled," for "that which can foresee with the mind is the naturally ruling and naturally mastering element, while that which can do these things with the body is the naturally ruled and slave" (*Politics* I.2.1252a (1984, p. 36)).[2] This argument is part of Aristotle's more general position concerning natural rule, which is ultimately derived from his teleological theory of nature: "For whatever is constituted out of a number of things—whether continuous"—e.g., soul and body in an individual human being—"or discrete"—e.g., master and slave—"and becomes a single common thing, always displays a ruling and ruled element" (1.5.1254a). In his ensuing discussion of natural slavery, Aristotle defines the natural slave in the following terms: "one who does not belong to himself by nature but is another's, though a human being, is by nature a slave" (1.4.1254a). Likewise, he concludes: "Accordingly, those who are as different from other men as the soul from the body or man from beast—and they are in this state if their work is the use of the body, and if this is the best that can come from them—are slaves by nature" (1.5.1254b).

Note that Aristotle's definition of the natural slave is not a statement about the actual existence of such beings, but a definition of what such a being would be. While Aristotle does conclude that *some* human beings meet his definition (how many is not clear), he wields his argument concerning natural slavery *against* the existing practice of slavery, arguing explicitly that someone being a slave by *law*, whether through purchase or conquest in war, for example, does not mean that they are slaves by *nature* (1.6.1255a–b). In this light, Aristotle's remark at the outset of his discussion of natural slavery is telling: "Let us speak first about master and slave, so that we may see … whether we cannot acquire something in the way of knowledge about these things that is better than current conceptions" (1.3.1253b). The interpretation of Aristotle's position on natural slavery, and on similar subjects such as women, is hotly contested (see, e.g., Dobbs 1994). Nonetheless, even if the ultimate thrust of his argument concerning slavery is more egalitarian than it may at first appear, his fundamental position on relations of authority between natural unequals remains intact.

In what respects equality and inequality among humans are relevant for politics and morals becomes thematic in Aristotle's investigation of the various political regimes. Aristotle outlines the six forms of regime, or the authoritative form of the city that determines who is allowed to participate in the offices of the city or who is a citizen, in terms of the number of citizens (one, few, many) and whether the aim of the regime is "correct"—that is, oriented toward the common advantage—or

[2] Subsequent references to Aristotle's *Politics* will include only the standard referents to book, chapter, and Bekker page number. I have also eliminated the brackets included by the translator to indicate words or phrases which he interpolates to make Aristotle's highly compressed prose make sense in translation.

"deviant." The three deviant forms are tyranny, oligarchy (essentially, the rule of the rich), and democracy (essentially, the rule of the poor). The three correct forms are kingship, aristocracy, and what he terms "polity," which is the rule of the many in a proper way and in practice a mixed regime of democracy, oligarchy, and aristocracy (3.7–8.1279a–1280a). Each of these regimes, he argues, espouses a certain understanding of justice in terms of competing notions of equality and inequality.

In order to examine the different claims by these contenders for rule, and especially oligarchs and democrats, since they are the two regimes he claims are empirically pervasive, Aristotle frames and then examines their claims in terms of their arguments concerning justice.

> It is necessary first to grasp what they speak of as the defining principles of oligarchy and democracy and what justice is from both oligarchic and democratic points of view. For all fasten on a certain sort of justice, but proceed only to a certain point, and do not speak of the whole of justice in its authoritative sense. For example, justice is held to be equality, and it is, but for equals and not for all; and inequality is held to be just and is indeed, but for unequals and not for all; but they disregard this element of persons and judge badly. The cause of this is that the judgment concerns them selves, and most people are bad judges concerning their own things (3.9.1280a).

In other words, both oligarchs and democrats are "partial" in the dispute, both in the sense of having a "partial" or interested point of view and in the sense of seeing only a part, and not the whole, of justice. In this context Aristotle references his treatise on ethics, to which I shall turn momentarily, but for the present he lets his claimants make their cases. "For the ones, if they are unequal in a certain thing, such as goods, suppose they are unequal generally, while the others suppose that if they are equal in a certain thing, such as freedom, they are equal generally. But of the most authoritative consideration they say nothing" (3.9.1280a). Aristotle explicitly rejects the oligarchs' claim, saying that their argument that their unequal possession of goods entitles them to an unequal share in rule would be correct if they were a joint business venture whose end was to make money, but it is incorrect because they mistake the end of the city (3.9.1280a). The end of the city is not "to live" but rather to "live well," meaning the full completion and exercise of human capacities, or "virtues," and thus happiness (3.9.1280b–1281a; see 1.2.1252b). Goods are necessary for "living," but they are only the necessary condition, if that, for the ultimate end of "living well." Aristotle does not explicitly reject the democrats' claim that their equal freedom entitles them to an equal share in ruling, but he would undoubtedly offer a similar argument about freedom being necessary but not sufficient for the true end of the political partnership. It is the aristocrats—aristocrats properly speaking, that is the virtuous—who in fact have the best claim to rule, but these just claimants do not tend to press their case (see 3.13.1283a). The theoretical argument for understanding justice in relation to political rule is clear: Those who are unequally suited to attaining the true end of the city, "living well," have the most just claim to rule. The case regarding merit that Aristotle raises in this context as being supposedly analogous is telling: "If someone were preeminent in flute playing … the outstanding flutes … ought to be given to him" (3.12.1282b–1283a). Thus, for Aristotle the just distribution of political power might in principle be quite unequal. Even if this conclusion is warranted in principle or in theory, however, it is superseded for Aristotle by the practical consideration that all but a vanishingly small number of cities contain elements (virtuous, rich, free) that have claims to participating in rule that are incommensurate in nature and are impractical or unsafe simply to ignore (3.12.1283a; 3.13.1283b). In sum, once again even if Aristotle's ultimate practical solution is to give equality its due in politics by advancing the democrats' case or by arranging for their participation in rule, the ultimate thrust of his argument concerning justice in political life is generally inegalitarian.

This brief examination of Aristotle's treatment in the political realm of justice understood as equality and inequality is useful for understanding how his conception of justice cashes out, and will also be useful when we turn to Hobbes in order to see how he challenges Aristotle's argument on behalf of equality. But it is Aristotle's systematic analysis of justice in the *Nicomachean Ethics* that is most important for understanding how he conceives the relationship between justice and equality. Aristotle's examination of the virtue of justice in the *Ethics* is rich and complex; and although the present analysis of how he conceives of justice in relation to equality will necessarily not do justice to his argument, it is still worth sketching out briefly.

At the outset of his discussion of justice in Book 5 of the *Ethics*, Aristotle remarks on the complexity of the concept, but he focuses immediately on the notion that justice is said to be a kind of equality and injustice a kind of inequality (5.1.1129a–b). Once again, in order to comprehend his point fully, we must recall that the word being translated as "equal" in this context is *isos,* which also means "fair." Since Aristotle casts his analysis of justice in mathematical terms, treating justice as a kind of middle term in a geometric proportion in the case of distributive justice or in an arithmetic proportion in the case of corrective justice, however, the sense of *isos* as "equal" is central to his discussion.

Distributive justice is Aristotle's first order of business, in large part because it is for him the most important consideration for politics and morals, and once again it is inequality, not equality, that is paramount. Aristotle describes distributive justice as a kind of geometric proportion between at least two things (people, goods, people and goods, etc.). In simplified form:

$$A{:}B :: c{:}d \quad \text{or} \quad \frac{c}{A}{:}\frac{d}{B}$$

Where $A$ and $B$ are persons, and $c$ and $d$ some sort of good. In this case, for example, if $A = 2B$, then $c = 2d$, *or* $A$ receives twice as much as $B$ of the relevant good. Alternatively, if $A =$ B, then $c = d$, *or* $A$ and $B$ receive an equal amount of the relevant good (3.3.1131a–b). The important thing to note with regard to Aristotle's discussion of distributive justice here is that equality is only a *special case* within a proportion that is otherwise not assumed to be equal. In other words, an equal distribution is just *only* in the case where the persons happen to be equal in the relevant respect. Equality understood as absolute or numerical equality has no privileged position in Aristotle's treatment of distributive justice, and in fact his treatment of distributive justice as a kind of proportion appears to assume inequality.

Equality does, however, play a central role in Aristotle's treatment of what he terms "corrective" justice. Corrective justice is either voluntary, as in commercial transactions or exchanges, or involuntary, as in punishing crimes. Rather than being akin to a geometric proportion, however, corrective justice is akin to an arithmetic proportion, which is concerned with absolute rather than proportional equality or differences in equality. "The just in transactions is a certain equality, and the unjust, a certain inequality, yet not in accord with the proportion just indicated but in accordance with an arithmetic one. For it makes no difference at all whether a decent person robs a base one, or a base person a decent one, or if a decent or a base person commits adultery. Rather, the law looks only at the difference that stems from the harm done, and it treats people as equals: if the one person acts unjustly, the other suffers injustice; and if the one did harm, the other was harmed" (5.4.1131b–1132a). Appealing to the sense of "unjust" as meaning "unequal," Aristotle treats corrective justice as one person creating an inequality through committing a wrong, for example when a thief robs someone of a certain amount of money so that the victim suffers a loss and the thief has an equivalent gain. This relationship might be represented in the following way:

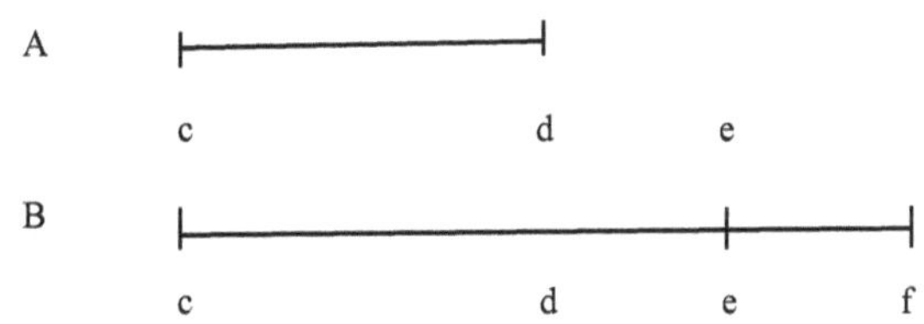


In this example, *A* and *B* are persons and the lines represent the amount of some good they each have after *B* has stolen a portion of *A's* amount of the good represented by the length of the line from e to f. *B's* theft has created an inequality where there was previously equality. The "just" thing to do in this case, then, would be to restore equality by restoring the portion of *B's* line from *e* to *f* to *A*. As Aristotle states, the law in this case is indifferent to any other attributes of the persons involved in the "transaction," *A* and *B*, and treats them both as equals. Aristotle examines "voluntary" exchanges such as commercial transactions in a similar way in this context, but the important point about this examination for the present analysis is that he similarly treats the two parties to the exchange as equals. Although Aristotle does not develop a concept of procedural justice in this context, one might rearticulate his theory of "corrective" justice in this manner, with the key point being that procedural justice likewise treats the parties to a dispute or a transaction as equals. Recasting his theory in this way helps prepare us for grasping the transformation of distributive and procedural justice that will happen in Hobbes' hands.

## *Hobbes on Equality*

If Aristotle's philosophy is premised on inequality, then Hobbes is perhaps the first philosopher to premise his thought on equality. Or so it seems at first. Closer examination of Hobbes' position on equality and justice reveals that his argument for equality is deceptive and is instead advanced for political purposes rather than as a substantive argument, or at least not as the substantive argument he initially seems to advance. Likewise, and related, his argument concerning distributive justice is meant to evacuate inegalitarian claims concerning justice, such as those found in Aristotle, of any meaning or force, again for political purposes. Hobbes instead converts essentially controversial and irresolvable questions of distributive justice into issues of procedural justice that take individuals as equal and are resolvable as matters of simple exchange or sovereign will or law.

Hobbes begins his famous chapter in *Leviathan* (1651) "Of the Natural Condition of Mankind" with a seemingly straightforward argument for the natural equality of human beings: "Nature hath made men so equal…" (1994 [1651], p. 74). The consequences of this argument are monumental: our natural equality contributes to making the state of nature a state of "war of all against all;" every human has an equal and unlimited right to self-preservation, and therefore the way out of the state of nature is a contract of everyone with everyone to relinquish those rights and obey a sovereign that has authority to make laws which everyone is obliged to obey. Many of these arguments are directed at Aristotle, for Hobbes denies that any particular human being has a natural authority or just claim to rule over others due to virtue or some other quality. He likewise asserts that "there is no such *Finis ultimus* (utmost aim) nor *Summum Bonum* (greatest good) as is spoken of in the books of the old moral philosophers" (1994 [1651], p. 57), Aristotle foremost among them. He thereby challenges Aristotle's teleological theory of nature, human nature, and politics, thus robbing anyone of the claim that they merit being rulers because they are most able to achieve the proper end of the political association, for there is no such end. Finally, and to similar effect, Hobbes denies Aristotle's claim that humans are by nature political animals (1994 [1651], p. 108). All this is true about Hobbes, but none of it is ultimately premised on an argument for human equality. Indeed, Hobbes' actual argument concerning human equality never establishes this equality, at least in the way it first seems. A closer examination of his argument is therefore necessary.

Hobbes' argument for equality comprises the first two paragraphs of the chapter "Of the Natural Condition of Mankind." He begins:

> Nature hath made men so equal in the faculties of body and mind as that, though there be found one man sometimes manifestly stronger in body or of quicker mind than another, yet when all is reckoned together the difference between man and man is not so considerable as that one man can thereupon claim to himself any benefit to which another may not pretend as well as he. For as to the strength of body, the weakest has strength enough to kill the strongest, either by secret machination, or by confederacy with others that are in the same danger with himself. (1994 [1651], p. 74)

Note first that Hobbes actually admits inequality of both body and mind: "though there be found one man sometimes manifestly stronger in body or of quicker mind than another…." His point, then, is not that humans are equal, but that the inequality among them does not matter decisively. No one is so unequal as to be able to "claim" anything for himself that everyone else might not claim. Or, to put this in the strongest possible terms, the terms Hobbes later uses in describing the state of nature: "in such a condition every man has a right to everything, even to one another's body" (1994 [1651], p. 80). In other words, every human has an equal natural right to everything, and therefore no one individual has an exclusive right or "claim" to anything—even himself! Hobbes thereby evacuates natural right or justice of any specific claim to anything. Hobbes' argument concerning our equality in terms of our bodies is likewise not quite what it at first seems. For while admitting inequalities in bodily strength, his point is that despite these inequalities everyone is equally physically *vulnerable,* that is, vulnerable to being killed. If fear of violent death is the greatest fear, according to Hobbes, then everyone ought to be equally afraid. Anyone who is not so afraid, for example because he is so prideful as to consider himself as so unequal in body or mind so as not to be vulnerable, is deceiving himself.

Having established our equal claim to everything and our equal physical vulnerability, Hobbes turns in the second paragraph to the qualities of mind:

> And as to the faculties of the mind– setting aside the arts grounded upon words, and especially … science (which very few have, and but in few things), as being not a native faculty (born with us), nor attained (as prudence) while we look after somewhat else– I find yet a greater equality amongst men than that of strength. For prudence is but experience, which equal time equally bestows on all men in those things they equally apply themselves unto…. (1994 [1651], pp. 74–75)

Note again that Hobbes does not argue that humans are in fact equal in mind, for at least some people acquire science and therefore potentially much great power of mind. Science is not a "native faculty," however, and Hobbes seems to imply that naturally all humans' mental faculties are equal before any acquisitions. However, in his discussion of intellectual virtues a few chapters earlier, he notes that people's minds differ in their quickness or "celerity" for various reasons (1994 [1651], p. 38). All humans are therefore not as equal in mental faculties as Hobbes seems at first to argue. His position on prudence, which seems to be directed at Aristotle in particular, is curious, for it seems an odd claim that prudence is simply experience, "which equal time equally bestows on all men in those things they equally apply themselves unto." His claim would make sense, however, if we take him quite literally as saying that individuals would *in principle* be equally prudent *if* they have equal "time" or experiences and especially *if* they equally apply their minds to matters requiring prudence. This position would be reconcilable with our actual experience that individuals are not in fact equally prudent. However this may be, the continuation of this passage is quite revealing about Hobbes' actual argument:

> … That which may make such equality incredible is but a vain conceit of one's own wisdom, which almost all men think they have in a greater degree than the vulgar, that is, than all men but themselves…. For they see their own wit at hand, and other men's at a distance. But this proveth rather that men are in that point equal, than unequal. For there is not ordinarily a greater sign of the equal distribution of anything than that every man is contented with his share. (1994 [1651], p. 75)

Rather than this proving that humans are in fact equal instead of unequal in terms of mind, Hobbes has in fact established that they are equally *vain.*[3]

In short, in his argument for equality, Hobbes has actually established that humans are equal in having an equal claim to everything, being equally vulnerable to death, and being equally vain. It is therefore no coincidence that, after this argument, Hobbes identifies the three principal causes that make the state of nature a state of war of all against all: competition, diffidence, and glory (1994 [1651], p. 75). These three causes of quarrel directly parallel the three respects in which humans are actually equal: There is competition in principle among humans because they all have an equal claim to everything; humans are "diffident" (that is, wary such that they anticipate threats and strike first) because they are equally vulnerable; and they are equally glory-seeking or prideful because they are equally vain about their own capacities. All of this is not to deny that Hobbes' actual arguments concerning human equality have no bearing, for they certainly do. They have a crucial bearing in at least two ways. First, the natural right of everyone to everything carries with it the proposition that no one has any natural authority over anyone else, which means that authority comes from contract, not nature, which is crucial to Hobbes' theory (and opposed to Aristotle's theory). Second, equal vulnerability and equal vanity are aspects of human nature that Hobbes believes we must acknowledge in order to be amenable to his solution of the social contract. The present point is that Hobbes does not actually argue what he at first seems to with regard to human equality, namely, that we are equal in some substantial way.

Why, then, does Hobbes offer a misleading argument about human equality? His purpose in doing so is one of necessity: in order to achieve the political outcome he believes necessary for the relief of man's natural estate. This purpose becomes clear two chapters later in his discussion of the laws of nature. "The question 'who is the better man?' has no place in the condition of mere nature, where (as has been shewn before) all men are equal," Hobbes begins his discussion of the sixth law of nature, against pride. He then reveals that it is Aristotle he is opposing: "I know that *Aristotle* (in the first book of his Politics, for a foundation of his doctrine) maketh men by nature, some more worthy to command (meaning the wiser sort, such as he thought himself to be for his philosophy), others to serve …, as if master and servant were not introduced by consent of men, but by difference of wit; which is not only against reason, but also against experience." Hobbes is referring to Aristotle's argument concerning natural slavery, and putting aside the ad hominem attack and unfair characterization of Aristotle's argument (whether he is aware that it is unfair

[3] Descartes makes the same misleading argument at the beginning of Part One of his *Discourse on Method.*

is unclear), Hobbes' main point is clear: Humans are naturally equal, not unequal. Nonetheless, Hobbes' phrasing of the conclusion of the argument seems to undermine the supposed premise: "*If* nature therefore have made men equal, that equality is to be acknowledged; or *if* nature have made men unequal, yet because men that think themselves equal will not enter into conditions of peace but upon equal terms, such equality must be admitted" (1994 [1651], pp. 96–97; emphasis added). In other words, *if* by nature humans are in fact unequal rather than equal, and we have good reason to believe they are, we should nonetheless "admit" such equality—that is, pretend that we are equal—in order to enter into the social contract that will get us out of the state of nature. Differently put, Hobbes must deny claims about human inequality and assert claims about human equality, even against the facts, because his political solution is threatened by those individuals who refuse to acknowledge their equality.

With Hobbes' deceptive argument concerning equality in mind, then, we can now turn to how he re-characterizes distributive justice. His examination of distributive justice also comes in his discussion of the laws of nature, specifically in his treatment of the third law of nature dictating equity:

> Justice of actions is by writers divided into *commutative* and *distributive*; and the former they say consisteth in proportion arithmetical; the latter in proportion geometrical. Commutative, therefore, they place in the equality of value of things contracted for; and distributive, in the distribution of equal benefit to men of equal merit (as if it were injustice to sell dearer than we buy, or to give more to a man than he merits)…. (1994 [1651], p. 94)

So far, Hobbes offers a brief and reasonable summary of Aristotle's understanding of distributive and commutative justice, or what was referred to above as "corrective" justice, but at least two things are already noteworthy. First, in characterizing distributive justice, Hobbes emphasizes equality ("equal benefit to men of equal merit") rather than, as in Aristotle, inequality. Second, his concluding parenthetical statement has a deflationary effect that will take over his discussion, for he snidely wonders why anyone would say it is unjust to offer too much for something in an exchange (the assumption being that offering too little is not an unjust offer but rather an offer that will not be accepted) and, more importantly, why anyone would say that it is unjust to give someone more than he merits (begging the question of whether it is unjust to offer someone less than he merits). The continuation makes it clearer where Hobbes is going with this:

> The value of all things contracted for is measured by the appetite of the contractors; and therefore the just value is that which they be contented to give. And merit (besides that which is by covenant, where the performance on one part meriteth the performance of the other part, and falls under justice commutative, not distributive) is not due by justice, but is rewarded of grace only. (1994 [1651], p. 94)

Hobbes thus transforms both distributive and commutative justice as they are understood by Aristotle. As for commutative justice, Hobbes transforms it into a matter of simple exchange, or a part of a much larger whole in Aristotle's discussion, and argues that such exchanges are not a matter of justice at all, but rather of the appetite of the contractors. The transformation of distributive justice is even more thoroughgoing. He first divides "merit" in two: that which is by covenant or contract and that which is done by "grace," namely the "grace" or free will of the sovereign. As for that part by covenant or contract, Hobbes argues that what is at issue is performance of contract by the parties, and that is equivalent to a kind of exchange and therefore not a matter of distributive justice at all. As for what remains of distributive justice, Hobbes argues that it is not a matter of justice either, but rather of the sovereign's unconstrained will or "grace." He completes his argument against Aristotle's distinction between distributive and commutative justice in this way:

> And therefore this distinction, in the sense wherein it used to be expounded is not right. To speak properly, commutative justice is the justice of a contractor, that is, a performance of covenant (in buying and selling, hiring and letting to hire…). And distributive justice is the justice of an arbitrator, that is to say, the act of defining what is just. (1994 [1651], p. 95)

What remains of distributive justice, then, is what Hobbes terms "the justice of an arbitrator," and principally "defining what is just," that is, making law. Since laws must be general in form and application for all citizens, according to Hobbes, distributive justice is simply what is properly speaking "equity," which dictates that individuals should be treated as equals.

In short, Hobbes has eliminated distributive justice as a cause for contention in politics, whereas it is perhaps *the* cause of conflict in politics for Aristotle. He has done so by effectively turning matters of distributive justice into matters of "corrective" justice, to use Aristotle's terminology, where the parties to an exchange or dispute are considered as equals. Differently put, Hobbes has converted matters of distributive justice, in which inequality is a persistent issue, into matters of procedural justice, where equality is presumed. Hobbes has effectively tried to sidestep the issues of inequality and distributive justice. Out of the hat of inequality, Hobbes has managed to pull the rabbit of equality.

## *Rawls on Pure Procedural Justice*

Hobbes' magic trick is successful because he misdirects his audience through a misleading argument about human equality, but his act is completed without the devilish glee by his successors within the liberal tradition of political and moral philosophy. In order to see something like the dénouement of this story, a brief examination of John Rawls will suffice. Rawls' *Theory of Justice*, first published in 1971, has proved to be the most influential work of political philosophy in the twentieth century and so far in the twenty-first century, at least in Anglo-American analytic philosophy, and so his theory may be taken for the present purposes as representative. In addition, Rawls is a useful place to conclude this examination of the relationship between distributive justice and equality because a number of scholars have attempted to test his propositions empirically (see Frohlich and Oppenheimer 1992; Mitchell et al. 1993; Michelbach et al. 2003). Rather than attempting to do justice to Rawls' theory of justice, for the present purposes I want to focus only on certain aspects of how it may be seen as the culmination of Hobbes' elision of inegalitarian claims with regard to distributive justice and his effective incorporation of distributive justice into procedural justice.

The basic outlines of Rawls' theory of justice are well-known. Rawls sees his theory as a continuation of the social contract tradition that includes Locke, Rousseau, and Kant (Rawls 1971, p. 11), and we might add Hobbes (even if Rawls says doing so "raises special problems" (Rawls 1971, p. 11 n.)). He terms his approach "justice as fairness, a theory of justice that generalizes and carries to a higher level of abstraction the traditional conception of the social contract." He explains: "The compact of society is replaced by an initial situation that incorporates certain procedural constraints on arguments designed to lead to an original agreement on principles of justice" (Rawls 1971, p. 3). Note the "procedural constraints," a point to which I shall return. This initial situation Rawls terms "the original position," or "the original position of equality," a hypothetical situation "characterized so as to lead to a certain conception of justice" (Rawls 1971, p. 12). In the "original position," we are to imagine ourselves as equal individuals deciding on the principles of justice by which we will govern ourselves in society, but without any substantive knowledge about our class position or social status, our natural assets and abilities, or even our conception of the good. Rawls terms this procedure of choosing principles of justice behind "a veil of ignorance" such that "no one is advantaged or disadvantaged in the choice of principles by the outcome of natural chance or the contingency of social circumstances (Rawls 1971). This last statement is later expanded by Rawls with an argument that the natural or other inequalities we possess are "arbitrary from a moral point of view," so that the unequal consequences of those unequal circumstances and abilities are undeserved or unmerited (Rawls 1971, p. 15). Finally, Rawls argues that these equal individuals in the "original position" will choose a set of lexically ordered principles of justice: First, equality of right to the most extensive basic liberty consistent with a similar liberty for others; second, an arrangement of any social and economic inequalities that may result from this liberty such that they are to the advantage of the "least well off," or what Rawls terms the "difference principle"; third, that positions and office are open to all, or the principle of "fair equality of opportunity" (Rawls 1971, p. 60). Rawls expands on all of these claims at length, both within the *Theory of Justice* and in his later works (see Rawls 1993, 1999, 2001), and there is a vast scholarly literature debating, criticizing, and defending all of these claims and their implications, but this summary will suffice for the present purposes.

Perhaps most noteworthy about Rawls' strategy for the present purposes is the fact that the whole set-up of the "original position" and the "veil of ignorance" is a procedural method that presumes equality of individuals. Let us begin with the presumption of equality. Rawls later defends his initial assumption of equality as follows: "It seems reasonable to suppose that the parties in the original position are equal. That is, all have the same rights in the procedure for choosing principles; each can make proposals, submit reasons for their acceptance, and so on. Obviously, the purpose of these conditions is to represent equality between human beings as moral persons, as creatures having a conception of their good and capable of a sense of justice" (1971, p. 19). This formal equality of individuals says nothing about actual inequalities among them, whether natural or acquired. As for those, as noted, Rawls argues that such inequalities and their results are "arbitrary from a moral point of view." All of these qualities are, Rawls contends, the result of a "natural lottery" that has no moral bearing (Rawls 1971, pp. 73–74). Rawls thus admits inequalities among humans, but denies that they have a bearing for morality or justice; he sweeps aside Aristotle's understanding of distributive justice. The results of these unequal qualities do, however, have a bearing for society as a whole, according to Rawls. The outcomes of these unequal attributes, even the extra earnings of those who work harder (as the desire and willingness to work harder is also, according to Rawls, the result of a natural lottery), are allowable only insofar as they benefit the "least advantaged" members of society. The results of unequal attributes are a matter of efficiency, not justice. Like Hobbes, Rawls aims to make inequality irrelevant as a moral claim within distributive justice and instead posits equality as the presumptive fact about human beings, although he does so with less finesse and seemingly with less appreciation for the alternative.

With Rawls' position on equality in mind, we can turn to the procedural character of his enterprise. The thrust of his strategy perhaps comes to light most clearly within his discussion of the last principle of justice that he argues will be adopted behind the "veil of ignorance," fair equality of opportunity. In his discussion of fair equality of opportunity, Rawls argues that the theory of justice as fairness suggests "the idea of treating the question of distributive shares as a matter of pure procedural justice" (1971, pp. 84–85). Rawls explains what he means by "pure procedural justice" by contrasting it to "perfect and imperfect procedural justice." "Perfect procedural justice" is where the procedure adopted for distribution directly implies a specific resulting distribution, or, more accurately, where there is a result that is pre-determined to be fair and the procedure is chosen accordingly. The classic example of "perfect procedural justice" is the division of a piece of cake: One person cuts and the other person chooses, with the presumptively just result being an equal division. "Imperfect procedural justice" is where a procedure is adopted beforehand without a determinant resulting distribution, such as in a criminal trial, where the defendant may or may not be justly condemned or acquitted. By contrast with these two other forms of procedural justice, "pure procedural justice" is where there is no pre-determined resulting distribution but where whatever distribution that results is regarded as being just or fair because it is a result of the procedure. Rawls adduces gambling as an example: As long as the procedures for the game are followed the results are regarded as just or fair, regardless of the outcome (Rawls 1971, pp. 85–86).

Rawls claims that his principle of fair equality of opportunity, and perhaps his entire approach to distributive justice, is akin to "pure procedural justice." If we grant him this, then the presumption is still one of equality within a procedural treatment of justice. We might nonetheless wonder whether it is not more akin in certain crucial respects to "perfect procedural justice," that is, like cutting a piece of cake. By taking the hypothetical parties to the "original position" as equal and by asserting that any actual inequalities among them are morally arbitrary, Rawls adopts a procedure that in important respects privileges equality. This is arguably the case even where he defends inequality through the "difference principle," though with regard to its contribution to efficiency and not justice itself. In this regard, when discussing the difference principle he imagines a situation where all primary goods are equally distributed and states, "This state of affairs provides a benchmark for judging improvements" (1971, p. 62). Rawls is clearly uncomfortable with inequality, and many of his fellow philosophers have criticized him for not being egalitarian enough, even on his own terms (especially Cohen 2001; compare Nozick 1977). In short, one might characterize Rawls and many of his fellow contemporary liberals of pressing the revolution in how equality and distributive justice are understood to at least one of its logical conclusions, by wanting to cut their cake and have it too when it comes to equality.

## *Equality and Distributive Justice in Empirical Studies of Justice Behavior*

As noted at the outset, equality is almost universally treated as a distributive justice or allocation principle in empirical studies of justice behavior over the past 50 years or so. Much of the scholarly literature within psychology and related work in political science, sociology, and elsewhere has been influenced by the work of Deutsch (1975, 1985). Deutsch opposed the then-dominant approach of equity theory, which analyzed distributive justice behavior and beliefs in terms of a proportion between inputs and outputs in an interaction (e.g., Adams 1965; Walster et al. 1973; Adams and Freedman 1976; Messick and Cook 1983), and instead proposed that distributive attitudes and behaviors could be explained by three principal distributive justice principles: equity, equality, and need. The "pluralist" approach advocated by Deutsch and others (e.g., Lerner 1974; Leventhal 1976; Mikula 1980; Schwinger 1980; Konow 2001) has, in its turn, largely dominated the experimental research into distributive justice. In the thousands of studies in this area over the past 40 years since Deutsch's initial statement of his approach, researchers have investigated the role of equality in a wide range of domains or contexts (cultural, societal, occupational, relational, etc.), in relation to procedural and corrective or retributive justice, etc. (for overviews, see Tyler et al. 1997; Miller 1999; Schwettmann 2009). Numerous nonexperimental studies such as surveys or interviews have also been conducted that investigate people's attitudes toward equality in relation to their attitudes about equity or merit, need, and other issues, both within the USA and across various countries (Hochshild 1981; Verba and Orren 1985; Kluegel and Smith 1986; Verba et al. 1987; Kluegel et al. 1995). Numerous other empirical studies could be cited, but they all have one thing in common: They assume that equality is a distributive justice principle.

The preceding examination of the role of equality in the history of political and moral philosophy had as its aim to raise the question of whether equality is in fact a distributive justice principle or, more modestly, to raise our suspicions about whether equality has the central role in distributive justice that empirical researchers and others assume it does. The purpose of the present section is to reexamine some recent experimental research with the questions raised by the preceding examination in mind, in order to propose alternative explanations of what is *really* going on when we see what appears to be egalitarian behavior in distributive justice research. This reexamination is meant to be for purposes of illustration alone, and will therefore be restricted to three recent studies in which the present author (and an editor of this volume) has participated, and even then only in summary form. The assumption here is that these studies are sufficiently representative of research more generally that the same approach could be taken in a more comprehensive examination of the empirical literature on distributive justice.[4]

The first two studies (Scott et al. 2001; Michelbach et al. 2003) to be examined are related and build on an earlier study (Mitchell et al. 1993). Both of these studies employ similar experimental designs in order to study distributive justice norms concerning income distribution under conditions of impartiality. More specifically, these studies examine how individuals use four allocation principles—equality, merit, need, and efficiency—in making judgments of income distributions under different conditions as well as what factors affect how individuals use these principles. The main question at issue in these experiments for the present purpose concerns the degree to which individuals' relative preferences for equality and efficiency (understood as the average income in the society as a whole) are mediated by the degree to which income is believed to be merited. The main prediction of these studies for these purposes is that individuals will be increasingly willing to trade off equality for efficiency as the degree to which merit is said to predict income increases. As is obvious from this summary of the goals of these experiments, we assumed at the outset that equality is a distributive justice principle.

In both experiments, participants are given a short description of a hypothetical society and are asked to imagine that they are outside observers giving their advice about a set of proposals that would have differing effects on the level and distribution of income in that society. The experimental manipulations are contained in the description of the society, with participants being assigned to one of six conditions ($3 \times 2$) that vary information about the relationship of income level to merit in that society (high, medium, and low) and about the poverty level in that society (high and low). More specifically, the relationship of income level to merit is operationalized as the degree to which income outcomes are said to be predicted by effort and ability as opposed to luck, connections, and other such factors in that society: 90 % of income outcomes due to merit, 50 % due to merit, and 10 % due to merit. After reading this description, participants then evaluate nine income distributions that vary in terms of the overall level and distribution of income by rating them on a scale from 0 ("very bad") to 10 ("very good"). Each income distribution is pre-

[4] On an autobiographical note, I want to add that the central question of this chapter as a whole—whether equality is a distributive justice principle—was first raised by James Konow after I presented the research contained in the first two of these studies in an invited talk in the Department of Political Science at University of California, Los Angeles (UCLA). My subsequent conversations with James on this subject led me to write this paper, and I want to acknowledge him in this regard.

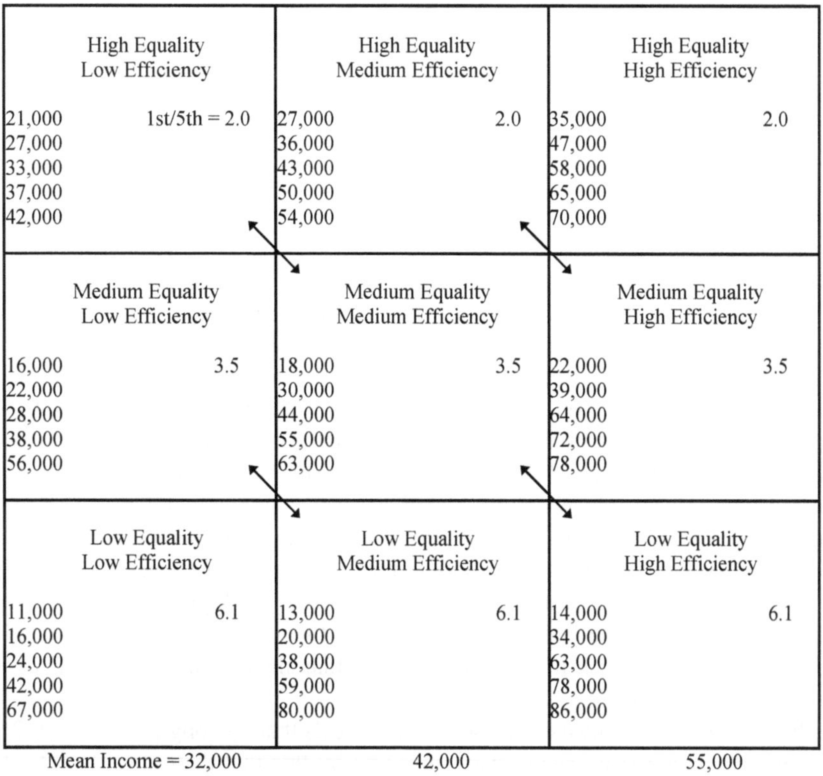


**Fig. 2.1** Income distributions for Scott et al. (2001)

sented as a bar graph that shows the average income for each income quintile along with information about the overall average income, the ratio of the incomes of the top and bottom quintiles (the "income inequality ratio"), and the poverty line. The principal difference between the two experiments is that the income distributions presented to participants differ.

In the first study (Scott et al. 2001), participants in the first experiment are presented with a randomized version of the income distributions displayed in Fig. 2.1. (The study consisted of three related experiments, but only the first one is under examination here.) As noted, these income distributions vary in terms of the level and distribution of income. The level of income (or level of "efficiency") within each of the three columns is constant, with a mean societal income of $ 32, 000 in the first column, $ 42, 000 in the second, and $ 55, 000 in the third. The level of income inequality within each of the three rows is similarly constant, with income inequality (operationalized as the ratio of the income of the highest quintile to the lowest) varying as low in the first row (2.0), medium in the second row (3.5), and high in the third row (6.1). These income distributions also pose participants with decisions about trading off equality for efficiency, represented by the four "diagonal" tradeoffs indicated in Fig. 2.1.

**Table 2.1** Results (mean ratings of income distributions) for Scott et al. (2001)

10% Merit Condition

| | | |
|---|---|---|
| 5.94 | 6.87 | 8.29 |
| 4.60 | 5.37 | 5.94 |
| 1.43 | 2.43 | 3.14 |

N = 63

50% Merit Condition

| | | |
|---|---|---|
| 5.68 | 6.93 | 8.47 |
| 4.71 | 5.53 | 6.63 |
| 1.90 | 2.97 | 3.15 |

N = 59

90% Merit Condition

| | | |
|---|---|---|
| 4.95 | 6.22 | 7.54 |
| 4.44 | 5.51 | 6.61 |
| 2.43 | 3.62 | 4.27 |

N = 63

The results of this first study (and here, for simplicity's sake, only for the condition in which "need" is not at issue because every income quintile has an income level above the poverty line in all the income distributions) are displayed in Table 2.1. Mere inspection of the mean ratings of the income distributions by inequality level (i.e., looking down from one row to the next) suggests that on average participants prefer more equality to less equality. This is evident by the fact that, on average, participants always give a higher rating to a more equal distribution when holding efficiency constant (that is, comparing ratings within each column). This is particularly evident in the first condition, in which the merit level is 10 % and in which the mean ratings of the income distributions in the high equality row, ranging from 5.94 to 8.29, are all higher than those in the medium equality row, ranging from 4.60 to 5.94, which in turn are all higher than those in the low equality row, ranging from 1.43 to 3.14.

Individual-level analysis of these ratings reveals that a strong minority (26.2 %) of participants are strict egalitarians, meaning by this that they always prefer the more equal income distribution to the less equal one in each of the tradeoffs with which they are confronted in evaluating distributions where they "get" an increase in average income or efficiency for a loss of equality, namely the four "diagonal" equality-efficiency tradeoffs. Since only 7.7 % of participants are strict efficiency-maximizers, meaning that they always prefer the more efficient (and less equal) income distribution to the less efficient (and more equal) one in each of these tradeoffs, then the remaining 66.1 % of participants, while not strict egalitarians, display at least some degree of preference for equality. The results in Table 2.1 also suggest that assumptions about the degree to which income is merited do affect individuals' relative preferences for equality and efficiency, with participants on average being more willing to accept the tradeoff of equality for efficiency as merit level increases, as predicted. Finally, analysis of participants' behavior at the individual level reveals that women are on average more concerned with equality than men, and likewise for liberals in comparison to conservatives, also consistent with previous studies.

Summarizing the results of this study with regard to equality, we stated: "Equality performed as a normal good with participants overwhelmingly preferring more equality over less while holding efficiency constant, frequently even at the cost of a considerable loss in efficiency" (Scott et al. 2001, p. 763). In short, we seemed warranted in our assumption that equality is indeed a distributive justice principle. So far, so good.

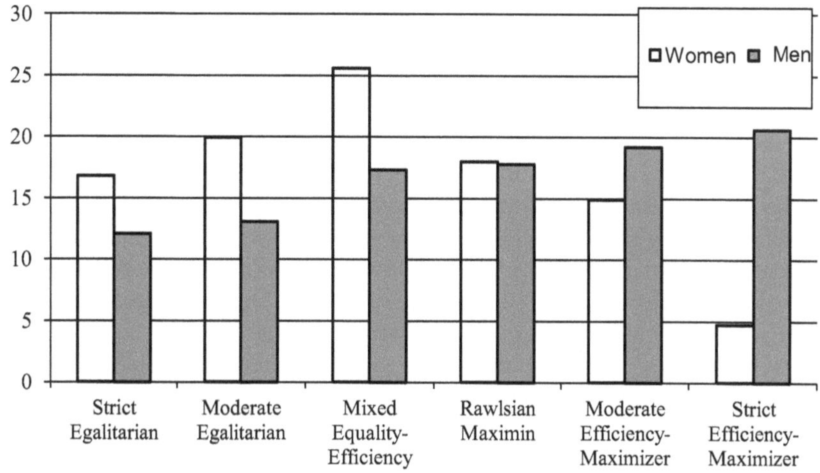


**Fig. 2.2** Categorization of Participants' Observed Behavior for Michelbach et al. (2003)

In the second study (Michelbach et al. 2003), we use the same experimental design but with different income distributions, designed in part to ascertain whether individuals would use a specifically Rawlsian maximin strategy in evaluating income distributions. The results of this experiment are consistent with those of the previous one, and for the present purposes a summary of the aggregate results in terms of the strategies participants employed will suffice. The categorization of participants' observed behavior as strictly egalitarian, etc., was done in a similar fashion as for the previous experiment, although with somewhat more fine-grained categories and also, of course, including a Rawlsian maximin strategy. These results are displayed in Fig. 2.2.

The results show that participants use a variety of strategies in assessing income distribution, including a strictly egalitarian one. The results are disaggregated by gender since we found that gender was the most important variable in explaining equality-efficiency preferences, also consistent with the previous experiment. Namely, we see a striking difference in the behavior of women and men regarding their use of egalitarian and efficiency-maximizing strategies. Women are more likely to be either strong or moderate egalitarians than males, and they are also more likely than men to use a mixed equality-efficiency strategy, which is still a relatively egalitarian strategy given the modest inequality of preferred outcomes. In turn, men are far more likely to be moderate efficiency-maximizers and especially strong efficiency-maximizers than women. In addition our results reveal that a substantial number of participants (18.0 %) have behavior consistent with a distinct Rawlsian maximin strategy, and in this case with no difference in behavior by gender.

With regard to equality in particular, we see that about 15 % of participants in the aggregate have strictly egalitarian preferences, while another 17 % or so have moderately egalitarian preferences and another 23 % or so have mixed equality-efficiency preferences, meaning that over half of participants seem to give equality at least a fair amount of weight in evaluating income distribution. Once again, summarizing our results with regard to equality, we concluded: "We found considerable evidence that most individuals use equality as an allocation principle, even preferring more equal income distributions at the cost of a considerable loss in efficiency" (Michelbach et al. 2003, p. 535). In short, once again we seemed warranted in our assumption that equality is indeed a distributive justice principle.

If our first two studies seem to exhibit a fair degree of egalitarian behavior, and thus confirm that equality is a distributive justice principle, the third and final study (Scott and Bornstein 2009) in this reexamination begins to raise some doubts. Whereas our previous experiments were macro-level analyses of distributive justice beliefs that focused on income alone, this third experiment is a micro-level study of allocation behavior involving decisions under different allocation contexts and qualitatively different goods. Specifically, we analyze allocation decisions across two allocation contexts—nonemergency and emergency conditions—and with regard to money, prescription medicine, and food. We theorize that distributive behavior would likely vary across context and good depending on how individuals weigh distinct and competing allocation principles: merit, need, and equality. We hypothesize that individuals would emphasize need over merit in the emergency context, and vice versa for the nonemergency context, and that they would also emphasize need over merit with regard to prescription medicine and food in comparison to money, across both allocation contexts. We had no specific expectations with regard to their use of equality.

In this experiment, participants are asked to imagine that they are administrators at a relief center who are to distribute various supplies. Participants are assigned one of six experimental conditions ($2 \times 3$) that vary both the allocation context and the supply (good) they are to distribute: an emergency condition (a flood where the recipients of the allocation are flood victims) and a nonemergency condition (where the recipients are working at the center in exchange for goods) for the two allocation contexts and money, prescription medicine, and food for the different goods. Participants then make a series of allocation decisions where they have to distribute a given good between two individuals (say, Smith and Jones) based on two items of information: the amount of work these individuals did that day (where they are said to have worked equal amounts of time and are equally able to do the work) and the amount of their (confirmed) need for the good. These different allocation decisions involve situations where the amount of work and the amount of need are contrasted. For example, Smith packed 90 boxes and needs 10 units of a given good, whereas Jones packed 10 boxes and needs 90 units of the same good. We vary these contrasts as 90 vs. 10, 75 vs. 25, and 66 vs. 34. In analyzing their behavior, we deem an allocation that rewards work to be based on merit and one that rewards need to be based on need, with mixed strategies also possible. Finally, we also include a scenario meant to detect specifically egalitarian behavior, where the work and need were not contrasted, so that Smith packed 75 boxes and needs 75 units of a given good and Jones packed 25 boxes and needs 25 units of the same good. Under this scenario, if a participant divides the good equally, 50–50, then he or she can only have done so

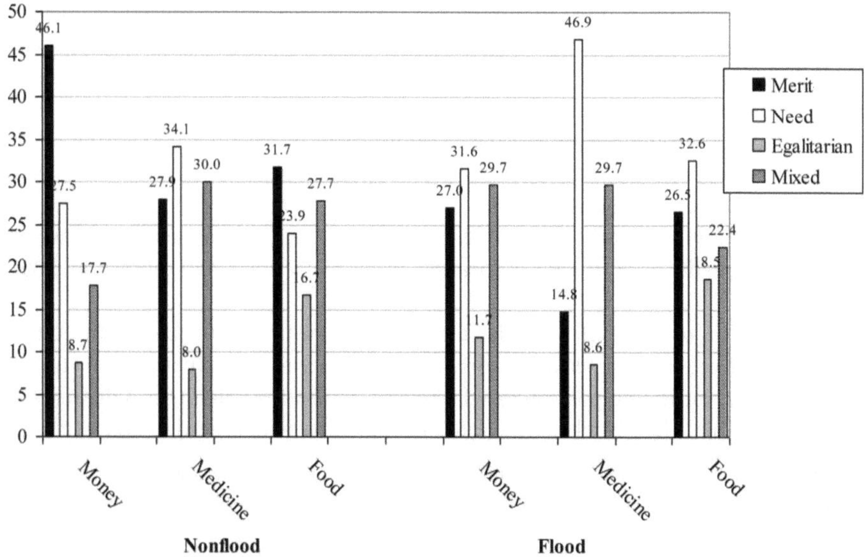


**Fig. 2.3** Predicted probabilities for allocation behavior for Scott and Bornstein (2009)

based upon equality, whereas in the scenarios where work and good are contrasted and decision to allocate the good 50–50 could mean that the participant is, for example, weighing merit and need equally.

Figure 2.3 presents the results of our experiment, categorizing participants' behavior (for the 75 vs. 25 contrasted scenario, using behavior in the non-contrasted scenario to identify egalitarian behavior) across allocation contexts and goods according to four allocation strategies: merit, need, equality, and mixed. As is evident, our major hypotheses concerning allocation behavior are confirmed, and to a striking degree. First, participants overall clearly emphasize merit in the nonemergency context across all goods and likewise clearly emphasize need in the emergency (flood) context, again across all goods. Second, participants overall emphasize merit more with regard to money and need more with regard to prescription medicine and food, across both allocation contexts, although with proportionately less emphasis on need in the nonemergency context and proportionately less emphasis on merit in the emergency (flood) context. But what about equality? We observe only about 8–12 % of participants exhibiting specifically egalitarian behavior for either money or prescription medicine, across both allocation contexts, and somewhat higher levels of egalitarian behavior for food, or on average about 17 % of participants in the aggregate. Finally, unlike in the earlier macro-level income distribution experiments, we found no difference in behavior between men and women in this micro-level experiment.

What to make of these results? First, with regard to equality, we did find some evidence of egalitarian behavior, especially with regard to the allocation of food.

However, this result is open to alternative explanations. As we say in our discussion of the results: "This result might be due to some participants having reasoned that all recipients have a general need for food whereas they have differential specific needs for prescription medicine. If so, then this finding would further increase doubts raised by some researchers (see Konow 2003, pp. 1232–1234) as to whether equality is indeed a separate allocation principle, or instead is either too closely related to need to be distinguishable or serves as a heuristic in the absence of relevant information. Clearly, further research is necessary to understand how—or whether—equality is a distinct allocation principle" (Scott and Bornstein 2009, p. 844).

Second, the *absence* of a gender difference in behavior, which is not consistent with our previous experiments or with most macro-level experimental studies, raises another intriguing possibility with regard to whether equality is a distributive justice principle. Here is what we wrote in conclusion with regard to this issue:

> One potential explanation for this result is that our experiment is a micro-level study where participants do not have to make assumptions or to extrapolate information about recipients or context, as opposed to most macro-level studies, or public opinion surveys, concerning views about the hypothetical or actual distribution of income or other goods across an entire society. In our study, participants in principle perfectly know all the relevant characteristics of the allocation context, good, and recipients because we stipulate these factors as part of the experimental manipulations themselves. Most importantly, we stipulate the main characteristics of the recipients: their demonstrated need for a given good and their contribution to the (same) productive task. Women and men participants in our study may therefore behave in the same way because they share the same information and assumptions. Other research has shown that in the absence of specific information participants tend to extrapolate or to make assumptions in making decisions or judgments (see Kahneman et al.1986). What the absence in our study of a difference of behavior between women and men may suggest, then, is that the observed gender differences in other studies regarding distributive justice behavior or core values determining public opinion could be due in large measure to the different assumptions women and men make concerning the overall distribution of goods in a society. Women and men may, for example, tend to make different assumptions about the characteristics of the recipients of social welfare programs: for instance, whether the economically disadvantaged are "deservingly" poor or not. If this conjecture is correct, the implication is that differences in the core beliefs and values of women and men are not the principal underlying cause for observed gender differences, but that assumptions concerning the features of the distributive context, as they interact with these core values, explain the observed gender gap in distributive justice behavior and support for social welfare policies. Our study thus suggests some obvious lines of research that would confirm or disconfirm this hypothesis about gender. (Scott and Bornstein 2009, p. 844)

In other words, it may be the case that the supposedly egalitarian behavior we witnessed in the first two experiments, or at least some of that behavior, was not in fact evidence that equality is a distributive justice *principle*, but instead that equality is a *heuristic*. Individuals might use equality as a heuristic when they lack any or enough relevant information to use a different principle or where they believe that conditions are such that another principle cannot be invoked, for example where "outputs" (e.g., income) are not the result of "inputs" (e.g., effort and ability) but are instead the result of luck or other arbitrary factors. In other words, the results of our micro-level study of distributive justice behavior may call into question how we have interpreted the results of our macro-level studies.

In sum, this brief reexamination of some (hopefully) representative studies of distributive justice beliefs and behavior has, I hope, at least raised questions about whether—or to what extent—they actually show individuals using equality as a distributive justice principle. Our interpretation of the results of the first two, macro-level, studies of judgments of income distribution as showing that equality is in fact an important distributive justice principle seems entirely reasonable, and the same could be said about the conclusions of numerous other empirical studies of distributive justice. However, in light both of the questions about equality and distributive justice raised by the review of the philosophical literature and of the results of the third, micro-level, study of distributive justice behavior, this interpretation seems open to debate. Could it be the case that equality is not in fact a distributive justice principle except under very specific conditions, if at all?

## Avenues for Future Research

The present critical examination of the relationship between equality and distributive justice in both the philosophical tradition from Aristotle to Rawls and recent experimental and other empirical research into distributive justice suggests several potentially fruitful avenues for future research. I will conclude with a brief discussion of four of these avenues.

The first and most obvious line of inquiry suggested by this examination is to explore whether equality is indeed a distributive justice principle, or, again more modestly, under what conditions it may be. In this regard, it would be important to distinguish between when equality is specifically being employed as a distributive justice *principle* as opposed to a heuristic of some kind. One route to pursue in this line of inquiry would be to vary the information concerning the allocation context. In the micro-level experiment concerning distributive justice behavior in different allocation contexts and different goods discussed above (Scott and Bornstein 2009), I noted that participants made allocation decisions with something like perfect information concerning the recipients. This experimental set-up therefore largely removed equality as a heuristic, in the sense of a rule of thumb when relevant information is lacking, and as such we saw very little specifically egalitarian behavior. This experimental design could be applied with more information being progressively added, for example from a baseline condition of providing no information at all about recipients where we would expect to see considerable egalitarian allocations and then progressively adding more relevant information that might move participants away from equal allocations.

A second line of inquiry concerns further investigation of the relationship between distributive and procedural justice. Such studies exist, notably by Tom Tyler and his collaborators (see Tyler et al. 1997), and they are generally designed to examine the relative weight individuals accord to distributive as opposed to procedural aspects of a decision regarding justice (e.g., legal proceedings) or distribution, and they broadly suggest that the perception of procedural justice is critical in individuals being willing to accept a given decision or allocation, even when they are on the short end of the stick in terms of the distributive outcome. The preceding review of the philosophical tradition and argument that modern theories of distributive justice tend to convert issues of distributive justice into more tractable issues of procedural justice are not inconsistent with these results. However, this review also suggests that we at minimum need to be sensitive to our potentially unwitting (or possibly witting) tendency to pose distributive justice decisions in a manner where the procedure effectively determines the result, as in the case of cutting a cake by the procedure of one person cuts and the other chooses.[5] That is, in designing studies of distributive justice we may need to be more sensitive to the procedural issues in the design if we want to isolate distributive justice beliefs and behaviors from procedural issues or, in turn, we may want to consciously design studies where we are precisely interested in manipulating the interaction between distributive and procedural aspects of an allocation situation.

A third avenue suggested by the preceding remarks is to undertake studies that examine the results of macro-level studies in light of those of micro-level studies, and vice versa. For example, in the review of our recent experimental studies, I suggested that the micro-level results where we do not see much egalitarian behavior might lead us to reinterpret the results of the macro-level studies where we do seem to see such behavior. As with the suggestions regarding the first avenue of inquiry suggested above, one route in this regard would be to more carefully examine and manipulate informational aspects of the allocation decision in order to determine whether equality is operating as a principle or as a heuristic. Another route in this regard would be to nest micro-level studies within macro-level studies in order to see how behavior at the micro-level is affected by certain characteristics of the macro-level environment. This route has been informally pursued insofar as allocation context can effectively represent a macro-level context within which a micro-level behavior is examined (e.g., Scott and Bornstein 2009), but perhaps this research design strategy should be adopted more self-consciously or systematically.

Finally, and most ambitiously, work needs to be done to develop a general theory of allocation or distributive justice behavior and beliefs. Currently, research into distributive justice is being done at a variety of levels, including micro- and macro-levels, and across a number of disciplines with somewhat different approaches and assumptions, such as psychology, political science, behavioral economics, etc., with little communication across disciplines and no common foundation. A first step toward such a goal might be a meta-analysis of research across these various arenas in order to suggest fruitful cross-pollinations and to begin to establish a common ground on which to further study distributive justice.

[5] For an approach that embraces the method of cutting the cake, see Brams and Taylor 1996.

## References


Adams, J. S. (1965). Inequity in social exchange. In L. Berkowitz (Ed.), *Advances in experimental social psychology*. New York: Academic.

Adams, J. S., & Freedman, S. (1976). Equity theory revisited: Comments and annotated bibliography. In L. Berkowitz & G. W. Walster (Eds.), *Advances in experimental social psychology* (pp. 43–90). New York: Academic.

Aristotle. (1984). *The politics* (trans: C. Lord). Chicago: University of Chicago Press.

Aristotle. (2011). *Aristotle's Nicomachean ethics* (trans: R. C. Bartlett & S. D. Collins). Chicago: University of Chicago Press.

Arneson, R. (1990). Liberalism, distributive subjectivism, and equal opportunity for welfare. *Philosophy and Public Affairs, 19,* 158–194.

Brams, S. J., & Taylor, A. D. (1996). *Fair division: From cake-cutting to dispute resolution*. Cambridge: Cambridge University Press.

Cohen, G. A. (1989). On the currency of egalitarian justice. *Ethics, 99,* 906–944.

Cohen, G. A. (2001). *If you're an egalitarian, how come you're so rich?* Cambridge: Harvard University Press.

Dahl, R. A. (1989). *Democracy and its critics*. New Haven: Yale University Press.

Daniels, N. (2003). Democratic equality: Rawls' complex egalitarianism. In S. Freeman (Ed.), *The Cambridge companion to Rawls* (pp. 241–276). Cambridge: Cambridge University Press.

Deutsch, M. (1975). Equity, equality, and need: What determines which value will be used as the basis for distributive justice? *Journal of Social Issues, 31,* 137–149.

Deutsch, M. (1985). *Distributive justice*. New Haven: Yale University Press.

Dobbs, D. (1994). Natural right and the problem of Aristotle's defense of slavery. *Journal of Politics, 56,* 69–94.

Dworkin, R. (1981). What is equality? *Philosophy & Public Affairs, 10,* 185–246.

Dworkin, R. (2000). *Sovereign virtue: The theory and practice of equality*. Cambridge: Harvard University Press.

Frohlich, N., & Oppenheimer, J. A. (1992). *Choosing justice: An experimental approach to ethical theory*. Berkeley: University of California Press.

Gosepath, S. (2011). Equality. In E. N. Zalta (Ed.), *The Stanford encyclopedia of philosophy*. Spring 2011 ed. http://plato.stanford.edu/entries/equality/. Accessed May 5 2012.

Hobbes, T. (1994 [1651]). *Leviathan* (E. Curley (Ed.)). Indianapolis: Hackett.

Hochshild, J. L. (1981). *What's fair? American beliefs about distributive justice*. Cambridge: Harvard University Press.

Kahneman, D., Knetsch, J. L., & Thaler, R. (1986). Fairness as a constraint on profit seeking: Entitlements in the market. *American Economic Review, 76,* 728–741.

Kluegel, J. R., & Smith, E. (1986). *Beliefs about equality: Americans' views of what is and what ought to be*. Hawthorne: Aldine de Gruyter.

Kluegel, J. R., Mason, D. S., & Wegener, B. (1995). *Social justice and political change*. New York: Aldine de Gruyter.

Konow, J. (2001). Fair and square: The four sides of distributive justice. *Journal of Economic Behavior and Organization, 46,* 137–164.

Konow, J. (2003). Which Is the fairest one of all? A positive analysis of justice theories. *Journal of Economic Literature, 41,* 1188–1239.

Lerner, M. J. (1974). The justice motive: 'Equity' and 'Parity' among children. *Journal of Personality and Social Psychology, 29,* 539–550.

Leventhal, G. S. (1976). The distribution of rewards and resources in groups and organizations. In L. Berkowitz & G. W. Walster (Eds.), *Advances in experimental social psychology* (pp. 92–131). New York: Academic.

Mellers, B. A. (1982). Equity judgment: A revision of Aristotelian views. *Journal of Experimental Psychology, General, 111,* 242–270.

Messick, D. M., & Cook, K. S. (Eds.). (1983). *Equity theory*. New York: Praeger.

Michelbach, P. A., Scott, J. T., Matland, R. E., & Bornstein, B. H. (2003). Doing Rawls justice: An experimental study of distributive justice norms. *American Journal of Political Science, 47,* 523–539.
Mikula, G. (1980). On the role of justice in allocation decisions. In G. Mikula (Ed.), *Justice and social interaction: Experimental and theoretical contributions from psychological research* (pp. 127–166). Bern: Hans Huber.
Miller, D. (1999). *Principles of social justice.* Cambridge: Harvard University Press.
Mitchell, G., Tetlock, P. E., Mellers, B. A., & Ordóñez, L. (1993). Judgments of social justice: Compromises between equality and efficiency. *Journal of Personality and Social Psychology, 65,* 629–639.
Nozick, R. (1977). *Anarchy, state, and utopia.* New York: Basic Books.
Nussbaum, M. (1992). Human functioning and social justice: In defense of Aristotelian essentialism. *Political Theory, 20,* 202–246.
Nussbaum, M. (2000). *Women and human development: The capabilities approach.* Cambridge: Cambridge University Press.
Rae, D. (1981). *Equalities.* Cambridge: Harvard University Press.
Rawls, J. (1971). *A theory of justice.* Cambridge: Harvard University Press.
Rawls, J. (1993). *Political liberalism.* New York: Columbia University Press.
Rawls, J. (1999). *A theory of justice (Revised edition).* Cambridge: Harvard University Press.
Rawls, J. (2001). *Justice as fairness: A restatement.* Cambridge: Harvard University Press.
Roemer, J. E. (1998). *Equality of opportunity.* Cambridge: Harvard University Press.
Schwettmann, L. (2009). *Trading off competing allocation principles: Theoretical approaches and empirical investigations.* Frankfurt a. M.: Peter Lang.
Schwinger, T. (1980). Just allocation of goods: Decisions among three principles. In G. Mikula (Ed.), *Justice and social interaction: Experimental and theoretical contributions from psychological research* (pp. 95–125). Bern: Hans Huber.
Scott, J. T., Matland, R. E., Michelbach, P. A., & Bornstein, B. H. (2001). Just deserts: An experimental approach to distributive justice. *American Journal of Political Science, 45,* 749–767.
Scott, J. T., & Bornstein, B. H. (2009). What's fair in foul weather and fair? Distribution principles across different allocation contexts and goods. *Journal of Politics, 71,* 831–846.
Sen, A. (1992). *Inequality reexamined.* Cambridge: Harvard University Press.
Tyler, T. R., Boeckmann, R. J., Smith, H. J., & Huo, Y. J. (1997). *Social justice in a diverse society.* Boulder: Westview.
Verba, S., & Orren, G. R. (1985). *Equality in America: The view from the top.* Cambridge: Harvard University Press.
Verba, S., Kelman, S., Orren, G. R., Miyake, I., Watanuki, J., Kabashima, I., & Donald Ferree, G. Jr. (1987). *Elites and the idea of equality: A comparison of Japan, Sweden, and the United States.* Cambridge: Harvard University Press.
Walster, E., Berscheid, E., & Walster, G. W. (1973). New directions in equity research. *Journal of Personality and Social Psychology, 25,* 151–176.
Weale, A. (1985). The welfare state and two conflicting ideals of equality. *Government and Opposition, 20,* 315–327.
Williams, B. (1973/1976). *The idea of equality. Reprinted in Bernard Williams, problems of the self* (pp. 230–249). Cambridge: Cambridge University Press.

# Part II
# Objectification and Discrimination

# Chapter 3
# A Psycholegal Model of Hostile Environments: The Role of Dehumanization

**Richard L. Wiener, Sarah J. Gervais, Ena Brnjic and Gwenith Nuss**

## Dehumanization and Hostile Environments

The Merriam-Webster dictionary defines "dehumanization" as "to deprive of human qualities, personality, or spirit" (http://www.merriam-webster.com/dictionary/dehumanization). While this simple phrase captures the social and natural language meaning of saying that an individual or a group of people dehumanizes another, it is silent about the ways in which one person may deprive another of the quality of humanness, what constitutes the qualities of being human, and how such deprivation can harm the spirit of the target. The primary goal of this chapter is to examine the concept of dehumanization from legal and psychological perspectives and ultimately to seek an integration of these two points of view. The secondary goals are to gain an understanding of what constitutes a dehumanizing situation and to describe some of the ways that the law can respond to the harms that dehumanization causes. We begin with two stories that appear uncontroversial on the surface in the sense that almost all readers would agree that the underlying themes involve at least some dehumanization.

Both stories are true summaries of events that took place at Lift Line, Inc., a division of the Rochester Genesee Regional Transportation Authority (RGRTA) starting in 1994 and continuing over a 14-year period, finally ending in 2008 (Rivera vs. Rochester Genesee Regional Transportation Authority 2012). As a subsidiary of the RGRTA, Lift Line provided transportation service for the elderly and the disabled who live in and around the Rochester New York area. The first story is about Enio Rivera, a man of Puerto Rican descent, who found out shortly after he came to work as a bus driver for Lift Line in 1994 that Dominic Folino, a senior mechanic at Lift Line was having an affair with Kimberly Rivera, Enio's wife. Enio and Kimberly divorced, Kimberly married Dominic, and Enio remarried another woman.

---

R. L. Wiener (✉) · S. J. Gervais · E. Brnjic · G. Nuss
Department of Psychology, University of Nebraska-Lincoln, Lincoln, NE, USA
e-mail: rwiener2@unl.edu

B. H. Bornstein, R. L. Wiener (eds.), *Justice, Conflict and Wellbeing*,
DOI 10.1007/978-1-4939-0623-9_3, © Springer Science+Business Media New York 2014

Between 2003 and 2007, Rivera claimed that Folino repeatedly referred to him as a "spic" and a "Taco Bell." On one occasion Folino and a coworker chanted to Rivera, "What's that smell, look at the fat fuc**r, there is Taco Bell" (Rivera vs. Rochester Genesee Regional Transportation Authority 2012, p. 690). During other times, Folino and coworkers intimidated and bullied Rivera. For example, on one occasion they confronted Rivera while he was driving out of the parking lot, cursing and staring at him menacingly and at another time, they meddled with his time card. Rivera claimed that Folino sprayed paint thinner at him, swerved his car toward him, and regularly posted pictures of expensive gifts that he had given to Rivera's son, who was then living with Folino and Kimberly (Rivera vs. Rochester Genesee Regional Transportation Authority 2012, p. 691). Rivera eventually filed a complaint with the Equal Employment Opportunity Commission (EEOC).

Another worker at Lift Line, Michael Talton who is an African–American also complained that he was the victim of harassment during an overlapping period of time (2004–2006) (Rivera vs. Rochester Genesee Regional Transportation Authority 2012). Lift Line hired Talton in 2004 as a "fueler-washer" whose job was to clean and service buses after the drivers returned with them at the end of their routes. A white mechanic, John Stiggins, as well as Talton's direct supervisor, John Tiberio referred to Talton on several occasions with the word "n****r" (Rivera vs. Rochester Genesee Regional Transportation Authority 2012, p. 691). On one occasion, Stiggins asked Talton to cover for him because Stiggins was trying to avoid the attention of one of the company dispatchers. When Talton failed to do so, Stiggins said to Talton, "I thought you was my boy….You know what I'm talking about n****r. You were supposed to look out for us." When Talton complained, Stiggins threatened Talton with a fistfight (Rivera vs. Rochester Genesee Regional Transportation Authority 2012, p. 691). On another occasion, Talton walked in on Stiggins conversing with another coworker and heard him tell the coworker that he and a second coworker named Sanhueza were out drinking and that Sanhueza "started talking about n****rs" and said "wished all you n****rs died." When Talton complained, his supervisor called him a "n****r" and told him to "get over it" (Rivera vs. Rochester Genesee Regional Transportation Authority 2012, p. 691). In 2005, Talton found a gun in the bus that Sanhueza was driving and reported it. Sanhueza threatened Talton by shaking his hand in the shape of a gun and said, "I'm going to kick your ass, n****r". Lift Line fired Sanhueza for keeping a gun in the bus but later reinstalled him as a fueler-washer to resolve a dispute with the union over the incident. Lift Line assigned Talton to the job of training Sanheuza who promptly responded by once again calling Talton a "n****r". Talton eventually filed a complaint with the EEOC.

While most readers will find the situations that Rivera and Talton confronted at Lift Line at least somewhat dehumanizing, the legal history of the case showed that it was unclear whether either of the complainants would have his day in court. Rivera and Talton jointly filed a lawsuit in the federal Western District Court of New York under Title VII complaining of racial harassment that created a hostile work environment only to find that the district court dismissed both claims (Rivera vs. Rochester Genesee Regional Transportation Authority 2011). The district court held that any harassment that Rivera suffered arose out of a personal conflict with another worker, not because of his national origin, and therefore was not a violation of the Title VII prohibition of hostile work environments. The district court judge also found that Talton's evidence based only upon crude language, spread out over a number of years, was insufficient to establish a claim under Title VII of the Civil Rights Act.[1] Together the stories and the legal responses to the complaints at the district court level raise some interesting and difficult questions about hostile environments, including:

1. What is a hostile environment?
2. How is dehumanization related to hostile environments?
3. What are sources of dehumanization in hostile environments?
4. When does dehumanization become a violation of civil law?
5. What do we know about the causes and psychological outcomes of dehumanization?

This chapter will analyze the issues that these questions pose and in the process provide a psycholegal model to answer the questions raised by these and other equally disturbing fact patterns. The chapter will describe situations when the law of hostile environments and the psychology of dehumanization agree, when they disagree, and in the end offer a theory of dehumanization to explain hostile environments at work, at school, and at home. Section II summarizes the law of hostile environments at work, at home, and at school that are due to discrimination based upon gender, race and ethnicity, national origin, age, and disability. Section III advances a theory of dehumanization that explains how environments become hostile. Section IV discusses some of the research that underlies the psychology of hostile environments and Section V will summarize the arguments, present the implications for law and psychology, and suggest new areas for additional theoretical and empirical work.

## The Law of Hostile Environments

In this section, we consider the most common types of hostile environments at work, at school, and in the home prohibited under federal law. The section is not exhaustive but summarizes the most common causes of action for sex, race, national origin, age, and disability. It is not exhaustive because we do not consider state statutes or local ordinances, which have extended the reach of civil rights laws both in areas covered under federal law (i.e., sex, race, religion, national origin, and disability) and in areas for which the federal law does not define a protected class (e.g., sexual orientation). Although the review is not exhaustive, the theories and approaches that the law uses to resolve federal violations are similar to the approaches

[1] Upon appeal, the Second Circuit Appellate Court disagreed with the summary judgment and sent the case back to the district court for further processing of the hostile work environment claim where it is still under litigation.

that states and local municipalities take to resolve these same or similar issues. Although a complete analysis of all the types of hostile environments is beyond the scope of this chapter, the review presented here tracks the main contours of the law and it allows us to draw some conclusions about the social psychology of hostile environments.

*Hostile Work Environments Based on Sex* Hostile environments occur at work, at home, and at school based upon misconduct around issues of race, sex, religion, national origin, age, or disability status of the target or on some combination of these factors. A hostile work environment is one that is "permeated with discriminatory intimidation, ridicule, and insult" Harris vs. Forklift (1993, p. 21). As stated in Title VII of the Civil Rights Act (CRA), "It shall be an unlawful employment practice for an employer … to fail or refuse to hire or to discharge any individual, or otherwise to discriminate against any individual with respect to his compensation, terms, conditions, or privileges of employment, because of such individual's race, color, religion, sex, or national origin" (42 U.S.C.A. sec 20003-2; 703). In Meritor Savings Bank vs. Vinson (1986, p. 2404), the US Supreme Court ruled that because the statute included "terms and conditions of employment," it was a violation for employers to subject workers to "hostile work environments." Vinson brought a sexual harassment complaint, which provided the Court the opportunity to delineate the elements of a hostile work environment due to sexual misconduct. As announced by the Court (p. 2404) and reaffirmed in 1993 in Harris vs. Forklift Systems, a hostile work environment is one in which one worker subjects another to unwelcome conduct which is based upon sex and which is "sufficiently severe or pervasive to alter the conditions of employment and create an abusive working environment." The abusiveness of the environment depends upon a totality of the circumstances test, which takes into consideration how frequently the discrimination occurred, the severity of the misconduct, whether it was humiliating and physically threatening or merely an isolated miscommunication, and whether it interfered with an employee's work performance (Faragher vs. City of Boca Raton 1998; Harris vs. Forklift 1993; Oncale vs. Sundowner Offshore Services, Inc. 1998). As Justice O'Connor stated in Harris (1993, p. 19), "…we can say that whether an environment is 'hostile' or 'abusive' can be determined only by looking at all the circumstances." Furthermore, the test of what constitutes a hostile work environment includes both a subjective prong, that is, the complainant actually perceived the environment as either sufficiently severe or pervasive to be abusive, and an objective prong, that is, a reasonable person or victim's reaction to a "similar environment under essentially like or similar circumstances" (Harris 1993, p. 21) would also find the conduct unwelcome and severe or pervasive enough to be abusive. This model of what constitutes a hostile work environment under the CRA has become the model not only for sexual harassment but also for other types of harassment due to race, ethnicity, disability, and age.

We consider an example of hostile work environment harassment due to gender, which results from sexual objectification (treating a human being not as a person but rather as a sexual object for one's own gratification, Nussbaum 1999) because it illustrates the legal elements with a gender example that speaks directly to our own research (Wiener et al. 2012). Josephine Chapple worked for Fahnestock & Co., a securities broker firm, as a sales assistant in Manhattan. Chapple's boss, Robert Pelham, reacted to Ms. Chapple in ways that most would consider less than professional, making inappropriate comments about her appearance, such as, "Oh, you always know when Josephine is coming. Her chest is always right in front of her" (Messer vs. Fahnstock & Co., Inc. 2008, p. 2). Not only did Pelham make these types of comments to others, he did so in front of Chapple herself. Furthermore, Chapple complained that she often looked up to find Pelham leering at her chest in a sexual way as if "he were undressing her with his eyes" (p. 2). Finally, Pelham made joking comments about Chapple suggesting that because of her special physical endowment, the company could pay her to entertain brokers at meetings. There was little disagreement that Chapple's complaint met the subjective prong of the hostile work environment test. Chapple found this sexual conduct unwelcome as evidenced by the fact that she complained to Pelham and broke into tears when he referred to and stared at her chest. She had a difficult time working with Chapple and eventually lodged a complaint with the EEOC, which concluded that Pelham had humiliated Chapple with his comments and associated behaviors. When Chapple filed a complaint against Fahnestock & Co. in district court, the judge agreed that the misconduct was serious enough to go forward to a jury to determine whether the leering and comments were sufficiently severe or pervasive in an objective sense to violate the CRA of 1991 in the form of a hostile work environment.

The way in which different federal jurisdictions set the severity or pervasiveness standard shows a good deal of variability in interpreting the totality of the circumstances. For example, in Garriga vs. Novo Nordisk, Inc. (2010) the 11th Circuit Court of Appeals affirmed a district court ruling that Vivian Garriga was not the victim of a hostile work environment due to sexual harassment at the hands of her boss, Brian Taylor. Taylor came to work for Novo Nordisk, a pharmaceutical distributing firm, after Garriga was already working for the company. During his early encounters with Garriga, Tayler bantered with her about sexual behavior asking her with which celebrity she wished to have sex. Garriga asked Taylor to stop but instead he put his arm around Garriga one day in the parking lot before a business trip and, according to Garriga, he leered at her breasts and backside on several subsequent occasions. The 11th Circuit upheld the district court's summary judgment concluding that Taylor's behavior failed the objective test for a hostile work environment, even if he had acted as Garriga claimed, because the conduct was neither severe nor pervasive enough to constitute an abusive work environment. Thus, there is some need to understand from both psychological and legal points of view the contours of hostile environments. We believe that a fuller understanding of dehumanization offers a fruitful path for understanding the characteristics of hostile environments that flow from discrimination.

*Hostile Work Environments Based on Race or National Origin* Congress enacted Title VII in 1964, a time in US history when the nation's minority populations forced the majority to face and try to ameliorate the high prevalence of discrimination based upon race and national origin. Nonetheless, the problem of discrimination at work based upon race, ethnicity, or national origin is still with us today. The model for hostile work environments due to race, color, and national origin follows a very similar theory as the one for hostile work environments due to sexual harassment. For example, in another transportation case, Massachusetts Bay Transportation Authority (MBTA) hired Chungchi Che, a man of Asian descent as a driver in and around the Boston area in 1982 (Che vs. Massachusetts Bay Transporation Authority 2003). Che worked hard and did well at his position so that MBTA sent Che to a training institute to learn about police work in 1988. During this training, Che learned about federal, state, and local law prohibiting discrimination and later came to believe that he was a victim of harassment on the job. Ultimately, he filed a complaint with the Massachusetts Commission Against Discrimination. The complaint stemmed from actions that began in 1993 at which time Che advanced at MBTA and became a chief inspector with the responsibility of monitoring the operation of the "Green Line." As chief inspector, Che reported directly to James Johnson, the superintendent of the Green Line. In 1994, Che and another employee were involved in an argument and Johnson demoted Che to a streetcar operator. At a meeting with the union representative to resolve the issue, Che suffered an anxiety attack and passed out. When the union representative asked Johnson to call for assistance, Johnson hesitated stating, "I think this Ch**k is faking it" (p. 35). The union negotiated a resolution with MBTA so that Che's punishment became a 3-day suspension. However, Che complained that following this incident Johnson had improperly disciplined him on a number of subsequent occasions. For example, Johnson wrote Che up for calling in an automobile accident using his telephone rather than a radio despite the fact that MBTA allowed employees to use either method to report. In November of 1995, Che noticed piles of leaves on the tracks of the Green Line on top of the heated coils that MBTA uses to clear the tracks of frost during the cold months. Che wrote in the assignment book that the heaters should remain off until workers cleaned the leaves from the track. When Johnson read that Che wrote in the assignment book without his permission, he again demoted Che for insubordination to the job of streetcar operator. Che fell ill after the incident, went on sick leave, and filed his complaint with the Massachusetts Commission Against Discrimination claiming among other issues that Che's supervisor used harsh discipline with him because of his national origin. Che claimed that MBTA's disciplinary actions were more severe for him than for other workers who were not Asian. Included in the complaint were other examples including evidence that his supervisors (i.e., Johnson) admonished Che for requesting meal breaks, that his supervisors allowed other workers to scream at Che with impunity, and that supervisors on a number of occasions referred to Che as a "Ch**k." After receiving a finding of reasonable cause Che went on to win a favorable outcome in federal district court, which MBTA unsuccessfully appealed to the First Circuit Court of Appeals.

The doctrine of hostile work environment harassment for race, national origin, color, or religion is clear and settled law. Complainants must show by a preponderance of the evidence that they are members of a protected class (based upon sex, race, religion, color, or national origin under Title VII) and that the employer subjected them to harassment because of the protected class status (in the case of Mr. Che, national origin). Furthermore, the harassment was sufficiently severe or pervasive to create an abusive work environment from the subjective perspective of the complainant and the objective point of view of a reasonable person. The First Circuit Court of Appeals upheld this formula in the Che case, citing the prior delineation of these factors at the district court level (PowerComm, LLC vs. Holyoke Gas & Electric Department 2010). The elements of a hostile work environment under Title VII are similar in all federal jurisdictions. While the law is settled on the elements of a hostile work environment, it leaves open for interpretation what factors may rise to the level of abuse and when the totality of circumstances does and does not cross that not so bright line. As we argue below, the psychology of dehumanization may offer an empirical approach to answering these questions.

*Hostile Work Environments Based on Age* The Age Discrimination in Employment Act (ADEA) prohibits employers from discriminating based upon an employee's age. Tracking closely the language in the CRA of 1964 amended in 1991, the ADEA states, "It shall be unlawful for an employer to fail or refuse to hire or to discharge any individual or otherwise discriminate against any individual with respect to his compensation, terms, conditions, or privileges of employment, because of such individual's age"[2] Sec. 4(623)(a)(1).

As a side issue, it is important to note that the US Supreme Court has interpreted the causality prong in disparate treatment cases to be different under the language of the ADEA than under the language of the CRA, ruling that the causality factor requires "but for" or direct causality under the ADEA (Gross vs. FBL Financial Services 2009). Disparate treatment cases, unlike hostile environment cases, require that the employer acted with intent to reach an adverse outcome for the employee based upon the protected factor. The CRA prohibits an employer from using gender, race, religion, color, or national origin as a contributory factor in reaching an employment decision (i.e., a mixed-motive theory of discrimination). However, in Gross (2009) the Court held that Congressional amendments to the CRA (1991) preserved the mixed-motive model but because there were no similar amendments to the ADEA, it required direct causality, compelling complainants to show that "but for" the age of the plaintiff, there would be a different employer decision. Nonetheless, the holding in Gross (2009) should not, and as of yet has not, impacted the availability of hostile work environment theories under the ADEA because hostile work environment cases under either theory do not require "but for" causality.

Consider, for example, Dediol vs. Best Chevrolet, Inc. (2011). Milan Dediol worked at Best Chevrolet during the summer of 2007 (June 1 until the end of August). Dediol, who was 65 years old at the time of his employment, complained that his supervisor, Donald Clay, treated him badly at work after he asked for a morning off to attend a volunteer church event. Clay responded to Dediol's request with the language, "You old mother fu**er, you are not going over there tomorrow" and "if you do go over there [I'll] fire your fu***ng ass." Dediol stated in his complaint that

[2] The ADEA considers individuals 40 years or older to be members of the protected class.

following the church incident, Clay stopped using Dediol's proper name and instead called him "old mother fu**er," "old man," and "Pops" several times each day that he was at work. Clay also spoke disparagingly of Dediol's religion with comments like, "God would not put food on your plate" and "Go to your fu***ng God and see if he can save your job" (p. 438).

According to Dediol's complaint, on several occasions Clay "stole" deals from him and offered them to some of the younger salespeople. Dediol also stated that on several occasions Clay picked fights with him and physically intimidated him with threats of physical violence. When Clay learned that Dediol asked the general manager to transfer him to the new car division to escape the bad treatment, Clay denied the request and responded with, "Get your old fu***ng ass over here. You are not going to work with new cars."

Dediol filed a complaint with the EEOC and received a "right-to-sue" letter but Best Chevrolet successfully filed for a summary judgment, which upon Dediol's appeal reached the Fifth Circuit Court of Appeals. The Fifth Circuit found that the ADEA did support a hostile work environment claim pointing to a similar holding in the Sixth Circuit (Crawford vs. Medina General Hospital 1996) and affirmed the plaintiff's right to relief. A hostile work environment claim due to age under the ADEA requires plaintiffs to show by a preponderance of the evidence that "(1) he was over the age of 40, (2) the employee was subjected to harassment, either through words or actions, based on age, (3) the nature of the harassment was such that it created an objectively intimidating, hostile, or offensive work environment, and (4) there exists some basis for liability on the part of the employer" (p. 441). Until the US Supreme Court rules otherwise, the law, at least in some jurisdictions, prohibits employers from creating hostile work environments because of an employee's age if the employee is over the age of 40. It is worth noting that similar to the CRA cases, despite the prohibition against harassment due to age, there is no specific standard for determining what constitutes a sufficient level of abuse to reach an actionable cause under the totality of circumstances test. Again, the law is gray on what does and does not cross that line. Before turning to the psychology of dehumanization to obtain some insight into this question, we first consider hostile work environments due to disability and hostile environments in contexts outside of work, specifically at home and at school.

*Hostile Environments Based upon Disability* Congress wrote the Americans with Disabilities Act in 1990 stating in part that "….no employer shall discriminate against a qualified individual with a disability because of the disability of such individual who, with or without reasonable accommodation, can perform the essential functions of the employment position, unless the accommodation would impose an undue hardship on the operation of the business of that employer" (42 U.S.C. §§ 12112(a), 12111(8), 12112(b)(5)(A)). The statute is more complex than either the CRA or the ADEA because it includes a complicated formula, which requires all plaintiffs filing under the ADA to demonstrate that they possess a qualified disability defined under the Act. Thus, individuals who argue that an organization subjected them to hostile work environments based on a disability must show that they possessed such a disability. Those claiming that an organization denied them a benefit or invoked a disciplinary action based upon their disability must also show that they were qualified for the job with or without reasonable accommodation and that any accommodations would not result in an "undue hardship" to the employer. Although workers bringing hostile work environment actions are less concerned with job qualifications and reasonable accommodations, they still need to establish that they are disabled under the Act. An individual with "a physical or mental impairment that substantially limits one or more of the major life activities..." is disabled (42 U.S.C. § 12102(2)(A)). Furthermore, a worker who does not suffer from an illness is also disabled under the law if the employer "regards" the worker as having such an impairment (42 U.S.C. §§ 12102(2)(B)-(C)). Early on, the law was unclear about what constitutes a major life activity, but Congress' 2008 Amendments to the Act compiled a non-exhaustive list of major life activities including, "caring for oneself, performing manual tasks, seeing, hearing, eating, sleeping, walking, standing, lifting, bending, speaking, breathing, learning, reading, concentrating, thinking, communicating, and working" (42 U.S.C. §§ 12102(2)(A)). Furthermore, the EEOC provided a broad definition of possible impairments to major life activities including, "any physiological disorder, or condition, cosmetic disfigurement, or anatomical loss affecting one or more of the following body systems: neurological, musculoskeletal, special sense organs, respiratory (including speech organs), cardiovascular, reproductive, digestive, genitor-urinary, hemic and lymphatic, skin, and endocrine; or (2) any mental or psychological disorder, such as mental retardation, organic brain syndrome, emotional or mental illness, and specific learning disabilities" (29 C.F.R. § 1630.2(h) (2004)).

The early litigation under the ADA struggled to determine whether complainants possessed disabilities covered by law or if they were disqualified because the claimed impairments did not limit a major life activity. This continues to be a hotly contested issue in current ADA litigation even under the broader 2008 Amendments, which codified the EEOC's list of impairments and expanded the definition of disability. Making the matter even more complex, the Supreme Court ruled in Sutton vs. United Air Lines, Inc. (1999) that in determining whether a plaintiff's impairment limited a major life activity, a lower court had to examine a complainant after considering all mitigating measures, that is, any medical or rehabilitative aids that reduce the functional limitation of the disability (e.g., medicines, orthopedic aids, and visual aids). Thus, in Sutton the Court held that the Act did not protect two women who wore corrective glasses and who had applied for, but did not receive pilot positions with United Airlines because the eyeglasses corrected their vision deficits. The law changed in 2008 when the Congressional Amendments to the Act extended protection of the ADA to include impairments that mitigating measures ameliorate (42 U.S.C. §§ 12102(4)(D)-(i-ii)).

What then of the viability of a hostile work environment claim under the ADA? In 2001, the Fifth Circuit Court of Appeals ruled that a hostile work environment claim was available under the ADA (Flowers vs. Southern Regional Physician Servs., Inc. 2001). Plaintiff Sandra Flowers was a medical assistant at Southern Regional Physician Services Inc. from September 1993 to November of 1995. Prior to 1995, Flowers was close socially with her supervisor, Margaret Hallmark, both on the job and outside of work. In early 1995, Hallmark discovered that Flowers had tested positive for HIV and soon changed her behavior toward the complainant. Hallmark stopped socializing with Flowers, started listening in on her telephone calls, eavesdropped on Flowers' conversations with other workers, and spent a great deal of time at Flowers' desk observing Flowers' work performance. Others in the organization also interacted differently toward Flowers including the president of the company refusing to shake hands with her and even avoiding her physical presence. Her supervisors required Flowers to take repeated random drug tests and on one occasion, the president reprimanded Flowers, called her a "bitch" and told her he was "fed up with her crap." Flowers filed with the EEOC and received a right to sue letter. She brought a case in federal court alleging among other charges that she was the victim of hostile work environment harassment under the ADA. A jury trial ensued and Flowers received a favorable verdict on the hostile work environment claim.

Upon appeal, the Fifth Circuit held that HIV was a qualifying disability under the ADA, and that the law allowed a hostile work environment claim based upon such a disability. The Court ruled that under the ADA, a plaintiff must show that an employer subjected the worker to unwelcome harassment because of the protected class status and that the harassment was sufficiently severe or pervasive to create a hostile work environment and unreasonably interfere with the worker's job performance (Flowers vs. Southern Regional Physician Servs., Inc. 2001). At least three other circuit courts have followed suit and have allowed a hostile work environment claim under the ADA: the Fourth Circuit (Fox vs. General Motors Corp. 2001), the Eighth Circuit (Shaver vs. Independent Stave Co. 2003), and the Tenth Circuit (Lanman vs. Johnson County, Kansas 2004).

In Lanman vs. Johnson County (2004, p. 1155), the Tenth Circuit Court of Appeals agreed with these other circuit courts based upon the fact that Congress used similar language in both Title VII and the ADA to prohibit discrimination against "…any individual with respect to his compensation, terms, conditions, or privileges of employment." Therefore, the court found that Congress had intended to make available the same hostile work environment claim for disability as it had for race, national origin, sex, and religion under Title VII. In this case, the Deputy Sheriff in Johnson County, Kansas treated Lanman as if she was mentally ill, calling her "nuts" or "crazy," and repeatedly making statements to her such as, "Oh Lanman, you are going off the deep end again," and "Are you off your medication?" (p. 1155). Despite these findings, the Tenth Circuit affirmed the summary judgment against Lanman because it did not believe she qualified under the ADA. Lanman claimed a disability because the Sheriff's office "regarded" her as if she had a mental illness, which is a viable argument under the Act. However, the court concluded that despite the many comments that her coworkers and supervisors made about her erratic behavior, the County did not actually mistake Ms. Lanman as being mentally impaired. Furthermore, even if the County did regard her as mentally ill, it is unlikely that the Sheriff's office believed that Lanman's impairment substantially limited her in a major life activity. The court preferred to interpret the statements and actions that the County engaged in to represent personality conflicts between Lanman and her coworkers, an area of conflict that the ADA does not address. Thus, while several courts have recognized the viability of a hostile environment under the ADA, the burden of plaintiffs to establish that they have a qualified disability under the law is difficult to meet.

*Hostile Environments in School* We turn next to consider whether the law prohibits hostile educational environments. To begin, Title IX of the Educational Amendments of 1972 states, "… no person in the United States shall, on the basis of sex, be excluded from participation in, be denied the benefits of, or be subjected to discrimination under any education program or activity receiving Federal financial assistance" (20 U.S.C. § 1681(a). While the language in Title IX explicitly outlaws discrimination in education due to sex, it does not provide language to specify redress in court for a private action against a school or school system. Nonetheless, over the last 40 years following the passage of the 1972 Amendment, the courts have extended the reach of Title IX (20 U.S.C.A. §§ 1681 (a)) to prohibit hostile environments in school, which arise out of unwelcome social sexual conduct that teachers and students direct toward students and classmates. First, in Cannon vs. University of Chicago (1979), the Supreme Court held that Congressional language and statutory intent did imply the existence of a cause of action for gender discrimination in school and it does allow private citizens to bring cases alleging hostile school environments. However, the Supreme Court was silent in Cannon about whether monetary damages that attach to a hostile environment theory under Title VII of the CRA were available under Title IX. Without the availability to seek remedies, the protection that Title IX provides against a hostile environment claim at school would be minimal. The Supreme Court took up the issue in Franklin vs. Gwinnett County Public School (1992), a case in which Christine Franklin, a high-school student attending a school that received federal funds, argued that a male coach at the school, Andrew Hill, repeatedly asked about her sexual experiences with her boyfriend. Hill went on to ask Franklin if she was interested in having sex with an older man, then forcibly kissed the girl in the school parking lot and finally took her into an abandoned office and coerced her into having intercourse. The trial court dismissed the civil case finding that Title IX did not allow monetary damages, but the Supreme Court disagreed and held that monetary damages are available for a private action enforceable under Title IX and remanded the case back to the lower courts.

Despite these initial cases, it was not until 1998 in Gebser vs. Lago Vista Independent School District that the Supreme Court formalized the required elements of a hostile school environment under Title IX. Alida Gebser, an eighth-grade girl, joined a book club at her middle school led by a teacher, Frank Waldrop, who made sexually suggestive comments to many of the students in the club. When Gebser advanced to high school the following fall, she found herself in Waldrop's classes where he continued to make inappropriate comments to her and eventually initiated sexual contact while the two were alone in his classroom. Waldrop had sexual intercourse with Gebser on multiple occasions into the following school year but never on school property. Although Gebser did not report the incidents, other students subjected to Waldrop's inappropriate comments did complain to school officials and several months later police caught Waldrop and Gebser engaged in intercourse and arrested the teacher. Although Waldrop did lose his teacher's license, the school district never initiated an official sexual harassment civil action against him. The district court granted summary judgment in favor of Lago Vista and the Fifth Circuit Court of Appeals affirmed that judgment holding that school districts are not liable under Title IX for teachers sexually harassing students unless a school official supervising the alleged harasser had actual knowledge of the abuse and failed to act to end the abuse. Only under those circumstances, does school policy come into play.

Upon appeal, the US Supreme Court agreed with the Fifth Circuit, stating "… in cases like this one that do not involve official policy of the recipient entity, we hold that a damage remedy will not lie under Title IX unless an official who at a minimum has authority to address the alleged discrimination and to institute corrective measures on the recipient's behalf has actual knowledge of discrimination in the recipient's programs and fails to adequately respond" (Gebser 1998, p. 1999). Although Waldrop did lose his teaching license and faced criminal charges, the action against the school district for tolerating a hostile environment due to sex was not successful.

Thus, under Title IX, if a teacher in a school that accepts federal funds creates a hostile environment due to sex through sufficiently severe or pervasive conduct, then the school (or school district) is liable for the harms that the discrimination caused if school officials knew about the actions and took no measures to address the problem. In short, schools must show deliberate indifference to hostile environments due to sex, in order for complainants to bring successful cases. This, of course, implies that schools can avoid liability for hostile environments if they act to address the complaints before they reach the level of court action. For our purposes, regardless of whether a complaint stops at the school level or goes through litigation, the impact of the law is to prohibit teachers from creating hostile environments due to sex by engaging in pervasive or severe sexual conduct toward students.

What happens when students sexually harass other students? In Davis vs. Monroe County Board of Education (1999), the parents of LaShonda D. brought a suit in federal district court for injunctive relief and monetary damages claiming that another student in a public elementary school harassed their daughter. The parents claimed that a fifth-grade classmate, G.F., tried to touch LaShonda's breasts and genital area while making comments such as, "I want to get in bed with you" and "I want to feel your boobs." This went on for many months despite LaShonda reporting the incidents to her parents and her parents, in turn, reporting the behavior to school officials. Although the school officials informed the principal, Bill Querry, about the incidents, the school took no disciplinary action. The incidents stopped only when authorities caught G.F. and charged him with sexual battery to which he pleaded guilty. The district court dismissed the civil case finding that Title IX did not allow a damage remedy for peer harassment in the public schools and the 11th Circuit Court of Appeals affirmed the dismissal. However, the US Supreme Court overturned the ruling holding that, under Title IX, a school receiving public funds may be liable for student-to-student sexual harassment if the school shows deliberate indifference to actual knowledge of a hostile environment due to sex, if the school has some control over the alleged harassment and it elects to take no action. Again, for our purposes, the impact of the law is to prohibit schools from allowing students to create hostile environments due to sex by engaging in unwelcome sexual conduct toward other students that is severe or pervasive.

There is some suggestion that schools might also be liable for hostile school environments based upon national origin or race. For example, in Howard vs. Feliciano (2008), the US District Court of Puerto Rico found that a teacher, Feliciano, subjected an Anglo student, Robert, to a hostile environment at school because of discriminatory comments that were sufficiently severe or pervasive to create an abusive educational environment. The court let stand a $ 1,000,000 jury award against the Puerto Rico Department of Education. In that case, the 11th-grade mathematics teacher at a public school displayed posters in his classroom with derogatory comments about American citizens referring to them as "gringos." The teacher referred to the plaintiff as a "son of a bitch American," "asshole," and "American jerk" while looking menacingly at the student. Robert earned A's in all his classes except a B in science and a C in mathematics. Feliciano had announced to the class, "I am going to give gringo Robert a C because he is an American" (Howard 2008, p. 257). The school principal took no action other than discussing the situation with Feliciano. The boy's parents went to court first for a restraining order against Feliciano because their complaints to the school officials went without any response. Finally, the boy's parents moved back to the US mainland to escape the harassing conduct.

The court relied upon Title VI (42 U.S.C. Sect. 2000d) which states, "No person in the United States shall on the grounds of race, color or national origin, be excluded from participation in, be denied the benefits of, or be subjected to discrimination under any program or activity receiving Federal financial assistance." The district court took notice that the Supreme Court of the US has consistently interpreted Title VI and Title IX in a similar manner (citing Barnes vs. Gorman 2002 ; Cannon vs. University of Chicago 1979). The district court, relying upon the Title IX hostile school environment logic, held that for the plaintiff to prevail, he needed to show that he was a student subjected to abusive conduct because of his national origin, and that the conduct was sufficiently severe or pervasive to create an abusive educational environment. However, following the *Gebser* case line, the district court held that the government was only liable if the plaintiff could show that an official who had the authority to remedy the situation was actually aware of the conduct and did not take the steps necessary to correct the misbehavior.

In Bryant vs. Indep. Sch. Dist. No. I-38 (2003), the Tenth Circuit Court of Appeals also seemed to indicate that there was a private cause of action available under Title VI prohibiting schools from allowing a hostile environment due to race. In that case, the plaintiffs were African-American students who claimed that their school suspended them, but not the Caucasian students involved in a fight. The plaintiffs alleged that the school officials allowed white students to carve offensive racial slurs, epithets, swastikas, and the letters KKK in school furniture. Furthermore, school officials ignored Caucasian students wearing T-shirts with confederate flags, which was against the school dress code. They claimed that the school officials were aware of the hostile environment but did not act to correct the situation, which eventually led to the fight between the African-American and Caucasian students (Bryant 2003). The Tenth Circuit held that in that jurisdiction, the lower courts should apply the US Supreme Court's test in Davis vs. Monroe County Board of Education (1999, p. 633), which allows a private suit for "deliberate indifference to known acts of student-to-student harassment," which can be "an intentional violation of Title IX capable of supporting a private damages action." Thus, until the Supreme Court rules differently, there is at least in the Tenth Circuit, and in Puerto Rico, a prohibition against hostile school environments due to national origin and race under Title VI, which applies similarly as does Title IX. It is only a matter of time until other plaintiffs bring similar cases in other jurisdictions.

*Hostile Environments under the Fair Housing Act* We have shown that under the right circumstances, federal law prohibits hostile work environments in our workplaces and schools. We turn now to consider hostile environments at home. As with other types of hostile environments, the model for establishing a hostile housing environment claim follows from the model of hostile working environment due to sex under Title VII of the Civil Rights Act. At least three federal appeals courts including the Seventh Circuit (DiCenso vs. Cisneros 1996), the Tenth Circuit (Honce vs. Vigil 1993), and the Eighth Circuit (Quigley vs. Winter 2010) recognize in the Fair Housing Act (42 U.S.C.A. Section 3601), a viable theory for hostile housing environments resulting from sexual harassment. The Fair Housing Act prohibits discrimination based upon sex in both the selling or renting of housing with language similar to that found in Title VII, " … It shall be unlawful: (a) To refuse to sell or rent after the making of a bona fide offer, or to refuse to negotiate for the sale or rental of, or otherwise make unavailable or deny, a dwelling to any person because of race, color, religion, sex, familial status, or national origin. (b) To discriminate against any person in the terms, conditions, or privileges of sale or rental of a dwelling, or in the provision of services or facilities in connection therewith, because of race, color, religion, sex, familial status, or national origin" (42 U.S.C.A. Section 3604(a)(b)).

Consider the recent case of Quigley vs. Winter (2010), in which renter Jaymie Quigley and her four children lived in one of many homes that aid of Dale Winter owned in Iowa with the Section 8 housing vouchers. Winter told Quigley that she was eligible to live in a larger house under the voucher system and drove her to view the home. Upon return to the car, Winter rubbed his hand down Quigley's arm and asked how she liked the house. Later, when Quigley's boyfriend moved out of her house, Winter entered the home without prior notice and moved Quigley's clothing around. When she complained, Winter told her he was in the house to fix a screen but the screen was not in need of repair at that time (Quigley 2010, p. 944). On another occasion, Winter came in to inspect Quigley's home at dinnertime, stood very close to Quigley and rubbed his crotch. On still another occasion, Winter entered Quigley's home at bedtime when her daughters were dressed in pajamas and he refused to leave until she forcefully asked him to leave a third time.

Shortly before Quigley's lease ended, Winter came by to find Quigley outside lying in the sun with her sister and a friend. Quigley asked Winter if she would be getting her deposit back. Winter responded by reaching down, "fluttering" his hand against Quigley's stomach and then saying, "My eagle eyes have not seen everything yet." Just before Quigley was about to move out, in part, to escape the unwelcome attention from her landlord, Winter came by to find Quigley's 14-year-old sister was visiting and at the time wearing shorts and a sport bra. Winter said to the girl, "You're really mature. How old are you?...Well, she looks a lot more mature than you [to Quigley]" (Quigley vs. Winter 2010, p. 945).

Quigley filed a complaint with the Sioux City Human Rights Commission and eventually in district court. Among the other claims that she brought was a hostile housing environment claim under the Fair Housing Act. The jury found in favor of Quigley. Upon appeal, the Eighth Circuit held that there was a viable hostile housing environment claim available under the Fair Housing Act. The Court went on to say, "In this case, there was sufficient evidence to support a hostile housing environment claim, if a reasonable jury could find Quigley provided by a preponderance of the evidence, that Winter subjected her to unwelcome sexual harassment, and that the harassment was sufficiently severe or pervasive so as to interfere with or deprive Quigley of her right to use or enjoy her home" (Quigley 2010, pp. 946–947). Thus, the law of hostile housing environments due to sex follows the law of hostile work environment sexual harassment under Title VII. However, a hostile housing environment must interfere or deprive plaintiffs of their right to use or enjoy the property that they have rented instead of creating an abusive work situation.

The extension of hostile housing environments to abusive environments due to other protected classes (e.g., race or disability) has been less successful.[3] Some courts have held that the Fair Housing Act only prohibits discrimination in the buying or renting of houses or apartments (including making loans) but is silent once the consumer lives in the house. In Halprin vs. The Prairie Single Family Homes of Dearborn Park Association (2004), Judge Posner of the Seventh Circuit held that the language in the Fair Housing Act coupled with Congressional intent only meant to prohibit owners and agents from discriminating against minority groups in selling or renting practices. He went on to say that the law did not target the future problems of protected class members after they occupied their places of residence. The US Department of Housing and Urban Development (HUD) has promulgated regulations that make it "unlawful to coerce, intimidate, threaten, or interfere with any person in the exercise or enjoyment of, or on account of his having exercised or enjoyed, or on account of his having aided or encouraged any other person in the exercise or enjoyment of, any right granted or protected by section... 3604... of this title." However, the Courts do not uniformly agree that HUD's rules are consistent with Congress's intentions under the Fair Housing Act. The issue is alive in the

[3] Note that there are many other claims that are actionable under the Fair Housing Act including claims for reasonable accommodations for disabled individuals and for unfair rent and loan policies practiced against all protected classes including race, color, religion, sex, familial status, and national origin.

courts and we will likely see additional litigation at the trial and ultimately appellate level of litigation. In the meantime, there is some law that prohibits hostile housing environments because of race under the FHA. The plaintiffs must show that they are members of a protected class, the conduct was unwelcome, the plaintiff's race caused the conduct, the conduct was sufficiently severe or pervasive to alter the living conditions and produce an abusive housing environment, and that the defendant knew or should have known about the abusive conduct (Smith vs. Mission Associates Limited Partnership 2002). A similar paradigm using hostile environments under the ADA led the Eighth Circuit to find a hostile housing environment action due to disability under the FHA and the Rehabilitation Act (Neudecker vs. Boisclair Corporation 2003).

## Dehumanization in Behavior Settings: A Theory of Hostile Environments

As Section II shows, the law prohibits hostile environments at work, at school, and in the home under certain limiting and qualifying conditions but does not universally protect people from having to endure abusive environments that result from discrimination based upon race, ethnicity, religion, gender, national origin, age, or disability. From a psychological perspective, each type of hostile environment shares defining characteristics, which in some circumstances are a violation of civil law but not so, under other circumstances, depending upon whether the subject of abusive conduct is a protected class under the law and upon how much protection the law provides.

Our theory of hostile environments makes use of the concept of behavior settings (Barker 1978), which started with the idea that the current environment influences the behavior of the inhabitants of those environments as much, if not more, than do the characteristics of the inhabitants. Although Barker advanced behavior setting theory to make sense of the repeated patterns of behaviors of children at school, social psychologist Alan Wicker (1987, 1992) borrowed the concept to examine the role of human cognition in the environment. Accordingly, behavior settings are miniature self-contained social systems made up of people and physical objects (Wicker 1992). Although they have space and time boundaries, behavior settings re-emerge repeatedly over time featuring the same patterns of behavior, known as the setting program (Wicker 1979). In other words, the setting program, an established sequence of interactions among the inhabitants of the setting in the context of their common environment, is the defining property of the setting. According to Wicker, behavior settings are social constructions that we use to make sense of the roles of other people and to negotiate behavioral interactions among the inhabitants of the settings. A setting becomes hostile if one or more of the inhabitants dehumanizes other inhabitants of the setting as a feature of the setting program. This leads to our major assertion: *A hostile environment whether at work, in school, or at home is one that features dehumanization as part of the setting program. That is, one or more people in the setting dehumanize others based upon a characteristic that defines a social category*. Federal law may or may not prohibit individuals from creating hostile environments depending upon whether the social category, which gives rise to the dehumanization, is a protected class and whether or not the law allows a cause of action in the specific context. The law treats behavior settings differently depending upon not only the extent of dehumanization present but also upon the reasons and purposes for the settings' existence in the first place.

Regardless of whether or not federal law prohibits a hostile environment, it is useful to consider in more detail what we mean by dehumanization in order to understand exactly what constitutes a hostile environment or a dehumanized behavior setting. Haslam (2006; Haslam et al. 2013) argues convincingly that before we can make sense out of the concept of dehumanization, it is first necessary to understand the common meaning of humanness. In other words, the way a reasonable person comes to know that an environment is hostile, that it is dehumanized, depends upon the perceiver's judgment about whether the environment denies one or more of the behavior settings' inhabitants the defining characteristics of being human. According to Haslam (2006; Haslam et al. 2013), our everyday understanding of being human is a mixture of uniquely human (UH) characteristics, which separate people from other animals, and human nature (HN) characteristics, which are attributes that are prototypical features at the core of being human and that distinguish people from inanimate objects. These attributes are not objective features that define a human being in a scientific sense; instead, they are common language characteristics that people use to think about humanness in their everyday lives. In other words, Haslam (2006; Haslam et al. 2013) asserts that in common discourse, people think of others as possessing a set of UH characteristics that form boundaries between humans and animals and that they intuitively identify other HN characteristics that define the central factors of being human. Haslam theorizes that these factors establish the common language meaning of humanness, which we believe are important from a social normative and from a legal perspective because they determine society's boundaries of being human and ultimately shape discrimination law.

UH characteristics emerge from socialization and culture and are therefore not universal but instead show substantial variation across cultures. As a result, people likely come to understand them later in their chronological development (Haslam 2006; Haslam et al. 2013). Haslam discusses both UH and HN features as a series of bipolar attributes, each on a continuum with presence on one side and absence on the other side. The UH dimensions are (1) civility vs. lack of culture, (2) refinement vs. coarseness, (3) moral sensitivity vs. amorality (no self-constraint), (4) rationality and logic vs. irrationality and instinct, and (5) maturity vs. childlikeness. In other words, in everyday social discourse, we consider people who show signs of civility, refinement, a strong sense of morality, thinking rationally, and acting in a mature manner as the most human. To dehumanize an individual and make the person appear more like an animal than a person (i.e., animalistic dehumanization), a perceiver would deny that person one or more UH characteristics. Therefore, one way in which behavior setting can be hostile is for people to treat other inhabitants as if they were less than human; that is, viewing them as if they were lacking in refinement, civility, self-control, maturity, and higher cognitive processes. We expect less human and more animal-like individuals to behave out of instinct or appetite rather than out of thoughtful deliberation. Thus, in Che vs. Massachusetts Bay Transportation Authority 2003), when Mr. Che's supervisor called him a "Ch**k" and applied unduly harsh punishment, he was treating the Asian man as less than human and more as an animal without culture or refinement, as one who needed external controls to offset his amoral nature. When we dehumanize others in an animalistic manner, we appraise them with the emotions of disgust and contempt (Haslam 2006), emotions that Mr. Johnson's behavior manifestly expressed toward Chungchi Che.

According to Haslam (2006), animalistic dehumanization features prominently in interethnic relations based upon factors such as race, national origin, ethnicity, or religion gone awry (see Che vs. Massachusetts Bay Transportation Authority 2003; Bryant vs. Indep. Sch. Dist. 2003). People who apply animalistic dehumanization see others as members of an out-group occupying a lower social stratum than their in-group. Thus in Bryant (2003), when the school principal allowed white students to carve offensive racial slurs, epithets, swastikas, and the letters KKK in school furniture and ignored Caucasian students wearing T-shirts with confederate flags, they clearly sent a message that Black students were subordinate to Whites in the school behavior setting. The norms of the environment or the program setting made it acceptable to treat African-American students as coarse, uncultured, and childlike in nature. In short, the school allowed the white students to deny the humanity of the Black students treating them more like animals than fellow humans.

HN attributes represent the biological bases of being human. According to Haslam (2006; Haslam et al. 2013), HN characteristics link people to the natural world and in that sense, most all cultures endorse them and they are prevalent in most social interaction. The HN dimensions are (1) emotionally responsive vs. inert, (2) interpersonal warmth vs. coldness, (3) cognitive openness vs. rigidity, (4) agency and individuality vs. passivity and fungibility, and (5) depth vs. superficiality. Universally, we consider people who are emotionally responsive, warm, cognitively open, active and deep in meaning as the most human in a biological sense. To dehumanize an individual and make the person appear more like an inanimate object than a living organism (i.e., mechanistic dehumanization), a perceiver would deny that person one or more HN characteristics. Therefore, a second way in which an environment can be hostile is for people to treat others as if they were inanimate objects viewing them as if they were inert, cold, rigid, superficial, and fungible. In other words, when we mechanistically dehumanize people, we treat them as if they were objects without their own purposes and autonomy. People who mechanistically dehumanize others see their existence as means to an end; that is, they exist more as objects in the behavior setting than as fellow human inhabitants. In the eyes of the dehumanizer, the role of such individuals in the behavior setting program is to satisfy the dehumanizer's own purposes and not to act as people with their own agency and individuality.

Thus, in Messer vs. Fahnstock & Co. (2008), when Robert Pelham stared at Josephine Chapple and stated, "Oh, you always know when Josephine is coming. Her chest is always right in front of her," he was viewing her an inert object, a fixture of the behavior setting, rather than as a fully human being with her own individuality, purpose, and agency. Pelham showed that he saw Chapple as superficial and fungible, an interchangeable part of the setting, when he suggested, presumably in jest, that the company could pay her to entertain brokers at meetings. That is, she was not a person with her own sense of meaning and her own motivations; instead, Pelham saw her as an inanimate object interchangeable with any one of a number of other women whose purpose was to serve only as an object of sexual desire. When we dehumanize others in a mechanistic manner, we show little emotion toward them at all regarding them with indifference or mild disregard. Certainly, Mr. Pelham saw Ms. Chapple as a cold and rigid fixture of the behavior setting and reacted toward her with indifference.

Haslam's (2006; Haslam et al. 2013) treatment of mechanistic dehumanization is very similar to philosopher Martha Nussbaum's (1999) classical discussion of objectification, which feminist scholars in psychology use almost synonymously with sexual objectification. According to Nussbaum, objectification means "...treating as an object what is really not an object, what is in fact, a human being" (p. 218). She went on to summarize seven ways in which one can objectify another focusing on sexual objectification of women. First, one can objectify through fungibility, which refers to situations when one person treats another as interchangeable with similar persons or other group members (e.g., one woman is indistinguishable from another woman). Second, one objectifies another through the denial of subjectivity, which refers to situations when one person sees another as lacking feelings and experiences (e.g., the sum total of a woman is her looks). Third, one can objectify another through perceptions of inertness, which refers to situations when one person treats another as lacking agency (e.g., a woman is to be acted upon and not herself an actor). Fourth, one can objectify through instrumentality, which refers to situations when one person treats another as an instrument for use (e.g., a woman's purpose is to satisfy men's needs). Fifth, one can objectify through violability, which refers to situations when one person can deny another person accepted boundaries (e.g., a woman's body can be violated or broken up). Sixth, one can objectify by feelings of ownership, which refers to situations when one sees another as a commodity (e.g., my car is similar to my woman). Finally, one can objectify another by denial of autonomy, which refers to situations when one person sees another as lacking independence and self-determination (e.g., a woman cannot make her own decisions). While it is an empirical question whether treating an individual in only one of these ways is sufficient to stand as objectification in a more general sense, feminist scholars agree in principle that to treat a human being in any one of these ways may constitute sexual objectification (Nussbaum 1999). In the language of behavior setting theory, one individual objectifies another to the extent to which the recipient becomes more like an inanimate object in the setting than like another human agent with her or his own motivations, intentions, and purposes.

We must point out that objectification need not always be dehumanizing, but in some way that depends upon the program of the behavior setting in which it occurs, the motivations of the target, and the motivations of the person doing the objectifying. For example, employers objectify their employees in most situations, hiring them to perform specific tasks, seeing them as somewhat fungible, and not always being concerned with their autonomy, sense of purpose, or with their subjectivity or sense of internal emotional satisfaction. Nonetheless, few of us, perhaps with the exception of those avidly opposed to market based economies (Marx 1964), would insist that a sales clerk in a store who sells cosmetics or accessories to consumers for a salary suffers from dehumanization. That is, we recognize that the behavior setting programs that define most businesses endorse a pattern of objectification because objectification is essential to the settings if they are to achieve their essential purpose of existence, namely to promote the development, sale, and delivery of products and services. Similarly, few of us would find consensual flirting at a local bar or pub among consenting adults dehumanizing, despite the fact that both actors may see the other as a source of sexual desire. In both of these examples, the objectified individual agrees either explicitly (the sales clerk) or implicitly by visiting a local bar (the consenting adults) to being treated as an instrument and fungible for others' purposes in at least some realms and for limited purposes. In other words, the purpose of the bar or pub behavior setting is to provide an opportunity for individuals to seek out the company of others with the potential for a possible romantic interlude. However, under other circumstances the experience of objectification quickly becomes mechanistic dehumanization. This is most likely to occur in behavior settings with programs that do not include objectification as a fundamental process necessary to achieve the settings' purpose. This is most evident when people reduce others to sexual objects even though others have not agreed to the unwelcomed sexual attention or when people objectify others according to their age, treating them as inanimate objects without their own sense of subjective well-being or agency. For example, in Quigley vs. Winter (2010), Jaymie Quigley's landlord repeatedly touched her in unwelcome ways rubbing his hand down her arm and stomach. When he went on to stare at her young daughters dressed in pajamas and to imply that he was interested in seeing Quigley undressed, Winter's unwelcomed attention targeted Quigley as a superficial and fungible sex object whose purpose was to satisfy his own desires. Quigley was only interested in the landlord-renter relationship and had not agreed tacitly or explicitly to any other type of arrangement. She entered the apartment setting only because she understood its program to be one that existed to satisfy her housing needs but not any romantic function. This is not dissimilar to the age-based objectification described in Dediol vs. Best Chevrolet, Inc. (2011), when Donald Clary, Dediol's supervisor, responded to the 65-year-old auto salesman's request to attend a volunteer church event by cursing him for being old. When Clary referred to Dediol as "old mother fu***r", "old man," and "pops" several times each day, there is little doubt that he saw him as someone lacking autonomy, fungible and indeed as something that is owned by another, and whose experience and feelings were irrelevant.

Once again, our major assertion is that a hostile environment is one in which the inhabitants of a behavior setting dehumanize one or more of other inhabitants based upon one or more of the target's immutable or nearly immutable social characteristics that define a social category. If the social category is a protected class and the settings and circumstances afford protection to the victims of dehumanization as specified under the appropriate statute and case law, then the dehumanized environment is a hostile environment intolerable to the norms, regulations, and laws of society. The dehumanization can occur at work, in school, or at home. The first step in creating a hostile work environment is to separate the inhabitants of behavior settings into social categories along social fault lines. Some differentiations that have been made within the context of the dehumanization literature (Haslam 2006, 2012) are unprotected under the law (other vs. self, social class, education, sexual orientation[4], and status/power) while others (race, national origin, gender, religion, age, and disability) are covered by federal statute. Thus, while dehumanization pertaining to the first set of factors could create a potential hostile environment from the target's perspective, denying humanness based upon these social factors will not result in a violation of civil rights as defined by federal law. However, we acknowledge that for some federally unprotected social dimensions such as sexual orientation, there are state and local protections so that dehumanization along those social fault lines could produce illegal hostile environments under limited state or local jurisdictions.

Second, dehumanization results when the inhabitants of behavior settings deny UH or HN factors to other inhabitants along the contours of these societal fault lines. The extent of dehumanization in a given environment is a function of the number and strength of UH or HN factors that inhabitants deny to others. The denial of some UH factors (e.g., morality and maturity) likely carries more meaning than the denial of others (e.g., civility and refinement) and the denial of some HN factors (e.g., agency and individuality) likely carries more meaning than other HN characteristics (e.g., cognitive openness and depth). Furthermore, if more than one person engages in the discriminatory behavior then the number and types of denied UH and HN factors will increase resulting in a more abusive hostile environment. Our third point follows from the first two. We see dehumanization as varying along a continuum from minimal or no dehumanization, where all inhabitants attribute all UH and HN characteristics to all other inhabitants of the behavior setting, to a maximum in which multiple inhabitants deny all or nearly all UH and HN factors to one or more in the behavioral setting. The fourth point in our model is that, in principle, researchers can measure the level of dehumanization and therefore hostility in an environment through cataloguing the number and type of UH and HN factors that inhabitants attribute and/or deny to targets in the setting. Following the law, measurement of dehumanization in an environment ought to focus on the properties of severity and pervasiveness. Here, severity (i.e., harsh and unsparing treatment of others) is the degree to which inhabitants of settings partially or completely deny UH or HN factors to others. This includes the number and type of denied human attributes. Pervasiveness pertains to whether others deny the UH or HN factors throughout the environment or only in limited situations or circumstances (see Fig. 3.1).

[4] As of the time of that we wrote this paper (April 2013), the federal courts had not accepted sexual orientation as a dimension that created protected classes as they have done under some circumstances for gender, race, national origin, religion, age, and disability.

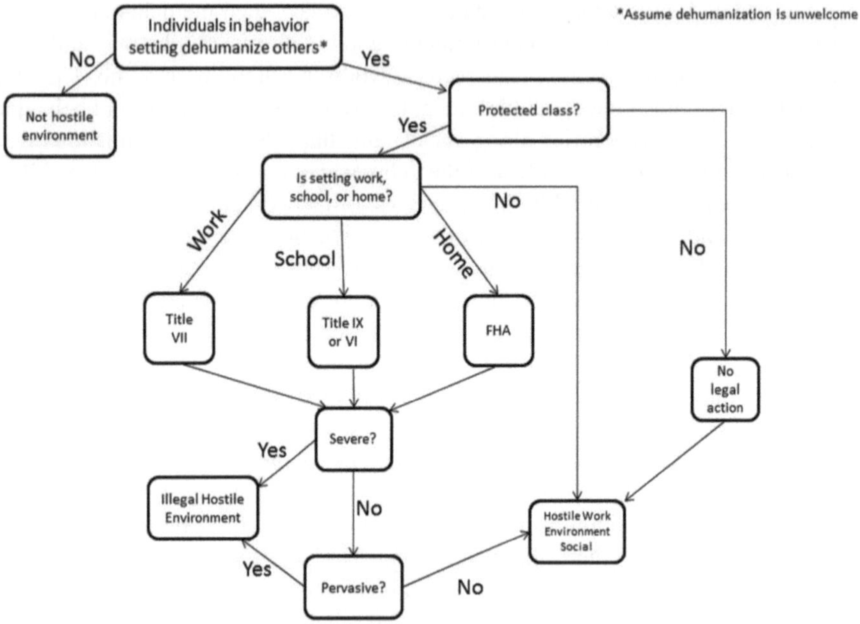


**Fig. 3.1** Determination of illegal hostile environment

We acknowledge that in real world behavior settings, there are probably few examples of pure forms of animalistic and mechanistic dehumanization. Most hostile environments likely contain elements of both types of dehumanization. Nonetheless, following the lead of Haslam (2006; Haslam et al. 2013), we expect that intergroup discrimination based upon race, national origin, religion, and sometimes gender where people make comparisons between in-groups and out-groups is most likely associated with animalistic dehumanization. Furthermore, discrimination that involves comparisons of the self to individual others along dimensions of gender, age, or disability, rather than comparisons to out-groups, features mechanistic dehumanization (see Fig. 3.2). Other types of mechanistic dehumanization such as denying HN characteristics based upon status, power, personality features, and education level are not legally actionable but may cause social problems that are just as debilitating. For example, treating poor people as cogs in an economic machine, denying them individuality, agency, interpersonal warmth, and emotional responsiveness is a serious political and social problem, but the law does not prohibit the creation of hostile work, school, or home environments based upon lack of wealth (see Fig. 3.3). In principle, it ought to be possible to measure animalistic and mechanistic dehumanization and test their associations with different types of hostile environments including those that the law prohibits and those for which the law is silent. However, if dehumanization in a behavior setting occurs along social fault lines that are protected under law (i.e., race, national origin, gender, religion, age, or disability) and the dehumanization is severe and/or pervasive, then the environment

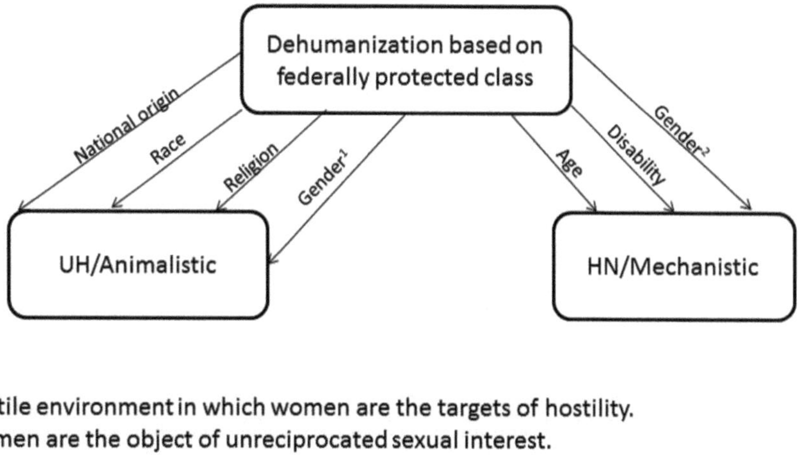


**Fig. 3.2** Type of illegal hostile environment

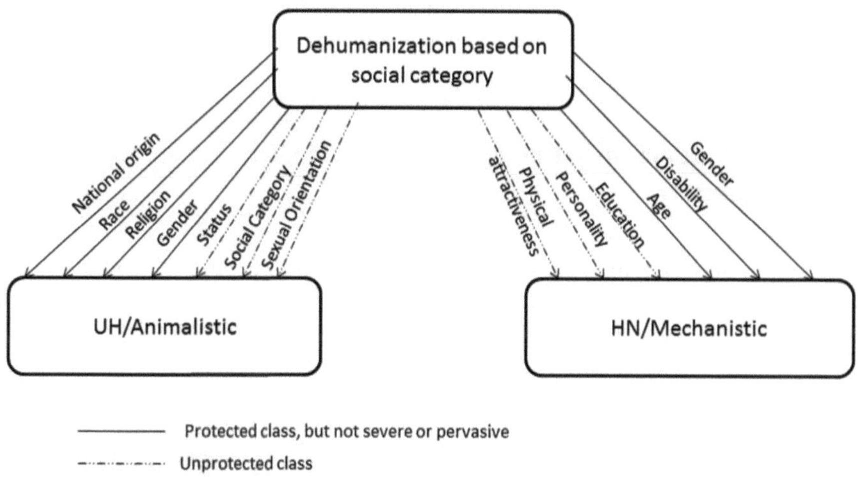


**Fig. 3.3** Type of social hostile environment

is hostile in a legally relevant sense provided that it occurs in circumstances that the law recognizes under existing statute and case law. Figure 3.1 is graphic depiction of our model of hostile environments due to dehumanization.

One more qualifying point is relevant to our model of hostile environments. The law of hostile work environments requires that the conduct in question is unwelcome. That is, disparaging comments or actions based upon an individual's race, national origin, gender, religion, age, or disability must be unwelcome to the recipient of the action. This issue is most relevant for hostile environments due to sexual harassment because in some environments social sexual conduct is part of the ongoing and accepted patterns in the behavioral setting. That is, sexual comments and flirting at work or even at home or in school occasionally may be welcome because gender is somewhat unique with regard to intergroup relations; heterosexual men and women are intimately interdependent (Rudman and Glick 2008) and sexual comments and flirting in work, home, or school settings may be perceived as a normal part of gendered interactions, despite the fact power and status differences often underlie such social sexual conduct in the workplace. While it is possible that other types of bantering based upon race, religion, or age may also be part of the accepted behavior of a setting, it is less likely that the recipient will welcome such comments even if they are part of the norms of the setting. Nonetheless, to prevail in any hostile environment action, a plaintiff must demonstrate that the action was unwelcome, often by demonstrating that the individual made a formal complaint at the time of the abusive conduct. Our model assumes that dehumanization is unwelcome. That is, denying an individual humanness—either UH or HN characteristics—is by definition an unwelcome action. It is difficult to imagine that anyone would welcome another person treating her or him as if she or he was lacking in refinement, civility, self-control, maturity, or higher cognitive processes or as if she or he was inert, cold, rigid, superficial, or fungible. In other words, one dimension of dehumanizing conduct is that it is unwelcome. Nonetheless, legally relevant research ought to demonstrate that the discriminatory conduct was indeed unwelcome.

## Research Underlying the Psychology of Hostile Environments

We propose that denying others UH characteristics or engaging in animalistic dehumanization explains hostile environment judgments for some protected classes. Most empirical research focusing on denying others UH characteristics shows that animalistic dehumanization of out-groups (and animalistic humanization of in-groups) is a robust phenomenon that emerges in intergroup relations, specifically perceiving people from different races, ethnicities, or national origins (e.g., Castano and Kofta 2009; Haslam 2006; Haslam et al. 2012, 2013; Leyens et al. 2003). For example, Vaes et al. (2003) found that Italians attributed UH emotions to other Italians (i.e., members of the in-group) compared to North Africans (i.e., members of an out-group). Extending this to traits, as well as other ethnicities or nationalities (e.g., Italians vs. Slavs, Italians vs. Belgians, or Italians vs. Japanese), Vaes and Paladino (2010; Paladino and Vaes 2009; Vaes et al. 2010; see also Viki and Calitri 2008, for comparison between Brits and Americans) also found that in-group traits were regarded as more UH than out-group traits. Perceptions of intergroup conflict and differences in status often contribute to these effects (Rohmann et al. 2009).

Other research has shown that animalistic dehumanization emerges for people from other groups, including women, immigrants, and indigenous people. Applied to the context of sexual objectification, for example, Vaes et al. (2011, see also Rudman and Mescher 2013; Viki and Abrams 2003) found that sexualized women were associated more with animals (vs. humans) on single-category implicit association tests (IATs) compared to sexualized men. Interestingly, Vaes and colleagues found evidence that sexual attraction triggered animalistic dehumanization of sexualized women for men, whereas social distance predicted animalistic dehumanization of sexualized women for women. Regarding immigrants with a focus on reducing intergroup conflict, Costello and Hodson (2010) found that factors related to reducing animalistic dehumanization and perceiving animals and humans similarly predicted greater immigrant humanization and empathy, which reduced prejudice toward immigrants. Similar attributions about indigenous people (Jahoda 1999; Haslam et al. 2013) showed that people were more likely to associate animal stimuli with Native Americans in the US and Aborigines in Australia (Castano and Giner-Sorolla 2006; Saminaden et al. 2010). Finally, these effects have also emerged cross-culturally with people associating less humanness to out-groups compared to in-groups across samples from countries such as Australia, China, and Italy (Bain et al. 2009, 2012; Haslam et al. 2008; Park et al. 2012).

Consistent with the notion that animalistic dehumanization may predict hostile environment harassment, attributing less UH emotions and traits to out-groups compared to in-groups has meaningful policy implications. For example, Zebel et al. (2008) found that animalistic dehumanization of out-groups reduced people's support for policies intended to repair harm toward the out-group caused by the in-group. Specifically, Dutch participants' support for the government making reparations to Muslims who were killed by Dutch UN soldiers during the war in the former Yugoslavia was negatively related to animalistic dehumanization. Regarding animalistic dehumanization for African Americans in the USA, implicitly associating Blacks with apes contributed to more endorsement of violence against Black suspects in the criminal justice system (Goff et al. 2008). Furthermore, news articles written about Blacks (vs. Whites) convicted of capital crimes were more likely to contain ape-relevant language, and when people of either race were implicitly associated with apes in the media, they were more likely to be executed by the state (Goff et al. 2008).

Individual differences related to support for different policies also appear to moderate animalistic dehumanization effects. For example, politically conservative Caucasians attributed less UH attributes to Hispanics, and this animalistic dehumanization predicted less aid to Hispanic families suffering from a natural disaster, compared to politically liberal Caucasians (DeLuca-McLean and Castano 2009). More generally, animalistic dehumanization tends to elicit disgust (Harris and Fiske 2006; Haidt 2007) as well as moral disengagement (Castano and Giner-Sorolla 2006). Applied to the present framework, animalistic dehumanization of people from protected classes determined by race, ethnicity, national origin, or religion should explain the relation between discrimination and hostile environment judgments.

Corresponding to our consideration of denying UH characteristics, we suggest that denying others HN characteristics or engaging in mechanistic dehumanization may explain hostile environment judgments for protected classes because of self vs. other comparisons such as those based upon sex, age, and disability. At the very least, people tend to humanize themselves more than they do others (Haslam et al.2005), and a host of psychological factors including egocentrism, focalism, and abstract construals of other people moderate these self-humanizing effects (Haslam and Bain 2007). These effects also emerge for in-groups more generally and even appear for undesirable, negative, HN flaws (Koval et al. 2012). This self-humanization bias, however, reverses with people denying themselves HN attributes when they feel others exclude (Bastian and Haslam 2010, 2011) or control (Moller and Deci 2010) them. Like human uniqueness denials, HN denial effects emerge cross-culturally when researchers compared people's reactions to robots (vs. humans) and found they perceived robots as lacking emotion and desire-related capacities across samples from many different countries (Bain et al. 2009, 2012; Haslam et al. 2008; Park et al. 2012).

Regarding denying HN to people from protected classes, mechanistic dehumanization has been linked to the perception of women, but not men. For example, utilizing a single category IAT, Rudman and Mescher (2012) found that women were likened to objects more than men were. That is, words describing women such as "woman," "female," "she," and "her" were implicitly associated with object words such as "object," "tool," "device," and "thing," whereas words describing men such as "man," "male," "he," and "his" were not. Interestingly, this mechanistic dehumanization of women predicted self-reported rape proclivity (though animalistic dehumanization and not mechanistic dehumanization predicted actual aggressive behaviors).[5] This finding is consistent with the more general notion that mechanistic dehumanization predicts interpersonal violence (Moller and Deci 2010). Applied to the present work, hostile environments related to sex discrimination, which can involve an element of interpersonal violence (e.g., microaggressions in the workplace), may be explained by the denial of HN. Although empirical evidence for denying others HN is limited, there is a substantial literature on a closely related construct—sexual objectification—which provides additional evidence that mechanistic dehumanization may underlie hostile environments.

Closely related to mechanistic dehumanization, which involves denying people HN characteristics, scholars across many disciplines have argued that people sometimes view and treat others as objects. This process is called objectification and occurs when a person's body parts, functions, or other characteristics are separated from the person, reduced to the status of instruments, or regarded as capable of representing the entire person (Bartky 1990; Fredrickson and Roberts 1997; Gruenfeld et al. 2008; MacKinnon 1987; Nussbaum 1995, 1999). For example, economists and philosophers have argued that in capitalism, employers objectify their employees, reducing their employees to their work qualities for their own use (Marx 1964). To the employer, the sum of the employees corresponds to their capacity to get the

[5] One possible explanation for the predictive power of animalistic dehumanization in this context is that people who associated women with animals did so because they saw women as an out-group. People who hold hostile sexist attitudes toward women (Glick and Fiske, 1996) likely do so because they see sexuality not as a characteristic that differentiates the self from others but because it differentiates an in-group (men) from an out-group (women).

job done (Gruenfeld et al. 2008). Likewise, in medicine, physicians may objectify a patient, reducing their patients to their symptoms (Barnard 2001; Foucault 1989). Sometimes, objectification may occur along stigmatized group membership lines. For example, people may reduce others to their race, age, or disability attributes, but of greatest familiarity and empirical examination, scholars have noted that both men and women commonly reduce women to their gender attributes and sexually objectify them in many contexts, with serious consequences (Bartky 1990; Code 1995; Fredrickson and Roberts 1997; LeMoncheck 1985; McKinley and Hyde 1996; Nussbaum 1999).

According to feminist scholars, objectification represents a fundamental issue in the lives of women; women are often viewed and treated as men's sexual objects and as less than human (MacKinnon 1989, 2006; Nussbaum 1995, 1999). As discussed above, Nussbaum (1999) developed more nuanced mechanisms and along with other feminist scholars applied these notions to sexual objectification more specifically. Although the origins of feminist considerations are in critiques of pornography (Dworkin 1989; MacKinnon 1987, 1989, 2006), more recent inquiries represent sexual objectification as a specific type of appearance-focus concentrated on sexual body parts that also emerges during everyday interactions (Gervais et al. 2011). Representing a form of body reduction (Langton 2009), sexual objectification emerges when people focus on women's appearances, bodies, sexual body parts, or sexual functions more than their faces and other non-observable attributes, such as thoughts, feelings, and desires. When people reduce women to their appearance, this contributes to the perceivers' dehumanized evaluations of others. For example, Heflick and colleagues (Heflick and Goldenberg 2009; Heflick et al. 2011) found that when people focused on appearance of others, they regarded women (but not men) as less competent and less warm than when they focused on others as people. Not only do we commonly reduce people to their appearance more generally but we also frequently reduce them to their bodies specifically (Archer et al. 1983; Langton 2009). Body-focus (e.g., presenting a woman's body without her face) has been associated with decreased perception of mind, less moral treatment, and less pain attribution (Loughnan et al. 2010; see also Gray et al. 2011), as well as more animalistic dehumanization (Vaes et al. 2011). Finally, people sometimes reduce others from their appearances and entire bodies to their sexual body parts (Gervais et al. 2012a). This results in piecemeal rather than holistic processing of women (Bernard et al. 2012, 2013; Gervais et al. 2012a), less focus on women's faces compared to their bodies (Gervais et al. 2012b, 2013), and perceiving women as fungible (or interchangeable) with women with similar bodies (Gervais et al. 2012b). Sexually objectifying behaviors resulting from this reduction of women to their sexual body parts may result in subtle and covert microaggressions such as inappropriate sexual innuendo, appearance comments, and objectifying gazes. These more subtle forms of objectification may be most likely to emerge in everyday interactions in employment, education, and housing contexts. When sufficiently severe and/or pervasive, these forms of objectification may represent hostile environments.

Objectification researchers have focused a great deal of attention on self-objectification, showing that one important consequence of sexual objectification is that women learn to be their first surveyors (see Moradi and Huang 2008 for review). That is, as a result of experiencing sexual objectification from others, women also persistently objectify themselves (Fredrickson and Roberts 1997; McKinley and Hyde 1996). This self-objectification has serious detrimental outcomes. When women self-objectify, they internalize an observer's perspective of their bodies and regard their appearance as more important to their self-concept than their other attributes (e.g., physical health, emotions, cognitions; Bartky 1990; Berger 1972; de Beauvoir 1952; Fredrickson and Roberts 1997; McKinley 1998, 2006; McKinley and Hyde 1996). Through sexual objectification experiences in the media and interpersonal interactions, girls and women learn that it is adaptive to focus on their appearance more than their other attributes to determine how they will be treated by others. For example, previous research has shown that women (vs. men) consider their observable physical appearance attributes (e.g., body measurements) as more central to their self-concept compared to less observable physical competence characteristics (e.g., strength; Noll and Fredrickson 1998) and persistently think about how they look (McKinley and Hyde 1996). A multitude of negative consequences are posited to result from objectification experiences through the self-objectification process, including appearance anxiety, body surveillance, body shame, and a diminished capacity for peak motivational states. These intermediary consequences set the stage for psychological disorders that disproportionately affect women compared to men, including unipolar depression, eating disorders, and sexual dysfunction (see Calogero et al. 2011; Moradi and Huang 2008, for reviews). As a result, women may come to accept sexual objectification of women (Rudman and Glick 2008) so that people often integrate such detrimental conduct into the programs of the most common behavior settings providing the stage for additional dehumanization and the emergence of hostile environments. Furthermore, it is possible but so far undocumented that women who do self-objectify are less likely to perceive and complain about hostile environments due to sexual harassment.

Although psychologists have primarily focused on self-objectification for women, like objectification more generally, our behavior setting analysis suggests that when objectification is an integral part of the behavior setting, program inhabitants of the setting may endorse objectification more broadly, resulting in objectified individuals adopting other people's perspectives of themselves (Fanon 1967; Marx 1964). To illustrate, the worker may reduce himself to his work-related capabilities, adopting the objectifying gaze of his employer. When supervisors reduce employees to illegal characteristics (e.g., gender, race, national origin, age, disability), employees may subsequently internalize the gaze of the employer and they may see themselves primarily in terms of their social group.

Recent findings from our collaborative research provide evidence for use of this framework for hostile work environment judgments. First, we focus on analogue studies in which people evaluate descriptions of environments that are more or less dehumanizing and predict hostile environment judgments. Wiener et al. (2010), for example, showed participants two video reenactments of dehumanized environments in two sexual harassment cases. Participants saw a video that was based on Faragher vs. Boca Raton (1998), in which male supervisors repeatedly subjected female lifeguards to "uninvited and offensive touching" and made lewd remarks, speaking of women in "offensive terms." They also saw a video based on Rabidue vs. Osceola Refining Co. ( 1986), in which men workers made crude and vulgar comments toward their women co-workers, downplayed the women's abilities, and displayed photographs of nude and scantily clad women in the workplace. Wiener et al. (2010) also manipulated which case came first and the complainant's behavioral tone. Specifically, they varied whether the complainant was aggressive (inconsistent with the female gender role), submissive (consistent with the female gender role), or neutral. Participants provided hostile work environment judgments (i.e., the extent to which the unwelcome sexual conduct was sufficiently severe or pervasive to create a hostile work environment). Case order, complainant tone, and participant gender interacted to predict hostile work environment judgments. When evaluating the first case, men participants were more likely to find the work environment to be hostile when the complainant was submissive than when she was aggressive. Women participants were insensitive to the tone of the complainant. If anything, the women were less sympathetic when the complainant was submissive because they found the work environment to be more hostile than men did, but not when the complainant was submissive. Interestingly, a different pattern of results emerged on the second case presented in which all complainants were neutral in tone. When evaluating the second case, men were insensitive to the behavioral tone of the complainant from the first case as they, in fact, should have been. The events in one case should not cross over to judgments of a second case. These are independent events and workers should see them that way. Most interesting, the women found the environment less hostile when the complainant in the first case was submissive. Reinterpreted through our framework, women expected the complainant to stand up for herself in the face of dehumanization and when she did not, our female participants held higher expectations for the ability of women to stand up for themselves. Thus, women workers blamed the victims in subsequent cases for the fact that women in prior episodes did not stand up for themselves. Women complainants may be in a double bind, with perceptions of hostile work environments in dehumanizing situations depending on their tone and the gender of the perceiver.

In a more recent investigation, we have used a similar analogue study and extended these considerations to age discrimination (Wiener et al. 2013). Specifically, we presented scenarios in which an interviewer reduced an older worker to his age attributes during a job interview, resulting in dehumanizing treatment. For example, a younger interviewer made several references to the older worker's age, noting that he was surprised that someone as old as the worker could remember details from the past and likened the older worker to his grandparents. The younger interviewer made several stereotypic comments, indicating that he believed the older worker would have difficulty with technology, would have trouble remembering high school and college activities, and needed the assistance of bifocals to read the interview materials. Finally, the interviewer was generally condescending, calling the older worker "Pops" and "old guy," smirking at the older worker, and acting with impatience toward the older worker. The control condition was exactly the same, except the younger interviewer did not focus on the older worker's age, make stereotypic comments, or treat the older worker in a condescending way.

After reading this scenario, participants predicted the degree to which the older worker was lacking HN and UH dimensions more generally (e.g., characteristics that are central to HN but not to objects and characteristics that humans experience but that animals do not) as well as specific attributes (Haslam et al. 2005; Haslam and Bain 2007). For example, "ambitious" represented both a UH and HN attribute; "broad-minded" represented a uniquely human, but not HN attribute; "active" represented a HN, but not UH attribute; and "contented" represented neither a UH nor HN attribute. Participants also reported the degree to which the older worker was subjected to a hostile work environment.

Interestingly, age discrimination (vs. control) caused greater perceptions of the older worker possessing less HN and UH dimensions and attributes as well as more hostile work environment judgments. Most importantly and consistent with our suggestion that mechanistic and not animalistic dehumanization should specifically explain age discrimination, attributing to the older worker fewer HN attributes and dimensions explained the relationship between age discrimination and hostile work environment judgments. The denial of UH characteristics was not a mediator of the relationship between age discrimination and judgments of a hostile work environment.

Second, we focus on studies in which we have directly manipulated mechanistic dehumanization in the context of sexual objectification with analogues to job interviews in the lab. Gervais et al. (2011) brought women and men into the lab for a study of how people work in teams. Following a rigged scoring of a leadership questionnaire, the participant was assigned to the role of worker, while an opposite-gender confederate was assigned to the role of leader. Leaders were responsible for interviewing the worker, selecting math problems, evaluating the answers, and forwarding a final team solution. Workers were responsible for answering interview questions and completing math problems. Following leader and worker assignments, a getting acquainted interview ensued in which Gervais et al. (2011) manipulated objectification. In the objectification condition, the confederate gazed from the head to waist and from waist to head in one sweeping motion when the participant entered the room. Then the confederate proceeded to ask five questions and before and after asking the first, third, and last question, the confederate briefly gazed at the participant's chest. To ensure that participants actually interpreted the gaze as objectifying, the confederate provided written feedback following the interview indicating that the participant was "looking good" and that he had selected the problems based on the way the participant looked. The control condition was exactly the same, except eye contact was maintained and participants received feedback indicating that they were "doing good" and their problems were selected based on their interview responses. Participants were then given 10 min to complete 12 math problems. Consistent with the notion that being treated in a mechanistically dehumanizing manner may negatively impact people from protected classes, namely women in a sexually objectifying context, women showed decreased performance compared to men when they were objectified, and decreased performance compared to women who were not objectified.

Adapting this paradigm to specifically examine hostile work environment sexual harassment, Wiener et al. (2012) brought women participants into the lab to presumably examine people's performance on different types of jobs. Upon arriving at the lab, the participant learned that she would complete either an interesting poster-creating task or a boring research article-sorting task. To ostensibly determine which task they would complete, a male research assistant conducted an interview in which he asked 10 questions of the woman participant. After asking the fourth, seventh, ninth, and tenth questions, the participant slowly gazed at the participant's chest for two seconds and nodded. Following the ninth question, he asked for further clarification and said, "That's a really unexpected answer for a woman as good looking as you" and ended the interviewing saying, "Okay, you're looking good." The control condition was identical, except the interviewer maintained eye contact. The male interviewer also said, "That's a really unexpected answer" after the ninth question and ended the interview by saying, "Okay, you're doing good." Following the objectifying manipulation, the women participants completed a modified version of the positive and negative affect schedule (PANAS-X; a mood measure), a modified version of the math problems from Gervais et al. (2011), and measures of hostile work environment sexual harassment (Wiener et al. 2010).

We also examined the predicted emotions, performance, and judgments of sexual harassment from people who observed the harassment or learned about the harassment after the fact. Specifically, we recorded the experiencer interactions and then asked a separate set of women participants to watch the interactions (i.e., observers) and a separate set of women participants to read transcripts describing the interactions (i.e., predictors). These participants then predicted what emotions the woman in the interaction might feel, predicted how she would perform on work tasks, and made judgments of sexual harassment. They also made the emotion and sexual harassment judgments based on self-referenced perspectives (i.e., imagining how they would feel and evaluate sexual harassment in the interaction if they had been the woman subjected to the social sexual conduct). Consistent with our theoretical framework based upon an affective forecasting model, which documents that people overestimate anticipated emotional consequences of especially negative events (Gilbert et al. 1998) and the Asymmetric Immune Knowledge hypothesis (AIK), which extended affective forecasting to show that people overestimated other's emotional reactions (Igou 2008), women who experienced objectification evaluated the interaction as more sexually harassing than women who did not. Interestingly, those predictors who read transcripts of the interactions evaluated the interaction as more sexually harassing than women who actually experienced objectification. Additionally, although experiencers showed no differences in negative emotions, predictors expected more negative emotions in the objectification condition than the control condition. Furthermore, self-referenced sexual harassment judgments and forecasted negative emotion were significant mediators explaining the relation between objectification and sexual harassment judgments for predictors. Interpreted through our current theoretical framework, the predicted negative emotions that emerged in the objectification condition may have stemmed from the notion that the male research assistant objectified the women in the interviews. We have also replicated these findings, but included more severe forms of sexual objectification (longer gazing and more negative appearance commentary) and found a similar pattern of results (Gervais et al. 2013). We are also currently examining more pervasive forms of sexual objectification (gazing from multiple sources), explicitly assessing both animalistic and mechanistic dehumanization, and expanding the predictor conditions beyond transcripts to EEOC-like interviews.

## Summary and Conclusions: Implications for Law and for Psychology

We started this paper with five basic questions: (1) What is a hostile environment? (2) How is dehumanization related to hostile environments? (3) What are sources of dehumanization in hostile environments? (4) When does dehumanization become a violation of civil law? And (5) What do we know about the causes and psychological outcomes of dehumanization? We believe our model offers potential answers to all of these questions and this line of research has the potential to provide a nuanced understanding of hostile environments, those that the law does and does not prohibit under federal statute. In doing so, this work has the potential to contribute to our understanding of how justice contributes to conflict resolution and ultimately to the well-being of people in a variety of behavior settings at work, at home, and in school. In that way, our model contributes directly to the theme of this volume, titled, *Justice, Conflict and Well-being*. It does so by helping us to understand what we mean from a psycholegal perspective when we speak about hostile environments.

Hostile environments can occur at work, home, or at school because of abusive treatment based upon unprotected factors (other vs. self, social class, education, sexual orientation, and status/power) or factors that have at least some protection under law (race, national origin, gender, religion, age, and disability). By law, hostile environments emerge from unwelcome misconduct that results because of a protected factor and which is sufficiently severe or pervasive to be abusive. When dehumanization is severe or when it permeates a behavior setting's program, so that it becomes a pervasive part of the setting norm, the outcome is a hostile environment. Two types of dehumanization result in hostile environments. The first type, animalistic dehumanization, is the act of denying UH characteristics, in other words, viewing people as "animal-like." Animalistic dehumanization frequently distinguishes in-groups from out-groups resulting in abusive conduct and hostile environments that can violate federal law if the dehumanization is based upon factors such as race, national origin, religion, or possibly gender. The second, mechanistic dehumanization, is the act of denying people fundamental attributes of HN, in other words viewing people as "object-like." Mechanistic dehumanization often distinguishes the self from the other and similarly can result in hostile environments as a result of abusive behavior due to gender, age, and disability.

We believe that research conducted to explore the antecedents and consequences of dehumanization can further our understanding of when and how hostile environments bring about negative consequences to the inhabitants of behavior settings. There are at least two ways to study dehumanized hostile environments within a social psychological framework in order to learn about the processes that create illegal and socially unacceptable hostile environments and to develop an understanding of how people determine what constitutes a hostile environment. The first involves manipulating the descriptions of the environments to vary levels of animalistic and mechanistic dehumanization and then measuring people's cognitive, motivational, emotional, and behavioral responses to the dehumanization. The second approach is to directly manipulate types of dehumanization through objectification or some other method of denying specific UH or HN factors and examining the effects of the dehumanization, again on the cognitions, motivations, emotions, judgments, and behavioral reactions of those who experience, observe, and predict the outcomes of the manipulations.

Our joint program of research has made a start at understanding the antecedents and consequences of dehumanization in behavior settings showing that (1) objectified experiencers perceive the environment as more hostile than do control experiencers, and (2) predictors (people learning about the objectification through indirect sources) anticipate that experiencers will find objectification more hostile than the experiencers actually find it. In fact, at low levels of sexual objectification (i.e., mechanistic dehumanization), the "objective" experience (in a legal sense) of hostile environments is actually more intense than is the "subjective" experience (again in a legal sense of subjectivity). This is perhaps due to the predictors' failure to take into consideration the coping system of the experiencers (i.e., Igou's AIK effect 2008) and as a result, they over-anticipate negative affect and self-referenced expectations (i.e., if I was objectified in this way, it would be dehumanizing). Furthermore, initial findings with our experimental paradigm (Wiener et. al. 2012), which simultaneously studies experiencers, observers, and predictors in objectified environments, shows that pervasive mechanistic dehumanization (i.e., objectifying gazes that permeate a behavior setting) results in similar experiencer effects and a similar gap between experiencers, on the one hand, and observers and predictors on the other. Finally, our efforts at manipulating descriptions of a setting in which an older worker was applying for a job by endorsing unfounded stereotypes of older people showed mechanistic dehumanization but not animalistic dehumanization mediated predictors' judgments of hostile environments. We believe that additional research examining animalistic and mechanistic dehumanization in work settings, school settings, and residential settings offers great promise for learning more about hostile environments from both psychological and legal perspectives.

We invite others to join in our efforts to provide additional and more refined answers to our initial questions and address other topics, such as how severe must dehumanization become for experiencers (i.e., plaintiffs), observers (i.e., witnesses), and predictors (i.e., jurors, EEOC workers, and judges) to detect a hostile environment? How pervasive must dehumanization become under conditions of both high and low severity for these same actors to detect a hostile environment? What is the effect of animalistic dehumanization both as a separate factor and in conjunction with mechanistic dehumanization? How does the law and how should the law respond to severe and pervasive dehumanization as it tries to deter and correct the negative consequences of hostile environments? In addition, our model raises many other interesting psycholegal questions that researchers may approach from both experimental and nonexperimental avenues. We believe that our psycholegal model has a great deal to offer to assist us in gaining an understanding of hostile environments and that other similar efforts at integrating social psychology and the law can bring additional insights to the study, prevention, and treatment of discrimination at work, at school, and in the home.

## References

Age Discrimination in Employment Act, 29 U.S.C. §§ 621–634.

Americans with Disabilities Act Regulations. (2008). 29 C.F.R. §§ 1630.1 et seq.

Americans with Disabilities Act of 1990 as amended in 2008 42 U.S.C. §§ 12102–12213.

Archer, D., Iritani, B., Kimes, D. D., & Barrios, M. (1983). Face-ism: Five studies of sex differences in facial prominence. *Journal of Personality and Social Psychology, 45,* 725–735. doi:10.1037/0022-3514.45.4.725.

Bain, P., Park, J., Kwok, C., & Haslam, N. (2009). Attributing human uniqueness and human nature to cultural groups: Distinct forms of subtle dehumanization. *Group Processes & Intergroup Relations, 12*(6), 789–805. doi:10.1177/1368430209340415.

Bain, P., Vaes, J., Kashima, Y., Haslam, N., & Guan, Y. (2012). Folk conceptions of humanness beliefs about distinctive and core human characteristics in Australia, Italy, and China. *Journal of Cross-Cultural Psychology, 43*(1), 53–58. doi:10.1177/0022022111419029.

Barker, R. G. (1978). Theory of behavior settings. In R. G. Barker (Ed.), *Habitats, environments, and human behavior: Studies in eco-behavioral science from the Midwest Psychological Field Station* (pp. 213–228). Stanford: Stanford University Press.

Barnard, A. (2001). On the relationship between technique and dehumanization. In R. C. Locsin (Ed.), *Advancing technology, caring, and nursing* (pp. 96–105). Westport: Auburn House.

Barnes v. Gorman. (2002). 536 U.S. 181 (2002).

Bartky, S. L. (1990). Femininity and domination: Studies in the phenomenology of oppression. New York: Routledge.

Bastian, B., & Haslam, N. (2010). Excluded from humanity: The dehumanizing effects of social ostracism. *Journal of Experimental Social Psychology, 46*(1), 107–113. doi:10.1016/j.jesp.2009.06.022.

Bastian, B., & Haslam, N. (2011). Experiencing dehumanization: Cognitive and emotional effects of everyday dehumanization. *Basic and Applied Social Psychology, 33,* 295–303.

Berger, J. (1972). *Ways of seeing.* London: Penguin.

Bernard, P., Gervais, S. J., Allen, J., Campomizzi, S., & Klein, O. (2012). Integrating sexual objectification with object versus person recognition: The sexualized-body-inversion hypothesis. *Psychological Science, 23*(5), 469–471. doi:10.1177/0956797611434748.

Bernard, P., Gervais, S. J., Allen, J., & Klein, O. (2013). Perceptual determinants are critical, but they don't explain everything a response to Tarr. *Psychological science, 24*(6), 1071–1073. doi:10.1177/0956797612474672.

Bryant v. Indep. Sch. Dist. No. I-38, 334 F.3d 928 (10 Cir. 2003).
Calogero, R. M., Tantleff-Dunn, S. E., & Thompson, J. (2011). *Self-objectification in women: Causes, consequences, and counteractions*. Washington, D.C.: American Psychological Association.
Cannon v. University of Chicago, 441 U.S. 677, 99 S.Ct. 1946, 60.
Castano, E., & Giner-Sorolla, R. (2006). Not quite human: Infrahumanization in response to collective responsibility for intergroup killing. *Journal of Personality and Social Psychology, 90*(5), 804–818. doi:10.1037/0022-3514.90.5.804.
Castano, E., & Kofta, M. (2009). Dehumanization: Humanity and its denial. *Group Processes & Intergroup Relations, 12*(6), 695–697.
Che v. Massachusetts Bay Transportation Authority, 342 F.3d 21, (1st Cir. 2003).
Civil Rights Act of 1964, Pub.L. 88–352, 78 Stat. 241 (1964).
Civil Rights Act of 1964, as amended in 1991, 42 U.S.C. § 2000, C-22, (1).
Code, L. (1995). *Rhetorical spaces: Essays on gendered locations*. New York: Routledge.
Costello, K., & Hodson, G. (2010). Exploring the roots of dehumanization: The role of animal—human similarity in promoting immigrant humanization. *Group Processes & Intergroup Relations, 13*(1), 3–22. doi:10.1177/1368430209347725.
Crawford vs. Medina General Hospital, 96 F.3d 830 (6th Cir. 1996).
Davis v. Monroe County Bd. of Educ., 119 S. Ct. 1661, (1999).de Beauvoir, S. (1952). The second sex (trans: H. M. Parshley). New York: Knopf.
Dediol v. Best Chevrolet, Inc., 655 F.3d 435 (5th Cir. 2011)
DeLuca-McLean, D., & Castano, E. (2009). Infra-humanization of ethnic minorities: The moderating role of ideology. *Basic and Applied Social Psychology, 31*(2), 102–108. doi:10.1080/01973530902880258.
DiCenso v. Cisneros, 96 F.3d 1004, (7th Cir. 1996).
Dworkin, A. (1989). *Pornography: Men possessing women*. New York: Plume.
Fair Housing Act of 1968, 42 U.S. 3601 et seq., (1968).
Fanon, F. (1967). *The wretched of the earth*. Ringwood: Penguin.
Faragher v. City of Boca Raton, 118 S. Ct. 2275, 1998.
Flowers v. Southern Reg'l Physician Servs., Inc., 247 F.3d 229 (5th Cir. 2001).
Foucault, M. (1989). *The birth of the clinic*. London: Routledge.
Fox v. General Motors Corp., 247 F.3d 169, (4th Cir. 2001).
Franklin vs. Gwinnett County Public Schools, 503 U.S. 60, (1992).
Fredrickson, B. L., & Roberts, T. A. (1997). Objectification theory. *Psychology of Women Quarterly, 21*(2), 173–206. doi:10.1111/j.1471-6402.1997.tb00108.x.
Garriga v. Novo Nordisk Inc., 390 Fed. Appx 952 (10th Cir. 2010).
Gebser v. Lago Vista Independent School Dist., 524 U.S. 274, (1998).
Gervais, S. J., Holland, A., & Dodd, M. D. (in press). *Sex Roles. My eyes are up here: The effects of appearance-focus and body shape on the objectifying gaze*.
Gervais, S. J., Vescio, T. K., & Allen, J. (2011). When what you see is what you get: The consequences of the objectifying gaze for men and women. *Psychology of Women Quarterly, 35*, 5–17. doi:10.1177/0361684310386121.
Gervais, S. J., Vescio, T. K., & Allen, J. (2012a). A test of the fungibility hypothesis from sexual objectification theory. *British Journal of Social Psychology, 51*, 499–513. doi:10.1111/j.2044–8309.2010.02016.x.
Gervais, S. J., Vescio, T. K., Förster, J., Maass, A., & Suitner, C. (2012b). Seeing women as objects: The sexual body part recognition bias. *European Journal of Social Psychology, 42*(6), 743–753. doi:10.1002/ejsp.1890.
Gervais, S. J., Wiener, R. L., Farnum, K., Kimble, K., & Allen, J. (2013, March). Sexual objectification in the workplace: When and why does it represent sexual harassment? Paper presented at the annual meeting of American Psychology and Law Society. Portland.
Gilbert, D. T., Pinel, E. C., Wilson, T. D., Blumberg, S. J., & Wheatley, T. P. (1998). Immune neglect: A source of durability bias in affective forecasting. *Journal of Personality and Social Psychology, 75*(3), 617–638. doi:10.1037/0022-3514.75.3.617.

Glick, P., & Fiske, S. T. (1996). The ambivalent sexism inventory: Differentiating hostile and benevolent sexism. *Journal of Personality and Social Psychology, 70*(3), 491–512. doi:10.1037/0022-3514.70.3.491.

Goff, P. A., Eberhardt, J. L., Williams, M. J., & Jackson, M. C. (2008). Not yet human: Implicit knowledge, historical dehumanization, and contemporary consequences. *Journal of Personality and Social Psychology, 94*(2), 292–306. doi:10.1037/0022-3514.94.2.292.

Gray, K., Knobe, J., Sheskin, M., Bloom, P., & Barrett, L.F. (2011). More than a body: Mind perception and the nature of objectification. *Journal of Personality and Social Psychology, 101,* 1207–1220. doi: 10.1037/a0025883.

Gross v. FBL Financial Services Inc., 557 U.S. 167 (2009).

Gruenfeld, D. H., Inesi, M. E., Magee, J. C., & Galinsky, A. D. (2008). Power and the objectification of social targets. *Journal of Personality and Social Psychology, 95*(1), 111–127. doi:10.1037/0022-3514.95.1.111.

Haidt, J. (2007). The new synthesis in moral psychology. *Science, 316,* 998–1001.

Halprin v. The Prairie Single Family Homes of Dearborn Park Association, 388 F.3d 327 (7th Cir. 2004).

Harris v. Forklift Systems, Inc., 114 S. Ct. 367 (1993).

Harris, L. T., & Fiske, S. T. (2006). Dehumanizing the lowest of the low neuroimaging responses to extreme out-groups. *Psychological Science, 17*(10), 847–853.doi:10.1111/j.1467-9280.2006.01793.x.

Haslam, N. (2006). Dehumanization: An integrative review. *Personality and Social Psychology Review, 10*(3), 252–264.

Haslam, N., & Bain, P. (2007). Humanizing the self: Moderators of the attribution of lesser humanness to others. *Personality and Social Psychology Bulletin, 33*(1), 57–68. doi:10.1177/0146167206293191.

Haslam, N., Bain, P., Douge, L., Lee, M., & Bastian, B. (2005). More human than you: Attributing humanness to self and others. *Journal of Personality and Social Psychology, 89*(6), 937–950. doi:10.1037/0022-3514.89.6.937.

Haslam, N., Kashima, Y., Loughnan, S., Shi, J., & Suitner, C. (2008). Subhuman, inhuman, and superhuman: Contrasting humans with nonhumans in three cultures. *Social Cognition, 26,* 248–258.

Haslam, N., Bastian, B., Laham, S. M., & Loughnan, S. (2012). Humanness, dehumanization, and moral psychology. In M. Mikulincer & P. Shaver (Eds.), *The social psychology of good and evil* (pp. 203–218). Washington, D.C.: APA Press.

Haslam, N., Loughnan, S., & Holland, E. (2013). The psychology of humanness. In S. J. Gervais (Ed.), *Objectification and (de)humanization: The 60th Nebraska Symposium on motivation* (pp. 25–51). New York: Springer.

Heflick, N., & Goldenberg, J. (2009). Objectifying Sarah Palin: Evidence that objectification causes women to be perceived as less competent and less fully human. *Journal of Experimental Social Psychology, 45*(5), 98–601. doi:10.1016/j.jesp.2009.02.008.

Heflick, N. A., Goldenberg, J. L., Cooper, D. P., & Puvia, E. (2011). From women to objects: Appearance focus, target gender, and perceptions of warmth, morality and competence. *Journal of Experimental Social Psychology, 47*(3), 572–581. doi:10.1016/j.jesp.2010.12.020.

Honce v. Vigil, 1 F.3d 1085 (10th Cir. 1993).

Howard v. Feliciano, 583 F.Supp. 2d 252 (U.S District Court of Puerto Rico 2008).

Igou, E. R. (2008). How long will I suffer? versus "How long will you suffer?" A self-other effect in affective forecasting. *Journal of Personality and Social Psychology, 95,* 899–917. doi:10.1037/a0011619.

Jahoda, G. (1999). *Images of savages: Ancient roots of modern prejudice in Western culture*. London: Routledge.

Koval, P., Laham, S. M., Haslam, N., Bastian, B., & Whelan, J. A. (2012). Our flaws are more human than yours: Ingroup bias in humanizing negative characteristics. *Personality and Social Psychology Bulletin, 38*(3), 283.

Langton, R. (2009). *Sexual solipsism: Philosophical essays on pornography and objectification*. Oxford: Oxford University Press.-295. doi:10.1177/0146167211423777.
Lanman v. Johnson, Kansas , 2004 WL 3017258 (10th Cir. 2004).
LeMoncheck, L. (1985). *Dehumanizing women: Treating persons as sex objects*. Totowa: Rowman and Allanheld Publishers.
Leyens, J. P., Cortes, B., Demoulin, S., Dovidio, J. F., Fiske, S. T., Gaunt, R., Paladino, M. P., Rodriguez, A., Rodriguez, R., & Vaes, J. (2003). Emotional prejudice, essentialism, and nationalism: The 2002 Tajfel Lecture. *European Journal of Social Psychology, 33*(6), 703–717.
Loughnan, S., Haslam, N., Murnane, T., Vaes, J., Reynolds, C., & Suitner, C. (2010). Objectification leads to depersonalization: The denial of mind and moral concern to objectified others. *European Journal of Social Psychology, 40,* 709–717. doi:10.1002/ejsp. 755.
MacKinnon, C. A. (1987). Feminism unmodified: Discourses on life and law. Cambridge: Harvard University Press.
MacKinnon, C. (1989). *Toward a feminist theory of the state*. Cambridge: Harvard University Press.
MacKinnon, C. (2006). *Are women human*? Cambridge: Harvard University Press.
Marx, K. (1964). *Economic and philosophic manuscripts of 1844*. New York: International Publishers.
McKinley, N. M. (1998). Gender differences in undergraduates' body esteem: The mediating effect of objectified body consciousness and actual/ideal weight discrepancy. *Sex Roles, 19,* 113–123.
McKinley, N. M. (2006). The developmental and cultural contexts of objectified body consciousness: A longitudinal analysis of two cohorts of women. *Developmental Psychology, 42*(4), 679–687.
McKinley, N. M., & Hyde, J. S. (1996). The objectified body consciousness scale: Development and validation. *Psychology of Women Quarterly, 20,* 181–215. doi:10.1111/j.1471-6402.1996.tb00467.x.
Meritor Savings Bank v. Vinson, 477 U.S. 57 (1986).
Messer v. Fahnestock & Co., Inc., 2008 WL 4934608 (E.D.N.Y. 2008).
Moller, A. C., & Deci, E. L. (2010). Interpersonal control, dehumanization, and violence: A self-determination theory perspective. *Group Processes & Intergroup Relations, 13*(1), 41–53. doi:10.1177/1368430209350318.
Moradi, B., & Huang, Y. (2008). Objectification theory and psychology of women: A decade of advances and future directions. *Psychology of Women Quarterly, 32,* 377–398. doi:10.1111/j.1471-6402.2008.00452.x.
Neudecker v. Boisclair Corp., 351 F.3d 361, 363 (8th Cir. 2003).
Noll, S. M., & Fredrickson, B. L. (1998). A mediational model linking self-objectification, body shame, and disordered eating. *Psychology of Women Quarterly, 22,* 623–636. doi:10.1111/j.1471–6402.1998.tb00181.x.
Nussbaum, M. (1995). Objectification. *Philosophy & Public Affairs, 24,* 249–291. doi:10.1111/j.1088-4963.1995.tb00032.x.
Nussbaum, M. C. (1999). *Sex and social justice*. New York: Oxford University Press.
Oncale v. Sundowner Offshore Services, Inc., 118 S. Ct. 998 (1998).
Paladino, M. P., & Vaes, J. (2009). Ours is human: On the pervasiveness of infra humanization in intergroup relations. *British Journal of Social Psychology, 48*(2), 237–251.
Park, J., Haslam, N., & Kashima, Y. (2012). Relational to the core lay theories of humanness in Australia, Japan, and Korea. *Journal of Cross-Cultural Psychology, 43*(5), 774–783. doi:10.1177/0022022111414417.
PowerComm, LLC v. Holyoke Gas & Electric Department, 746 F. Supp, 2d 325 (D. Mass. 2010).
Quigley v. Winter 598 F.3d 938 (8th Cir. 2010).
Rabidue v. Osceola Refining Co., 805 F. 2d 611 (6th Cir. 1986).
Rivera v. Rochester Genesee Regional Transportation Authority, 761 F.Supp. 2d 54 (W.D.N.Y. 2011).
Rivera v. Rochester Genesee Regional Transp. 702 F.3d 685 (2d Cir. 2012)

Rohmann, A., Niedenthal, P. M., Brauer, M., Castano, E., & Leyens, J. P. (2009). The attribution of primary and secondary emotions to the in-group and to the out-group: The case of equal status countries. *The Journal of Social Psychology, 149*(6), 709–730. doi:10.1080/00224540903348253.
Rudman, L. A., & Glick, P. (2008). *The social psychology of gender: How power and intimacy shape gender relations*. New York: Guilford.
Rudman, L. A., & Mescher, K. (2013). Penalizing men who request a family leave: Is flexibility stigma a femininity stigma? *Journal of Social Issues, 69*(2), 322–340. doi:10.1111/josi.12017.
Saminaden, A., Loughnan, S., & Haslam, N. (2010). Afterimages of savages: Implicit associations between primitives, animals and children. *British Journal of Social Psychology, 49*(1), 91–105. doi:10.1348/014466609×415293.
Shaver v. Independent Stave Co., 350 F.3d 716, (8th Cir. 2003).
Smith v. Mission Associates Limited Partnership, 225 F. Supp. 2d 1293 (U.S. District Court Kansas 2002).
Sutton v. United Air Lines, Inc., 527 U.S. 471 (1999).
Title IX of the Education Amendment of 1972, 20 U.S.C. § 1681.
Title VI of the Civil Rights Act of 1964, 42 U.S.C. § 2000d et seq., (1964).
Title VII of the Civil Rights Act of 1964, 42 U.S. C. Section 2000c-(a)(1) (1964).
Vaes, J., & Paladino, M. P. (2010). The uniquely human content of stereotypes. *Group Processes & Intergroup Relations, 13*(1), 23–39.
Vaes, J., Paladino, M. P., Castelli, L., Leyens, J. P., & Giovanazzi, A. (2003). On the behavioral consequences of infrahumanization: the implicit role of uniquely human emotions in intergroup relations. *Journal of Personality and Social Psychology, 85*(6), 1016–1034. doi:10.1037/0022-3514.85.6.1016.
Vaes, J., Heflick, N. A., & Goldenberg, J. L. (2010). "We are people": Ingroup humanization as an existential defense. *Journal of Personality and Social Psychology, 98*(5), 750–760. doi:10.1037/a0017658.
Vaes, J., Paladino, P., & Puvia, E. (2011). Are sexualized women complete human beings? Why men and women dehumanize sexually objectified women. *European Journal of Social Psychology, 41*(6), 774–785. doi:10.1002/ejsp.824.
Viki, G. T., & Abrams, D. (2003). Infra-humanization: Ambivalent sexism and the attribution of primary and secondary emotions to women. *Journal of Experimental Social Psychology, 39*(5), 492–499.
Viki, G. T., & Calitri, R. (2008). Infrahuman outgroup or suprahuman ingroup: The role of nationalism and patriotism in the infrahumanization of outgroups. *European Journal of Social Psychology, 38*(6), 1054–1061. doi:10.1002/ejsp.495.
Wicker, A. W. (1979). Ecological psychology: Some recent and prospective developments. *American Psychologist, 34*(9), 755–765.
Wicker, A. W. (1987). Behavior settings reconsidered: Temporal stages, resources, internal dynamics, context. In D. Stokols & I. Altman (Eds.), *Handbook of environmental psychology* (pp. 613–653). New York: Wiley.
Wicker, A. W. (1992). Making sense of environments. In W. B. Walsh, K. H. Clark & R. H. Price (Eds.), *Person-environment psychology: Models and perspectives* (pp. 158–191). Hillsdale: Lawrence Erlbaum Associates.
Wiener, R. L., Reiter-Palmon, R., Winter, R. J., Richter, E., Humke, A., & Maeder, E. (2010). Complainant behavioral tone, ambivalent sexism and perceptions of sexual harassment. *Psychology, Public Policy, and Law, 16*, 56–84.
Wiener, R. L., Gervais, S. J., Allen, J., & Marquez, A. (2012). In the eye of the beholder: The role of sexual objectification and affective forecasting on sexual harassment judgments. *Psychology, Public Policy, and the Law, 19*(2), 206–221. doi:10.1037/a0028497.
Wiener, R. L., Gervais, S. J., Brnjic, E., & Nuss, G. (2013). Hostile work environment harassment due to age: Dehumanizing older workers (unpublished manuscript in preparation).
Zebel, S., Zimmermann, A., Tendayi Viki, G., & Doosje, B. (2008). Dehumanization and guilt as distinct but related predictors of support for reparation policies. *Political Psychology, 29*(2), 193–219. doi:10.1111/j.1467-9221.2008.00623.x.

# Chapter 4
# Exploring the Dark Matter of Objectification

**Thomas Lee Budesheim**

## Exploring the Dark Matter of Objectification

Physicists study matter ranging from electrons to galaxies, all of which they can detect by the light or energy the matter emits. But in recent years, most physicists have come to believe that the vast majority of the universe is made up of "dark matter" that emits neither light nor energy, and hence has gone undetected and unstudied. Similarly, social psychology has its own "dark matter" to deal with, and one that until recently was largely unstudied. While we have spent decades studying the thoughts, feelings, and behaviors we can readily detect, we have often overlooked the absence of thoughts, feelings, and behavior between people. Yet the absence of thought about another person's mind (objectification), the absence of feeling or empathy for another person (dehumanization), and the absence of behavioral interaction with another person (ostracism) are all dark matters that underlie many of the injustices, conflicts, and threats to well-being with which human societies struggle. The deprivation of personal and positive attention from our fellow human beings is implicated in a number of social ills, ranging from sexual harassment to genocide, and it is the desire to ameliorate these problems that motivate psychologists, policy-makers, and legal scholars to understand the causes and consequences of these dark matters in our daily lives.

Because we humans are intensely social animals that interact with each other in many elaborate ways, our ability to survive and thrive is largely dependent upon the quality of our relationships with others. As a result, deciding who to befriend and who to avoid, who to trust and who to distrust is a fundamental part of our encounters with others (Cuddy et al. 2007). Nevertheless, we can also be thoughtless and callous when dealing with others, giving little attention to those among us that we deem unworthy of our careful attention. This thoughtlessness and callousness is at the heart of social psychology's longstanding efforts to understand stereotypes and

T. L. Budesheim (✉)
Department of Psychology, Creighton University, 2500 California Plaza, 68178 Omaha, NE, USA
e-mail: budesh@creighton.edu

B. H. Bornstein, R. L. Wiener (eds.), *Justice, Conflict and Wellbeing*,
DOI 10.1007/978-1-4939-0623-9_4, 

prejudice, and it is at the heart of legal efforts to combat and control various forms of discrimination. As our understanding of these phenomena has increased, however, there has been a proliferation of related concepts and terms used in the research literature, including objectification, dehumanization, and infra-humanization, among others.

In this chapter, I focus on one particular "dark matter," namely objectification. I discuss the various definitions of objectification, both in terms of how it has been defined conceptually by philosophers and psychologists, and in terms of how it has been defined operationally in experimental research. I ultimately offer my own working definition of what objectification is, and in doing so, attempt to distinguish it from the two main pillars of social cognition, namely individuation and stereotyping. I also propose three different forms that objectification can take. Finally, I discuss new avenues for moving forward in our collective investigation of objectification, with a particular emphasis on the social context and the social dynamics between the objectifying perceiver and the objectified target, which may play a determining factor in whether or not objectification has a deleterious effect.

## Philosophical Perspectives on the Definition of Objectification

Objectification has been examined within several academic disciplines and from a number of different perspectives (Berger 1972; Calogero 2013; Dworkin 1985; Heldman and Wade 2011; Jeffreys 2005). However, some of the most detailed analyses of objectification have come from philosophers dating as far back as Immanel Kant (Kant et al. 1997). Recent examinations of this topic by feminist philosophers have been particularly influential. Nussbaum (1995) provided perhaps the most detailed consideration of what constitutes objectification. She argued that in all forms of objectification, "one is treating as an object what is really not an object, what is, in fact, a human being" (p. 257). Nussbaum identified seven aspects of treating something as an object:

1. *Instrumentality*: The objectifier treats the object as a tool for his or her own purposes.
2. *Denial of Autonomy*: The objectifier treats the object as lacking in autonomy and self-determination.
3. *Inertness*: The objectifier treats the object as lacking in agency and perhaps also in activity.
4. *Fungibility*: The objectifier treats the object as interchangeable (a) with other objects of the same type, and/or (b) with objects of other types.
5. *Violability*: The objectifier treats the object as lacking in boundary integrity, as something that it is permissible to break up, smash, break into.
6. *Ownership*: The objectifier treats the object as something that is owned by another, can be bought or sold, etc.
7. *Denial of subjectivity*: The objectifier treats the object as something whose experience and feelings (if any) need not be taken into account.

In contrast, feminist scholars such as Bartky (1990) had a decidedly narrower approach to objectification, asserting that objectification "occurs when a woman's sexual parts or functions are separated out from her person, reduced to the status of mere instruments, or else regarded as they were capable of representing her" (p. 35). Merging these different viewpoints, Langton (2009) has since expanded Nussbaum's list by adding three additional considerations:

8. *Reduction to body*: The treatment of a person as identified with their body, or body parts.
9. *Reduction to appearance*: The treatment of a person primarily in terms of how they look, or how they appear to the senses.
10. *Silencing*: The treatment of a person as if they are silent, lacking the capacity to speak.

This lengthy list of notions as to what constitutes objectification raises the troubling possibility that objectification is a "catch-all" term representing a nebulous concept that is used to describe a variety of reprehensible behaviors. Philosophers themselves seem uneasy with the concept, such as when Papadaki (2010) argued that while objectification "is a notion central to contemporary feminist theory… [it] has not yet been adequately defined" (p. 16). More specifically, Papadaki believes that Nussbaum's (1995) conception of objectification:

> … encompasses too much to be useful, and there is great uncertainty as to when to apply this concept. People will apply the concept differently, often relying solely on their intuitions, and there will be much disagreement and confusion as to what really counts as objectification. (p. 29)

Certainly, Langton's additions only exacerbate this problem. Papadaki is by no means the only philosopher concerned about how objectification is defined and how the term is used. For example, Cahill (2011) noted:

> Objectification per se has received surprisingly little attention by feminist thinkers. Although often deployed, it is rarely considered directly and in depth… The number of feminist thinkers who have employed the notion of objectification (without explicitly and in some detail articulating its meanings)… is enormous. (p. 1)

To be fair, Nussbaum herself acknowledged that objectification is "a relatively loose cluster-term, for whose application we sometimes treat any one of these features as sufficient" (Nussbaum 1995, p. 258). Nevertheless, the looseness with which this term can be applied is problematic. For example, consider the first criterion of instrumentality. As social animals, we rely on one another in many ways; people are inherently useful and can serve some purpose for us in almost any context. Papadaki (2010) articulates the crux of this problem:

> Consider what would happen if every time we treated each other instrumentally, without such treatment denying humanity in any way, we called this 'objectification'. It would mean that in our everyday lives we objectify nearly everyone: partners, teachers, taxi drivers, waiters, plumbers, and everyone else we use as a means to achieve our ends… We use each other, as well as ourselves, instrumentally all the time, and it seems unreasonable to want to call all such instrumental treatment objectification. (p. 28)

Perhaps, you might think, I am unfairly dwelling on the role of instrumentality in determining what is or is not objectification. Perhaps some other criterion is more central to determining when objectification does or does not occur. Let us consider a couple of other criteria, such as the denial of subjectivity (the failure to consider the experiences or feelings of another person) and fungibility (the person is treated as interchangeable with another person). Think back to the last time you went grocery shopping. You took your cart full of food to the checkout stand where someone scanned your items, told you the amount you owed, took your money or credit card, and bagged your food. What was your impression of this person? Did you give much thought as to what he or she was experiencing? Would it have mattered to you if that person had been replaced with someone else to perform that task? In this example, we typically regard the cashier as fungible, fail to consider their subjectivity, and focus on them as instrumental to our purpose of acquiring food while avoiding the risks associated with simply stealing it. This is not an exceptional case, but rather is typical of many superficial interactions with other people. The concept of objectification, and the interest we have in understanding it, would be greatly diluted if we were to regard so much of our routine, everyday interactions as objectification, while at the same time regarding more serious acts of dehumanization, such as sexual harassment, as objectification as well.

Papadaki (2010) comes to a similar conclusion, and therefore chooses to constrain the concept of objectification to apply only when the treatment of others is morally objectionable. She therefore defines objectification as follows:

> Objectification is seeing and/or treating a person as an object (see and/or treating them in one or more of these seven ways: as an instrument, inert, fungible, violable, owned, denied autonomy, denied subjectivity, in such a way that denies this person's humanity. A person's humanity is denied when it is ignored/not properly acknowledged and/or when it is in some way harmed.

Papadaki also suggests that we refine the notion of objectification by delineating different forms that objectification can take. She outlines four different forms of objectification that result from two basic factors: (1) Does the objectifier intend to deny (either by harming, ignoring, or not fully acknowledging) the objectified individual's humanity or is it done unintentionally? (2) Is the objectified person's humanity (rational capacities) harmed or diminished in some way (reductive objectification), or is it merely ignored or not fully acknowledged (non-reductive objectification)? The combination of these factors results in four different forms of objectification: intentional reductive objectification, intentional non-reductive objectification, unintentional reductive objectification, and unintentional non-reductive objectification. The first form is clearly the most morally reprehensible while the last form of objectification is the least reprehensible.

Papadaki emphasizes the distinction between intentional and unintentional forms of objectification, in part, because it influences which strategies may be most effective in correcting the problem. She also suggests that unintentional objectification may be far more common than people realize, and that both women and men are prone to this form of objectification.

From this brief and selective review of how philosophers conceptualize objectification, it is clear that no general consensus has emerged and that the concept of objectification continues to be debated and refined. Nevertheless, psychologists are already hard at work studying objectification, and a variety of perspectives on objectification have emerged.

## Psychological Perspectives on the Definition of Objectification

### *Objectification Theory and Self-Objectification*

Objectification was largely neglected as a topic of psychological investigation throughout most of the twentieth century. A dramatic shift occurred following the publication of the seminal work by Fredrickson and Roberts (1997), entitled "Objectification Theory: Toward Understanding Women's Lived Experiences and Mental Health Risks." This work inspired a tidal wave of research, as indicated by the fact that their article had been cited in the PsycINFO database over 600 times as of the time this chapter was written. However, if the reader is a relative newcomer to this area of research, do not be fooled by the title of their article. Far from providing an overarching theory of objectification in general or resolving the philosophers' debate over how objectification should be defined, their theory is more narrowly focused on the resulting negative consequences sexual objectification has for women. As they put it:

> Distinct from attempts to uncover why objectification occurs, objectification theory takes as a given that women exist in a culture in which their bodies are—for whatever reasons—looked at, evaluated, and always potentially objectified. The theory limits its aim to illuminating the psychological and experiential consequences that sexual objectification might have in many women's lives. (Fredrickson and Roberts 1997, p. 177)

Fredrickson and Roberts accept as given that there exists in American culture (and in other societies as well) a high degree of sexual objectification of women. They, like Bartky (1990) and Langton (2009), emphasize body focus as the defining feature of objectification, stating that "when objectified, women are treated as bodies—and in particular, as bodies that exist for the use and pleasure of others" (p. 175). They argue that sexual objectification occurs in three general ways. First, women are objectified in face-to-face social encounters, with women's bodies being the target of men's "objectifying gaze" and, in many instances, accompanied by explicit commentary. Second, the media socialize and perpetuate this sexual objectification by repeatedly highlighting objectifying social interactions in films, advertisements, and other visual media where men are depicted as focused on women's bodies. Third, the visual media often "spotlight" women's bodies and body parts such that the viewer is automatically put in the position of having an objectifying gaze upon the women depicted.

Without explicitly stating so, Fredrickson and Roberts conceptualize objectification as an active process, as something that a perceiver (e.g., a man) does to the target (e.g., a woman), presumably in such a way that (a) the target becomes aware of this objectification (e.g., through a leering gaze accompanied by whistling, catcalls, or other explicit commentary), and/or (b) it has a demonstrable effect on the target by altering the perceiver's behavior toward the target or judgments of the target. The presumption about this objectifying encounter is that the perceiver's attention to the target's body is (a) excessive or in some other way inappropriate relative to the amount of attention paid to other qualities of the person, (b) unwelcome by the target of that attention, and (c) damaging to the target's psychological state of mind and/or disruptive to the target's ongoing behavior.

This latter point is the focus of Fredrickson and Roberts' research and that of many other researchers their work has influenced. Women's frequent experiences as the target of objectification can lead them to engage in self-objectification, which in turn can lead to a variety of psychological difficulties, such as body shame, anxiety, depression, and disordered eating behavior (for a review, see Calogero et al. 2011). Self-objectification is conceptualized as an individual-difference variable that reflects to what extent a woman has internalized society's obsession with women's physical beauty and sexual attractiveness.

Studies of self-objectification have relied heavily on two self-report measures: the Objectified Body Consciousness Scale (OBCS) developed by McKinley and Hyde (1996), and the Self-Objectification Questionnaire (SOQ) developed by Noll and Fredrickson (1998). The SOQ asks individuals to rank ten body attributes from most important to least important to their physical self-concept. Five of the attributes are regarded as observable appearance-based attributes (i.e., physical attractiveness, physical measurements, weight, sex appeal, firm/sculpted muscles). The other five attributes are less directly observable and are regarded as physical competence-based attributes (i.e., strength, coordination, fitness level, energy level, and health). Ranking the appearance-based attributes more highly presumably indicates a greater concern with how one appears to others as more important than one's own sense of physical well-being. Similarly, the OBCS asks women to indicate their level of agreement or disagreement along a 7-point scale to 24 items that measure (a) self-surveillance (e.g., "I often worry about whether the clothes I am wearing make me look good"), body shame (e.g., "When I am not the size I think I should be, I feel ashamed"), and (c) control beliefs (e.g., "I think a person can look pretty much how they want to if they are willing to work at it").

In addition to being regarded as a stable individual difference variable, self-objectification can also be treated as a state that can be manipulated by situational factors. In the laboratory, state self-objectification has been manipulated in a number of ways, including (a) having women try on either a swimsuit or a sweater in front of a full-length mirror (Fredrickson et al. 1998), (b) exposing women to media images featuring thin, sexualized images of other women's bodies such as Victoria Secret ads (Harper and Tiggemann 2008), (c) priming words related to objectified bodies, such as sexiness or thinness (Roberts and Gettman 2004), and (d) giving women the mere anticipation of having a face-to-face interaction with a man (Calogero 2004).

Ironically, despite the fact that objectification is prototypically described as something that men "do" to women, none of these manipulations directly involve men doing anything. In fact, the closest men come to being involved in these studies is when women were threatened with the possibility of actually having to interact with a man. Simply put, the studies on self-objectification tell us very little about objectification itself. In actual interactions between men and women, what constitutes objectification? Does a glance at someone's physique constitute objectification? How do we know when objectification has or has not occurred? Is objectification "in the eye of the beholder" or is it "in the eye of the beholden?" How is objectification harmful? When is it harmful and when is it not harmful? We are far from answering these questions, but the next set of studies I will review brings us closer to at least addressing these questions.

## *Experimental Studies of Sexual Objectification*

There are two main types of experimental investigations of sexual objectification. In the first type, participants are experimentally put in the role of the objectifier, either by (a) manipulating how the target person is depicted, and thereby manipulating the participants' attentional focus and thought process, or (b) directly instructing the participants to focus their attention on the target in different ways and thereby manipulating their thought process. The second and most recent form of experimental investigation of sexual objectification is to expose the participants to instances of objectification performed by a confederate of the experimenter, and then assess the impact of this objectification on the participants.

*Participants as Objectifiers* This line of research is fundamentally concerned with how focusing on a target person's body or appearance alters one's judgments of, and behaviors toward, the target. In a classic example of this form of objectification research, Gurung and Chrouser (2007) randomly assigned participants to (a) view photographs of women athletes depicted in either their normal sports attire or (b) view these same women provocatively dressed in minimal clothing. After viewing the pictures, participants made a series of judgments about the targets related to (a) objectification (attractiveness, sexually experienced, desirable), (b) capabilities (strength, determination, capability), and (c) personal characteristics (self-respect, intelligent, feminine). Consistent with their expectations, provocatively dressed targets were rated as more attractive, more sexually experienced, more desirable, and more feminine than athletically dressed targets. Furthermore, the provocatively dressed women were judged as lower in strength, determination, capability, intelligence, and self-respect than when they were athletically dressed.

Gurung and Chrouser (2007) concluded that the provocative clothing increased objectification, as indicated by the decreased perceptions of their personal capabilities and higher ratings of their physical attributes. In other words, the participants "objectified" the provocatively dressed women. But as one ponders over the nature of objectification and how it takes place, one might wonder where exactly did "objectification" occur in this study? One could argue that the objectification took place well before the participants made their judgments. After all, the researchers selected these pictures for presentation to the participants. Like the objectifying media that Fredrickson and Roberts (1997) and other social critics have commented upon, the act of depicting the women in this fashion is regarded as objectifying. One might even say that the women athletes themselves did the objectifying, because they allowed themselves to be photographed in this provocative fashion.

It is neither clear that Gurung and Chrouser's (2007) results nor other studies like it (Johnson and Gurung 2011), tell us much about the process of objectification, which they described as follows: "when objectified, a women's body, or parts of her body, are separated from other personal characteristics" (p. 91). By providing participants only with pictures of each woman's body, and in some cases, stripping the women of most of their outer clothing, which might have provided some useful clues about them, the "separation from other personal characteristics" was arguably done for the participants already. Considering the fact that participants were asked to form an impression of these women under informationally impoverished circumstances, such that all they learned about each target was conveyed through a photograph of either a provocatively (un)dressed woman or an athletically dressed woman, I think participants' assumptions about these women were reasonable and represent their best efforts under the circumstances. A provocative photograph of a scantily clad woman does covey more information about the woman's physical beauty and her sexual desirability than it does about her intelligence or capability, and consequently participants rated these women more strongly in these areas. Likewise, a photograph of a woman engaged in an athletic competition does convey more information about her strength and determination than it does about her physical attractiveness and desirability, and consequently participants rated these women more strongly in those areas. In fact, both sets of images might have evoked different stereotypic subtypes of women that differ in their evaluative implications. This possibility raises the question of whether or not "objectification" is just a form of stereotyping of women based on appearance. Hence, what was intended as a straightforward attempt to experimentally demonstrate objectification may have demonstrated instead that different appearances evoke different stereotypes, which in turn result in different judgments of the target.

Heflick and Goldenberg (2009) also placed participants in the role of the objectifier and examined how this objectification affected their judgments of the target. At the outset, they provide what has become the almost obligatory definition, which is that "objectification refers to construing an individual as an object" (p. 599), but they do not clarify what the precise nature of this construal process is. They simply note that "by virtue of this, targets of objectification are likely to be perceived as less fully human" (p. 599). Contrary to Gurung and Chrouser's (2007) methodology, Heflick and Goldenberg did not provide images of their targets (Sarah Palin and Angelina Jolie) but rather manipulated the participants' focus when thinking about these familiar targets. This approach has the decided advantage of more closely simulating how objectification might happen in everyday life. For example, a man might encounter a woman and choose to focus on her body, whereas another man might simultaneously encounter the same woman but choose to think about what the woman was doing and what she was thinking. The woman has the same presentation to both men, but the first man would be described as objectifying her, while the second man would not. In their experimental conditions, Heflick and Goldenberg asked participants to write about either Sarah Palin or Angelina Jolie, focusing on their thoughts and feelings about this person's appearance. In the control conditions, they asked participants to write about either Sarah Palin or Angelina Jolie, focusing on their thoughts and feelings about this person.

On average, participants rated the women as significantly less competent when their focus was on the women's appearances than when their focus was on the women as persons. While this difference was small (a mean difference of half a point on a 7-point scale), it nevertheless indicates that focusing on appearances (presumably to the exclusion of other information available about a person) can have a detectable negative effect on judgments of a target person. But what exactly did the appearance-focus manipulation do in the Heflick and Goldenberg (2009) study to result in less positive judgments of the targets? One possibility is that it primed a subset of the known information about the target person, creating a different informational basis for making subsequent judgments of the target. The appearance focus manipulation may have led participants to activate in memory more superficial information about the target (magazine photos, depictions on TV, etc.), thereby making that information relatively more accessible than information about the target's actions, expressed attitudes, and goals, etc. The result, not surprisingly, would be that the judgments of the target would be subtly influenced by what information was more accessible about the target. Another possibility is that the appearance focus served to activate gender stereotypes of these women as less competent (Eagly et al. 1991).

Heflick, Goldenberg, Cooper, and Puvia (2011) attempted to address some of the alternative explanations that arose for the Heflick and Goldenberg (2009) results. For example, they specifically tackled the notion that the effects of appearance focus on judgments of women's competence may have been due to the activation of gender stereotypes rather than due to objectification and dehumanization. They asked participants to focus either on a person's appearance during a brief video clip or on the person's performance during the same video clip. In some conditions, the person in the video was a man (news anchorman Brian Williams, or an unknown male weather forecaster) and in other conditions, the person was a woman (morning newsperson Robin Meade, or an unknown female weather forecaster). They reasoned that if appearance focus on women activated the gender stereotype of women, the women would be rated as warmer, but less competent. On the other hand, if objectification and not stereotype activation was created by the appearance focus, then women would be rated lower in both warmth and competence. In fact, across three different studies, Heflick et al. (2011) found that appearance focus consistently lowered perceptions of a woman's competence, warmth, and morality, but that appearance focus did not result in significant changes in the judgments of men. Their conclusion was that appearance focus resulted in the objectification of women but did not result in the objectification of men.

While there is much to commend about these studies, there is a conceptual slipperiness here that I find troubling and which I have pointed out in a previous commentary on this work (Budesheim 2011). It is unclear if objectification is operationally defined as the focus on a person's appearance or whether it is operationally defined as the resulting decrease in the evaluations of the person's personal qualities. Or perhaps, it is some combination of the two, which is hinted at by the authors' statement that "objectification should occur for any person whose worth is strongly or solely linked to their appearance" (Heflick et al. 2011, p. 580). This way of defining objectification is problematic, as it opens the door to circular reasoning, in which objectification is viewed as both cause and effect. Consider the following two ways that someone might describe Heflick et al.'s (2011) results: (1) "Focusing on Sarah's appearance caused her to be objectified. We know that she was objectified (and that the men were not) because she was judged as lower in competence, warmth, and morality (and the men were not)." This view portrays objectification as the effect of appearance focus. (2) "Sarah's worth/humanness was diminished because she was objectified. We know that the manipulation of appearance focus caused them to judge her as lower in competence, warmth, and morality." This view equates objectification with appearance focus, and thus portrays objectification as the cause of the diminished judgments. Logically, objectification cannot be both cause and effect. Yet the research literature in this area is typically ambiguous, leaving unresolved which view of objectification is preferable. It is as if objectification researchers currently are stuck viewing objectification as not exclusively cause or effect, but rather "objectification = appearance focus + reduced perceptions of personal qualities." This formulation is agnostic with regard to why appearance focus sometimes is associated with lowered perceptions of personal qualities (e.g., when judging women) and sometimes not (e.g., when judging men). It simply labels the co-occurrence of these events as "objectification." A deeper understanding of the phenomenon of objectification, however, demands that we try to uncover why or how these effects occur. If appearance focus, in and of itself, is insufficient to reduce perceptions of personal qualities, then what other factors are involved?

What is needed is a more detailed understanding of the cognitive processes that underlie appearance focus and how these processes may differ when that focus is on women than when that focus is on men. Fortunately, some recent research by Sarah Gervais and her colleagues has begun to do just that (Bernard et al. 2012; Gervais 2012a, b). The proverbial "elephant in the room" that objectification researchers have tip-toed around is the question "What is meant by 'viewing sexualized women as objects'?" (Bernard et al. 2012, p. 469). Using work in cognitive psychology that identifies configural processing (perceiving the relations of the constituent parts of a stimulus and the resulting configurations) as a prominent part of person recognition, in contrast to analytic processing (perceiving the constituent parts of a stimulus but not their configural relationships), they employed a method that can test which type of processing is taking place. Specifically, the inversion effect, which occurs when inverted stimuli are harder to recognize than upright stimuli is specifically associated with configural processing and is particularly prominent in face recognition (Maurer et al. 2002; Yin 1969). Male and female participants were briefly presented with a mixture of inverted and upright photographs of sexualized men and women (i.e., just wearing swimsuits or underwear), with each photograph flashed onto the screen for 250 ms followed by a blank screen presented for 1-s. After each presentation, the participants were given a recognition test in which two images were presented (the actual image and a left-right mirror image) and asked which one they had seen. Only the inverted sexualized images of men resulted in significantly lower recognition memory, whereas the inverted sexualized images of women did not. This result would seem to indicate that the sexualized images of women, in contrast to those of men, engaged more analytical and less configural processing, which is consistent with viewing the women in a more object-like fashion.

Research examining the cognitive processes underlying objectification, such as that done by Bernard et al. (2012), represents an important step in the right direction, but more work remains. In order to advance a deeper understanding of objectification, we should utilize a multi-method approach that incorporates some of the more sophisticated tools available to us. For example, future research might employ eye-tracking technology to reveal how men are viewed versus how women are viewed. For example, despite the fact that Bernard et al. (2012) displayed both male and female stimuli in a sexualized manner, it is possible that participants still focused on men's faces to a greater extent than on women's faces, which is to say that they focused more on the women's bodies than on the men's bodies. This difference might account for why configural processing was engaged to a greater extent with male stimuli than with female stimuli, even though both were displayed in a sexualized manner. Research indicates men's faces are often displayed in a more prominent fashion in the media, whereas women are more likely to be displayed as a full body (Archer et al. 1983; Konrath and Schwarz 2007; Schwarz and Kurz 1989). Perhaps as a result of this "face-ism" bias, we habitually pay more attention to men's faces than to women's faces, and this cognitive habit carries over into situations where there is an option of focusing on the body or focusing on the face.

*Participants as the Target of Objectification* As noted earlier, there is considerable work on how state self-objectification can be created, but there is generally no actual interaction with an objectifier, and hence almost no empirical investigation of being the target of another person's "objectifying gaze." A notable exception is the recent work by Gervais et al. (2011; Wiener et al. 2013). They randomly assigned male and female participants to experience either no objectifying gaze or a brief series of objectifying gazes from a confederate of the opposite sex during a brief interview. In the objectifying gaze conditions, the confederate would look at the participant as they walked in for the interview, visually scanning down to their waist and then back up to their face. In addition, each confederate was trained to gaze at the participant's chest for a couple of seconds at three different points during the interview, and immediately after the interview to make verbal comments that reinforced this visual focus (e.g., "From the looks of you, I thought you would do these problems best").

Gervais et al. found that the objectifying gaze adversely affected women's subsequent performance on a math test, but did not affect men's performance. Surprisingly, those female participants who had been objectified expressed greater motivation to interact with the interviewer in future situations. Further, no significant differences were observed in women's body shame, body surveillance, or body dissatisfaction as a result of the objectifying gaze manipulation. By operationally defining objectification as the manipulated exposure to an interviewer's objectifying gaze (and comments), these researchers avoid the definitional ambiguity of whether objectification is to be regarded as the cause or the effect in the study. Clearly, the objectifying gaze was the causal factor in this study, and interestingly, it did not have ubiquitously negative consequences, suggesting that there is "more than meets the eye" to objectification.

## Expanding the Concept of Objectification

Moradi (2011) has reviewed the theory and research on objectification and suggested possible avenues for extending this work. In doing so, she raised the question, "What is a non-sexually objectifying environment, and where do such environments exist?" (p. 158). Moradi's question acknowledges the possibility that sexually objectifying environments are just one form of objectifying environment. Similarly, Calogero (2011) noted that an extension of objectification theory and research "to other social domains beyond the sexual arena… is timely and imperative" (p. 42).

### *Stereotyping, Mind Perception, and Objectification*

Objectification is of interest to social psychologists and relevant to the mainstream theories of social perception, though it has not been explicitly incorporated into their models. For example, in their stereotype content model (SCM), Susan Fiske, Amy Cuddy, Peter Glick, and their colleagues (Cuddy et al. 2007, 2008, 2009; Fiske et al. 1999, 2002; Fiske 2011) make the case that what we think and feel about others, and how we behave toward them, is largely shaped by two fundamental judgments: the first is warmth ("Is the person friend or foe?") and the second is competence ("Does this person have the ability to help me or hurt me?"). We typically judge our in-groups as high in both warmth and competence, whereas we judge our most despised out-groups as low in both warmth and competence. Groups that are judged low in both warmth and competence (e.g., the homeless) are frequently the targets of active harm (e.g., abusive treatment) and passive harm (e.g., neglect and ostracism). Such scorned groups are likely to incur more unjust treatment and experience deeper suffering than others in a society. And yet scorn is often overlooked, because, as Fiske (2011) astutely observed, "we are often unaware… of scorning others; precisely because scorn is thoughtless, it does not bother us" (p. 15). Scorn often takes the form of turning our backs on others, physically and mentally. Simply put, we do not give scorned individuals a second thought.

Our lack of thought about those we scorn is a form of objectification. Nussbaum (1995) called this the denial of subjectivity. Objects are treated as if they have no feelings or experiences that we should pause to consider. For example, I do not reflect on what my chair is feeling when I sit on it, or what it might think as I leave it each evening to spend the night alone in the dark until I return the following morning. It is a chair, and it never has occurred to me (until this moment) to wonder about its thoughts or feelings. But when the "object" is a person that we know can think and feel at some level, and yet we fail to consider their thoughts and feelings, then this is objectification in its purest and simplest form.

To think about the thoughts and feelings of another person is referred to as mind perception. Intriguing work on mind perception indicates that perceivers are likely to think about the contents of another's mind when (a) they have a desire for social connection with that person, and/or (b) are motivated to understand, predict, or even control the other person's behavior (Waytz et al. 2010). Both of these motivations are often lacking when interacting with strangers, but particularly so if they are viewed as having little or nothing to offer with regard to warmth or competence. Waytz et al. (2010) assert that mind perception is key to the moral status of the individual. When people are thought of as incompetent and incapable of rationality and civility, then their freedoms are restricted and they must be confined or constrained. When one regards a person, or group of persons, as lacking in warmth and human kindness, then they are to be either avoided or attacked. Those individuals unlucky enough to be regarded in this way are often vulnerable to having their liberties and their equal rights in the society stripped from them.

Social neuroscience provides even further evidence that we think about these individuals in fundamentally different ways. Neuroimaging research has determined that the medial prefrontal cortex is particularly active when one engages in person perception rather than object perception (Mason and Macrae 2004). With this result in mind, Harris and Fiske (2006) conducted a functional magnetic resonance imaging study in which participants viewed 48 photographs of individuals representing groups in each of the four combinations of (a) low or high warmth, and (b) low or high competence. They found that pictures of people who fell into the low warmth—low competence quadrant elicited significantly less activation of the medial prefrontal cortex. That is, perceivers viewing a person from the low warmth—low competence quadrant had significantly less of the neural activity associated with forming impressions of a person, and thus neurologically appeared as if they were forming an impression of an object.

One of the particular benefits of using such an approach for the study of objectification and dehumanization is that it does not rely on self-reports, which are subject to biased responding. In addition, the low-tech self-report approach to objectification research suffers from a particularly ironic flaw. Consider studies in which participants are in the role of a perceiver who objectifies the target. If the experimental task elicits objectification, participants will have formed little to no impression of the target person's inner qualities, but rather will regard the person in a much more superficial way (e.g., as a useful tool, as a pleasing body, or as an unpleasant object to be avoided). But having elicited this objectification of the target, researchers typically then ask the participants to judge the objectified target on the very same trait scales that they would use in most studies of individuated person impressions. In other words, after actively discouraging participants from forming a detailed impression through one's manipulations, or after presenting participants with a target person to whom they are averse to giving much thought, the experimenter then asks the participants to make a series of judgments that demands that they form an impression of the target individual's inner qualities on the spot.

The commonly used tools of the trade for impression formation research, such as self-report scales for trait judgments, in and of themselves, are ill-suited for adequately identifying and measuring objectification. They are a heuristic measure used when other more sophisticated measures are unavailable. I refer to them as a heuristic measure, because, like other heuristics (e.g., the availability heuristic), they are susceptible to the logical fallacy of affirming the consequent (If A, then B. B occurs. Therefore A.). We start with the premise that objectification causes people to judge others as less warm and less competent (if A, then B). If our measures indicate that a person was judged less warm and less competent (B occurs), we assume that objectification was the cause (therefore, A). The causal process is inferred from the outcome without sufficient regard to the possibility that the same outcome could have arisen from a variety of different processes other than objectification. Social neuroscience provides one exciting new way to explore these questions. In addition, eye-tracking technology, reaction time tasks, and a variety of other more sophisticated tools need to be employed that more directly measure the processes underlying objectification.

## *Power and Objectification*

Another productive avenue of research in this area concerns the role that power can play in objectification. A variety of research suggests that those with power pay less attention to the relatively powerless or regard them in a more stereotypical fashion (Barreto et al. 2010; Dépret and Fiske 1999; Fiske 1993; Russell and Fiske 2010). Goodwin, Gubin, Fiske, and Yzerbyt (2000), for example, found that powerful perceivers shift their attention to stereotype-consistent information and pay less attention to specific traits of the target person. Similarly, Galinsky, Magee, Inesi, and Gruenfeld (2006) found that individuals made to feel more powerful were less likely to take into account other people's perspectives. Power may create a greater focus on one's own goals, which in turn results in less attention to the feelings, experiences, and points of view of those around us. Having power promotes using less powerful others to serve one's own goals while neglecting to consider their subjective experiences (Chen et al. 2001; Overbeck and Park 2006).

Gruenfeld, Inesi, Magee, and Galinsky (2008) assert that, of the seven characteristic features of objectification that Nussbaum (1995) identified, the most essential element is instrumentality. In short, objectification is best described as viewing people and interacting with people in a manner that primarily regards them as a tool for satisfying one's own goals. Gruenfeld and her colleagues go on to point out that "the notion of instrumentality helps to distinguish objectification from other, related constructs, such as dehumanization and stereotyping, both of which tend to be associated with negative appraisals and a desire to distance oneself from the target" (Gruenfeld et al., p. 112).

This latter point raises a difficult issue. What exactly is the difference between stereotyping, objectification, and dehumanization? In this next section, I provide a possible answer to that question.

## In Search of a Synthesis

Although the exploration of objectification has taken place on many fronts, ranging from feminist philosophy to social neuroscience, a common assumption across these perspectives is that objectification involves a certain way of thinking about another person. The research and theorizing about sexual objectification and self-objectification has emphasized our obsessive attention to the body as the defining feature of objectification. Research and theorizing about mind perception, on the other hand, has emphasized the absence of thinking about another person's mind (denial of subjectivity) as the defining feature of objectification. And research and theorizing about power has emphasized instrumentality (thinking about the person as a tool for furthering our own ends) as the defining feature of objectification. These are not mutually exclusive ways of thinking, and in fact, are likely to operate in concert. For example, if I was focused on my own goals, I might regard someone in terms of their instrumentality and minimize thoughts of their mental life. As a result, I might be unlikely to attend to their facial expressions, or look them in the eye at all, as I do not feel the need to look for clues as to what they are thinking and feeling. To the extent that I might focus on their physical form at all, it would be more for my own pleasure, or for making more basic assessments about the person's usefulness (e.g., "Do they appear physically capable of doing what I need them to do?").

One way to try to define what objectification is, is to determine what objectification is not. How does objectification differ from other ways of thinking about persons? The classic dual processing theories of person perception (Brewer 1988; Fiske and Neuberg 1990) contrast category-based processing (i.e., stereotyping) with piecemeal or attribute-based processing (i.e., individuation). Objectification bears some similarities to stereotyping, in that it does not involve careful consideration of all individual qualities. Both the "body focus" view of objectification and the "denial of subjectivity" view of objectification would suggest that relatively little thought is given to the person's inner mental life and qualities: the target's feelings, traits, attitudes, and goals are irrelevant to the perceiver. However, category-based processing (stereotyping) is not equivalent to forming little or no impression of a target's inner qualities. Rather, stereotyping means the basis for an impression comes from one's prior knowledge or expectations about the category of people to which the target is assumed to belong.

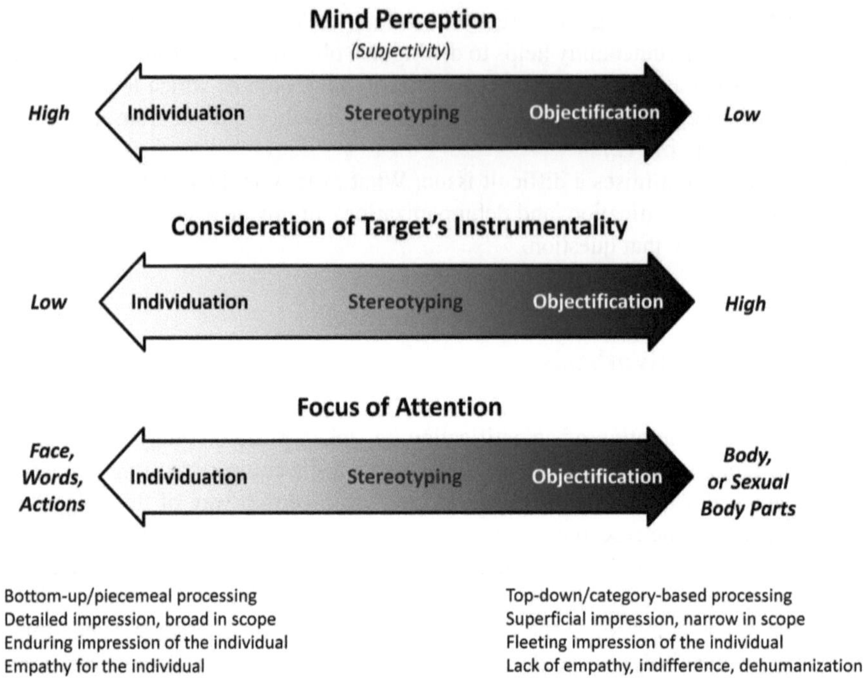


**Fig. 4.1** Impression formation process active as a function of mind perception, consideration of instrumentality, and focus of attention

The dual-processing view argues that forming impressions can occur via two routes. Individuation is the route that requires effortful information gathering and the construction of an impression that is tailor-fit to the unique qualities of the individual target. Stereotyping, on the other hand, is the route in which little to no new information is gathered, but rather one "pulls off the rack" a previously formed impression based on the category or categories in which the target is judged to fit. This is a one-size-fits-all approach that minimizes the work involved in forming an impression of the target individual.

Objectification is different from both individuation and stereotyping, in that it represents (at least in its purest form) the absence of any personal impression of the individual's inner qualities. If one were to adapt the Fiske and Neuberg (1990) continuum model to include objectification, objectification would be the true polar opposite of individuation, with stereotyping falling somewhere in between (see Fig. 4.1). There are no sharp lines dividing objectification and stereotyping, just as there are no sharp lines dividing stereotyping from individuation. Nevertheless, it might help to think of these as three distinct processes in the impression formation process. We can at times engage in any of these three ways of thinking about people, and we may vacillate between these three modes relatively quickly. Like a recipe for a meal, the impressions we cook up will differ, depending on how much of these various ingredients we add. How much of our impression of a person was based on their individual attributes? How much of it was based on category-based assumptions? And how much of it was based on judging the person's utility for our own goals? Each impression we form of another human being may reflect some combination of these three ingredients.

Consider your last encounter with the cashier at the grocery store again. If you were rushed, thinking about the dinner you needed to cook, or distracted by your child's insistent pleas for a candy bar conveniently displayed at their eye level, I doubt your impression of the cashier went much beyond the automatic registration of their gender, age, race, and general physical appearance. And even though certain category-based information was automatically activated in your mind, you may have given no effort to stitch that information together in your working memory and actively form and store an impression of him or her. If you formed an impression, it may well have narrowly focused on the speed and efficiency with which the cashier could scan your items and bag your groceries. Whatever "impression" you had, it likely dissolved away as your short-term memory of the encounter faded. Now consider how much of our lives are filled with such superficial encounters, many of them even less meaningful than the one you had with the cashier. In urban environments, people encounter countless strangers, forming almost no impression at all. Such is the "dark matter" that fills much of our social lives.

An intriguing look into the routine nature of our daily social contact with others comes from a series of studies by Simons and colleagues (Levin et al. 2002; Simons and Levin 1998). In these studies, they arranged for a brief conversation between two people, one of them being a confederate of the experimenter, and the other being an unwitting participant. The key element of their studies was that they cleverly switched the confederate with whom the participant was talking in the middle of their conversation. In one situation, the confederate stopped a person walking across campus and asked for directions. While they were talking, two workers (also confederates) who were carrying a door walked between the participant and the confederate. While the door passed between them, the conversation partner was surreptitiously switched with one of the workers carrying the door. Only 50 % of the participants noticed the switch. In another version of this study, participants arrived at a counter to receive instructions for where to go to participate in a research study. During the brief conversation, the confederate reached down to get a consent form from under the counter, but it was a different confederate who popped up with the form and continued with the directions. Only 25 % of the participants noticed the switch. It is noteworthy that these researchers originally studied this phenomenon of change blindness for objects in a scene and then extended this work to human interactions. Without intending to do so, they provided an excellent example of how, at least some of the time, we think about others as superficially as we think about objects, even to the point that those others are unconsciously interchangeable (i.e., fungible).

If objectification is a common social experience, as suggested by the scenarios and research studies I have just described, how are we to reconcile this with the view of objectification as a harmful, even dehumanizing experience, as so much of the research on sexual objectification would indicate? Nussbaum (1995), Cahill (2011), and others have argued that objectification need not always be the devastating insult to one's humanity that some scholars portray it to be. It can occur in rather benign and even positive forms.

Should the concept of objectification be applied to extreme events such as dehumanization, as well as to the mundane and mindless interactions of everyday social life? Papadaki (2010) explicitly constrained the concept to those encounters with negative dehumanizing results, thereby declassifying the other "objectifying" events as objectification. I am not comfortable with this approach for three reasons. First, Papadaki's recommendation requires defining objectification in terms of certain ways of treating or viewing others (i.e., a process) that result in a negative and dehumanizing judgment of them (i.e., an outcome). Thus, by limiting the definition of objectification in this way, she potentially treats objectification as both cause (process) and effect (outcome). Second, the benign and malevolent forms of objectification appear to be close cousins conceptually, and artificially tossing some forms of objectification aside because they pose difficulties for our theories is scientifically suspect. Third, the benign and malevolent forms of objectification may interact or have carry-over effects from one to the other. For example, a malevolent form of objectification (e.g., sexual harassment) may have a more detrimental impact in an environment in which benign forms of objectification are absent. That is to say, the more one has experienced benign forms of objectification, the more psychologically immunized one may be to the more malevolent forms of objectification. Another possibility may be that the frequency with which one engages in benign forms of objectification may increase the likelihood of engaging in more malevolent forms of objectification, perhaps as a result of procedural priming (e.g., Förster et al. 2009; Neumann 2000). Though these conjectures are purely speculative at this point, including the full range of objectification in our conceptualizations and theories allows us to empirically examine these possibilities.

Nevertheless, as a single unitary construct, objectification may have too much weight to bear. The use of the same term for such a diversity of events may reflect our discipline's lack of conceptual development and clarity in this area. As we move forward, the terms and concepts we use need to help articulate and explain the differences we identify as important. Recall that Papadaki (2010) suggested that we delineate different forms of objectification, and it is this suggestion that I will take up next. My own conceptual framework for objectification, which I offer here, is far from some "grand theory" of objectification. Instead, I offer it as an opening volley, which I hope others will take up and return, with critiques and refinements of their own.

I propose three broad categories of objectification (see Fig. 4.2) which follow from an assessment of the target person's instrumentality, the variable that Nussbaum (1995) and Gruenfeld et al. (2008) pegged as the key element in objectification. Perceived instrumentality drives which form objectification will take,

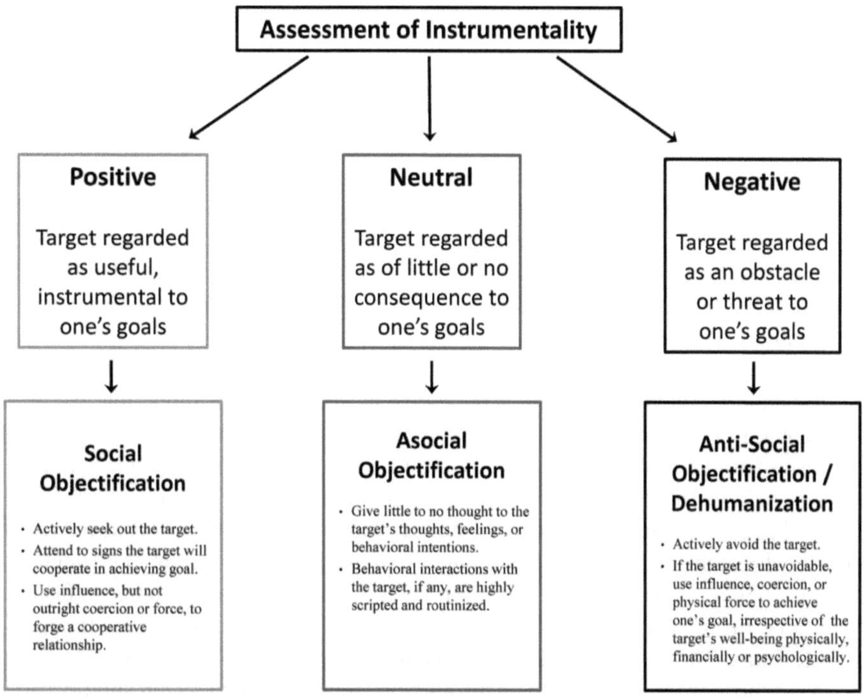


**Fig. 4.2** The relationship between instrumentality assessment and type of objectification

with three general ways we can view others' instrumentality (positive, neutral, or negative), resulting in three different forms of objectification (social objectification, asocial objectification, and anti-social objectification, respectively).

*Social objectification* occurs when there is a positive appraisal of a person's instrumentality, in that the person is perceived as useful to us. This form of objectification is likely to occur when (a) one is focused primarily on one's own goal, (b) the attainment of that goal is dependent on the cooperation of others, and (c) others are not required by their social roles to offer assistance. In such a situation, one must attend to indications that another person has the ability, knowledge, or other resources you require, and is willing (or potentially willing with some persuasion) to provide the assistance needed. This form of objectification is closest to stereotyping or individuation, in that one is forming an impression of the target individual with respect to his or her particular qualities and his or her state of mind. However, because there is a narrow focus, such that it is limited to considering only those aspects of the person's mind that bear directly on one's goal, it is more a form of objectification than not. There is little to no interest in a deeper and more elaborate impression of the objectified target person. Furthermore, interactions of this type are relatively brief, focused on the tasks at hand, and lasting only long enough to satisfy the objectifier's goals.

*Asocial objectification* occurs when there is a neutral appraisal of a person's instrumentality, in that the person is judged (perhaps in many cases quickly and automatically) to be of little or no consequence to us. This form of objectification is likely to occur when we encounter others (a) who are of little or no consequence to us, and/or (b) in contexts in which we can mindlessly follow well-established behavioral scripts requiring no thought, no plan for coordinating our actions, and hence no need to wonder what the other person will or will not do. For example, the exchange of money for a hamburger at your local fast food restaurant is so well scripted that both the customer and the server engage in mindless, asocial objectification of the other. In short, asocial objectification occurs when the social world is operating on autopilot.

*Anti-social objectification* occurs when there is a negative appraisal of a person's instrumentality, in that he or she is perceived as an obstacle or threat that we must overcome to reach our goals. There is a robust literature relating the perception of threat to various forms of prejudice (Cottrell and Neuberg 2005), and it is reasonable to believe that it plays a role in objectification as well. Because the target is viewed as a hindrance to one's goals, one is focused on how to (a) avoid the target and the threat they pose to achieving your goals, or (b) control the target through coercion or force so that their threat is eliminated. Acting in this self-interested fashion would be difficult if one gave consideration to the target's experiences, thoughts, and feelings. The result is, at best, a thoughtlessness and callousness that leads us to avoid those we find troubling or disquieting, such as turning a cold shoulder to a homeless panhandler who asks for money. At worst, it results in the demonization of those that we perceive as enemies and untethers us from the restraints of our moral compass and social norms. It is in these worst cases that we actively treat others as less than human, and in doing so become less than human ourselves.

I deliberately limit the use of the term "dehumanization" to this category of anti-social objectification. Just as the word "objectification" has been asked to cover too much conceptual ground, the word "dehumanization" has been used more widely as well. In recent empirical studies, for example, where the perceiver's attention might be manipulated to focus on the body instead of the face, the resulting small decrease in judgments of certain traits regarded as key to humanness (Haslam 2006) has led researchers to label this body-focused form of objectification as a subtle form of dehumanization. If the conceptual language of "dehumanization" is used to describe sexual assault, slavery, or genocide, should we use the same linguistic concept to describe such a minor shift in trait judgments? Furthermore, I think there is an important conceptual difference between the absence of individuation and dehumanization, with the former being more passive and unintentional, while the latter is more active and deliberate. Some experimental procedures may create an absence of individuation, which in turn results in a small but statistically significant diminution in trait judgments related to "humanness," but this is qualitatively different from the active and intentional dehumanization of a fellow human being.

## The Social Dynamics of Objectification in Context

In her groundbreaking treatise on objectification, Martha Nussbaum (1995) noted that "context is everything…in many cases if not all cases, the difference between an objectionable and a benign use of objectification will be made by the overall context of the human relationship in question" (p. 271). This observation is remarkably similar to that of Justice Sandra Day O'Connor in her landmark opinion on sexual harassment in Harris vs. Forklift (1993, p. 19), in which she wrote that "whether an environment is 'hostile' or 'abusive' can be determined only by looking at all the circumstances." The subjective nature of this assessment requires that we investigate the factors that influence whether an environment is judged to be hostile or abusive. If we accept that some forms of objectification (e.g., sexual harassment) are morally objectionable and legally actionable, then what are the characteristics of the contexts/environments that create these malevolent forms of objectification? Wiener, Gervais, Brnjic, and Nuss (this volume) provide an excellent review of (a) the legal parameters of hostile environments and (b) the psychological research and theory on objectification and dehumanization. Merging these two perspectives, they have developed an intriguing psycholegal model of hostile environments.

To this point, I have emphasized three key elements of objectification—instrumentality, denial of subjectivity, and body focus—all of which have been the focus of research efforts in psychology. Yet even the combination of all three of these elements would not inherently define a particular encounter as a negative form of objectification, or the environment as "hostile" or "abusive" in a legal sense. Consider a scenario in which two individuals cross paths at a local bar where they hoped to meet potential sexual partners. They may view each other instrumentally, with a focus on each other's body, and with little interest in each other's mental life beyond the other person's apparent willingness to "hook up." Though some may question this behavior on other grounds, this behavior is socially tolerated and certainly legal. In this example of social objectification, one key aspect of the situation is the reciprocity or symmetry between the expectations of both individuals. Both apparently regard the situation to be one in which objectification by the other was expected and accepted.

Three key elements in each interaction are: (a) the expectations Person #1 has for how he or she would/should be treated in this situation, (b) the expectations Person #2 has for how she or he would/should be treated in this situation, and (3) the expectations for how people in general are treated and should be treated in such contexts ("behavior settings," see Wiener et al., this volume). Now imagine that one of these elements was switched. Suppose the first person shows up to the bar not expecting that people would be there looking to "hook up" with someone else. The sexual objectification she might experience from the second person would be unwelcome and potentially offensive and upsetting. Nevertheless, in the court of public opinion at least, the second person would not be blamed for their objectifying behavior, which was in accordance with what he and most others would expect in that situation, unless it persisted once it became apparent that the first person did not reciprocate.

Expectations and context matter in actual social interactions, yet the experimental research on objectification rarely has examined actual interactions, let alone the expectations of those involved or the context of their interactions. Wiener, Gervais, and their colleagues (Wiener et al. 2013) have developed a research paradigm for studying sexual objectification, in which they can examine how different individuals perceive the objectifying encounter. They examine the reactions of those who directly experienced the objectification, those who observed it secondhand (videotape of the encounter) and those who read a transcript of the encounter. Interestingly, those who experienced the objectification found it less problematic than those who witnessed it or heard about it. Certainly, the perspective one has when viewing the event (experiencer vs. observer) may have an influence (Taylor and Fiske 1975), but a variety of other social dynamics may be involved as well. What is particularly exciting about their research paradigm is that it is amenable to manipulating some of the parameters of the situation. Experimenters can provide participants with expectations about what the encounter will be like. Experimenters can manipulate the goals of the individual participants placed in the setting, and they can manipulate the behavior of an experimental confederate to be either consistent or inconsistent with those goals. Hence, one can create situations in which any objectification that occurs is either symmetrical (expected and conducted by both parties to the interaction), or asymmetrical (expected and conducted by one party but not by the other). When the experience of asymmetrical objectification occurs in a context in which objectification is not expected and is not the norm, it may result in (a) greater recognition that one is being objectified, (b) greater psychological distress in the objectified party, and (c) greater likelihood of resisting the objectification by speaking out, filing a complaint, or taking other active steps to eliminate or combat any recurrence of the objectification.

The manner in which the objectification occurs can also be manipulated. Gervais, Wiener, and their colleagues (Gervais et al. 2011; Wiener et al. 2013) have done this with their use of an objectifying gaze at a person's chest for various lengths of time during a face-to-face interview. While the person may have felt objectified, it may have been unclear as to whether that was the objectifier's intention. But in many cases of workplace harassment, it is quite clear what the intention of the objectifier was. It is one thing for an objectifier to stare at a woman's body, and it is another for the objectifier to stare at her body in such a way as to make it obvious to the woman that she is being viewed in this way, like it or not. The objectifier's intention introduces into discussion some elements that have been missing from our discussion of objectification: violability and denial of autonomy. When a man gawks at a woman's body in an obviously intentional fashion and draws even further attention to this objectification through his explicit verbal commentary on her body, the woman is robbed of control over how she is viewed. To the extent that this type of interaction is repeated and the woman is unable (or at least feels unable) to stop such encounters, a loss of autonomy and a sense of violation will emerge.

The perception of intent is crucial to determining how we should respond, both socially and legally (Malle and Nelson 2003; Weiner 2001). Unintentional objectification may be more easily tolerated by those who experience it, as it may seem less personally hurtful or rejecting. Unintentional objectification may be more likely to elicit a positive constructive response from the objectified person, designed to educate and change the objectifier's behavior. Intentional objectification, on the other hand, is likely to be the most socially and psychologically damaging, and more likely to be the subject of legal dispute.

## In Conclusion

The work summarized in this chapter is but a sample of the tremendous volume of research being conducted on objectification in its various forms. Each individual study may have its limitations and flaws, but they have all helped the field to make significant strides in understanding what objectification is, why it happens, and what the consequences of it are for our relationships with others and for our own well-being. There is much more to be done. At the conceptual level, we should refine our understanding of what objectification is and what it is not. These refinements could entail a more careful consideration of how objectification is different from other forms of person perception (e.g., stereotyping and individuation), as well as delineating the multiple facets of objectification into different subtypes of this phenomenon. At the methodological level, we need more sophisticated research strategies to (a) circumvent the reliance on measures of impression formation, which are ill-suited as measures of objectification, and (b) gain a greater understanding of the cognitive processes involved in objectification. Lastly, we need to examine the social dynamics of objectification (e.g., the expectations that the perceiver and the target have of each other and the setting; how the individuals actually interact with one another in an objectifying encounter), which may largely determine the psychological and legal ramifications of such experiences. I hope the ideas I have contributed here provide a useful lens through which to view where we have been, as well as where we might go next on this exploration of objectification.

## References

Archer, D., Iritani, B., Kimes, D. D., & Barrios, M. (1983). Face-ism: Five studies of sex differences in facial prominence. *Journal of Personality and Social Psychology, 45*(4), 725–735. doi:10.1037/0022-3514.45.4.725.

Barreto, M., Ellemers, N., & Fiske, S. T. (2010). What did you say, and who do you think you are? How power differences affect emotional reactions to prejudice. *Journal of Social Issues, 66*(3), 477–492. doi:10.1111/j.1540-4560.2010.01657.x.

Bartky, S. L. (1990). *Femininity and domination: Studies in the phenomenology of oppression.* New York: Routledge.

Berger, J. (1972). *Ways of seeing.* London: BBC and Penguin Books.

Bernard, P., Gervais, S. J., Allen, J., Campomizzi, S., & Klein, O. (2012). Integrating sexual objectification with object versus person recognition: The sexualized-body-inversion hypothesis. *Psychological Science, 23*(5), 469–471. doi:10.1177/0956797611434748.

Brewer, M. B. (1988). A dual process model of impression formation. In T. K. Srull & R. S. Wyer Jr. (Eds.), *Advances in social cognition* (pp. 1–36). Hillsdale: Lawrence Erlbaum Associates, Inc.

Budesheim, T. L. (2011). Going out on a limb in an underdeveloped branch of objectification research. *Sex Roles, 65*(3–4), 165–172. doi:10.1007/s11199-011-9999-z.

Cahill, A. J. (2011). *Overcoming objectification: A carnal ethics*. New York: Routledge.

Calogero, R. M. (2004). A test of objectification theory: The effect of the male gaze on appearance concerns in college women. *Psychology of Women Quarterly, 28*(1), 16–21. doi:10.1111/j.1471-6402.2004.00118.x.

Calogero, R. M. (2011). Operationalizing self-objectification: Assessment and related methodological issues. In R. M. Calogero, S. Tantleff-Dunn, & J. K. Thompson (Eds.), *Self-objectification in women: Causes, consequences, and counteractions* (pp. 23–49). Washington, DC: American Psychological Association. doi:10.1037/12304-002.

Calogero, R. M. (2013). Objects don't object: Evidence that self-objectification disrupts women's social activism. *Psychological Science, 24*(3), 312–318. doi:10.1177/0956797612452574.

Calogero, R. M., Tantleff-Dunn, S., & Thompson, J. K. (Eds.). (2011). *Self-objectification in women: Causes, consequences, and counteractions*. Washington, DC: American Psychological Association. doi:10.1037/12304-000.

Chen, S., Lee-Chai, A., & Bargh, J. A. (2001). Relationship orientation as a moderator of the effects of social power. *Journal of Personality and Social Psychology, 80*(2), 173–187. doi:10.1037/0022-3514.80.2.173.

Cottrell, C. A., & Neuberg, S. L. (2005). Different emotional reactions to different groups: A sociofunctional threat-based approach to 'prejudice'. *Journal of Personality and Social Psychology, 88*(5), 770–789. doi:10.1037/0022-3514.88.5.770.

Cuddy, A. J. C., Fiske, S. T., & Glick, P. (2007). The BIAS map: Behaviors from intergroup affect and stereotypes. *Journal of Personality and Social Psychology, 92*(4), 631–648. doi:10.1037/0022-3514.92.4.631.

Cuddy, A. J. C., Fiske, S. T., Glick, P., & Mark, P. Z. (2008). Warmth and competence as universal dimensions of social perception: The stereotype content model and the BIAS map. *Advances in Experimental Social Psychology, 40,* 61–149. (Academic Press).

Cuddy, A. J. C., Fiske, S. T., Kwan, V. S. Y., Glick, P., Demoulin, S., Leyens, J., & Ziegler, R. (2009). Stereotype content model across cultures: Towards universal similarities and some differences. *British Journal of Social Psychology, 48*(1), 1–33. doi:10.1348/014466608X314935.

Dépret, E., & Fiske, S. T. (1999). Perceiving the powerful: Intriguing individuals versus threatening groups. *Journal of Experimental Social Psychology, 35*(5), 461–480. doi:10.1006/jesp.1999.1380.

Dworkin, A. (1985). Against the male flood: Censorship, pornography, and equality. *Harvard Women's Law Journal, 8,* 1–29.

Eagly, A. H., Ashmore, R. D., Makhijani, M. G., & Longo, L. C. (1991). What is beautiful is good, but…: A meta-analytic review of research on the physical attractiveness stereotype. *Psychological Bulletin, 110*(1), 109–128. doi:10.1037/0033-2909.110.1.109.

Fiske, S. T. (1993). Controlling other people: The impact of power on stereotyping. *American Psychologist, 48*(6), 621–628. doi:10.1037/0003-066X.48.6.621.

Fiske, S. T. (2011). *Envy up, scorn down: How status divides us*. New York: Russell Sage.

Fiske, S. T., & Neuberg, S. L. (1990). A continuum of impression-formation, from category-based to individuating processes: Influences of information and motivation on attention and interpretation. *Advances in Experimental Social Psychology, 23,* 1–74. doi:10.1016/S.065-2601(08)60317-2

Fiske, S. T., Xu, J., Cuddy, A. C., & Glick, P. (1999). (Dis)respecting versus (dis)liking: Status and interdependence predict ambivalent stereotypes of competence and warmth. *Journal of Social Issues, 55*(3), 473–489. doi:10.1111/0022-4537.00128.

Fiske, S. T., Cuddy, A. J. C., Glick, P., & Xu, J. (2002). A model of (often mixed) stereotype content: Competence and warmth respectively follow from perceived status and competition. *Journal of Personality and Social Psychology, 82*(6), 878–902. doi:10.1037/0022-3514.82.6.878.

Förster, J., Liberman, N., & Friedman, R. S. (2009). What do we prime? on distinguishing between semantic priming, procedural priming, and goal priming. In E. Morsella, J. A. Bargh, & P. M. Gollwitzer (Eds.), *Oxford handbook of human action. Social cognition and social neuroscience* (pp. 173–192). New York: Oxford University Press.

Fredrickson, B. L., & Roberts, T. (1997). Objectification theory: Toward understanding women's lived experiences and mental health risks. *Psychology of Women Quarterly, 21*(2), 173–206. doi:10.1111/j.1471-6402.1997.tb00108.x.

Fredrickson, B. L., Roberts, T., Noll, S. M., Quinn, D. M., & Twenge, J. M. (1998). That swimsuit becomes you: Sex differences in self-objectification, restrained eating, and math performance. *Journal of Personality and Social Psychology, 75*(1), 269–284. doi:10.1037/0022-3514.75.1.269.

Galinsky, A. D., Magee, J. C., Inesi, M. E., & Gruenfeld, D. H. (2006). Power and perspectives not taken. *Psychological Science, 17*(12), 1068–1074. doi:10.1111/j.1467-9280.2006.01824.x.

Gervais, S. J., Vescio, T. K., & Allen, J. (2011). When what you see is what you get: The consequences of the objectifying gaze for women and men. *Psychology of Women Quarterly, 35*(1), 5–17. doi:10.1177/0361684310386121.

Gervais, S. J., Vescio, T. K., & Allen, J. (2012a). When are people interchangeable sexual objects? The effect of gender and body type on sexual fungibility. *British Journal of Social Psychology, 51*(4), 499–513. doi:10.1111/j.2044-8309.2010.02016.x.

Gervais, S. J., Vescio, T. K., Förster, J., Maass, A., & Suitner, C. (2012b). Seeing women as objects: The sexual body part recognition bias. *European Journal of Social Psychology, 42*(6), 743–753. doi:10.1002/ejsp.1890.

Goodwin, S. A., Gubin, A., Fiske, S. T., & Yzerbyt, V. Y. (2000). Power can bias impression processes: Stereotyping subordinates by default and by design. *Group Processes & Intergroup Relations, 3*(3), 227–256. doi:10.1177/1368430200003003001.

Gruenfeld, D. H., Inesi, M. E., Magee, J. C., & Galinsky, A. D. (2008). Power and the objectification of social targets. *Journal of Personality and Social Psychology, 95*(1), 111–127. doi:10.1037/0022-3514.95.1.111.

Gurung, R. A. R., & Chrouser, C. J. (2007). Predicting objectification: Do provocative clothing and observer characteristics matter? *Sex Roles, 57*(1–2), 91–99. doi:10.1007/s11199-007-9219-z.

Harper, B., & Tiggemann, M. (2008). The effect of thin ideal media images on women's self-objectification, mood, and body image. *Sex Roles, 58*(9–10), 649–657. doi:10.1007/s11199-007-9379–x.

Harris, L. T., & Fiske, S. T. (2006). Dehumanizing the lowest of the low: Neuroimaging responses to extreme out-groups. *Psychological Science, 17*(10), 847–853. doi:10.1111/j.1467-9280.2006.01793.x.

Haslam, N. (2006). Dehumanization: An integrative review. *Personality and Social Psychology Review, 10*(3), 252–264. doi:10.1207/s15327957pspr1003_4.

Heflick, N. A., & Goldenberg, J. L. (2009). Objectifying Sarah Palin: Evidence that objectification causes women to be perceived as less competent and less fully human. *Journal of Experimental Social Psychology, 45*(3), 598–601. doi:10.1016/j.jesp.2009.02.008

Heflick, N. A., Goldenberg, J. L., Cooper, D. P., & Puvia, E. (2011). From women to objects: Appearance focus, target gender, and perceptions of warmth, morality and competence. *Journal of Experimental Social Psychology, 47*(3), 572–581. doi:10.1016/j.jesp. 2010.12.020

Heldman, C., & Wade, L. (2011). Sexualizing Sarah Palin. *Sex Roles, 65*(3), 156–164. doi:10.1007/s11199-011-9984-6.

Jeffreys, S. (2005). *Beauty and misogyny: Harmful cultural practices in the west*. New York: Routledge.

Johnson, V., & Gurung, R. A. R. (2011). Defusing the objectification of women by other women: The role of competence. *Sex Roles, 65*(3–4), 177–188. doi:10.1007/s11199-011-0006-5.

Kant, I., Heath, P., & Schneewind, J. B. (1997). *Lectures on ethics*. Cambridge: Cambridge University Press.

Konrath, S. H., & Schwarz, N. (2007). Do male politicians have big heads? Face-ism in online self-representations of politicians. *Media Psychology, 10*(3), 436–448. doi:10.1080/15213260701533219.

Langton, R. (2009). *Sexual solipsism: Philosophical essays on pornography and objectification.* United Kingdom: Oxford University Press.
Levin, D. T., Simons, D. J., Angelone, B. L., & Chabris, C. F. (2002). Memory for centrally attended changing objects in an incidental real-world change detection paradigm. *British Journal of Psychology, 93*(3), 289–302. doi:10.1348/000712602760146224.
Malle, B. F., & Nelson, S. E. (2003). Judging mens rea: The tension between folk concepts and legal concepts of intentionality. *Behavioral Sciences & the Law, 21*(5), 563–580. doi:10.1002/bsl.554.
Mason, M. F., & Macrae, C. N. (2004). Categorizing and individuating others: The neural substrates of person perception. *Journal of Cognitive Neuroscience, 16*(10), 1785–1795. doi:10.1162/0898929042947801.
Maurer, D., Le Grand, R., & Mondloch, C. J. (2002). The many faces of configural processing. *Trends in Cognitive Sciences, 6*(6), 255–260. doi:10.1016/S. 364-6613(02)01903-4.
McKinley, N. M., & Hyde, J. S. (1996). The objectified body consciousness scale: Development and validation. *Psychology of Women Quarterly, 20*(2), 181–215. doi:10.1111/j.1471-6402.1996.tb00467.x.
Moradi, B. (2011). Objectification theory: Areas of promise and refinement. *The Counseling Psychologist, 39*(1), 153–163. doi:10.1177/0011000010384279.
Neumann, R. (2000). The causal influences of attributions on emotions: A procedural priming approach. *Psychological Science, 11*(3), 179–182. doi:10.1111/1467-9280.00238.
Noll, S. M., & Fredrickson, B. L. (1998). A mediational model linking self-objectification, body shame, and disordered eating. *Psychology of Women Quarterly, 22*(4), 623–636. doi:10.1111/j.1471-6402.1998.tb00181.x.
Nussbaum, M. C. (1995). Objectification. *Philosophy & Public Affairs, 24*(4), 249.
Overbeck, J. R., & Park, B. (2006). Powerful perceivers, powerless objects: Flexibility of powerholders' social attention. *Organizational Behavior and Human Decision Processes, 99*(2), 227–243. doi:10.1016/j.obhdp. 2005.10.003.
Papadaki, L. (2010). What is objectification? *Journal of Moral Philosophy, 7*(1), 16–36. doi:10.1163/174046809×12544019606067.
Roberts, T., & Gettman, J. Y. (2004). Mere exposure: Gender differences in the negative effects of priming a state of self-objectification. *Sex Roles, 51*(1–2), 17–27. doi:10.1023/B:SERS.0000032306.20462.22.
Russell, A. M., & Fiske, S. T. (2010). Power and social perception. In A. Guinote & T. K. Vescio (Eds.), *The social psychology of power* (pp. 231–250). New York: Guilford.
Schwarz, N., & Kurz, E. (1989). What's in a picture? The impact of face-ism on trait attribution. *European Journal of Social Psychology, 19*(4), 311–316. doi:10.1002/ejsp.2420190405.
Simons, D. J., & Levin, D. T. (1998). Failure to detect changes to people during a real-world interaction. *Psychonomic Bulletin & Review, 5*(4), 644–649. doi:10.3758/BF03208840.
Taylor, S. E., & Fiske, S. T. (1975). Point of view and perceptions of causality. *Journal of Personality and Social Psychology, 32*(3), 439–445. doi:10.1037/h0077095.
Waytz, A., Gray, K., Epley, N., & Wegner, D. M. (2010). Causes and consequences of mind perception. *Trends in Cognitive Sciences, 14*(8), 383–388. doi:10.1016/j.tics.2010.05.006.
Weiner, B. (2001). Responsibility for social transgressions: An attributional analysis. In B. F. Malle, L. J. Moses, & D. A. Baldwin (Eds.), *Intentions and intentionally: Foundations of social cognition* (pp. 331–344). Cambridge: MIT Press.
Wiener, R. L., Gervais, S. J., Allen, J., & Marquez, A. (2013). Eye of the beholder: Effects of perspective and sexual objectification on harassment judgments. *Psychology, Public Policy, and Law, 19*(2), 206–221. doi:10.1037/a0028497.
Yin, R. K. (1969). Looking at upside-down faces. *Journal of Experimental Psychology, 81*(1), 141–145. doi:10.1037/h0027474.

# Part III
# Justice and Conflict Involving People with Mental Illness

# Chapter 5
# Therapeutic Jurisprudence and Recovery from Severe and Disabling Mental Illness

**William D. Spaulding, Elizabeth Cook and Andrea Avila**

The principles derived from the concepts of conflict, justice, and well-being are broad but fundamental, as the contributions to this volume collectively demonstrate. This contribution is about how those principles play out in a particular domain of application, treatment, and rehabilitation for severe and disabling mental illness.

The concept of therapeutic jurisprudence (TJ; Wexler and Winick 1991) provides a useful epistemological bridge between the legal scholarship on conflict, justice, and well-being and the science and clinical methods pertinent to mental health and mental illness. Elsewhere in this volume, Professor David Wexler, universally recognized as a founding figure in TJ, provides an account of TJ from the perspective of legal scholarship and practice. The perspective in this chapter combines that of the research psychopathologist, primarily concerned with the causes of mental illness, and the clinical practitioner, primarily concerned with effective application of helpful treatments and other interventions. TJ informs those perspectives, and vice versa, with implications for the scientific agenda, for clinical practice, and for development of TJ itself as a body of legal and scientific scholarship. These implications are directly pertinent to resolving conflict, promoting justice, and enhancing well-being in the face of the challenges of severe and disabling mental illness.

From the psychopathologist and practitioner's perspective, the promise of TJ derives in large part from a reframing of mental illness itself. Traditionally, mental illness is understood as a condition that creates risks to individuals and the general public, sometimes requiring legal constraints on the individual liberties of the identified patient, informed by scientific expertise and practitioners' professional opinions. The TJ perspective broadens this understanding, without necessarily competing with it, to address and resolve conflicts created by mental illness. These conflicts occur at four relatively distinct levels:

1. Between individuals with mental illness vs. the public interest
2. Between individuals vs. other family members

W. D. Spaulding (✉) · E. Cook · A. Avila
Department of Psychology, University of Nebraska-Lincoln, Lincoln, NE 68588-0308, USA
e-mail: wspaulding1@unl.edu

B. H. Bornstein, R. L. Wiener (eds.), *Justice, Conflict and Wellbeing*,
DOI 10.1007/978-1-4939-0623-9_5, © Springer Science+Business Media New York 2014

3. Between individuals vs. clinical practitioners
4. Between individuals vs. the mental health services industry

All these conflicts have features in common with comparable conflicts not involving mental illness, but mental illness also creates distinctive features, in the conflicts themselves and in possible resolution strategies. Psychopathology and the technology of clinical practice inform methods for resolving these conflicts, much as they (arguably) inform traditional legal/judicial decision-making.

Professor Wexler identifies "soft spots" in the legal infrastructure that represent opportunities for deference to individual circumstances and problems, to be exploited in TJ. From the practitioner's perspective, there are also "squishy spots" where legal considerations (i.e., justice) overlap and interact with the imperatives of clinical practice (i.e., pursuit of well-being). This is where the TJ philosophy leads most directly to implications for treatment. Contemporary treatment and rehabilitation of severe mental illness generate six such "squishy spots:"

1. Proxies, directives, and relapse prevention;
2. Contracts, contingencies, and behavior modification;
3. Mediation and family therapy;
4. Outpatient commitment and treatment planning;
5. Daubert evidentiary principles, involuntary treatment, and evidence-based practice;
6. Right to treatment and mental health reform.

The remainder of this discussion will consider in turn these opportunities to enhance treatment outcome through application of TJ. But first, it is important to consider two other factors that have significantly reframed severe mental illness in ways that complement TJ, psychiatric rehabilitation and the recovery movement.

Psychiatric rehabilitation (Anthony 1979; Spaulding et al. 2003; Liberman 2008) is a holistic, integrated approach to treatment. Although its conceptual roots can be traced to the early twentieth century (e.g., Beers 1921), it took on its contemporary form in the 1970s through translation of the psychology of physical rehabilitation (e.g., of paraplegia and comparable disabilities) into the psychiatric context. Its key principle is an understanding of mental illness as a type of disability to be overcome, rather than a disease to be cured. Consistent with the legacy of rehabilitation psychology, psychiatric rehabilitation also emphasizes rigorous, objective measurement of the various domains of human personal and social functioning and application of treatment modalities known through experimental study to benefit functioning in those domains.

The recovery movement is a consumerist social movement energized primarily by people with mental illness and their families and advocates (Bellack 2006). It also has extensive historical roots and a close association with psychiatric rehabilitation (Anthony 1993). The recovery movement found a voice in two important national policy documents, a report of the US Surgeon General (US Public Health Service 1999) and of a presidential commission (President's New Freedom Commission on Mental Health 2004). Both were pointed indictments of the American mental health system, especially its failure to serve people with severe and disabling mental illness. Some in the recovery movement view any kind of technological perspective on SMI as suspect, and therefore do not distinguish between psychiatric rehabilitation and the conventional "medical model" practices that are the targets of indictment. However, the mainstream view in both the psychiatric rehabilitation community and the recovery movement is that psychiatric rehabilitation represents a toolbox of modalities that collectively address the values and goals of the recovery movement on a person-by-person basis. Together, psychiatric rehabilitation and the recovery movement have created a mandate for mental health services that go beyond traditional medically oriented treatment outcomes, i.e., suppression of psychiatric symptoms with drugs, to enhance self-worth, quality of life, and participation in the social community. These new treatment goals are particularly relevant to the contributions of TJ.

## Psychiatric Advance Directives, Relapse Prevention, Recovery, and Wellness

Unlike developmental disorders such as autism or mental retardation, severe mental illness tends to be episodic, meaning episodes of exacerbated illness punctuate a higher and more stable level of baseline functioning. For some people, the difference between higher and more stable functioning vs. exacerbated illness is small, and therefore a relatively less crucial consideration. In others, the difference is great, even so as to cross legal criteria of competence to make decisions. There are familiar legal mechanisms to ensure that a person's interests are protected during periods of legal incompetence, e.g., power of attorney and advance directives. They are quite distinct from mechanisms usually used to protect the interests of people whose legal incompetence does not fluctuate, e.g., guardianship. Over the past several years, as consumer interests associated with SMI have come to the attention of the general public and the legal community, there has been increasing interest in use of power of attorney and advance health care directives during temporary periods of legal incompetence.

In the US 25 states recognize advance directives in statute (National Resource Center on Psychiatric Advance Directives 2011). Arguably, in all remaining states, the purposes of advance directives are served by conventional power of attorney. The difference is that an advance directive necessarily includes specifications about the type of treatment or other dispositions to be provided, in those situations where a legally competent choice is required of the identified patient. A power of attorney may lack such specificity, but generally it may also be granted with the stipulation that certain procedures are to be followed in its execution.

In an extensive program of research studies based at Duke University, 70% of participants with SMI said they would like to have an advance directive in anticipation of future exacerbations of their illness, although only 10% actually had them (Swanson et al. 2006). The discrepancy is not due to resistance from the health care industry or professional communities. The hospital standards of the Joint Commission (former Joint Commission on Accreditation of Healthcare Organizations, JCAHO) require that hospital staff enquire about patients' advance directions upon admission. The standards of the federal Center for Medicare and Medicaid Services (CMS) require that providers seeking reimbursement from those sources respect valid advance health care directives. The Duke studies indicated that health care professionals are generally accepting of the idea of advance directives, but are often unsure of how the law and ethical codes might constrain their use (Elbogen et al. 2006; Van Dorn et al. 2008; Kim et al. 2008)

In principle, there is no dispute that people's interests are served when they gain a degree of control over what happens at times when they cannot make legally competent decisions. In practice, it is unclear how much control advance psychiatric directives really provide. Psychiatric directives address complex, ongoing clinical judgments about treatment selection that may remain subject to the discretion of health care providers. The personal choices are different from those involved in the difficult but straightforward and familiar choices reflected in such advance directives as "Do Not Resuscitate" (e.g., Wilder et al. 2007). Often, the circumstances that would activate an advance directive have already activated other mechanisms that severely limit courses of action, e.g., civil commitment. Currently there is insufficient research evidence to be confident that advance psychiatric directives really do improve quality of life or otherwise benefit people with SMI. Without strong evidence, and without the resources in mental health systems to make advance directives happen, their impact is seriously limited. Research that could facilitate better use of advance directives and related mechanisms would address:

- Staff training practices around assisting consumers with development and implementation of psychiatric advance directives
- Agency and staff characteristics that affect psychiatric advance directive implementation
- Statistics regarding number of psychiatric advance directives that are implemented effectively vs. not effectively
- Whether there are certain parts of psychiatric advance directives that are typically implemented well vs. not well
- Impact of implementation (or lack thereof) of psychiatric advance directives on consumer quality of life, etc.

One of the "squishy areas" where legal concepts and processes overlap with clinical ones is between advance directives and relapse prevention. Exploration of this overlap leads to new ideas about how to make the benefits of advance directives more meaningful and more available to people with SMI.

The term "relapse" is often used when a person's functioning is significantly impaired by episodic exacerbations of SMI. It is used generally in medicine to describe recurrence or exacerbation of an illness, although in mental health the meaning is less clear and specific. For example, in the alcoholism treatment community, "relapse" means recurrence of alcohol use, sometimes reflecting an ideological commitment to viewing alcoholism as a disease that must be managed through absolute abstinence. More circumspect views of alcoholism hold that moderate, socially acceptable alcohol use is a legitimate treatment goal, but such views still appropriate the idea of relapse as crossing a boundary between moderate use and abuse. These ideas led to the development of relapse prevention as a distinct and coherent approach to treatment of alcoholism, with the goal of preventing "relapse" however it might be defined. Psychiatric rehabilitation appropriated the idea and applied it to relapse of mental illness, with the goal of preventing episodic exacerbations, also known as psychotic episodes. Our modern understanding of schizophrenia as extremely sensitive to stress and related environmental conditions gives relapse prevention additional meaning and focus.

Today relapse prevention is a core modality in the psychiatric rehabilitation toolbox (e.g., Alvarez-Jimenez et al. 2011; Gumley 2011; Ziedonis et al. 2007). It is a combination of didactic and interactive education about the nature of episodic disorders, identification of individual's "warning signs" of an impending psychotic episode, training in methods of forestalling relapse through stress management skills and adherence to medication, and detailed planning for what to do and when, during an impending relapse.

Preventing psychotic relapse in SMI usually involves ongoing participation in an array of treatment and rehabilitation, and in that sense is inseparable from a person's comprehensive strategy for achieving a better life. This holistic dimension of relapse prevention intersects with the values and priorities of the recovery movement, which has generated similar modalities designed for use outside professional auspices. An early version was called Wellness and Recovery Action Plan (WRAP; Copeland 2001), and WRAP soon became a generic term for such modalities. WRAP groups have evolved to function somewhat like Alcoholics Anonymous, organized and operated by consumers, outside of but complementing the professional mental health system. There is insufficient outcome research on consumer-organized WRAP, but at least one controlled trial has appeared (Cook et al. 2011), showing improvements on measures of symptom severity, hope, and quality of life, compared to a group receiving "treatment as usual" with no wellness/relapse prevention of any kind. There is also considerable research on the various formal components of relapse prevention, indicating effectiveness in reducing frequency of relapses and improving personal and social functioning (e.g., Lee et al. 2010; Klingberg et al. 2010; Ziedonis et al. 2007). WRAP ideas have also influenced relapse prevention for SMI, toward being increasingly holistic and recovery-oriented, to the degree that "relapse prevention" is now one dimension of a broader, individualized wellness and recovery regimen. Interestingly, WRAP modalities have begun to include components that explicitly address construction of advance directives. This creates an even more direct connection between WRAP and TJ and indicates the importance of systematic input from legal scholarship on development of clinical modalities.

From the clinical perspective, an advance directive is one component of relapse prevention. Developing the directive can and should be part of the broader education and recovery process necessary for a plan that all understand and endorse. Issues addressed in developing the directive are often crucial aspects of the broader rehabilitation and recovery process. For example, a directive requires that all involved must find a way to agree that there are times when the identified patient loses or is at risk of losing the ability to make competent decisions. Failure to recognize one's own illness ("lack of insight" in psychiatric jargon) is a notoriously detrimental feature of SMI, and this sometimes includes failure to recognize the role of psychotic episodes in one's own life. This creates a conflict between the identified patient, family, caregivers, and the public interest represented in this context by the judicial system. The conflict is needlessly complicated when "insight" means the patient understands and agrees with the psychiatric diagnostic system, an object of strenuous controversy even within psychiatry.

"Insight" is also addressed in relapse prevention and related rehabilitation modalities. Conflict can usually be skirted or defused by a systematic focus on the symptoms and functional consequences, without arguing about the validity of the diagnostic system. Surprisingly to some, people often accept the idea that they can gain control of symptoms, and that specific treatments are useful for that purpose, without agreeing that they have a mental illness. The heavy social stigmatization of "mental illness" partly accounts for this phenomenon. In addition, there are rational reasons to fear acknowledgement of a condition that defers so much to professional opinion. An advance directive that depends too much on diagnosis and professional opinion has less chance of resolving the conflict. An advance directive developed in conjunction with recovery-oriented rehabilitation and relapse prevention builds consensus as development proceeds.

Unfortunately, the techniques of conflict resolution embedded in relapse prevention are not commonly in the repertoire of the professionals who serve people with SMI. This is because psychiatric rehabilitation is relatively new and new techniques disseminate slowly in mental health care (Lehman, Kreyenbuhl, Buchanan, et al. 2004). Also, rehabilitation skills are different and even inconsistent with some conventional psychiatric practices. This may be as much a reason for professionals' passivity about advance directives as their lack of legal background. Ironically, patients with the least "insight" are probably in greatest need of advance directives. The solution for underuse of advance directives may therefore be to augment relapse prevention and related modalities to include systematic development of an advance directive, using the techniques that have proven effective in overcoming conflicts over "insight" and related problems.

This solution is consistent with national policy that addresses dissemination problems in mental health. Substance Abuse and Mental Health Services Administration (SAMHSA), the federal agency responsible for fostering quality in mental health and substance abuse services, has developed a network for developing new rehabilitation modalities and packaging them for real-world application (SAMHSA 2012). This includes materials to support on-the-job training necessary to use the new modalities. Service providers can download these packages and use them to develop local capabilities. A new relapse prevention modality incorporating the capacity to develop advance directives would fit quite easily into that dissemination pipeline. In addition to the conflict resolution, skills already inherent in relapse prevention, the package would train the skills necessary to engage appropriate legal processes when the advance directive is complete, and the wellness plan is ready to implement. It remains only for TJ scholars to collaborate with treatment developers to create the modality. For the purposes of research, the outcome measures that could demonstrate superiority of relapse prevention modalities enhanced by TJ-informed advance directives include:

- The patient's experience of dignity and personal empowerment
- Relapse rate
- Fidelity of advance directive implementation after relapse
- Severity of the course of the illness and the long-term outcome

## Clinical Decision-Making in Advance Directives and Other TJ Applications

Inclusion of relapse prevention and related approaches creates a very different advance directive, compared to the conventional format of specifying or prohibiting particular medications and other actions. The conventional format identifies specific decisions made in the course of "medical model" clinical practice that predated contemporary psychiatric rehabilitation, and constrains practitioners to specific choices, e.g., type of medication or other treatments. Clinical decision-making has a different quality in psychiatric rehabilitation. Decisions do not stem solely from diagnosis or risk considerations. They result from interactions between patient, practitioner, and others in which technical considerations are continuously reassessed in the context of the patient's personal preferences and changing circumstances.

Ultimately, anticipating such complex contingencies may be too much to expect from an advance directive. Even in conventional psychiatry, attempts to formalize medication prescription as a rational process that can be fully represented by syllogistic algorithms have been disappointing (Kashner et al. 2006). If we could identify and understand the key decision points and processes in psychiatric rehabilitation, and codify them as algorithms, the algorithms themselves could be included in advance directives. Instead of specifying particular choices, they could specify the process for making key decisions, and the assumptions or preferences upon which the algorithms operate. This would make the advance directive more sensitive to momentary or unanticipated circumstances, and therefore more likely to produce a desirable outcome. Research on judgment and decision-making applied to mental health practice has just begun (Spaulding and Deogun 2011). The first step will be to simply identify the points, either in the course of illness or the process of treatment where the advantages of an advance directive (or any other TJ application) can be determined. The next step will be to apply or not apply specific decision algorithms and processes at those points in controlled experiments. The outcome variables in such experiments could include some that are specific to the advance directive, e.g., the satisfaction of the patient and professionals involved in the process, and in the longer term, the reliability of implementation when the criteria in the directive are met. In addition, the general outcome variables for TJ research described above would apply.

Short of comprehensive algorithms for decision-making, psychiatric rehabilitation has evolved new methods for managing the complexity of recovery from SMI (Spaulding et al. 2003). These include functional assessment, case formulation, and integrated treatment planning. Functional assessment, a familiar technique in clinical psychology, is a systematic approach to identifying and measuring key abilities, including those that are impaired by SMI. Case formulation, adapted from its origins in cognitive behavioral therapy, is a method for putting assessment data together to form a comprehensive understanding of the factors that limit a person's functioning, for the purpose of informing treatment strategy. Treatment planning, adapted from its origins in health care regulations, is a method for organizing and coordinating complex treatment regimens. Together these three methods provide a practical framework for (1) identifying the decisions that need to be made, (2) collecting data to support making those decisions, and (3) evaluating the outcome. As the following discussion demonstrates, this framework usefully guides development of other TJ-based approaches as it does in the case of advance directives.

## Contingencies, Contracts, and Behavior Modification from the Bench

An early landmark in the history of TJ was Professor Wexler's (1973) review, "Token and taboo: Behavior modification, token economies and the law." It was an analysis of the justice implications of a new genre of psychiatric treatment based on the psychology of learning and motivation, especially timely because research had shown dramatic effectiveness of that treatment in people institutionalized with SMI (e.g., Ayllon and Azrin 1968). The innovation in the approach was systematic use of rewards ("reinforcement" in psychology terminology) to establish and maintain basic adaptive behavior. Over the ensuing decades, the approach evolved into a broad range of interrelated techniques, collectively known as contingency management because they have in common systematic use of reward contingencies, natural and contrived, to promote adaptive behavior.

The original approach was used with involuntary and/or legally incompetent patients in institutions. The reinforcements were tokens that could be used to purchase goods in a "token store." As psychiatric rehabilitation expanded beyond the institutions, money and other natural reinforcements took the place of tokens. Increasingly, the approach was adapted for use with voluntary patients where it evolved into techniques for negotiating, instead of imposing, reward contingencies. One variant of the original technique is literally called contingency contracting (Heinssen et al. 1995).

The recovery movement brought concerns about the coercive dimensions of the original institutional versions of contingency management, but coercion became a complex and unresolved problem in mental health law and practice (Molodynski et al. 2010). Today, social learning theory has matured to the point that we understand all human behavior as operating in a complex psychological economy where individuals continually engage in social contracts, using contingencies they control to obtain outcomes they desire. Social interactions in the mental health system are no different. Mental health professionals have the same responsibility as everyone else, in fact more so, to not use the contingencies they control in coercive or exploitative ways. In addition, in accordance with the methods of rehabilitation and the values of recovery, practitioners increasingly have the theoretical rationale and the tools to make the contingencies they control serve the interests and desires of the identified patient.

Mental illness does not destroy one's ability to participate in the psychological economy, but it limits one's ability to apprehend and respond to contingencies that are abstract or temporally distant. This effect is so universal and pervasive that it has been formulated as a broad theory of schizophrenia, the immediacy hypothesis (Salzinger 1984), wherein the functional deficits of schizophrenia are understood to be the product of responding to contingencies that are abnormally concrete or immediate. This is arguably an old idea in psychology, related to the psychoanalytic idea of delay of gratification, but cast in the more precise and measurable terms of learning theory and cognitive psychology. The clinical technique of contingency management works because people with SMI who cannot respond normally to abstract or distant consequences can respond normally when the behavioral contingencies on those consequences are engineered to be more concrete and/or immediate.

A related idea lies at the heart of problem-solving courts (Casey and Rottman 2003), an innovation in judicial practice associated with TJ. Problem-solving courts extend the goal of justice beyond punishing unacceptable behavior, to rewarding adaptive behavior through the behavioral contingencies that the law creates. Drug courts (Belenko 2002) and mental health courts (Watson et al. 2000) are specialized forms of problem-solving courts, tuned to the special circumstances of substance abuse and severe mental illness, respectively. In practice, there is a striking correspondence between the key features of these courts and the key features of clinical contingency management:

- Treatment services are coordinated with natural and contrived contingencies on the identified patient's behavior
- Non-adversarial problem-solving is applied in pursuit of the joint goals of justice and the well-being of the identified patient
- Specific behaviors of interest (abstinence, treatment adherence, occupational functioning) are rigorously defined and measured
- Consequences related to the behaviors of interest are clearly and measurably specified
- There is a built-in process for measuring progress toward individual patients' objective goals

Clinical contingency management is difficult, even in institutions where the clinician has considerable control over contingencies highly salient to the identified patient (e.g., mobility, access to desired activities and persons). Effectiveness requires a lot of training and experience. A judge, applying contingency management from the bench, arguably has greater control over contingencies than clinicians, who have to negotiate interpersonal contracts while minimizing coercion. However, it is not just about controlling contingencies. It includes identifying and correcting skill deficiencies that prevent access to natural reinforcements, taking into account the patient's unique assets and liabilities, strategically progressing from very immediate consequences for very specific behaviors to more natural consequences for increasingly complex behaviors and skills, weighing trade-offs between treatment and recovery imperatives vs. the patient's experience of coercion, and avoiding inadvertent reinforcement of maladaptive behavior (surprisingly difficult, especially in institutional settings).

In drug courts, these vicissitudes are arguably eclipsed by relatively straightforward behaviors and contingencies. The target behavior is abstinence and adherence to treatment, and the contingency is prosecution for drug violations. In mental health courts, the situation is less straightforward. Clinical outcome cannot be measured by a urine test, as it can be in drug courts. In mental health courts, the crime that makes prosecution a contingency is not so directly related to the target behaviors or the treatment; i.e., substance abuse is both symptom and crime—not so with psychotic hallucinations, impaired social cognition, and other features of severe mental illness. Justice demands that consequences are proportionate to the seriousness of the offense. In mental health courts, especially for first offenders, the offense may be relatively minor, e.g., public nuisance, trespassing. The implications of requiring adherence to treatment for such offenses, which often will involve using prescriptive medications with significant medical side effects and risks, are not necessarily comparable to requiring abstinence from illegal drugs. On the other hand, in both drug and mental health courts, there is usually an array of intermediate steps toward solution of the problem that precipitated the court's involvement, e.g., therapy attendance. In both cases, there must be a judicial determination that the consequences of not adhering to treatment are justified by the long-term implications, independent of a separate criterion with a priori validity such as substance abuse. This requires an advanced level of clinical assessment skill. So, do mental health court judges need practitioner-level training in clinical contingency management?

Collaborative education and training are core features of problem-solving courts. The relatively slow spread of mental health courts, compared to drug courts, may be attributable to the more complex contingency management that mental health court judges have to learn to do. So far, the training and education is somewhat limited, and derives mostly from narrowly medical understandings of mental illness—"take your medication and go to therapy." A rehabilitation and recovery perspective recognizes a much more diverse array of target behaviors and contingencies, including social consequences controlled by family members and others besides the judge (this is arguably true in drug courts as well, although treatment is qualitatively different). Logically, a degree of sophistication by the judge, and close collaboration with experts in clinical contingency management, would improve the outcome of mental health courts beyond those achieved with the training and collaboration protocols that typify problem-solving courts. Exactly what degree of sophistication, and exactly what kinds of collaboration, remains unclear.

There are some controversies about mental health courts (Bazelon Center for Mental Health Law 2012). An example is criteria for participation. A "guilty" plea is usually required for diversion from the conventional court process. This may create a coercive contingency, leading some to plead guilty who otherwise would not. For some in underserved areas, it may create a perverse incentive to engage in criminal behavior in order to access mental health services, although there are no research findings to support this concern. A related problem is the seriousness of the offense in question. Mental health courts usually deal exclusively with lower-level offenses, but some have focused on felonies (Fisler 2005). There is concern that mental health courts may impose more consequences on lower-level offenders, i.e., greater restrictions on liberties, than they would otherwise experience, even leading to incarceration for not adhering to treatment. This would normally be counterbalanced by due process considerations, but relaxation of due process in pursuit of problem-solving is one of the overarching concerns about problem-solving-type courts. For felonies, the consequences are arguably already approximated by the long-term court supervision of treatment associated with Not Guilty By Reason of Insanity adjudications.

Whether the controversies are resolved or not, controlled outcome trials of mental health courts are beginning to appear, showing lower rearrest rates and lower jail time, and also some patient features that appear to moderate outcome (Steadman et al. 2011). However, it remains unknown what specific characteristics or features of mental health courts contribute to such outcomes. Methodologically, the next step to experimental validation of treatment interventions requires a treatment manual. Treatment manuals are precise directions for conducting psychotherapy and related procedures, and there are formal guidelines for their development and essential components (e.g., Carroll and Nuro 2002; Rounsaville et al. 2001). When subjective or clinical judgment is required, the manual specifies the grounds for making the judgment and when it is to be made. Establishing fidelity to the manual, i.e., that the therapist is actually following its directions, is a prerequisite to testing a treatment against something else (a placebo, a competing treatment, nothing, etc.). It's possible to envision treatment manuals for mental health courts. Experimental comparisons of different treatment manuals could reveal which outcomes are attributable to which specific features or procedures, and also what patient characteristics predict better response to one or another manual. Once again, a collaborative effort between clinical psychologists and legal scholars could produce one.

## Mediation and Family Therapy

Mediation is increasingly of interest among legal scholars as a conflict resolution approach that potentially avoids the stress, expense, and other adverse consequences of trials and related conventional mechanisms (e.g., Folberg and Taylor 1984).

Instead of an adversarial process refereed and decided by a judge, mediation is explicitly collaborative. The mediator's role is partially that of a referee, but in pursuit of maintaining a non-adversarial, problem-solving process. Compromise and accommodation are expected to be the key features of conflict resolution. Mediation is often a formal alternative to adjudication, and failure to resolve the dispute leads to a trial or other conventional processes. Mediation is almost by definition a voluntary process, requiring the consent and participation of all parties in the conflict. It is generally assumed this is what gives it certain advantages over conventional adjudication.

Mediation has become an especially important approach to family conflicts, e.g., conflicts about specific child custody and visitation arrangements in the wake of divorce. This is probably because adult family members are usually balancing their personal interests, desires, and values against the long-term welfare of the children, and so are more often willing to compromise and accommodate to avoid exposing the children to a protracted and stressful legal battle.

The idea of mediated resolution to internal family conflict is complementary to the rationale and purpose of modern family therapy specialized for families that include a member with SMI (e.g., Falloon et al. 1984; Goldstein 1991). Modern family therapy for SMI began in the 1960s when researchers found that measures of a family's emotional climate were powerfully predictive of whether the member with SMI would experience a relapse. Emotional climate was measured as levels of expressed emotion derived from objective counts of various kinds of utterances during family interactions. Negative effects of expressed emotion can be reduced through education about the nature of SMI and through conventional behavioral psychotherapy techniques, and this leads to the observed reduction in relapse rate. Nevertheless, education and conventional therapy do not necessarily resolve all the conflicts between the person with SMI and the other family members. These conflicts include:

- The family cannot tolerate certain behaviors
- The member with SMI is dependent on other family members
- The member with SMI refuses to acknowledge having an illness
- The member with SMI is violating family expectations for achievement
- The member with SMI refuses to take medication or participate in other treatment

Obviously these conflicts can be seriously detrimental to family functioning, yet fall short of meeting criteria for civil commitment or other means of imposing solutions. It is unknown whether a mediation approach (whether legal mediation or a less formal version) might reduce or resolve conflicts that remain after conventional family education or therapy has contributed all it can. A research agenda for addressing this question would have to pursue a hierarchical set of hypotheses:

1. Mediation effectively resolves conflicts in families with a member who has SMI
2. Mediation's benefits are comparable to those of modern family therapy for SMI, making it a potential alternative to family therapy

3. Mediation complements the benefits of family therapy by resolving conflicts that are not resolved by education or cognitive behavioral therapy
4. Different families benefit optimally from different combinations of mediation and therapy

We already know that a simple, relatively inexpensive course of family education confers large benefits for many families, while other families require more intensive therapy, focused on reducing familial expressed emotion. A comparable situation may obtain for mediation. On the other hand, a mediation approach may be more accessible or otherwise more effective for some families, while for others a therapy approach may be better. Ultimately, the research needs to tell us how to match individual families with the optimal combination of education, therapy, and mediation, based on measurable features of the family, the member with SMI, and the nature of the conflicts.

## Outpatient Commitment and the Treatment Plan

The concept of involuntary outpatient commitment (IOC) is rooted in the era of deinstitutionalization, and took shape as the recovery movement began to transform American mental health policy (e.g., Allen and Smith 2001; Petrila, 2003; Schopp 2003). As deinstitutionalization proceeded, and expectations about antipsychotic medication went unchecked, failure to adhere to a medication regimen appeared to many to be the main barrier to functioning in community settings for people with SMI. The conventional concept of civil commitment was modified so that people could escape institutionalization by adhering to prescribed medication. This was a big step away from the traditional criterion of "imminent danger to self or others" required for conventional commitment and affirmed by US Supreme Court rulings over three decades. The change was seen by some as an unconscionable lowering of the threshold for invoking involuntary treatment, and by others as a less restrictive alternative for those that had been passed over by deinstitutionalization. Either way, 44 states now have an outpatient commitment law.

The first American IOC laws were instituted in the 1990s. After more than a decade, they remain controversial (Kahan et al. 2010). The controversy is less about whether IOC reduces rehospitalization, improves outcome or enhances public safety, and more about whether the costs to individual liberties are justified. In addition, there is variability in outcome, attributable to variability in state laws, variability in implementation of existing laws, and availability of treatment. An early analysis (Ridgely et al. 2001) identified variability in service availability and enforcement as critical barriers to conclusive findings about IOC outcomes. Subsequent research tends to support the hypothesis that IOC leads to improved clinical outcomes (Link et al. 2011; Phelan et al. 2010; Swarz et al. 2010), although variability in procedures, enforcement, quality of services, and other contextual factors clearly have a moderating effect (Christy et al. 2009; Petrila and Christy 2008; Segal and Burgess

2006; Pollack et al. 2005). Ironically, one moderating factor is a self-serving fatalism among practitioners about the prospects of recovery in SMI. This has been observed more generally in the context of hostility toward psychiatric rehabilitation, especially among practitioners who espouse a narrow "medical model" view of SMI (Spaulding et al. 2010; Tarasenko, Sullivan, Ritchie, and Spaulding, 2013).

The current position of the Bazelon Center, a prestigious and respected center for protection of civil rights among people with disabilities, is that there is insufficient evidence of effectiveness to justify its use. The New York Civil Liberties Union opposes IOC on the grounds that it is disproportionately used with members of minority groups. There is no direct research support for this concern, and one empirical study (Galon et al. 2012) found no difference between African-Americans and Whites, in the rate at which IOC was applied or in the use of assertive community treatment, a clinical approach associated with IOC. There was a differential effect on perceptions of coercion and negative pressure, with diminished influence in African-Americans. IOC is opposed by various consumer advocacy groups on the grounds that antipsychotic drugs have serious and potentially lethal side effects (IOC laws often mandate adherence to medication, and sometimes little else).

Despite the controversy, IOC has become a stable feature of mental health systems. There are clearly several reasons for this. First and perhaps foremost, there is sustained popular concern about public safety, arguably another consequence of stigmatization and stereotyping of people with SMI (Penn and Martin 1998; Penn et al.1999; Wylie et al. 2012). This is reflected in the nickname given to IOC statutes based on the New York version, "Kendra's Law," named for the victim of a person who clearly should not have been released from psychiatric care. Ironically, the New York case was not one of simple refusal of treatment. The perpetrator had reportedly sought treatment but was unsuccessful. Accordingly, some analysts suggest that if there is any benefit to IOC statutes, it is that they may stimulate more effective and accountable mental health services. However, that leads to the argument that if the solution is better services, better services should be pursued through better public policy, not legal sanctions directed at the patients. In fact, IOC may have detrimental effects on services available to voluntary patients (Swanson et al. 2010). Unfortunately, better services come at a cost, at least in the public's perception. As a result, policy in this area is driven by media sensationalism and political reaction as much as by clinical research.

If IOC is here to stay, a TJ perspective guides us toward its most therapeutic use (Winick, 2003). Early in the evolution of IOC laws, TJ scholars recognized that requiring participation in treatment in return for greater civil liberties (e.g., avoiding institutional incarceration) is yet another form of contingency management (Elbogen and Tomkins 2000). In that regard, the implications are about the same as for problem-solving courts and mental health courts. Contingency management is generally recognized as a beneficial and effective tool for treatment and rehabilitation of SMI, but to be effective, it must be based on a systematic analysis of the patient's individual characteristics and socio-environmental circumstances. An added complication is that different IOC laws allow and/or require different kinds of contingencies. The most common is the contingency between treatment non-adherence and inpatient commitment, but in any mental health system there are numerous other situations that potentially represent incentives toward recovery. Using them optimally in a personalized IOC requires close collaboration between the presiding judges or other entities (mental health boards in some states) and practitioners with relevant training and expertise.

Recognition of the contingency management dimension of IOC is the first step toward recognition of the broader role of psychosocial (i.e., non-pharmacological) treatment and rehabilitation for SMI. While IOC laws focused on medication adherence were proliferating in the 1990s and 2000s, the psychiatric rehabilitation research community was producing a widening array of evidence-based treatments having demonstrated benefits for the problems and disabilities associated with SMI (Lehman et al. 2003). Importantly, these new treatments address functional impairments, e.g., in self-care, emotional regulation, interpersonal skills, and occupational functioning. Research on the course of SMI revealed that such impairments are at least as important as the symptoms (e.g., hallucinations, delusions, anxiety) that are the primary targets of psychiatric medication. People with SMI have individually specific constellations of symptoms and functional impairments. Optimal recovery requires a personalized selection of specific treatments from an increasingly broad and varied array, including individual psychotherapy, family therapy, interpersonal skills training, living skills training, and occupational/vocational support (Spaulding et al. 2003; Spaulding and Deogun 2011).

Research on the impact of IOC reflects the importance of psychosocial treatments in particular and comprehensive psychiatric rehabilitation in general. A key conclusion of the Rand analysis was that IOC is only beneficial if there is a sufficient array of treatment beyond medication. Subsequent findings suggest that a period of 6 months or more is necessary to produce measurable benefits. This is well beyond the time frame that medication exerts its effects on symptoms. The additional time is required to acquire the skills and overcome the disabilities that psychosocial treatments address.

The need for sufficiently personalized treatment regimens means that the central idea of IOC, an agreement to adhere to treatment, is dependent on a credible plan that identifies, organizes, and coordinates that regimen. As with advance directives, psychiatric rehabilitation and recovery introduce new demands, but also new opportunities for effectiveness. Today, we know much more about what is required than when IOC laws were first implemented. Adhering to a medication regimen is expected to be insufficient in the large majority of SMI cases. A credible treatment, rehabilitation, and recovery plan must be based on a comprehensive functional assessment of the patient's abilities and disabilities, strategic management of reward contingencies to optimally support adherence to the plan, clear assignment of specific decision-making and treatment responsibilities to specific practitioners and providers, and systematic, quantitative measurement of progress toward treatment goals. Unfortunately, these are rarely features of treatment anywhere in the mental health system, let alone the special circumstances of IOC. In practice, IOC "treatment plans" do little more than identify practitioners and providers without even specifying what they are to decide or provide.

Experience with problem-solving courts, drug courts, and mental health courts should suggest to us that education and training is a critical component of beneficial IOC. Perhaps, the need for special knowledge and skill is less obvious with IOC, because early versions so simply required adherence to medication and other medically focused treatment. There is great implicit deference to practitioners and providers to "do whatever needs to be done." Some IOC laws recognize the need for training but insufficiently or problematically specify the mechanisms. For example, Nebraska's IOC law specifies that training be provided to mental health board members by the state Department of Health and Human Services (HHS). However, the judiciary, county prosecutors, and defense attorneys view the state HHS as an interested party in IOC actions. The content of the training is susceptible to the political agenda of the incumbent executive branch, and therefore not impartial. IOC laws that specify the content of training focus on the legal criteria of dangerousness and generalities about the nature of mental illness and none are informed by the demands of contemporary psychiatric rehabilitation and recovery.

We need a joint effort of the legal and mental health communities toward producing a modern, evidence-based "manual" for IOC processes. We should expect that such a manual would emphasize ongoing collaboration between legal and clinical professionals. The key organizational principle should be the validity and credibility of the treatment plan, because the treatment plan defines the critical contingency of the IOC process—patients must adhere to the treatment plan to preserve civil liberties. The research suggests that if the treatment plan is insufficient, IOC is not beneficial. We know what optimal recovery-oriented treatment and rehabilitations plans should look like. There is no reason to doubt that the relevant criteria could be codified in IOC procedures and implemented with reliability and fidelity. Arguably, formal outcome trials are not required to establish the superiority of IOC processes based on formulation of sufficient and appropriate treatment plans. We already know what the active ingredients are. The problem is to ensure that IOC procedures generate treatment plans that incorporate a personalized regimen based on valid assessment and evidence-based practice and reliable mechanisms for measuring service provision and outcome. This will require not just an effective training system, but also a process that ensures the integrity of the training and insulation from politicization.

The rehabilitation and recovery perspective also raises a neglected question about involuntary treatment: what about the training and education of the patient? Research on coercion has revealed that patients often know or understand very little about their legal situation or the relevant mechanisms. Even when practitioners are better informed (which is not always the case), they do not necessarily share this information with patients. Even when they do, they may not communicate effectively. Defense attorneys seldom have the time or clinical skills to help people with SMI reach an adequate level of understanding. In the context of traditional inpatient commitment, specially designed educational approaches can effectively inform patients, and this leads to higher adherence to treatment. In the IOC context, such approaches could either be incorporated in the IOC procedures themselves or provided as a specific component of the comprehensive treatment plan (Strachan 2004). This equivalence of legal and clinical processes is an emergent principle of therapeutic jurisprudence.

## Daubert Evidentiary Principles, Involuntary Medication, and Evidence-Based Practice

Application of TJ to IOC raises issues of coercion and negative pressure, but application to involuntary medication, i.e., physically compelling injection of toxic drugs, requires consideration of the difference between "restrictiveness" and "intrusiveness." In Washington vs. Harper, a 1990 US Supreme Court decision, the Court held that it is permissible to forcibly medicate a prison inmate with mental illness "if the inmate is dangerous to himself or others and the treatment is in the inmate's medical interest." This decision was expanded 2 years later by Riggins vs. Nevada, when the Court held that the "essential" or "overriding" state interest must be coupled with a showing that medication is medically appropriate and essential, after considering less intrusive means.

In 2003, Washington and Riggins were combined in Sell vs. US, when the Court further articulated that physically forcing medication requires a finding that there are no alternative, less intrusive treatments likely to achieve substantially the same result. Judgments about comparability of treatment effects and less intrusive alternatives are critical, but ultimately to make this determination, courts must rely on testimony that is the opinion of mental health experts.

In a different context, but very relevant to involuntary treatment, Daubert vs. Merrell Dow Pharmaceuticals set the standards for admissible expert opinion testimony. These include whether it is based on theory generally accepted in the scientific community, based on findings subjected to peer review, whether it is testable with an acceptable rate of error, whether it is supported by research independent of the current litigation, and whether it is relevant to the proceedings.

Under Sell, individuals faced with forced medication are entitled to a court's careful weighing of their constitutionally protected interests. Under Daubert, this determination must be based on scientifically supported expert testimony. This gives the defendant an opportunity to present scientific evidence contradicting what has become a long-standing assumption in the legal community: forced medication is the necessary and the most effective solution. In its most familiar form, scientific knowledge is a universal principle supported by the scientific methods. However, scientific knowledge is also that which is observed or measured scientifically in individual cases. So, a clinical practitioner's opinion about whether a particular patient has benefitted from treatment may only be admissible if the treatment has generated scientific data about that particular patient. Even a treatment that has produced statistical effects in laboratory studies is not expected to benefit every single patient. The principle of evidence-based treatment is complemented by the principle of treatment-based evidence, i.e., that the process of treatment must generate self-validating data case by case.

Playing out the implications of Sell coupled with Daubert leads to striking conclusions. The principle that involuntary treatment must be the least intrusive necessary for effectiveness is universally endorsed, but there is no universal criterion for effectiveness. In psychiatry, involuntary treatment invariably means drug treatment (incarceration via civil commitment is not considered "treatment;" additional court orders are usually required to forcibly administer drugs to committed patients). Psychological treatments are inherently less intrusive than drugs. Potentially, forcible administration of drugs is only permissible if credible practice-based evidence shows that evidence-based psychological alternatives have failed. Psychological alternatives are almost never available in the settings where drugs are or can be forcibly administered. Assertive invocation of these US Supreme Court decisions in courts adjudicating involuntary psychiatric treatment could, at least theoretically, precipitate a revolution in institutional practice. This would be the result of the close alliance between TJ and clinical science.

## Right to Treatment and Mental Health Reform

Evidence-based psychological alternatives are almost never available in institutional psychiatric settings. They tend to be incompatible with guild interests and other interests inherent to institutions. Since the 1960s, the predominant treatment approach in psychiatric institutions has been the "medical model," which emphasizes pharmacological treatment prescribed by physicians (psychiatrists), behavioral management of patients by nurses, and overall direction by psychiatrists operating in a "disease model" of mental illness. In the 1970s and 1980s, comparative outcome trials showed psychological treatment approaches strikingly superior to medical model treatment in psychiatric institutions (Paul and Lentz 1977; Paul and Menditto 1992). Nevertheless, institutional practices have not substantially changed. Efforts to modernize continue to be blocked and even rolled back by institutional interests. A recent case study of elimination of modern psychiatric rehabilitation in an institutional setting (Tarasenko et al. 2013) documented subsequent declines in quality of care and outcomes, radiating throughout the mental health service system.

In previous decades, it was hoped that this anomaly would be obviated by deinstitutionalization (Bachrach 1999). It is true that many have escaped institutionalization, but there is growing consensus that there remains a residual "difficult to discharge" population who need treatment in protective and restrictive settings for extended periods of time, i.e., months rather than days (Fisher et al. 2009). This residual population continues to be subjected to a demonstrably inferior treatment approach.

The conflict here is between the patient's right to treatment and the mental health industry's right to provide what its constituents want to provide (Magaro et al. 1978). A landmark US Supreme court decision, O'Connor vs. Donaldson (1975), established that institutionalized individuals must be given a reasonable opportunity to "improve [their] mental condition," only implicitly linking "reasonable opportunity" to the quality of treatment. This was echoed in Ohlinger vs. Watson (1980), an appellate court finding requiring institutions to provide adequate and effective treatment. Youngberg vs. Romeo (1982) affirmed institutionalized patients' right to treatment, but set the criterion as generally accepted standards and practices, not evidence-based treatment. An appellate court ruling, D.W. vs. Rogers (1997), affirmed that a constitutional right to psychiatric care and treatment is triggered by physical confinement of a person with mental illness, but did not change the standards of practice criterion.

It has become apparent that deferring to "standards of practice" has not compelled effective treatment for institutionalized people. The economic and political forces that might ordinarily resolve the conflict do not obtain. People who are institutionalized have very little social clout. Their families often have little more, but are further hobbled by fear that activism may bring retribution to their vulnerable institutionalized members. The public has an interest in cost-effective public mental health services, but stigmatization and media sensationalism direct public attention to safety rather than quality of care. The public is willing to pay any price for safety, but incarceration, not treatment, is the perceived solution. It is left to humanitarian legislation and litigation to create a more equitable resolution of the conflict.

In Olmstead vs. L.C. (1999), the Supreme Court found that under the Americans With Disabilities Act (ADA), individuals with mental disabilities have the right to live in the community rather than institutions. This arguably raised the "standards of practice" criterion to an operational level, i.e., that treatment must be good enough to improve patients' functioning such that they can live safely in a less restrictive setting. Successful Olmstead-based litigation has put more pressure on public bureaucracies to develop better community-based services, but mental health professionals are still allowed to determine who is "appropriate" for those services. It is prohibitively difficult to prove that a patient's institutional status is the result of bad institutional treatment, as opposed to inadequate community-based support services. As a result, Olmstead has not had a direct effect on the quality of treatment within the institutions. In fact, in the Tarasenko et al. (2013) case study, the state mental health administration used Olmstead to justify closing its evidence-based state hospital rehabilitation program. Similarly, it remains unclear whether Olmstead requires the state to provide for a decent and normalized life in "community settings." Formerly institutional populations now often live in decrepit residential facilities, with no access to community-based rehabilitation, and with a quality of life and level of community participation that are no better than what they had in the institution.

The Civil Rights of Institutionalized Persons Act of 1980 (CRIPA) was a forceful effort to overcome the most egregious consequences of vested institutional interests. The act authorized the US Department of Justice to bring suit against state institutions for violation of patients' constitutional rights, and created a Special Litigation Section within the Department to do the work. Many state hospitals across the country became targets. Litigation continues to this day. So far, the outcome of CRIPA in redressing the conflict has been analyzed only anecdotally (Lampson 1983). In the near future, as cases are settled and become accessible for research, more quantitative analysis may be possible. Meanwhile, from a TJ perspective, critical features of CRIPA are expected to render it less than effective.

CRIPA was passed before evidence-based practice became a national concern, before psychiatric rehabilitation and recovery were known beyond a few researchers and social reformers, before Daubert, and even before TJ itself had taken shape. Like Youngberg, the bar is set rather low for requiring validated, quality treatment. CRIPA also requires a pattern of abuse and "grevious harm" for litigation to proceed. Institutions have thus been indicted under CRIPA not because of ineffective treatment models but because of inhumane conditions unacceptable in any treatment model. This did not prevent advocacy for evidence-based treatment by individuals in some cases, but neither did it prevent preservation of demonstrably ineffective institutional models in others. As a result, in some cases enormous cost yielded dubious improvements.

Were CRIPA to be rewritten today, incorporating a modern TJ perspective, its demand for reform would be more effectively guided by outcome research and by practice-based evidence generated by the reforming institutions. Short of new legislation, TJ-informed scrutiny of ongoing CRIPA litigation should be expected to support and enhance evidence-based reform.

## Conclusion

The principles and research base of psychiatric rehabilitation provide fertile ground for application of therapeutic jurisprudence. Conceptualizing problems associated with SMI as conflicts between individuals, family, the public, and the mental health industry leads to a clear agenda for empirical research to identify the most effective TJ approaches. Applications range from design of treatment procedures to innovation in judicial procedure to legislation and litigation. Realization of TJ's promise will require close collaboration between legal scholars, clinical researchers, and policy makers, not only to develop effective solutions but also to ensure that such solutions are accessible to the people that need them.

## References

Allen, M., & Smith, V. F. (2001). Opening pandora's box: The practical and legal dangers of involuntary outpatient commitment. *Psychiatric Services, 52,* 342–346.

Álvarez-Jiménez, M. P. A., Hetrick, S., McGorry, P., & Gleeson, J. (2011). Preventing the second episode: A systematic review and meta-analysis of psychosocial and pharmacological trials in first-episode psychosis. *Schizophrenia Bulletin, 37,* 619–630.

Anthony, W. A. (1979). *Principles of psychiatric rehabilitation*. Baltimore: University Park Press.

Anthony, W. (1993). Recovery from mental illness: The guiding vision of the mental health service system in the 1990s. *Psychosocial Rehabilitation Journal, 16,* 11–23.

Ayllon, T., & Azrin, N. H. (1968). *The token economy*. New York: Appleton-Century-Crofts.

Bachrach, L. (1999). The state of the state mental hospital at the turn of the century. In W. Spaulding (Ed.), *The state hospital in the 21st century. New directions for mental health services* (Vol. 89). San Francisco: Jossey Bass.

Bazelon Center for Mental Health Law. (2012). The role of mental health courts in system reform. Bazelon Center website, http://www.bazelon.org/LinkClick.aspx?fileticket=xQf5_1grKcI%3d&tabid=104 Accessed 1 June 2014.

Beers, C. (1921). *The mental hygiene movement*. New York: Longmans.

Belenko, S. (2002). Drug courts. In F. Tims (Ed.), *Treatment of drug offenders: Policies and issues* (pp. 301–318). New York: Springer.

Bellack, A. S. (2006). Scientific and consumer models of recovery in schizophrenia: Concordance, contrasts, and implications. *Schizophrenia Bulletin, 32*(3), 432–442.

Carroll, K. M., & Nuro, K. F. (2002). One size cannot fit all: a stage model for psychotherapy manual development. *Clinical Psychology, 9,* 396–406.

Casey, P., & Rottman, D. (2003). Problem solving courts: models and trends. National Center for State Courts website. http://www.ncsconline.org/wc/publications/comm_ProSolProbSolvCtsPub.pdf Accessed 1 June 2014.

Christy, A., Petrila, J., McCranie, M., & Lotts, V. (2009). Involuntary outpatient commitment in Florida: Case information and provider experience and opinions. *The International Journal of Forensic Mental Health, 8,* 122–130. E.

Cook, J., Copeland, M., Jonikas, J., Hamilton, M., Razzano, L., Grey, D., et al. (2011). Results of a randomized controlled trial of mental illness self-management using wellness recovery action planning. *Schizophr Bull* Advance online publication. doi:10.1093/schbul/sbr012.

Copeland, M. (2001). Wellness recovery action plan: A system for monitoring, reducing and eliminating uncomfortable or dangerous physical symptoms and emotional feelings. In C. Brown (Ed.), *Recovery and wellness: Models of hope and empowerment for people with mental illness* (pp. 127–150). New York: Hawthorne.

Elbogen, E., Swartz, M., Van Dorn R., Swanson, J., Kim, M., & Scheyett, A. (2006). Clinical decision making and views about psychiatric advance directives. *Psychiatric Services, 57,* 350–355.

Elbogen, E., & Tomkins, A. (2000). From the psychiatric hospital to the community: Integrating conditional release with contingency management. *Behavioral sciences and the law, 18,* 427–444.

Falloon, I. R. H., Boyd, J. L., & McGill, C. W. (1984). *Family care of schizophrenia: A problem-solving approach to the treatment of mental illness*. New York: Guilford.

Fisler, C. (2005). Building trust and managing risk: A look at felony mental health court. Psychology. *Public Policy & Law, 11,* 587–604.

Fisher, W., Geller, J., & Pandiani, J. (2009). The changing role of the state psychiatric hospital. *Health Affairs, 28,* 676–684.

Folberg, J., & Taylor, A. (1984). *Mediation: A comprehensive guide to resolving conflicts without litigation*. San Francisco: Jossey-Bass.

Galon, P., Wineman, N., & Grande, T. (2012). Influence of race on outpatient commitment and assertive community treatment for persons with severe and persistent mental illness. *Archives of Psychiatric Nursing, 26,* 202–213.

Goldstein, M. (1991). Schizophrenia and family therapy. In B. Beitman & G. Klerman (Eds.), *Integrating pharmacotherapy and psychotherapy*. Washington D.C.: American Psychiatric Press.

Gumley, A. (2011) Staying well after psychosis: A cognitive interpersonal approach to emotional recovery and relapse prevention. In R., Hagen, D., Turkington, T., Berge, & R. W. Gråwe (Eds.) *CBT for psychosis: A symptom-based approach* (pp. 128–143). New York: Routledge/Taylor & Francis.

Heinssen, R., Levendusky, P., & Hunter, R. (1995). Client as colleague: Therapeutic contracting with the seriously mentally ill. *American Psychologist, 50*(7), 522–532.

Kahan, D., Braman, D., Monohan, J., Callahan, L., & Peters, E. (2010). Cultural cognition and public policy: The case of outpatient commitment laws. *Law and Human Behavior, 34,* 118–140.

Kashner, T. M., Rush, A. J., Crismon, M. L., Toprac, M., Carmody, T. J., Miller, A. L., et al. (2006). An empirical analysis of cost outcomes of the Texas Medication Algorithm Project. *Psychiatric Services, 57*(5), 648–659.

Kim, M., Scheyett, A., Elbogen, E., Van Dorn R., McDaniel, L., Swartz, M., Swanson, J., & Ferron, J. (2008). Front line workers' attitudes towards psychiatric advance directives. *Community Mental Health Journal, 44,* 28–46.

Klingberg, S., Wittorf, A., Fischer, A., Jakob-Deters, K., Buchremer, G., & Wiedemann, G. (2010). Evaluation of a cognitive behaviourally oriented service for relapse prevention in schizophrenia. *Acta Psychiatrica Scandinavica, 121,* 340–350.

Lampson, M. (1983). Senate subcommittee reviews justice department's enforcement of section 504 and CRIPA. *Mental Disability Law Reporter, 7,* 492–493.

Lee, S., Choi, T., Sug, S., Kim, Y., Kim, B., Lee, E., et al. (2010). Effectiveness of a psychosocial intervention for relapse prevent in patients with schizophrenia receiving risperidone via long-acting injection. *Psychiatry Research, 175,* 195–199.

Lehman, A. F., Buchanan, R. W., Dickerson, F. B., Dixon, L. B., Goldberg, R., Green-Paden, L., et al. (2003). Evidence-based treatment for schizophrenia. *The Psychiatric Clinics of North America, 26*(4), 939–954.

Lehman, A. F., Kreyenbuhl, J., Buchanan, R. W., Dickerson, F. B., Dixon, L. B., Goldberg, R., et al. (2004). The Schizophrenia Patient Outcomes Research Team (PORT): Updated treatment recommendations 2003. *Schizophrenia bulletin, 30*(2), 193–217.

Liberman, R. P. (2008). *Recovery from disability: Manual of psychiatric rehabilitation*. Washington D.C.: American Psychiatric Press.

Link, B., Epperson, M., Perron, B., Castille, D., & Yang, L. (2011). Arrest outcomes associated with outpatient commitment in New York State. *Psychiatric Services, 62,* 504–508.

Magaro, P., Gripp, R., McDowell, D., & Miller, I. (1978). *The mental health industry: A cultural phenomenon*. New York: Wiley.

Molodynski, A., Rugkasa, J., & Burns, T. (2010). Coercion and compulsion in community mental health care. *British Medical Bulletin, 95,* 105–119.

National Resource Center on Psychiatric Advance Directives. (2011). http://www.nrc-pad.org. Accessed 1 June 2014.

Paul, G. L., & Lentz, R. J. (1977). *Psychosocial treatment of chronic mental patients: Milieu vs. social learning programs*. Cambridge: Harvard University Press.

Paul, G., & Menditto, A. (1992). Effectiveness of inpatient treatment programs for mentally ill adults in public psychiatric facilities. *Applied and Preventive Psychology, 1*(1), 41–63.

Petrila, J., & Christy, A. (2008). Law & psychiatry: Florida's outpatient commitment law: A lesson in failed reform? *Psychiatric Services, 59,* 21–23.

Petrila, J., Ridgely, M. S., & Borum, R. (2003). Debating outpatient commitment: Controversey, trends and empirical data. *Crime and Delinquency, 49,* 157–172.

Penn, D., & Martin, J. (1998). The stigma of severe mental illness: Some potential solutions for a recalcitrant problem. *Psychiatric Quarterly, 69*(3), 235–247.

Penn, D., Kommana, S., Mansfield, M., & LInk, B. (1999). Dispelling the stigma of schizophrenia: II. The impact of information on dangerousness. *Schizophrenia Bulletin, 25*(3), 437–446.

Phelan, J., Sinkewicz, M., Castille, D., Huz, S., Muenzenmaier, K., & Link, B. (2010). Effectiveness and outcomes of assisted outpatient treatment in New York State. *Psychiatric Services, 61,* 137–143.

Pollack, D., McFarland, B., Mahler, J., & Kovas, A. (2005). Outcomes of patients in a low-intensity, short-duration involuntary outpatient commitment program. *Psychiatric Services, 56,* 863–866.

President's New Freedom Commission on Mental Health. (2004). Report to the President. http://www.mentalhealthcommission.gov/reports/reports.htm. Accessed 15 Oct 2004.

Ridgely, M. S., Borum, R., & Petrila, J. (2001). *The effectiveness of involuntary outpatient treatment: Empirical evidence and the experience of eight states*. Santa Monica: RAND.

Rounsaville, B. J., Carroll, K. M., & Onken, L. S. (2001). A stage model of behavioral therapies research: getting started and moving on from stage I. *Clinical Psychology*, *8*, 133–142.

Salzinger, K. (1984). The immediacy hypothesis in a theory of schizophrenia. In W. Spaulding & J. Cole (Eds.), *Theories of schizophrenia and psychosis: The Nebraska Symposium on Motivation* (Vol. 31). Lincoln: University of Nebraska Press.

Schopp, R. F. (2003). Outpatient civil commitment: A dangerous charade or a component of a comprehensive institution of civil commitment? *Psychology, Public Policy, and Law, 9,* 33–69.

Segal, S., & Burgess, P. (2006). The utility of extended outpatient civil commitment. *International Journal of Law and Psychiatry, 29,* 525–534.

Spaulding, W., & Deogun, J. (2011). A pathway to personalization of integrated treatment: Informatics and decision science in psychiatric rehabilitation. *Schizophrenia Bulletin, 37*(suppl 2), S129–137.

Spaulding, W., Sullivan, M., & Poland, J. (2003). *Treatment and rehabilitation of severe mental illness*. New York: Guilford.

Spaulding, W., Sullivan, M., Poland, J., & Ritchie, A. J. (2010). State psychiatric institutions and the left-behinds of mental health reform. *American Journal of Orthopsychiatry, 80*(3), 327–333.

Steadman, H. J., Redlich, A., Callahan, L., Robbins, P. C., & Vesselinov, R. (2011). Effect of mental health courts on arrests and jail days: A multisite study. *Archives of general psychiatry, 68*(2), 167–172.

Strachan, E. (2004). Evaluation of education and skill training regarding involuntary hospitalization for psychiatric inpatients. Doctoral dissertation, University of Nebraska—Lincoln, Lincoln NE.

Substance Abuse and Mental Health Services Administration (SAMHSA). (2012) Evidence-based practices KITs. http://store.samhsa.gov/list/series?name=Evidence-Based-Practices-KITs. Accessed 1 June 2014.

Swanson, J., Swartz, M., Feron, J., Elbogen, E, & Van Dorn, R (2006). Psychiatric advance directives among public mental health consumers in five U.S. cities: Prevalence, demand, and correlates. *Journal of the American Academy of Psychiatry and the Law, 34,* 43–57.

Swanson, J., Van Dorn, R., Swarz, M., Cislo, A., Wilder, C., L, M., et al. (2010). Robbing Peter to pay Paul: Did New York state's outpatient commitment program crowd out voluntary service recipients? *Psychiatric Services, 61,* 988–995.

Swarz, M., Wilder, C., Swanson, J., Van Dorn, R., Robbins, P., Steadman, H., et al. (2010). Assessing outcomes for consumers in New York's assisted outpatient treatment program. *Psychiatric Services, 61,* 976–981.

Tarasenko, M., Sullivan, M., Ritchie, A., & Spaulding, W. (2013). The effects of eliminating psychiatric rehabilitation from the secure levels of a psychiatric service system. *Psychological Services, 10,* 442–51.

U.S. Public Health Service (1999). Mental health: A report of the Surgeon General. http://www.surgeongeneral.gov/library/mentalhealth.

Van Dorn, R., Swanson, J., Swartz, M., Elbogen, E., & Ferron, J. (2008). Reducing barriers to completing psychiatric advance directives. *Administrative Policy in Mental Health, 35,* 440–448.

Watson, A., Luchins, D., Hanrahan, P., Heyman, M., & Lurigio, A. (2000). Mental health court: promises and limitations. *Journal of the American Academy of Psychiatry and the Law, 28,* 476–482.

Wexler, D. (1973). Token and taboo: Behavior modification, token economies, and the law. *Behaviorism, 1,* 1–24.

Wexler, D., & Winick, B. (Eds.) (1991). *Essays in therapeutic jurisprudence*. North Carolina: Carolina Academic Press.

Wilder, C., Elbogen, E., Swartz, M., Swanson, J., & Van Dorn, R. A. (2007). Effect of patients' reasons for refusing treatment on implementing psychiatric advance directives. *Psychiatric Services, 58,* 1348–1350.

Winick, B. (2003). Outpatient commitment: A therapeutic jurisprudence analysis. *Psychology, Public Policy & Law, 9,* 107–144.

Wylie, L. E., Brank, E. M., & King, C. M. (2012). *Incompetent and dangerous? The Stereotype Content Model and involuntary outpatient commitment*. Paper presented at the Annual meeting of the American Psychology-Law Society, San Juan, Puerto Rico.

Ziedonis, D., Yanos, P., & Silverstein, S. (2007). Relapse prevention for schizophrenia. In K. Witkiewitz & G. Marlatt (Eds.), *Therapist's guide to evidence-based relapse prevention*. San Diego: Elsevier.

# Chapter 6
# Mental Illness, Dangerousness, and Police Power Interventions in Pursuit of Justice and Well-being

**Robert F. Schopp**

## Introduction

Mental health courts (MHCs) have been described as courts for offenders whose crimes are "more a product of mental illness than of criminality."[1] They are designed to prevent crime by providing offenders with treatment that ameliorates the mental illness that was a causal factor contributing to their crimes. Thus, they promote the well-being of the offenders by ameliorating the disorder that contributed to their offenses and by reducing the risk that they will commit further crimes and elicit further criminal punishment. In this manner, MHCs also promote the well-being of the public by reducing the risk of recidivism by those offenders.[2] Civil commitment and post-insanity acquittal commitment provide two additional forms of coercive police power interventions directed toward mentally ill individuals who endanger the public.[3]

The presence of MHCs, civil commitment, and post-insanity acquittal commitment as three alternative institutions for the application of the police power to individuals who are mentally ill and endanger the protected interests of others raises a series of questions regarding the most defensible interpretation of the legitimate functions of these institutions and of the significance of mental illness and dangerousness for the application of each institution. What type and degree of impairment and of risk should qualify as mental illness and as dangerousness that justify the application of each of these interventions to specific individuals in specific circumstances? What considerations other than type and degree of impairment and of risk justify the application of the police power through one of these institutions, rather than the others, to specific individuals with mental illness who harm or endanger

[1] Stefan, S., & Winick, B. J., A dialogue on mental health courts, 11 Psychol., Pub., Pol., & L 507 (2005).

[2] See infra § II.

[3] See infra § III D.

R. F. Schopp (✉)
College of Law, University of Nebraska-Lincoln, Lincoln, NE, 68583-0902 USA
e-mail: rschopp1@unl.edu

B. H. Bornstein, R. L. Wiener (eds.), *Justice, Conflict and Wellbeing*,
DOI 10.1007/978-1-4939-0623-9_6, © Springer Science+Business Media New York 2014

the protected interests of others? What is the appropriate form and range of expert testimony regarding mental illness and dangerousness for the application of each of these interventions to a specific individual in specific circumstances? In what way might research advance our abilities to: understand the relevant conceptions of and relationships between mental illness and dangerousness, justify appropriate forms of intervention for particular individuals in specified circumstances, and provide relevant testimony in individual cases that applied these interventions?

The current chapter identifies and clarifies some of the central considerations relevant to the most defensible applications of these institutions to individuals who manifest mental disorders and endanger others. It does not purport to provide a formula for application. Rather, it identifies some central principles and considerations relevant to selecting the most justifiable applications to specific individuals. The analysis proceeds in the following manner. The section "Mental Health Courts" provides a brief summary description of MHCs and of two hypothetical offenders who illustrate the central concerns relevant to the justified application of MHCs. The section "Police Power and Mental Illness" pursues an analysis of the central considerations that justify the application of the police power to psychologically impaired individuals through the criminal justice system (CJS) or civil commitment. The section "Expert Testimony and Research Regarding Psychological Impairment and Culpability" addresses the appropriate form and range of psychological expert testimony regarding mental illness, and it identifies some aspects of further research that might inform that testimony. The section "Expert Testimony and Research Regarding Dangerousness" addresses the appropriate form of expert testimony regarding dangerousness, and it identifies some aspects of further research that might inform that testimony. The section "Conclusion" concludes the analysis.

## Mental Health Courts

The specific range of offenses and offenders addressed by MHCs can vary across jurisdictions. As generally discussed, they function as specialty courts in the CJS designed to reduce recidivism by promoting effective treatment for offenders who manifest mental disorder that contributed to their criminal offenses. One primary purpose of the CJS, including MHCs, is to reduce crime. MHCs are designed to reduce recidivism by promoting effective treatment of offenders whose crimes are "more a product of mental illness than of criminality."[4] The specific applications and procedures of MHCs vary across jurisdictions. They frequently require guilty pleas from mentally ill offenders, apply criminal sentences, suspend those sentences, place the offenders on probation, and require as a condition of probation that those offenders participate in treatment designed to reduce the risk of recidivism by ameliorating the disorders that contributed to their criminal conduct. If the offenders do not participate in the treatment required as a condition of probation,

[4] See supra note 1.

incarceration for brief periods is applied to enforce treatment participation. Some jurisdictions allow criminal records to be expunged for offenders who complete their conditions of probation.[5] MHCs are designed to promote the well-being of society and of the mentally ill offenders by providing treatment expected to ameliorate the impairment that contributed to the criminal offenses committed by these offenders. Insofar as the treatment is effective, it can reasonably be expected to reduce the risk of recidivism and of punishment.

Consider two similar but different offenders as hypothetical examples of individuals who manifest psychological impairment that contributes to their criminal offenses. Anderson has been diagnosed with a chronic schizophrenic disorder that varies in severity across time and circumstances.[6] He voluntarily participates in treatment during periods of relatively less severe impairment. When his impairment exacerbates, however, his capacities to accurately perceive reality, to reason coherently, and to make reasoned judgments deteriorate. During these periods, he receives hallucinatory orders from God to stop participating in treatment because Satan's agents are using the medication to prevent him from doing God's work. He abandons treatment in response to these hallucinatory orders, and his cognitive deterioration exacerbates. He then conforms to hallucinatory orders from God by breaking into his neighbor's house and destroying the neighbor's furnace because God's voice told him that the neighbor was using the furnace to beam Satan's mind waves into his brain.[7]

Baker experiences chronic, severe depression involving sadness, fatigue, pessimism, and anhedonia.[8] Although his depression is severe, it does not include psychotic distortion of his ability to recognize reality. He spent extended periods lying dormant in bed preoccupied with his own judgments that he is worthless and that there is no hope that he will improve. He lost his job and his apartment because he has been unable to work with minimum adequacy during the worst periods of depression. Since losing his job, he resides in homeless shelters, under highway overpasses, and in alleys. He sometimes steals food when he is hungry and unable to secure food from assistance agencies. When he has not eaten for several days, he breaks into a neighbor's basement to steal food. He understands that this conduct is contrary to law, to generally accepted societal standards, and to his own standards of acceptable behavior. His depression deepens further as he breaks into his neighbor's basement because he interprets his own conduct as reaffirming his worthlessness.[9]

---

[5] Problem Solving Courts (Wiener, R. L., & Brank, E. M., eds.); John Petrila, Mental health courts: Do they work? And does it matter?, Chap. 8 in Problem Solving Courts; Redlich, A. D., The past, present, and future of mental health courts, Chap. 9 in Problem Solving Courts.

[6] American Psychiatric Association, Diagnostic and Statistical Manual of Mental Disorders 298–313 (4th ed. Text Revision 2000). The appendix provides brief descriptions of the hypothetical offenders in the order in which they appear.

[7] For an earlier version of Anderson, see Schopp, R. F., Mental health courts: Competence, responsibility, and proportionality, Chap. 10 in Problem Solving Courts, supra note 5.

[8] American Psychiatric Association, supra note 6, at 349–352, 371–382. (Anhedonia refers to the inability to experience pleasure in activities that are normally pleasurable.)

[9] Schopp, supra note 7, providing an earlier version of Baker.

Baker presents an example of a defendant appropriate for MHC because his psychological impairment was sufficiently serious to reduce his culpability, but that impairment did not preclude competence to proceed in the criminal process or criminal responsibility for the offense. Thus, he is competent to plead guilty in the MHC, and a suspended sentence with participation in treatment as a condition of probation is proportionate to his limited culpability and reasonably expected to promote his well-being and the public well-being by ameliorating the disorder that contributed to his offense. The use of brief periods of punishment to enforce Baker's participation in mandated treatment can be justified if Baker remains criminally responsible and thus is accountable for his failure to conform to the conditions of probation. Baker's failure to meet the conditions of probation, including participation in treatment, might not justify punishment, however, if his failure to participate is a result of deterioration into a more severe condition of impairment that renders him not responsible for his conduct.

Compare Baker to Anderson, who is not appropriate for MHC because his psychotic disorder renders him: incompetent to plead guilty, not guilty due to insanity, and, therefore, not deserving of a criminal sentence as a matter of retributive justice. Because he does not deserve a criminal sentence, that sentence cannot justly be applied and suspended as a condition for probation, and he cannot justly be required to serve jail time for failure to conform to treatment as a condition of probation.[10] In addition, he does not deserve incarceration for failure to conform to those conditions of probation unless his impairment has improved to the degree that he is justly held responsible for his failure to conform.

Anderson's impairment and circumstances that render him inappropriate for MHC should lead us to ask whether he is more appropriately subject to criminal trial, acquittal under the insanity defense, and post-acquittal commitment, or to civil commitment as the most appropriate form of police power intervention. What reasoning justifies one intervention or the other as the most consistent with the purpose and justification of the relevant doctrine? Similarly, although Baker is eligible to participate in the MHC, what reasoning would justify the decision to apply the MHC to Baker rather than civil commitment or an ordinary criminal court with the possibilities of an insanity defense and post-acquittal commitment or of reduced sentencing due to the mitigating effect of his disorder?

[10] I do not claim here that he could not be found guilty in a jurisdiction that did not have an insanity defense or that he could not be competent to plead guilty if his treatment ameliorated his impairment to the degree that rendered him competent to proceed. I claim only that a guilty verdict and criminal punishment would be inconsistent with the underlying principles of retributive justice.

## Police Power and Mental Illness

### *Police Power, the Criminal Justice System, and MHCs*

The police power is the source of the state's authority to enact and apply law "to preserve the public security, order, health, morality, and justice."[11] The legitimate function of the police power is "to secure and promote the public welfare, and it does so by restraint or compulsion."[12] The primary function of the police power is to protect the interests of the public, and it often does so by intervening coercively in the conduct of individuals or entities. States ordinarily exercise the police power through the CJS for those who culpably commit crimes and through the civil commitment system for those who are mentally ill and harm or endanger others. Severely impaired individuals, such as Anderson, lack the capacities of responsible agency that would render them competent to proceed in the criminal process and criminally responsible for their conduct. Other impaired individuals, such as Baker, retain the capacities required for competence to proceed and for criminal responsibility, but their impairment reduces their blameworthiness for their conduct and, thus, the severity of justified punishment.

MHCs provide a component of the CJS designed to address offenders, such as Baker, who are appropriately subject to the criminal law but manifest impairment that renders them less blameworthy than most offenders who commit similar offenses and more amenable to interventions that promote their well-being and the public well-being by ameliorating their impairment and reducing the risk that they will recidivate. Reduced severity of punishment for these offenders promotes well-being in a manner consistent with justice because relatively less severe sentences for these offenders are proportionate to their reduced culpability. Insofar as MHCs accurately identify and address these offenders, they apply the police power through the CJS in a manner that advances the preventive purpose of that institution and conforms to the justification of criminal punishment.

Insofar as MHCs function as designed, four important applications of the values for justice and well-being converge. The first two applications address the value for the well-being of those affected by legal institutions. First, MHCs that provide effective treatment promote the well-being of the offenders by ameliorating the mental disorders that are disrupting their lives, promoting their criminal behavior, and rendering them subject to coercive state intervention. Second, by promoting this treatment, the MHCs promote the general well-being of the public by reducing the risk of criminal recidivism by these individuals.

The third and fourth applications address the principles of retributive justice pursued by the CJS. As ordinarily understood, justice requires that each individual is treated as that person is due according to the applicable principles. Retributive justice requires that each offender receive the punishment that is consistent with

[11] Black's Law Dictionary 1276 (Garner, B. R., ed., 9th ed. 2009).

[12] *Id.*

the applicable principles of justified punishment.[13] The Supreme Court's opinions do not provide a single consistent theory of justified punishment under the Eighth Amendment, but several of those opinions identify retribution as an important purpose or limit of punishment.[14] A retributive justification of punishment prescribes punishment in proportion to the desert of the offender.[15] Supreme Court opinions apply the retributive purpose of punishment as addressing punishment in proportion to the severity of the offense and the culpability or blameworthiness of the offender. The Eighth Amendment proscribes excessive punishment, rather than prescribing specific punishments. Thus, these opinions discuss retributive limits on the severity of punishment.[16]

The principle of comparative justice requires that the criminal justice process treat similar offenders alike and relevantly different offenders differently in proportion to their relevant differences.[17] Courts that consistently apply the same defensible principles of retributive justice to a variety of offenders and offenses conform to the requirement of comparative justice. Consistent application of the applicable principles of retributive justice would apply similar sentences to offenders who commit offenses of similar severity with similar degrees of culpability. Consistent application of those principles would generate differences in severity of punishment, however, when applied to offenders who differed in the severity of their offenses or in their degree of culpability for their offenses. These differences would reflect variation in punishment proportionate to these offenders and offenses, rather than arbitrary or discriminatory departures from the principled application of punishment. Several concurring opinions in Furman vs. Georgia establish the importance of comparative justice in the Eighth Amendment doctrine by emphasizing the significance of arbitrary or discriminatory variations in capital sentencing as a justification for their reversal of three capital sentences.[18]

By applying interventions less severe than would ordinarily be applied to offenders who committed similar offenses but lacked similar impairment, the MHCs apply the principle of proportionality in retributive justice because they apply punishment of reduced severity that is proportionate to the degree to which each offender's impairment reduces that individual's culpability. Thus, they apply punishment that is consistent with non-comparative retributive justice because the severity of punishment in each case reflects the degree of culpability appropriately attributed to the specific offender and offense. Insofar as these courts accurately identify criminally responsible offenders whose impairment renders them less culpable than

[13] The Cambridge Dictionary of Philosophy 759 (Audi, R. ed., 2nd ed. 1999).

[14] Roper vs. Simmons, 125 S.Ct. 1183, 1194–1196 (2005); Atkins vs. Virginia, 536 US 304, 319 (2002); Gregg vs. Georgia, 428 US 153, 183–184 (1976).

[15] The Cambridge Dictionary of Philosophy, supra note 13, at 759.

[16] Roper vs. Simmons, 125 S.Ct. 1183, 1194–1196 (2005); Atkins vs. Virginia, 536 US 304, 319 (2002); Gregg vs. Georgia, 428 US 153, 183–184 (1976).

[17] Joel Feinberg, Rights, Justice, and the Bounds of Liberty 265–287 (1980).

[18] Furman vs. Georgia, 408 US 238, 242–257 (Douglas, J., concurring), 274–277 (Brennan, J., concurring), 308–310 (Stewart, J., concurring), 364–366 (Marshall, J., concurring).

unimpaired offenders who commit similar offenses and consistently apply principles of proportionality to the full range of offenders, they promote comparative justice by applying punishments of different severity that express different degrees of condemnation in proportion to the morally relevant differences among offenders.

## *Criminal Responsibility, Culpability, and Psychological Impairment*

Recall Anderson, who is not appropriately addressed through the MHC because the guilty plea, suspended sentence, and periods of incarceration to enforce participation in treatment violate the applicable principles of retributive justice due to mental illness that precludes culpability for the offense.[19] What reasoning justifies civil commitment or criminal trial, an insanity defense, and post-insanity acquittal commitment as the more justified approach for Anderson?

Civil commitment ordinarily requires that he meet the criteria of mental illness and dangerousness.[20] Is Anderson dangerous to others? His offense did not involve violence toward any other persons, but it did involve destruction of property, possible harm to others if destroying the furnace resulted in fire or toxic fumes, and possible harm to others or to self if the residents of the house became aware of his presence and exercised force in resistance. His conduct would seem to meet the dangerousness criterion in a jurisdiction that explicitly included dangerousness to property, and the potential for harm to the residents would arguably be sufficient to meet the requirement of a statute requiring dangerousness to other persons.[21]

What interpretation of "mental illness" or of "mental disease" would support addressing his impairment and conduct as appropriate for civil commitment or for criminal trial resulting in an insanity defense and post-acquittal commitment? If his impairment is sufficient to constitute mental illness for civil commitment and a mental disease for an insanity defense, what reasoning justifies application of either path as most consistent with the purposes and justifications of these provisions as components of a comprehensive body of law designed to guide and discipline the exercise of the police power?

As discussed previously, MHCs pursue convergence of four applications of the values for well-being and retributive justice. Insofar as civil commitment and an insanity defense followed by post-acquittal commitment are accurately applied to those who are not criminally responsible for harming or endangering others, retributive justice precludes punishment. Thus, appropriate application of these institutions of police power intervention requires explicit identification of additional societal values that justify application of each institution, a clear explanation regarding the type and degree of impairment that would render a person appropriate for the

---

[19] See supra text accompanying notes 6–7.

[20] Michael L. Perlin, I Mental Disability Law § 2A (2nd ed. 1998).

[21] *Id.* at §§ 2.4–4.2, 4.8

application of each doctrine consistent with the applicable justification, and a clear statement of the type and degree of risk that should qualify as dangerousness according to these justifications.

Common standards for the insanity defense excuse offenders who fulfilled the offense elements for a criminal offense but, due to a mental disease or defect, did not know (or appreciate) that their conduct was wrong.[22] This inability to know that one's conduct is wrong is ambiguous, however, in that a specific jurisdiction might interpret the insanity standard as addressing the ability to know that one's conduct violates law, widely accepted societal standards of morality, or one's personal standard of moral wrongfulness.[23]

Consider two variations of Anderson. Anderson1 believes that his conduct is in violation of law, but he believes that he is morally obliged to conform to God's command to violate that law. He also believes that most members of society would agree that his conduct was morally required if they were aware of the information he had received from God regarding the evil effects of the furnace and understood that he was acting in response to God's command. Anderson2 believes that his conduct is in violation of law and of generally accepted societal standards, but he believes that widely held moral standards in society are a result of the pervasive influence of Satan on the population. Thus, he is morally obliged to perform this conduct that is contrary to law and generally accepted societal morality because God commands it as necessary to free this household of Satan's influence.

Anderson1 would qualify for an insanity defense in a jurisdiction that interpreted that defense as applying to individuals who were unable to know that their conduct was wrong by widely accepted societal standards of moral wrongfulness or by their personal moral standards. He would not qualify for the insanity defense in a jurisdiction that interpreted the defense as applying only to those who were unable to know that their conduct was contrary to law. Anderson2 would not qualify for the insanity defense in jurisdictions that applied either the standard of wrongfulness embodied in law or the standard of wrongfulness according to widely accepted societal moral judgments. He would qualify for an insanity defense, however, if the jurisdiction applied a standard of personal knowledge that the conduct is morally wrong.

Compare East, who qualifies for a clinical diagnosis of pedophilia on the basis of an ongoing pattern of sexual fantasies regarding prepubescent children and a series of incidents in which he has subjected children to sexual activity.[24] He is criminally charged with committing sexual offenses against children.[25] He is aware that sexual activity with children is contrary to law and societal standards of morality, but he believes that pedophilia is not wrong because it reflects love of children. Thus, he

---

[22] Model Penal Code § 4.01 (Proposed Official Draft 1962); Wayne R. LaFave, Criminal Law§ 7.2 (5th ed. 2010).

[23] LaFave, *id.* at § 7.2(b; 4).

[24] American Psychiatric Association, supra note 6, at § 3.02.2, p 572.

[25] Model Penal Code, supra note 22, at Article 213.

qualifies for a clinical diagnosis, and he does not believe that his conduct is wrong by his personal moral standards.

Compare Frant, who qualifies for a clinical diagnosis of antisocial personality disorder on the basis of an extended pattern of criminal conduct, aggression, and lack of empathy or remorse.[26] While in prison for a series of crimes, he becomes a member of the Church of The Aryan Father.[27] After release, he sets fire to a house occupied by an interracial couple because his newly adopted religion teaches that God forbids miscegenation. Almost everyone he talks with agrees, so he is sure that only "Washington elites" disagree. Frant qualifies for a clinical diagnosis, and he does not believe that his conduct is wrong by his personal moral standards or by widely held societal standards.

Assume that most courts and readers would agree that East and Frant should be held responsible for their crimes, rather than acquitted due to insanity. What reasoning justifies acquittal through the insanity defense for Anderson1 or Anderson2, but not for East or Frant? All qualify for clinical diagnosis of mental disorder, and none believe that their conduct is wrong, although all are aware that it violates law. Anderson2 and East are also aware that their conduct is wrong by widely held societal standards of morality although they believe that those standards are contrary to correct morality.

Frant differs from Anderson1 and Anderson2 in that Anderson1 and Anderson2 qualify for an Axis I clinical diagnosis, but Frant qualifies for an Axis II clinical diagnosis.[28] An Axis I clinical diagnosis would not be sufficient to fulfill the requirements of the insanity defense, however, because East also fulfills the criteria for an Axis I clinical diagnosis.[29] What reasoning differentiates these offenders for the purpose of an insanity defense? If one applies knowledge of widely held societal standards of morality, neither East nor Anderson2 qualify for the insanity defense. Frant might have an arguable claim, however, insofar as he believes that his moral judgment is consistent with widely held societal judgments. Although all four offenders qualify for clinical diagnosis, they vary substantially in the type and severity of impairment that qualifies them for their diagnoses. It seems very unlikely that a court or jury would consider East or Frant appropriate for acquittal under the insanity defense, but clearly articulating the basis for that conclusion is important in order to responsibly address Anderson1 and Anderson2, as well as to maintain the integrity of the process. In order to accurately assess the criminal responsibility of each individual, we must shift attention from clinical diagnostic categories to the specific functional impairment manifested by each offender and to the manner in which that impairment influenced the criminal conduct at issue.

---

[26] American Psychiatric Association, supra note 6, at § 301.7.

[27] To my knowledge, there is no church by this name. I intend it to represent a fictional church based on the belief that the members are obliged to protect racial purity consistent with God's design.

[28] American Psychiatric Association, supra note 6, at 27–37.

[29] *Id.* at 28.

Compare Anderson3, who resembles Anderson2 in that he believes that his conduct is contrary to law and societal standards, but he also believes that his conduct is wrong by his personal moral standards. He also believes that he is morally obliged to perform that conduct, however, because he has experienced auditory hallucinations commanding him to perform that conduct. He understands these hallucinations as commands from God, and he believes that God is omnipotent, omniscient, and omni-benevolent. Thus, conformity to God's commands is morally mandatory. That is, he holds directly contradictory beliefs that his conduct is morally wrong and that it is morally mandatory because it is commanded by the morally infallible God. His ability to hold these obviously contradictory beliefs without questioning whether he might be mistaken regarding at least one of these beliefs is the product of a severe thought disorder that distorts his ability to direct his conduct through the minimally coherent processes of practical reasoning that are necessary to participate in the CJS that governs the behavior of responsible agents in the public domain of a democracy.[30]

Compare Anderson1 and Anderson2 to Anderson3. All three are aware that their conduct is contrary to law. Anderson2 and Anderson3 differ from Anderson1 in that they are aware that their conduct violates generally accepted societal standards of moral wrongfulness. It is not clear that this standard justifies differential treatment regarding criminal responsibility and punishment, however, because this standard would exempt Anderson1 and Frant from criminal responsibility while holding Anderson2 and Anderson3 responsible. Yet, all three variations of Anderson differ from Frant in that they reveal serious distortion of psychological process that arguably precludes culpability. The central impairment that all three have in common is distortion of thought process that prevents them from directing their behavior through decision making as minimally competent practical reasoners. Their distorted beliefs regarding moral wrongfulness by societal or personal standards are important to criminal responsibility primarily because these distorted beliefs reflect impaired capacities of comprehension and reasoning that prevent them from directing their conduct through a minimally competent process of practical reasoning. Thus, they are unable to participate in the CJS as responsible agents. Each fails to recognize that his conduct is wrong by some interpretation of the wrongfulness standard because each lacks the capacities necessary to engage in a minimally competent process of practical reasoning regarding wrongfulness. This shared impairment of cognitive process undermines the justification for subjecting them to harsh treatment and the explicit expression of condemnation that constitutes criminal punishment.[31]

Compare East, whose diagnosis of pedophilia reflects a disorder of sexual desire and sexual behavior with children but does not involve disorder of comprehension or reasoning.[32] He knows his conduct is wrong by legal and generally accepted societal standards. He disagrees with those standards, but he possesses the capacities

---

[30] *Id.* at 297–313; Robert F. Schopp, Competence, Condemnation, & Commitment 144–151 (2002).

[31] Schopp, *id.* at 144–151.

[32] American Psychiatric Association, supra note 6, at 571–572.

of comprehension and reasoning that enable him to direct his behavior according to legal and societal standards through a minimally coherent process of practical reasoning, and thus, to function as a responsible participant in the society ordered by law. Thus, his disagreement regarding the wrongfulness of his sexual exploitation of children is reasonably interpreted as a result of his desire to pursue his sexual preferences and avoid confronting the exploitative nature of those preferences.

Compare Frant, whose diagnosis of antisocial personality disorder reflects a pattern of criminal conduct involving deceitfulness, aggression, and impulsivity. He demonstrates a lack of remorse for his criminal conduct and a lack of empathy for those who suffer injury from his behavior.[33] He manifests no impairment of the minimal capacities of comprehension or practical reasoning that qualify him as a responsible agent in the CJS. His belief that his criminal conduct is not wrongful by widely held societal standards is a product of his selective interaction with others who share his beliefs, his inclination to accept propositions that are personally convenient, and his preference for beliefs that facilitate his abilities to rationalize his desired behavior and deny responsibility. It may be difficult to determine whether his recently acquired religious beliefs are sincerely held or merely a convenient rationalization for his ongoing criminal conduct. Religious beliefs can blur the boundary between thought disorder and ordinary cognitive process insofar as we culturally accept religious beliefs based on faith in the absence of reason or evidence that would ordinarily be expected as the basis for nonreligious beliefs.[34] Thus, it can be difficult to clearly explain the distinction between some beliefs that reflect thought disorder and some beliefs grounded in religion. Insofar as we recognize that the significance of mental disorder for criminal responsibility rests upon impaired thought process, rather than merely on inaccurate beliefs, however, Frant's belief that his conduct is not wrong should not exculpate him in the absence of substantial distortion of cognitive process.

Individuals such as East and Frant arguably differ from individuals with severe thought disorders for the purpose of criminal responsibility because they possess the capacities of practical reasoning that enable them to determine that their conduct is wrong by standards of law or generally accepted societal mores. Thus, they are responsible for their failure to ascertain and conform to those mores. In contrast, some individuals with severe impairment of cognitive process associated with psychotic disorders lack the capacities of comprehension and reasoning that would enable them to understand or to reason competently about standards of wrongfulness embodied in law or societal mores. Thus, they lack the capacities necessary to reason competently regarding these standards or their obligations to conform to these standards. Due to impaired capacities of comprehension and reasoning, they are not justly held accountable for their failure to direct their conduct according to the applicable standards of law or societal mores.

Consider, in contrast, the competent conscientious objector who recognizes that his conduct violates law but concludes through competent processes of practical

---

33 *Id.* at 701–706.

34 The Sloane-Dorland Annotated Medical-Legal Dictionary 187 (Sloane, R., ed. 1987).

reasoning that he is justified in violating that law because it is unjust. In each particular case, various observers might agree or disagree with that individual's decision and conduct, but he differs from the seriously cognitively impaired person in that he possesses the cognitive capacities that render him able to engage in a decision-making process that qualifies him as responsible for that decision. Whether he decides to violate law because he concludes that the law is unjust according to his religious beliefs or according to his own critical moral reasoning, he acts as a responsible agent because he retains the capacities to engage in at least minimally adequate practical reasoning regarding the decision to violate law.

Compare East and Frant to East2. East2 is 20 years old and has been consistently diagnosed with mild mental retardation. He has consistently scored at approximately 60–65 on intelligence tests and demonstrated corresponding impairment in social skills and adaptive functioning.[35] He has been arrested and charged with several counts of sexual offenses for engaging in consensual sexual activity with 13- and 14-year-old girls.[36] East2 is aware that this conduct is forbidden, but due to his impairment and the willing participation of the girls, he is not aware of the seriousness of the potential harm to the girls, of potential pregnancy, or of the criminal punishment he could receive.

East2 and East are both subject to clinical diagnosis and are at least arguably competent to proceed in the criminal process and criminally responsible. It would be at least plausible to contend, however, that East2 differs from East in that his clinical diagnosis reflects impairment that substantially reduces his culpability and renders him appropriate for a suspended sentence and probation on the condition that he participates in monitored training designed to promote his conformity to societal standards of acceptable behavior. Thus, the most justified societal response to East, Frant, and East2 through ordinary criminal courts or the MHC varies with the specific type and severity of functional impairment they manifest and the manner in which their impairment influences their degree of culpability and the risk that they will engage in further criminal conduct.

In short, the CJS provides the primary institution for the exercise of the police power in response to conduct that culpably harms or endangers others. Individuals who culpably harm or endanger others are subject to criminal prosecution and punishment. Some of those individuals such as East and Frant qualify for clinical diagnoses, but they remain subject to criminal prosecution and punishment because they retain the capacities of criminal competence and responsibility. Furthermore, their clinical diagnoses do not reflect impaired capacities of a type that renders them substantially less culpable than ordinary offenders by societal standards embodied in law. Thus, comparative justice requires criminal sentences similar to those applied to other offenders who commit similar offenses under similar conditions.

In contrast, MHCs provide an alternative to the ordinary approach to criminal prosecution and punishment for individuals, such as Baker and East2, who suffer mental disorder that contributes substantially to their criminal conduct in a manner

---

[35] American Psychiatric Association, supra note 6, at 41–49.

[36] Model Penal Code, supra note 22, at §§ 213.3(1)(a), 213.4(b).

that does not preclude competence to proceed in the criminal process or criminal responsibility but does render them substantially less culpable than most ordinary criminals who commit similar offenses. Thus, MHCs provide an alternative path through the CJS for these individuals, rather than an alternative to the CJS. In this manner, MHCs seek integration of mental health interventions into the criminal justice process. Insofar as MHCs accurately identify criminally responsible offenders who manifest impairment that contributes to their criminal behavior in a manner that renders them less culpable than unimpaired offenders, they can promote treatment interventions that protect the well-being of the individual and the public while remaining consistent with the applicable principles of justice. In many circumstances, accurately identifying individuals whose impairment contributed to their criminal conduct requires competent clinical assessment. Thus, integrating the MHC process with local clinical resources is an important step in promoting the MHC's ability to promote individual and societal interests in integrating effective treatment with the applicable principles of justice. Civil commitment or post-insanity acquittal commitment provide two alternative interventions for those who harm or endanger others due to serious psychological impairment. In contrast to MHCs, neither involves a finding of guilt nor a criminal sentence.

## *Post-insanity Acquittal Commitment and Civil Commitment*

Assuming that the justification for applying standard criminal conviction and punishment to East and Frant but providing MHCs as an alternative path through the CJS for Baker and East2 is persuasive, what reasoning justifies civil commitment or criminal prosecution, an insanity defense, and post-acquittal commitment as the most justified approach to Anderson? Civil commitment under the police power would apply to individuals who provided clear and convincing evidence that they suffer significant psychological impairment and endangered others, although they had not yet engaged in criminal conduct.[37] Consider, for example, Peter who manifests a chronic schizophrenic disorder involving delusions and hallucinations. During periods of exacerbation, he hears the hallucinatory voice of God. During one period, this voice told him that he was John, the Baptist, who was returned to earth because he had failed to baptize some of the Jewish people. Peter began sprinkling water on people leaving Jewish temples in order to baptize them in accordance with God's orders. The police removed him, but he was not civilly committed because he had not endangered anyone. Recently, Peter has been referring to himself as Abraham and approaching small boys in the local park. He has addressed them as Isaac and told them that the need for sacrifice is greater now than ever. The police responded to calls from parents, and the county attorney has initiated civil commitment proceedings.[38]

---

[37] Perlin, supra note 20, at §§ 2A–3, 4.

[38] Schopp, supra note 30, at 159–165.

In circumstances such as these, civil commitment with appropriate treatment would promote the treatment interests of the impaired individuals and society's interest in reducing the risk of harm to others associated with their mental illness. Thus, it would promote individual and societal well-being in a manner consistent with retributive justice because it would not apply a criminal trial or punishment to a person who had not engaged in criminal conduct. It would involve an intrusion into ordinarily protected liberty, but it would not carry the expression of condemnation inherent in criminal punishment. Neither would it violate the ordinary right to make self-regarding decisions because Peter's psychotic disorder that renders him a danger to others justifies state intervention under the police power to prevent that harm.[39]

A criminal trial with an insanity defense and post-acquittal commitment would resemble civil commitment in that it would provide a path to commitment and treatment, rather than punishment. This path would subject an individual, such as Peter, who has not yet engaged in criminal conduct, to an unjustified criminal charge and trial, however, because there is no legitimate basis for filing a criminal charge or for pursuing a criminal trial. If the court applied the law appropriately, a trial would result in a verdict of not guilty, rather than not guilty due to insanity. Thus, it would not result in post-acquittal commitment. If the trial resulted in a verdict of not guilty due to insanity and a post-acquittal commitment, it would undermine the discipline on the state's exercise of coercive force through the criminal justice process. This dilution of discipline on the state's exercise of coercive force undermines the integrity of the process and threatens the well-being of the public generally. Similarly, MHC would not apply because neither a criminal charge a guilty plea nor the application of a suspended sentence as a condition of probation would be consistent with the applicable principles of retributive justice. Thus, application of the MHC would converge with pursuit of criminal charges against Peter in ordinary criminal court insofar as both subject Peter to unjustified criminal charges, and both undermine the integrity of the process in a manner that endangers the public by diluting the discipline on state intrusions into protected liberties through the rigorous application of substantive standards and procedures.

Consider a variation of Peter in which Peter2 approaches the synagogue because his hallucinatory voice of God orders him to convert the Jewish members. When ordered to leave the property, he threatens to "smite the heathens" while waving his staff in a threatening manner. He would then be subject to a criminal charge of terroristic threats.[40] He might reasonably be expected to be incompetent to proceed at trial, however, requiring a period of commitment for treatment to restore competence followed by an acquittal due to insanity and a post-acquittal commitment. MHC would not provide a justified alternative because his competence to proceed and plead guilty is highly questionable, and the guilty plea would be inappropriate for one who lacked the capacities of criminal responsibility at the time of the

[39] See supra notes 11–12 and accompanying text regarding the police power.

[40] Model Penal Code, supra note 22, at § 211.3.

conduct. Thus, a criminal sentence would not conform to the applicable principles of retributive justice.

Practical concerns about facilitating access to a coordinated clinical treatment program and avoiding costly and time-consuming criminal procedures might support civil commitment, rather than the criminal process, in circumstances such as these in which the conduct establishing dangerousness could support a criminal charge. Thus, civil commitment might promote the public interest in efficiency and the converging interests of Peter2 and the public in timely application of effective treatment.

In pursuing civil commitment, rather than the criminal process, however, we should be aware of the risk that this alternative process might promote unjustified limitations on liberty due to relatively less rigorous procedures and the tendency to think of commitment and treatment as positive interventions that we do for the individual, rather than intrusions that we inflict upon individual. Thus, well-meaning participants in the civil commitment process might tend to interpret the commitment criteria of mental illness and dangerousness relatively broadly when it appears that the subject of the commitment process would benefit from treatment. The criminal trial process, in contrast, is likely to apply rigorous adversarial proceedings to clearly establish the conduct and required culpability elements that constitute the crime because conviction carries substantial punishment and condemnation rather than the apparent benefit of clinically appropriate treatment. Thus, the criminal process is designed to rigorously discipline state intrusions into protected individual liberty.

The expressive function of criminal trials for serious crimes might provide persuasive reason to pursue criminal prosecution, especially in circumstances in which the conduct that establishes dangerousness constitutes a serious offense against the victim. Criminal conviction and punishment condemns the crime as a wrong and the offender as a culpable wrongdoer.[41] An acquittal due to a successful insanity defense exculpates the defendant as one who is not responsible for his crime, but in doing so, it affirms that the conduct was a criminal wrongdoing. Thus, the verdict reaffirms the condemnation of the conduct as a criminal wrong, and it vindicates the standing of the victims by condemning the defendant's conduct as a criminal wrong against the victims.

Applying the criminal trial process arguably serves another important expressive function because subjecting each psychologically impaired offender to the criminal trial process expresses respect for the standing of the general category of people with mental disorders. By requiring a criminal trial and persuasive evidence that this defendant's disorder renders this individual not responsible for this specific conduct, we collectively avoid implicitly suggesting that all people with mental disorders lack the capacities of criminal responsibility. Thus, we avoid a categorical implication of non-responsibility that denies full standing to people with psychological impairment. Subjecting psychologically impaired defendants to the criminal trial process clearly differentiates mental disorders generally from those specific forms and degrees of impairment that render a specific individual not responsible

---

[41] Schopp, supra note 30, at 144–148.

for the specific criminal conduct that was related to his impairment in a manner that undermines criminal responsibility. By applying criminal law and punishment to those who manifest disorder but remain criminally responsible, we reaffirm the standing of persons with mental illness generally as responsible agents. By exempting only a subset of impaired individuals who manifest severe impairment that renders them unable to function as responsible agents regarding the conduct at issue, we reject a categorical denial of full standing for mentally ill individuals generally.

## *Summary*

The CJS provides the primary institution designed to protect the well-being of the public and individual liberty by reducing the rate of crime through a process that applies principles of retributive justice to those who possess the capacities of responsible agency. Criminal punishment of those who have culpably engaged in criminal conduct infringes upon the liberty and well-being of those who are convicted of crimes, but individuals who culpably commit crimes forfeit their claim to equal liberty and consideration. Insofar as MHCs are appropriately limited to those individuals who manifest impairment that reduces their culpability as compared to ordinary offenders who commit similar offenses but does not preclude competence to proceed or criminal responsibility, they provide an institutional structure designed to provide effective treatment for impaired offenders while explicitly reaffirming that these individuals are responsible agents but significantly impaired in a manner that reduces their culpability. Thus, MHCs provide an alternative path through the CJS that promotes comparative justice and treatment expected to promote the well-being of the offenders and of the public. Furthermore, this alternative path explicitly rejects any implicit suggestion that all individuals with mental disorders lack standing as responsible agents.

Civil commitment or a criminal trial leading to a successful insanity defense and post-acquittal commitment provide two alternative institutional structures for the application of the police power to those who endanger others and manifest serious psychological impairment. Civil commitment provides the appropriate institutional structure for individuals, such as Peter, who demonstrate serious impairment and endanger others but have not engaged in criminal conduct. The application of commitment in these circumstances raises concern regarding the risk that we collectively might tend to intrude into protected liberty without sufficiently rigorous standards and procedures if we tend to interpret commitment as an intervention that provides treatment for the individual, rather than as an intrusion into protected liberty.

A criminal trial resulting in an insanity acquittal and post-acquittal commitment can reasonably be expected to promote rigorous application of the legal standards of criminal responsibility and to avoid the implication that all psychologically impaired individuals lack full standing as responsible agents. This process also explicitly recognizes and condemns the criminal wrong inflicted upon the victim. The extended process might have adverse effects on individual and societal well-being, however, by delaying the application of a comprehensive treatment program. Thus, applying the civil commitment process, rather than the criminal justice process, to individuals such as Peter2, who commit relatively mild offenses, might represent a reasonable alternative to the criminal justice process insofar as it promotes the converging well-being of the public and of the individual without undermining respect for the victims or for the general category of people who experience psychological impairment.

In short, individuals can manifest various forms and degrees of impairment that render them most appropriate for police power interventions through civil commitment or through the criminal trial process, including MHCs or the insanity defense and post-acquittal commitment. Recognizing that individuals who endanger others due to psychological disorder can be appropriately addressed through a variety of legal processes draws attention to the need for further clarification regarding the categories and degrees of functional impairment that justify the application of specific institutions of police power intervention to specific individuals.

## Expert Testimony and Research Regarding Psychological Impairment and Culpability

Assume for the sake of this analysis that most courts and juries would agree that Anderson's disorder described previously as Anderson3 renders him a reasonable candidate for the insanity defense because it renders him unable to know that his conduct is wrongful.[42] Assume further that most courts and jurors would agree that the disorders manifested by East and Frant do not render them reasonable candidates for the insanity defense. What differentiates Anderson's disorder from that of East and Frant, such that Anderson is unable to know that his conduct is wrong but East and Frant are able to know that their sexual offenses against children (East) and arson (Frant) are wrong, although they believe that their conduct is not wrong?

Compare Anderson3, East, and Frant to a member of a criminal gang who believes it is wrong to talk to the police, but it is not wrong to kill members of a rival gang or witnesses to his criminal conduct who would talk to the police. Regarding each of these individuals, expert testimony and relevant psychological research might advance the ability of jurors, judges, or other legal actors to address the following questions. What, if any, kind of functional psychological impairment does this individual manifest? How did that impairment influence his understanding, reasoning, and decision making regarding the specific conduct at issue? What is the significance of these effects for the defendant's ability to meet the legal standards of criminal competence, responsibility, and culpability at issue in the specific case?

To the extent that relevant information is available, expert witnesses can provide descriptive and explanatory testimony that informs legal decision makers. Further

[42] See Appendix regarding Anderson3.

research can pursue more complete understanding of the relevant psychological processes and impairment. In most circumstances, neither psychological research nor expert testimony can provide conclusive answers to the relevant legal determinations for two reasons. First, the legal standards often lack clarity regarding the psychological capacities or impairment that are required. Some commentators assert that standards for the insanity defense addressing the ability to appreciate wrongfulness differ from standards addressing one's ability to know that one's conduct is wrongful, for example, but they do not provide clear explanations regarding the relevant differences.[43] Similarly, in Panetti vs. Quarterman, the Court has recently referred to a requirement of rational understanding as necessary to fulfill the retributive function in the context of competence to face execution.[44] The opinion provides no clear explanation, however, regarding either the type or degree of comprehension that qualifies as rational understanding for this purpose or the reasoning that justifies requiring rational understanding as the most appropriate standard for competence to face execution.[45]

Panetti had been diagnosed with a psychotic disorder involving delusions.[46] He reportedly believed that the government wanted to kill him to prevent him from preaching the gospel.[47] Compare him to a hypothetical variation of Frant who was convicted of two counts of murder when the fire he set at the home of the interracial couple caused the deaths of both members of that couple.[48] Frant qualifies for a diagnosis of antisocial personality disorder, rather than a psychotic disorder. Frant believes that the government wants to kill him to suppress the growing political influence of the Church of the Aryan Father. It seems very likely that the Courts would reject any claim that Frant's personality disorder and beliefs would render him incompetent to face execution, but the Court's opinions provide no clear explanation that describes or justifies an appropriate standard of rational understanding for this purpose.

Second, in addition to lacking clarity, some legal standards, such as appreciation or lack of rational understanding, may contain justificatory components that extend beyond psychological expertise. The Panetti opinion, for example, suggests that Panetti's delusional beliefs render him incompetent to face execution at least partially because they prevent the execution from serving the retributive purpose.[49] The opinion provides no clear account of that retributive purpose or explanation regarding the quality or degree of understanding that would fulfill that purpose. Thus, it provides no clear guidance regarding the quality or degree of cognitive capacity that constitutes competence for this purpose. Arguably, the decision maker must make the justificatory judgment that the offender understands the reason for his execution

---

[43] LaFave, supra note 22, at § 7.5.

[44] Panetti vs. Quartermann, 127 S.Ct. 2842 (2007).

[45] *Id.* at 2860–2862.

[46] *Id.* at 2862.

[47] *Id.* at 2859.

[48] See supra text accompanying notes 26–27.

[49] Panetti, 127 S.Ct., at 2860–2862.

in a manner and to a degree that justifies execution. Thus, psychological research and testimony can promote understanding of the individual's psychological capacities and impairment, but it can rarely provide a sufficient basis for expert opinions that the defendant does, or does not, meet the applicable legal standard because such conclusions almost always require justificatory judgments that extend beyond clinical expertise. These justificatory judgments require integration of the psychological research and assessment that experts can provide with judgments regarding the significance of that research and assessment for justifications of punishment embodied in a specific legal institution. The latter integration extends beyond the expertise of expert witnesses.

In some circumstances, expert testimony explaining how the individual developed the impairment and the individual's awareness of its potential effects might also be relevant. In People vs. Decina, a driver was criminally convicted for the death of pedestrians who were killed by the car he was driving when he experienced a seizure, lost control of the car, and the car ran into the pedestrians on the sidewalk. Although his seizure impaired consciousness and motor control at the time of the accident that caused the deaths, his decision to operate the motor vehicle with awareness that he was subject to unanticipated seizures constituted criminal negligence regarding the causation of the deaths.[50] If a court were to consider only a defendant's psychological state at the time of the offense, his impaired consciousness and motor control at the time of the seizure might reasonably have prevented him from fulfilling any culpability element or the voluntary act requirement.[51] He was held criminally responsible, however, because the court considered his history of seizures that rendered him aware of the serious risk he was creating at the time he chose to drive the car despite his ongoing vulnerability to seizures that impaired his consciousness and his ability to competently direct his decision making and his physical behavior. In circumstances such as these, expert testimony that informs the decision maker regarding the nature and degree of impairment at the time of the event, the risk that such impairment would occur, and the circumstances that might provide the individual with notice that he was at risk for a seizure would be relevant to the determination of various levels of culpability, such as knowing, reckless, or negligent mental states.[52]

Consider also common approaches to intoxication as a defense to criminal conviction and punishment. As a general matter, involuntary intoxication can serve as a defense to a criminal charge if it negates the mental state required by the offense definition or if it causes the individual to fulfill the requirements of the insanity defense in that jurisdiction.[53] Voluntary intoxication, in contrast, exculpates only if it prevents the individual from fulfilling the mental state required by the offense definition.[54] Voluntary intoxication carries narrower exculpatory significance than

[50] People vs. Decina, 138 N.E. 2d 799, 802–804 (1956).

[51] Model Penal Code, supra note 22, at §§ 2.01, 2.02.

[52] *Id.* at § 2.02.

[53] *Id.* at § 2.08; LaFave, supra note 22, at § 9.5 (g).

[54] *Id.* at § 2.08 (1); LaFave, *id.* at 9.5–9.5(c).

involuntary intoxication because the individual is responsible for inducing the impaired state. This rule arguably resembles the decision in Decina insofar as both Decina and the voluntarily intoxicated individual are held responsible for creating the condition that contributed to the resulting harm.[55] Voluntary intoxication differs from Decina's circumstances in that the voluntarily intoxicated defendant created his impaired capacity. Decina, in contrast, did not create his seizure disorder, but he culpably created the risk to others by driving with awareness of the risk that he would experience a seizure that would render him unable to maintain safe control of the vehicle. Thus, Decina and the voluntarily intoxicated offender consciously made informed decisions that created the circumstances in which they endangered others and in which their impaired capacities rendered them unable to responsibly prevent themselves from causing the harm.

In both cases, relevant expert testimony might inform the legal decision maker regarding the nature and severity of the impairment, the probability and severity of the risk created, and the individual's ability to accurately anticipate that risk. The conclusion that the conduct involved in becoming intoxicated or in deciding to drive with the risk of seizures was sufficient to constitute negligence or recklessness, however, requires an assessment of the sufficiency of the risk required to justify holding the defendant criminally culpable. Regarding recklessness, the defendant must have consciously disregarded "a substantial and unjustifiable risk."[56] Regarding negligence, the failure to perceive the risk must have involved "a gross deviation from the standard of care that a reasonable person would observe in the actor's situation."[57] Thus, descriptive and explanatory expert testimony regarding the degree of risk, the defendant's awareness of that risk, and the manner in which that risk was generated by the offender might inform the decision maker's understanding of the relevant matters. Expert testimony that either defendant was or was not reckless or negligent would extend beyond the range of expertise, however, because these determinations require justificatory judgments that fall within the responsibility of the court or the jury and beyond the range of expert testimony.

Similar consideration of the manner in which a person develops psychological impairment might be considered relevant to the degree to which the disorder alters, or does not alter, the individual's blameworthiness for acting in a manner consistent with that disorder. Assume, for example, that East gradually developed his sexual attraction to children and his inclination to act upon that attraction by viewing child pornography and then approaching and engaging children in activities that involved increasing physical contact. East is of average intelligence, and this pattern of conduct provides him with increasingly explicit awareness that he is developing stronger sexual attraction to children and engaging in gradually more intimate contact, culminating in overtly sexual contact. Contrast East to the mildly mentally retarded East2, who goes to a playground that is often occupied by young adolescents and gradually becomes involved in consensual sexual activity with 13- and 14-year-old

[55] LAFAVE, *id.* at § 9.5 (c).

[56] MODEL PENAL CODE, supra note 22, at § 2.02(2; c).

[57] *Id.* at § 2.02 (2; d).

girls.[58] In contrast to East, East2 lacks the capacities needed to recognize relatively early in the process that he is gradually approximating criminal activity. He also lacks the capacities needed to recognize the seriousness of his misbehavior and of the potential harm it might cause.

A sentencing court might reasonably conclude that East and East2 both fulfill the offense elements for sexual offenses against children, but that court might conclude that they differ substantially in their degree of blameworthiness.[59] The court might reach that conclusion in part because East gradually developed his pedophilia in circumstances that provided him with explicit notice that he was engaging in conduct that promoted his sexual attraction to children and the willingness to act upon that attraction. East2, in contrast, lacked the capacity to recognize the manner and degree to which he was developing these inclinations. Although he was aware that the conduct was forbidden, he also lacked the capacities to understand the potential severity of the harm caused and of the criminal punishment. Thus, expert testimony that informs the court regarding the manner in which each of these defendants developed their sexual attraction to children and gradually increased their willingness to act upon that desire has the potential to improve the ability of the courts to assess their degree of blameworthiness for the specific offenses and for developing the sexual inclinations that increased the risk that they would commit these offenses. A putatively expert opinion that the individual was or was not sufficiently culpable to meet the requirements of an offense definition or a specific degree of punishment would extend beyond professional expertise, however, because it would require assessment of the justificatory significance of the defendant's condition.

In short, relevant expert testimony might provide the courts with description and explanation regarding the nature and degree of impairment, the manner in which that impairment influenced the criminal conduct, and the manner in which that individual developed that impairment. Research that advanced the understanding of various categories of impairment, including the factors that contribute to the development of that impairment and the manner in which it influences behavior in various circumstances, has the potential to enhance the quality of expert testimony. The courts might apply that expertise as relevant to the appropriate form of intervention and to the severity of punishment that is proportionate to the blameworthiness of each individual who is convicted of a criminal offense.

## Expert Testimony and Research Regarding Dangerousness

I have argued previously that when dangerousness is addressed as a criterion that justifies a specific form of legal intervention into protected liberty, the determination of dangerousness requires empirical and justificatory judgments. The empirical assessment of risk includes estimates of the probability and severity of risk of

[58] See supra text accompanying notes 35–36.

[59] Model Penal Code, supra note 22, at §§ 213.3 (1; a), 213.4 (6).

harm presented by this person in the circumstances as well as explanation regarding the manner in which this person generates this risk and regarding the reasonably expected effects of various interventions designed to manage that risk. The justificatory components of the determination of dangerousness require the quantitative judgment that the risk is sufficient in probability and severity to justify the specific legal intrusion at issue and the qualitative judgment that the individual generates that risk in a manner that justifies that specific intervention.[60]

Some civil commitment statutes require dangerousness due to mental illness as a necessary condition to justify commitment. Other statutes require mental illness and dangerousness but do not explicitly require the causal connection between mental illness and dangerousness.[61] Insofar as they are interpreted and applied as written, statutes in the first category require an explicit finding of a causal connection between the individual's impairment and the risk he presents, but the statutes in the second category require only the concurrence of mental illness and dangerousness.

Consider Gant, who has a long criminal history involving substance abuse, selling illegal drugs, and violence. He eventually develops a delusional disorder associated with his extended pattern of drug abuse and his ongoing conflict with competing drug dealers and law enforcement.[62] His disorder includes delusions regarding a conspiracy among competing drug dealers and some of his family members to steal his drugs and accumulated money. He is unable to ascertain which family members are involved, but he is certain that some have conspired against him with rival drug gangs. He develops complex plans to conceal his drugs and money from family members. He monitors various family members in an ongoing effort to identify the conspirators. He continues committing crimes for profit as before. These crimes involve drug sales and criminal violence to intimidate drug users, witnesses, and members of rival drug gangs who are competitors in sales.

His delusional disorder and criminal violence would be sufficient to establish civil commitment in a jurisdiction that required mental illness and dangerousness. Arguably, his delusional disorder and violence should not be sufficient for civil commitment in a jurisdiction that required dangerousness due to mental illness because his violence appears to be the product of the same motives and conditions that produced his extended pattern of criminal conduct. Thus, he is seriously impaired and dangerous, but he is not dangerous due to his psychological impairment.

Arguably, a criminal trial would be more consistent with the applicable principles of justice because he commits serious crimes, and his disorder does not undermine his culpability for those crimes. Thus, his offenses merit the condemnation inherent in criminal punishment and he merits condemnation as a culpable offender.

---

[60] Schopp, R. F., Two-edged swords, dangerousness, and expert testimony in capital sentencing, 30 L. & Psychology Rev. 57, 72–80 (2006).

[61] See e.g., Revised Statutes of Nebraska § 71–908 (2009; requiring a causal connection between mental illness and dangerousness); Wisconsin Statutes Annotated § 51.20 (1; 2008; requiring mental illness, drug dependence, or developmental disability and dangerousness, but not explicitly requiring a causal connection).

[62] American Psychiatric Association, supra note 6, at 323–329.

Furthermore, there is no evidence to suggest that treatment to ameliorate his disorder would reduce his inclination to commit crimes because his pattern of criminal behavior began before he developed his disorder and continues during his current period of impairment. Thus, a criminal trial and sentence appears more likely than treatment to promote the well-being of the public because incarceration promotes incapacitation.

Suppose Gant murders the city police chief because he has accurately learned that the chief has identified him as a target for arrest and prosecution. Gant is convicted of premeditated murder in a jurisdiction that authorizes capital punishment for a limited number of offenses, including premeditated murder. The state statute requires the finding of at least one statutory aggravating factor to render the offender eligible for capital punishment, and those factors include the killing of a law enforcement officer and dangerousness.[63] Gant's attorney presents evidence of his delusional disorder and argues that this disorder qualifies as a mitigating factor for the purpose of capital sentencing for the murder of the police chief.[64]

Gant's case raises a series of questions regarding the significance of mental illness and dangerousness for capital sentencing. First, what type and degree of psychological impairment should carry mitigating significance for sentencing? Second, in what manner should that impairment be related to the crime in order to mitigate the appropriate punishment for that crime? Third, what degree of risk, including probability and severity, should be sufficient to qualify as dangerousness for the purpose of capital sentencing? Fourth, are the aggravating factor of dangerousness and the mitigating factor of mental illness most defensibly interpreted as independent or as related? That is, should dangerousness be a legitimate aggravating factor for capital sentencing regardless of the explanation for the risk presented by the offender? Should it matter for the purpose of capital sentencing whether the risk presented by the offender is a product of his psychological impairment that distorts his capacities of responsible agency, such as a response to paranoid delusions, or whether his dangerousness is due to personality factors, such as lack of empathy, that do not distort his capacity for comprehension or reasoning? Similarly, should various forms of psychological impairment fulfill legitimate mitigating functions, regardless of their specific form or whether they were a causal factor in the murder?

Although capital punishment draws attention to these considerations, they are relevant to noncapital sentencing and in other contexts. Compare, for example, capital sentencing with civil commitment. Are there good reasons why dangerousness and mental illness should be addressed as independent criteria or as related criteria for each purpose? What justificatory significance do mental illness and dangerousness carry in each context, and what relationship between mental illness and dangerousness, if any, does that justification require? Psychological research that promotes the ability to understand the manner in which risk is exacerbated by various forms of psychological inclinations or impairment might inform the ability to

[63] See e.g., Wyo. Stat. Ann. §§ 6-2-102 (h; viii), (xi; 2011).

[64] *Id.* at § 6-2-102 (j; vi; 2011).

accurately assess the degree to which an individual's psychological traits or impairment increases or decreases his responsibility for the risk he presents.

Consider Gant2, who is similar to Gant, except that he had delusional beliefs that the police chief he murdered was targeting him for arrest and prosecution because the chief was running the police department as a competing drug supplier. According to Gant2's delusional interpretation of events, each arrest of a drug dealer and seizure of illegal drugs was part of the chief's effort to eliminate competition and to secure a greater supply of drugs that the chief could then sell on the streets. Each news report of a drug-related arrest confirms his delusional belief that all law enforcement officers, including the police chief and prison guards, are part of the conspiracy to kill him in order to eliminate competition in the illegal drug market.

Gant and Gant2 are similar in that both engage in similar patterns of criminal activity, including the recent murder of a law enforcement officer, and both experience ongoing delusional disorders. It seems likely that reasonable jurors would agree that Gant knew that his killing of the police chief was wrong according to standards embodied in law or according to widely held societal standards of wrongfulness. It might be less clear whether reasonable jurors would agree that Gant2 knew that his conduct was wrong for the purpose of applying the insanity defense. If jurors concluded that both Gant and Gant2 were guilty of capital offenses, they could confront decisions regarding dangerousness as part of the capital sentencing determinations in some jurisdictions.[65] Insofar as risk assessment research is available, experts might be able to provide relevant testimony regarding the rate of recorded violence by convicted murders generally or by those with delusional disorders. Expert testimony might be able to provide some explanation regarding the process through which delusions influence the risk of violence in identifiable circumstances and the likely effects of treatment or risk management on that risk.

The judgment that a particular level of risk is, or is not, sufficient to justify a determination of dangerousness for the purpose of applying capital sentencing to a particular individual extends beyond the scope of expertise, however, because that determination requires a justificatory judgment that the probability and severity of risk, as well as the source of that risk, is sufficient to justify enhanced punishment. Reasonable jurors might conclude, for example, that Gant's willingness to kill on the basis of his delusional belief that he was targeted by the police chief for arrest and prosecution supports a determination of dangerousness for the purpose of capital sentencing and provides no mitigation. In contrast, reasonable jurors might conclude that Gant2's delusional belief that the police chief was conspiring to kill him for criminal purposes mitigates his culpability for capital sentencing although it might also support the conclusion that he presents an elevated risk to others. I do not claim here that these conclusions are necessarily the most appropriate conclusions. Rather, the central point is that these conclusions involve justificatory judgments regarding the significance of the level of risk and the manner in which the offender generates that risk for a specific legal determination. Such judgments extend beyond clinical expertise or empirical research. Thus, descriptive and explanatory

[65] See e.g., notes 63–64 and accompanying text.

testimony reflecting appropriate research and clinical assessment can inform these judgments, but conclusions for specific legal applications extend beyond clinical or empirical expertise.

Similarly, some Supreme Court capital punishment opinions include retribution as one legitimate purpose of punishment and require only that punishment serve some legitimate purpose. Other opinions appear to address retribution as a limiting principle that defines the maximum severity of punishment.[66] Arguably, if retribution is a limiting principle and if the offender is dangerous due to mental illness that impairs his capacities of criminal responsibility and that he is not responsible for developing, then his dangerousness should not serve as an aggravating factor. If retribution is a limiting principle and the offender is dangerous due to personality traits that do not undermine responsibility, or for which he is responsible for developing because, for example, he was aware that those traits are a predictable product of abusing certain substances that he continued to abuse, then the risk he presents is an aggravating factor for which he is responsible. Alternately, if retribution and incapacitation are two independent justifications for punishment, and this offender is dangerous due to his mental illness that does not preclude criminal responsibility, then the risk he presents serves as an aggravating factor relevant to capital sentencing intended to serve the purpose of incapacitation.

These examples illustrate a more general point. Appropriately designed and executed risk-assessment research can provide a reliable basis for descriptive and explanatory expert testimony relevant to determinations of dangerousness for various legal purposes. In addition to investigating the correlation between various categories of impairment and risk of harm in various circumstances, appropriate research can enhance our ability to explain the manner in which various types of functional impairment contribute to the risk presented by individuals who experience such impairment. Even if the most reliable research supported the conclusion that East and East2, or Gant and Gant2, represented similarly elevated risk of recidivism, however, the differences in their psychological capacities and pathology that contributed to that risk might justify different forms or degrees of legal intervention. Similarly, different explanations regarding the manner in which they developed the psychological propensities that contribute to their elevated risk might justify different patterns of legal intervention. Conclusions regarding the most justified form and degree of intervention necessarily extend beyond the scope of empirical research and testimony, but research that advances understanding of the manner in which various types of impairment develop and contribute to risk can enhance the ability of expert witnesses to provide relevant explanatory testimony and the ability of legal decision makers to pursue just outcomes and appropriate dispositions.

The sentencer must evaluate this information for the purpose of deciding whether the risk the offender presents is quantitatively and qualitatively sufficient to justify capital punishment for Gant or Gant2. Similarly, legal decision makers must make corresponding decisions for the purpose of noncapital sentencing, diversion

[66] Compare, e.g., Gregg vs. Georgia, 428 US 153, 182–186 (1976; plurality opinion) with California vs. Brown, 479 US 538, 545 (1987; O'Connor, J., concurring).

to MHCs, civil commitment, or other alternative interventions. In each case, expert testimony might provide descriptive and explanatory information regarding the degree and severity of the risk, the relationship between that risk and various characteristics of the individual and the circumstances, and the likely effectiveness of various risk-prevention strategies. Empirical research might enhance the understanding that provides the basis for that testimony. Case-specific legal decision makers must determine whether the risk presented by this individual justifies the specific legal intervention at issue according to the applicable legal standards and principles. Legislators can consider relevant research in formulating legislation that sets the applicable rules in that jurisdiction.

## Conclusion

The CJS, MHCs, and civil commitment are institutional structures designed to apply the police power in order to protect the well-being of the public in a manner that conforms to the applicable principles of justice. Individuals who manifest significant psychological impairment and harm or endanger others raise important concerns regarding interventions designed to protect the public well-being in a manner that conforms to the applicable principles of justice as well as other values and practical concerns raised by these interventions. MHCs provide an alternative path through the CJS for offenders who are competent to proceed and criminally responsible but suffer impairment that renders them less blameworthy than unimpaired offenders who commit similar offenses. Insofar as MHCs develop an ongoing cooperative relationship with mental-health clinicians who can provide assessment and treatment, they enhance the ability of the courts and the treatment providers to cooperatively promote the well-being of the offender and of the public consistent with the applicable principles of justice.[67]

Civil commitment provides an appropriate institutional structure for those, such as Peter, who present a substantial risk of harm to others due to mental illness but have not yet committed a criminal offense.[68] A more complex set of considerations becomes relevant regarding the most appropriate form of coercive intervention for those who commit criminal offenses associated with significant psychological impairment. To the extent that an offender's impairment renders him incompetent to proceed in the criminal process or not criminally responsible for the conduct at issue, a guilty plea and criminal sentence in MHC subjects the offender to unjustified punishment and undermines the integrity of the process. Following restoration of competence to proceed, a criminal trial resulting in a verdict of not guilty due to insanity and post-acquittal commitment arguably results in the most justified outcome and maintains discipline on the exercise of coercive force under the police power. Furthermore, the verdict of not guilty due to insanity vindicates the standing of the

---

[67] Schopp, supra note 7.

[68] See supra notes 38–40 and accompanying text addressing Peter.

victim by affirming that the offender's conduct was a criminal wrong against the victim. Finally, by addressing most individuals with mental disorders who engage in criminal conduct through the CJS, we vindicate the standing of the general category of individuals with mental disorders as responsible agents.

The criminal process can continue for an extended period, however, especially if the offender requires treatment to restore competence to proceed. Thus, particularly for relatively minor offenses, civil commitment might provide a more efficient path to treatment expected to promote the well-being of the offender and of the public. In short, selecting the most defensible application of the police power to individuals who manifest significant psychological impairment and harm or endanger others requires consideration of at least the following: the applicable principles of retributive and comparative justice; the individual's competence to proceed and responsibility for the harm done; the severity of the harm done to the victim and the importance of the expressive function of criminal trial and verdict as condemnation of the criminal conduct and vindication of the standing of the victim; respect for the standing of people with mental disorders by applying the CJS to those who retain the relevant capacities of competence and responsibility; and maintaining discipline on the government application of coercive force.

## Appendix: Offender Examples

The offenders are listed in the order in which they initially appear in the text:

Anderson: schizophrenic disorder; destroys furnace in response to hallucinatory orders from God

Baker: severe but not psychotic depression; steals food from neighbor's basement

Anderson1: schizophrenic disorder; God's commands; society would agree

Anderson2: schizophrenic disorder; God's commands; society would not agree due to Satan's influence

East: pedophilia; sex offenses against children; aware that law and society condemn as wrong; disagrees

Frant: antisocial personality disorder; criminal history; prison; arson to prevent miscegenation

Anderson3: schizophrenic disorder; God's commands; conduct is wrong and morally required

East2: mild mental retardation; sex offenses with 13- and 14-year-old girls

Peter: schizophrenic disorder; God's commands; baptizing Jews; "Abraham and Isaac"

Peter2: schizophrenic disorder; God's commands; baptizing Jews; waves staff; "smite the heathens"

Gant: recent delusional disorder; ongoing pattern of criminal conduct; murders police chief to avoid arrest

Gant2: recent delusional disorder; ongoing pattern of criminal conduct; murders police chief to prevent chief from killing him

# Chapter 7
# That's What Friends Are For: Mentors, Lawyers Assistance Program (LAP) Lawyers, Therapeutic Jurisprudence, and Clients with Mental Illness

**David B. Wexler**

This chapter serves first to introduce briefly the concept of therapeutic jurisprudence (TJ)—the study of the impact of the law, legal procedures, and the role of legal actors on the emotional well-being of those affected by the law. It explains how TJ practices of lawyers and judges often find application in special problem-solving or 'solution-focused' courts—such as drug treatment courts, mental health courts, domestic violence courts, DWI courts, and most recently veterans courts. Many of those courts also have volunteers—often clients who have themselves successfully completed programs in such courts—who now serve as mentors for clients newly-admitted to those courts.

The chapter continues, however, by taking the "mentor" concept to the professional level: speaking of lawyers and judges who have themselves confronted issues of drug and alcohol addiction and mental illness. In prior work, the author opened up this topic principally in the context of drug and alcohol addiction. Here, that work is summarized but the analysis is broadened to focus principally on lawyers who have had their own struggles with mental illness—a newer area of consideration opened up principally by a few law professors brave enough to come forth and to tell their stories of struggles with mental illness.

The chapter then compares these lawyers and their "mentoring" opportunities with the work of lawyers with addiction issues and begins a discussion of how they

The International Network on Therapeutic Jurisprudence maintains a website (with an extensive bibliography) at www.therapeuticjurisprudence.org and an active facebook page at www.facebook.com/TherapeuticJurisprudence. Thanks to Marjorie Silver, Michael Perlin, and Peggy Hora for comments on an earlier draft.

D. B. Wexler (✉)
School of Law, University of Puerto Rico, P.O. Box 23349, UPR Station, San Juan, PR 00931-3349, USA
e-mail: davidBwexler@yahoo.com

University of Arizona, Tucson, USA

B. H. Bornstein, R. L. Wiener (eds.), *Justice, Conflict and Wellbeing*,
DOI 10.1007/978-1-4939-0623-9_7, © Springer Science+Business Media New York 2014

may serve, often in a "second chair" advisory capacity, in civil commitment cases, mental health court cases, veterans court cases, and the like.

The field of inquiry of Therapeutic Jurisprudence (TJ)[1] developed at about the same time as Drug Treatment Courts (DTCs), but from different sources. TJ began in legal academia in 1987, with law and psychology scholarship that would have a hoped-for-real-world application.[2] DTCs, by contrast, began in Dade County, Florida in 1989, and originated atheoretically by frustrated, practical, creative, intuitive judges eager to find an alternative to revolving door justice in the area of addicts and resulting criminality. The two developments were brought together in 1999, in a law review article by DTC judges Peggy Hora and William Schma,[3] and the perspectives have been intimately connected ever since.

Because of this symbiotic relationship, DTCs apply many principles consistent with or indeed directly derived from TJ.[4] But TJ principles, though comfortably employed in DTC and other similar "problem-solving" or "solution-focused" courts, are not "tied" to such courts, and I have repeatedly urged their *general* judicial application, especially in criminal cases.[5] For example, one of the most important sections of my edited book, *Rehabilitating Lawyers*: *Principles of Therapeutic Jurisprudence for Criminal Law Practice*,[6] gathers actual techniques used by lawyers practicing TJ.[7]

A number of these practices are what I have called "family-friendly,"[8] meaning they draw on family, friends, and neighbors to facilitate a disposition requested by a

[1] See references and resources in note 1, supra.

[2] See David B. Wexler, Therapeutic Jurisprudence Forum: The Development of Therapeutic Jurisprudence: From Theory to Practice, 68 Rev. Jur. U.P.R. 691, 693 (1999; first essay written in 1987); David B. Wexler, Therapeutic Jurisprudence: The Law as a Therapeutic Agent (1990); David B. Wexler & Bruce J. Winick, Essays in Therapeutic Jurisprudence (1991).

[3] Peggy Hora, et al., Therapeutic Jurisprudence and the Drug Treatment Court Movement: Revolutionizing the Criminal Justice System's Response to Drug Abuse and Crime in America, 74 Notre Dame L. Rev. 439 (1999).

[4] Susan Goldberg, Judging for the Twenty-first Century: A Problem-Solving Approach (2005), online version available at: http://www.nji.ca/nji/Public/documents/Judgingfor21scenturyDe.pdf; Michael S. King, Solution Focused Judging Judicial Bench Book (2009), online version available at: http://www.aija.org.au/Solution%20Focused%20BB/SFJ%20BB.pdf; David B. Wexler & Michael S. King, Promoting Societal and Juridical Receptivity to Rehabilitation: The Role of Therapeutic Jurisprudence (2013), online version available at: http://papers.ssrn.com/sol3/papers.cfm?abstract_id=1722278.

[5] A case I typically use as a TJ criminal law practice teaching tool is Riggs, involving a client with paranoia. USA vs. Riggs, 370 F.3d 382 (4th Cir. 2004), vacated by 125 S. Ct. 1015 (2005). The case is used as a springboard for discussion in David B. Wexler (ed.), Rehabilitating Lawyers: Principles of Therapeutic Jurisprudence for Criminal Law Practice (2008), hereinafter cited as Rehabilitating Lawyers. The author, along with US Judge Michael Jones and Australia Magistrate Pauline Spencer, is now involved in a "Mainstreaming TJ" project with a Hague Institute Innovating Justice Project known as "Integrating the Healing Approach to Criminal Law," available at: http://www.innovatingjustice.com/innovations/integrating-the-healing-approach-to-criminal-law.

[6] Id.

[7] Id. at 143–255. As will discuss later, my hope is to open TJ practice and service opportunities to attorneys both in and out of the area of problem-solving courts.

[8] David B. Wexler, Therapeutic Jurisprudence and Family-Friendly Criminal Law Practice, 17 Barry Law Review 7 (2011), online version available at: http://ssrn.com/abstract=1753265. See

client and his or her lawyer. In the book, for example, one illustration details how the law firm representing a defendant sought a "community" sanction (along the lines of probation) by submitting letters signed by neighbors that they would have no problem with such a disposition and that, in fact, they would be willing to report the defendant if he were not in compliance with the imposed conditions.[9] Another example, by a lawyer representing young adult clients suffering from fetal alcohol spectrum disorder, explains how the lawyer gathers together a community support group to help insure the compliance of the client with imposed probation conditions.[10] And in an example to be discussed in a bit more detail in a later section, Dallas attorney John McShane writes about how, at the behest of the family of a jailed family member with drug and alcohol problems, McShane conducted what he calls a "jailhouse intervention," speaking to the client about treatment options and then facilitating the incarcerated person's release on a treatment bond from jail to a high-quality treatment center.[11]

Nonetheless, despite their increasing use in general judicial contexts, TJ principles remain particularly popular in problem-solving or solution-focused courts. One such court is mental health court, which unlike the atheoretical origin of DTCs, arose explicitly as an application of TJ principles to persons with apparent mental health issues charged with the commission of rather minor offenses.[12]

TJ principles are now widely employed in DTCs, mental health courts, domestic violence courts,[13] and, more recently, in the newly formed veterans courts.[14] Veterans courts are interesting and important because they typically deal with the issues confronted by each of the previously mentioned courts: posttraumatic stress

also Susan L. Brooks & Robert G. Madden, Relationship-Centered Lawyering: Social Science Theory for Transforming Legal Practice (2010).

[9] Rehabilitating Lawyers, supra note 6, at 185 (contribution by Karine Langley).

[10] Id. at 186 (contribution by David Boulding).

[11] Id. at 193 (contribution by John McShane).

[12] In the words of Judge Ginger Lerner-Wren: "The first (TJ) problem-solving court of its kind in the country, the primary goal of The Mental Health Court was diversion from the criminal justice system into community based care, whenever possible. Yet, the court needed a philosophical and pragmatic construct through which its goals, standard of practice and values could effectively be communicated and understood. TJ was adopted for that purpose." Hon Ginger Lerner-Wren, Justice Speaks: Applying Therapeutic Jurisprudence (TJ) in a Court of General Jurisdiction, Guest Column, May 2008, www.therapeuticjurisprudence.org. Note that the fact that mental health courts began as an application of TJ does not suggest that mental health courts were "derived" from a normative framework of TJ. See Lea Johnston, Theorizing Mental Health Courts, Washington University Law Review, Vol. 89, version available online at: http://ssrn.com/abstract=1710882. Simply stated, if, for whatever reason, the establishment of a mental health court appears to be a worthwhile idea, the use of TJ principles can aid in the effective functioning of such a court.

[13] Bruce J. Winick, Applying the Law Therapeutically in Domestic Violence Cases, 69 UMKC L. Rev. 33 (2000). See also Judging in a Therapeutic Key: Therapeutic Jurisprudence and the Courts 116–123 (Bruce J. Winick & David B. Wexler, eds; 2003; contributions by Randal Fritzler and Leonore Simon). And see Carrie J. Petrucci, The Judge-Defendant Interaction: Toward a Shared Respect Process, in id at 148–155.

[14] William H. McMichael, The Battle on the Home Front: Special Courts Turn to Vets to Help Other Vets, ABAJ, Nov. 2011, online at: http://www.abajournal.com/magazine/article/the_battle_on_the_home_front_special_courts_turn_to_vets_to_help_other_vets/.

disorder (PTSD), a condition widely suffered by veterans, often leads to issues of drug and alcohol abuse, driving while intoxicated (DWI), domestic violence, homelessness, and similar legal problems.[15]

As I hope will become clear later on, my discussion of TJ both in and out of special courts is designed to introduce the reader to TJ ideas and to their application *generally*; my goal, as will be seen, is to recruit additional lawyers to TJ practice opportunities and *pro bono* activities, whether in special courts or otherwise.

## Mentors

Many of the problem-solving courts recruit mentors to help clients navigate their way through the court process. Indeed, having a veteran mentor seems an essential feature of the new veterans courts.[16]

But other problem-solving courts—like DTCs and dependency drug courts (where the clients are not facing criminal charges but are threatened with losing their parental rights)—draw on 12-step and AA insights and practices and use as mentors persons who have *themselves* successfully navigated their way through and who have successfully *graduated* from such courts. Many DTCs, for example, have formed "alumni associations" of former clients who wish to express their gratitude by volunteering to assist new clients. Some—like the court in Toronto—even employ a "peer support worker." And dependency drug courts and family wellness courts have made excellent use of "mentor moms"[17] and "mentor parents"[18] who orient and help new clients—many of them addicted single mothers threatened with the loss of their children—to live drug-free, to improve their parenting skills, and to reunite with their children.

These sorts of mentors have empathy with the new clients and have knowledge and experience to share with them. Their past histories likewise give them credibility with their clients; they can serve as excellent role models, can be a support system, can give practical and important advice, and can serve as a source of hope—a remarkably important therapeutic ingredient in successful recovery.[19] And as we

[15] In fact, American Civil Liberties Union (ACLU) has objected to the special treatment accorded veterans, as opposed to the population at large, facing legal charges relating to drugs, alcohol, mental health issues, and domestic violence. Id.

[16] Id. Ethnic mentors are often important too. Thus, in New Zealand, where Maori are dramatically overrepresented in the criminal justice and parole system, proposals have emerged to have Maori elders orient Maori prisoners to the correctional system and to be involved in the parole or reentry planning of such inmates. Valmaine Toki, Are Parole Boards working or is it time for an Indigenous Reentry Court? International Journal of Law, Crime and Justice 39 (2011), pp. 230–248.

[17] Judging in a Therapeutic Key, supra note 14, at 39, 41 (contribution of Judge Leonard P. Edwards).

[18] Thanks to Allen Korenstein, a lawyer with the Dependency Advocacy Center in San Jose, California, for providing information on that court's mentor parent program and the valuable role that fathers have brought to the process.

[19] Michael D. Clark, A Change-Focused Approach for Judges, in Judging in a Therapeutic Key, supra note 14, at 137, 142–144.

will see in the section immediately following, *lawyers and judges* may sometimes themselves satisfy all of these roles: I am speaking of lawyers in recovery.

## Lawyers in Recovery

Client hope has also been boosted by hearing success stories of members of the legal profession who have themselves struggled with issues of alcoholism and drug use. For example, a recent *Chicago Tribune* piece tells the story of Elizabeth Johnson, now a Will County Assistant State's Attorney, but, 10 years earlier, herself a client in Will County's drug court.[20] According to the article,

> When the next group of Will County's drug court participants graduate in March, Assistant State's Attorney Elizabeth Johnson will be the one to tell them the charges against them have been dropped. For Johnson, it will be a special moment. The newly hired prosecutor will be able to tell the graduates that just over 10 years ago, she was one of them.[21]

And in the Philadelphia area, drug court graduates heard from—and gave a standing ovation to—John Duffy, a 76-year-old criminal defense lawyer, 35 years sober, who received an award for his "tireless efforts to assist others with recovery."[22]

There are moving and inspiring stories from judges as well. With considerable trepidation, Judge Michael J. Murphy wrote of his long-standing struggle with alcoholism.[23] The trepidation came in part because "there is always the fear of a possible relapse,"[24] and he could, after all, "remain anonymous and not be subject to the watchful eyes and the judgment of others."[25] But he wrote—on a website for lawyers and then on a state supreme court website—in the hope that "those who read this who suffer from the disease of addiction will see themselves, and seek help."[26] Similarly, the Hon. Sarah L. Krauss, a judge in New York City, wrote, "My journey from alcoholism to sobriety, recovery and the bench,"[27] recounting her life with alcohol from her teenage years—including being a mother at age 17—through her recovery efforts, her successful election to the New York bench, and finally her development of a "close, loving relationship with {her} daughter."[28]

---

[20] Alicia Fabbre, From Drug Court Participant to Assistant State's Attorney, Chicago Tribune, January 19, 2011.

[21] Id.

[22] Kathleen Brady Shea, Clean and sober Chesco lawyer commended for helping addicts, Philadelphia Inquirer, May 19, 2009.

[23] http://www.supremecourt.ohio.gov/Boards/OJFN/resources/murphyM.asp. His story was originally published in 2008 in www.thecompletelawyer.com.

[24] Id.

[25] Id.

[26] Id.

[27] 34 Tennessee Bar Journal, no. 6, Nov–Dec 1998, reprinting "A Personal Story," which appeared in the American Bar Association's Bar Leader, May 1996.

[28] Id.

## LAP Programs

In their respective essays, both Judge Murphy and Judge Krauss underscored their involvement in Lawyer Assistance Programs (LAP), programs designed to "offer hope and help to the impaired attorney, law student, or judge."[29] Murphy noted that "all the help and hope is given in the strictest of confidence,"[30] that "I had never heard of a breach of such confidence", and that, through the program, "I have seen professions saved. I have seen families saved. I have seen lives saved."

As a member on the national level of what is today known as the American Bar Association (ABA) Commission on Lawyer Assistance Programs (CoLap),[31] Judge Krauss (currently the commission chair) encouraged lawyer readers of her essay "to address the problem of alcoholism and drug addiction among lawyers" and "to get involved in your local or state bar association lawyer's assistance committee."[32]

A recent symposium issue of the *North Carolina State Bar Journal* is dedicated to the LAP program in that state.[33] The symposium explains the functioning of the program and traces its history since the late 1970s, when the Positive Action for Lawyers (PALS) Committee was formed. Among other functions, PALS provides confidential peer support to impaired lawyers through lawyer volunteers—typically themselves in recovery—who "support those suffering from similar conditions by sharing their own experiences and successes."[34]

The principal purpose of LAP is, of course, for these volunteer LAP lawyers to counsel and to serve as role models for other lawyers needing support. But there is another incredibly valuable potential secondary function for LAP lawyers, especially as they begin to use the principles they have honed in recovery and, in 12-step language, to "practice these principles in all of {their} affairs."[35] Since law practice is obviously a major component of their "affairs," LAP lawyers can begin expressly to introduce therapeutic jurisprudence into their practices and can seek to include in their client base some clients with alcohol and drug problems.

As detailed in one section of my edited book *Rehabilitating Lawyers: Principles of Therapeutic Jurisprudence for Criminal Law Practice*,[36] some attorneys—like John McShane of Dallas, Texas—are already doing just that. Earlier, I alluded to McShane's "jailhouse intervention,"[37] and to how McShane visited a jail inmate and offered to help secure the inmate's transfer from jail to a treatment facility. Besides

---

[29] Murphy, supra note 24.

[30] Id.

[31] http://www.americanbar.org/groups/lawyer_assistance.html.

[32] Supra note 28. There is also a National Helpline for Judges Helping Judges: http://www.caljudges.org/news_detail.php?n=60.

[33] North Carolina State Bar Journal, Fall 2010.

[34] Barbara B. Weyher, Help is a Confidential Phone Call Away, id at 5. The California lawyer support group adds a dose of levity through its name: The Other Bar. See www.otherbar.org.

[35] www.aa.org.

[36] Supra note 6.

[37] Text accompanying note 12 supra.

recounting the successful resolution of that situation—a favorable plea bargain and a client in recovery living a satisfying life—the anecdote included another crucially important aspect of McShane's client counseling: McShane is himself a recovering addict, now many years clean and sober. Moreover, McShane shared with the defendant "how the attorney's life was almost destroyed by alcohol and drugs, the availability of treatment for addiction, and the promise of a rich, full, and joyful life if recovery is embraced."[38]

McShane's story led me to write an essay for the journal *Court Review*, the official journal of the American Judges Association, entitled Lawyer-*Assistance-Program Attorneys and the Practice of Therapeutic Jurisprudence*,[39] in which I noted that "LAP volunteer lawyers have a special strength and skill to offer" and that "that special strength and skill can also be of great assistance to a great many people caught up in the criminal justice and mental health systems."[40]

There are obviously many ways in which the additional skills—and the enhanced credibility—of PALS can be used by those LAP lawyers in their client counseling and representation. Jailhouse interventions themselves may be particularly appropriate for LAP lawyer participation. Indeed, LAP programs routinely engage in interventions with lawyers,[41] and, as John McShane has demonstrated, intervention skills (such as self-disclosure and piercing through denial and deception) can readily be transferred from a population of impaired lawyers to the context of jailed clients with drug and alcohol issues. In addition, LAP lawyers might make arrangements to participate in some cases in the various problem-solving courts noted earlier. For a powerful example, consider how a lawyer (especially a woman lawyer)[42] with the background of Judge Sarah Krauss—once a teenage alcoholic mother and today a prestigious member of the legal profession (in her case a judge) with a loving relationship with her daughter—could function as a client advocate (even as a *pro bono* "second chair") in dependency drug court or family wellness court. A lawyer with such a background could also function well coordinating with a public defender office and visiting jailed clients to discuss the possibility of being bailed into a treatment facility.

## A New Direction

My earlier essay focused primarily on LAP lawyers who volunteer as PALS—lawyers in long-term recovery from drug and alcohol issues—and their value to the practice of TJ with clients facing addiction issues. What I would like to address here

---

[38] Rehabilitating Lawyers, supra note 6, at 200.

[39] Court Review, Vol. 47, p. 64 (2011), online version available at: http://ssrn.com/abstract=1876065.

[40] Id.

[41] See Hawaií Supreme Court Rule 16 (1)(b)(2)(discussing "intervention" component of state LAP program).

[42] Judge Krauss made a special point to reach out to women lawyers—who she saw as often too terrified to seek help. See note 33, supra.

is the role of LAP lawyers who, to use the North Carolina LAP terminology, are FRIENDS rather than PALS. In the North Carolina structure, PALS is focused on addiction, whereas FRIENDS "provides peer assistance in the areas of depression and mental health."[43] Because I find the separate categorization of substance abuse and mental health helpful in thinking about practice and *pro bono* opportunities for LAP attorneys, I will continue to use the North Carolina terminology even if it is not in wide use nationally.

There are some encouraging signs that we may actually be entering an era where we might make a dent in the stigma associated with mental illness[44]—or in "sanism,"[45] as the damning stereotype is referred to by Professor Michael Perlin. The New York Times, for example, has recently run a number of touching pieces on persons suffering from—and coping admirably with—serious mental illness. In the words of the New York Times, it is "a series of profiles about people who are functioning normally despite severe mental illness and have chosen to speak out about their struggles."[46]

Some of these pieces relate to accomplished professionals holding prestigious and influential positions, such as Keris Myrick, featured in a piece entitled *A High-Profile Executive Job as Defense Against Mental Ills*, who suffers from schizoaffective disorder (closely related to schizophrenia) and obsessive-compulsive disorder.[47] Moreover, the series began with a profile highly relevant to our present purposes: Dr. Marsha Linehan, a psychology professor at the University of Washington, known worldwide for creating a highly respected treatment for helping severely suicidal people—and herself a person with borderline personality disorder.[48] Linehan's public disclosure came after a patient, noticing faded burns and cuts on the doctor's arms, asked, "Are you one of us? Because if you were, it would give all of us so much hope."[49]

---

[43] Weyher, supra note 5. Of course, there is often a connection between addiction and mental illness, as North Carolina noted when it decided to follow a *unified* administrative structure to evaluate all lawyers seeking help: "Many individuals suffering from addiction also had symptoms of depression, and …often a person who identified as having a depression problem had, in the background, an unrecognized addiction issue." Jerry Leonard & Don Carroll, The Lawyer Assistance Program Story, North Carolina State Bar Journal 8, 10 (Fall 2010). John McShane's jailhouse intervention client suffered from addiction and depression, Rehabilitating Lawyers, supra note 6, at 194. And John McShane himself, before seeking treatment for his alcohol addiction, was on the verge of committing suicide. See Steve Keeva, Passionate Practitioner, at: http://www.law.arizona.edu/depts/upr-intj/pdf/Passionate_Practitioner.pdf.

[44] Danielle Andrewartha, Words Will Never Hurt? Media Stigmatisation of People with Mental Illnesses in the Criminal Justice System, 35 Alternative Law Journal 4 (2010), available online at: http://ssrn.com/abstract=1945538.

[45] Michael L. Perlin, Baby Look Inside Your Mirror: The Legal Profession's Willful and Sanist Blindness to Lawyers with Mental Disabilities, 69 U. Pitt. L. Rev. 589 (2008), available online at: http://ssrn.com/abstract=1111596.

[46] E.g., NY Times, Oct. 23, 2011, at A1.

[47] See the article by that title by Benedict Carey in NY Times, Oct. 23, 2011, at A1.

[48] Benedict Carey, Expert on Mental Illness Reveals Her Own Fight, NY Times, June 23, 2011, at A1.

[49] Id.

To explode some of the myths, to help destigmatize mental illness, to show that people with mental illness can lead productive and fulfilling lives, and to give the all-important ingredient of hope to people suffering from mental illness, these profiled people and others have begun to "come out," with startling stories that, in turn, lead still others to share their own life ventures.

Highly meaningful revelations have recently sprung from the legal academy, most notably through the remarkable book by a first-rate legal scholar, Professor Elyn Saks of the University Of Southern California School Of Law. Saks' *The Center Cannot Hold*[50] recounts her life with schizophrenia, the most serious of the thought disorders. She details her fierce struggles with doctors, hospitals, medications, her deep valleys and severely psychotic episodes, *and* her academic and professional accomplishments as a Vanderbilt University valedictorian, a prestigious Oxford University fellowship holder, a Yale Law Journal member, and, now, the holder of an endowed professorship at the University of Southern California law school where she is a mental health law institute director and a major force in mental health law scholarship and reform.

Saks 'revelation is joined by an essay in the *Journal of Legal Education* by University of Louisville law professor James Jones, who wrote of his long-term battle with bipolar disorder, a serious mood disorder—and Professor Jones has now published a fascinating book on his story.[51]And most recently, Touro law professor Marjorie Silver followed suit and wrote her story of life with episodic depression.[52] "Luckily," writes Silver, "unlike that of Professor James Jones or Elyn Saks, my story is one of episodic, not chronic, mental illness."[53] Noting that she has suffered six episodes of major clinical depression over a three-decade period, Silver is explicit about her purpose for writing:

> I share my story here for several reasons. One is to join Professors Jones' and Saks' brave campaigns to help de-stigmatize, to *normalize*, mental illness generally, and among the legal academy in particular. Another is my supposition that there are more law professors who have suffered from clinical depression similar to what I have experienced than have coped with either schizophrenia or bipolar disorder. Finally, I hope to inspire others who have borne mental illness to use their own experiences, when feasible, to help their students, colleagues, and the practicing bar.[54]

Silver's supposition that more law professors—and likely more lawyers—have suffered from clinical depression than from schizophrenia or bipolar disorder, while not backed by hard data, is consistent with the manner in which depression is underscored in, for example, the North Carolina LAP literature. Thus, FRIENDS "pro-

---

[50] Elyn R.Saks, The Center Cannot Hold (2007).

[51] James T. R. Jones, Walking the Tightrope of Bipolar Disorder: The Secret Life of a Law Professor, 57 J. Legal Ed. 349 (2007), online version available at: http://ssrn.com/abstract=1087129. Jones'book is James T. R. Jones, A Hidden Madness (2011).

[52] Marjorie A. Silver, A Transformational Melancholy: One Law Professor's Journey through Depression, at: http://ssrn.com/abstract=1908992.

[53] Id.

[54] Id.

vides peer assistance in the area of depression and mental health,"[55] and "depression and other mental illnesses" seems to be the customary way of describing mental health issues among the bar.[56] Moreover, a major resource in the field is the website *Lawyers with Depression*.[57]

In any case, Silver has shared her experience and insights in discussing pertinent mental health issues in her Professional Responsibility course, in counseling law students suffering serious anxiety or depression, and, more recently, in a LAP program involving both lawyers and law students.[58] Silver's role in LAP has included an effort to "broaden {the LAP program's} efforts with respect to mental illness."[59]

In New York, as in North Carolina, LAP was formed originally to support lawyers in recovery from substance abuse.[60] In New York, the program began to deal with drug and alcohol abuse and was later broadened to include mental health issues.[61]

LAPs in New York apparently receive a large number of inquiries from lawyers suffering from depression as well as from those with problems of substance abuse. Yet, in Silver's words, "the membership of many LAPs is composed primarily of those who are in recovery from the latter. When I attended the annual NYS Bar Association LAP retreat in 2008, I had the interesting experience of being a member of a distinct minority…among an overwhelming number of lawyers who had suffered from alcohol and other drug dependency, some of whom resented the expansion of the LAPs' mission."[62]

This lag time regarding the inclusion of mental health issues—and the resentment of some about the expansion of the LAP mission—may well reflect the special stigma still attached to mental illness. But the increasing scope of the LAP mission now seems certain, and, especially in light of the revelations and the efforts of Saks, Jones, Silver, and others, we are likely to see many more lawyers and law students seeking support with mental health issues. And, in time, we are likely to see many more lawyers with personal experience with mental illness volunteering to offer their stories and insights, as Silver is now doing.

---

[55] Weyher, supra note 5.

[56] E.g., Mark Merritt, A Hard Look in the Mirror, North Carolina State Bar Journal 6, 10 (Fall 2010); Leonard & Carroll, supra note 44, at 9 ("the mission of the Lawyer Assistance Program was expanded to include helping lawyers with depression and other mental health issues….").

[57] See www.lawyerswithdepression.com. As this important website reveals, the personal stories of mental illness have not come solely from the legal academy. Some courageous practicing lawyers—persons without the protective cloak of university tenure—have also gone public, contributing, I hope, to the destigmatization of mental health problems.

[58] Silver, supra note 53.

[59] Id.

[60] In North Carolina, the program was extended to mental illness in 1999, 20 years after its formation. See Leonard & Carroll, supra note 44, at 8, 9.

[61] Silver, supra note 53.

[62] Id See also Perlin, supra note 46, discussing the legal profession's prejudice toward persons in their ranks with mental illness.

Above and beyond sharing their stories with lawyers now in emotional crisis, these "Friends," to use the North Carolina terminology, may "give back" by bringing their knowledge and experience into their law practices. Even before going to law school, Saks gave back by volunteering in a mental hospital.[63] And her decision to attend law school, instead of pursuing studies in philosophy, came when she "wondered if there were a role I could play in the lives of people who suffered in a way I understood so well."[64] In fact, during and after law school—before entering academia—Saks worked in a legal capacity with some hospitalized mental patients.[65]

Silver is supportive of lawyers using their skills—and special knowledge and insights—in their practices: "I hope my students will have the courage not only to share their stories with me, but as they proceed on the journey that will become their legal careers, they will use their experiences to help clients who are suffering as well."[66]

Silver continues: "Whether an attorney should share personal details about herself with a client is a sensitive issue, dependent on the attorney, the client, and the circumstances. When done, however, for the benefit of the client, to improve the client's therapeutic outcome, it constitutes good lawyering."[67]

The disclosure issue has two components. First, the lawyer needs to assess whether he or she is sufficiently secure to disclose without suffering in professional prestige and opportunities—something not that worrisome, perhaps, for accomplished, tenured professors like Saks, Jones, and Silver. The other issue is whether, given the stigma of mental illness—even among persons with mental illness themselves—disclosure to the client may sometimes turn out to be harmful rather than helpful.

These matters and many related ones need to be considered carefully by LAP lawyers and others—and such considerations ought to be the subject of scholarship in the therapeutic jurisprudence field.[68] For instance, in contrast to PALS (those in long-term recovery from substance abuse), do FRIENDS lack a clear counterpart to being "X years clean and sober?" Or does the contrast between substance abuse and mental illness break down when one considers the trepidation, expressed earlier by Judge Michael Murphy in the context of abstinence from alcohol, that "there is always the possibility of a relapse," and that watchful eyes might always be in

[63] Saks, supra note 51, at kindle edition location 1654-61.

[64] Id at kindle edition location 1602-9.

[65] Id at kindle edition location 3010-17, 3017-23; 3139-47.

[66] Silver, supra note 53.

[67] Id. See also Susan L. Brooks, Using Therapeutic Jurisprudence to Build Effective Relationships with Students, Clients and Communities, 13 Clinical L. Rev. 213 (2006; discussions, among other matters, of boundary and limit-setting).

[68] David B, Wexler, From Theory to Practice and Back Again in Therapeutic Jurisprudence: Now Comes the Hard Part, 37 Monash Univ. L. Rev. 33 (2011), online version available at: http://ssrn.com/abstract=1580129.

pursuit?[69] And, in the context of mental illness, might lawyers profitably resort to Marjorie Silver's words that although the "chances are high that I will experience one or more breakdowns during the remainder of my years," it is nonetheless true that "the future is uncertain for all of us," and that "all any of us has for sure is *now.*"[70]

As I noted in my previous essay in the context of substance abuse, "LAP lawyers in long-term recovery who….feel comfortable talking about their personal histories…will immediately achieve an added credibility with courts and clients."[71] In the present essay, we must ask if that same statement would at the moment carry as much strength in the context of mental illness. If not, can a particular type of disclosure language be developed—maybe along the lines of Silver's words above—to narrow the credibility gap between the two situations?

In any case, the following statement, again from the prior essay relating to substance abuse, *would* clearly apply with equal force in the area of mental health: "But lawyers who wish to keep such personal matters personal may still have much to add."[72] Even without disclosure, in other words, lawyers who have battled mental illness will often better understand matters such as the experience of hospitalization and medications, may know much about treatment options and particular programs and treatment centers, may be particularly well equipped to have meaningful discussions with clients, with mental health professionals, and much, much more.

## Legal Opportunities for FRIENDS

We need to think carefully about how and where FRIENDS may be most helpful. One clear area would be by representing respondents in *civil commitment* hearings, an area where representation is often dreadful,[73] and where LAP lawyers could perform admirably, especially in counseling their clients and in keeping them fully informed of options and consequences. With meaningful representation, in-

---

[69] Murphy, supra note 24.

[70] Silver, supra note 53.

[71] Supra note 40.

[72] Id.

[73] Judge Bazelon wrote of the representative lawyers in such proceedings as "walking violations of the Sixth Amendment." David L. Bazelon, The Defective Assistance of Counsel, 42 U. Cin. L. Rev. 1, 2 (1973). And, except for a handful of jurisdictions, matters haven't improved much in the nearly 40 years since Judge Bazelon wrote. See Michael L. Perlin, "I Might Need a Good Lawyer, Could be Your Funeral, My Trial": Global Clinical Legal Education and the Right to Counsel in Civil Commitment Cases, 28 Wash. U. J. L. & Polý 241 (2011), version available online at http://ssrn.com/abstract=1090997. There are, however, some stellar examples of representation in the mental health area, such as the Law Project for Psychiatric Rights (PsychRights), a public interest law firm, directed by Alaska attorney Jim Gottstein, devoted to opposing forced psychiatric drugging. http://psychrights.org. LAP lawyers who have themselves experienced and objected to forced drugging (a major struggle of Elyn Saks) might wish to involve themselves in work along the lines of that engaged in by PsychRights.

voluntary commitment can often be avoided and other acceptable treatment possibilities might be invoked. Even if a hearing takes place and results in an order of commitment, there is TJ literature on the importance of procedural justice in these proceedings and of the therapeutic as well as the due process benefit of providing it[74]—something the lawyer can be attentive to even if the judge, without counsel's intervention, might not be.[75] And there is also value that comes to the *attorney* from participating in civil commitment hearings: the skills and sensitivity one develops that is transferable to many other TJ-like practice settings—an excellent learning experience specifically noted by North Carolina deputy public defender Robert Ward, who branched out from that avenue to many others, including becoming a leading figure in DTC representation.[76]

---

[74] Judging in a Therapeutic Key: Therapeutic Jurisprudence and the Courts 131 (Bruce J. Winick & David B. Wexler, eds.)(2003).

[75] If outcome is not much in doubt, judges may tend to cut corners, but this would be a mistake in terms of perceptions of fairness and even with later cooperation with doctors and the like. Another role a TJ volunteer lawyer might play is analogous to the role played in the criminal justice sphere by Georgia Justice Project lawyers: to "defend people accused of crimes and, win or lose, stand with them while they rebuild their lives." http://gjp.org/about I am indebted to Marjorie Silver for this insight, and believe it will likely be of particular interest to FRIENDS and clients with mental health issues. Indeed, armed with that insight, I was reminded of Saks' long-term involvement with a client named Jefferson: "One of my favorite cases, involving someone I would end up working with on and off for six years, was Jefferson, a young man barely out of his teens. When we first met him, Jefferson had been on a back ward in a state mental hospital for many years….In addition to having been diagnosed as mentally ill, Jefferson was moderately mentally retarded. And therein lay the problem: Retardation is not equivalent to mental illness, and there seemed to be no current evidence that he was still mentally ill. And if he wasn't, a state mental hospital was absolutely the last place he should have been living." Saks, supra note 51, kindle edition location 3140-47-55. One important function a LAP FRIEND lawyer could perform when dealing with a client in a civil commitment or mental health court matter is discussing—and perhaps preparing—an advance directive instrument relating to possible future psychiatric care. This function would be especially useful if the lawyer adheres to the Georgia Justice Project model mentioned above and is willing to work with the client even after hospitalization and release. Upon release, for example, the lawyer might ask the client if he or she wishes to prepare an advance directive instrument to be followed if serious psychological matters occur later on. See Bruce J. Winick, Foreword: Planning for the future through Advance Directive Instruments, 4 Psychology, Public Policy, and Law 579 (1998). Surveys reveal that many persons support the use of advance directive instruments but, because of time and other logistical considerations, few of them actually prepare one. See J. Swanson et al., Psychiatric Advance Directives Among Public Mental Health Consumers in Five US Cities: Prevalence, Demand, and Correlates, 34 J. American Acad. Of Psychiatry & Law 43 (2006). See generally William P. Spaulding, Therapeutic Jurisprudence: A View From the Trenches (this volume). LAP FRIENDS could function to lessen the above noted logistical problems.

[76] Rehabilitating Lawyers, supra note 6, at 207 (contribution of Robert Ward)("I began my work at the Public Defender's Office by representing clients facing civil involuntary commitments and regular misdemeanors. Knowledge gained there later helped me with the more serious cases. I learned much from clients and the hospital staff, particularly how to identify the symptoms of common illnesses such as schizophrenia and bipolar disorder. I learned how to speak with them as I would any other client. Essentially, the key was to be aware of their condition and then work with them to develop an action plan").

Participating in *mental health court* proceedings is another natural forum for LAP FRIENDS. Much of the legal work in that setting is actually conducted *before* court hearings in conversations between counsel and client about the decision to enter into the mental health court program, what it means, and what consequences would flow from choosing or declining program participation.[77] Although courts are supposed to explain these choices to new candidates, the judges often do this in group settings, and many who enter mental health court turn out to believe that they were never given a clear explanation and choice.[78] Since, as we have already seen,[79] these clear and respectful communications have a therapeutic as well as a legal effect, counsel can play a highly important role here, and a role in which LAP FRIENDS should feel especially comfortable: speaking with persons in emotional crisis, explaining the actual functioning of the offered programs, making sure the prospective enrollee understands the costs and benefits of participation and non-participation.[80]

The newly established *veterans courts* should be another rewarding source of professional work for these LAP lawyers—especially since so many clients of such courts are returning combat veterans with PTSD.[81] These courts will often see cases where a veteran's PTSD has led to drug and alcohol problems, to driving while intoxicated (DWI) charges, or to domestic violence or other assault charges. If the client is in treatment for PTSD, the lawyer can, with the client's consent, help co-ordinate appointments with the client's therapist—the kind of communication that a LAP FRIEND should find familiar and comfortable. Coordination is especially important because if a client is, for example, receiving a type of "exposure therapy," the therapy itself may actually temporarily *heighten* the client's stress and anxiety; thus, a court appointment or legal counseling session should surely not follow on the heels of such a therapy session.[82] Coordination is also important because litigation clearly adds to the client's stress—sometimes even pushing particularly

---

[77] "Although observations of mental health court reveal 'there is little that reflects traditional 'lawyering' as the attorneys are relegated to relatively minor roles in the hearings,' pre-selection legal advice and counseling are essential." Rehabilitating Lawyers, supra note 6, at 26.

[78] Id.

[79] Supra, note 75.

[80] In the analogous area of drug court enrollment, lawyer Martin Reisig underscores the importance of taking pains to explain the program and of avoiding a rush to judgment on the part of the client. Such is especially the case because a number of clients in drug court fail to complete the program and are returned to court to await sentencing on a charge to which they have already pled guilty. Such clients often experience a "double whammy" and feel "sold out" by their hurried lawyers. See Rehabilitating Lawyers, supra note 6, at 156–162 (contribution by Marin Reisig).

[81] Supra note 15. See also Capt. Evan Seamone, Attorneys as First-Responders: Recognizing the Destructive Nature of Posttraumatic Stress Disorder on the Combat Veteran's Legal Decision-Making Process, 202 Military L. Rev. 144 (2009)(hereinafter Seamone I); Capt. Evan Seamone, The Veterans' Lawyer as Counselor: Using Therapeutic Jurisprudence to Enhance Client Counseling for Combat Veterans with Posttraumatic Stress Disorder, 202 Military L. Rev. 185 (2009) (hereinafter Seamone II).

[82] Seamone I, supra note 81, at 171.

troubled clients to suicide[83]—and a LAP lawyer could perform an important service explaining to the therapist the legal situation of the client so that the therapist can take into account of that in providing the necessary psychological services.[84]

Capt. Evan Seamone, a military lawyer, has written a couple of excellent articles relating to therapeutic jurisprudence, legal counseling of veterans, and PTSD.[85] In the course of his comprehensive exposition of the issues, he discusses some aspects of a lawyer's role that overlap substantially with what a psychologist might do professionally. For example, he provides a PTSD checklist designed by the military for rather simple and straightforward use, and suggests it can—and should—be used by lawyers when they suspect a veteran may have PTSD.[86] Seamone convincingly likens the task to the commonly accepted practice of attorneys using a Competency Screening Test to assess a client's mental capacity to stand trial.[87]

But then Seamone suggests something not conventionally in the bailiwick of barristers: using simple, basic psychological techniques such as relaxation exercises to calm a client before a stressful interview and the like.[88] Seamone examines the statutes on the lawful and unlawful practice of psychology, and concludes that the techniques and practices he notes do not constitute unlawful practice when performed by other professionals—lawyers are specifically mentioned in some of the statutes[89]—in the course of *their* professional practices.[90] Thus, instead of postponing to another date the interviewing or counseling of a stressed client, a lawyer might appropriately consider a relaxation exercise to be part and parcel of the lawyer's professional task.

Seamone cautions lawyers who decide to engage in these simple psychological practices to explain clearly and carefully to the client that the lawyer is not a psychologist, and to secure the client's consent.[91] It is also important to underscore that the practices discussed here are indeed simple and find their way into standard and well-regarded "self-help" books.[92]

Of course, not all lawyers—LAP or otherwise—will be inclined to engage in these basic psychological techniques. But it may well be that a number of LAP

---

[83] Id at 150.

[84] Id at 178, 181.

[85] Supra note 82.

[86] Seamone II, supra note 82, at 207, 212.

[87] Id at 215.

[88] Id at 228.

[89] Id at 203.

[90] Id.

[91] Id at 243.

[92] Id at 228, 243. It might be a good practice for lawyers interested in this work to create a committee of psychologists to "vet" such self-help books. Indeed, one can imagine a respected psychologist or group of psychologists writing a book especially for lawyers to use with clients. By analogy, consider the excellent book by Martin Seligman, a former president of the American Psychological Association, entitled What You Can Change…. and What You Can't: The Complete Guide to Successful Self-Improvement (1994).

FRIENDS will indeed be attracted to including this work in their practice. How, then, can the logistics be worked out to facilitate interested LAP FRIENDS engaging in these as well as the earlier mentioned practice areas?

## Logistics and Concluding Remarks

In my earlier paper dealing with LAP principally in the area of PALS (substance abuse), I addressed certain basic issues. For instance, "representation in problem-solving courts is overwhelmingly engaged in by public defender offices,"[93] thus in practice excluding other lawyers—LAP and others—from practicing in those courts. Special arrangements might be made with such public defender offices to designate a group of "special deputy public defenders" and thereby allow some volunteer lawyers—from LAP programs or, perhaps, from recent law school graduates eager to gain some experience practicing in settings particularly conducive to honing TJ skills.[94] Similar efforts may be appropriate to widen the pool of talent handling civil commitment cases.[95] The earlier essay concluded by stating that "the next step, therefore, is for interested persons and groups—including the courts and the bar—to brainstorm how these practice avenues may be opened to interested lawyers, and to provide training, materials, and overall encouragement to lawyers—LAP and otherwise—wishing to serve others in achieving a rich and full life."[96]

The opening up of these opportunities to volunteer lawyers *generally*, rather than to LAP lawyers exclusively, would serve an additional purpose: "if the volunteer lawyers are drawn not only from LAP programs but are broadly-based, confidentiality of LAP status may be preserved for those who wish to preserve it"[97]—a matter that, as we have discussed earlier, may turn out to be even more important for FRIENDS than for PALS.

But this discussion brings us back to the earlier discussion of disclosure, and how the work of Saks, Jones, and Silver may encourage others in the legal profession to be willing to speak of their struggles and successes. While much good work by LAP FRIENDS can be accomplished by thinking through and implementing the reforms noted immediately above, still other rewarding and very helpful practice avenues can be opened to LAP FRIENDS who follow in the disclosure footsteps of the above legal academics.

---

[93] Supra note 40.

[94] Id. Another model, a bit different from the special deputy public defender model, would be to consider whether interested attorneys could form part of the panels of lawyers ordinarily called upon when the public defender office has a conflict of interest. Such a model would also allow for appointed attorneys to receive a modest fee from public funds—a not insignificant matter in tough economic times.

[95] Supra note 40.

[96] Id.

[97] Id.

Imagine, for example, that, instead of individual LAP lawyers volunteering to take cases in specific practice settings, there were committees of LAP volunteer lawyers that could be called upon by other lawyers—including public defenders or perhaps law school clinics[98]—to associate in particular cases involving clients with substance abuse or mental health issues. Thus, a lawyer called upon by a family to represent a jailed family member with drug and alcohol issues might well contact the LAP program for a volunteer PAL who could be called upon to engage with the client in a "jailhouse intervention." Likewise, an attorney working with a combat veteran charged with assault might request the involvement of a FRIEND to conduct a PTSD screening test, and, if PTSD seems a likely diagnosis, to refer the veteran for mental health treatment, to coordinate matters with the mental health professional, to explore the option of moving the case to veterans court, perhaps to engage the client in relaxation exercises before further counseling sessions with the principal lawyer, and so on.

Moreover, if a LAP lawyer is to serve as an independent attorney in an area outside his or her prior practice experience, the plunge into a TJ practice may seem appealing but intimidating. But if one has the opportunity to engage in a TJ practice in the capacity of a "second chair" or as a consultant with some special knowledge, skills, and credibility, the opportunity to "give back" by venturing into the TJ world may be much more palatable[99]—and may then attract more and more of such lawyer volunteers. The entire issue of training of LAP lawyers—and of introducing them comfortably and gradually into TJ practice—is an interesting one worthy of attention.

The issues explored in this essay are by necessity given a very preliminary treatment. My hope is that interested LAP lawyers can consider these issues in more depth, and can discuss them with lawyers and judges involved in problem-solving courts, in civil commitment cases, and with the TJ community in general. Such cooperative exchanges are destined to result in improved service to clients and to new rewarding practice and *pro bono* opportunities for LAP lawyers and for their relatively new FRIENDS. Moreover, as interesting TJ literature suggests, engaging in this type of practice is likely to add professional satisfaction to the life of the lawyer.[100] And as if that were not enough, a recent study suggests that "giving back" in an altruistic way may even, in and of itself, be good for one's health, even increasing longevity.[101]

---

[98] E.g., Gregory Baker & Jennifer Zawid, The Birth of a Therapeutic Courts Externship Program: Hard Labor but Worth the Effort, 17 St. Thomas L. Rev. 711 (2005).

[99] This arrangement may also prove to be more palatable to the clients. Earlier, we mentioned that the stigma of mental illness may extend to persons who themselves have mental health problems—including clients facing civil commitment or proceedings in mental health court. But if a disclosing LAP lawyer is serving in an advisory or "second chair" capacity, an adverse reaction by the client would seem to be most unlikely. And this process itself may also serve gradually to lessen the stigma attached to mental illness.

[100] E.g., Deborah Chase & Hon. Peggy Fulton Hora, The Best Seat in the House: The Court Assignment and Judicial Satisfaction, 47 Family Court Rev. 209 (2009), available online at: http://www.judgehora.com/FCH_Hora_Chase_03_2009.pdf.

[101] Volunteering to Help Others Could Lead to Better Health, Medical News Today, Sept. 7, 2011, at: http://www.medicalnewstoday.com/releases/233972.php.

# Part IV
# Political Conflict, Policy Solutions, and Citizens' Well-being

# Chapter 8
# After Violent Conflict: Justice, Well-being, and International Criminal Courts

**Patrice C. McMahon and Jennifer L. Miller**

## Introduction

In international politics, conflict resolution is difficult to achieve. Conflict resolution generally signifies that disputants have resolved their differences with little likelihood of future conflict—violent or otherwise (Diehl 2008). After violence occurs, conflict resolution is almost impossible, and this is particularly true when the violence is sustained for long periods of time and affects large numbers of people. Nonetheless, international peace operations in the 1990s asserted that the management of conflict was not enough; instead, international actors like the United Nations (UN) needed to address the "root causes of conflict" and transform hostile environments. This assumption and practice—about resolving and transforming violent conflicts—is fairly new to international politics, and many trace these ideas to the UN's 1992 Agenda for Peace that acknowledges both the challenges and opportunities in the post-Cold War era (UN document A/47/277–S. 24,111, 1992). This document, and many others that followed, put into place the UN's peace operations that include a continuum of activities, from preventive diplomacy to post-conflict peacebuilding.

Of these peace operations, post-conflict peacebuilding was the most comprehensive and ambitious. Broadly defined, peacebuilding includes any "actions to identify and support structures which will tend to strengthen and solidify peace in order to avoid a relapse into conflict;" and this involves various top-down and bottom-up mechanisms aimed at changing structures and attitudes related to peace (Keating and Knight 2006, p. xxxv). This chapter focuses on the role and impact of the International Criminal Tribunal for the Former Yugoslavia (ICTY) to understand the long-term effects of peacebuilding initiatives in the southern Balkans (which includes the countries of the former Yugoslavia: Croatia, Bosnia and Herzegovina, Serbia, Kosovo, Slovenia, Macedonia, and Montenegro). Put differently,

P. C. McMahon (✉)
Department of Political Science, University of Nebraska-Lincoln, Lincoln, NE 68588, USA
e-mail: pmcmahon2@unl.edu

J. L. Miller
School of Government and Public Policy, University of Arizona, 315 Social Science Bldg., Tucson, AZ 85721, USA

B. H. Bornstein, R. L. Wiener (eds.), *Justice, Conflict and Wellbeing,*
DOI 10.1007/978-1-4939-0623-9_8, 

after violent conflict and the intentional use of this legal mechanism (as well as other tools), is conflict resolution transpiring? Using Balkan countries as comparative case studies, we argue that although justice and well-being are difficult to achieve in the wake of violent international conflict, these outcomes are not impossible. Almost two decades after the violence started and 15 years since the international community intervened, Balkan countries are moving, albeit slowly, toward justice and peace.

The strife that enveloped the former Yugoslav republic from 1992–1995 resulted in ethnic cleansing, concentration camps, and some 100,000 people killed. In 1993, the United Nations Security Council (UNSC) established the ICTY to prosecute individuals responsible for war crimes, crimes against humanity, and genocide in the Yugoslav wars. However, as the UNSC resolution also states, the court was created with other, broader political and social purposes in mind, specifically "to contribute to the restoration and maintenance of peace" (UN Resolution 827 1993). Thus, the long-term and ambitious goals of the international court were to promote justice, well-being, and conflict resolution in the Balkans. After more than a dozen years of activity, some 161 indictments, 64 arrests and 47 surrenders, the ICTY has accomplished a good deal in terms of its prosecutorial task. But what of its other secondary goals related to the restoration and maintenance of peace? Are progressive changes underway that reflect these broader goals? Finally, what does this strategy, which focuses on individual accountability and legal prosecution, suggest about the prospects for conflict resolution in other war-torn countries?

To answer these questions, this paper compares different sectors associated with the ICTY's multidimensional mandate. We argue that although there were, initially, significant differences among Balkan states over the establishment of the court, changes associated with the court's long-term mission, or what we call transitional justice outcomes, are relatively uniform. For example, in Bosnia and Kosovo, where elites were more predisposed to the ICTY's goals and where external actors hold significant sway, we should expect better transitional justice outcomes. Conversely, in Serbia, where elites have been consistently opposed to the ICTY and where international actors have less power, transitional justice outcomes should be less evident. We suggest that if the ICTY and this strategy have really had any discernible impact on conflict resolution, there should be some clear differences in outcomes in the Balkans; and yet, there are not. Instead, we find that outcomes are fairly uniform, and even though they do not suggest that international conflict resolution is easy or quick, improvements are possible and disputants can resolve their differences with little likelihood of future conflict.

Early writings on the ICTY, largely those of legal scholars, claimed that the creation of an international tribunal was an essential ingredient of peacebuilding in the former Yugoslavia (Hampson 1996; Akhavan 1998). According to this view, the ICTY would not only end impunity, but it would help rebuild judicial capacity and foster respect for human rights and the rule of law (Bass 2000; Thoms et al. 2008). The ICTY was, thus, essential to conflict resolution. The ideas of these so-called judicial romantics[1] were contested by "judicial skeptics," who doubted the import of international institutions and insisted that the ICTY in particular would have little bearing on states' behavior (Mearsheimer 1994/1995; Mendeloff 2004; Cobban 2006). Some even argued that the existence of an international court would do more harm than good, provoking a negative backlash especially within Serbia (Vinjamuri and Snyder 2004).

In the last few years, there has been a noticeable shift toward more empirically grounded research on transitional justice and the ICTY (Kerr 2005; Meernik 2005; Orentlicher 2008; Peskin 2008; Subotić 2009; Lamont 2010; Orentlicher 2010). And while there is widespread agreement on the need to move away from a priori legalistic assertions and toward empirical studies, scholars readily acknowledge the significant methodological hurdles to establishing causality and evaluating outcomes (Lundy and McGovern 2008; Van der Merwe et al. 2009; Nettelfield 2010; Olsen et al. 2010). Studies of transitional justice in the Balkans, therefore, tend to examine these issues quite narrowly in terms of cooperation with the ICTY and largely as it relates to arrests and prosecutions (Peskin 2008; Subotić 2009; Lamont 2010). Since these scholars are interested in assessing the ICTY's primary, short-term task of prosecution—and not the more diffuse, long-term goal of peace and security—other transitional justice outcomes are ignored.[2]

Defining and measuring broader outcomes requires some creativity, because of problems of causal inference, a plurality of causes, as well as the diffuse nature of the ICTY's mandate (King et al. 1994; Nettelfield 2010; Olsen et al. 2010). Acknowledging these complications, we use the concept of "transitional justice outcomes" to examine what is happening on different fronts, including: criminal accountability, democratization, rule of law, and attitudes toward transitional justice and peace. These empirical proxies allow us to test the arguments and predictions of both judicial romantics and skeptics. To be clear, we do not suggest that transitional justice outcomes are due solely to the ICTY and international criminal justice; rather, our intention is to examine whether assumed and broad processes associated with the ICTY's creation are, in fact, evident across similar cases (George and Bennett 2005; Gerring 2007).

Based on our findings, we make two claims. First, Balkan countries have, indeed, moved beyond prosecution, and the other, secondary goals of the ICTY related to justice and conflict resolution are transpiring, albeit slowly. Second, given that certain behaviors—like the arrest of high-profile war criminals—can only be linked directly to other actors and stimuli, like the European Union (EU) and conditionality, the ICTY plays only an indirect role in encouraging progressive outcomes by informing the policies of other more powerful actors that are more capable of effectuating change. By necessity, our analysis is largely qualitative and interpretive and relies on data from various primary and secondary sources.

---

[1] On the concept of judicial romanticism, see Forsythe (2006), Chap. 4.

[2] There are two notable exceptions: the research and interviews conducted by Diane F. Orentlicher in Serbia and Bosnia (see Orentlicher 2008, 2010).

Our research makes three contributions to existing literature in political science and public policy. First, it addresses important and expensive policies adopted by the international community under the guise of conflict resolution that, thus far, lack empirical confirmation. We, therefore, ask whether the existence of this international court has proven essential to fostering the rule of law and restoring and maintaining peace in the Balkans. We believe that our findings—or lack of findings—have relevance for conflict resolution in other post-conflict settings. Although we find no evidence that the ICTY has seriously harmed outcomes or provoked a sustained backlash, we also garner little evidence that this international institution alone has had a discrete impact on the outcomes and behavior we observe. At best, this international court can be seen as one actor, among many, that is contributing in certain, but indirect ways, to promoting positive liberal changes and resolving conflict. Thus, if the international community genuinely wants to engage in conflict resolution after violent conflict, the importance of reinforcing actors and strategies cannot be overlooked.

Second, this work adds to the academic research on the role and effectiveness of the ICTY. Much of the empirical research on the ICTY argues that compliance with the ICTY, when it occurs, is largely instrumental because Balkans leaders "hijack" transitional justice to further their own political agendas (Subotić 2009). Our research does not necessarily disagree with this finding, but we do show that even while this elite behavior is occurring, other political and social changes are underway which are in line with the court's broader long-term goals. We repeat what is both surprising and important: positive political and social changes are happening throughout the Balkans, and all countries are moving toward accountability, liberal democracy, improved rule of law, and peace—at roughly the same pace and regardless of elite posturing. To be sure, liberal democracy at the national level does not guarantee peace and conflict resolution, but it does bode well for the future of both.

Finally, this project contributes to empirical studies of transitional justice outcomes by establishing various benchmarks of political and social change. Using the concept of transitional justice outcomes, this comparative study of democratization focuses on the nuanced changes and policies related specifically to the goals and expectations of transitional justice. By bringing together quantitative indicators and qualitative research, this research helps establish a framework for evaluating the long-term impact of efforts at conflict resolution. Admittedly, these broader, more protracted outcomes do not attract the same amount of attention as the arrests of war criminals, but they do point in the same direction: toward mission accomplished.

## The Multiple Goals of Transitional Justice

The use of international criminal courts to address legacies of conflict or repression reflects different motivations and embodies various goals (Kritz 1995; Minow 1998; Elster 2004). In the short-term, courts are sometimes regarded as an effective strategy for ending bloodshed, holding criminals accountable, and deterring future atrocities. In the medium- to long-term, accountability through prosecution allegedly builds trust among citizens, promotes societal reconciliation, and helps foster a democratic culture based on the rule of law (Orentlicher 1991). Or so it is claimed; the true test, but also the toughest one for the ICTY, rests on its ability to foster institutions and practices that address the past and lay the foundation for a democratic future (Van der Merwe et al. 2009). Methodologically, it is easy neither to measure the ability of the ICTY "to foster institutions and practices," nor to prove its impact on outcomes. States' compliance with judicial mandates is an important part of transitional justice, but this is just one aspect of a broader, multi-pronged, multi-institutional mission to promote economic reform, democracy, and stability in the region (UN Resolution 827 1993; Kelley 2004; Vachudova 2005; McMahon 2007). It is these broader transitional justice outcomes that we seek to address conceptually and assess empirically.

Recently, a great deal has been written on the challenges of measuring transitional justice effects, with a particular focus on disaggregating contextual factors and developing baseline characteristics (Van der Merwe et al. 2009; Nettelfield 2010; Olsen et al. 2010). The field is maturing quickly, with research that employs both quantitative and qualitative techniques. The Transitional Justice Data Base, the Truth Commission Database Project, and the Human Rights Prosecutions Database Project now all make large-scale quantitative analysis possible (Dancy et al. 2010; Olsen et al. 2010; Kim and Sikkink 2010). Although this research advances what we know about when and why certain transitional justice mechanisms are adopted and their achievements, these datasets focus either on domestic transitional justice mechanisms or include international criminal courts and the Balkans to a limited extent (Olsen et al. 2010).

Excellent qualitative work has also been done on transitional justice and the Balkans that uses thick description[3] to explain state compliance with the ICTY (Peskin 2008; Subotić 2009; Lamont 2010). These studies focus on the demand for arrests and the transfer of indicted war criminals, evaluating only these specific outcomes and the ICTY's goals in this one area. This is neither surprising nor fundamentally flawed, but it is incomplete; arrests are an important sign of cooperation with the ICTY, but they are only one indicator, and focusing solely on criminal accountability can distort or overlook broader aggregate outcomes (Forsythe 2011). In Serbia, for example, international actors that demanded "cooperation with the ICTY" gauged achievements exclusively by the number of suspects Serbian authorities arrested and transferred to The Hague (Subotić 2009, p. 44). However, this measure can only be considered a partial test of the achievements in international criminal justice, especially since many of the arrests were linked to other actors, like the EU or the US, and the policy of conditionality, rather than the ICTY and its legal arguments (Subotić 2009; Lamont 2010). It is also true that in all Balkan countries, other outcomes were expected and, indeed, promised with the ICTY's creation.

[3] Within the social sciences, "thick description" broadly refers to an examination of behavior, which includes historical, cultural, and social context as a portion of the explanation.

As Neil Kritz suggests, there are four basic objectives of any transitional justice program: truth, justice, rule of law, and durable peace (1995). These outcomes, however, are not agreed upon and are difficult to measure because no exact proxies exist that capture these outcomes. We contend that if these are the standards by which transitional justice policies are evaluated, benchmarks of progress must be established and outcomes evaluated. Bringing together the benefits of comparative research and relying on both quantitative and qualitative research, we provide a preliminary way of measuring transitional justice outcomes by examining criminal accountability, democratization, rule of law, and attitudinal and social changes. This is neither comprehensive nor definitive, but the following are based on the claims made about the broad benefits of international criminal justice. These categories and how they are measured are conceptualized as follows:

(i) *Criminal accountability*: The creation of an international court reflects a basic belief in the importance of punishing lawbreakers and societies' need to establish a just order (Huyse 1995). Arrests, along with other efforts to establish individual accountability, are evidence that states accept the primary and most immediate objective of the ICTY. We, thus, examine arrest records, especially the arrests of high-profile war criminals, as initial apprehensions tended to be "middle management" rather than the "big guns" (Bohlander 2003).

(ii) *Democratization*: Prosecution is supposed to strengthen fragile democracies by providing protection against "spoilers" who might exploit the country's precarious political environment (Huyse 1995). Democracy requires time to take root, but there are several widely accepted sources that measure democratic change over time. We use Freedom House[4] data which measures eight different aspects of democracy and provides a composite state score. However, since political change cannot be interpreted simplistically or formulaically, we also analyze briefly the content of elite discourse for illiberal ethnic nationalism as it relates specifically and solely to cooperation with the ICTY. This is done through content analysis of news sources accessed via LexisNexis from 1996 to 2010.[5]

(iii) *Rule of law*: The prosecution of war criminals, allegedly, fosters domestic practices and new norms associated with strengthening rule of law (Vinjamuri and Snyder 2004). We use both Freedom House rankings of judicial independence and the World Bank's World Governance Indicators (WGI) to assess changes in rule of law for each of the states in this study. While the former measures judicial capacity, the latter captures perceptions of confidence in the rules of society, and in particular the quality of contract enforcement, property rights, the police, and the courts. In addition to these different measures of judicial capacity, we also address the development of domestic criminal courts and, when available, the devolution of specific criminal cases and legislation relating to cooperation with the ICTY.[6]

---

[4] Reports used in this research can be found at www.freedomhouse.org; the locations of specific reports used are included in the bibliography.

[5] For Kosovo, it was from 2008–2010.

[6] For discussion of the World Governance Indicators, see http://info.worldbank.org/governance/wgi/pdf/rl.pdf.

(iv) *Attitudes toward transitional justice and peace*: International criminal justice should also affect public opinion (Huyse 1995, p. 341). The existence of the ICTY should have some impact on beliefs related to criminal accountability, reconciliation, and future peace (Hagan 2003; Elster 2004; Stromseth et al. 2006). Some public opinion data on the ICTY exist, but they are either dated or unavailable for all Balkan countries (Olsen et al. 2010, p. 160). Although no cross-national surveys of attitudes toward transitional justice exist, interviews conducted by Diane Orentlicher in Serbia (2008) and Bosnia (2010), as well as earlier interviews conducted by the International Center for Transitional Justice in Croatia, provide insight into public attitudes toward transitional justice and the goals of the ICTY (Cruvellier and Valinas 2006). In addition to existing surveys and interviews, we examine activities within civil society that relate to transitional justice and the ICTY.

## Balkan Comparisons

For those hoping that the ICTY's creation would have an immediate impact on the disintegrating Yugoslav state, the outcome was both obvious and disappointing; it neither stopped the bloodshed nor deterred violent behavior (Akhavan 1998, p. 751). In the medium- to long-term, Serbia and Croatia are generally known for resisting ICTY dictates while elites in Bosnia and Kosovo are considered to be supportive of international criminal justice and the court. The following in-depth examination demonstrates that despite these positions, transitional justice outcomes are not that different and political and social changes have occurred at roughly the same pace throughout the region. Whereas quantitative indices provide some evidence of these outcomes, we are also interested in other, more nuanced changes, as well as perceptions of change that make qualitative, interpretive analysis necessary.

### *Criminal Accountability*

The presence of 36,000 North Atlantic Treaty Organization (NATO)-led troops in Bosnia in January 1996 augured a bright future for criminal accountability; however, since the Americans in particular were bent on avoiding causalities, the "arrest of war criminals was the one thing that they most opposed" (Bass 2000, p. 239). It was not until July 1997 that NATO's Stabilization Force in Bosnia (SFOR) began arresting indicted war criminals (Bass 2000). In general, Bosniaks cooperated with the ICTY's dictates while Bosnian Serbs and Croats resisted. By mid-2010, SFOR had made 27 arrests and Bosnian authorities 3. The existence of the ICTY did encourage Bosnian surrenders, including former Republic of Srpska (RS) President Biljana Plavsic in 2001. Nonetheless, the ICTY's ineffectiveness in the RS is noteworthy; as of 2004, it was the only Balkan authority that had not handed over a single suspect to the Tribunal (International Center for Transitional Justice, 2004).

Croatia has similarly had a mixed record of cooperation with the ICTY's goals in this area. Public approval of the "Croatian Homeland War" meant there was little initial internal pressure to hand over indicted criminals. Yet, investigations and transfers of Bosnian Croats were often collaborative, particularly with low-level offenders. Such cooperation did not materialize in cases targeting high-ranking Croatian army members or that garnered little international scrutiny. Some suspects even received state support; according to one attorney, the Croatian military helped relocate and cover-up the whereabouts of four suspects between 1997 and 2000 (Wood 2006). After campaigning to improve relations with the ICTY, Ivica Račan's government was tested in the summer of 2001 with the indictments for Ante Gotovina and Rahim Ademi (Fisher 2006). Ademi "surrendered" and was quickly transferred, but government officials delayed in arresting Gotovina, allowing him time to escape (McLean and Simons 2005). Račan's refusal to transfer Janko Bobetko in 2002, on account of the general's poor health, reinforced Croatia's deteriorating image (Fisher 2006).

Nevertheless, a 2004 Security Council Report noted that "cooperation on the part of the Croatian authorities has improved considerably" from previous administrations (HINA 2004). By February 2005, nine individuals were transferred to The Hague and the government began seriously pursuing Gotovina (Wood 2005). Gotovina was finally arrested in December 2005 by Spanish authorities; extensive cooperation between Croatian intelligence and ICTY field officials attested to the government's newfound willpower (McLean and Simons 2005). At the same time, the Croatian government continued to provide financial support to many arrested individuals, leading the ICTY to characterize its behavior as taking "sides with the accused" (HINA 2006).

Of the 161 indictments issued, only 7 were for Kosovar Albanians. All of those charged have been affiliated with the Kosovo Liberation Army (KLA). Early attempts to investigate Kosovar Albanians were thwarted by the Serbian administration; even in June 1999, when control of Kosovo was already transferred to the United Nations Mission in Kosovo (UNMIK), Serbian officials tried to deny access to the ICTY's Prosecutor (Kerr 2007). UNMIK's control over the region allowed the NATO-led Kosovo Force (KFOR) to arrest two Kosovar Albanians while others surrendered or were arrested by different authorities. To date, Kosovo has created the most inhospitable environment for accused war criminals in the Balkans (though some members of the KLA have served as leaders in the government). Direct cooperation between Kosovar elites and the ICTY has occurred at the highest levels. Ramush Haradinaj, for example, was a former KLA leader who served as prime minister (2004–2005) but stepped down due to his indictment by the ICTY for crimes against humanity. The reopening of war crimes cases by the European Union Rule of Law Mission in Kosovo (EULEX), also suggests some support for transitional justice (Koha Ditore 2008). Closed war crimes files that were sealed due to their potential for destabilization are now being reexamined, with the hope that information about missing persons will finally be revealed.

Approximately 65 % of the indicted war criminals were ethnic Serbs, though only 13 % were Serbian citizens (Orentlicher 2008). Serbia has arrested and handed over four of the highest-profile war criminals—Slobodan Milošević in 2001,

Radovan Karadžić in 2008, Ratko Mladić in May 2011 and Goran Hadžić in June 2011. Although the international community feared that these arrests would generate a violent backlash, they did not and news of Milošević's arrest even ignited "jubilant celebrations in the streets of Belgrade" (UN 2001). After Karadžić's arrest, special forces were deployed and several Karadžić supporters were arrested after attacking reporters in front of the war crimes court (Stojanovich 2008). Mladić's arrest prompted demonstrations but no large-scale violence. Given that these indictments came in 1995 (for Karadžić and Mladić) and 1999 (for Milošević), it is clear the ICTY alone did not produce a change in Serbia's behavior. And these important arrests aside, Serbia's record of holding war criminals accountable is quite poor. As of early 2009, the Serbian government arrested only 12 of its citizens, though dozens of Serbs have surrendered (ICTY n.d., "The Cases").

## *Democratization*

An examination of some of the similarities in democratization can be made through a comparison of Freedom House scores since 1999. As Table 8.1 shows, Balkan states have trended together toward democratic change. Although there are some exceptions and movement is slow, all Balkan states have "transitional" or "hybrid" regimes, meaning that democratic institutions are still fragile throughout the Balkans. Importantly, in Serbia and Croatia, there is greater movement toward becoming semi-consolidated democracies, and Freedom House analyses even highlight these progressive changes within Serbia, starting in 2009, noting its increasing cooperation with the ICTY (Freedom House 2010, p. 426). The in-depth country summaries further demonstrate that political developments cannot be interpreted simplistically and that outcomes, such as the election of nationalist parties, still need to be examined alongside other developments and over a longer time period.

Politics has indeed changed significantly in Bosnia, but democratization has not advanced as quickly as hoped, and illiberal ethnic nationalistic rhetoric remains a problem (McMahon and Western 2009). Bosniaks are "bitterly" divided between those who see the current structure as "a temporary system, hardly worthy of their attention," and moderates who accept that structure and call for an "end to the philosophy of victimhood and self-pity" (International Crisis Group 2009, p. 6). Some contend that the Dayton Peace Accord itself, and the political structure it created, have contributed to the reification of ethnicity and the enduring appeal of ethnic nationalism (Chandler 1999; Bose 2002). The October 2006 elections, deemed the most important since the war's end because of the scheduled departure of the UN's Office of the High Representative (OHR), were fraught with nationalist rhetoric and threats by leaders to split the country apart (Lippman 2006; International Crisis Group 2007; International Crisis Group 2009). In fall 2008, Bosnia's leading political parties reached an agreement that many hoped would pave the way for constitutional reform. Instead, the process fueled yet another political crisis, as Bosnian Serbs debated Montenegrin-style secession and Bosnian Croats

**Table 8.1** Freedom House scores. (Source: Freedom House Nations in Transit Country Reports (n.d.). Note that the ratings are based on a scale of 1–7. A value of 1 indicates the highest level of democratic progress, which embodies "the best policies and practices of liberal democracy" while a value of 7 indicates the lowest level of democratic progress, or consolidated autocracies with widespread rights violations (Freedom House 2012). For further information on each of these measures, see the "Nations in Transit: Methodology" web page (Freedom House 2012).)

| Score Components | 1999–2000 | 2001 | 2002 | 2003 | 2004 | 2005 | 2006 | 2007 | 2008 | 2009 | 2010 |
|---|---|---|---|---|---|---|---|---|---|---|---|
| *Bosnia* | | | | | | | | | | | |
| Civil society | 4.50 | 4.50 | 4.25 | 4.00 | 3.75 | 3.75 | 3.75 | 3.50 | 3.50 | 3.50 | 3.50 |
| Independent media | 5.00 | 4.50 | 4.25 | 4.25 | 4.25 | 4.00 | 4.00 | 4.00 | 4.25 | 4.50 | 4.50 |
| National governance | 6.00 | 6.00 | 5.50 | 5.25 | 5.00 | 4.75 | 4.75 | 4.75 | 5.00 | 5.00 | 5.25 |
| Local governance | 6.00 | 6.00 | 5.50 | 5.25 | 5.00 | 4.75 | 4.75 | 4.75 | 4.75 | 4.75 | 4.75 |
| Corruption perceptions | 6.00 | 5.75 | 5.50 | 5.00 | 4.75 | 4.50 | 4.25 | 4.25 | 4.25 | 4.50 | 4.50 |
| Democracy score | 5.42 | 5.17 | 4.83 | 4.54 | 4.29 | 4.18 | 4.07 | 4.04 | 4.11 | 4.18 | *4.25* |
| *Croatia* | | | | | | | | | | | |
| Civil society | 3.50 | 2.75 | 2.75 | 3.00 | 3.00 | 3.00 | 2.75 | 2.75 | 2.75 | 2.75 | 2.75 |
| Independent media | 5.00 | 3.50 | 3.50 | 3.75 | 3.75 | 3.75 | 3.75 | 4.00 | 3.75 | 4.00 | 4.00 |
| National governance | 4.00 | 3.50 | 3.50 | 3.75 | 3.75 | 3.50 | 3.50 | 3.50 | 3.25 | 3.50 | 3.50 |
| Local governance | 4.00 | 3.50 | 3.50 | 3.75 | 3.75 | 3.75 | 3.75 | 3.75 | 3.75 | 3.75 | 3.75 |
| Corruption perceptions | 5.25 | 4.50 | 4.50 | 4.75 | 4.75 | 4.75 | 4.75 | 4.75 | 4.50 | 4.50 | 4.50 |
| Democracy score | 4.46 | 3.54 | 3.54 | 3.79 | 3.83 | 3.75 | 3.71 | 3.75 | 3.64 | 3.71 | *3.71* |
| *Kosovo* | | | | | | | | | | | |
| Civil society | 5.25 | 4.00 | 3.00 | 2.75 | 4.25 | 4.00 | 4.25 | 4.25 | 4.00 | 4.00 | 3.75 |
| Independent media | 5.75 | 4.50 | 3.50 | 3.25 | 5.50 | 5.50 | 5.50 | 5.50 | 5.50 | 5.50 | 5.50 |
| National governance | 5.50 | 5.25 | 4.25 | 4.25 | 6.00 | 5.75 | 5.75 | 5.75 | 5.50 | 5.25 | 5.50 |
| Local governance | 5.50 | 5.25 | 4.25 | 4.25 | 6.00 | 5.50 | 5.50 | 5.50 | 5.50 | 5.25 | 5.00 |
| Corruption perceptions | 6.25 | 6.25 | 5.25 | 5.00 | 6.00 | 6.00 | 6.00 | 6.00 | 5.75 | 5.75 | 5.75 |
| Democracy score | 5.67 | 5.04 | 4.00 | 3.88 | 5.50 | 5.32 | 5.36 | 5.36 | 5.21 | 5.11 | *5.07* |

**Table 8.1** (continued)

| Score Components | 1999–2000 | 2001 | 2002 | 2003 | 2004 | 2005 | 2006 | 2007 | 2008 | 2009 | 2010 |
|---|---|---|---|---|---|---|---|---|---|---|---|
| *Serbia* | | | | | | | | | | | |
| Civil society | 5.25 | 4.00 | 3.00 | 2.75 | 2.75 | 2.75 | 2.75 | 2.75 | 2.75 | 2.75 | 2.50 |
| Independent media | 5.75 | 4.50 | 3.50 | 3.25 | 3.50 | 3.25 | 3.25 | 3.50 | 3.75 | 3.75 | 4.00 |
| National governance | 5.50 | 5.25 | 4.25 | 4.25 | 4.00 | 4.00 | 4.00 | 3.75 | 4.00 | 4.00 | 3.75 |
| Local governance | 5.50 | 5.25 | 4.25 | 4.25 | 4.00 | 3.75 | 3.75 | 3.75 | 3.75 | 3.75 | 3.50 |
| Corruption perceptions | 6.25 | 6.25 | 5.25 | 5.00 | 5.00 | 5.00 | 4.75 | 4.50 | 4.50 | 4.50 | 4.50 |
| Democracy score | 5.67 | 5.04 | 4.00 | 3.88 | 3.83 | 3.75 | 3.71 | 3.68 | 3.79 | 3.79 | *3.71* |

pushed for territorial autonomy—a demand Bosniaks and Serbs rejected outright. Haris Silajdžić, the Bosniak representative to the country's 3-person presidency, even called for the dissolution of the RS and the restructuring of Bosnia's political structure (Bilefsky 2008b). Meanwhile, Milorad Dodik, the Prime Minister of the RS, has continued to use his power base to increase the authority of the entities. Data from Freedom House confirm both the country's democratic progress and its stagnation, if not backsliding, since 2006. At the time of this writing in early 2012, Bosnian democratization is quite mixed, and it remains a unified but fragile country still burdened by the past and nationalistic appeals.

Croatian democratization has also been slow but has progressed steadily. Until 1999, Franjo Tuđman and the Croatian Democratic Part (HDZ) dominated Croatian politics and "despite paying lip service to joining Western institutions, the Tuđman regime did little to respect international norms" (Peskin and Boduszyński 2003, p. 1124). Tuđman's death in 1999 and the resounding victory of Račan's coalition in 2000 appeared to herald a new democratic era in Croatia; "Tudjmanism—the mixture of authoritarianism, nationalism and socialism—[was] dead with its creator" (Wood 2003; Erlanger 2000, Para. 5). By 2002, Croatia was deemed a pioneer of international justice (Pond 2006). Yet, these positive reports quickly gave way when Račan aligned himself with the nationalist position on the Homeland War and 2 years after the democratic era broke out in Croatia, there were anti-ICTY protests. By 2003, Ivo Sanader became Prime Minister and declared that his primary goals were democratization and membership in NATO and the EU (Pond 2006, p. 134). Sanader's leadership brought liberalization and cooperation with the ICTY and although Croatian politics became more transparent, certain trends deterred significant changes toward transitional justice. Namely, a new political approach was embraced that prioritized "short-term personal gains over longer-term transparent institution building" (Freedom House 2007, p. 6). Even with these setbacks, elections in 2007 were the most transparent, free, and fair in Croatia's history, and different measures, particularly those related to cooperation with the ICTY, improved (Freedom House 2008a). Croatia's progress, and specifically its cooperation with the ICTY, were rewarded in 2011 when Croatia signed a Treaty of Accession with the EU.

In June 1999, UNMIK was established as an interim authority in the territory of Kosovo. Domestic actors slowly became part and parcel of the international network responsible for security and governance, and every administration that has led Kosovo has been both pro-western and pro-liberal (Rezun 2001). Unable to push the international community to resolve Kosovo's status, in 2008 the Assembly proclaimed that Kosovo was "an independent and sovereign state" (Bilefsky 2008a, p. 1). Although Kosovar structures have taken on greater responsibility, NATO and UNMIK continue to handle security and supervision of the country. Despite internal disputes over transitional justice, Kosovo's governments and most of the political parties have adopted a moderate approach toward criminal accountability that underscores cooperation with the ICTY and the need for broader political and judicial changes. Freedom House data confirm that significant political changes are underway in Kosovo, and in almost every category related to democratization Kosovo remains—like the other countries in the region—a hybrid regime.

Serbian politics and democratization can be divided into two periods: the Milošević and post-Milošević eras. Milošević lost power in Serbia in September 2000, though 7 years after the ICTY was established and only after elections that he called. Serbia's so-called democratic revolution had little sustained effect; ridding the country of Milošević was an important step forward, but it was insufficient for liberal change to take hold. Although the short-term impact of Milošević's departure did not result in an immediate liberal shift, signs of progress were apparent from 2000–2003. With the assassination of Serbia's Prime Minister Zoran Đinđić, in the spring of 2003, there was a return of nationalist politics, with the Serbian Radical Party (SRS) winning the greatest number of votes. Yet, the return of the SRS and the Socialist Party of Serbia (SPS) to the political scene was not a total setback for liberal democracy, as both parties adopted pro-European slogans. With the January 2008 presidential elections and parliamentary elections 4 months later, more moderate, pro-European parties were back in power. Freedom House indices, especially in 2009 and 2010, reflect these progressive changes. This, along with the summer 2011 arrests of Mladić and Hadžić by Serb authorities, suggest that although Serbia remains a hybrid regime, it is one that is coming to terms with the past and on the road to democracy.

## *Rule of Law*

Tables 8.2 and 8.3 provide some indication of how the rule of law is changing throughout the region. Freedom House regards judicial developments in Balkan countries quite similarly, as does the World Bank, which reveals that perceptions of rule of law and the courts have improved in all Balkan states since 1998. The following summaries provide details of the positive judicial developments in these countries, as well as some of the challenges.

Significant resources have gone into strengthening rule of law in Bosnia, and a new, if highly complex court structure currently exists, with national, state, and the Brcko District courts (Barria and Roper 2008). This reflects Dayton's institutional structure, but it means the country's judicial system suffers from numerous design problems, with competing legal authorities undermining fair and effective trials (Human Rights Watch 2006; Lowry and McMahon 2010). In July 2002, the State Court of Bosnia and Herzegovina (State Court) was established to create a unified national legal system; however, the State Court becomes involved only "upon request from any of the Entity courts or Brcko courts," leaving a legal vacuum because no court is viewed as superior (Barria and Roper 2008, p. 321). Bosnia's special War Crimes Chamber (WCC) was created within the State Court in 2003 for the specific purpose of handling cases transferred from the ICTY. The underlying philosophy for the court's creation was clear: "accountability for gross violations of human rights… ultimately remains the responsibility of the people of Bosnia"

**Table 8.2** Freedom House judicial independence scores. (Source: Freedom House Nations in Transit Country Reports (n.d.). Note that the ratings are based on a scale of 1–7, with 1 indicating the highest and 7 indicating the lowest level of judicial independence. Judicial independence measures examine "constitutional reform, human rights protections, criminal code reform, judicial independence, the status of ethnic minority rights, guarantees of equality before the law, treatment of suspects and prisoners, and compliance with judicial decisions" (Freedom House 2012).)

| Judicial Independence Scores | 1999–2000 | 2001 | 2002 | 2003 | 2004 | 2005 | 2006 | 2007 | 2008 | 2009 | 2010 |
|---|---|---|---|---|---|---|---|---|---|---|---|
| *Bosnia* | 6.00 | 5.50 | 5.25 | 5.00 | 4.50 | 4.25 | 4.00 | 4.00 | 4.00 | 4.00 | 4.00 |
| *Croatia* | 4.75 | 3.75 | 3.75 | 4.25 | 4.50 | 4.50 | 4.25 | 4.25 | 4.25 | 4.25 | 4.25 |
| *Kosovo* | 5.75 | 5.50 | 4.25 | 4.25 | 6.00 | 5.75 | 5.75 | 5.75 | 5.75 | 5.75 | 5.75 |
| *Serbia* | 5.75 | 5.50 | 4.25 | 4.25 | 4.25 | 4.25 | 4.25 | 4.25 | 4.50 | 4.50 | 4.50 |

**Table 8.3** World Governance Indicators Rule of Law Rankings

| | 1996 | 1998 | 2000 | 2002 | 2003 | 2004 | 2005 | 2006 | 2007 | 2008 | 2009 |
|---|---|---|---|---|---|---|---|---|---|---|---|
| Bosnia | | 32.4 | 32.4 | 27.1 | 23.3 | 33.3 | 34.8 | 39.5 | 40.0 | 42.1 | 43.9 |
| Croatia | 31.9 | 50.5 | 57.1 | 56.7 | 57.1 | 59.5 | 56.7 | 53.3 | 55.2 | 56.5 | 60.4 |
| Kosovo | N/A | N/A | N/A | N/A | 14.8 | 19.0 | 18.6 | 19.5 | 24.8 | 34.0 | 37.3 |
| Serbia | 16.2 | 9.0 | 10.5 | 20.0 | 18.6 | 30.0 | 22.9 | 36.2 | 39.5 | 36.8 | 42.5 |

0th-10th percentile
10th-25th percentile
25th-50th percentile
50th-75th percentile

(Human Rights Watch 2006, p. 2). Although the WCC has faced many challenges, it has received significant support and in-kind assistance from the ICTY. In fact, the planning and creation of this domestic court was the result of a "joint plan of action" by the ICTY and Bosnia's Office of the High Representative (OHR) (Orentlicher 2010, p. 21)

The WCC represents a valuable opportunity to build respect for the rule of law, but there has been little progress in terms of trial completion. Some achievements should not be overlooked, including the promotion of regional cooperation in war crimes cases. In July 2005, the WCC entered into agreements with Croatian, Serbian, and Montenegren authorities to enhance cooperation (Human Rights Watch 2006). The limited mandate and resources of the WCC continue to undermine its effectiveness, and even under the best circumstances, this court can only try a few cases each year (Barria and Roper 2008). Throughout its existence, however, the WCC has worked closely with the ICTY, enjoying ongoing technical support from this international institution as well as others, like the OSCE and the UN (Orentlicher 2010).

With Croatia's establishment of special war crimes chambers in various district courts, rule of law has progressed, if slowly. By 2007, over 800 war crimes trials had been carried out with another 1500 investigations underway (Drumbl 2007). These numbers, however, conceal a disturbing trend: a disproportionate number of those prosecuted are Serbs and ethnic bias remains rampant. The Croatian Supreme Court has consequently had to overturn between 55 and 90% of trial court verdicts (Drumbl 2007). At least some progress has been made with new witness protection laws and the dismissal of numerous unsubstantiated charges against minorities (OSCE 2005). Another report noted that in handling cases that were transferred to local courts, the Croatian courts were displaying "increased responsibility and activity" (OSCE 2007). As in the case of Bosnia, Croatia's domestic courts have benefited from the assistance they have received from the ICTY, as well as other international institutions. Although the ICTY worked with Croatia's State Attorney General to help develop the country's domestic capacity to try cases transferred from The Hague, ICTY officials acknowledged the court's lack of preparedness in this area. As a former ICTY prosecutor explained, "The ICTY was not designed to help institutions;" yet, given the circumstances, the money and resources already spent by the ICTY and the lack of alternatives, providing advice and transferring knowledge became yet another way that the ICTY tried to improve rule of law (Cruvellier and Valinas 2006).

While the general conduct of Croatian courts has been positive, a significant number of witnesses have failed to appear due to threats and intimidation (Freedom House 2008b). However, national courts and the Supreme Court, where ethnic bias is less severe, have made positive gains and are becoming increasingly professionalized, whereas the local court system "still suffers from significant abuse of office and political influence from Zagreb" and has fewer staff (Freedom House 2008b, Para. 69). According to Freedom House analyses, although the situation is improving, problems continue to plague Croatia's judicial system that are unlikely to disappear overnight, including a dearth of resources, excessive trial length, and lack of enforcement of trial decisions (Freedom House 2006, 2008a).

Improving rule of law in Kosovo has been more challenging because Serbian control over this territory included its judicial institutions. With Serbia's retreat, any semblance of a functioning legal system disappeared since most individuals working as judges, attorneys, and staff had been Serbs. In June 1999, the Special Representative to the Secretary General issued an emergency decree, creating the Joint Advisory Council on Provisional Judicial Appointments to fill positions left open after NATO's intervention. The Council subsequently recommended 55 candidates to fill the openings and move forward with court restructuring. Yet, after years of exclusion, many of the Albanians recommended to serve in the courts had lost a decade of professional development and those who ultimately accepted the positions also lacked experience. Since assembling the tangible and intangible necessities to create a judicial system proved to be a massive task, the UN created internationalized hybrid courts (better known as the Regulation 64 Panels), which utilized both foreign and domestic judges (Drumbl 2007). Primary jurisdiction for criminal cases, however, remains with the ICTY. Although these courts are criticized by both local and international advocates, they have proven more successful and impartial than many local courts in the region.

As elsewhere in the region, there have been important legal developments in Serbia. In July 2003, the Law on the Organization and Justification of State Organs in Proceedings against Perpetrators of War Crimes created a special judiciary organ to prosecute war crimes. This law was initially discounted because the members of Serbia's War Crimes Court were selected by the Serbian Assembly; yet by the end of 2005, eight trials were held before this court and all were deemed "professional" (Amnesty International 2005). In April 2007, a surprising ruling by the War Crimes Court convicted four Serbs of war crimes against civilians, and in its first ruling related to Srebrenica, the Belgrade judge said that guilt for these crimes was proven beyond any doubt, suggesting that the country's judiciary might indeed be heading in the right direction (Wood 2007). Although the ICTY did not have a direct hand in creating this Serbian court, interviews in Serbia suggest that it still played an important indirect role. As Orentlicher notes, "Everyone we interviewed in Serbia believes that such a court could not have functioned in Serbia until the political transition following the fall of Milošević—and most believe that the WCC would not exist but for the ICTY" (Orentlicher 2008, pp. 19–20). The Tribunal, thus, was useful in allowing reformist elements within Serbia a political space to begin addressing the past. Even a spokesman for the Serbian War Crimes Prosecutor agrees that the ICTY paved the way for the WCC because there was no will in Serbia to prosecute war crimes alone; the process in The Hague thus pushed Serbs to address the past on their own (Orentlicher 2008)

## *Attitudes Toward Transitional Justice and Peace*

Given the lack of consistent public opinion polls in the Balkans, it is difficult to say with any certainty what patterns exist. However, interviews with interlocutors in Bosnia, Serbia, and Croatia indicate that although many are dissatisfied with many aspects of the ICTY and the progress of transitional justice, the ICTY has been a "much needed tool to keep questioning the official discourse until society, or the authorities, showed more readiness to think critically" (Cruvellier and Valinas 2006, p. 11).

The international community in Bosnia is a concoction of disparate organizations, all of which have made reconciliation and peacebuilding central to their missions. Yet, Bosnian attitudes toward the international community and its goals are mixed. There is considerable support for the EU; in a 2006 poll, 48 % "agreed strongly" that their country should be an EU member; by 2008, 66 % of Bosnians indicated that membership is good thing (Gallup 2008).[7] Among international organizations in 2002, the ICTY was the least trusted, with 51 % of Bosnians in the Federation but only 4 % in the RS indicating that they had trust in the court (IDEA 2002).[8] Interviews with individuals in Bosnia from June 2006 to July 2009, however, suggest that although attitudes toward the court are still heavily shaped by ethnic identity, views are changing, and individuals in all three major ethnic groups (Serbs, Croats, and Muslims) indicated that the ICTY has promoted justice for its own sake, helped communities establish truth, and provided an "inestimably important measure of justice for victims" (Orentlicher 2010, p. 18). A recent Gallup poll reflects some of these positive changes, with almost half of the country (49 %) indicating that there is "certainly not" a chance for armed conflict in the Balkans in the next 5 years, a significant change from 2006 when only 24 % said this (Balkan Monitor 2010).[9] The ICTY alone cannot be credited for producing such optimism about peace in the region, but according to Orentlicher, among the Bosnians she interviewed there was "a nearly universal belief" that however imperfect the performance of the ICTY, when thinking about both justice for individuals and society, it was absolutely necessary to establish the ICTY (2010, p. 36).

Bosnian society also boasts an impressive number of international and national NGOs working throughout the country, although most assessments conclude that Bosnian civil society remains weak and the NGO sector has changed little since

[7] Based on face-to-face interviews with 2000 adults between December 2006 and January 2007. Margin of error estimated at ±2 % points.

[8] The South Eastern Europe (SEE) involved a total of 10,000 face-to-face interviews conducted during January and February 2002 in Serbia, Montenegro, and Kosovo, and also in Bosnia and Herzegovina (with two separate surveys, one for the Federation and one for Republika Srpska), Croatia, Macedonia, Bulgaria, and Romania.

[9] Based upon interviews with 1000 or more individuals in each respective state.

the late 1990s (US Agency for International Development, 2007; McMahon and Western 2009). US government evaluations characterize the non-governmental organization (NGO) sector as between "mid-transition" and "early transition," with NGOs just starting to play a role in policy issues by 2009 (Freedom House 2009). The 2005 creation of RECOM, a coalition of grassroots NGOs that seeks to develop a regional commission devoted to human rights violations, however, is a reminder that the number of organizations is perhaps less important than the focus and strength of these organizations. Three human rights organizations spearheaded the RECOM effort: the Research and Documentation Center in Bosnia-Herzegovina, Dokumenta in Croatia, and the Humanitarian Law Center in Serbia. The organizers of this regional, grassroots effort explain that although they support the formal judicial mechanisms for punishing war criminals, these mechanisms cannot satisfy the victims' need for information and truth-telling, and any efforts to establish a comprehensive understanding of human rights abuses during the wars needs to adopt a regional approach.[10]

Croatian political elites have often adopted a more liberal tone than the masses with respect to the ICTY and transitional justice. In fact, although some Croatian leaders (Račan and Mesić) initially enjoyed substantial public approval, their policies toward the ICTY and justice found considerably less support among the populace. In particular, veterans of the Homeland War, an active civil society organization, became the most vocal opponent of government cooperation with the ICTY. Public opinion in Croatia has become more favorable to both EU and NATO membership, indicating that citizens wish to be less isolated from the rest of the world, but this does not necessarily extend to the ICTY. Eurobarometer polls from 2005, for example, demonstrate that when EU membership was tied to cooperation with the ICTY, public support for joining the former declined (European Commission 2005).

Yet, even those who vigorously criticize the ICTY acknowledged its positive effects on Croatian society. As a member of one political party put it in December 2005, "Even if people say there was too much pressure on Croatia, this constant presence of prosecutions has helped a lot in limiting the myth of the hero. The ICTY has kept the debate open [which] would have probably not happened without [its presence]. Institutionally, we were not strong enough. It was helpful to have [prosecutions take place] outside [Croatia]" (Cruvellier and Valinas 2006, p. 11). This pragmatism toward the ICTY may be shaping attitudes about the future. Croatians are, in fact, quite optimistic that war will not return to the region; 88 % of those polled in 2010 indicated that armed conflict will "certainly not" or "probably not" happen anywhere in the Balkans in the next 5 years (Balkan Monitor 2010). What's more, almost half of the country (47 %) thinks that ties to its neighbors in the region are "not strong enough" (Balkan Monitor 2010).

In terms of activities in society, positive changes are also evident, with the focus of many NGOs shifting from human or minority rights to democratization and transparency, mirroring the priorities of the EU and donor directives. And although

[10] Author interviews in Sarajevo and Brcko, Bosnia and Pristina, Kosovo May 2011. See also the website on the Rekom initiative at: http://www.zarekom.org.

the number of NGOs in Croatia is declining, many are increasingly active and involved in transitional justice with numerous organizations claiming membership in RECOM.[11] A report for the International Center for Transitional Justice highlights the important work of local and international NGOs: "besides the important but limited contributions of the trials of the ICTY and the work of domestic courts, the most visible truth-seeking efforts have been pursued by local and international NGOs" (Cruvellier and Valinas 2006, p. 26).

Turning to Kosovo, public attitudes have in some ways changed quickly; data suggest that 1 year after the war, the level of hatred among Albanians for Serbs dropped precipitously, from 88.7 % in 1999 to 54 % in 2000 (Cardozo et al. 2005).[12] However mistrust between the groups has not declined. The debates over Kosovo's independence widened the chasm between the majority and minority groups; Serbs view Kosovo's independence as destabilizing, whereas Albanians adopt the opposite position (Nyiri and English 2008). This divide is also reflected in attitudes about international intervention and transitional justice. Perceptions of international institutions, including the ICTY, are not surprisingly more positive among Albanians than Serbs—over 50 % of Albanians see the ICTY as fair, in contrast with only 8 % of Kosovar Serbs (Gallup 2007).[13] As in most countries in the region, however, the citizens of Kosovo are becoming more optimistic about the future, with almost half of the Kosovars polled (47 %) indicating that they did not expect armed conflict in the Balkans soon (Balkan Monitor 2010). Kosovar NGO activity remains high and has expanded substantially; in 2000, for example, USAID registered 400 NGOs working within Kosovo, although only 100 were regarded as "active" (2001). Although Kosovo has been receptive to NGOs, it is not clear that they necessarily embody positive or progressive attitudes about transitional justice or peace.

As elsewhere in the region, polls tracking Serbian attitudes toward transitional justice and peace are scarce. The polls that do exist demonstrate both continued ambivalence and growing acceptance of the ICTY's mandate and its place in broader Western efforts to push for change. Only 11 % of the Serbs polled in 2003 completely approved of cooperation with the ICTY, but by January 2006, 16 % felt this way, with 46 % viewing cooperation as a "necessarily evil" (International Republican Institute 2006). Distrust of the ICTY may be a result of ignorance; in fact, in 2003, 64 % of Serbs indicated that they knew "a little" or "very little" about the ICTY (Belgrade Centre for Human Rights 2003). In 2004, 42 % of those polled indicated that they did not know that there were special judicial institutions for war crime trials in Serbia, and 89 % of citizens did not or very rarely followed any war crimes trials (Belgrade Centre for Human Rights 2004).[14] Despite not knowing what the ICTY

[11] See the extensive list on the Rekom initiative at: http://www.zarekom.org.

[12] The authors employed a cross-sectional cluster sample survey. The survey was administered to 1,399 Kosovar Albanians living in 593 randomly selected households.

[13] Results based on face-to-face interviews conducted in February 2007 with randomly selected samples of about 1000 residents aged 15 and older in Kosovo, Serbia, and Albania. Margin of error estimated at ±4 %.

[14] As in 2003, a 3-stage stratified sample was utilized; face-to-face interviews were conducted with 1245 individuals over age 18 in August 2004.

does, Serbs have a clear opinion about this international institution; in December 2009—although half of those polled had no or little knowledge of the ICTY—72% still held mostly or extremely negative views of the court (OSCE 2009).[15] Interviews in Serbia indicate that even though many Serbs do not agree with how the court has behaved, they still believe that Serbian society must acknowledge that atrocities were committed, and that "the ICTY plays a crucial and necessary role in this process" (Orentlicher 2008, p. 40). Moreover, the ICTY has helped educate the public on certain legal processes and what defendants are entitled to when they are brought before a court (Orentlicher 2008, p. 51).

In Serb society, there are also important grassroots organizations that have aligned their organization's mission with those Western actors and the ICTY in particular, hoping to change public attitudes toward transitional justice and addressing the past. After significant growth in the 1990s, the nongovernmental sector stagnated by 2005; yet, according to USAID, the most successful and well-known NGOs are those that are focused on reconciliation and human rights (USAID 2010). Since 2003, Freedom House has given Serbian civil society a rating of 2.75—almost within the range for a consolidated democracy. Several NGOs stand out in their attempt to confront Serbia's nationalist past, including the Humanitarian Law Center (HLC). Without exaggerating the importance of any single organization, it is fair to say that attitudes are shifting and progressive changes are underway in Serb society.

## Conclusion

Although the ICTY was slated to complete its mandate by December 2010, its work continues today. As ICTY prosecutor Serge Brammertz explained, "there is still much left to be done and the progress must be faster" (ICTY 2010, Para. 5). Given that the primary prosecutorial aims of the court have nearly been met, it is important to consider what effect the court has had upon the larger goals of conflict resolution. While this study does not constitute a comprehensive examination of all possible transitional justice outcomes, it does indicate that the secondary goal of restoring and promoting peace is being witnessed at a slow but rather uniform pace across the region. It may be too early to declare that conflict resolution has been obtained, but the movement toward positive results, as reflected in democratization trends, expanded rule of law, and changing attitudes toward justice and peace, is palpable.

In this chapter, our larger argument mimics that of Jelena Subotić and touches upon many of the central themes noted in her work on expanding accountability. As Subotić argues, the current approach to and conceptualization of accountability is inadequate to address the underlying causes of mass violence perpetrated in cases such as that which transpired in the Yugoslav Wars. We similarly view the approach to

[15] This survey was conducted in partnership with the Belgrade Centre on Human Rights. A 3-stage, stratified, representative sampling process was utilized; 1400 face-to-face interviews were conducted with individuals over the age of 16. The sample was expanded for groups of particular interest, including the young (16–23), Albanians, and Bosniaks.

measuring transitional justice outcomes as too limited—the mandates of institutions such as the ICTY envision a greater role for these courts than simple prosecution. If scholars continue to focus solely upon immediate compliance in terms of arrest records or trials, academic research misses the opportunity to see a larger web of interconnected outcomes that emanate from the pursuit of justice and peace. Although international courts (and the states involved) may suffer from a limited approach to accountability or may have failed to deliver the level of progress that they promised, this does not mean that important changes are not taking place or that the significant challenges which arise after violent conflict make justice and well-being impossible.

A secondary but related theme which emerges from Subotić's work is that of engaging in "more substantive, sustained, and deep transitional justice projects" (see Subotić, Chap. 10). Our attempt to do just that has led us to a new research question: to what degree do institutions such as the ICTY contribute directly to outcomes associated with justice and well-being? As we have already acknowledged throughout this analysis, it is impossible to attribute any changes directly to the ICTY alone. However, it is also important to note that international courts themselves foster and develop deep transitional justice projects through their relationships with powerful political actors; in the case of the ICTY, this has come about through alliances with the US, EU, UN, and World Bank among others. Diane Orentlicher has asserted that the ICTY has been crucial to positive developments within Serbia and Croatia (2008). The productive and interpretive power of the ICTY (not to mention its considerable level of expertise) have positioned it to be a unique contributor to the attainment of justice and well-being in the Balkans. In a network of actors working to achieve these outcomes, the ICTY appears to have served as an agent of change through its networked agenda-setting power.

To conclude, this analysis strongly suggests that research on transitional justice, particularly international criminal courts, should consider other, broader outcomes in addition to arrests and prosecutions. As the Balkans and other regions move beyond adjudication, it is this broader criterion that scholars and policymakers alike need to adopt in assessments both of transitional justice mechanisms and the aftermath that follows. With respect to conflict resolution, it appears that any mechanisms that are adopted by international actors will require extensive cooperation with powerful state actors. Networked power, like that employed by the ICTY, will be a necessity to ensure any level of success in terms of accountability, justice, or well-being.

## References

Akhavan, P. (1998). Justice in the Hague, peace in the former Yugoslavia? A commentary on the United Nations war crimes tribunal. *Human Rights Quarterly, 20*(4), 737–816.

Amnesty International. (2005). Amnesty international's concerns on the implementation of the "completion strategy" of the International Criminal Tribunal for the Former Yugoslavia. http://www.amnesty.org/en/library/info/EUR05/001/2005/en. Accessed 15 August 2012.

Balkan Monitor. (2010). Survey data: Next 5 yrs: Armed conflict in the Balkans. http://www.balkan-monitor.eu/index.php/dashboard. Accessed 15 August 2012.

Barria, L., & Roper, S. (2008). Judicial capacity building in Bosnia and Herzegovina: Understanding legal reform beyond the completion strategy of the ICTY. *Human Rights Review, 9*(3), 317–330.

Bass, G. (2000). *Stay the hand of vengeance: The politics of war crimes tribunals*. Princeton: Princeton University Press.

Belgrade Centre for Human Rights. (2003). Attitudes towards the International Criminal Tribunal for the Former Yugoslavia (ICTY). http://english.bgcentar.org.rs/images/stories/Datoteke/attitudes%20towards%20the%20international%20criminal%20tribunal%20for%20the%20former%20yugoslavia%20icty%202003.pdf. Accessed 15 August 2012.

Belgrade Centre for Human Rights. (2004). Attitudes towards the International Criminal Tribunal for the Former Yugoslavia (ICTY). http://english.bgcentar.org.rs/images/stories/Datoteke/attitudes%20towards%20the%20international%20criminal%20tribunal%20for%20the%20former%20yugoslavia%20icty%202004.pdf. Accessed 15 August 2012.

Bilefsky, D. (2008a). Kosovo declares its independence from Serbia. New York Times [online], 18 February. http://www.nytimes.com/2008/02/18/world/europe/18kosovo.html. Accessed 15 August 2012.

Bilefsky, D. (2008b). Fears of new ethnic conflict in Bosnia. New York Times [online], 14 December. http://www.nytimes.com/2008/12/14/world/europe/14bosnia.html. Accessed 15 August 2012.

Bohlander, M. (2003). Last exit Bosnia: Transferring war crimes prosecutions from the international tribunal to domestic courts. *Criminal Law Forum, 14*, 59–99.

Bose, S. (2002). *Bosnia after Dayton: Nationalist partition and international intervention*. New York: Oxford University Press.

Cardozo, B., Kaiser, R., Gotway, C., & Agani, F. (2005). Mental health, social functioning, and feelings of hatred and revenge of Kosovar Albanians one year after the war in Kosovo. *Journal of Traumatic Stress, 16*(4), 351–360.

Chandler, D. (1999). The limits of peace-building: International regulation and civil society development in Bosnia. *International Peacekeeping, 6*(1), 109–125.

Cobban, H. (2006). Think again: International courts. Foreign Policy [online]. http://www.foreignpolicy.com/articles/2006/02/17/think_again_international_courts. Accessed 15 August 2012.

Cruvellier, T., & Valinas, M. (2006). Croatia: Selected Developments in Transitional Justice. *International Center for Transitional Justice Occasional Paper Series*. December 2006. http://wcjp.unicri.it/proceedings/docs/ICTJ_Croatia%20developments%20tr%20justice_2006_eng.PDF.

Dancy, G., Kim, H., & Wiebelhaus-Brahm, E. (2010). The turn to truth: Trends in truth commission experimentation. *Journal of Human Rights, 9*(1), 45–64.

Diehl, P. (2008). *Peace operations*. Cambridge: Polity.

Drumbl, M. (2007). *Atrocity, punishment, and international law*. Cambridge: Cambridge University Press.

Elster, J. (2004). *Closing the books: Transitional justice in historical perspective*. New York: Cambridge University Press.

Erlanger, S. (2000). Croatian victors fret about what awaits them. New York Times [online], 6 January. http://www.nytimes.com/2000/01/06/world/croatian-victors-fret-about-what-awaits-them.html. Accessed 15 August 2012.

European Commission. (2005). Executive summary: Croatia. *Standard Eurobarometer, 63*.

Fisher, S. (2006). *Political change in the post-communist Slovakia and Croatia: From nationalist to Europeanist*. New York: Palgrave MacMillan.

Forsythe, D. (2006). *Human rights in international relations* (2nd edn.). Cambridge: Cambridge University Press.

Forsythe, D. (2011). Human rights and mass atrocities: Revisiting transitional justice. *International Studies Review, 13*(1), 85–95.

Freedom House. (n.d.). http://freedomhouse.org/report-types/nations-transit#.U4bNefldWSo. Accessed 28 May 2014.

Freedom House. (2006). Freedom in the world country report 2006: Croatia. http://www.freedomhouse.org/template.cfm?page=22&year=2006&country=6946.

Freedom House. (2007). Nations in transit 2007: Croatia. http://www.freedomhouse.org/report/nations-transit/2007/croatia#.U4bN_vldWSo. Accessed 28 May 2014.

Freedom House. (2008a). Freedom in the world country report 2008: Croatia. http://www.freedomhouse.org/template.cfm?page=22&year=2008&country=7377.

Freedom House. (2008b). Nations in transit 2008: Croatia. http://freedomhouse.org/report/nations-transit/2008/croatia#.U4bOYPldWSo. Accessed 28 May 2014.

Freedom House. (2009). Bosnia-Herzegovina. http://www.freedomhouse.org/template.cfm?page=22&year=2009&country=7571. Accessed 15 August 2012.

Freedom House. (2010). Nations in transit: Serbia, 2010. http://www.freedomhouse.org/report/nations-transit/2010/serbia. Accessed 15 August 2012.

Freedom House. (2012). Nations in transit: Methodology. http://www.freedomhouse.org/report/nations-transit-2012/methodology. Accessed 15 August 2012.

Gallup. (2007). UN, EU viewed far more positively by Kosovar Albanians than Serbs. http://www.gallup.com/poll/27679/UN-Viewed-Far-More-Positively-Kosovar-Albanians-Than-Serbs.aspx. Accessed 15 August 2012.

Gallup. (2008). Many in Bosnia and Herzegovina support EU membership. http://www.gallup.com/poll/107284/Many-Bosnia-Herzegovina-Support-Membership.aspx. Accessed 15 August 2012.

George, A., & Bennett, A. (2005). *Case studies and theory development in the social sciences*. Cambridge: MIT Press.

Gerring, J. (2007). *Case study research principles and practices*. Cambridge: Cambridge University Press.

Hagan, J. (2003). *Justice in the Balkans: Prosecuting war crimes in the Hague tribunal*. Chicago: University of Chicago Press.

Hampson, F. O. (1996). *Nurturing peace: Why peace settlements succeed or fail*. Washington, DC: USIP Press.

HINA News Agency. (2004). Croatian government has objections to latest Hague indictments-premier. 2 April. Lexis-Nexis Academic.

HINA News Agency. (2006). Hague tribunal rules against referral to Croatia of generals' trials. 12 September. Lexis-Nexis Academic.

Human Rights Watch. (2006). Looking for justice. http://www.hrw.org/en/reports/2006/02/07/looking-justice. Accessed 15 August 2012.

Huyse, L. (1995). On the choices successor elites make in dealing with the past. In N. Kritz (Ed.), *Transitional justice: How emerging democracies reckon with former regimes* (pp. 337–349). Washington, DC: USIP Press.

International Center for Transitional Justice (ICTJ). (2004). Serbia and Montenegro: Selected developments in transitional justice. http://www.ictj.org/sites/default/files/ICTJ-Former-Yugoslavia-Serbia-Developments-2004-English_0.pdf. Accessed 28 May 2014.

International Criminal Tribunal for the Former Yugoslavia (ICTY). (n.d.). The cases. http://www.icty.org/action/cases/4. Accessed 15 August 2012.

International Criminal Tribunal for the Former Yugoslavia (ICTY). (2010). Press releases: Prosecutor Brammertz's address before the UN security council. http://www.icty.org/sid/10560/en. Accessed 15 August 2012.

International Crisis Group. (2007). Ensuring Bosnia's future: A new international engagement strategy. http://www.crisisgroup.org/~/media/Files/europe/%20180_ensuring_bosnias_future.ashx. Accessed 15 August 2012.

International Crisis Group. 2009. Bosnia's incomplete transition: Between Dayton and Europe. http://www.crisisgroup.org/~/media/Files/europe/198_bosnias_incomplete_transition___between_dayton_and_europe.pdf. Accessed 28 May 2014.

International Institute for Democracy and Electoral Assistance (IDEA). 2002. South East Europe public agenda survey. http://www.idea.int/europe_cis/balkans/. Accessed 28 May 2014.

International Republican Institute. 2006. Poll: Serbia January 2006. Available from the authors.

Keating, T., & Knight, W. A. (2006). Building Sustainable Peace. New York: Academic Foundations.

Kelley, J. (2004). International actors on the domestic scene: Membership conditionality and socialization by international institutions. *International Organization, 58*(3), 425–457.

Kerr, R. (2005). The road from Dayton to Brussels? The International Criminal Tribunal for the Former Yugoslavia and the politics of war crimes in Bosnia. *European Security, 14*(3), 319–337.

Kerr, R. (2007). Peace through justice? The International Criminal Tribunal for the Former Yugoslavia. *Southeast European and Black Sea Studies, 7*(3), 373–385.

Kim, H., & Sikkink, K. (2010). Explaining the deterrence effects of human rights prosecutions for transitional countries. *International Studies Quarterly, 54*(4), 939–963.

King, G., Keohane, R., & Verba, S. (1994). *Designing social inquiry: Scientific inference in qualitative research*. Princeton: Princeton University Press.

Koha Ditore. (2008). EULEX to reopen Kosovo war crimes files. 17 October. Lexis-Nexis Academic.

Kritz, N. (Ed.). (1995). *Transitional justice: How emerging democracies reckon with former regimes* (Vol. 1). Washington, DC: USIP Press.

Lamont, C. (2010). *International criminal justice and the politics of the compliance*. Burlington: Ashgate.

Lippman, P. (2006). Srebrenica's search for justice. http://www.opendemocracy.net/conflict-yugoslavia/srebrenica_3851.jsp. Accessed 15 August 2012.

Lowry, R., & McMahon, P. (2010). Home court advantage? Domestic trials and transitional justice in Bosnia-Herzegovina. In L. Barria & S. Roper (Eds.), *The development of the institutions of human rights: A comparative study*. New York: Palgrave McMillan.

Lundy, P., & McGovern, M. (2008). Whose justice? Rethinking transitional justice from the bottom up. *Journal of Law and Society, 35*(2), 265–292.

McLean, R., & Simons, M. (2005). Croatian suspect in war crimes is arrested in Canary Isles. New York Times [online], 9 December. http://www.nytimes.com/2005/12/09/international/europe/09croatia.html. Accessed 15 August 2012.

McMahon, P. (2007). *Taming ethnic hatred: Ethnic cooperation and transnational networks in eastern Europe*. Syracuse: Syracuse University Press.

McMahon, P., & Western J. 2009. The death of Dayton: How to stop Bosnia from falling apart. *Foreign Affairs, 88*(5). http://www.foreignaffairs.com/articles/65352/patrice-c-mcmahon-and-jon-western/the-death-of-dayton. Accessed 15 August 2012.

Mearsheimer, J. (1994/1995). The false promise of international institutions. *International Security, 19*(3), 5–49.

Meernik, J. (2005). Justice and peace? How the international criminal tribunal affects societal peace in Bosnia. *Journal of Peace Research, 42,* 271–289.

Mendeloff, D. (2004). Truth-seeking, truth-telling, and postconflict peacebuilding: Curb the enthusiasm? *International Studies Review, 6*(3), 355–380.

Minow, M. (1998). *Between Vengeance and forgiveness: Facing history after genocide and mass violence*. Boston: Beacon.

Nettelfield, L. (2010). *Courting democracy in Bosnia and Herzegovina: The Hague tribunal's impact in a postwar state*. New York: Cambridge University Press.

Nyiri, Z., & English, C. (2008). Kosovo's declaration of independence carries risk. http://www.gallup.com/poll/104416/kosovos-declaration-independence-carries-risk.aspx. Accessed 15 August 2012.

Olsen, T., Payne, L., & Reiter, A. (2010). *Transitional justice in balance: Comparing processes, weighing efficacy*. Washington, DC: USIP Press.

Orentlicher, D. (1991). Settling accounts: The duty to prosecute human rights violation of a prior regime. *The Yale Law Journal, 100*(8), 2537–2615.

Orentlicher, D. (2008). *Shrinking the space for denial: The impact of the ICTY in Serbia*. New York: Open Society Institute.

Orentlicher, D. (2010). *That someone guilty should be punished*. New York: Open Society Institute.

Organization for Security and Co-operation in Europe Mission in Croatia (OSCE). (2005). Background report: Domestic war crime trials in 2004. www.osce.org/zagreb/14425. Accessed 15 August 2012.

Organization for Security and Co-operation in Europe Mission in Croatia (OSCE). (2007). Background report: Domestic war crimes proceedings 2006. www.osce.org/zagreb/28339. Accessed 15 August 2012.

Organization for Security and Co-operation in Europe Mission in Croatia (OSCE). (2009). Public perception in Serbia of the ICTY and the national courts dealing with war crimes.

http://wcjp.unicri.it/proceedings/docs/OSCESrb_ICTY_Perception_in_Serbia.pdf. Accessed 28 May 2014.

Patrice C. McMahon and Jon Western, "The Death of Dayton" Foreign Affairs September/October 2009

Peskin, V. (2008). *International justice in Rwanda and the Balkans*. Cambridge: Cambridge University Press.

Peskin, V., & Boduszyński, M. (2003). International justice and domestic politics: Post-Tuđman Croatia and the International Criminal Tribunal for the Former Yugoslavia. *Europe-Asia Studies, 55*(7), 1117–1142.

Pond, E. (2006). *Endgame in the Balkans: Regime change, European style*. Washington, DC: Brookings Institution Press.

Rezun, M. (2001). *Europe's nightmare: The struggle for Kosovo*. Westport: Praeger.

Stojanovich, D. (2008). Radovan Karadžić captured in Serbia. Huffington Post [online], 21 July. http://www.huffingtonpost.com/2008/07/21/radovan-karadzic-captured_n_114156.html. Accessed 15 August 2012.

Stromseth, J., Wippman, D., & Brooks, R. (2006). *Can might make right? Building the rule of law after military interventions*. Cambridge: Cambridge University Press.

Subotić, J. (2009). *Hijacked justice: Dealing with the past in the Balkans*. Ithaca: Cornell University Press.

Thoms, O., Ron, J., & Paris, R. (2008). The effects of transitional justice mechanisms: A summary of empirical research findings and implications for analysts and practitioners. Centre for international policy studies working paper.

Tom Keating and W. Andy Knight, Building Sustainable Peace (New York: Academic Foundations 2006).

United Nations. (1993). Security council resolution 827. http://daccess-dds-ny.un.org/doc/UNDOC/GEN/N93/306/28/IMG/N9330628.pdf?OpenElement. Accessed 15 August 2012.

United Nations. (2001). Slobodan Milošević arrested, charged with corruption. UN Wire, 2 April.

United States Agency for International Development (USAID). (2001). 2000 NGO sustainability index for central and eastern Europe and Eurasia. http://pdf.usaid.gov/pdf_docs/pnacn876.pdf. Accessed 15 August 2012.

United States Agency for International Development (USAID). (2007). 2006 NGO sustainability index for central and eastern Europe and Eurasia. http://pdf.usaid.gov/pdf_docs/pnadk556.pdf. Accessed 15 August 2012.

United States Agency for International Development (USAID). (2010). 2009 NGO sustainability index for central and eastern Europe and Eurasia. http://www.icnl.org/research/resources/regional/NGOSICEE2009.pdf. Accessed 28 May 2014.

Vachudova, M. (2005). *Europe undivided: Democracy, leverage, & integration after communism*. Oxford: Oxford University Press.

Van der Merwe, H., Baxter, V., & Chapman A. (Eds.) (2009). *Assessing the impact of transitional justice: Challenges for empirical research*. Washington, DC: USIP Press.

Vinjamuri, L., & Snyder, J. (2004). Advocacy and scholarship in the study of international war crimes tribunals and transitional justice. *Annual Review of Political Science, 7*(1), 345–362.

Wood, N. (2003). Croatian nationalists poised for a comeback in elections. New York Times [online], 23 November. http://www.nytimes.com/2003/11/23/world/croatian-nationalists-poised-for-a-comeback-in-elections.html. Accessed 15 August 2012.

Wood, N. (2005). Europe union upsets Croatia with demands. New York Times [online], 28 February. http://www.nytimes.com/2005/02/28/international/europe/28croatia.html. Accessed 15 August 2012.

Wood, N. (2006). Croat's case offers guide to finding Bosnian Serb fugitives. New York Times [online], 2 January. http://www.nytimes.com/2006/01/02/international/europe/02croatia.html. Accessed 15 August 2012.

Wood, N. (2007). Serbian court convicts 4 in Srebrenica massacre. New York Times [online], 10 April. http://www.nytimes.com/2007/04/10/world/europe/10cnd-serbia.html. Accessed 15 August 2012.

# Chapter 9
# Complexity of Accountability for Mass Atrocity

Jelena Subotić

## The Impact of International Criminal Trials: The Long View

In a wonderful addition to the ever-strengthening field of transitional justice, the chapter by Patrice McMahon and Jennifer Miller (see Chap. 8.) joins the debate by arguing, forcefully, that any evaluation of international transitional justice mechanisms, specifically those implemented by the International Criminal Tribunal for the Former Yugoslavia (ICTY), needs to take a long view. Too many studies, McMahon and Miller argue, were quick to pass judgment on the impact of ICTY trials on the states and societies of the former Yugoslavia. Previous scholars have been either too optimistic or forgiving in their accounts of the ICTY's impact, or were too quick to point to flaws in the design of these international institutions and the continuing, intractable cycle of ethnic mistrust and democratic instability in the region.

In arguing for a long view, McMahon and Miller propose that we look at four specific factors in evaluating the impact of the ICTY in the Balkans: seriousness and independence of criminal prosecutions of war crimes suspects; level of democratization; rule of law; and attitudes toward transitional justice in the former Yugoslav states. If there is improvement along these four dimensions, McMahon and Miller argue, we can begin to trace the positive outcomes of international criminal trials as the seeds of not only justice but also democratic institution building as well as sustainable peace.

---

Some of the material in this paper appeared, in a different form, in my article "Expanding the scope of postconflict justice: Individual, state and societal responsibility for mass atrocity." Journal of Peace Research, *48*(2), 157–169 (2011).

---

J. Subotić (✉)
Department of Political Science, Georgia State University, Atlanta, USA
e-mail: jsubotic@gsu.edu

B. H. Bornstein, R. L. Wiener (eds.), *Justice, Conflict and Wellbeing*,
DOI 10.1007/978-1-4939-0623-9_9, © Springer Science+Business Media New York 2014

In their excellent empirical sections, the authors find quite a bit of evidence that there has been significant, although perhaps not fully satisfactory, improvement along these four dimensions. What is most interesting, perhaps, is the relatively similar degree of progress in otherwise quite different political environments in the four states the paper covers: Bosnia, Croatia, Serbia, and Kosovo. Nonetheless, several questions need to be further explored. First, against what point in time and place are we comparing these states? In other words, there is progress compared to the immediate postwar years, but not as much progress as the countries themselves promised, nor as much progress as international actors, such as the European Union (EU), expected as they continue to deliver carrots of hope for EU membership. Second, what exactly is the role of the EU and EU conditionality (cooperation with the ICTY in exchange for EU membership), and how did EU pressures differ across these different cases? Third, some states have clearly made more progress (e.g., Croatia) than others (e.g., Bosnia). With Croatia's accession to the EU this year, will the difference in Croatia's level of progress be even more manifest, or will the issue of dealing with the past completely disappear from the Croatian political agenda?

Finally, how do we measure the rule of law? While there are clearly positive developments such as the regional cooperation between war crimes prosecutors that the paper mentions, the problems of judicial independence continue to plague the region. Political appointment of judges, the control by political parties of these judicial appointments, and the pervasive corruption of both the judicial sector and the political parties themselves continue to be of great concern. Even the most successful of the four states, Croatia, has to deal with the embarrassment of having a former prime minister, Ivo Sanader—himself instrumental in cooperation with the ICTY—currently on criminal trial for corruption. The rule of law, it seems to me, has a long way to go.

And so while I applaud and appreciate the work done on this issue by McMahon and Miller and others, I want to shift gears somewhat and analyze ways in which we can complicate this story. I want to argue that whatever the impact of international trials may be, the problem with the way we currently conceptualize accountability for mass atrocity is the focus on individual criminal accountability. I will argue that we need to open up that space to include two other levels of accountability or atrocity—state and societal accountability. I believe that only with such a multilayer accountability for atrocity will the path to justice truly begin.

## The Paradox of Accountability for Mass Atrocity

When Radovan Karadzic, the Bosnian Serb wartime leader accused of genocide, crimes against humanity and war crimes by the ICTY, was arrested in Belgrade in July 2008, Human Rights Watch declared the arrest "a step toward redress for Bosnian victims and families who have suffered horribly" (Human Rights Watch 2008). After more than a decade in hiding, the man accused of some of the worst atrocities in Europe since World War II was finally to face justice.

This arrest was also very useful politically. Since Serbia is required by the EU to fully cooperate with the ICTY as condition for its member candidate status, the Serbian government placed the arrest in the context of its European accession plans. Karadzic's arrest demonstrated that the Serbian government had a "very ambitious European agenda," Serbia's foreign minister declared (B92, July 22, 2008). The EU officials also claimed credit, arguing that the arrest was the result of sustained European pressures on Serbia, its clever use of European "soft power" (Smyth 2008).

Karadzic's arrest, however, did little to change the understanding of the past in Serbia. So many years after the end of the war in Bosnia, with so much evidence of Serbian crimes presented in war crimes trials at The Hague, the Serbian public still refused to accept that horrific crimes were committed in their name. A survey conducted right after Karadzic's arrest discovered that a third of the respondents saw Karadzic as a hero, and only 17% as a war criminal; while the vast majority (86%) considered the ICTY biased against the Serbs (B92, July 25, 2008). Furthermore, the Serbian government portrayed this arrest as the event that would finally put an end to international demands for Serbia to address its violent past. "The Hague story must end" (Radio Free Europe, April 13, 2009), said a Serbian government minister.

I argue in this chapter that the main reason postconflict justice often has disappointing domestic outcomes is that the contemporary justice framework that is based fundamentally on individual criminal accountability is poorly suited for collective crimes such as crimes against humanity. It also leads to undesirable consequences, as governments will support individual trials in order to protect the state and society from accountability for them. To remedy this paradox, I propose a post-conflict justice framework that includes individual, state, and societal responsibility for mass atrocity.

After offering a short overview of the contemporary paradigm of individual criminal accountability, I present reasons why we need additional levels of responsibility—state and societal—to deal with legacies of mass violence more completely.

## Contemporary Transitional Justice Framework

The broad field of transitional justice is anchored in the assumption that finding out the truth about past atrocities, identifying the perpetrators, and punishing them appropriately achieves justice by ending impunity (Mendeloff 2004).[1] Human rights trials such as those at The Hague are significant because they serve a retributive function of justice, and can also deter potential human rights abusers from committing atrocities in the future. This increasingly strong expectation at the international

[1] While many of the mechanisms I describe below could more precisely be described as mechanisms of international criminal justice, I use the term "transitional justice" to incorporate a much wider variety of tools for addressing past wrongs. International criminal justice, as has developed over the past few decades, uses primarily the mechanisms of trials (of individuals, and increasingly less often, states). The mechanisms of transitional justice with many non-trial-type instruments offer a broader spectrum of possibilities that I want to explore.

level that postconflict states will legally deal with legacies of past violence has produced a number of separate justice mechanisms. Transitional justice processes have been carried out through international and domestic trials of human rights violators, truth commissions, as well as reparations, lustration, museums or sites of commemoration, apologies, community initiatives, or other unofficial mechanisms (Roht-Arriaza and Mariezcurrena 2006). In fact, so unprecedented has the proliferation of various transitional justice mechanisms been that more than two-thirds of all transitional states in the past 20 years have instituted or debated instituting some mechanism of transitional justice (Sikkink and Walling 2007).

In the case of human rights trials, the individual accountability demanded is criminal and the justice delivered retributive. Some truth commissions and community initiatives understand accountability to be primarily moral (Gutmann and Thompson 2000). Other community efforts, for example the *gacaca* trials in Rwanda, produce yet different kinds of sanctions, such as community service (Daly 2002). In all these different mechanisms, however, the principal focus of the postconflict justice process is the individual accountability of the perpetrator. In fact, such is the dominance of individual approaches to transitional justice that we are possibly witnessing the institutionalization of individual accountability as the primary regulatory mechanism in human rights, with the International Criminal Court as the pinnacle of this dramatic change (Sikkink 2009).

Individual criminal accountability provides for punishment that is effective and enforceable, an improvement over vague sanctions historically placed on the state. For too many years, perpetrators of gross human rights violations, often including heads of state, were shielded by the state or were immune to prosecution under norms of sovereignty (Lutz and Reiger 2009). The focus on individual criminal responsibility has made impunity for mass violence much more difficult to tolerate, and governments have found that their own citizens are asking for more accountability for serious human rights abuses occurring beyond their borders (Lutz and Sikkink 2001).

The pointed focus on individual criminal accountability, however, leads to several paradoxical outcomes. While a significant step toward ending impunity and offering a sense of justice for the victims, governments can use it to protect the state from its own responsibility for crimes. If individuals are convicted of atrocities, this may remove the pressure from states to issue apologies or reparations or other types of redress. While West Germany did pay considerable reparations to Holocaust survivors and state reparations to Israel (Honig 1954), and the Nuremberg trials of individual Nazi officers did not create obstacles for reparations, the historical moment in which these reparations were offered was unique and has not been repeated since. The reparations agreement was signed in 1952, when the memories of the Holocaust were fresh, and the international community was willing to support massive and expensive financial commitments (West Germany in the early 1950s was financially supported through the Marshall Plan, hence Germany's generosity toward Israel was in large part underwritten by American money). Partly as the result of the perceived success of the Nuremberg trials, the individual accountability model has, since the end of World War II, and especially since the 1980s, taken considerable precedence over other justice models, including mechanisms of reparative justice, such as state apologies or state reparations (Lutz and Reiger 2009; Sikkink 2011).

More important for my argument, the focus on individual criminal accountability may remove the urgency of addressing the causes of crimes and the policies that produced them. Governments can point to trials of high-profile perpetrators and argue that justice has been done, and it is time to move on (Cohen 2003). In fact, this is exactly the strategy that the governments of Serbia and Croatia have used in supporting the trials of high ranking officials accused of genocide and crimes against humanity. By supporting individual trials, the governments were able to preempt calls for state responsibility, and even use the trials to put forward the narrative of individual, isolated crimes that are removed from Serbian and Croatian state wartime efforts (Subotić 2009).

The claim that individual criminal accountability is becoming the principal regulation of mass atrocity may, therefore, be premature as well as undesirable from the perspective of postconflict justice goals. In addition to individual prosecutions, states are still filing claims against each other for crimes against humanity in front of international courts. For example, Bosnia recently filed a genocide claim against Serbia in front of the International Court of Justice (ICJ), a lawsuit that created great international attention and significant political consequence in the region (Dimitrijević and Milanović 2008). In 2007, the court found that Bosnian Serb troops, and not the Serbian state had committed genocide in Bosnia. The Serbian state, therefore, was found not guilty of committing genocide, but it was deemed responsible for failing to prevent the genocide from happening since it had direct links with the political and military leadership of the Bosnian Serbs and, presumably, was aware of impending atrocities. The verdict was interpreted in Serbia as vindication, followed by massive financial relief since Serbia would not be responsible for paying any reparations to Bosnian victims. Bosnian survivors and political elites were disappointed, even outraged at the verdict, because they assumed enough incriminating evidence against Serbian leaders had already been recovered at the prior ICTY trials. The issue of financial compensation was further disappointing, because the Bosnian press widely circulated the expected payoff to be in the vicinity of US$ 100 billion (Numanovic 2006). The already tense relations between Bosnia and Serbia have only been exacerbated in the aftermath of the ruling.

In the next section, I discuss both theoretical and normative reasons for why state accountability for mass atrocity should remain part of international regulatory mechanisms in the field of human rights.

## State Accountability for Mass Atrocity

The most obvious reason to keep state accountability as part of the postconflict justice framework is that serious human rights abuses are quite often crimes of the state—not isolated incidents by rank and file soldiers, but efforts so massive in scale that they can only be successfully implemented by an organized state apparatus (Lang 2007). Focusing only on individual perpetrators therefore disconnects the crime from a broader state policy that made the atrocities possible in the first place. The importance of maintaining state accountability for most serious human rights violations is also clear in the many postconflict justice mechanisms states use that require at least a degree of state responsibility: offering state apologies or reparations to victims are principally state actions which implicitly accept the responsibility of the state for past violence.

It is important to differentiate here the state from the regime. I define the state in a Weberian sense, as an entity that claims monopoly on the legitimate use of violence on a given territory. I define regimes in this context as periods of continuous control of the state apparatus by a single political faction or leader. Institutions of the state, therefore, go beyond individual regimes. A political transition, therefore, is not the end of the state; it is the end of the regime. The state continues to function and use its monopoly of force to carry on its policies. If the new regime takes over state instruments of power, it can also use these instruments to deal with past wrongs.

State accountability for mass atrocity is not a novel idea. Thomas Franck argued that "when the state commits a great evil, it cannot be allowed to escape responsibility by the punishment of a few leaders" (Franck 2007, p. 569). Lang claimed that individual accountability for mass atrocity is insufficient as individuals in warfare act as and through institutional structures of the state (Lang 2007). Individuals during war rarely make decisions with complete autonomy from the state and outside a specific political context. Instead, "they act based on a social understanding of war and their particular role in that collective enterprise" (Crawford 2007, p. 190). They act on behalf of the state that has devised the specific policy that led to atrocity. In fact, contemporary research on mass atrocity has provided ample evidence that mass killings, such as those in Nazi Germany, Stalinist Soviet Union, or Maoist China were the direct result of state power and were carried out with limited active support of broader society (Valentino 2004).

The dependence on individual criminal accountability for mass atrocity is, therefore, not sufficient to deal with the complex relationship between the individual and the state during mass violence. Individuals should, of course, be held accountable for crimes they have committed. But so should the states that ordered, organized, and implemented the policies of violence. Accountability for atrocity should be official if it is to matter. Something good should come from a history of violence—official state apology, reparations, or state supported commemorations and sites of memory. These projects will not be produced in trials of individual perpetrators if the state disconnects itself from the policy the perpetrator put in practice.

This, however, is still not enough. Neither the individual perpetrators nor the state act in a vacuum. Even the most totalitarian of states are to some degree products of their social environments and contexts, which allowed for the institutionalization of a totalitarian regime to happen. What is needed, therefore, is another level of accountability for mass crimes carried out by individuals on orders by the state. This is the societal responsibility for atrocity, the third pillar in the current architecture of postconflict justice theory and policy.

## Societal Responsibility for Mass Atrocity

I define society as an enduring social group whose members have developed organized and institutionalized patterns of relationships through interaction with one another, and who act under the structural constraints of the state in which they live. I clearly distinguish the concept of "society" from that of the "nation," which is an imagined community of people who share a belief in common culture, traditions, interests, and purpose. This differentiation is important because my conceptualization of societal responsibility involves responsibility of citizens of offending states on the basis of citizenship and societal membership, and not on the basis of their national identity or other kinds of "deeply rooted" cultural similarities. Citizens of Nazi Germany or 1990s Serbia are responsible for atrocities of their state because they provided a permissive social and political environment for the atrocities to take place, and did not do enough to prevent them. Their responsibility does not come from some inherent national flaw or genocidal intent. This is my primary point of departure from cultural explanations of mass atrocity (for example, Goldhagen 1996).

In order for society to have responsibility, it must have agency. Since the state is the agent or representative of its citizens, members of society can also bear some responsibility for creating, approving, or building a social and political context in which state-led atrocities could have taken place (Parrish 2009). Citizens can also be held responsible for agreeing to and materially supporting—for example, through taxation—state policies that led to mass atrocity. These citizens, even in democracies, have either allowed these policies to move forward, or have failed to stop them. They can be held morally accountable because they failed to distance themselves from such criminal practices. They bear societal responsibility for mass atrocity.

Individual leaders, I argue, should not be the only ones responsible for mass violence since their actions did not appear out of thin air. They created their policies on a societal receptivity to violent claims that were broadly accepted, normalized, and routinized in society and provided criminal policies with a patina of legitimacy. This normalization of violence creates a "complicity cascade"—a social and political environment where carrying out acts of mass violence "becomes a product of conformity and collective action, and not delinquency and individual pathology" (Drumbl 2007, p. 8).

Adding a third dimension of accountability is also significant from the perspective of international law. The selection of a few individuals to be punished for systemic mass violence does not adequately address the problem that victims of mass atrocity are brutalized because of their group belonging (e.g., ethnicity, religion, gender, race), and usually by perpetrators who act on behalf of their groups. This centrality of the individual in international criminal law often in practice means that "the enemy of humankind is punished no differently than a car thief" (Drumbl 2007, p. 5). The centrality of the individual therefore leaves bystanders, people actively or tacitly complicit in atrocities or benefiting materially or socially from atrocity, completely outside the reach of international criminal law (Fletcher 2005).

From the perspective of normative postconflict justice goals, societal responsibility is necessary to fight denial of atrocity in the society of perpetrators. Exclusive focus on individualizing guilt is in direct tension with the goal of countering denial of broad social complicity in mass crimes (Leebaw 2008). In fact, if individualizing guilt is successful, it offers society a way out, an opportunity to project the responsibility to a few select individuals and deny one's own culpability for massive crimes that were committed in one's name. This is how "myths of collective innocence" are created and perpetuated (Fletcher and Weinstein 2002, p. 580).

The inadequacy of individual criminal accountability to fully deal with mass atrocity should by now be clear. While philosophy and political theory have dealt with problems of collective and social responsibility at length and in depth (May and Hoffman 1991; Radzik 2001), contemporary postconflict justice scholarship has been resistant to incorporating these ideas into theory and practice. This is perhaps understandable strategically, as the concepts of collective responsibility have often been incorrectly conflated with collective guilt—a proposition that at times makes liberal internationalists uncomfortable (Branscombe and Doosje 2004). Practically, as well, designing policies to deal with societal responsibility is difficult and very much prone to politicization and backlash. Postconflict justice advocates may therefore fear that by dealing with responsibility of everyone, they may end up with responsibility of no one. While I take these objections seriously, the negative consequences of conceptualizing responsibility for mass atrocity as being solely, or primarily, in the domain of individual criminal accountability, are greater than the complications that will inevitably follow as we design mechanisms to deal with societal responsibility for mass atrocity. The focus on individual accountability is not only inevitably limiting in scope—only a few individuals will ever stand trial—but individualization of accountability will almost certainly be used as an escape hatch for bystanders, conflict architects, and everyday citizens who supported, approved of, and cheered for success of the criminal endeavor.

I therefore argue for a three-tier framework that would address different aspects of mass atrocity, and possible mechanisms of dealing with atrocity legacies.

Individual criminal accountability should be the option of first resort. Direct perpetrators, leaders, and officials who ordered the atrocity, as well as political architects of the criminal policy should be held criminally liable. There are many debates within postconflict justice and international law on how these trials should be designed, where they should be located, and what should be the appropriate punishment of the convicted (Roper and Barria 2006). The precise mechanisms of trials are not of my immediate interest here. I am more concerned with ensuring that as many perpetrators of all ranks—from rank and file to heads of state—are prosecuted in an appropriate and proportional manner.

The second pillar of any postconflict justice policy should be attribution of state responsibility for mass atrocity. For example, victim states can file claims for reparations in front of international courts. A preferred mechanism would be for the state implicated in mass crimes to offer apologies or provide reparations on its own prompting, without the instruments of international law. This may not be that far-fetched to imagine. A willingness to engage state responsibility for past violence can be politically useful for new governments, as they use postconflict justice to demonstrate a clear break with the past.

The third pillar of transitional justice—societal responsibility for mass atrocity—is the most important. It is only through a societal reckoning with the criminal past that the pernicious ideologies that produced the atrocity could be delegitimized. Societal responsibility provides "normative discontinuity with the bad past" (Dimitrijević 2006a). Victims of atrocities should know that the group in whose name atrocity was carried out has come to realize that what was done was wrong and would not be repeated. And it is particularly necessary, indeed imperative, for the perpetrator society to come to an understanding that what was done was wrong, that it was not how a decent society operates, and that politics must change. In the absence of this type of accountability, political ideologies will remain the same and a new cycle of violence can begin.

The truth commission model can be especially useful to this kind of endeavor. This public body would collect evidence from victims, broadly disseminate these testimonies, and put them in a proper political context of the time when atrocities were committed. The commission could systematically articulate why the policies of the past were criminal, and what were possible political alternatives to the choice of engaging in violence. This could be an opportunity to debunk chauvinistic or exclusionary ideologies and replace them with a normative framework of civic engagement and tolerance. What a national commission or a similar institution that would systematically deal with legacies of the past would offer is more than transitional justice. It would offer "transformative justice," where principal social norms, values, beliefs, and understandings are shifted so that society can be just and decent again (Allen 1999).

Finally, postconflict states should implement comprehensive education reform, which includes textbook and curriculum reform that clearly presents evidence of crimes committed, the nature of the conflict, and the political environment that made the atrocities possible and even popular among wide segments of society. They should promote media professionalization, specialization, and education in the field of transitional justice—how to investigate war crimes, how to write about them, how to present evidence, and how to protect the victims. Postconflict states should also create national days of memory for victims of atrocities their own troops have committed, and set up museums or other types of memorial sites to remember victims and survivors. Regardless of the model chosen, systematically addressing societal norms, values, beliefs, and practices should be a priority of any postconflict government.

To conclude, my goal in this chapter was twofold. First, I aimed to analytically distinguish three categories of responsibility for mass atrocity: individual, state, and societal. Second, I argued that the central focus of transitional justice on individualizing responsibility is misguided, inadequate, and counterproductive.

I have advocated a maximalist interpretation of transitional justice, which includes all three types of responsibility and designs proper policy mechanisms to address them. Expanding the scope of transitional justice to seriously include state and societal culpability is important for the victims of atrocity, but it is also essential for the society that produced the perpetrators. It is important for the health of the nation to distinguish right from wrong. It is important for the society to accept that human rights abuses, war crimes, and genocide are wrong. Understanding and acknowledging the difference between appropriate and inappropriate ways to act in politics and manage conflict is necessary for bringing back a lost sense of justice in the society that was complicit in massive human rights abuses (Dimitrijević 2006b).

Transitional justice scholars and policymakers should engage in more substantive, sustained, and deep transitional justice projects beyond merely counting the number of individual indictments and length of convictions and sentences. They should promote comprehensive education and media reform in the field of human rights more generally, and transitional justice specifically. Domestic political leaders can be socialized, persuaded, and rewarded for opening the black box of the past in a way that is politically responsible. New generations of political elites can be educated to understand and appreciate the significance of separating right from wrong for the future of their country.

Finally, political elites—domestic and international—should do all they can to strengthen the political culture of human rights. Whether or not a state cooperates with an international tribunal and conducts domestic trials is not the best indicator of a state's commitment to human rights. Only when stories of the past are wide open—when people can talk about what happened, how, and why—will the path to justice truly begin.

## References

Allen, J. (1999). Balancing justice and social unity: Political theory and the idea of a truth and reconciliation commission. *University of Toronto Law Journal, 49*(3), 315–353.

Branscombe, N. R., & Doosje, B. (2004). *Collective guilt: International perspectives*. Cambridge: Cambridge University Press.

Cohen, D. (2003). *Intended to fail: The trials before the ad hoc human rights court in Jakarta*. New York: International Center for Transitional Justice.

Crawford, N. (2007). Individual and collective moral responsibility for systemic military atrocity. *Journal of Political Philosophy, 15*(2), 187–212.
Daly, E. (2002). Between punitive and reconstructive justice: The Gacaca courts in Rwanda. *New York University Journal of International Law and Politics, 34*(2), 355–396.
Dimitrijević, N. (2006a). Justice beyond blame: Moral justification of (the idea of) a truth commission. *Journal of Conflict Resolution, 50*(3), 368–382.
Dimitrijević, N. (2006b). Moral responsibility for collective crime. *Belgrade Circle Journal* 1–4.
Dimitrijević, V., & Milanović, M. (2008). The strange story of the Bosnian genocide case. *Leiden Journal of International Law, 21*(1), 65–94.
Drumbl, M. A. (2007). *Atrocity, punishment, and international law*. Cambridge: Cambridge University Press.
Fletcher, L. E. (2005). From indifference to engagement: Bystanders and international criminal justice. *Michigan Journal of International Law, 26,* 1013–1095.
Fletcher, L. E., & Weinstein, H. M. (2002). Violence and social repair: Rethinking the contribution of justice to reconciliation. *Human Rights Quarterly, 24,* 573–639.
Franck, T. (2007). Individual criminal liability and collective civil responsibility: Do they reinforce or contradict one another? *Washington University Global Studies Law Review, 6,* 567–573.
Goldhagen, D. J. (1996). *Hitler's willing executioners: Ordinary Germans and the Holocaust*. New York: Alfred A. Knopf.
Gutmann, A., & Thompson, D. (2000). The moral foundations of truth commissions. In R. I. Rotberg & D. Thompson (Eds.), *Truth vs. justice: The morality of truth commissions*. Princeton: Princeton University Press.
Honig, F. (1954). The reparations agreement between Israel and the Federal Republic of Germany. *The American Journal of International Law, 48*(4), 564–578.
Human Rights Watch. (21 July 2008). Bosnia: Karadzic arrest a blow against impunity. http://www.hrw.org/en/news/2008/07/20/bosnia-karadzic-arrest-blow-against-impunity. Access 29 May 2014
Lang, A. F. (2007). Crime and punishment: Holding states accountable. *Ethics and International Affairs, 21*(2), 239–257.
Leebaw, B. A. (2008). The irreconcilable goals of transitional justice. *Human Rights Quarterly, 30*(1), 95–119.
Lutz, E. L., & Reiger, C. (2009). *Prosecuting heads of state*. Cambridge: Cambridge University Press.
Lutz, E. L., & Sikkink, K. (2001). The justice cascade: The evolution and impact of foreign human rights trials in Latin America. *Chicago Journal of International Law, 2*(1), 1–34.
May, L., & Hoffman, S. (1991). *Collective responsibility: Five decades of debate in theoretical and applied ethics*. Savage: Rowman & Littlefield.
Mendeloff, D. (2004). Truth-seeking, truth-telling, and postconflict peacebuilding: Curb the enthusiasm? *International Studies Review, 6*(3), 355–380.
Numanovic, S. (2006). *Pocinje historijski proces protiv agresorske SCG* [The Historic Trial Against Aggressor Serbia-Montenegro Begins]. Sarajevo: Dnevni avaz.
Parrish, J. M. (2009). Collective responsibility and the state. *International Theory, 1*(1), 119–154.
Radzik, L. (2001). Collective responsibility and duties to respond. *Social Theory and Practice, 27*(3), 455–471.
Roht-Arriaza, N., & Mariezcurrena, J. (Eds). (2006). *Transitional justice in the twenty-first century: Beyond truth vs. justice*. Cambridge: Cambridge University Press.
Roper, S. D., & Barria, L. A. (2006). *Designing criminal tribunals: Sovereignty and international concerns in the protection of human rights*. Aldershot: Ashgate.
Sikkink, K. (2009). From state responsibility to individual criminal accountability: A new regulatory model for core human rights violations. In W. Mattli & N. Woods (Eds.), *The politics of global regulation* (pp. 121–150). Princeton: Princeton University Press.

Sikkink, K. (2011). *The justice cascade: How human rights prosecutions are changing world politics*. New York: WW Norton.
Sikkink, K., & Walling, C. B. (2007). *The impact of human rights trials in Latin America. Journal of Peace Research, 44*(4), 427–445.
Smyth, J. (2008). Karadzic's arrest hailed as victory for EU enlargement policy. *Irish Times*.
Subotić, J. (2009). *Hijacked justice: Dealing with the past in the Balkans*. Ithaca: Cornell University Press.
Valentino, B. A. (2004). *Final solutions: Mass killing and genocide in the twentieth century*. Ithaca: Cornell University Press.

# Part V
# Justice Outside of Court: Alternative Dispute Resolution

# Chapter 10
# Advancements in Arbitral Immunity and Judicial Review of Arbitral Awards Create Ethical Loopholes in Arbitration

**Kristen M. Blankley**

## Introduction

A colleague practicing law once asked me: Is it ethical to destroy documents in arbitration? I was surprised by the question. Why *would* it be ethical or just to destroy documents simply because the dispute resolution forum is something other than litigation? Would not the same rationale for preservation of documents apply equally to litigation as arbitration? Similarly, what about the rules regarding truthful testimony? Do those need to be followed in the arbitral forum? What makes arbitration so different that licensed attorneys had questions about whether or not fundamental rules of fairness and justice applied to conflicts in the arbitral forum?

After looking into the issue, I found that the answers to these questions surprised me even more than the questions did. An examination of the criminal statutes and the common law developments over the years shows that arbitration, in some respects, has taken on some characteristics of litigation while other, complementary characteristics have yet to be applied in the arbitral forum. I discovered that the justice expected in the litigation system might not be the same as that afforded in arbitration.

Consider, for example, the issue of absolute, or "judicial," immunity—which is the immunity granted not only to judges but also to all participants in the judicial forum that prevents litigation participants from being sued for defamation and other torts based on the testimony given in court. Applying this concept to arbitration makes wise sense. The policies underlying "judicial" immunity include giving fact-finders needed information for decision-making, encouragement for those seeking redress of wrongs, and personal security for those who would give testimony. These policies apply equally—if not more so—to the arbitral forum.

Thanks to the Program of Excellence for allowing me to present this work at the December 2011 conference. Thanks, also, to Dean Susan Poser, Richard Moberly, Bob Schopp, Brian Bornstein, Charlie Hendrix, and Karlus Cozart for their helpful comments on earlier drafts. Thanks to Mike Douglass for his love and support.

K. M. Blankley (✉)
College of Law, University of Nebraska-Lincoln, Lincoln, NE 68583-0902, USA
e-mail: kblankley2@unl.edu

B. H. Bornstein, R. L. Wiener (eds.), *Justice, Conflict and Wellbeing*,
DOI 10.1007/978-1-4939-0623-9_10, © Springer Science+Business Media New York 2014

Courts, through the common law, have rightly begun to extend this doctrine to the arbitral forum.

Bestowing judicial immunity on the court system, however, has never given litigation participants the right to lie with impunity or otherwise act in an unjust manner. The criminal law serves as an important backstop to punish those who commit wrongdoing within the judicial system and deter people from so doing. In other words, if a person gives false and defamatory testimony during a trial, the victim of the alleged defamatory statement cannot sue the declarant for money damages—but that person could talk with the local prosecutor and try to have perjury or other charges[1] brought against the declarant under the criminal law.

For arbitration, however, these criminal laws do not apply. Presumably, then, arbitration participants (other than attorneys who are bound by certain ethical standards) may be able to lie or destroy evidence without any consequence whatsoever. This disconnect is what I consider to be the "loophole" in arbitration ethics, creating an injustice in the arbitral system. One obvious way to close this loophole would be to extend the criminal laws to the arbitral forum. By extending the criminal law to arbitration, the punitive and deterrent effects of the criminal law would close the loophole created by the bestowing of immunity on the arbitral process.

This loophole, however, is exacerbated by an odd development in the law regarding judicial review of fraudulent conduct within the judicial forum. The Federal Arbitration Act (FAA) contains very limited grounds for judicial review, largely relating to issues outside of the arbitral process. Grounds for review of arbitration awards generally relate to bias, misconduct, or arbitrators acting outside of their scope of authority. For the most part, courts review arbitration awards on a de novo basis to determine if the award fits within one of these limited standards of review. With respect to party misconduct, or "fraud," the courts have instituted an extraordinarily high burden on the party seeking to have the award vacated. This burden is unlike any of the other grounds for review of arbitration awards. Making a uniform burden of proof for vacatur of arbitral awards would alleviate some of this burden and incentivize a fairer arbitral forum.

This chapter explores these issues in greater detail. Part II of this chapter demonstrates how evolutions in the area of arbitral immunity and the difficulties regarding judicial review make the arbitral forum particularly ripe for ethical violations to occur without redress. Part III of this chapter demonstrates that state laws dealing with witness tampering and lying under oath do not currently apply to the arbitral forum, concluding that minor modifications to existing criminal law would make arbitration a fairer and more just forum. Part IV examines the standards of judicial review available for arbitral awards for participant misconduct, compared to other types of judicial review, concluding that the review for fraud should be the same as the review for every other type of arbitral award. By closing these "loopholes," the arbitral forum will help resolve conflict in a more just manner.

[1] Other types of laws, such as obstruction of justice, might also apply.

## The Evolution of Arbitral Immunity Creates an Ethical Loophole

The application of absolute or judicial[2] immunity to the arbitral forum inadvertently creates an ethical loophole for those participating in the arbitral forum. Judicial immunity is a concept that immunizes litigation participants from suits for defamation based on statements made in the litigation.[3] Most often, the concept of judicial immunity applies to bar defamation suits, but the immunity applies to any civil cause of action that "sounds in defamation"[4] such as intentional infliction of emotional distress, unfair competition, conspiracy, and many other types of actions based on harms stemming from words used in official forums, like courtrooms.[5]

Under the defense of absolute immunity, the intention of the speaker and the extent of the harm do not matter. As the California Court of Appeals once noted: "the immunity of a suit for damages at issue is not dependent on the severity of the misconduct."[6] The otherwise defamatory statement could be an oral statement, or

---

[2] This chapter will use the terms "judicial immunity" and "absolute immunity" interchangeably. Different jurisdictions use different names for the immunity. Essentially, the type of immunity is the same. The immunity afforded is to be absolutely free from suit for statements made while in a judicial proceeding.

[3] See, e.g., *Kidd vs. Superior Nursing Care, Inc.*, 2008 WL 2945960, at *2 (D.N.J. 2008) ("A statement made in the course of judicial, administrative, or legislative proceedings is absolutely privileged and wholly immune from liability.") (citation omitted); *Schultea vs. City of Patton Vill.*, 2006 WL 3063457, at *3 (S.D. Tex. October 27, 2006) ("Statements made in the due course of a quasi-judicial proceeding cannot serve as the basis of a civil action for defamation regardless of the negligence or malice with which they were made.") (quotation marks and citation omitted).

[4] *Mahoney & Hagberg vs. Newgard*, 712 N.W.2d 215, 219 (Minn. Ct. App. 2006) ("Even if the claim is not for defamation, if it sounds in defamation, absolute immunity applies. The judicial immunity rule is not to be 'scuttled' by pleadings which allege that the wrongful acts resulted from a conspiracy rather than from defamation") (internal quotation marks and citation omitted). The *Mahoney & Hagberg* court noted that most often, the defense of absolute immunity arises in the context of a defamation claim. *Id.* ("Respondent claims that judicial immunity applies only to defamation claims. Traditionally, judicial immunity has applied to protect participants in the judicial process against claims of defamation. [D]efamatory matter published in the due course of a judicial proceeding is absolutely privileged and will not support a civil action for defamation. In Minnesota, nearly all assertions of judicial immunity involve underlying claims for defamation") (internal quotation marks and citations omitted) (citing *Prosser & Keaton on Torts* § 113, at 816–17 (5th ed. 1984)).

[5] *Asset Mgmt. Sys. Inc. vs. White, Zuckerman, Warsavsky & Luna*, 2002 WL 72925, at *8-9 (Cal. Ct. App. April 20, 2002) (dismissing all of the causes of action on the basis of immunity, including the causes of action for abuse of process and unfair business practice).

[6] *Soliz vs. Williams*, 74 Cal. App. 4th 577, 589 (1999) (involving a claim for defamation against a judge who, in the hallway of the courthouse, told plaintiffs in one of his cases that their settlement demand was "bullshit" and that they had "shit for brains"). The *Soliz* court also noted that immunity is not "overcome by allegations of bad faith or malice." *Id.* at 592. In comparison, if the privilege were only qualified (i.e., not absolute), then the privilege may be defeated by such a showing of malice or even recklessness.

it could be a written communication, such as a brief or a pleading.[7] Whether the speaker intends to commit harm and the amount of resulting harm is immaterial under an immunity inquiry. Provided that the statements fit within the common law immunity exemption, the immunity is, as its name suggests, "absolute."

Keep in mind, however, that not all statements made in a judicial proceeding are *per se* immune. The speaker must have made the statement as part of a judicial proceeding, and it must be pertinent or material to the redress or relief sought for the statements to be covered by an absolute privilege.[8] Off-handed and immaterial comments are not covered by the privilege. Therefore, judicial participants cannot institute lawsuits and use the protection of judicial privilege just to defame others and cause harm.[9] This chapter does not examine the contours of the test for absolute privilege, but it does examine the underlying policies to demonstrate why the privilege has been applied—and should continue to apply—to the arbitral forum.

Several important policies underlie this common law theory. In particular, those policies include the ability for courts to obtain and weigh evidence, the ability for judicial participants to speak in proceedings without fear of redress by the opponent, and as a curb for endless satellite litigation. These next sections discuss those policy reasons.

## *Immunity Encourages Candor and Promotes the Tribunal's Truth-Seeking Function*

Traditional litigation relies on an impartial, public third-party tribunal to decide cases brought before the tribunal. The third-party neutral, i.e., the judge, must render a decision based on the evidence presented. The judge is asked to consider conflicting evidence and testimony in order to determine the truth and the applicable rights and responsibilities among the parties before the court. Presumably, the more evidence the judge can consider, the more likely that the judge will come to the truth of the matter. Stated another way, potential repercussion for those who submit evidence or arguments to a court does not support the court's truth-seeking objectives.

---

[7] *Gallegos vs. Escalon*, 993 S.W.2d 422, 424 (Tex. Ct. App. 1999) ("All communications, oral or written, made in the due course of a judicial proceeding are absolutely privileged.").

[8] *Harmon vs. Bennett*, 103 Wash. App. 1045 (2000) ("Allegedly libelous statements, spoken or written by a party or counsel in the course of a judicial proceeding, are absolutely privileged if they are pertinent or material to the redress or relief sought, whether or not the statements are legally sufficient to obtain that relief.") (citing *McNeal vs. Allen*, 621 P.2d 1285 (Wash. 1980)).
Note that if the statement made is not pertinent or material to the redress or relief sought, then the statement is not covered by the absolute privilege and the speaker may be liable for a cause of action in defamation. See *Post vs. Mendel*, 507 A.2d 351, 356 (Pa. 1986) (holding that a letter sent by an attorney was not privilege because it was not relevant to the redress or relief sought by the client).

[9] Of course, other remedies exist if a person files a frivolous lawsuit, such as sanctions under the federal Civil Rule 11 (or state rule) or common law claims for frivolous conduct.

Absolute immunity serves this truth-seeking function of the courts. Absolute immunity "is intended to protect the integrity of the process itself and to insure that the decision-making body gets the information it needs, whether the speaker deserves the privilege or not."[10] In other words, the common law values the information received and deliberated upon by courts over the right to sue the speaker in civil court for potential wrongs occurring during the judicial process.[11] To serve this end, the absolute immunity applies to both parties and witnesses. Witnesses have even less at stake in litigation than parties and should not be deterred from giving testimony and other evidence in court.[12] In fact, some states recognize a distinct privilege for statements made by witnesses because "witness immunity fosters the truth-finding function within the context of the adversarial process."[13]

Because of the emphasis on the truth-seeking function of the court, the court system prefers to encourage people to give testimony and offer evidence. If people were held civilly liable for damages occurring by the statements or actions of one party or witness in a court case, then the law would have a chilling effect and discourage people from setting forth all of the evidence a court may need in order to do its job of determining the truth and promoting justice. Judicial (or absolute) immunity, then, helps encourage people to put evidence before the court, even if the consequence of the immunity is that some individuals may be harmed—in fact, they may suffer extensive damages—based on something said or presented to the tribunal. This is the trade-off associated with judicial immunity—that a court will have the information it needs, even if some amount of damage may be done to the citizenry at large.

Critics might wonder why the court should encourage and protect the admission of all evidence—including evidence that is blatantly false and spoken with intent to deceive (or at least spoken recklessly). Granting immunity for one action necessarily involves a balancing act and allows some individuals to suffer harm. Here, the policies for immunity—including the court's truth-seeking mission—outweigh the potential for the court's receipt of knowingly false testimony. Without such a grant of immunity, participants may be less likely to present evidence in court or even bring claims—both of which are discussed below. A frightened public does not advance courts' need for receiving evidence, and the courts could not determine the rights of individuals without parties and attorneys bringing evidence before the tribunals. If people are too hesitant to bring evidence, the courts will lose *truthful* evidence from those veracious witnesses otherwise too scared to testify. This need for evidence, then, outweighs the possibility that someone would lie and the result-

---

[10] *Id.* at 424 (citing *Reagan vs. Guardian Life Ins. Co.*, 166 S.W.2d 909 (Tex. 1942)).

[11] *Id.* at 912 ("Stated in another way, where there is an absolute privilege, no action in damages for language, oral or written, will lie; and this is true even though the language is false and uttered or published with express malice.... The falsity of the statement or the malice of the utterer is immaterial, and the rule of nonliability prevails even though the statement was not relevant, pertinent and material to the issues involved in the case.").

[12] *Gallegos*, 933 S.W.2d at 425 (noting that the "administration of justice" is best served if witnesses "are not deterred by fear of lawsuits").

[13] *Blevins vs. Hudson & Keyse, Inc.*, 395 F. Supp. 2d 662, 667 (S.D. Ohio 2004).

ing harm thereof. Undoubtedly, some untruthful testimony will enter into the courts, but this detriment will be outweighed by the additional truthful information that witnesses will divulge when they feel comfortable enough to testify.

Although a wronged party cannot seek civil redress against the speaker of such a defamatory statement, the wronged party still has the option to pursue criminal remedies against the declarant. In other words, although immunity exists, that does not mean that a declarant is *allowed* to lie. In fact, the criminal law serves as an ethical back-stop to ensure that the court hears only truthful (or at least perceived truthful) testimony, submissions, and briefs. This criminal law ensures a just process.

## *Immunity Encourages Wronged Parties to Seek Redress*

As noted just above, judicial privilege encourages parties to bring lawsuits to seek redress for apparent wrongs without the fear of being sued for bringing such action. Whereas the previous justification focused on the court's need for evidence, this justification focuses on parties—particularly plaintiffs.[14] One of the purposes of the absolute privilege is to allow parties to "speak truly…without fear of personal liability or an expensive lawsuit."[15] In other words, the absolute privilege helps

---

[14] This rationale applies equally to defendants filing cross-claims and counterclaims.

[15] Dan B. Dobbs, *The Law of Torts* § 412 (2001); *see also* Paul T. Hayden, *Reconsidering the Litigator's Absolute Privilege to Defame*, 54 Ohio St. L.J. 985, 1027 (1993) ("We should recognize, in other words, that the absolute privilege, much like constitutional protections for speech, provides "breathing room" allowing for speech without fear."); *Harvey vs. Montgomery Cty., Tex.*, 2012 WL 12530, at *6 (S.D. Tex. January 3, 2012) ("Policy interests justifying immunity include the fact that the fear of suit may cause the prosecutor to shade his decisions instead of exercising the independence of judgment required by his public trust."); *Ims vs. Town of Portsmouth*, 32 A.3d 914, 928 (R.I. 2011) ("The doctrine of absolute privilege exists because it is more important that witnesses be free from the fear of civil liability for what they say than that a person who has been defamed by their testimony have a remedy.") (internal quotation marks and citation omitted); *Simms vs. Seaman*, 23 A.3d 1, 13 (Conn. App. Ct. 2011) ("While no civil remedies can guard against lies, the oath and the fear of being charged with perjury are adequate to warrant an absolute privilege for a witness' statements.") (citation omitted); *Viviano vs. CBS, Inc.*, 597 A.2d 543, 549 (N.J. Super. Ct. 1991) ("An absolute privilege for words spoken in the course of a judicial proceeding was thought necessary to promote testimonial candor by shielding witnesses from fear of subsequent civil suits; criminal penalties were deemed sufficient sanctions against perjury."); *In re Raspanti*, 8 So. 3d 526, 533–34 (La. 2009) ("Louisiana jurisprudence has consistently held that communications made in judicial or quasi-judicial proceedings carry an absolute privilege so that witnesses, bound by their oaths to tell the truth, may speak freely without fear of civil suits for damages."); *Hopkins vs. O'Connor*, 925 A.2d 1030, 1042 (Conn. 2007) ("Participants in a judicial process must be able to testify or otherwise take part without being hampered by fear of defamation suits."); *Mahoney & Hagberg*, 712 N.W.2d at 219 ("The absolute immunity of witnesses and parties from claims for damages arising out of their trial testimony is premised on public policy concerns that favor "ascertainment of truth" over self-censorship that may result from witnesses' "fear of subsequent liability.""); *Sinrod vs. Stone*, 2004 WL 60396596, at *2 (N.Y. Sup. Ct. March 30, 2004) ("The public interest in maintaining high standards among members of the bar, and the necessity that persons be given a forum in which to lodge complaints without fear of being sued for libel, warrants that absolute privilege be maintained, even at the risk that some attorneys will

protect freedom of speech and allows parties the freedom to seek redress for wrongs without fear of being sued for the mere act of filing a lawsuit.[16] As noted above, the inquiry involves a careful balancing of interests—here the right to speak freely in the course of judicial proceedings compared to the harm of defaming another person, causing damages.[17]

The litigation privilege protects not only litigation parties but also litigation advocates. As the Ohio Supreme Court held: "While the imposition of an absolute privilege in judicial proceedings may prevent redress of particular scurrilous and defamatory allegations that tend to harm the reputation of the person defamed, a contrary rule, in our view, would unduly stifle attorneys from zealously advancing the interests of their clients in possible violation" of the ethical codes governing attorneys.[18] Advocates also need a wide flexibility to use strategy to determine the best way of attempting to secure justice for individual clients.[19] The fear of repercussion—either in the form of disciplinary action or a defamation lawsuit—by other parties in litigation would have a chilling effect on the practice of law entirely. Rational actors would not enter the practice of law if they would be open to suit in every losing venture, and attorneys would not be able to afford malpractice insurance because of the significant increase of exposure. In these ways, absolute immunity protects not only judicial participants but also those who work to advocate on their behalf.

Thus, the judicial privilege protects all litigation participants to seek redress for wrongs and to defend themselves in litigation activities without fear of facing suit for damages in a defamation action. Without this rule, the losing party in *every*

---

be falsely or maliciously accused of wrongdoing."); *Boyd vs. Bressler*, 18 F. App'x 360, 365 (6th Cir. 2001) ("In determining whether the writings or statements are reasonably related to the matter of inquiry, Ohio courts construe the absolute privilege with great liberality to assure that parties or their attorneys are not deterred from prosecuting an action vigorously for fear of personal liability.").

[16] The First Amendment of the Constitution preserves "the right of the people peaceably to assemble, and to petition the Government for a redress of grievances." US Const. Am. 1.

[17] *Business Defamation and Disparagement, 19 No. 5 Bus. Tort Rep.* 134, 140 (March 2007) ("Judicial proceedings have been held an appropriate setting for application of an absolute privilege. As a matter of public policy, the possible harm caused persons unable to recover for defamatory statements made in connection with judicial proceedings is deemed to be outweighed by the need to encourage parties and other participants in litigation to speak freely in the course of the proceedings. It has thus been held that a statement made in the course of legal proceedings is absolutely privileged if it is at all pertinent to the litigation. The privilege applies to all parties involved *141 in such proceedings, i.e., judges, jurors, counsel, witnesses, and the parties.").

[18] *Surace vs. Wuliger*, 25 Ohio St. 3d 229, 235 (1986).

[19] Monica R. Nuckolls, *Torts*, 54 Wayne L. Rev. 439, 465 (2008) (noting that absolute privilege exists to promote the public policy of securing to attorneys as officers of the court the upmost freedom in their efforts to secure justice for their clients) (citations and quotation marks omitted). Ronald S. Canter & Manuel H. Newburger, *Common Law Immunity for Litigation Activities Under the Fair Debt Collection Practices Act, 61 Consumer Fin. L. Q.* 29, 39 (Spring 2007) (discussing the importance of attorneys exercising "sound legal perspective" as part of their duty as officers of the court and needing immunity from attempting to help clients achieve representation for their colorable legal claims).

*disputed suit*—and that party's attorney—could face a colorable claim of defamation. Winning plaintiffs could sue losing defendants who mounted a vigorous defense or asserted counterclaims on the basis of defamation. Winning defendants could sue plaintiffs for the mere act of bringing their complaints. Sound policy dictates that the courts should be open to redress grievances without fear of repercussion simply for engaging in litigation activity, even if the ultimate result is that some parties suffer serious damages and consequences as a result of wrong and hateful accusations levied.

Stated another way, lawsuits for defamation are too strong of a disincentive for lying—especially at the fringes. If defamation lawsuits were available for every litigant, then no one would want to testify in court. Those witnesses who second-guess their own stories will not want to testify out of fear of losing a large judgment in a post-lawsuit defamation action. The court would, in effect, lose a lot of truthful information by making defamation lawsuits available. Thus, the balance of interests weighs in favor of making perjury solely a criminal law, and not also a civil tort.

## *Immunity Prevents Endless Satellite Litigation*

Building on the above, judicial or absolute immunity also serves the court system by preventing endless satellite litigation. Without the judicial privilege, victors in litigation would have colorable causes of action for defamation against opposing parties, witnesses, experts, and their attorneys. Each lawsuit could lead to another handful of lawsuits, which would have the potential to multiply exponentially even after just a handful of litigated cases.

Courts simply do not have the capacity to deal with such lawsuits. Without a litigation privilege, the courts would be clogged with "a multitude of lawsuits based upon alleged defamatory statements made in other judicial proceedings."[20] The litigation privilege, thus, prevents a "proliferation of lawsuits" stemming from the filing of one, single lawsuit.[21] A system without such a privilege would feel like the next generation of *Bleak House*[22] with generations upon generations of disputants creating new and endless disputes based on a single transaction from decades prior.

[20] *Surace*, 25 Ohio St. 3d at 235.

[21] *Lambert vs. Carneghi*, 158 Cal. App. 4th 1120, 1138 (2008) (quoting *Mattco Forge, Inc. vs. Arthur Young & Co.*, 5 Cal. App. 4th 392, 402 (1992)). The *Lambert* case involved the application of immunity for a party-appointed expert witness in an arbitration. The California court did not extend the absolute privilege to those expert witnesses hired by the party to provide testimony in an arbitration (or litigation, for that matter).

[22] Charles Dickens, *Bleak House* (1852). The Dickens novel involves the lawsuit of *Jarndyce vs. Jarndyce*, a complex probate case dealing with the inheritance of a large estate. The lawsuit, however, drags on over the course of several generations, and ultimately, the legal fees associated with litigating a case for so many years deplete the estate.

The mathematical possibilities for the creation of new lawsuits and the stresses on the current system would be nothing less than mind-numbing.

The court system is intended to be a system that resolves disputes with final judgments.[23] Although many scholars criticize the American system of justice as a lengthy and costly process,[24] the process largely results in finality, even if that finality results, in some cases, only after many years and many appeals. In this way, the absolute privilege serves to "promote finality of judgments by discouraging endless collateral litigation."[25] Without finality, disputes cannot be resolved, and conflict among parties will likely escalate, perhaps causing multigenerational rifts between (or worse among) families.[26]

A system of endless litigation would inevitably lead to inconsistent results. Inconsistent results are bad both for the litigants and for the judicial system. For the litigants, multiple lawsuits could leave parties with inconsistent obligations, offsetting judgments, and confusing standards—all of which could be compounded by the passage of time as endless lawsuits drag on and on. In addition, inconsistent judgments across jurisdictions or within a jurisdiction are harmful for society as a whole. In a common law system that relies upon the principle of *stare decisis,*[27] consistency with past precedent is of the utmost importance. Having a multitude of

---

[23] In fact, at the termination of every lawsuit is a decree known as a "final judgment." See, e.g., Fed. R. Civ. P. 58. As a general matter, only "final judgments" can be appealed. 28 U.S.C. § 1291 (2006).

[24] See, e.g., Jacob Macfarlane, Note, How Many Cooks Does It Take To Spoil A Soup? *San Juan County vs. U.S. and Interventions In R.S. 2477 Land Disputes, 29 J. Land Res. & Environ.* L 227, 244 (2009) ("Over the past few decades, a consensus has emerged that traditional litigation is an inefficient way to resolve disputes. Litigation is costly, drawn-out, adversarial, and fails to produce long-term solutions to problems."); Ossie Ravid & William Hayes Weissman, *Cash Management Activities and the Sales Factor: When is Gross Really Gross and a Receipt Really a Receipt?, 10 St. & Local Tax Law.* 93, 146 (2005) ("Thus, litigation is an inefficient and expensive way to resolve these issues."); Norman I. Silber, *Commercial Litigators Reveal All: Exploring Commercial Litigation in New York State Courts*, 25 Hofstra L. Rev. 235, 246 (1996) ("It is no wonder that litigation looks inefficient and unpredictable to outsiders: the profession's own guidebook describes it this way to insiders.").

[25] *Lambert*, 158 Cal. App. 4th at 1143 (discussing finality).

[26] Scholar John Lande has written extensively on dispute resolution design and how design can de-escalate conflict, compared to the escalation of conflict that often occurs in traditional litigation. See John Lande, *The Revolution in Family Law Dispute Resolution, 24 J. Am. Acad. Mat. Law.* 441, 445 (2012) (noting that many families do not like resorting to the litigation system because litigation has the potential to escalate conflict in the name of dispute resolution); John Lande, *The Movement Toward Early Case Handling in Courts and Private Dispute Resolution*, 24 Ohio St. J. on Disp. Resol. 81, 82 (2008) ("Being in a dispute in an adversarial disputing culture is enough to bring out the brute in many people. Even though many parties and lawyers are not generally nasty, they may act that way in response to their perception of nastiness by the other side. This can lead to a cycle of escalating conflict, which prolongs the agony.").

[27] *Stare decisis* is a system in which judges respect and act consistently with earlier precedents. The term stems from the Latin maxim: "*Stare decisis et non quieta movere*," meaning "to stand by decisions and not disturb the undisturbed."

lawsuits creates increased opportunity for inconsistent results and makes the system unpredictable. An unpredictable legal system imposes increased costs on litigants—particularly relating to the costs associated with the inability of parties and their legal counsel to assess the risks of litigation.[28]

For all of these reasons, the application of judicial immunity to litigation parties makes perfect sense. Judicial immunity rightly extends to litigation parties, witnesses, judges, and attorneys.[29] Judicial immunity serves the court system by preserving the judicial inquiry for the truth and preventing satellite litigation from clogging the courts' already busy dockets. Judicial immunity serves witnesses by allowing them to feel free to testify truthfully without any civil recourse by the parties against whom they are testifying. The doctrine serves attorneys by allowing them to represent clients zealously and without fear of facing civil litigation by opposing parties. And judicial immunity protects parties' abilities to seek redress for civil wrongs without fear and preserves the finality that accompanies a final judgment or settlement.[30]

### *The Policies Underlying Judicial Immunity Apply Equally—If Not More So—to Arbitration*

The policies mentioned above apply equally, if not more so, to arbitration. Arbitrators, like judges, need to seek the truth of situations to best achieve justice. Witnesses and parties benefit from the ability to speak freely. Attorneys can work within the bounds of the ethical guidelines without fear of disciplinary action. All arbitration participants benefit from the prevention of endless satellite litigation—as does the traditional court system.[31]

---

[28] See, e.g., Kathleen R. Guzman, *Intents and Purposes*, 60 U. Kan. L. Rev. 305, 307 (2011) ("Unpredictable outcomes encourage inefficient litigation and impose unnecessary economic and human costs on parties to it.").

[29] As noted supra note 28, the litigation privilege should not extend so far as to apply to a party's own hired attorneys or expert witnesses. Judicial immunity does not serve as a bar to attorney malpractice suits or to suits against the expert witnesses hired by the parties. These situations are markedly different than the situation involving an opponent or neutral who utters words thought to be defamatory.

[30] Of course, under some circumstances, litigants may be liable for sanctions based on litigation conduct. Attorneys who violate Civil Rule 11 can be sanctioned. Statutes exist allowing recovery for the filing of frivolous or vexatious litigation. Thus, the concept of judicial immunity is not absolute, and these are a few of the exceptions to judicial immunity, other than perjury, which is discussed elsewhere in this chapter.

[31] Because arbitration is a creature of contract, only those parties and those disputes governed by the arbitration agreement would actually be subject to the use of the arbitral forum to resolve the dispute. See, e.g., 9 U.S.C. § 2 (2002). Claims of defamation against arbitrators, witnesses, and opposing counsel would likely all fall outside of the contract between the arbitration claimants and respondents (the arbitration equivalent of plaintiffs and defendants). Claims of defamation against

Because these policies benefit the arbitration participants in the same manner as litigation participants discussed above, this chapter does not address these again in the context of arbitration. Instead, this section discusses some reasons why justice in arbitration is served to an even greater degree by the absolute privilege. First, this section discusses how the benefit of finality in the context of alternative dispute resolution serves the participants' interest. Second, this section discusses how the truth-seeking function of the arbitrator may be particularly heightened given the limited discovery available during the arbitration process.

### Absolute Immunity Serves Arbitration Participants' Interest in Finality

Arbitration, and indeed most forms of alternative dispute resolution, seek to give participants a final resolution to their conflict.[32] Some of arbitration's hallmarks include confidentiality,[33] efficiencies in both time and money,[34] informality in

---

an arbitral opponent may or may not fall within the arbitration agreement. If the disputes fall outside of existing arbitration agreements and the parties do not choose to arbitrate the new dispute, these cases will be heard in court. In other words, the proliferation of potential claims would most likely be claims in litigation and not claims in arbitration.

[32] Different forms of alternative dispute resolution (ADR) achieve finality in different ways. Mediation and negotiation seek to end conflict through the use of a binding, contractual settlement. Such a settlement becomes an enforceable contract and ends the litigation process (if the parties had already instituted litigation). Arbitration, by contrast, seeks finality through a streamlined adjudicatory procedure with limited ability to appeal.

[33] Arbitration is a private, i.e., nonpublic, process, but it is not necessarily confidential. See Bert K. Robinson, *Arbitration: The Quest for Confidentiality*, 58 La. B.J. 180, 181 (October/November 2010) ("Absent statute or contract, there is no confidentiality attaching to arbitration.... Feelings of confidentiality are perhaps created by the fact that arbitrations are, by their very nature, private and not public."). Of course, parties interested in confidentiality can simply include a confidentiality provision in their agreement to arbitrate or even to execute a separate confidentiality agreement. Arbitral demands, filings, and hearings are not part of the public record.

[34] Parties can streamline the arbitral process in order to resolve problems with less discovery, less motions, shorter hearings, and less delay than compared to traditional court processes. See *Folkways Music Publ'sh'rs, Inc. v. Weiss*, 989 F.2d 108, 111 (2d Cir. 1993) ("Arbitration awards are subject to very limited review in order to avoid undermining the twin goals of arbitration, namely, settling disputes efficiently and avoiding long and expensive litigation."). The commercial rules for the American Arbitration offer a prime example of the types of procedures often employed in arbitration, specifically the treatment of discovery issues in arbitration. See American Arbitration Association, Commercial Arbitration Rules and Mediation R-21, at http://www.adr.org/sp.asp?id=22440. Because the parties have the freedom to design the arbitral process, parties could always contract for more or less discovery, hearings, motions, etc., if in the best interests of the parties.

procedure,[35] finality in the resulting award,[36] and the possibility for the parties to continue their relationships with each other (working, professional, or otherwise) after the arbitrator resolves the dispute.[37] These benefits flow from arbitration's large independence from the traditional legal system in the USA,[38] which is presumably a reason why parties choose to be in arbitration in the first place.[39]

Parties choose arbitration, at least in part, because of the promise of finality that the process brings. Arbitration brings finality primarily because of the limited scope of judicial review available for arbitration awards.[40] Under the FAA, arbitration awards can only be vacated (i.e., overturned) if the party seeking review can show one of the following limited circumstances:

> (1) where the award was procured by corruption, fraud, or undue means; (2) where there was evident partiality or corruption in the arbitrators, or either of them; (3) where the arbitrators were guilty of misconduct in refusing to postpone the hearing, upon sufficient cause shown, or in refusing to hear evidence pertinent and material to the controversy or any other misbehavior by which the rights of any party have been prejudiced; or (4) where the arbitrators exceeded their powers, or so imperfectly executed them that a mutual, final, and definite award upon the subject matter submitted was not made.[41]

---

[35] Arbitration has flexible and informal procedures compared to traditional, American litigation. Arbitral hearings often occur in conference rooms, not court houses. Hearings occurring over multiple days may not occur consecutively if spreading out the hearing process over time is advantageous to one or more of the parties (or the arbitrator, for that matter). Arbitrators also have greater involvement in the merits' presentation compared to judges, often engaging in questioning of witnesses and asking additional information of attorneys.

[36] As noted above, the ability to review an arbitration award is quite limited. The primary purpose for the limited review is to ensure finality of the arbitration award. Because review is limited, the parties to arbitration have little incentive to challenge an arbitration award, thus ending the process before spending additional time and money in the appeals process.

[37] This benefit of continuing a relationship between the parties will depend on the nature of the relationship of the parties at the onset. If, for example, the parties are a primary contractor and a subcontractor working on a project under a short deadline, then the ability to resolve disputes quickly and get back to a working relationship maybe of the utmost importance. In fact, the construction industry primarily uses arbitration to resolve disputes arising in a project. Construction projects often involve parties that must work together to meet deadlines, and these parties must continue to work with each other even after a dispute arises. If, on the other hand, the parties are a consumer and a national cell-phone company, the ability to return to a lasting relationship may not be important.

[38] This paper is limited to a discussion of arbitrations occurring within the USA. International arbitration involves a whole host of ethics issues not covered here.

[39] Arbitration is a consensual process. If the parties do not agree to be in arbitration, then they do not have to participate. Agreement to arbitrate, however, can take place before a dispute even arises. In fact, most agreements to arbitrate are pre-dispute contracts to arbitrate. These arbitration agreements occur in any number of contexts, including commercial (business) contracts, consumer contracts with businesses for products or services, and employment contracts. For more information regarding arbitration as a consensual process, see Kristen M. Blankley, *Taming the Wild West of Arbitration Ethics*, 60 U. Kan. L. Rev. 925 (2012) (describing the disconnect between arbitration and the court system and the consensual nature of the process).

[40] Arbitration "awards" are the equivalent of a court judgment.

[41] 9 U.S.C. § 10 (a).

Even a cursory examination of the grounds for review demonstrates that Congress intended on not prying into an arbitrator's decision on its merits. These four grounds deal with factors well outside the arbitral process. The first three of these grounds for review consider whether *outside* influences, bias, or misconduct entered into the hearing, thus resulting in an award not worth affirming. The final ground for review examines whether the arbitrator even had the authority to rule in the manner demonstrated by the award.

Not surprisingly, demonstrating that any of these circumstances exist is a difficult task for a party dissatisfied with an arbitration award. Because so few reasons exist for vacating an arbitration award,[42] the rate of vacating arbitration awards hovers in the single digits.[43] The limited grounds for review, coupled with an extremely low reversal rate, demonstrate the finality that arbitration provides participants.

Arbitration awards often do not include a reasoned award, but only a determination of who wins, who loses, and the continuing obligations of the parties (i.e., monetary damages, an order to reinstate, etc.).[44] Unreasoned awards are virtually unreviewable, as the reviewing court has little to consider when determining if the limited circumstances justifying review even apply.[45] This arbitration custom or

---

[42] Interestingly, when examining these grounds for review, none of them concern whether the arbitrator was right or wrong in deciding the case. See R. Wilson Freyermuth, *Foreclosure by Arbitration?*, 37 Pepp. L. Rev. 459, 474 (2010) ("By contrast, an arbitration award is, for the most part, substantively unreviewable."). In fact, arbitration awards will often not be vacated if the arbitrator ruled incorrectly on the law or made a seemly erroneous factual determination. See Yondan Li, *Applying the Doctrine of Unconscionability to Employment Arbitration Agreements, With Emphasis on Class Action/Arbitration Waivers*, 31 Whittier L. Rev. 665, 700 (2010) ("The FAA contains no guidance on the subject of whether or how arbitrators' findings of fact or conclusions of law can be reviewed.").

[43] See Sarah R. Cole, *Let the Grand Experiment Begin: Pyett Authorizes Arbitration of Unionized Employees' Statutory Discrimination Claim*, 14 Lewis & Clark L. Rev. 861, 880 (2010) (noting that the rates of reversal of arbitration awards is actually similar to the reversal rates of lower court decisions on appeal) (citing Christopher R. Drahozal, *Is Arbitration Lawless?*, 40 Loy. L.A. L. Rev. 187, 214 (2006) (conducting study of arbitration awards)); See also Robert B. Hamilton, When An Arbitration Ruling Must Be Overturned: The Commonwealth Court's Proper Application of the "Essence Test" in *Slippery Rock vs. APSCUF, 17 Wid. L. J.* 508 (2008) (noting that a more searching review of arbitration awards could cause a higher rate of reversal, which would make "a contractual arbitration provision almost meaningless" and simply a step to take prior to litigation).

[44] Currently, no research exists regarding the rate of reasoned awards compared to awards simply determining a winning party and obligations owed. See Drahozal, *Is Arbitration Lawless?*, supra, at 212 ("I know of no empirical evidence on the extent to which arbitration awards are reasoned or what proportion of reasoned awards are published").

[45] See, e.g., Edward Brunet & Jennifer J. Johnson, *Substantive Fairness in Securities Arbitration*, 76 U. Cin. L. Rev. 459, 490 (2008) (noting that judicial review can be extraordinarily difficult given the "paucity of reasoned awards"); *Leanne Montgomery, Expanded Judicial Review of Commercial Arb. Awards—Bargaining for the Best of Both Worlds: Lapine Tech. Corp vs. Kyocera Corp.*, 130 F.3d 884 (9th Cir. 1997), 68 U. Cin. L. Rev. 553 (2000) ("Furthermore, there are practical difficulties for a court reviewing an unreasoned or unwritten award which was arrived at through different procedural rules than those employed by the courts."); see also *Univ. Commons-*

norm, then, also encourages the finality of arbitration by leaving the courts with little to review following the issuance of the award.

Because the arbitration system already includes mechanisms to ensure the finality of decisions and efficiency in resolving disputes, the policy of absolute immunity is particularly well suited for this forum. All of these mechanisms for efficiency and finality would be defeated if the parties could simply reopen cases by asserting new defamation actions in court following an arbitration hearing. Thus, providing immunity to the actions in the arbitral forum makes sense and serves these policies.

## Arbitrators Hear Cases Based on a Less-Developed Factual Record Than Judges, Which May Heighten the Truth-Finding Requirements of Arbitrators

Civil trials often occur after the attorneys involved develop a large factual record. Attorneys regularly engage in extensive discovery, especially if the case involves high dollars in damages or important issues to be resolved. The discovery file typically involves deposition transcripts, written interrogatory questions and answers, documents obtained as a result of document requests or subpoenas, and expert witness reports and depositions, among other types of factual and legal development. When attorneys develop such a large file prior to trial, they are armed with information to question witnesses on the stand, demonstrate contradictory statements, and impeach questionably untruthful witnesses. Creating such a discovery file, however, can take years of pretrial time and be extraordinarily costly.[46]

In contrast, the arbitration process is intended to be significantly more streamlined and efficient. One of arbitration's biggest efficiencies (aside from the limited review discussed above) is the ability to scale down significantly the amount of pre-hearing discovery. Failing to take advantage of these cost- and time-saving opportunities "runs counter to the purposes for which arbitration was originally conceived—as a swift and efficient alternative dispute resolution process."[47] Without wasting clients' valuable time and money on discovery and motion practice, cases can be brought before arbitrators swiftly, and the parties can receive an award quickly that likely will not be overturned (or even challenged) in court.

---

*Urbana, Ltd. vs. Universal Constructors Inc.*, 304 F.3d 1331, 1337 (11th Cir. 2002) (stating that when arbitration awards are unreasoned, courts have a nearly impossible task on judicial review).

[46] By and large, discovery is the most costly portion of a civil case. Even the US Supreme Court noted the expense of discovery in the 2007 case *Bell Atl. Corp. vs. Twombly,* 550 U.S. 544, 558 (2007). The Twombly Court heightened the pleading requirements for plaintiffs such that only "plausible" cases can survive a motion to dismiss and move into the realm of discovery practice. Motion practice in civil litigation is also costly and timely. Arbitration largely does not have the same motion practice (if at all) as seen in civil litigation, so the parties in arbitration can save substantial time and money bypassing that stage of the process.

[47] Edna Sussman & Victoria A. Kummer, *Drafting the Arbitration Clause: A Primer on the Opportunities and the Pitfalls, 67-Apr. Disp. Resol. J.* 30, 35 (February–April 2012); See also Judy Rost et al., Cmoparative International Perspective of Arbitration in the Franchising Context, 31-NTR Franchise L.J. 124, 127 (Winter 2012) (noting that discovery can be expensive in US litigation and that the arbitration procedure is intended to cut down on much of that cost).

If little discovery occurs prior to the arbitration hearing, then the arbitrator must be ready to take an active role in the truth-seeking process. When parties testify at an arbitration who have never been deposed, there exists no previous sworn statement against which the neutral can determine if the witness is testifying consistently.[48] Similarly, if document discovery prior to the hearing is not robust, then the arbitrator might need to rely on testimonial evidence to a greater degree than judges in court.

In practice, many arbitrators are aware of their role as truth-seekers in a dispute with limited discovery. Arbitrators are often keenly aware of the discovery schedule and the relatively short amounts of time needed for these cases to reach a hearing. Arbitrators tend to consider all evidence—even evidence that judges would find objectionable—in order to determine the best resolution for the situation.[49] Unlike most judges, arbitrators are active participants in the evidence-gathering process. Arbitrators routinely ask questions of the witnesses and lawyers if the presentation of evidence still leaves the decision-makers with questions.

Given this great truth-seeking function of arbitrators, absolute immunity serves an important purpose in the arbitration process. The protection of absolute privilege should encourage witnesses to speak without fear of reprisal, thus giving the arbitrators greater information upon which to make their rulings. In this way, the search for truth might be even greater in the arbitral forum with a less robust discovery file upon which to double-check the veracity of witnesses and truthfulness in written records. Given the fact that absolute immunity serves to encourage the truth-seeking function of tribunals, this policy is particularly important in the arbitral forum.

## *Recognizing the Benefits of Judicial Immunity to Arbitration, Many Jurisdictions Already Apply Immunity to the Arbitral Forum*

Because the policies surrounding absolute immunity apply equally, if not more so, to the arbitral forum, many courts have rightly begun to apply the privilege to defamation and other tort claims arising out of conduct occurring in the arbitral forum. This section discusses some recent cases applying arbitral immunity to the arbitral context, focusing on the policy reasons for the decisions.

In 2007, the Florida Court of Appeals applied the doctrine of absolute immunity to the actions of an arbitration party in *Kidwell vs. General Motors Corp.*[50] That case

---

[48] Cross-examination in court based on inconsistent statements is one of the most common courtroom techniques. The rules of evidence generally allow the use of previous sworn statements to come in to evidence as showing the witness's inconsistent testimony. Such use of prior statements is simply not considered hearsay. See *Fed. R. Evid. R.* 801 (d 2011) (1).

[49] In fact, if an arbitrator fails to admit certain evidence, under the FAA, an award is subject to vacatur in court. 9 U.S.C. § 10 (a) (2006)

[50] *Kidwell vs. General Motors Corp.*, 975 So. 2d 503, 504 (2007) (Fl. Ct. App. 2007) ("[W]e agree with the trial court that Nichols had immunity for his alleged wrongful actions because they occurred during an arbitration proceeding").

involved a Better Business Bureau (BBB) arbitration concerning alleged damages relating to the purchase of a Chevrolet pickup truck.[51] Following the arbitration, Kidwell instituted a lawsuit against General Motors (GM) claiming that the defendant's employee lied under oath and committed other intentional misconduct preventing him from recovering damages during the arbitration.[52] Here, the court applied the doctrine of judicial immunity because the arbitration forum provided Kidwell with all of the protections that he would have had in court. Specifically, the court held that Kidwell had "the opportunity to testify, present evidence, and cross-examine witnesses," and the ability to appeal the arbitrator's decision to the Florida New Motor Vehicle Arbitrator Board.[53] Because the alleged tortious statements and activity had some relation to the proceeding, GM could successfully invoke the doctrine of absolute immunity.[54] By focusing on the similarities of procedures afforded in the arbitral forum, the court had little difficulty in extending immunity to the arbitral forum.[55]

The *Bushell vs. Caterpillar*[56] employment case from the Illinois Court of Appeals specifically applies the policies underlying the doctrine of immunity in dismissing a post-arbitration defamation lawsuit. The basis for Bushell's lawsuit was testimony at his grievance arbitration hearing accusing Bushell of sleeping on the job and falsifying employment records.[57] The court recognized the competing policies at issue

[51] 9 U.S.C. § 10 (a).

[52] *Id.* Kidwell complained that the GM employee denied him rights under Florida's "Lemon Law," and that the law specifically requires arbitration as a prerequisite for anyone seeking to make a claim in court under that law. See Fla. Stat. § 681.109 (2005).

[53] *Id.* (citing Fla. Stat. § 681.109). The decision also notes that Kidwell failed to so appeal the adverse award. *Id.* Additionally, the Florida Division of Consumer Services and the Department of Agriculture and Consumer Services audits the BBB Auto Line Arbitration Program on a yearly basis. 9 U.S.C. § 10(a).

[54] *Id.* § 505.

[55] The opinion does not state whether an appeal on these same grounds would have been successful.

For other cases involving arbitral immunity, see R., supra. *Mahallati Dental Corp. vs. Adelman*, 2011 WL 2811328, at *8 ("The litigation privilege protects witnesses from tort liability, with the exception of malicious prosecution, for any communication made in judicial or quasi-judicial proceedings by litigants and other participants to achieve the objects of the litigation. Statements made in the course of a private, contractual arbitration proceeding are protected by the litigation privilege") (internal citations omitted); *W. Mass. Blasting Corp. vs. Metro. & Cas. Ins. Co.*, 783 A.2d 389, 403 (R.I. 2001) ("To the extent that these assertions against Western were published in the context of an arbitration proceeding, we agree with those courts holding that such communications are privileged"); *Dunn vs. Ladenburg Thalmann & Co.*, 686 N.Y.S.2d 471, 473 (App. Div. March 1999) ("The challenged arbitration award operates to completely negate the compelling public policy concerns underlying the privilege, i.e., the need to encourage the free and open disclosure of information relevant to potential securities violations."); *Duke vs. Domtar*, 2006 WL 2228830, at *8 (W.D. Ark. August 3 2006) ("To the extent Duke and Maxey allege witnesses' testimony given during their grievance and arbitration proceedings were defamatory, the law is crystal clear that such testimony is absolutely privileged as well"); *Blanchard vs. Lithia Rose-FT, Inc.*, 2004, at 1WL 2331816, *1 (D. Ore. October 15, 2004) ("Such says nothing about confidentiality, but refers to communications in the course of or incident to the qausi-judicial proceeding of the arbitration. Such communications can have an absolute privilege attached to them under Oregon law for claims such as defamation").

[56] *Bushell vs. Caterpillar*, 693 N.E.2d 1286 (1997) (Ill. Ct. App. 1997).

[57] *Id.*

when deciding to apply the absolute immunity. Specifically, the court noted that the ability to testify at an arbitration hearing free from fear "is acting in furtherance of some interest of social importance, which is entitled to protection even at the expense of uncompensated harm to the plaintiff's reputation."[58] In this case, the court described the social interest as the "free and unhindered flow of information."[59] Thus, the defendant could rely on the "absolute immun[ity] from suit for communications made in plaintiff's arbitration hearing."[60] Based on this analysis, the Illinois court relied on the important policies discussed above—particularly the policy regarding witness freedom to testify in a manner without the fear of being sued and the policy of preserving the free flow of information so that the arbiter can make the best decision possible.

The Maryland case of *Odyniec vs. Schneider*[61] also involves a court that specifically applied the policies promoting judicial immunity in deciding a case involving the arbitral forum. The *Odyniec* plaintiffs, and respondent doctors in the underlying arbitration, sued an opposing expert witness for defamation based on statements made during a medical malpractice arbitration.[62] At the arbitration hearing, the expert witness made pre-hearing statements that these doctors made false statements and performed needless surgery with respect to the arbitration claimant.[63] With respect to the application of the privilege, the Maryland court recognized: "Because the need for participants to speak freely during judicial proceedings is so essential to the judicial process, the individual's right to redress for defamation is necessarily curtailed."[64] Similar to the Illinois case, the Maryland court determined that "social

[58] *Id.*

[59] 683 N.E.2d at 1287. The court also relied on the Restatement (Second) of Torts for authority that arbitral proceedings should be covered by absolute privilege. Id. at 1288 (citing Restatement (Second) of Torts, 9 U.S.C. §§ 587, 588). The court found arbitration to constitute a "quasi-judicial" tribunal under Illinois law. Id. at 1288 ("Under Illinois law, a tribunal is quasi-judicial when it possesses powers and duties to (1) exercise judgment and discretion; (2) hear and determine or ascertain facts and decide; (3) make binding orders and judgments; (4) affect the personal or property rights of private persons; (5) examine witnesses, compel the attendance of witnesses, and hear the litigation of issues on a hearing; and (6) enforce decisions or impose penalties") (citing *Adco Servs., Inc. v. Bullard*, 256 Ill. App. 3d 655 (1993)).

[60] *Id.* at 1289.

[61] *Odyniec vs. Schneider*, 588 A.2d 786 (Md. 1991).

[62] Note that this case involved a lawsuit against the opponent's expert witness, unlike the cases discussed above involving a suit against one's own hired witness (or attorney). As noted above, immunity should apply in cases involving opposing witnesses, including experts—but that immunity should not extend to cases involving one's own hired representatives and witnesses.

[63] *Id.* at 787.

[64] *Id.* at 790, 793 ("That Dr. Schneider's defamatory statement may have been gratuitous, unsolicited, and in part irrelevant to the purpose for which he was employed, and was not made during the actual hearing before the arbitration panel, does not defeat the absolute privilege. Whatever Dr. Schneider's motivation may have been, he made his verbal statement to Ms. Ensor, a party in the then-pending arbitration proceeding, while he was conducting a medical examination of her in preparation for his participation in that proceeding. It was thus made in the course of his participation in that pending proceeding and therefore, without regard to its relevance, the verbal statement is accorded the same absolute privilege as if it had been made by a witness during the arbitration hearing itself").

benefit derived from free and candid participation by potential witnesses in the arbitration process is essential to achieve the goal of a fair and just resolution of claims of malpractice against health-care providers."[65] Again, the courts recognize the benefits of immunity applied in the arbitration context. Here, the Maryland court explicitly recognizes the witness' need to speak freely and without fear of recourse, as well as the arbitrator's need to be able to resolve disputes based on being able to consider all of the relevant evidence.

Thus, courts have already begun to recognize that the policies underlying the doctrine of judicial immunity apply equally—if not more so—to the arbitral forum. So far, however, none of these cases recognizes *any* repercussions for bad behavior in arbitration. The next section considers this issue in more detail.

## *Dealing with Bad Behavior in Arbitration in The Midst of Absolute Immunity*

At this point, the law appears clear that no civil cause of action exists for defamation or other torts based on bad behavior occurring in the arbitral forum. What happens, then, when a party, witness, or attorney[66] lies or otherwise wrongs another party or witness in the arbitral forum? Take, for example, the situation involving Floyd Landis, 2006 winner of the Tour de France. Landis, a US cyclist, seemed to have fallen behind the pack in Stage 16, only to make a miraculous comeback in Stage 17 of the Tour and ultimately to win the competition.[67] Thereafter, the International Cycling Union determined that Landis took performance-enhancing drugs during the race, in violation of the rules.[68] Landis denied the allegations and challenged the finding in an arbitration against the US Anti-Doping Agency (USADA) under the World Anti-Doping Code.[69] Landis engaged in a highly public arbitration taking place

[65] *Id.*; see also *Yeung vs. Maric*, 232 P.3d 1281, 1285 (2010) (Ariz. App. Ct. 2010) (extending privilege to a physician witness in an arbitration, and stating: "These principles support a corresponding immunity for witnesses who participate in arbitration proceedings. Arbitrators perform quasi-judicial functions, and arbitration proceedings are quasi-judicial in nature. Witnesses in private, contractual uninsured/underinsured motorist coverage arbitration proceedings should generally be covered by the absolute privilege regarding defamatory statements, assuming the statements are related to the proceeding and basic procedural safeguards… are present in the proceeding").

[66] Questions about arbitrator misconduct are not considered in this chapter. Unlike parties, arbitrators must often abide by a code of ethics. The doctrine of absolute immunity, however, applies equally to arbitrators as to other participants, provided that the arbitrators are acting in their official capacity as arbitrators in the case.

[67] See 2 Maureen Weston, *Anatomy of the First Public International Sports Arbitration and the Future of Public Arbitration After USADA vs. Floyd Landis, in Yearbook on Arbitration and Mediation*, at 234–36 (Vandeplas Publishing 2010).

[68] *Id.* at 235.

[69] *Id.* at 236. At the time, the USADA had never lost a doping case to an athlete. Unlike standard procedure, Landis requested that his hearings be public. *Id.* at 237. The USADA rules specifically

at Pepperdine University, during which he maintained his innocence, claiming he never took any performance-enhancing drugs. Ultimately, the arbitrators ruled 2 – 1 that Landis had, in fact, taken performance-enhancing drugs and should be stripped of his title as Tour de France winner. More than 2 years later, Landis admitted in an interview with ESPN to using banned substances, detailing "extensive, consistent use of the red blood cell booster erythropoietin (commonly known as EPO), testosterone, human growth hormone and frequent blood transfusions, along with female hormones and a one-time experiment with insulin, during the years he rode for the U.S. Postal Service and Switzerland-based Phonak teams."[70] To date, no serious allegations have arisen that Landis committed perjury because he lied under oath in an arbitral—but not litigation—forum.[71]

In traditional litigation, parties can appeal incorrect decisions and they can try to convince prosecutors to institute perjury proceedings. These options, however, are significantly more limited in arbitration. As will be discussed below, the availability of judicial review—already limited in arbitration—is even more limited in the context of claims of fraud occurring in the arbitration proceedings. As for criminal liability, the laws simply do not extend to the arbitral forum. The juxtaposition of arbitral immunity against the backdrop of the limited review and lack of criminal consequences in arbitration creates the possibility of an arbitral ethical loophole.

## A Survey of Criminal Laws Dealing with the Litigation Process Shows That the Criminal Law Does Not Extend to the Arbitral Process

Thus, the criminal law serves as the ethical "check" to prevent litigation participants from committing wrongdoing and injustice in the arbitral forum. The criminal law provides a deterrent for those who might otherwise lie, bribe, or destroy evidence. The criminal law also provides an avenue for prosecuting wrongdoers who cannot be held civilly liable for their misconduct. In other words, without the criminal

allow for such a public procedure. American Arbitration Association, *Supplementary Procedures for the Arbitration of Olympic Sport Doping Disputes Rule*, American Arbitration Association, *Supplementary Procedures for the Arbitration of Olympic Sport Doping Disputes Rule* 12 (May 1, 2009), available at www.ard.org/sp.asp?id=28627 ("The athlete….shall have the sole right to request that the hearing be open to the public subject to such limitations as may be imposed by the arbitrator(s)").

[70] Bonnie D. Ford, "Landis Admits Doping, Accuses Lance," ESPN.com, May 21, 2010, available at http://sports.espon.go.com/oly/cycling/news/story?id=5203604 (last visited June 15, 2011). Even more recently, Lance Armstrong has now publically admitted his extensive use of performance-enhancing drugs during his cycling career, forfeiting all of his Tour de France titles.

[71] Admittedly, because Landis lost his arbitration, his case might not make the best test-case for perjury within the arbitral forum. Whether a person convinces the decision-maker of the false statements, however, should not be part of the calculus in determining whether perjury occurred.

law, absolute immunity would shield the litigation process from repercussion from wrongdoing. What, then about the arbitral forum?

As a general matter, most states have adopted a set of criminal laws based on the chapter of the Model Penal Code (MPC) dealing with "Offenses Against Public Administration" to criminalize offenses occurring before bodies such as courts and legislatures and involving people such as police.[72] Although most of this MPC chapter is inapplicable to the realm of civil litigation,[73] the sections dealing with perjury and tampering could have some easy application to the arbitral forum. This section shows how the perjury and tampering laws currently do not extend to the arbitral forum, creating the arbitral "loophole" noted above.

## *Perjury Laws Generally Only Apply to "Official Proceedings," Which Do Not Include the Arbitral Forum*

Although a lay person might expect that lying at an arbitration is illegal, the criminal laws surrounding lying in proceedings largely do not extend to the arbitral forum. But the laws criminalizing lying should apply to arbitration. After all, "[p]erjury strikes at the very heart of our system. When people lie in court, it undermines the whole process. The problem is so bad that it is severely evaporating confidence people have in the court system."[74] Lying in arbitration would have the exact same outcome, undermining the arbitral process, and evaporating confidence in the arbitration system.

A large number of states follow the MPC definition of "perjury," which occurs when a person who, in any "official proceeding," makes a "false statement under oath or equivalent affirmation, or swears or affirms the truth of a statement previously made, when the statement is material and [the speaker] does not believe it to be true."[75] The Model Penal Code defines "official proceedings" as follows: "[A] proceeding heard or which may be heard before any legislative, judicial, administrative or other governmental agency or official authorized to take evidence under oath, including any referee, hearing examiner, commissioner, no-

[72] See *Model Penal Code Articles* §§ 240, 241, 242, 243 (1962).

[73] For instance, the sections dealing with law enforcement, obstruction of justice, escape, bail jumping, and abuse of office are not applicable to this discussion.

[74] Mark Curriden, *The Lies Have It*, 81 A.B.A. J. 68, 69 (May 1995) (quoting former ABA Section of Litigation chair David Weiner); see also John L. Watts, To Tell The Truth: A Qui Tam Action for Perjury in a Civil Proceeding is Necessary to Protect the Integrity of the Civil Judicial System, 79 Temp. L. Rev. 773, 784 (2006) ("While this reluctance to criminally prosecute perjury in civil cases may be understandable, it is regrettable because perjury undermines the real and perceived legitimacy of the civil judicial system").

[75] Fla. Stat. § 241.1 (1972)(1).

tary or other person taking testimony or deposition in connection with any such proceeding."[76] The terms "arbitration" and "arbitrator" are not found anywhere in this definition.

The following states have adopted the MPC or similar definition: Alabama,[77] Colorado,[78] Connecticut,[79] Florida,[80] Hawaii,[81] Illinois,[82] Kansas,[83] Kentucky,[84] Maine,[85] Missouri,[86] Montana,[87] Nebraska,[88] New Hampshire,[89] New Mexico,[90] North Dakota,[91] Ohio,[92] Pennsylvania,[93] Utah,[94] and Washington.[95] These statutes are ambiguous, at best, as to whether they apply in arbitration. Although arbitration is commonly considered a "proceeding" of sorts, whether it falls within the criminal law is quite unclear. Although some creative lawyers might make arguments that the definition of "official proceedings" applies to the arbitral forum, the law would be much improved by explicitly adding "arbitration" to the list of official proceedings.

---

[76] *Id.* § 240.0 (4).

[77] Ala. Code § 13A-10-100, -101 (2010).

[78] Colo. Rev. Stat. § 18-8-501, -502 (2010).

[79] Conn. Gen. Stat. § 53a-146, -156 (2010).

[80] Fla. Stat. Ann. § 837.02, -0.11 (2010).

[81] Hawaii. Rev. Stat. § 710-1000, -1060 (2010).

[82] 720 I.L.C.S. 5/32-3 (a) (2010).

[83] Kan. Stat. Ann. § 21-5903 (a)(1) (2010).

[84] Ky. Rev. Stat. Ann. § 523.010 (3), -.020 (2010).

[85] 17-A Maine Rev. Stat. Ann. §§ 451 (1), 451 (5) (2010) (defining perjury). Maine also has a civil cause of action for perjury—the only state to have such a statute. 14 Maine Rev. Stat. Ann. § 870 (2010). Whether this statute would apply to arbitration is also questionable.

[86] Mo. Ann. Stat. § 492.040 (West 2010); Mo. Ann. Stat. § 575.010 (2010).

[87] Mont. Code Ann. § 45-7-201 (2010).

[88] Neb. Rev. Stat. § 29-915(1), -916 (2010).

[89] N.H. Rev. Stat. Ann. § 641:1 (I, II) (2010).

[90] N.M. Stat. Ann. § 30-25-1; N.M. Stat. Ann. § 30-1-12 (G) (2010).

[91] N.D. Cent. Code § 12.1-11-01 (2010) (defining perjury).

[92] Ohio Rev. Code Ann. § 2921.01(D), -.11(A) (2010).

[93] 18 Pa. Stat. Ann. § 4902 (West 2010).

[94] Utah Code Ann. § 76-8-501(1), -502 (2010).

[95] *Id.* §§ 9A.72.010 (4)-.020 (2010). The Washington perjury laws, like some other state laws, require that the oath taken be an oath mandated by law. Wash. Rev. Code Ann. § 9A.72.010 (3) (defining "oath"). Because arbitration does not involve a statutory mandate to give testimony under oath, these perjury statutes would not apply to arbitration.

Another handful of states prohibit lying under oath more generally. These states include: Alaska,[96] Arizona,[97] Arkansas,[98] California,[99] Delaware,[100] District of Columbia,[101]

[96] *Id.* § 11.56.200 (2010) ("A person commits the crime of perjury if the person makes a false sworn statement which the person does not believe to be true"); Alaska Stat. § 11.56.240 (2010) ("defining "sworn statement" as statement knowingly given under oath or affirmation attesting to the trust of what is stated, including a notarized statement"). These statues apply to arbitration proceedings. *Gilbert vs. Sperbeck*, 126 P.3d 1057, 1060 (Alaska 2005) (assuming, without deciding, that perjury rules apply to arbitration proceedings).

[97] 683 N.E.2d at 1287. The court also relied on the Restatement (Second) of Torts for authority that arbitral proceedings should be covered by absolute privilege. *Id.* at 1288 (citing Restatement (Second) of Torts), 9 U.S.C. §§ 13-2702 ("A person commits perjury by making either: 1. A false sworn statement in regard to a material issue, believing it to be false"); Ariz. Rev. Stat. § 13-2701 (LexisNexis 2010) (defining "sworn statement" as "any statement knowingly given under oath or affirmation attesting to the truth of what is stated"). Arizona courts, similarly, applied perjury laws to attorney fee arbitrations. *State vs. Self*, 135 Ariz. 374 (Ct. App. 1983) (holding that the "sworn statement" language in the perjury statute facially applies to arbitration, and finding that an arbitration hearing before the State Bar Committee constituted an "official proceeding" for the tampering charges).

[98] Ark. Code Ann. § 16-2-103 (2010) ("In all cases in which an oath is required or authorized by law, it may be taken in any of the forms prescribed in this chapter. Every person swearing, affirming, or declaring in any such form, or any form authorized by law, shall be deemed to have been lawfully sworn and to be guilty of perjury for corruptly and falsely swearing, affirming, or declaring, in the same manner as if he or she had sworn by laying his or her hand on the Gospels and kissing them")

[99] Cal. Penal Code § 118 (Deering 2010) ("Every person who, having taken an oath that he or she will testify, declare, depose, or certify truly before any competent tribunal, officer, or person, in any of the cases in which the oath may by law of the State of California be administered, willfully and contrary to the oath, states as true any material matter which he or she knows to be false, and every person who testifies, declares, deposes, or certifies under penalty of perjury in any of the cases in which the testimony, declarations, depositions, or certification is permitted by law of the State of California under penalty of perjury and willfully states as true any material matter which he or she knows to be false, is guilty of perjury").

[100] Del. Stat. Tit. 11, 9 U.S.C. § 1221 (2010) ("A person is guilty of perjury in the first degree when the person swears falsely and when the false statement consists of testimony and is material to the action, proceeding or matter in which it is made"). Delaware, however, defines "testimony" as "oral statement made under oath in a proceeding before any court, body, agency, public servant or other person authorized to conduct the proceeding and to administer the oath or cause it to be administered." *Id.* (2010).

[101] D.C. Code § 22-2402(a) (2010) (A person commits the offense of perjury if: ("(1) Having taken an oath or affirmation before a competent tribunal, officer, or person, in a case in which the law authorized such oath or affirmation to be administered, that he or she will testify, declare, depose, or certify truly, or that any written testimony, declaration, deposition, or certificate by that person subscribed is true, wilfully and contrary to an oath or affirmation states or subscribes any material matter which he or she does not believe to be true and which in fact is not true").

Idaho,[102] Indiana,[103] Iowa,[104] Maryland,[105] Michigan,[106] Minnesota,[107] Mississippi,[108] New York,[109] Oklahoma,[110] Oregon,[111]

---

[102] Idaho Code Ann. § 18-5401 (2010) ("Every person who, having taken an oath that he will testify, declare, depose, or certify truly, before any competent tribunal, legislative committee, officer, or person in any of the cases in which such an oath may by law be administered, willfully and contrary to such oath, states as true any material matter which he knows to be false, is guilty of perjury").

[103] Ind. Code § 35-44-2-1 (a)(1) (2010) ("A person who makes a false, material statement under oath or affirmation, knowing the statement to be false or not believing it to be true").

[104] Iowa Code Ann. § 720.2 (West 2010) ("A person who, while under oath or affirmation in any proceeding or other matter in which statements under oath or affirmation are required or authorized by law, knowingly makes a false statement of material facts or who falsely denies knowledge of material facts, commits a class "D" felony"). This statute applies to workman's compensation arbitrations. Continental Fire Sprinkler Co. vs. Hoolandt, *2002 WL 700977, at *2* (Iowa App. Ct. 2002).

[105] Md. Crim. Code, 9 U.S.C. §§ 9-101(a) ("A person may not willfully and falsely make an oath or affirmation as to a material fact: (1) if the false swearing is perjury at common law").

[106] Mich. Comp. Law Ann. § 750.423 (West 2010) ("Any person authorized by any statute of this state to take an oath, or any person of whom an oath shall be required by law, who shall wilfully swear falsely, in regard to any matter or thing, respecting which such oath is authorized or required, shall be guilty of perjury, a felony").

[107] Minn. Stat. Ann. § 609.48 (1) (West 2010) ("Whoever makes a false material statement not believing it to be true in any of the following cases is guilty of perjury and may be sentenced as provided in subdivision 4: (1) in or for an action, hearing or proceeding of any kind in which the statement is required or authorized by law to be made under oath or affirmation")

[108] Miss. Code Ann. § 97-9-59 (2010) ("Every person who shall willfully and corruptly swear, testify, or affirm falsely to any material matter under any oath, affirmation, or declaration legally administered in any matter, cause, or proceeding pending in any court of law or equity, or before any officer thereof, or in any case where an oath or affirmation is required by law or is necessary for the prosecution or defense of any private right or for the ends of public justice, or in any matter or proceeding before any tribunal or officer created by the Constitution or by law, or where any oath may be lawfully required by any judicial, executive, or administrative officer, shall be guilty of perjury, and shall not thereafter be received as a witness to be sworn in any matter or cause whatever, until the judgment against him be reversed").

[109] N.Y. Penal Code § 210.15 (2010) ("A person is guilty of perjury in the first degree when he swears falsely and when his false statement (a) consists of testimony, and (b) is material to the action, proceeding or matter in which it is made"). This statute applies to National Association of Securities Dealers (NASD) arbitrations. *People vs. Cohen*, 773 N.Y.S.2d 371, 385 (App. Div. 2004) (affirming perjury conviction).

[110] 21 Okla. St. Ann. § 491 (2010) ("Whoever, in a trial, hearing, investigation, deposition, certification or declaration, in which the making or subscribing of a statement is required or authorized by law, makes or subscribes a statement under oath, affirmation or other legally binding assertion that the statement is true, when in fact the witness or declarant does not believe that the statement is true or knows that it is not true or intends thereby to avoid or obstruct the ascertainment of the truth, is guilty of perjury. It shall be a defense to the charge of perjury as defined in this section that the statement is true").

[111] Ore. Rev. Stat. § 162. 065 (1) (2010) ("Whoever, in a trial, hearing, investigation, deposition, certification or declaration, in which the making or subscribing of a statement is required or authorized by law, makes or subscribes a statement under oath, affirmation or other legally binding assertion that the statement is true, when in fact the witness or declarant does not believe that the statement is true or knows that it is not true or intends thereby to avoid or obstruct the ascertainment of the truth, is guilty of perjury. It shall be a defense to the charge of perjury as defined in this section that the statement is true").

Rhode Island,[112] South Carolina,[113] South Dakota,[114] Tennessee,[115] Texas,[116] and Virginia.[117] These varying definitions of criminal lying under oath appear to have broader applicability to the arbitral forum.[118] A clearer, more explicit definition, however, would leave no question as to the laws' applicability to the arbitral forum.

A small minority of states have perjury laws specifically referencing arbitration. In Wisconsin, a person commits perjury by making a false material statement under oath before "[a]n administrative agency or *arbitrator* authorized by statute to determine issues of fact."[119] This statute, however, likely does not apply to private, contractual arbitrations because these arbitrations authorized by statutes fall in the public sector, not the private sector. New Jersey law utilizes the MPC definition of perjury,[120] but the definition of "official proceeding" includes arbitration.[121] Under the circumstances noted in the statutes, perjury liability would apply to arbitral proceedings in these jurisdictions.

---

[112] R.I. Gen. Laws § 11-33-1(a) (2010) ("Every person under oath or affirmation who knowingly makes any false material declaration or makes or uses any other information, including any book, paper, document, record, recording, or other material, knowing it contains any false material declaration, shall be deemed guilty of perjury").

[113] S.C. Code Ann. § 16-9-30 (2010) ("It is unlawful for a person to willfully and knowingly swear falsely in taking any oath required by law that is administered by a person directed or permitted by law to administer such oath").

[114] S.D. Comp. L. § 22-29-1 (2010) ("Any person who, having taken an oath to testify, declare, depose, or certify truly, before any competent tribunal, officer, or person, in any state or federal proceeding or action in which such an oath may by law be administered, states, intentionally and contrary to the oath, any material matter which the person knows to be false, is guilty of perjury").

[115] Tenn. Code Ann. § 39-16-702 (a)(1) (2010) ("A person commits an offense who, with intent to deceive… makes a false statement, under oath").

[116] Tex. Code Ann., Penal Code § 37.02 (a) (2010) ("A person commits an offense if, with intent to deceive and with knowledge of the statement's meaning: (1) he makes a false statement under oath or swears to the truth of a false statement previously made and the statement is required or authorized by law to be made under oath").

[117] Va. Code Ann. § 18.2-434 (2010) ("If any person to whom an oath is lawfully administered on any occasion willfully swears falsely on such occasion touching any material matter or thing… he is guilty of perjury").

[118] See *Gilbert*, 126 P.3d at 1060 (assuming, without deciding, that the perjury rules apply equally to arbitration proceedings); *Self*, 135 Ariz. 374 (holding that the "sworn statement" language in the perjury statute facially applies to arbitration, and finding that an arbitration hearing before the State Bar Committee constituted an "official proceeding" for the tampering charges); Hoolandt, supra (acknowledging perjury in a worker's compensation arbitration); *Scott vs. Commonwealth*, 416 S.E.2d 47, 49 (Va. Ct. App. 1992) (Neither Code § 18.2-434 nor Code § 18.2-435 expressly restricts "testimony" to testimony given in judicial proceedings. In fact, Code § 18.2-434 provides that it is perjury to swear falsely when an oath is lawfully administered "on any occasion").

[119] Wis. Stat. Ann. § 946.31 (d) (West 2010) (emphasis added).

[120] N.J. Stat. Ann. § 2C:28-1 (a) (West 2010) ("Offense defined. A person is guilty of perjury, a crime of the third degree, if in any official proceeding he makes a false statement under oath or equivalent affirmation, or swears or affirms the truth of a statement previously made, when the statement is material and he does not believe it to be true").

[121] Id. § 2C:277:1 (d) (2010).

A final minority of states limit perjury to judicial proceedings. In Georgia, perjury only applies to "judicial proceedings."[122] In Louisiana, perjury applies only in a judicial or legislative proceeding.[123] Massachusetts law applies solely in a "proceeding in a court of justice,"[124] and not to arbitrations.[125] Nevada perjury law applies to statements made in a judicial proceeding or when required by law.[126] North Carolina law similarly only applies when the witness is "*required* to be sworn or affirmed."[127] Vermont perjury law applies to court and agency proceedings.[128] West Virginia perjury law applies only at trial or felony grand jury proceedings.[129] The Wyoming perjury law applies only to statements in "judicial, legislative or administrative proceedings."[130] Federal perjury law similarly applies in situations in which an oath is required by law to be administered.[131] These laws, then, clearly do not apply to the arbitral forum, and legislative change would be necessary to make these statutes apply to arbitration.

### *Tampering Statutes Similarly Do Not Apply to Arbitrations, but Arbitrators Acknowledge Penalties for Wrongdoing Within Individual Arbitrations*

Tampering with documents and physical evidence, like lying, also has a devastating effect on the litigation and arbitral processes, weighing heaving on issues of just conflict resolution. Consider the post-September 11, 2001 actions of Morgan

[122] Ga. Code Ann. § 16-10-70 (a) (2010).

[123] La. Rev. Stat. Ann. § 14:123 (2010).

[124] Mass. Gen. Law Ann. 268, § 1 (West 2012) ("Whoever, being lawfully required to depose the truth in a judicial proceeding or in a proceeding in a court of justice, willfully swears or affirms falsely in a matter material to the issue or point in question, or whoever, being required by law to take an oath or affirmation, willfully swears or affirms falsely in a matter relative to which such oath or affirmation is required, shall be guilty of perjury").

[125] *Ezekiel vs. Jones Motor Co.*, 372 N.E.2d 1281, 1285 (Mass. 1978) (not applying perjury to a labor arbitration).

[126] Nev. Rev. Stat. § 199.120 (2010). Nevada case law emphasizes that an oath must be required by law (i.e., not voluntary). *Licata vs. State*, 661 P.2d 1306, 1307 (Nev. 1983) ("We construe the language of the statute to mean that a perjury charge may be sustained only where the false statement was made in a judicial or other setting where an oath or affirmation is legally required. Appellant's voluntary statement taken in the insurance company lawyer's office does not fall within the purview of the statute and thus, appellant could not have been found guilty of perjury in this case").

[127] N.C. Gen. Stat. Ann. § 14-209 (West 2010).

[128] Vt. Code Ann. § 2901 (2010).

[129] W. Va. Code § 61-5-1 (a) (2010).

[130] Wyo. Stat. Ann. § 6-5-301 (a) (2010).

[131] 18 U.S.C. § 1621 (1) (2012).

Stanley. Following the terrorist attacks on the World Trade Center, Morgan Stanley intentionally withheld evidence from arbitration claimants, falsely claiming that certain electronic evidence was destroyed in the twin towers. The documents were not destroyed but, in fact, preserved at a different location. Morgan Stanley withheld these documents from several *thousand* claimants in arbitration. In 2007, the Financial Industry Regulatory Authority (FINRA) sanctioned Morgan Stanley US $12.5 million for this scandalous conduct.[132] In contrast, Morgan Stanley suffered a US $1.4 *billion* dollar jury verdict based on its same lies in civil litigation cases.[133] Arguably, Morgan Stanley only suffered arbitration penalties because of its association with FINRA, and not because the law required such sanctions.

If Morgan Stanley and other participants could hide or destroy documents without serious repercussion (and many would argue that Morgan Stanley's FINRA sanctions were not "serious" in light of rhe company's overall net worth), then the arbitral forum loses all credibility. Like perjury, the MPC has a model statute on tampering that most states have adopted. Like the MPC perjury laws, the tampering laws only apply in "official proceedings."[134] As discussed above, statutes referencing official proceedings do not clearly apply to arbitrations and require additional clarification.

Most states follow the MPC definition of tampering: Alabama,[135] Alaska,[136] Arizona,[137] Arkansas,[138] Colorado,[139] Connecticut,[140] Delaware,[141] the District of Columbia,[142] Hawaii,[143] Idaho,[144] Kentucky,[145] Michigan,[146] Mississippi,[147]

[132] FINRA News Release, "Morgan Stanley to Pay $ 12.5 Million to Resolve FINRA Charges that it Failed to Provide Documents to Arbitration Claimants, Regulators," September 27, 2007.

[133] Richard L. McConnell et al., "Compliance Readiness—Law Firms: Discovery of Electronic Information: The Scylla of Excessive Cost and the Charybdis of Potential Sanctions," at http://www.metrocorpcounsel.com/current.php?artType=view&artMonth=October&artYear=2006&EntryNo=5741 (last viewed June 14, 2011).

[134] Ohio Rev. Code Ann. § 241.7 (2007).

[135] Ala. Code § 13A-10-129 (2010).

[136] Alaska Stat. § 11.56.610.

[137] Ariz. Rev. Stat. § 13-2809.

[138] Ark. Code Ann. § 5-53-111 (2010).

[139] Colo. Rev. Stat. Ann. § 18-8-610 (West 2010).

[140] Conn. Gen. Stat. Ann. § 53a-155 (West 2010).

[141] 11 Del. Code § 1274 (2010).

[142] D.C. Stat. § 22-723 (2010).

[143] Haw. Rev. Stat. § 710-1076 (2010).

[144] Idaho Code Ann. § 18-2603 (2010).

[145] Ky. Rev. Stat. Ann. § 524.100 (West 2010).

[146] Mich. Comp. Laws Ann. § 750.483a (5).

[147] Miss. Code Ann. § 97-9-125 (2010).

Montana,[148] Nebraska,[149] New Hampshire,[150] New Jersey,[151] New York,[152] North Dakota,[153] Ohio,[154] Oklahoma,[155] Oregon,[156] Pennsylvania,[157] South Dakota,[158] Tennessee,[159] Texas,[160] Utah,[161] and Washington.[162] Legislative changes to the definition of "official proceedings" to include arbitration would then have a sweeping effect and apply to both perjury and tampering laws.

Unlike perjury, some states recognize a civil cause of action based on evidence tampering.[163] The states of Alaska, District of Columbia, Florida, Kansas, Ohio, Illinois, Indiana, Louisiana, Montana, New Mexico, West Virginia, and New Jersey recognize this tort.[164] Generally speaking, a plaintiff establishes a cause of

[148] Mont. Code Ann. § 45-7-207 (2010).

[149] Neb. Rev. Stat. §§ 45-7 to -207 (2010).

[150] N.H. Rev. Stat. Ann. § 641:6.

[151] N.J. Stat. Ann. § 2C:28:6 (2010).

[152] N.Y. Penal Law § 251.40 (West, 2010).

[153] N.D. Cent. Code § 12.1-09-03 (2010).

[154] Ohio Rev. Code Ann. § 2921.12 (2010).

[155] 21 Okla.Stat. Ann. § 454 (2010).

[156] Ore. Rev. Stat. § 162.295 (2010).

[157] 18 Pa. Stat. Ann. § 4910.

[158] S.D. Comp. Laws § 19-7-14 (2010) (using the term "proceeding," not "official proceeding").

[159] Tenn. Code Ann. § 39-16-503 (2010).

[160] Tex. Penal Code Ann. § 37.09 (West 2010).

[161] Utah Code Ann. § 76-8-510.5 (2010) (including a catchall provision of "examination under oath").

[162] Wash. Rev. Code Ann. § 9A.72.150.

[163] Comment, Cecelia Hallinan, *Balancing the Scales After The Evidence is Spoiled: Does Pennsylvania's Approach Sufficiently Protect the Injured Party?*, 44 Vill. L. Rev. 947, 956 (1999) (describing the cause of action). Note that some jurisdictions require the completion of the underlying cause of action before raising a claim of spoliation.

[164] See *Nichols vs. State Farm Ins. & Cas.Co.*, 6 P.3d 300 (Alaska 2000) (recognizing tort of intentional spoliation of evidence); *Holmes vs. Amerex Rent-A-Car*, 710 A.2d 846 (D.C. 1998) (establishing tort); *Dardeen vs. Kuehling*, 821 N.E.2d 227, 2321 (Ill. 2004) (establishing tort); *Clotzbach, CPA vs. Froman*, 827 N.E.2d 105, 108 (Ind. App. 2005) (establishing tort); *Desselle vs. Jefferson Hosp. Dist. No. 2*, 887 So. 2d 524, 534 (La. Ct. App. 2004) (recognizing a tort of intentional spoliation); *Gentry vs. Douglas Hereford Ranch, Inc.*, 962 P.2d 1205 (Mont. 1998) (establishing tort); *Manorcare Health vs. Osmose Wood*, 336 N.J. Super. 218, 226, 764 A.2d 475, 479 (App. Div. 2001) (noting that destruction of evidence could result in a separate tort for spoliation, discovery sanctions, or an adverse inference); *Smith vs. Howard Johnson Co.*, 67 Ohio St. 3d 28, 29, 615 N.E.2d 1037 (1993) (applying tort); *Hanna vs. Heeter*, 584 S.E.2d 560, 563–64 (W. Va. 2003) (noting elements); *DiDomenico vs. C & S Aeromatik Supplies*, 252 A.D.2d 41, 682 N.Y.S.2d 452 (2d Dep't 1998) (noting availability of tort, but holding tort not established in the particular case).

Some states expressly reject this tort. *Tobel vs. Travelers Ins. Co.*, 988 P.2d 148, 156 (Ariz. Ct. App. 1999); *Cedars-Sinai Med. Ctr. vs. Sup.Ct.*, 18 Cal. 4th 1, 74 Cal. Rptr. 2d 248, 258, 954 P.2d 511 (1998); *Lucas vs. Christiana Skating Ctr., Ltd.*, 722 A.2d 1247, 1250 (Del. 1998); Lucas vs. Christiana Skating Center, Ltd., 722 A.2d 1247, 1250 (1998); *Owens vs. Am. Refuse. Sys., Inc.*, 244 Ga. App. 780, 536 S.E.2d 782 (2000); *Monsanto Co. vs. Reed*, 950 S.W.2d 811, 815 (Ky.

action by showing: (1) the existence of a potential civil action, (2) defendant's knowledge, (3) destruction of evidence, (4) intent, (5) inability to prove the original claim (i.e., proximate cause), and (6) damages. Some states also recognize a tort of negligent spoliation of evidence when the parties have a duty to preserve evidence.[165] Whether this cause of action applies to arbitration is largely an open issue.[166] The arbitrator's jurisdiction makes these claims particularly difficult to prove,[167] especially when courts consider these claims to be post-arbitration collateral attacks.[168]

Thankfully for arbitration parties, arbitrators are considering issues of document destruction in the arbitral forum. Arbitrators who find that tampering occurs punish wrongdoing parties with a wide variety of sanctions, similar to the authority of courts.[169] Case law suggests that arbitrators are implementing sanctions such as drawing adverse inferences against the wrongdoing party, meaning that the arbitrator will simply assume that the documentary evidence now lost would have

1997).); *Fletcher vs. Dorchester Mut. Ins. Co.*, 437 Mass. 544, 773 N.E.2d 420 (2002); *Panich vs. Iron Wood Prods. Corp.*, 445 N.W.2d 795 (Mich. Ct. App. 1989); *Federated Mut. Ins. Co. vs. Litchfield Precision Components, Inc.*, 456 N.W.2d 434, 437 (Minn. 1990); *Dowdle Butane Gas Co. vs. Moore*, 831 So. 2d 1124, 1135 (Miss. 2002).; *Patel vs. OMH Med. Ctr., Inc.*, 987 P.2d 1185 (Okla. 1999); *Elias vs. Lancaster Gen. Hosp.*, 710 A.2d 65, 68 (Pa. Super. Ct. 1998); *Malinowski vs. Documented Vehicle/Drivers Sys., Inc.*, 66 F. App'x 216, 222 (R.I. 2003). *Trevino vs. Ortega*, 969 S.W.2d 950, 951 (Tex. 1998); Estate of Neumann ex rel. *Rodli vs. Neumann*, 242 Wis. 2d 205, 244–49, 626 N.W.2d 821, 840–43 (Wis.App., 2001).

165 See *Holmes vs. Amerex Rent-A-Car*, 710 A.2d 846 (D.C. 1998) (establishing torts for both intentional and negligent spoliation); *Dardeen vs. Kuehling*, 821 N.E.2d 227, 2321 (Ill. 2004) (holding that the tort of negligent spoliation fit within traditional negligence law); Clotzbach, CPA, 827 N.E.2d at 108 (requiring the finding of a duty whether the claim is for intentional or negligent spoliation); *Gentry*, 962 P.2d 1205 (recognizing claim for intentional and negligent spoliation); *Smith*, 67 Ohio St. 3d at 29, 615 N.E.2d 1037 (recognizing the tort of negligent spoliation, provided that the parties have a special relationship).

166 Arbitrability issues can arise in this area with courts considering whether the arbitrator has jurisdiction over this question in the first instance. See *Clyde Bergemann, Inc. vs. Sullivan, Higgins & Brion, PPE, L.L.C.*, 2008 WL 2116908 (D. Or. May 14, 2008) (compelling spoliation claim to arbitration); *Positive Software Solutions, Inc. vs. New Century Mortgage Co.*, 259 F. Supp. 2d 561 (N.D. Tex. 2003) (same); *Dantz vs. Apple Ohio, L.L.C.*, 277 F. Supp. 2d 794 (N.D. Ohio 2003) (same).

167 Some arbitral opinions evidence that parties have asked for damages for a cause of action for spoliation. See *In the Matter of Arbitration Between Name of Claimants Daniel G Parsons Ellen M. Petri vs. Name of Respondent The Prudential Ins. Co. of Am.*, 1999 WL 681,721 (N.A.S.D. July 8 1999); *In the Matter of Arbitration Between Name of Claimant Brenda Rose Names of Respondents Lehwald Orosey Pepe, Inc.*, 1998 WL 11,78726 (N.A.S.D. August 5, 1998)

168 See, e.g., *Ungerland vs. Morgan Stanley & Co.*, 2010 WL 1795628 (Conn. Super. Ct. April 5, 2010) (dismissing cause of action for spoliation as a collateral attack on the arbitration award).

169 Nearly every jurisdiction in the USA recognizes some types of sanctions for spoliation of evidence. Those sanctions can range from drawing an adverse inference against the alleged spoliator to an award of attorney's fees to outright dismissal of a claim.

been favorable to the other party.[170] Arbitrators also use adverse presumptions to help support awards of punitive damages.[171] Case law also suggests that arbitrators will dismiss claims brought by a party found to have destroyed evidence.[172] These arbitration decisions demonstrate that arbitrators are beginning to address these important issues within the arbitral forum, which is at least a start in helping to ensure ethical behavior in arbitration.

## *Professional Ethics Laws Already Extend to the Arbitral Forum, and the Criminal Law has Not Yet Caught Up*

Although the criminal law relating to the administration of justice does not apply to the arbitral forum, the attorney ethics rules have recently been updated to apply to the arbitral forum. The ethical rules dealing with an attorney's conduct in the administration of justice were updated in 2002. While the criminal laws apply generally to "official proceedings," the ethical rules discuss behavior appropriate before a "tribunal." Part of these changes included defining the term "tribunal" to include binding arbitration.[173] The ethical rules dealing with truthfulness and proper

[170] See, e.g., *Jones vs. PPG Indus.*, 2010 WL 3565731 (3d Cir. September 15, 2010). Interestingly, the Jones court involved a claim in which the arbitrator found an adverse inference against the respondent party and then still ruled in favor of the respondent. The trial court and Third Circuit confirmed the arbitral award based a review of the extensive record in the case.

[171] See, e.g., *Davis vs. Reliance Elec.*, 104 S.W.3d 57 (Tenn. Ct. App. 2002). In Davis, the arbitrator had grave concerns regarding the respondent-employer's failure to provide certain critical documents, so the arbitrator awarded punitive damages against the employer based on a portion of the employer's net worth.

[172] See, e.g., *AmeriCredit Fin. Serv., Inc. vs. Oxford Mgmt. Serv.*, 627 F. Supp. 2d 85 (E.D.N.Y. 2008) (confirming award dismissing counterclaims when the party asserting the counterclaims destroyed documents relevant to the claim).

[173] *Model Rules of Professional Conduct, Rule 1.* 0 (m 2010) ("'Tribunal' denotes a court, an arbitrator in a binding arbitration proceeding or a legislative body, administrative agency or other body acting in an adjudicative capacity. A legislative body, administrative agency or other body acts in an adjudicative capacity when a neutral official, after the presentation of evidence or legal arguments by a party or parties, will render a binding legal judgment directly affecting a party's interests in a particular matter"); see also W. Suflas, *The Role of Ethics in ADR Leading Lawyers on Understanding the Ethical Obligation of Attorneys Engaging in Alternative Dispute Resolution, Aspatore,* at *3 (November 2011) ("A 'tribunal' is defined broadly to specifically include 'an arbitrator in a binding arbitration proceeding'"). Non-binding arbitration proceedings are exempt from these ethical rules.

States adopting this definition of tribunal include (found in Rule 1.0 of the respective state's model rules, unless otherwise noted): Arizona; Colorado; Connecticut; Delaware; District of Columbia; Georgia (unnumbered Terminology section); Idaho; Indiana; Iowa (Rule 32:1.0); Kansas; Kentucky (SCR 3/130 (1.0)); Louisiana; Maine; Maryland; Minnesota; Missouri (Rule 4-1.0); Montana; Nebraska (Rule 3-501.0); Nevada; New Hampshire; New Jersey; New Mexico (Rule 16-100); New York; North Carolina; North Dakota; Ohio; Oklahoma; Oregon; Pennsylvania; Rhode Island; South Carolina; South Dakota; Tennessee; Texas (undefined definitions' section); Utah; Vermont; Washington; Wisconsin; and Wyoming.

relations among adversaries all apply to the arbitral forum—unlike the criminal law. Ethics Rule 3.3, dealing with Candor toward the Tribunal, reads:

a. A lawyer shall not knowingly:

   1. *make a false statement of fact or law to a tribunal* or fail to correct a false statement of material fact or law previously made to the tribunal by the lawyer;
   2. offer evidence that the lawyer knows to be false. If a lawyer, the lawyer's client, or a witness called by the lawyer, has offered material evidence and the lawyer comes to know of its falsity, the lawyer shall take reasonable remedial measures, including, if necessary, *disclosure to the tribunal.* A lawyer may refuse to offer evidence, other than the testimony of a defendant in a criminal matter, that the lawyer reasonably believes is false.[174]

In addition, an attorney cannot knowingly procure false testimony from a witness, and if a witness gives false testimony, the attorney must remediate the situation, including disclosing the untruthfulness of the statement(s) to the tribunal.[175]

Attorneys are also prohibited from tampering with documents and evidence. Model Rule 3.4 prohibits an attorney from "unlawfully obstruct[ing] another party's access to evidence or unlawfully alter[ing], destroy[ing] or conceal[ing] a document or other material having potential evidentiary value. A lawyer shall not counsel or assist another person to do any such act."[176] Most states have adopted variations

A number of states have not adopted any definition of tribunal. Those states include: Alabama, Alaska, Arkansas, Florida, Illinois, Michigan, Mississippi, Virginia, and West Virginia. Massachusetts defines "tribunal" only as a "court or other adjudicatory body." Mass. R. Prof. Resp., R. 9.1 (o). Presumably, arbitration is an "adjudicatory body" because the purpose of arbitration is to make final and binding determinations of law and fact. The New York law does not contain a limitation on binding arbitrations, but it applies to all arbitration proceedings. NY Rules of Professional Conduct, R. 1.0 (w). Hawaii proposed an amendment to its rules of professional conduct that would include the above definition of the word "tribunal." Proposed HRPC Final Version, at http://www.hsba.org/resources/1/HRPC/Proposed%20HRPC%20Final%20Version.pdf.

[174] Model Code of Professional Responsibility, R. 3.3 (a) (2002) (emphasis added). The following states adopted this, or a substantially similar rule (found in Rule 3.3 of the respective state's model rules, unless otherwise noted): Alabama; Alaska; Arizona; Arkansas; Colorado; Connecticut; Delaware; District of Columbia; Florida (Rule 4-3.3); Georgia; Hawaii; Idaho; Illinois; Indiana; Iowa (Rule 32:3.3); Kansas; Kentucky (SCR 3.130 (3.3)); Louisiana; Maine; Maryland; Massachusetts; Michigan; Minnesota; Mississippi; Missouri (Rule 4-3.3); Montana; Nebraska (Rule 3-503.3); Nevada; New Hampshire; New Jersey; New Mexico (Rule 16-303); New York; North Carolina; North Dakota; Ohio; Oklahoma; Oregon; Pennsylvania; Rhode Island; South Carolina; South Dakota; Tennessee; Texas (Rule 3.03); Utah; Vermont; Virginia; Washington; West Virginia; Wisconsin; and Wyoming. See also Restatement (Third) of The Law Governing Lawyers § 120 (2000).

[175] *Model R. Prof. Conduct R.* 3. 3 (b) (2002).

[176] Model Rule of Professional Conduct R. 3.4; See also Restatement (Third) of The Law Governing Lawyers § 117. The following states adopted a version of Model Rule of Professional Conduct 3.4 dealing with candor towards opposing counsel and parties (labeled as Rule 3.4, unless otherwise noted): Alabama, Alaska, Arizona, Arkansas, Colorado, Connecticut, Delaware, District of Columbia, Florida, Georgia, Hawaii, Idaho, Illinois, Indiana, Iowa, Kansas, Kentucky, Louisi-

on these rules and similarly prohibit attorneys from lying and interfering with evidence. Given the broad language of these ethical rules, they apply to the arbitral forum—unlike their criminal law counterparts.

The ethical rules for attorneys have clearly caught up with modern ADR practice. These rules recognize that attorneys must be bound to certain baselines of ethical behavior even when they are not representing clients before a court. Although having strong ethical rules governing the arbitral forum is important, having ethical rules alone is not enough. These ethical rules only govern the conduct of parties. They do not apply to the conduct of non-attorneys, including witnesses, experts, non-attorney clients, and pro se parties. In other words, they are extremely limited in their application. Given the limited scope of the current ethical rules and the incredible range of conduct that these rules do not—and cannot—reach, this chapter calls for a legislative change that would extend the criminal law to the arbitral forum, as discussed in the next section.

## *A Simple Recommendation to Close the Loopholes*

This chapter recommends a very simple legislative change that would close the ethical loophole and help ensure that all arbitration participants engage in a fair process free of corruption, lies, deception, and fraud. If the criminal state statutes dealing with the "administration of justice" added "binding arbitration" to the list of "official proceedings," then the entire chapter would apply to arbitration—including the statutes dealing with perjury, false statements, document tampering, and witness tampering. In other words, adding two words to one definition would, in one fell swoop, create a fairer system of arbitration by disincentivizing unethical behavior and creating the potential for criminal liability for engaging in wrongdoing.

This change to the criminal law is long overdue. Most states' laws regarding the administration of justice date back to the 1960s, when the MPC was first promulgated. Arbitration looked significantly different in the 1960s than it does today. In the 1960s, arbitration largely involved arms-length agreements to arbitrate between business entities. Arbitrators usually heard fact-intensive cases dealing with the quality of goods, delivery of goods, and other similar issues. Arbitrators, at that time, often did not possess a law degree. In fact, parties often chose these arbitrators because of their technical expertise in industry. Arbitration today looks considerably different. Pre-dispute arbitration agreements are common in any number of contracts in the commercial, consumer, and employment contexts. Many arbitrations now resolve statutory claims of all types—which is a relatively new develop-

ana, Maine, Maryland, Massachusetts, Mississippi, Missouri, Montana, Nebraska, Nevada, New Hampshire, New Jersey, New Mexico, New York, North Carolina, North Dakota, Ohio, Oklahoma, Oregon, Pennsylvania, Rhode Island, South Carolina, South Dakota, Tennessee, Texas, Utah, Vermont, Washington, West Virginia, and Wyoming.

ment in arbitration law.[177] In addition, far more attorneys participate in arbitration now than in the 1960s, both as advocates and as arbitrators. This changing nature of arbitration requires additional safeguards governing the process, to ensure that the process is fair for all participants, given the increasing "legal" nature of arbitration.

As noted above, the increased application of absolute immunity to the arbitral forum practically requires that the criminal law governing crimes against the administration of justice apply to arbitration. The policy reasons for immunity apply equally to the arbitral forum as the judicial forum (if not more so), but immunity was always intended to involve a trade-off. The grant of immunity does not mean that a fact-finding and rights resolving forum should become lawless. To the contrary, the grant of immunity only makes sense if the criminal law exists as a back-stop so that justice can be served in dispute resolution. A system of immunity without criminal consequences has the potential to breed lawlessness. In this situation, extending the criminal law regarding the administration of justice to the arbitral forum would close the loophole created by the widespread grant of absolute immunity in the arbitral forum.

Although criminal prosecutions for crimes relating to the administration of justice are relatively rare,[178] the change to the criminal law would serve additional purposes than simply pressing criminal charges against those who commit wrongdoing in the arbitral forum. The criminal law serves as a powerful deterrent. Having a criminal law on the books applicable to the arbitral forum would presumably discourage parties, witnesses, and other arbitration participants from considering engaging in unethical conduct out of the fear of criminal prosecution.

Finally, making this change to the criminal law would instill ethical requirements without disturbing the authority or power of the arbitrators. Slightly modifying the criminal law in this manner would not require any invasive changes to the arbitration process. In fact, it would not require any changes to the arbitration process at all. The authority of the arbitrator would not change and no changes would be required to occur in the arbitral process. What would change is the availability of post-arbitration relief through criminal sanctions. As discussed below, the scope of judicial review is already incredibly limited for arbitration participants—especially for those who attempt to have an award vacated on the basis

[177] The nature of consumer and employment arbitration changed in 1991 when the Supreme Court decided the case *Gilmer v. Interstate Johnson*, 500 U.S. 44, 50 (1991). The Gilmer Court held that a party could enforce a pre-dispute agreement to arbitrate statutory claims, such as discrimination claims under the Age Discrimination in Employment Act. Following *Gilmer*, the floodgates opened and many large companies began requiring consumers and employees to agree to arbitrate all claims, including statutory claims.

[178] Erin Murphy, *Manufacturing Crime: Process, Pretext, and Criminal Justice*, 97 Geo. L.J. 1435, 1489 (2009) (noting that, while perjury charges are hard to quantify, sources indicate that as little as 0.2 % of all federally filed felonies are perjury charges, and noting that perjury charges are more likely filed in high-profile cases or cases involving difficult cases other than the process crimes).

of fraud.[179] The expansion of the criminal law to arbitration participants would simply give arbitration participants the opportunity to petition the local prosecutors to levy criminal charges against the wrongdoers.

The fundamental nature of arbitration would not change as a result of this proposal. The proposal would not impose any changes to the structure of arbitration itself, and arbitrators and parties would maintain arbitration's benefits of flexibility, finality, and informality. Parties will still have strong incentives to take claims of wrongdoing directly to the arbitrator as soon as they are aware of such problems given the very stringent standards of review and the possibility of a challenge for waiver. Arbitrators will still have full authority over the process, and this change to the criminal law would not have any impact on the way individual arbitrations are run.

In sum, the development of arbitral immunity to arbitration participants serves valid and lofty policies, while promoting justice in resolving conflicts in the arbitral forum. The extension of immunity, however, without a corresponding change in the criminal law is creating a wide gap, or a loophole, in the area of arbitration ethics. Extending the criminal law regarding the administration of justice would fill this gap while preserving the integrity of the arbitral process and arbitration's independence from the court systems.

## The Extraordinarily High Burden of Proof for Vacatur for Fraud Prevents Wrongfully Procured Awards from Being Overturned

In addition to the loophole explained above relating to the extension of the immunity doctrine, the evolution of the judicial review available in instances of participant fraud has created another ethical loophole. Unlike any other form of judicial review of arbitration awards, the common law development for review for "fraud" go beyond the statutory text and require a showing of "clear and convincing" evidence of fraud before vacating an arbitration award. This burden of proof is unjustified compared to the burdens of proof of other grounds for vacatur of arbitration awards and out of line with how the judicial system normally reviews such issues. For these reasons, this chapter advocates that the common law abandon the heightened pleading standard and simply consider whether the standard for vacatur has been met to overturn an arbitration award.

[179] As will be demonstrated below, a showing of fraud requires a "clear and convincing" evidentiary burden, unlike the burden of proof for any other standard of review.

## *Judicial Review Generally Under the Federal Arbitration Act and Common Law Development*

Judicial review of arbitral awards is limited by statutory design. Limited review promotes finality, one of the hallmarks of arbitration law and policy.[180] In light of the federal and state policies in favor of arbitration, limited review "thereby discourages litigation."[181] Litigation is discouraged because parties will understand that their chance for vacatur is low and so they will not use their limited resources to fight a likely losing battle. When as few as one in seven awards are vacated across the country, losing arbitration parties should consider very carefully whether they will pursue review in court.[182]

The grounds for review are extraordinarily narrow. Federal law recognizes four grounds for review. Those grounds are:

1. where the award was procured by corruption, fraud, or undue means
2. where there was evident partiality or corruption in the arbitrators, …
3. where the arbitrators were guilty of misconduct in refusing to postpone the hearing, upon sufficient cause shown, or in refusing to hear evidence pertinent and material to the controversy; or of any other misbehavior by which the rights of any party have been prejudiced or
4. where the arbitrators exceeded their powers, or so imperfectly executed them that a mutual, final, and definite award upon the subject matter submitted was not made [183]

These four statutory grounds for review are limited in that they do not deal with the award itself, but externalities that would cause the court not to have faith in the arbitration *process*. Consider some of the things not reviewable, including the correctness of the award, the arbitrator's evidentiary rulings, the arbitrator's rulings on motions, the arbitrator's factual findings, the arbitrator's findings with respect to credibility, and the legal soundness of the award. When viewing arbitration from a contract standpoint, these limitations make sense. Parties voluntarily contract with one another to resolve disputes outside of the traditional legal system. Limited review protects the contractual arrangement of the parties by elevating the importance of finality over the importance of a "correct" decision. Such balancing aims at preserving the parties' contractual wish to resolve the dispute through an appointed third-party arbitrator.

More recently, the common law has developed new, slightly expanded forms of judicial review of arbitral awards. These additional grounds for review are not

---

[180] See *supra Section II* (D) 2010 (1).

[181] *Low vs. Minichino*, 267 P.3d 683, 689 (Haw. 2011) (reversing the decision of the court below confirming an award challenged on the basis of fraud so that the lower court can hold an evidentiary hearing on the issue).

[182] Stephen K. Huber & Maureen A Weston, *Arbitration: Cases and Materials, by Huber, 2nd Edition* (2006).

[183] 9 U.S.C. § 10 (a) (2002).

accepted in all jurisdictions, and the Supreme Court has not definitively ruled on whether they are proper grounds for review.[184] The most commonly employed non-statutory ground for review is a review of an award for an arbitrator's "manifest disregard of the law." An arbitrator manifestly disregards the law when the arbitrator was aware of the applicable law (usually because a party supplied the arbitrator with such law) and the arbitrator ignored the law.[185] Mere misapplication of the law is insufficient to warrant vacatur. The line between "manifest disregard" and a substantively wrong decision is extraordinarily difficult to define, but relatively few decisions are vacated under the "manifest disregard" standard. Given the Supreme Court's ambiguous statements in *dicta* regarding "manifest disregard" in the *Hall Street* and *Stolt-Nielsen* cases about the viability of the manifest disregard standard, the federal circuit courts are currently split on the continuing availability of this standard of review.[186]

In addition to "manifest disregard," some courts will vacate an award on the basis that the award contravenes public policy. The "public policy" ground considers whether the public policy is clearly defined and the arbitration award is in contravention to that clearly defined policy. Mere "inconsistency with a court's generalized view of public policy" is not sufficient to vacate an arbitration award.[187] Courts most often utilize the public policy exception when labor arbitrators award reinstatement of a person not fit for the workplace—such as an airline pilot with a documented history of alcoholism and drinking on the job.[188] As with the exception for manifest disregard, the Supreme Court expressed some doubt as to the continuing sustainability of the public policy exception in a recent decision.[189] Whether or

[184] Over the past few years, the Supreme Court has given indications that only the four enumerated grounds for review listed in Sect. 10 (a) of the FAA can be used to vacate an arbitration award. In *Hall St. Assocs. vs. Mattel, Inc.*, 552 US 576 (2008), the Supreme Court held that parties could not contract for a standard of review greater than that proscribed in Sect. 10 (a). The Court left open the possibility that courts could review an award based on standards other than those in the statute. The Court acknowledged, but did not resolve this issue again in *Stolt-Nielsen, S.A vs. Animal-Feeds Int'l*, 130 S. Ct. 1758 (2010). For the purposes of this chapter, whether these grounds exist is immaterial because these grounds of review deal with an arbitrator's award, as opposed to the conduct of an opposing party or witness.

[185] See, e.g., *Wachovia Sec., L.L.C. vs. Brand*, 671 F.3d 472, 481 (4th Cir. 2012) ("Before Hall Street, we stated that for a court to vacate an award under the manifest disregard theory, the arbitration record must show that '(1) the applicable legal principle is clearly defined and not subject to reasonable debate; and (2) the arbitrator[ ] refused to heed that legal principle'") (citation omitted).

[186] See *Wachovia Sec.*, 671 F.3d at 481–83 (discussing the Supreme Court's decisions and the resulting circuit split).

[187] *Lagstein vs. Certain Underwriters at Lloyd's, London*, 607 F.3d 634, 641 n.4 (9th Cir. 2010).

[188] See, e.g., *Delta Air Lines, Inc. vs. Air Line Pilots Ass'n*, 861 F.2d 665 (11th Cir. 1988) (finding a violation of public policy when a labor arbitrator awarded reinstatement of a pilot who flew a passenger aircraft while intoxicated).

[189] In the 2012 decision of *Marmet Health Care Ctr., Inc. vs. Brown*, 565 U.S. ___ (2012), the US Supreme Court reversed a decision by the West Virginia Supreme Court invalidating certain nursing home contracts as violative of public policy. While never stating that the public policy exception does not exist, the Court struck down the West Virginia decision as preempted by the

not this exception continues to exist, finding a court to vacate a decision on public policy grounds is still rare.

Unlike the statutory grounds listed above, these two additional grounds delve deeper into the arbitrator's decision-making power. Arguably, whether an award is in manifest disregard of the law or violates public policy concerns the "correctness" of the award. The review, however, is still not searching (i.e., party perceived "incorrect" decisions will likely still be upheld). And the likelihood of successfully achieving a vacated decision is still slim. In sum, all of the grounds for judicial review are difficult to achieve, and the courts have not expressed much willingness to vacate awards liberally.

## *The Evolution of Judicial Review in the Case of Awards Challenged for "Fraud"*

Examining these grounds for review, the most plausible grounds for review based on a party's or witness's misconduct would be to challenge the award under Sect. 10 (a) (1) for corruption or fraud or undue means for the bad actions of the arbitration party or other participant (i.e., witnesses and attorneys). In fact, Sect. 10 (a) (1) has been the vehicle by which courts have considered whether a party's misconduct should warrant vacatur.

Unlike Sect. 10 (a) (1), every other ground for review deals with the *arbitrator's* conduct—not the conduct of any other participant. The text of Sect. 10 (a) (1) does not specify how the award was procured by corruption, fraud, or undue mean. Given that the other sections specify that the arbitrator must have committed the conduct worthy of vacatur, established theories of statutory interpretation would dictate that if Sect. 10 (a) (1) does not limit *who* commits the corruption, fraud, or undue means, then that conduct could have been done by either the arbitrator or another person. Reading the statute, then, Sect. 10 (a) (1) does not require any wrongdoing on the part of the arbitrator. In fact, the arbitrator can be innocent of actually committing wrongdoing, but another party's wrongdoing—here an opposing party or witness—has led to an award that is corrupt, fraudulent, or rendered by undue means because of the bad conduct of another arbitration participant.[190] Because Sect. 10 (a) (1) is the *only* ground for vacatur not premised on arbitrator misconduct, this section would be the only grounds available for arbitration participants who seek to vacate an award on the misconduct of a party, witness, or attorney.

---

Federal Arbitration Act—thus leaving in doubt whether any public policy exception based on state law would not be preempted.

[190] The FAA has a handful of limited grounds for vacatur, but the one most often invoked in situations involving perjury or tampering is the exception for fraud. See, e.g., *Trans Chem. Ltd. vs. P.R.C. Nat. Mach. Imp. & Exp. Corp.*, 161 F.3d 314, 319 (5th Cir. 1998) ("Willful destruction or withholding of evidence constitutes fraud under the FAA").

Fraud, however, is extraordinarily difficult to prove in the arbitration context.[191] Unlike any other judicial review under Sect. 10 (a), the burden of proving vacatur under Sect. 10 (a) (1) is higher than the burden of proving any other grounds under Sect. 10 (a) or under the limited common law grounds for vacatur noted above. The common law developed the following test to prove fraud in the context of vacating an arbitration award: "the fraud was (1) not discoverable upon the exercise of due diligence prior to the arbitration, (2) materially related to an issue in the arbitration, and (3) established by *clear and convincing* evidence."[192] The "clear and convincing" standard is one of the highest burdens of proof in civil litigation. In comparison, the common *de novo* standard gives the reviewer the discretion to review anew and make decisions without any deference to the prior decision-maker.

Plaintiffs asserting fraud based on alleged misconduct of parties and witnesses have not been very successful in post-arbitration motions to vacate, in part because of the high burden of proof.[193] In addition, courts examining the issue also tend to distinguish between cases in which the complaining party addressed the issue of fraud with the arbitrator during the hearing and those cases in which the parties ad-

[191] Fraud is difficult to prove in any context. A cause of action for fraud requires a heightened pleading standard, see, e.g., Fed. R. Civ. P. 9 (b), and a higher burden of proof. Fraud in the context of *FAA* § 10 (a)(2007) (1) is different than fraud generally, but it is still difficult to prove.

[192] *Lafarge Conseils Et Etudes, S.A. vs. Kaiser Cement & Gypsum Corp.*, 791 F.2d 1334, 1339 (9th Cir. 1986) (emphasis added) (affirming confirmation of an arbitration award despite allegations of document falsification because the information was discoverable with the exercise of due diligence); see also *Smith West, LLC vs. Mognach Payne Inc.*, 2010 WL 2471051, *2 (Ariz. App. Div. June 17, 2010) ("[A] party seeking to vacate an arbitration award claiming fraud must show 'that the fraud was (1) not discoverable upon the exercise of due diligence prior to the arbitration, (2) materially related to an issue in the arbitration, and (3) established by clear and convincing evidence'") (citing *Lafarge Conseils Et Etudes, S.A.*, 791 F.2d at 1339). This test appears to be the test that a majority of the courts employ when confronted with a motion for vacatur on the grounds of fraud. Other tests are employed in a minority of jurisdictions. See, e.g., 6 C.J.S., Arbitration § 151, p. 400 ("As a general rule any fraud or misconduct having a tendency to affect the award improperly will vitiate it and render it subject to impeachment"); *Prof'l Builders, Inc. vs. Sedan Floral, Ind.*, 819 P.2d 1254, 1258 (Kan. Ct. App. 1991) (same).

[193] *Molten Metal Equip. Innovations vs. Pyotek, Inc.*, 2010 WL 2639912, at *2 (N.D. Ohio June 29, 2010) (articulating same test and holding that no clear and convincing evidence of fraud existed that was not already presented to the arbitrator and noting that the reason for the rule is because a broader review would "undermine a substantive determination made by the arbitrator"); *Site, Inc. vs. Peabody Const. Co.*, 872 N.E.2d 841 (Mass. App. Ct. 2007) ("In addition, the court held that perjury itself does not constitute fraud for the purposes of vacating a judgment where the moving party cannot demonstrate that the judicial process itself was corrupted by the perjury"); *Artco, Inc. vs. DiFruscia*, 5 Mass. App. Ct. 513, 518 (1977) ("There is no fraud on the court where a judgment has been obtained with the aid of a witness who, on the basis of after-discovered evidence, is believed possibly to have been guilty of perjury"); *Groves vs. Merrill, Lynch, Pierce, Fenner, & Smith, Inc.*, 2006, at *4WL 2059514 (N.J. Super. A.D. 2006) (finding movant did not establish fraud based on alleged document tampering when the arbitrator considered the issue in the first instance); *Thomas vs. Lusk*, 27 Cal. App. 4th 1709 (1994) (reversing judgment in favor of plaintiff, client, in an action for legal malpractice when the plaintiff alleged that his counsel allowed evidence kept at plaintiff's workplace to spoilate prior to an arbitration when both parties had equal access to the evidence).

dress the issue of fraud for the first time on appeal. Both situations involve significant limitations on a party's ability to have an award vacated based on participant fraudulent conduct.

If an arbitrator considered the issue of fraud and ruled against the party now claiming vacatur, courts are particularly reluctant to overturn an issue an arbitrator already considered. In those cases, the arbitrator heard evidence on the issue and ruled. Courts are quite hesitant to overturn a decision that has been considered and decided by an arbitrator—especially because the arbitrator would have considered the witness testimony first hand or otherwise personally observed the complained of conduct.[194] Because telling the truthfulness of a witness or determining the wrongfulness of conduct necessarily involves a credibility assessment and determination of the subjective intent of the alleged wrongful actors, courts are significantly more likely to defer to the arbitrator's assessment of the participants' motivations and actions.[195]

If a party first raises the issue of party misconduct at the point of a motion for vacatur of the award, that party faces a significant challenge overcoming an allegation of waiver—which is embodied within the test for fraud, as noted above. The party instituting the motion for vacatur will have a high burden of proving that the party was not aware of the alleged fraudulent conduct during the course of the proceeding such that the arbitrator could have ruled on the issue in the first instance.[196] If at all possible, the court would rather the arbitrator determine these issues first given the issues of credibility and subjective intent. In addition, requiring an arbitrator to hear these complaints in the first instance prevents parties from having "two bites" at the

[194] See *Jones vs. Dykstra*, 2008 WL 4901080 (November 17, 2008) (affirming confirmation of award because under California law, even if the losing party could show fraud with respect to document destruction, such fraud is "intrinsic" fraud and not a basis upon which an arbitration award may be vacated).

[195] Sometimes the arbitrator finds that a witness lied or that a party committed misconduct during the hearing. The awards in cases in which an arbitrator found participant misconduct are equally difficult to vacate (here, by the party who allegedly engaged in the misconduct). See, e.g., *Hendrik Delivery Serv., Inc. vs. St. Louis Post-Dispatch L.L.C.*, 2007 WL 3071827 (E.D. Mo. October 19, 2007) (confirming an award in which an arbitrator awarded punitive damages, in part, because of the respondent's destruction of documents and failure to create a record of information pertinent to the upcoming arbitration).

[196] See, e.g., *Clyde Bergemann, Inc. vs. Sullivan, Higgins & Brion*, 2008 WL 4279632 (D. Or. September 18, 2008) ("ARC also argues that it is prejudiced by defendants' delay in seeking arbitration because of defendants' alleged spoliation of evidence. I am unpersuaded by ARC's contention that the arbitrator cannot appropriately remedy the situation, if he concludes that the allegations are true"); *Gateway Funding Diversified Mortg. Serv., L.P. v. Field*, 2008 WL 2758877 (E.D. Pa. July 10, 2008) (confirming arbitration award despite arguments that one party destroyed documents when the arbitrator considered the issue on a full record and refused to apply an adverse inference); *Banc of Am. Inv. Serv., Inc. vs. Plycraft Indus.*, 2005 WL 905927 (Cal. Ct. App. April 20, 2005) (enjoining a claim of spoliation from proceeding in arbitration under the doctrine of res judicata when the plaintiff failed to bring such a claim in a first arbitration against Bank of America in a claim involving investment advice and when the plaintiff actually used evidence of the "missing" documentation in the first arbitration).

apple if the fraud could have been discovered at the time of the hearing.[197] Thus, courts are quick to find that a party has waived the ability to bring a challenge for fraud. Even if the party can survive the waiver hurdle, the party still has the relatively high burden of proving fraud by clear and convincing evidence.

While this "clear and convincing" evidentiary burden likely stems from the burden of proof for civil fraud,[198] requiring such a high burden of proof in the arbitration context makes little sense.[199] Parties seeking to vacate an arbitration award on the basis of fraud are not trying to prove a *cause of action* for fraud resulting in damages. Instead, these parties seek only to have a previously issued award vacated on review.[200] The movant's request, or "prayer," to the court is simply that the award be vacated. This is the exact same type of relief that parties would seek under *any* of the grounds for review. Because the relief is the same and the party requesting relief is not instituting an affirmative cause of action, this heightened review makes little sense in the arbitral forum.

Although the waiver requirement may make sense, the heightened standard of review does not. The waiver requirement is a good incentive that arbitrators hear and decide these issues in the first instance, with the ability to weigh evidence (perhaps as it occurs) and consider the credibility of witnesses involved. The waiver requirement also encourages parties to deal with wrongdoing as it happens in the first instance, rather than waiting until an arbitrator decides the case on the merits and taking the award up on review by a court. This requirement further supports the

---

[197] *Id.* at 691 ("The second element [of the test for fraud] prevents the movant from taking a 'second bite at the apple' if the fraud could have been discovered at arbitration"). The Low court also recognized that the test for vacatur on the basis of fraud "sets a high standard in order to deter motions that merely seeks to relitigate issues that were already—or could have been—presented to the arbitrator. The test therefore preserves the parties' bargain for the judgment of the arbitrator." *Low*, 267 P.3d at 692.

[198] See, e.g., *Kelly vs. VinZant*, 197 P.3d 803 (2008) (requiring a plaintiff to prove the following elements of fraud by clear and convincing evidence: (1) a false statement of material fact; (2) that was known to be false or was recklessly made without knowledge concerning falsity; (3) the representation was intentionally made for the purpose of inducing another party to act; (4) the other party reasonably relied and acted upon the representation made; and (5) resulting in damages); *Fleges, Inc. vs. Truserv Corp.*, 2009 WL 424813 (Ky. February 19, 2009) (requiring a plaintiff to prove by clear and convincing evidence that: (1) statement of material fact, (2) that was false, (3) that declarant knew to be false or made recklessly, (4) that declarant induced plaintiff to act upon the misrepresentation, (5) that plaintiff relied upon the misrepresentation, and (6) that the misrepresentation caused damages); *Cowburn vs. Leventis*, 619 S.E.2d 437 (S.C. Ct. App. 2005) (requiring clear and convincing evidence to prove fraud).

[199] Worth noting is the fact that arbitration is a non-public proceeding that may or may not be transcribed or recorded. The amount and type of record in an arbitration might change from case to case, depending on the amount at stake and the financial resources of the parties involved. Proving fraud on the basis of an incomplete record may be difficult, logistically, to do. An additional constraint on the process could be issues of confidentiality, and whether the parties are even at liberty to discuss what happened at the arbitration.

[200] To be sure, some financial repercussion will result if an award is vacated. Typically, the movant seeks to vacate in order to not pay money that is awarded to the non-movant. The movant in this action typically seeks not to get money but to prevent paying out money.

contractual agreement of the parties. The parties agreed to have a dispute resolved by an arbitrator—not a court. Allowing a court to step in and resolve a side dispute pertaining directly to the merits of the dispute before the arbitrator would impose on the province of the arbitrator and likely lengthen the time of dispute resolution, thus cutting against the efficiency of the process. For these reasons, the waiver requirement imposed by the common law makes infinite sense and should be maintained.

To the contrary, the higher burden required for vacatur under Sect. 10(a)(1) does not make sense. As will be demonstrated below, this burden is unlike any other burden imposed on parties seeking to vacate arbitration awards. This standard—an apparent carryover from the civil claim for fraud—has little application in the review of arbitration awards, given the fact that neither party seeks an affirmative judgment for damages, but only a review of a decision made by a third-party neutral.

## *The Standard for Review under Sect. 10 (a) (1) is Inconsistent and Significantly More Burdensome than any other Review Under the Federal Arbitration Act*

This standard of review is unlike any other under the FAA. None of the other grounds for review requires a heightened pleading standard. On the contrary, the courts review arbitration awards on a *de novo* basis to determine whether the plaintiff can show that the arbitration award fits within one of the other four narrow categories (or one of the two common-law categories).[201] This section considers the standards of review for all of the other grounds of review for the FAA, as well as the common law standards of manifest disregard and contrary to public policy. As will be shown, the standard required under Sect. 10 (a) (1) is far more burdensome than any other.

### The Standard of Review Under Sect. 10 (a) (2) Simply Requires a "Reasonable Showing"

Section 10 (a) (2) of the FAA allows a court to vacate an arbitration award if there was "evident partiality or corruption" in the arbitrators.[202] The common law devel-

[201] Courts often conflate the grounds for review with the standard of review. Although the grounds are limited, the burden of proving these grounds is typically analyzed on a *de novo* basis. See, e.g., *Allstate N.J. Ins. Co. vs. Driscoll*, 2011 WL 408837, at *2 (N.J. Super. Ct. App. Div. February 19, 2011) ("Where, as here, a party seeks to vacate an award pursuant to N.J.S.A. 2A:23A-13c(3), the trial court 'shall make an independent determination of any facts relevant [to the application for vacating the award] de novo, upon such record as may exist or as it may determine in a summary expedited proceeding'"); *Braata, Inc. vs. Oneida Cold Storage Co.*, 251 P.3d 584, 588 (Colo. App. 2010) ("The latter issue is explicitly assigned to the court to decide by section 13–22–206(2), C.R.S.2009, and each of the other bases to vacate necessarily requires de novo findings by a court").

[202] 9 U.S.C. § 10 (a)(2).

opment for the standard of review under this section is significantly more lenient than the standard of review noted above under Sect. 10 (a) (1). The disconnect serves no real purpose given that the statute makes no distinction in the burdens of proof among the grounds for vacatur.

Consider the California case of *Ardalan vs. Macy's, Inc.*[203] This case involved a claimant's motion to vacate following a losing arbitration. The arbitration between the parties was heard over nine hearing days, and the arbitrator issued a "lengthy" 22-page award.[204] The claimant/plaintiff made several arguments in the case falling under many of the grounds listed under Sect. 10 (a). The court easily dismissed the claim under Sect. 10 (a) (1) for fraud under the "clear and convincing" burden of proof.[205] After dismissing the argument under Sect. 10 (a) (1), the arbitrator considered the claim under Sect. 10 (a) (2). Although the court did not vacate the arbitration award, the court applied a very different standard of review. When considering if the award should be vacated based on an arbitrator's bias, the court only required a "reasonable impression" of bias—a far lower standard than "clear and convincing" evidence of bias.[206] Because the plaintiff could not show bias even under the lower standard, the court upheld the award.[207] The court did not make any distinctions among the standards, but simply applied different standards to the different grounds for review.

Similarly, in *Urban Associates, Inc. vs. Standard Electronics, Inc*,[208] the Eastern District of Michigan ruled under a very similar standard of vacatur under Sect. 10 (a) (2). The case involved a breakdown of a long-term arrangement between the two companies and resulting commissions due under various contracts. The parties agreed to arbitrate shortly before trial, and participated in a lengthy arbitration process including extensive pre-hearing motions and briefing.[209] The losing party sought to vacate the award based on any number of grounds, including Sect. 10 (a) (2).[210] The court's test under that section was whether a party could present evidence showing that "a reasonable person would have to conclude that an arbitrator was partial to the other party to the arbitration."[211] The types of evidence the court sought consisted primarily of undisclosed relationships with the parties that would

---

[203] 2012 *WL* 25,03972 (N.D. Cal. June 28, 2012).

[204] *Id.* at *1.

[205] *Id.* at *2–3 (citing the heightened standard of review and then finding the award did not evidence any corruption, fraud, or undue means).

[206] *Id.* at *3 ("[Plaintiff] must show that specific facts create a reasonable impression of bias").

[207] *Id.* at *4.

[208] 2012 *WL* 10,79723 (E.D. Mich. Feb. 17, 2012).

[209] *Id.* at *6–8. Prior to the arbitration, the court ruled on summary judgment motions that was later appealed to the Sixth Circuit. *Id.*

[210] The plaintiff did not move for vacatur under Sect. 10 (a)(1).

[211] *Urban Assoc., Inc.*, 2012 WL 1079723, at *10 (quoting *Uhl vs. Komatsu Forklift Co.*, 512 F.3d 294, 306–07 (6th Cir. 2003)).

have created an impression of bias.[212] In this case, the plaintiff's only evidence of bias was a series of rulings against the party—which was utterly insufficient.[213] As with the California court, the Michigan court here did not require any heightened burden of proof. The plaintiff was only to provide "evidence," not "clear and convincing evidence" or any other heightened standard of evidence to prove evident partiality under Sect. 10 (a) (2).

These two cases are typical of cases decided under Sect. 10 (a) (2). Many other courts apply this very standard as well.[214] These cases demonstrate a very different standard between Sect. 10 (a) (2) and Sect. 10 (a) (1), despite the fact that the statute specifies no specific standard of review—much less different standards of review for different sections. Under Sect. 10 (a) (2), the courts simply require that the party seeking vacatur provide evidence (or reasonable evidence) that the statute is satisfied. This standard is significantly less burdensome than a "clear and convincing" evidentiary burden. The lower standard is sufficient to satisfy the goals of arbitration (such as finality and contractual intent) without creating an artificially high burden of proof.

## Courts State no Specific Burden Under Sect. 10 (a) (3) but Simply Consider Whether Parties Present Evidence Meeting the Narrow Grounds for Vacatur

Section 10 (a) (3) of the FAA allows a court to vacate an arbitration award if the arbitrator's conduct deprives a party of a fair hearing. The statute specifically mentions arbitrator misconduct such as failure to postpone reasonable requests for hearings and failure to admit evidence, provided the party alleging the wrongdoing can show prejudice.[215] Again, the statute mentions no specific evidentiary burden of

---

[212] Typically, the types of information that would create bias would be personal or financial relationships between the arbitrator and one of the parties, witnesses, or counsel.

[213] Id. at *10 ("The fact that the majority arbitrators ruled against plaintiff, even repeatedly, does not establish improper motives and thus provides no evidence of evident partiality").

[214] See, e.g., *Freedom Investors Corp. vs. Hadath*, 2012 WL 383944, at *4 (S.D.N.Y. Feb. 7, 2012) ("An arbitrator is disqualified only when a reasonable person, considering all of the circumstances, would have to conclude that an arbitrator was partial to one side"); *Cont'l Cas. Co. vs. Staffing Concepts, Inc.*, 2001 WL 7459781 (M.D. Fla. Dec. 20, 2011) (requiring evidence of an undisclosed conflict of interest or an actual conflict of interest); *Nw. Direct Teleservices, Inc. vs. Zweizig*, 2011 WL 7331297 (D. Or. Nov. 18, 2011) ("To show evident partiality in an arbitrator, a party either must establish specific facts indicating actual bias toward or against a party or show the arbitrator failed to disclose to the parties information that creates a reasonable impression of bias") (internal quotation marks and citation omitted); *Vinco Painting, Inc. vs. Painters Dist. Counsel No. 30,* 2010 *WL* 28,91685 (N.D. Ill. July 19, 2012) ("[E]vident partiality" exists where a "reasonable person would… conclude that an arbitrator was partial") (citation omitted). These are a mere sampling of recent cases ruling on the issue of evident partiality.

[215] Section 10 (a)(3) allows vacation "where the arbitrators were guilty of misconduct in refusing to postpone the hearing, upon sufficient cause shown, or in refusing to hear evidence pertinent and material to the controversy; or of any other misbehavior by which the rights of any party have been prejudiced."

proof before this standard is available to the parties. As demonstrated in the cases below, the courts have not applied a higher burden to cases under Sect. 10 (a) (3), even though they do require such a burden under Sect. 10 (a) (1).

The Texas case of *MPJ vs. Aero Sky, L.L.C.*[216] examined the standard set forth under Sect. 10 (a) (3) for procedural fairness. The underlying contract called for Aero Sky to perform certain maintenance on MPJ airplanes, and a dispute arose regarding certain scheduled maintenance.[217] The arbitrator awarded more than US $ 450, 000 in damages to MPJ.[218] MPJ moved to confirm the award,[219] and Aero Sky moved to vacate the award on multiple grounds. Aero Sky moved for vacatur under Sect. 10 (a) (1) based on the alleged misconduct of one of MPJ's principals. The court rejected the argument, finding that Aero Sky could not, among other things, meet the "clear and convincing" evidentiary burden.[220] Aero Sky also argued that the arbitrator prohibited it from providing certain evidence, thus requiring vacatur under Sect. 10 (a) (3).[221] The court articulated the standard for vacatur as follows: "To constitute misconduct requiring vacation of an award, an error in the arbitrator's determination must be simply not an error of law, but which so affects the rights of a party that it may be said that he was deprived a fair hearing."[222] Although this standard is *narrow*, the court does not impose any increased *evidentiary burden* on the party requesting vacatur—such as a "clear and convincing" burden. The court ultimately concluded that Aero Sky could not meet the "extraordinarily narrow" grounds for review.[223] Again, this case demonstrates the differing evidentiary burdens required by parties seeking vacatur under different sections of the FAA without any discussion or rationale as to how two standards under the same statute with *no guidance* at all on the evidentiary burden of the parties apply vastly different burdens for different sections.

The New York case of *In re Arbitration Before New York Stock Exchange*[224] also considered the Sect. 10 (a) (3) hearing. The case involved a dispute over who should receive a stock dividend when the sale order came at roughly the same time as the payment of a dividend. The investor received the dividend, and Merrill Lynch initiated an arbitration in order to receive that dividend back. After an arbitration hearing involving a significant amount of live testimony and attorney arguments,

---

[216] 673 F. Supp. 2d 475 (W.D. Tex. 2009).

[217] *Id.* at 483.

[218] *Id.* at 482.

[219] MPJ moved to confirm the award under Sect. 9 of the FAA, which mandates that courts confirm an arbitration award if it is not vacated or modified under Sects. 10 and 11 of the FAA. 9 U.S.C. § 9.

[220] 673 F. Supp. 2d at 494.

[221] *Id.* at 498.

[222] *Id.* (citing *Laws vs. Morgan Stanley Dean Witter*, 452 F.3d 398, 399 (5th Cir. 2006)) (internal quotation marks omitted).

[223] *Id.* at 499.

[224] 2004 *WL* 2072460 (S.D.N.Y. Sept. 5, 2004).

the panel issued an award in favor of Merrill Lynch.[225] The investor moved to vacate the award under multiple grounds. In discussing the fairness of the hearing under Sect. 10 (a) (3), the court stated that "except where fundamental fairness is violated, arbitration determinations will not be opened up to evidentiary review. A fundamentally unfair proceeding may result if the arbitration panel does not give each of the parties to the dispute an adequate opportunity to present its evidence and argument."[226] In this case, the court considered the investor's objection to the recall of a key witness, but ultimately determined that the arbitration proceeding was fundamentally fair.[227] Again, the court did not require any heightened burden, just a showing of specific facts that would establish a party's inability to present its own argument and evidence. Other cases impose very similar burdens for this section of the FAA.[228]

Although the grounds for vacatur under Sect. 10 (a) (3) are narrow, the burden of proof appears to be one of *de novo* review, with the reviewing court, in the first instance, determining whether the plaintiff has evidence to support the ground for vacatur. In this instance, the court seeks to determine whether the arbitrator admitted all of the material evidence and gave the parties equal time to put on their proofs. The parties are not required to show these types of misconduct by clear and convincing evidence—they only need to show the misconduct with evidence. Like Sect. 10 (a) (2), the burden of proof under Sect. 10 (a) (3) is significantly lower and not the heightened burden of clear and convincing evidence now required under Sect. 10 (a) (1).

## *Section 10 (a) (4) Similarly Contains No Burden of Proof and Courts Review These Cases on a De Novo Basis*

The final statutory grounds for relief is found in Sect. 10 (a) (4), which allows for vacatur if the arbitrators "exceeded their powers."[229] As noted above, arbitration is a creature of contract, and all arbitrators acquire their powers to resolve the dispute

---

[225] *Id.* at *4.

[226] *Id.* at *10 (citing *Tempo Shane Corp. vs. Bertek, Inc.*, 120 F.3d 16, 20 (2d Cir. 1997) (internal quotation marks omitted).

[227] *Id.* at *10–11.

[228] See, e.g., *Stone v. Bear, Sterns & Co.*, ___ F. Supp. 2d ___, 2012 WL 1946938, at *13 (E.D. Pa. May 29, 2012) (requiring a plaintiff to show that the aggrieved party did not receive a "fundamentally fair" hearing); *New York City Dist. Council of Carpenters vs. Dufour Grp. Inc.*, 2012 WL 13,72122 (S.D.N.Y. Apr. 19, 2012) (requiring vacatur if the proceeding is "fundamentally unfair"); *Bajaj vs. Fisher Asset Mgmt., L.L.C.*, 2012 WL 1293169 (D. Del. Apr. 10, 2012) (granting vacatur only if the evidence not allowed in the hearing deprives the complaining party of a "fair hearing"); *Wells Fargo Advisors, L.L.C. vs. Watts*, ___ F. Supp. 2d ___, 2012 WL 831878 (W.D.N.C. Mar. 12, 2012) (refusing to vacate because the plaintiff could not show any "gross misconduct" with respect to evidentiary and other procedural issues).

[229] 9 U.S.C. § 10 (a) (4).

from the agreement to arbitrate. Because arbitration is a contractual agreement, arbitrators can only resolve the claims the parties agreed to submit to the process. Parties are not required to submit to arbitration anything that they did not so agree.[230] Thus, Sect. 10 (a) (4) protects the parties' agreements to arbitrate and courts can award vacatur if the arbitrators go beyond the powers given to them by contract.

Of all of the Sect. 10 (a) grounds for vacatur, review for "exceeding authority" is considered the most generous review afforded to the parties, likely because of the flexibility and "wiggle room" within the text of the statute. Even this ground for review is limited, however, and few courts actually overturn awards on this basis.[231] The following cases illustrate the operation of Sect. 10 (a) (4).

In 2010, the US Supreme Court discussed the operation of Sect. 10 (a) (4) in an unlikely situation—the discussion of class action status. A little background on this case is helpful. Over the last few decades, many large companies began using arbitration agreements in their consumer agreements for products such as credit cards, cellular telephones, and mortgages.[232] Questions arose regarding the operation of class actions within the world of arbitration. The Supreme Court first addressed the issue of class action arbitrations in the 2003 case of *Bazzle vs. Green Tree*.[233] The plurality opinion in *Bazzle* found that arbitrators, not courts, should determine the suitability of class actions based on the contract language.[234] Following *Bazzle*, the AAA and other arbitral providers began providing class arbitration services in which the arbitrators, following *Bazzle*, would determine if the contract language allowed for a class procedure. Indeed, most arbitrators who ruled on the issue found that a contract that was "silent" as to class actions (i.e, neither prohibited nor explicitly permitted class actions) were still suitable for class procedures.[235]

The *Stolt-Nielsen* case arose from this newly created system. The Stolt-Nielsen parties were sophisticated businesses who contracted to rent certain space on a ves-

---

[230] See, e.g., *First Options of Chi., Inc. vs. Kaplan*, 514 U.S. 938 (1995) (holding that a party who did not sign an arbitration agreement did not have to arbitrate the dispute because the evidence did not show that the party who did not sign the agreement had actually agreed to arbitrate the matter in dispute).

[231] *Harper Ins. Ltd. vs. Century Indem. Co.*, 819 F. Supp. 2d 270, 276 (S.D.N.Y. 2011) ("The Second Circuit has consistently accorded the narrowest readings to the FAA's authorization to vacate awards pursuant to § 10(a)(4)") (internal quotation marks and citations omitted).

[232] New research suggests that fewer companies use widespread arbitration agreements in consumer contracts than originally suggested. See Peter B. Rutledge & Christopher R. Drahozal, *Contract and Choice*, __ *B.Y.U.L.R.* ___ (2012) (finding that arbitration agreements are not as widespread in consumer contracts as the literature suggests and finding that many businesses use arbitration in their business-to-business contracts).

[233] *Green Tree Fin. Corp. vs. Bazzle*, 539 U.S. 444 (2003).

[234] *Id.* In *Bazzle*, the South Carolina courts, not the arbitrators, decided that class status was appropriate. The Court reversed for the arbitrators to make this determination in the first instance.

[235] *Stolt-Nielsen, S.A*, 130 S. Ct. at 1770.

sel for the transportation of liquids.[236] A large number of companies who contracted to ship relatively small amounts of liquids instituted an arbitration against the vessel as a class action. The arbitrator held that the contract language was broad enough to support a class action, falling in line with a long line of similar arbitration awards in a wide variety of situations.[237] The Supreme Court held that the arbitrators erred in the class action ruling because the arbitrators "exceeded their powers" under Sect. 10 (a) (4). The Court reiterated how arbitration is a matter of contract and that the parties can choose how they want to arbitrate and with whom they choose to arbitrate. The Court concluded that "it follows that a party may not be compelled under the FAA to submit to class arbitration unless there is a contractual basis for concluding that the parties *agreed* to do so."[238] Ultimately, the Court concluded that the nature of bilateral (i.e., two party) arbitration was so incredibly different from the nature of multiparty arbitration (including class arbitration), that an agreement to arbitrate bilaterally does not, on its own, imply a right to proceed in a class arbitration.[239] Thus, a truly "silent" agreement on the issue of class action arbitration cannot, under Sect. 10 (a) (4), be read to include class arbitration.

Although this recent holding invokes Sect. 10 (a) (4), the Court did nothing to explain the contours of this section and how a litigant would prove that an arbitrator exceeded powers under the section. Despite the Court's lack of guidance, the Court did *not* employ any type of heightened evidentiary standard or require that the plaintiffs establish meeting the standard by clear and convincing evidence or any other heightened standard. Accordingly, no such heightened pleading standard seems to exist under Sect. 10 (a) (4), while such a standard does exist under Sect. 10(a)(1). Similar cases demonstrate that no heightened evidentiary standard exists under this section.[240]

As these sections demonstrate, no other subsection of Sect. 10 (a) has been interpreted to have a heightened evidentiary burden similar to the one employed under

---

236 *Id.* at 1764–65.

237 The AAA published all documents in the class action docket. Something of an anomaly in arbitration law, arbitrators in the class action docket could conduct an electronic search for similar awards. Given the accessibility of awards by fellow arbitrators, a type of arbitral "common law" began to develop in which the majority of "silent" arbitration awards were interpreted to support a class action procedure. See *Stolt-Nielsen, S.A*, 130 S. Ct. at 1176.

238 *Id.* at 1775 (emphasis in original).

239 *Id.* at 1775–76.

240 See, e.g., *Agility Pub. Warehousing Co. K.S.C. vs. Supreme Foodservice GmbH*, ___ F. Supp. 2d ___ (S.D.N.Y. 2011) (citing Stolt-Nielsen and not applying any particular burden of proof with respect to the claim under Sect. 10 (a) (4)); *S. Comm. Servs., Inc. vs. Thomas*, 829 F. Supp. 2d 1324 (N.D. Ga. 2011) (post-Stolt-Nielsen case finding that the arbitrator did not exceed powers in interpreting the law and the parties' contract to find that a cellular telephone agreement permitted class action relief); *Morgan Keegan & Co. vs. Garrett*, 816 F. Supp. 2d 439 (S.D. Tex. 2011) (vacating award on the basis of exceeding powers because an arbitrator heard claims by parties not subject to the arbitration agreement as well as claims not covered by the arbitration agreement and applying no particular burden in conducting this analysis); *Priority One Servs., Inc. vs. W & T Travel Servs., L.L.C.*, 825 F. Supp. 2d 43 (D.D.C. 2011) (analyzing the case under Sect. 10 (a)(4) without applying any type of heightened evidentiary burden).

Sect. 10 (a) (1). No good reason exists for the heightened burden as to cases involving allegations of fraudulent conduct when all of the other narrow grounds for vacatur are examined on a *de novo* basis. This chapter recommends putting Sect. 10 (a) (1) back in line with the other statutory grounds for vacatur and eliminating the heightened evidentiary burden for vacatur. The following two sections consider the burdens of proof for vacatur under the two non-statutory grounds of review, that is, for manifest disregard and vacatur for being contrary to public policy.

## *The "Manifest Disregard" Standard of Vacatur, to the Extent it is Still a Viable Source of Review, Requires a Simple Evidentiary Standard*

Although the viability of the "manifest disregard" standard of vacatur is currently in flux, when applied, the courts do not require a heightened evidentiary standard similar to the grounds for review under Sect. 10 (a) (1). Instead, they apply a rather standard, two-part test with no discussion regarding the evidentiary burden on the part of the party seeking vacatur. The court looks at the "exceedingly narrow" circumstances in which an arbitrator "knew the relevant legal position" and appreciated its applicability, yet still "willfully flouted the governing law by refusing to apply it."[241] Although this grounds for review is narrow, the courts do not require a heightened burden of proof before the court to vacate an award.

The following case illustrates the difference between the narrowness of the grounds and the evidentiary burden in this context. In *Rame, LLC vs. Popovich*,[242] an arbitrator determined that claimants could proceed as a class in a suit against their employer. The employer moved to vacate the opinion on multiple grounds, including the grounds that the arbitrator acted in manifest disregard of the law—particularly the *Stolt-Nielsen* decision. The court noted that the Second Circuit recognized the continuing validity of the "manifest disregard" standard as a "judicial gloss" on the FAA and thus survives *Hall Street*.[243] With respect to the standard of review for this standard, the court noted:

> "[A]wards are vacated on grounds of manifest disregard only in those exceedingly rare instances where some egregious impropriety on the part of the arbitrator is apparent." Such impropriety requires "more than error or misunderstanding with respect to the law, or an arguable difference regarding the meaning or applicability of law urged upon an arbitrator." The two part showing requires the court to consider, first, "whether the governing law alleged to have been ignored by the arbitrator was well defined, explicit, and clearly applicable," and, second, "whether the arbitrator knew about the existence of a clearly governing legal principle but decided to ignore it or pay no attention to it."[244]

---

[241] *Langlais vs. PennMont Ben. Servs., Inc.*, 2012 WL 2849414, at *3 (E.D. Pa. July 11, 2012) (citations omitted).

[242] 878 F. Supp. 2d 439, 2012 WL 2719159 (S.D.N.Y. July 9, 2012).

[243] *Id.* at *4.

[244] *Id.* (citations omitted).

In this case, the court found that the party seeking vacatur could not meet this narrow test. The arbitrator in this case considered over eighty pages of legal memoranda regarding the availability of class action arbitration following the *Stolt-Nielsen* decision and distinguishing this case from the Supreme Court precedent.[245] Accordingly, the court did not overturn the arbitrator's reasoned decision that considered and addressed all of the proper legal issues.

The *Rame* decision illustrates how even a grounds for review described as successful in the "exceedingly rare" circumstance still has a lower burden of proof than seeking vacatur under Sect. 10 (a) (4). Indeed, following the *Stolt-Nielsen* decision, many courts interpreted that decision as meaning that all clauses that did not specifically allow class arbitration could not support a class action procedure. Here, this arbitrator found a way to distinguish this Supreme Court precedent, despite the factual similarities in the two cases. Although the decision was upheld, the court only required that the moving party establish that the arbitrator knew what the law was and that the arbitrator disregarded the law. The court did not require that either of these elements be proven by a standard other than a preponderance, or *de novo* standard, unlike the "clear and convincing" burden required under Sect. 10 (a) (1). Similar cases demonstrate that no special evidentiary burden must be proven to succeed on a claim under the "manifest disregard" standard.[246]

## *Review for Violation of Public Policy Similarly Does Not Require a Heightened Evidentiary Burden*

The final widely recognized ground for review is if the award would be contrary to public policy. As with the other grounds for review noted above, the review for being contrary to public policy is a *narrow* ground for review, but the movant need not prove entitlement to vacatur by any higher standard than a preponderance of the evidence. The courts follow a rather simple test without requiring a higher evidentiary burden of proof.

Most commonly, awards will be vacated on the grounds of violation of public policy when an award requires a party to do something other than pay money. As noted above, certain types of reinstatements can be subject to vacatur on public policy grounds, especially if an arbitrator reinstates an employee with a history of substance abuse to a position involving public health and safety, such as a pilot or bus driver. Unsurprisingly, most awards challenged on public policy grounds stem

---

245 *Id.* at *13.

246 See *Langlais*, 2012 WL 2849414, at *3 (applying two-part test without any discussion of the burden of proof); *Ardalan vs. Macy's Inc.*, 2012 WL 2503972, at *6 (N.D. Cal. June 28, 2012) (same); *Williams vs. Nat'l Football League*, 2012 WL 2366636, at *7 (D. Colo. June 21, 2012) (same).

from labor and employment arbitrations. The following cases demonstrate the operation of this ground for vacatur.

For instance, in *Crozer-Chester Medical Center vs. Crozer-Chester Nurses Association*,[247] the arbitrator awarded reinstatement for a nurse, finding that her workplace infraction did not warrant termination.[248] The nurse improperly connected electronic monitoring equipment to a patient such that the patient's vital signs were not being recorded, and no one was alerted when the patient died.[249] The nurse had previously received discipline on a number of occasions, so the employer terminated her employment following this incident. The nurse followed the grievance procedure, which eventually led to arbitration of the dispute over the nurse's discipline. The court noted that the standard for vacating an award for a violation of public policy is if the award "violates a well defined and dominant public policy discernible by reference to the laws and legal precedents and not from general considerations of supposed public interest."[250] The arbitrator based the award on the principles of progressive discipline and the fact that a failure to properly use the monitoring equipment did not appear on the employer's own list of "immediate termination" actions.[251] Given the arbitrator's careful consideration of the arguments and evidence, the court confirmed the award. This case, like the others discussed above, demonstrates that courts do not apply a higher burden of proof for any other grounds for vacatur other than under Sect. 10 (a) (1).

In *Williams vs. National Football League*,[252] the plaintiff player received a 6-game suspension after the plaintiff's urine drug test uncovered that the player's urine was tampered with and not, in fact, human urine.[253] The plaintiff appealed the suspension, and an arbitrator heard the case. Ultimately, the arbitrator upheld the plaintiff's suspension.[254] At the arbitration, the plaintiff established some irregularity with the collection and testing of the sample, but the arbitrator determined that any irregularities did not interfere with the correct test results.[255] The plaintiff challenged the award on multiple grounds, including a violation of public policy. With respect to the public policy argument, the plaintiff argued that the arbitration award contravened the "established laws of the international sports community and the

[247] 2012 *WL* 25,00930 (E.D. Pa. June 29, 2012).

[248] *Id.* at *2.

[249] *Id.* at *1.

[250] *Id.* at *5 (internal quotations and citations omitted).

[251] *Id.*

[252] *Williams*, 2012 WL 2366636 (D. Colo. June 21, 2012).

[253] *Id.* at 1.

[254] *Id.*

[255] *Id.* at *3 (noting how the arbitrator was troubled by the procedures followed in the arbitration, but that "the deviations from established protocol in this case did not materially affect the validity of the test").

public policy underlying those laws."[256] In evaluating this argument, the court applied the following standard: "[F]or a court to determine that an award contravenes public policy, the policy must be well defined and dominant, and is to be ascertained by reference to the laws and legal precedents and not from general considerations of supposed public interests."[257] The plaintiff argued that precedent from the Court of Arbitration for Sport (CAS) established something of a "strict liability" for drug cases involving tampered samples. The plaintiff also noted that, on one occasion, Major League Baseball vacated a 50-game suspension because of a tampered urine sample.[258] Despite this "precedent," the court still upheld the arbitration award on the basis that the law cited by the plaintiff was not clearly established enough to warrant vacatur. Pointing to a single MLB example and a questionable line of precedent by CAS was simply not enough. Here, the court employed a narrow, difficult-to-establish standard, but the court did not require any type of increased burden of proof for the plaintiff to establish entitlement to vacatur. Other cases follow suit.[259] Thus, these cases fall in line with the long line of cases that do not require a heightened standard unless the movant brings the case under Sect. 10 (a) (1). In other words, only Sect. 10 (a) (1) for fraud has a heightened burden of proof.

## *The Common Law Should Eliminate the "Clear and Convincing" Standard Under Sect. 10 (a) (1)*

As the preceding sections demonstrate, all of the grounds for vacating an arbitration award are considerably narrow and hard to establish. In practice, most arbitration awards are confirmed, and few awards are vacated. Section 10 (a) (1), however, stands alone in adding a "clear and convincing" burden of proof upon an already narrow test to meet for vacating an arbitration award. This elevated burden of proof evolved through the common law, and the common law should now reverse course and eliminate this requirement.

No legitimate reason exists for the heightened evidentiary standard. Section 10 (a) makes no mention of evidentiary burdens of proof, and none of the other grounds for review have a heightened burden of proof. The common law grounds

---

256 *Id.* at *6.

257 *Id.* (internal quotation marks and citations omitted).

258 *Id.* The case involving the vacated suspension involved the steroid scandal of Ryan Braun.

259 *Bradford vs. Union Pac. R. Co.*, ___ F. Supp. 2d ___, 2012 WL 1969319 (D. Ariz. June 1, 2012) (requiring public policy to be well established, but not requiring any type of heightened evidentiary standard); *Zoom Elec., Inc. vs. Int'l Broth. Of Elec. Workers, Local 595*, 2012 WL 951778, at *6 (N.D. Cal. Mar. 20, 2012) ("Similarly, to vacate an arbitration award on public policy grounds, a court must find: (1) that an explicit, well-defined and dominant public policy exists, and (2) that the policy is one that specifically militates against the relief ordered by the arbitrator") (internal quotation marks and citations omitted); *Chi. Bears Football Club, Inc. vs. Haynes*, 816 F. Supp. 2d 534, 537 (N.D. Ill. 2011) (noting that the standard to vacate for public policy reasons is narrow, but saying nothing with respect to the burden of proof of showing that the party meets the standard).

for review, too, do not require a heightened evidentiary burden. In other words, Sect. 10 (a) (1) is an anomaly.

No legitimate reason exists for this anomaly. All four subparts of Sect. 10 (a) (as well as the common law grounds for vacatur) deal with misconduct of some type, and Sect. 10 (a) (1) is the only subsection that even arguably applies to participant conduct, as opposed to arbitrator misconduct. From a statutory interpretation standpoint, no reason exists to add a heightened burden of proof to one subsection and not the rest. In fact, the rules of statutory interpretation would counsel courts to treat all of the subsections the same. By adding a heightened burden of proof to Sect. 10 (a) (1) and not any of the other subsections of Sect. 10 (a), the courts are effectively re-writing the statute and adding words to the statute that clearly are not there. The way to correct this problem would be simply to eliminate the heightened burden and treat all of the subsections in a similar manner.

In addition, arbitrator misconduct is not dissimilar from participant (mis)conduct such that policy would require a different evidentiary standard for participant misconduct but not arbitrator misconduct. Whether or not an arbitrator or other participant commits the misconduct does not matter. In both situations, the victim is harmed and the resulting award may be influenced by improper conduct. Also, no matter who commits the misconduct, the arbitration process is tarnished and the reputation of arbitration everywhere suffers. Participant misconduct should be treated in a similar manner as arbitrator misconduct, and a party seeking vacatur of an award for participant misconduct should not be held to a higher burden of proof. Removing the heightened evidentiary standard to vacate an award for participant misconduct would demonstrate that all misconduct should be handled in a similar manner and that one type of misconduct (i.e., arbitrator misconduct) is not more serious than another type (i.e., participant misconduct).

Removing the "clear and convincing" requirement would not make vacatur under Sect. 10 (a) (1) any easier than any other standard of vacatur that already exists. In other words, this minor modification would hardly "open the floodgates" for lawsuits or for vacatur of arbitrator awards. Certainly, the finality of an arbitrator's decision would still be intact because proving a case of fraud—even without the "clear and convincing" burden of proof—is still a difficult showing for a party seeking vacatur. The party would still have to prove the other grounds for fraud, including that the fraud was (1) not discoverable upon the exercise of due diligence prior to the arbitration, and (2) materially related to an issue in the arbitration. The waiver and materiality requirements would still exist under this proposal, and only the burden of proof would change. Because of the slight modification suggested, the grounds for review would still be narrow—similar to all of the other grounds for vacatur, only Sect. 10 (a) (1) would not have a high burden of proof in addition to the narrow circumstances under which vacatur can be obtained.

Perhaps most importantly, this change would further encourage ethical conduct by arbitration participants. As it stands now, arbitration participants can essentially engage in misconduct, provided that one party does not have "clear and convincing" evidence of that misconduct. The heightened pleading standard thus incentivizes overly zealous behavior on the part of parties, witnesses and attorneys, further exacerbating the ethical loophole that already exists in the criminal law. Thus, this chapter urges courts to abandon the requirement for "clear and convincing" evidence for vacatur under Sect. 10 (a) (1) in order to encourage ethical conduct in the arbitration process.

## Conclusion

The application of ethical rules to the arbitral process over the last century has been piecemeal, at best. As this chapter demonstrates, serious loopholes exist in arbitration's structure as a conflict resolution mechanism, with few enforcement opportunities. Two of the most serious loopholes dealing with participant misconduct include the inapplicability of criminal laws to arbitration participants as well as the heightened burden of proof required to vacate an award that was procured by participant fraud.

This Chapter recommends two changes that would have a large impact on arbitration ethics and thereby improve the wellbeing of all parties involved. The first change would be to modify the criminal law such that the definition of "official proceedings" would include binding arbitration. This small change would make all of the criminal laws dealing with official proceedings, such as perjury, tampering, bribery, and others, applicable to the arbitral forum. The second change would be to eliminate the "clear and convincing" burden of proof for motions to vacate under Sect. 10 (a) (1) for fraud. No legitimate reason exists to single out fraudulent conduct for more stringent review compared to all of the other grounds for vacatur. Eliminating the higher burden of proof would further encourage ethical conduct in arbitration and promote justice by providing relief for parties who have suffered mistreatment or abuse because of misconduct by an arbitration participant.

While these two changes appear relatively minor, they would potentially have a large impact on arbitration ethics. These changes would clearly articulate that unethical conduct will not be tolerated in the arbitral forum, and that if parties were to act in an unethical manner, criminal sanctions and vacatur of arbitral awards could result as consequence. These changes would also signal to arbitration participants, and the world, that arbitration is a fair and just process for dispute resolution.

# Chapter 11
# Retired to Greener Pastures: The Public Costs of Private Judging

**Maureen A. Weston**

## The Public Justice System

The US Constitution establishes the framework for the operation of public governmental authority and the protection of rights in the country.[1] Under this federalist system of government, law is established and enforced through representatives of the federal government, as empowered and circumscribed in the Constitution, and otherwise by individual state governments. At both the state and federal levels, powers are separated among the executive, legislative, and judicial branches of government—in order to ensure a balance of power and function, as well as independence of the judiciary.[2] The Constitution also accords the right to access the public justice system, which guarantees citizens certain due process protections including the right to have a case heard by a judge or jury, proceedings open to the public, rules of procedure and evidence, as well as rights to present and confront witnesses, to a reasoned decision, and to appellate review.[3] The trial process is a formal hearing, presided over by a public judge who decides the case on the basis

[1] US Const. art. I–III.

[2] The separation of powers doctrine balances the legislature's constitutional power to determine public policy, the judiciary's inherent power over its own proceedings, and the executive branch's enforcement powers, and precludes undue interference by one of the other branches into the authority of the other two branches. See John F. Manning, *Separation of Powers As Ordinary Interpretation*, 124 Harv. L. Rev. 1939 (2011).

[3] It is axiomatic that "[a] fair trial in a fair tribunal is a basic requirement of due process." Caperton v. Massey, 129 S. Ct. 2252, 2264 (2009) (citing In re Murchison, 349 U.S. 133 (1955).

The author would like to thank participants and organizers of the University of Nebraska-Lincoln Conference on Justice, Conflict, and Well-Being and Pepperdine law student Jeff Salvesen for his helpful research assistance.

M. A. Weston (✉)
School of Law, Pepperdine University, 24255 Pacific Coast Highway, Malibu, CA 90263, USA
e-mail: Maureen.Weston@pepperdine.edu

B. H. Bornstein, R. L. Wiener (eds.), *Justice, Conflict and Wellbeing*, 
DOI 10.1007/978-1-4939-0623-9_11, 

of law.[4] The public justice forum also entitles parties to the discovery of relevant information and the joinder of claims and parties, including the right to bring cases in a representative capacity in the form of a class action.[5]

The public court system is designed to provide a forum for a fair trial that vindicates rights, and is integral enough to our democracy to be publicly funded. As public institutions, courts serve an important public function in preserving the rule of law as needed for a just and ordered society. Judges, as public officials, provide a central role in the protections of the public justice system.[6] Despite procedural protections designed to ensure fairness and access to information, the public court system is under attack and criticized for its delay, clogged dockets, and costs.[7] According to Chief Justice Roberts in his 2011 Year-End Report on the Federal Judiciary, judges, who serve as guardians to this public justice system, are underpaid, overworked, and increasingly migrating to the greener pastures of private industry and private judging.[8]

Mechanisms for the private resolution of disputes have evolved and taken root since the early 1980s as alternatives to address the costs, delays, and uncertainties of the public justice system.[9] The "Alternative Dispute Resolution" Movement (ADR) has brought processes for private justice and dispute resolution to mainstream use. Arbitration and mediation are the most common forms of ADR, although ADR can encompass a variety of mixed and customized processes.[10] Arbitration is a private adjudicative process where the parties select the arbitrator to render a final and binding award.[11] Mediation is an informal, consensual process where a mediator, as

[4] Owen Fiss, *Against Settlement*, 93 Yale L. J. 1073, 1090 (1984) ("[A]djudication uses public resources, and employs not strangers chosen by the parties but public officials chosen by a process in which the public participates. These officials, like members of the legislative and executive branches, possess a power that has been defined and conferred by public law, not by private agreement. Their job is not to maximize the ends of private parties, not simply to secure the peace, but to explicate and give force to the values embodied in authoritative texts such as the Constitution and statutes: to interpret those values and to bring reality into accord with them….").

[5] *See, e.g.*, Fed. R. Civ. P. 1, 18, 26, 23.

[6] *See* Richard A. Posner, *The Role of the Judge in the Twenty-First Century*, 86 B.U. L. Rev. 1049 (2006); Fiss, *supra* note 4, at 1084 (emphasizing the "guiding presence of the judge" in balancing disparities in power and guarding the fairness).

[7] Charles Silver, *Symposium: What We Know and Do Not Know About the Impact of Civil Justice on the American Economy and Policy: Does Civil Justice Cost Too Much?*, 80 Tex. L. Rev. 2073, 2103–2104 (2002) (reporting on the increase in private ADR caseloads and private arbitration providers).

[8] Id. See also U.S. Supreme Court Chief Justice, 2011 Year End Report on the Federal Judiciary (Dec. 31, 2011),

http://www.supremecourt.gov/publicinfo/year-end/year-endreports.aspx.

[9] For a description of the history and uses of ADR, see 1 Alternative Dispute Resolution Practice Guide § 1:1.

[10] Med-arb, arbitration-mediation, mini-trial, early neutral evaluation, ombuds. *See* 1 Litigating Tort Cases § 11:75.

[11] *See* Carrie J. Menkel-Meadow, *Ethics Issues in Arbitration and Related Dispute Resolution Processes: What's Happening and What's Not*, 56 U. Miami L. Rev. 949 (2002) (defining arbitra-

a neutral third party, facilitates the parties in attempting to reach a negotiated resolution. Parties to mediation also typically select and hire the mediator. Although ADR processes are generally conducted completely outside the court system and pursuant to a contractual provision, courts are also embracing ADR by referring, and at times ordering, parties in litigated cases to seek resolution via a private ADR process.[12] Increasingly, private mediators and arbitrators are commissioned to administer justice in public and privately filed cases.

Speed, efficiency, lower costs, party control, and finality are the lauded hallmarks of ADR processes.[13] While those features are increasingly questioned as arbitration in particular becomes more formalized and characterized as "the new litigation," the market for ADR services continues to grow.[14] Although arbitration has been used for centuries in specialized commercial industries, arbitration provisions have now become standard features of commercial and consumer contracts in the USA.[15]

This "alternative" private means for resolving disputes differs significantly from the public courts. Agreements to arbitrate are enforceable under state and federal law.[16] The Federal Arbitration Act (FAA) provides for the enforcement of agreements to arbitrate and is the source of substantial power preempting state initiatives that may seek to regulate arbitration in the interests of protecting consumers and the public.[17] Regarding the FAA as federal policy favoring arbitration, the US Supreme Court has held that the enforceability of arbitration agreements extends to federal and state statutory claims and applies to all contracts involving interstate commerce, including consumer and employment.[18] Arbitration contracts can even be enforced when written to deny consumers or employees from seeking collective relief, such as in a class action, in court or in arbitration. In *AT&T v. Concepcion,* the Court held that the FAA's mandate to enforce arbitration contracts as written preempts state law which invali-

---

tion as "[u]sually (but not always) a private process of adjudication in which the parties in dispute with each other choose decision-makers (sometimes one, often a panel of three) and the rules of procedure, evidence, and decision by which their disputes will be settled").

[12] *See* Donna Shestowsky, *Disputants' Preferences for Court-Connected Dispute Resolution Procedures: Why We Should Care and Why We Know So Little*, 23 Ohio St. J. on Disp. Resol. 549, 625 (2008).

[13] *See* Allied-Bruce Terminix Cos. v. Dobson, 513 U.S. 265, 280 (1995) ("The advantages of arbitration are many: it is usually cheaper and faster than litigation; it can have simpler procedural and evidentiary rules; it normally minimizes hostility and is less disruptive of ongoing and future business dealings among the parties....").

[14] *See, e.g.*, Thomas J. Stipanowich, *Arbitration: The "New Litigation,"* 2010 U. Ill. L. Rev. 1 (2010).

[15] *See, e.g.*, Soia Mentschikoff, *Commercial Arbitration*, 61 Colum. L. Rev. 846 (1961) (describing historical use of arbitration in trade industries); Timothy F. McCurdy, *The Doctor Will See You Now (If You Signed the Arbitration Agreement)*, 65 J. Mo. B. 232 (2009).

[16] *See Federal Arbitration Act*, 9 U.S.C. § 2.

[17] *See, e.g.*, AT&T Mobility LLC, 131 S. Ct. 1740 (2011) (holding that the FAA preempted California's rule classifying most collective-arbitration waivers in consumer contracts as unconscionable); Southland Corp. v. Keating, 465 U.S. 1, 16 (1984) (by enacting the FAA, "Congress intended to foreclose state legislative attempts to undercut the enforceability of arbitration agreements.")

[18] *See e.g.*, Gilmer v. Interstate Johnson, 500 U.S. 20 (1991); Circuit City v. Adams, 532 U.S. 105 (2001).

dates such bans on class actions as unconscionable.[19] Arbitration awards are final and binding, subject to extremely narrow judicial review unrelated to the merits of the decision.[20] Thus, a party's access to the public justice system may be displaced by virtue of a simple declaration in any contract which provides for legal claims and disputes to be brought to arbitration and, in effect, a waiver of rights to a judicial forum.[21]

ADR has become so widely used, promoted, and accepted as to spawn an entire industry of private dispute resolution.[22] This trend has created the professional opportunity for individuals to secure employment as "private judges" or neutrals, and correspondingly, a market for private businesses to provide arbitration support and administrative services (provider institutions).[23]

The phenomenon of the "vanishing trial" and steep reduction in the number of civil trials is attributable not only to expensive trial costs and complexity, but also to the diversion of cases to ADR.[24] Given the opportunities for higher salaries and career mobility in private dispute resolution, a considerable number of public judges at the state and federal courts have opted to leave the bench and embark on a career as a private neutral and to associate with one of the many private dispute resolution provider companies or organizations, notably Judicial Arbitration and Mediation Services (JAMS) or the American Arbitration Association (AAA), or simply to self-administer a case as an arbitrator or neutral.[25] News reports of public judges leaving

[19] AT&T Mobility LLC v. Concepcion, 131 S. Ct. 1740 (2011) (holding that the FAA preempted California's rule classifying most collective-arbitration waivers in consumer contracts as unconscionable); Doctors' Ass'n. v. Casarotto, 517 U.S. 681, 687 (1996); Allied-Bruce Terminix Cos. v. Dobson, 513 U.S. 265, 281 (1995); Southland Corp. v. Keating, 465 U.S. at 8–9.

[20] *See Federal Arbitration Act*, 9 U.S.C. § 10 (enumerating a limited category of grounds upon which a court may vacate an arbitral award, such as for fraud, arbitrator misconduct, or arbitrator abuse of authority).

[21] 9 U.S.C. § 2 (providing for the enforcement of agreements to arbitrate).

[22] Alternative Dispute Resolution, 2020, Hous. Law., at 37 (Sept./Oct. 2000). As stated by William K. Slate, CEO and President, American Arbitration Association, the "[u]se of arbitration and, more recently, mediation [has grown] by leaps and bounds…." American Arbitration Association, 2011 Presidents Letter and Financial Statements, http://www.adr.org/aaa/ShowProperty?nodeId=%2FUCM%2FADRSTG_019403&revision=latestreleased.

[23] *See* Maureen A. Weston, *Reexamining Arbitral Immunity in an Age of Mandatory Arbitration and Professional Arbitration*, 88 Minn. L. Rev. 449 (2004) (noting that major provider institutions, such as the American Arbitration Association (AAA), and Judicial Arbitration and Mediation Services (JAMS), continue to report growth in caseload and neutral membership). *See also infra* Sect. II.B. Obtaining an exact count or complete listing of the number of ADR or arbitration service providers is difficult because no one place collects such information and many operate locally or regionally. A link on the website for the American Bar Association, Section on Dispute Resolution lists national ADR organizations. *See* American Bar Association, Links of Interest, http://www.americanbar.org/groups/dispute_resolution/resources/links_of_interest.html; *see e.g.*, Federal Arbitraiton, Inc., ("FedArb's former and retired federal judges will bring you the highest quality, precedent-based, on-time arbitration decisions."), http://www.fedarb.com/.

[24] Mark Galanter, *The Vanishing Trial: An Examination of Trials and Related Matters in State and Federal Courts,* 1 J. Empirical Legis. Stud. 459, 461 (2004). Criminal cases, by contrast, are on the rise, and not referred to ADR involving a private third-party neutral.

[25] Stephen B. Burbank, Jay S. Plager & Gregory Ablavsky, 1 *Leaving the Bench, 1970–2009: The Choices Federal Judges Make, What Influences Those Choices, and Their Consequences* 12 (2012) [hereinafter Leaving the Bench].

the bench cite the lure of higher pay in the private ADR industry as a primary reason for their departure.[26] In short, private dispute resolution has become big business, and judges are a valued asset.[27]

The trend to privatize justice and the loss of judges from the public court system to the higher pay opportunities and flexibility in the private ADR industry raises important concerns about the quality of justice, due process, and well-being of the public justice system.[28] This chapter explores the impact of this development—the benefits and costs—on the access to quality and meaningful justice. Part II examines the process for judicial selection and appointment, the role of the judge in a public justice system, and the compensation packages typically offered to public judges, while also reporting attrition and retirement from the bench. Part III considers the reasons motivating public judges to leave the bench for work in the private ADR sector and attendant effects on the public courts. While recognizing the benefits of private dispute resolution, Part IV counsels for limitations on the marketing of one's status and service as a public judge while pursuing work as a paid private neutral and proposes adoption of a canon of ethics for former judges serving as private arbitrators and mediators. The chapter concludes with a call for increased public investment toward improvements in the public court system in order to renew the calling to judicial service and to preserve a meaningful foundation of access to public justice.

## The Role of the Judge in a Public Justice System

### *Function of the Judiciary*

#### Selection, Retention, and Discipline

Article III, Sect. 1 of the US Constitution provides that "[t]he judicial Power of the United States, shall be vested in one supreme Court, and in such inferior Courts

[26] *See* Molly McDonough, *NY Judge Quits for ADR Job, Cites Pay as Reason*, ABA J., (Aug. 16, 2012) (reporting on a state court judge leaving a $ 168,600 annual income for a 17% pay increase to work for JAMS); http://www.abajournal.com/news/article/ny_judge_quits_for_adr_job_cites_pay_as_reason/. *See also* Charisma L. Miller, *Justice Ariel Belen to Leave Bench; Longtime Brooklyn Jurist Cites Pay Issue*, Brooklyn Daily Eagle, (Aug. 16, 2012), *available at* http://www.brooklyneagle.com/articles/justice-ariel-belen-leave-bench-longtime-brooklyn-jurist-cites-pay-issue.

[27] *See supra* note 21.

[28] Public policy strongly favors the private negotiation and settlement of litigated disputes; however, the expectation that parties who submit their disputes to the courts, which are public institutions funded by public resources and designed to serve a public function, must comport with the standards of the judicial process, the needs of the rule of law, and orders of the court is equally availing. Mark Thompson, Rented Justice, CAL. LAW., Mar. 1988, at 42 (noting that over 150 California judges had "gone private," lured by the growing demand and good pay); Mark Dubois, *Private Judging, Private Justice*, Conn. Law Tribune (Oct. 19, 2012) (expressing concerns about a development of two systems of justice, notably private justice for the wealthy), *available at* http://www.ctlawtribune.com/PubArticleCT.jsp?id=1202575677512.

as the Congress may from time to time ordain and establish."[29] Justices of the US Supreme Court and judges of other Article III federal courts are appointed by the President, with the advice and consent of the Senate.[30] Article III judges are appointed for a life term, provided "good behavior," and hold their seats until they resign, die, or are removed from office.[31] The purpose of lifetime tenure is to ensure judicial independence.[32] Selection of judges at the state court level depends on respective state constitutions, which may provide either for (1) appointment by state legislature or governor; (2) judges running for election; or (3) initial gubernatorial appointment and then retention or rejection by voters.[33]

Federal judges are classified either as those who are in regular active service, retired but in senior status, retired from the office, or former judges who have resigned, relinquishing the office prior to eligibility for retirement.[34] Active and senior status judges are bound by the Code of Judicial Conduct and are therefore prohibited from practicing law or serving as a private neutral for compensation. Judges whose combination of age and years of service totals at least 80 are eligible to retain senior status on the bench, a form of semi-retirement, or to retire fully. In either case, judges who satisfy the "Rule of 80" receive a pension in the form of an annuity equal to the judge's salary at the time of retirement without that income being subject to taxes for Social Security or Medicare. Congress enacted this option, known as the Rule of 80, in 1984 in an effort to retain experienced members of the judiciary by broadening the availability of senior status judicial service for retired federal judges.[35] Senior status judges remain available for service on the bench and subject to judicial ethics rules, whereas retired judges are free from such prohibitions, including the prohibition against practicing law.[36] Fully retired judges, like judges who resign and relinquish office, are free to pursue outside employment.

---

[29] U.S. Const. art. III, § 1.

[30] *Id.*

[31] *Id.* Federal judges can be removed from office by impeachment but are subject to discipline in less drastic ways by a committee of federal judges. Non-Article III judges—including US magistrate judges and judges of the US bankruptcy courts, US Tax Court, US Court of Federal Claims, and US territorial courts—are appointed for specified terms of office.

[32] Richard A. Posner, *The Role of the Judge in the Twenty-First Century*, 86 B.U. L. Rev. 1049 (2006) (noting that elected judges likely exhibit less political independence that the relative freedom of the federal judges, with lifetime tenure).

[33] *See* Peter D. Webster, *Selection and Retention of Judges: Is There One "Best" Method?*, 23 Fla. St. U. L. Rev. 1 (1995). http://media.law.fsu.edu/journals/lawreview/issues/231/webster.html.

[34] 28 U.S.C. § 371(2012). Leaving the Bench, *supra* note 25, at 13.

[35] Leaving the Bench, *supra* note 25, at 7. The Rule of 80 allows federal judges to retain senior status or retire at or after age 65, provided the combination of his or her age and years of service totals at least 80. *Id.*

[36] 28 U.S.C. § 371(e)(1). Senior status judges receive the "salary of the office," including cost-of-living-adjustments (COLAs) and any subsequent pay increases, provided they satisfy the service requirements. *See* Leaving the Bench, *supra* note 25, at 61.

A similar structure operates at the state level, with the distinction that in some states, retired judges are eligible to serve on an *ad hoc* basis for fill-in assignments,[37] but otherwise are free to engage in private employment.[38]

## Public Judges as Guardians of Justice

Judges play a central role as guardians of justice in the public legal system. Foremost, judges are impartial decision-makers. Judicial impartiality, fairness, and independence are fundamental to the assurance of Constitutional due process.[39] These principles are embedded in the Judicial Code which mandates the disqualification of any federal court justice, judge, or magistrate judge "[i]n any proceeding in which his *impartiality might reasonably be questioned*."[40] Disqualification is also required where a judge:

1. [h]as a personal bias or prejudice concerning a party, or personal knowledge of disputed evidentiary facts concerning the proceeding;
2. [i]n private practice [] served as lawyer in the matter in controversy…;
3. [h]as served in governmental employment and in such capacity participated as counsel, adviser, or material witness concerning the proceeding or expressed an opinion concerning the merits of the particular case in controversy; or
4. [k]nows that he, individually or as a fiduciary, or his spouse or minor child residing in his household, has a financial interest in the subject matter in controversy or in a party to the proceeding, or any other interest that could be substantially affected by the outcome of the proceeding….[41]

Public judges are also held accountable to standards of ethical conduct in the performance of their judicial roles. Federal judges are expected to abide by the Code of Conduct for US Judges, a set of ethical principles and guidelines enacted by the Judicial Conference, a policy-making organization of the federal judiciary headed by the

[37] *See* Mark S. Hurwitz & Drew Noble Lanier, *Diversity in State and Federal Appellate Courts: Change and Continuity Across 20 Years*, 29 The Justice System J. 1, 52 (2008); HL 272, House of Lords Committee on the Constitution, 25th Report of Session 2010–2012 at note 330.

[38] *See infra* Sect. IV.A (citing examples of active judges engaging in outside private judging).

[39] Constitutional due process requires judge recusal where a judge has a direct financial interest in the outcome of a case, presides over a criminal contempt case which resulted from the defendant's hostility toward the judge, or where there is a "serious risk of actual bias" where a party "had a significant and disproportionate influence in placing the judge on the case by raising funds or directing the judge's election campaign when the case was pending or imminent." Caperton v. Massey, 129 S. Ct. 2252, 2264 (2009) (deeming a "serious risk of actual bias—based on objective and reasonable perceptions," where a party's campaign efforts had a significant and disproportionate influence in placing the presiding judge on the case). *See also* Aetna Life Ins. v. Lavoie, 475 US 813 (1986) (invalidating state appellate judgment in a civil matter where a state judge had a direct financial interest in the outcome); Liljeberg v. Health Services Acquisition Corp., 486 U.S. 847 (1988).

[40] 28 U.S.C..§ 455(a) (2012) (emphasis added).

[41] *Id.* (emphasis added) (extending rule to "a person within the third degree of relationship to either of them, or the spouse of such a person").

Chief Justice of the USA.[42] The Code of Conduct guides full-time judges on issues of "judicial integrity and independence, judicial diligence and impartiality, permissible extrajudicial activities, and the avoidance of impropriety or even its appearance."[43]

Judicial conduct rules likewise govern state court judges similar to the principles of the Model Code of Judicial Conduct.[44] These ethical precepts pronounce five broad canons, requiring that:

| | |
|---|---|
| Canon I | A Judge Shall Uphold the Integrity and Independence of the Judiciary. |
| Canon II | A Judge Shall Avoid Impropriety and the Appearance of Impropriety in All of the Judge's Activities. |
| Canon III | A Judge Shall Perform the Duties of Judicial Office Impartially and Diligently. |
| Canon IV | A Judge Shall So Conduct the Judge's Extra-Judicial Activities as to Minimize the Risk of Conflict with Judicial Obligations. |
| Canon V | A Judge or Judicial Candidate Shall Refrain From Inappropriate Political Activity.[45] |

In both the courtroom and their personal lives, judges are expected to maintain high standards of conduct. More specifically, "[t]he duties of judicial office, as prescribed by law, shall take precedence over all of a judge's personal and extrajudicial activities."[46] This also means that judges are not permitted to engage in other private employment or the practice of law. Both the federal and state model codes of judicial conduct specifically preclude judges from serving as private mediators and arbitrators while serving on the bench. [47]

---

[42] *See also* US Courts, Code of Conduct for United States Judges, 1, 17–19 (2012), *available at* http://www.uscourts.gov/Viewer.aspx?doc=/uscourts/RulesAndPolicies/conduct/Vol02A-Ch02.pdf (last visited Nov. 8, 2012). *See also* 28 U.S.C. § 331 (West. 2012) (establishing the Judicial Conference of US Judges).

[43] US Courts, Code of Conduct for United States Judges (2012), *available at* http://www.uscourts.gov/Viewer.aspx?doc=/uscourts/RulesAndPolicies/conduct/Vol02A-Ch02.pdf (last visited Nov. 8, 2012). Part-time, temporary, and retired judges may be exempt from complying with Canon IV of the Code of Conduct, which governs extrajudicial activities that are consistent with the obligations of judicial office. *Id.*

[44] American Bar Association, Model Code of Judicial Conduct (2012), *available at* http://www.americanbar.org/groups/professional_responsibility/publications/model_code_of_judicial_conduct.html.

[45] Model Code of Judicial Conduct (2012), United States Courts, *Code of Conduct for United States Judges*, 1, 17–19 (2011), *available at* http://www.uscourts.gov/RulesAndPolicies/CodesOfConduct/CodeConductUnitedStatesJudges.aspx. Part-time, temporary, and retired judges may be exempt from complying with Canon IV of the Code of Conduct, which governs extrajudicial activities that are consistent with the obligations of judicial office. *Id.*

[46] American Bar Association, Model Code of Judicial Conduct, Canon 2, R. 2.1 (2012), *available at* http://www.americanbar.org/groups/professional_responsibility/publications/model_code_of_judicial_conduct/model_code_of_judicial_conduct_canon_2.html.

[47] *Id.* at Canon 3, R. 3.9 ("A judge should not act as an arbitrator or mediator or otherwise perform judicial functions apart from the judge's official duties unless expressly authorized by law"). Code of Conduct for United States Judges , *supra* note 43, at 12 (Canon 4[A][4] [same]).

Professional ethics rules governing lawyers apply to judges who leave the bench to the extent they remain relevant to the judge's role. Thus, Model Rule of Professional Conduct 1.12, addressing conflicts of interest that arise when a judge leaves the bench and moves into private practice, precludes a lawyer from representing anyone in a matter in which he participated personally and substantially as a judge.[48] Rule 1.12 also precludes a lawyer from negotiating for employment with a party where the lawyer had participated as a judge, adjudicative officer, or as an arbitrator, mediator or third-party neutral.[49]

## Judicial Retention, Attrition, and the Private Alternatives

Appointment to judicial service is considered among the highest callings and honors in the legal profession. Yet, a shortage of judges and attrition from the bench are persistent concerns at both the federal and state levels. While the constitutional provisions for lifetime tenure intend to ensure the independence and stability of the federal judiciary, this goal is at risk due to failures in the confirmation process, inadequate judicial pay, and attrition on the federal bench.[50] Chief Justice Roberts echoes this theme in his 2006 annual report on the federal judiciary where he stated that federal judges "accept difficult work, public criticism [and] even threats to their personal safety," and while they may be willing to accept less than what could be earned in the private sector, "[t]hey can rightly expect, however, to be treated more fairly than they have been."[51]

The Judicial Conference conducts a biennial survey of the federal courts' judgeship needs and presents recommendations to Congress on whether to increase or decrease the number of federal judgeships in a particular judicial district.[52] As of 2012, the federal judiciary consisted of 9 Supreme Court Justices, 179 circuit courts of appeals judges, 677 district courts judges, and 9 posts on the Court of International

[48] Model Rules of Prof'l Conduct R. 1.12 (providing that "[a] lawyer shall not represent anyone in connection with a matter in which the lawyer participated personally and substantially as a judge or other adjudicative officer or law clerk to such a person or as an arbitrator, mediator or other third-party neutral, unless all parties to the proceeding give informed consent, confirmed in writing").

[49] Model Rules of Prof'l Conduct R. 1.12(b).

[50] *See* American Bar Association, *Standing Committee on Federal Judicial Improvements Annual Meeting* 1 (Aug. 3, 2012), *available at* http://www.americanbar.org/content/dam/aba/administrative/federal_judicial_improvements/12am_scfji_agendabk.authcheckdam.pdf.

[51] C.J. John Roberts, 2006 Year-End Report on the Federal Judiciary, United States Courts (Jan. 2007), http://www.uscourts.gov/News/TheThirdBranch/07-01-01/2006_Year-End_Report_on_the_Federal_Judiciary.aspx.

[52] United States Courts, http://www.uscourts.gov/Common/FAQS.aspx (last visited Oct. 16, 2012). The Judicial Conference considers the number of weighted filings per judgeship, geography, the number of senior judges, and the mix of cases as factors in making its judgeship recommendations to Congress. There are no specific qualifications set forth for recommended potential nominees; however, members of Congress have developed their own informal criteria.

Trade, for a total of 874 authorized Article III judgeships.[53] As of 2012, there were a total of 17,489 state court judges in the USA.[54] Despite these posts, the number of vacancies and departures from the bench is problematic, even considered at the "crisis" level.[55] The effect is an increased workload and significant trial delays all around the USA, with some civil cases having up to 3-year delays.[56]

In a comprehensive study and report entitled *Leaving the Bench,* researchers documented the rates of retirement of public judges and examined the underlying causes for attrition on the bench.[57] According to the study, between 1970 and 2009, 80 federal judges resigned from office.[58] The researchers found that most resignations during this period were not due to age or health, but rather to pursue private employment, other employment, and higher salary. According to the study, "[v]irtually all resignations involve dissatisfaction" with their work as federal judges.[59] Fourteen judges entering private practice during this period cited inadequate salary as an explicit reason prompting their judicial resignation.[60] Compensation was also a likely factor for another 28 judges pursuing private employment upon resignation, as their salaries reportedly doubled or tripled upon resignation.[61] Congress failed to grant cost-of-living adjustments and salary increases for 20 years until 1991.[62] This salary increase in 1991 had at least a temporary positive impact on promoting retention, as the retirement rate from 1990 to 1999 decreased.[63] Resignation rates again increased from 2000 to 2009.[64] As Congress has not provided salary increases or cost-of-living adjustments since 1991, more judges are opting to retire rather

[53] United States Courts, www.uscourts.gov (last visited Oct. 16, 2012).

[54] 2012 National Association of Women Judges, *2012 Representation of United States State Court Women Judges*, (Dec. 23, 2011), http://www.nawj.org/us_state_court_statistics_2012.asp (citing The American Bench: Judges of the Nation, Forster-Long, Inc., (2012 ed.).

[55] Jerry Markon & Shaleigh Murray, Federal Judicial Vacancies Reach Crisis Point, http://www.washingtonpost.com/wp-dyn/content/article/2011/02/07/AR2011020706032.html?hpid=topnews
(reporting that "there are now 101 vacancies among the nation's 857 district and circuit judgeships. At least 15 more vacancies are expected this year, according to the administrative office of the U.S. Courts. When Obama took office in 2009, 54 judgeships were open").

[56] Id.

[57] Leaving the Bench, *supra* note 25.]

[58] Leaving the Bench, *supra* note 25, at 14.

[59] Leaving the Bench, *supra* note 25, at 17 (noting overloaded dockets, lack of support services, Sentencing Guidelines' constraints on judges.

[60] Leaving the Bench, *supra* note 25, at 18.

[61] Leaving the Bench, *supra* note 25, at 19.

[62] Leaving the Bench, *supra* note 25, at 14, 18. "Although 27 federal judges resigned from 1980–1989 (3.9% of average authorized judgeships), and 23 federal judges resigned from 2000–2009 (2.8%), only 10 resigned from 1990–1999 (1.2%)."

[63] Leaving the Bench, *supra* note 25, at 19.

[64] Leaving the Bench, *supra* note 25, at 72. *Id.* at 37 (noting that "there have been no salary increases for federal judges, whatever their status, since 1991").

than assume senior status, or simply to resign.[65] Absent additional improvements, the long-term trend is toward an increasing number of judicial resignations.

## *The Private Judging Career*

Private dispute resolution, in forms such as arbitration and mediation, has been used for centuries.[66] Traditionally, arbitrators were members of a particular trade or industry who served on a volunteer basis.[67] Modern day private arbitration or mediation can be a career in itself. Unlike attorneys who must be licensed to practice law and held to comply with rules of professional conduct, private neutrals are not licensed or subject to regulatory oversight. Leading arbitration and mediation providers, however, have promulgated recommended standards of conduct for neutrals and established criteria to serve on panel rosters.[68]

The private judging industry offers a service to parties to privately resolve disputes, free of the rigor and arguable morass of standards of the public legal system. It also offers a reprieve from the overworked and underpaid experience as a public judge, and the potential for lucrative fees. *Leaving the Bench* notes that "[a] whopping 83 %" of retired judges surveyed reported working as either an arbitrator, mediator, or in a similar capacity for pay post retirement, including work for JAMS or other ADR providers.[69] The availability of former judges for private hire has increased dramatically. JAMS, for example, started in 1979 with a single retired judge. Employing 230 retired judges in 1993 and over 300 full-time neutrals in 2012, JAMS neutrals administer an average of 10,000 cases each year.[70] JAMS' annual revenue has been on an upward trajectory since 1987 at US $2.7 million,

[65] Leaving the Bench, *supra* note 25, at 38. While judges typically do not disclose explicit reasons for retiring, one focus group revealed that without the additional teaching income available in senior status, at least one judge would have retired and taken up ADR, and a number of respondents made similar comments. *Id.* at 61.

[66] *See, e.g.*, Soia Mentschikoff, *Commercial Arbitration*, 61 Colum. L. Rev. 846 (1961) (describing traditional uses of arbitration).

[67] *Id. See also* Maureen A. Weston, *Reexamining Arbitral Immunity in an Age of Mandatory Arbitration and Professional Arbitration*, 88 Minn. L. Rev. 449 (2004). *See, e.g.*, American Bar Association and AAA, Code of Ethics for Arbitrators in Commercial Disputes; AAA Commercial Arbitration Rules, Rules 12–20 (including standards for recruitment, training, conflicts of interest, and similar matters related to selection of persons for arbitrator panels and for assignment to particular disputes).

[68] See Carrie Menkel-Meadow, *Ethics Issues in Arbitration and Related Dispute Resolution Processes: What's Happening and What's Not*, 56 U. Miami L. Rev. 949, 955 (2002). Am. Arb. Ass'n., Qualification Criteria for Admittance to the AAA National Roster of Neutrals 1 (listing criteria) (last visited Nov. 3, 2012), available at http://www.adr.org/aaa/ShowPDF?doc=ADRSTG_003878.

[69] Leaving the Bench, *supra* note 25, at 92. JAMS was founded by the Hon. H. Warren Knight in 1979 and originally included only former judges and stood for the acronym Judicial Arbitration and Mediation Services. It has since expanded and panels include attorneys as well as former judges. http://www.jamsadr.com/about-the-jams-name/.

[70] JAMS, *About JAMS,* http://www.jamsadr.com/aboutus_overview/

to US $24 million in 1991, US $50 million in 1998, US $70 million in 2003, and reportedly reaching US $80 million in revenue for 2004.[71] JAMS purports to be the largest ADR provider in the world.[72] Not far behind, the AAA reported nearly US $77 million in 2010 revenues from its annual case administration fees.[73]

Judges serving as private ADR professionals generally charge from US $ 300 to US $ 500 an hour, although some popular judges command per diem fees in excess of US $ 10,000.[74] A 2007 study of four major ADR firms in California, including JAMS, concluded that of 483 individual neutrals affiliated with one of the firms, 288 of them were retired judges, charging an average of about US $ 400 per hour.[75] A similar migration from the public bench to private neutral work is occurring at the state level.[76] A report listing its assessment of the 500 leading judges included "[t]he vast realm of alternative dispute resolution presided over by retired judges, arbitrators and mediators, of which there are more than an estimated 20,000 nationwide. Unlike their counterparts in public service, the best private judges are well paid and highly sought after for high-stakes, complex cases…."[77]

Reports of judges leaving the bench to pursue private judging cite the recurring theme of finances and the need to pay children's college tuition as primary reasons for leaving.[78] For example, after 17 years of judicial service, New York Judge Belen left his US $168,600-per-year judge post to pursue a position with JAMS, citing the [relative] lack of a pay raise as the main force driving his decision to retire.[79]

---

[71] Marie Beaudette, *Neutral Territory*, ADR Law Notes (April 2004), *available at* http://www.landandmaritime.dla.mil/…/adr/…/ADR_Lawnotes_April.

[72] JAMS, *About JAMS,* http://www.jamsadr.com/aboutus_overview; *see also* American Arbitration Association, 2010 President's Letters and Financial Statements, *available at* http://www.adr.org/aaa/ShowProperty?nodeId=%2FUCM%2FADRSTG_004001&revision=latestreleased

[73] American Arbitration Association, 2010 Presidents Letter and Financial Statements, 4 (2010) (reporting nearly US $ 77 million revenues from case administration fees), *available at* http://www.adr.org/aaa/ShowProperty?nodeId=%2FUCM%2FADRSTG_004001&revision=latestreleased.

[74] Anne S. Kim, *Rent-A-Judges and the Cost of Selling Justice*, 44 Duke L. J.166, 175 (1994).

[75] Sara Laufer Batinovich, *Neutrals In California: Descriptive Findings On A Study of Retired Judges And Practicing Attorneys*, Mediate.com (Mar. 2009), http://www.mediate.com/articles/batinovichSL1.cfm.

[76] Capturing Excellence, The Lawdragon 500: Leading Judgesin America, http://www.lawdragon.com/images/uploads/pdf/LD500_Leading_Judges2.pdf 18, 30 (listing, *inter alia*, former Utah Supreme Court Justice Michael Zimmerman, retired in 2000, former federal district court judge Layn R. Phillips (Fmr), and J. Lawrence Irving, among the most prominent and sought-after commercial arbitrators and mediators).

[77] Id.

[78] Roy A. Schotland, *Judges Pay: A Chasm Worse Than Realized*, 82 Ind. L. J. 1273 (2007) (arguing that "[l]ow salaries guarantee a revolving door of judges that will erode the quality of justice. As judges' children grow older, experienced and talented judges will be forced to leave the bench to meet tuition obligations. Therefore, only young judges who view the bench as a stepping stone to other ambitions, and older judges who have independent means, will remain").

[79] Molly McDonough, *NY Judge Quits for ADR Job, Cites Pay as Reason*, ABA Journal (Aug. 16, 2012), http://www.abajournal.com/news/article/ny_judge_quits_for_adr_job_cites_pay_as_reason/. *See also* Dan Krisch, *Judges Jump Ship in Growing Numbers* (noting that "[w]hile $ 146,780 a year isn't chump change, especially given the current state of the economy, it's also about the

Announcements of judges resigning for private practice also emphasize the benefits of ADR.[80] Specializing in ADR permits a retired judge to continue using the skills and experience of a judge in a less adversarial process, earn many times his or her judicial salary, and enjoy a flexible work schedule.[81]

## Effects of Judicial Migration Toward Commercialized ADR

The increased availability of judges choosing early retirement, or simply resigning, to pursue commercialized ADR seemingly enhances the availability of qualified and experienced neutrals to participants in a private ADR process. Parties tend to select a former judge as a private neutral for that expertise and ability to provide a realistic evaluation and adjudication that would approximate trial. In addition to providing increased access to ADR services, former judges may facilitate higher resolution rates, participant satisfaction, reduced overall workload, and collaborative efforts with the courts.[82] Despite these recognizable benefits, the trend carries the potential to threaten the quality and integrity of both the public and private justice systems.[83]

### *Brain Drain and Closed Proceedings*

The loss of public judges to commercialized private ADR practice presents a range of concerns for the public justice system. A frequently cited negative effect of private ADR on the courts is that it is luring judges from the public bench to pursue

salary of a senior associate at a big firm—and one-half or even one-third of what many successful partners at those firms make").

[80] *See e.g.*, Dan Krisch, *Judges Jump Ship in Growing Numbers,* Conn. Law Tribune (Sept. 28, 2012) (expressing concern about the "trickling exodus" of judges to private practice and ADR and that "[m]any of our best judicial minds are embracing new, less adversarial models of civil litigation"); Thomas B. Scheffey, *Another Big Hitter Leaves the Bench*, Conn. Law Tribune (July 27, 2012) (reporting on Superior Court Judge Robert Holzberg's resignation from the bench to become a partner and mediator in a private law firm), *available at* http://www.ctlawtribune.com/PubArticleCT.jsp?id=1202564755043&Another_Big_Hitter_Leaves_The_Bench&slreturn=20120917215400; Retired circuit court judge, full-time ADR neutral, available at http://dlir.state.hi.us/labor/hlrb/arbitrators/resumes/McConnell,%20E.%20John%20%20Resume.pdf;

[81] See Ann S. Kim, *Rent-a-Judge and The Cost of Selling Justice*, 44 Duke L. J. 166, 175–176 (1994).

[82] Alternative Dispute Resolution In Civil Cases: The Report Of The Task Force On The Quality Of Justice Subcommittee On Alternative Dispute Resolution And The Judicial System, at 37–48. (Aug. 1999) [hereinafter Alternative Dispute Resolution In Civil Cases].

[83] *See* Lauren K. Robel, *Private Justice and the Federal Bench*, 68 Ind. L. J. 891 (1993) (stating that "alternatives to public courts-notably private judges and the proliferation of alternative dispute resolution providers-are threatening public judges' place in dispute resolution"); Kim, 44 Duke L. J. at 189 (discussing public policy implications).

careers as private ADR providers, thereby drawing the "best and brightest" from the public bench.[84] As one commentator notes,

> [t]here is a serious brain drain going on in our courts-especially, although not exclusively, in state courts. We are losing many of our most experienced jurists. They are leaving the bench in large numbers and joining alternative dispute resolution firms (such as JAMS), are simply going out on their own to act as neutrals (mediators and arbitrators), or are returning to private practice.[85]

In his plea for an increase in judicial pay, Chief Justice Roberts warned that "judges are no longer drawn primarily from among the best lawyers in the practicing bar" and "[i]f judicial appointment ceases to be the capstone of a distinguished career and instead becomes a stepping stone to a lucrative position in private practice, the Framers' goal of a truly independent judiciary will be placed in serious jeopardy."[86]

In addition to concerns of attracting and retaining a highly qualified judiciary, the trend toward private justice restricts public transparency and precedent development. Judges who retire for commercialized ADR no longer have authority to interpret the rule of law or establish precedent to ensure the protection of legal rights. As more judges choose earlier retirement, newly appointed judges have fewer senior judges to serve as their mentors to assist with difficult decisions affecting public policy. Rather than set forth clear pronouncements of legal doctrine, private judges have more of an incentive to be accommodating, vague, or inconsistent in their rulings in order to remain palatable to both sides for future appointments.[87] As a result, parties' ability to structure their conduct, business, and affairs to conform with legal standards is impaired.

## *Conflicts of Interest: Apparent, Potential, and Actual*

Judicial migration toward private neutral work also poses concerns about potential, actual, or the appearance of, conflicts of interest and misuse of judicial status for private commercial purposes.[88] This concern exists both while judges are on the bench considering the prospect of private judging employment options, and while

---

[84] Alternative Dispute Resolution In Civil Cases, *supra* note 79, at 27.

[85] Rex S. Heinke, *The Case for Raising Judicial Salaries*, LA Lawyer (Feb. 2001), *available at*, http://www.lacba.org/showpage.cfm?pageid=1198. *See also* Roy A. Schotland, *Judges Pay: A Chasm Worse Than Realized*, 82 Ind. L. J. 1273 (2007).

[86] Id.

[87] *See e.g.,* Kim, 44 Duke L.J. at 189–194 (asserting that "[p]rivate judges tend to avoid creating a coherent set of precedents; predictability could destroy a rent-a-judge's appeal to potential customers....").

[88] Caperton, 129 S.Ct. at 2264 (noting that "impermissible conflicts arise not only from a judge's pecuniary interest in a case, but also from the "possibility" of a temptation to disregard neutrality"). Even an amorphous "probability of bias," will itself bring our judicial system into undeserved disrepute, and diminish the confidence of the American people in the fairness and integrity of their courts). *Id.*

off the bench, in continuing to use the title and status as a former judge in the marketing and practice of private judging.

## On the Bench: Negotiations and Assignment Selection

Concerned that the allure of private judging could create a conflict of interest for judges seeking to use the public justice system as a revolving door to private industry, California enacted legislation providing for the disqualification of any judge who has arranged for future employment or other compensated service as a dispute resolution neutral.[89] The California legislation reported findings that certain judges were requesting assignments to hear types of cases where referral to private ADR was widely used.[90] In other cases, some judges in transactions with parties either solicited or indicated an interest in possible employment or service as an ADR neutral.[91]

Such a disqualification motion was ordered in *Rossco Holdings Inc. v. Bank of America,*[92] regardless of any showing of actual bias. In *Rossco,* the judge who presided over a lawsuit between a bank and holding company had participated in substantial negotiations with dispute resolution providers regarding possible employment during the time the bank moved to compel arbitration. Although the Legislature had amended the governing statute in response to a judicial ruling on that statute, the statute continued to disqualify judges,[93] such as *Rossco's* presiding judge, who participated in "substantial" negotiations for employment as a dispute resolution neutral.[94]

The plaintiffs in *Great Western Mining & Mineral v. Fox Rothschild* alleged in a conspiracy claim that certain Pennsylvania state court judges who had presided over their lawsuit in state court denied them the right to be heard in an impartial forum because the judges hoped to secure future employment as arbitrators with ADR Options, Inc., a private dispute resolution company, after leaving the bench and thus

---

[89] Cal. Civ. Proc. Code § 170.1 (West).

[90] *See generally* Reynolds Holding, *Private Justice: Millions Are Losing Their Rights, S.F. Chronicle,* Oct. 7 at A1, Oct. 8 at A15, Oct. 9 at A13 (2000) (four-part series on mandatory arbitration in California), *available at,* http://www.sfgate.com/news/article/PRIVATE-JUSTICE-Millions-are-losing-their-legal-2872314.php#ixzz2C40KwMCc (reporting, among the concerns of mandatory arbitration, that judges may be compromised by the "[s]oaring demand and potentially high pay [which] have lured an increasing number of sitting judges into arbitration—particularly in California—and pressured some to act in ways that may impress arbitration firms but weaken public confidence in the courts").

[91] Cal. Civ. Proc. Code § 170.1(a)(8)(A) (West).

[92] Rossco Holdings Inc. v. Bank of Am.,149 Cal.App.4th 1353, 1361–1363 (2007).

[93] Cal. Civ. Proc. Code § 170.1(a)(8)(A) (West) ("A judge shall be disqualified if any one or more of the following are true: The judge has a current arrangement concerning prospective employment or other compensated service as a dispute resolution neutral or is participating in, or, within the last two years has participated in, discussions regarding prospective employment or service as a dispute resolution neutral….").

[94] Rossco Holdings Inc., 149 Cal.App. 4th at 1362.

had an incentive to rule in the defendant company's favor. Although the Third Circuit recognized that "[f]or a judge to approach a party for whom he or she has just ruled to discuss the possibility of working for that party certainly creates a strong appearance of impropriety," it dismissed the conspiracy claim against the defendant because the alleged conduct indicated unilateral action on the part of certain judges, as opposed to specific misconduct by the non-judicial actor defendant.[95]

### Potential Repeat Player Bias

Another concern raised by the prospect of judges leaving to pursue private ADR involves the risk that judges may favor a party that is likely to generate repeat business. The "repeat player," whether in court or private arbitration, is generally the corporate party with greater resources than an individual claimant. Although private neutrals are likely to comply with ethical standards of impartiality, the economic incentive to favor the party likely to supply future business can affect perceptions about commercialized ADR services.[96]

## Prescriptions for Commercialized Judging

### *The California Approach: Requiring Judges to Choose*

Addressing the criticism that the trend to privatize justice is creating a two-tiered system of justice, one for the rich and one for the poor, California—which has led the nation in "private judging" since the 1980s—is forcing retired judges to choose between the two systems.[97] As of January 31, 2012, retired judges in California must decide whether they would accept fill-in assignments on the bench or work as private neutrals, but they cannot do both.[98] As a result of this rule, California court

[95] Great W. Mining & Mineral Co. v. Fox Rothschild LLP, 615 F.3d 159 (3rd Cir. 2010) (dismissing complaint for failure to state a claim based on insufficient factual allegations suggesting a conspiracy between the party and presiding judge).

[96] Despite the protection of lifetime tenure accorded to federal judges, federal judicial salaries have lagged below compensation packages of private industry. Moreover, where compensation is a primary motivator influencing judges' retirement decisions, the private judges in highest demand may only choose to pursue the most lucrative form of ADR, and thereby dilute the availability of other, otherwise effective forms of ADR. Amy Litkowitz, *The Advantages of Using a Rent-a-Judge System in Ohio*, 10 Ohio St. J. on Disp. Resol. 491, 494 (1998).

[97] Martin Kasindorf, *Rent-A-Judges Forced Out of California Courts*, USA Today (April 24, 2003), *available at*, http://usatoday30.usatoday.com/news/nation/2003-04-24-rentajudge-usat_x.htm.

[98] *Id.* California incorporates the use of private judging in its court system, permitting retired judges and attorneys to serve as private judges on pending cases. Under the California Constitution, litigants have the option to have their case heard by a private judge, paid by the parties. See Cal. Const. art. VI, § 21. *See* Amanda Bronstad, *"Private judges" alter legal landscape*, National

officials anticipated as much as 80 % of the 381 retirees who volunteered bench duties in 2012 to instead pursue the greener pastures of private judging.[99] The pastures are literally greener for California's retired judges, because it is a choice between earning US $ 512.76 a day accepting fill-in assignments, or as much as US $ 10,000 a day deciding outside disputes.[100]

The California decree requiring judges to choose between fill-in assignments and the private sector was implemented because retired judges' "private work affected their work in courts."[101] Some part-time judges had been "touting themselves" in courthouse chambers to draw in outside business, and one Los Angeles judge even recessed a jury trial for several days while he adjudicated a private case.[102] The California rule seeks to guard against judges potentially favoring one party who may be in a position to hire or appoint the judge in a future private ADR proceeding.

## *Enforce Ethical Restrictions Regarding Public Judges and Private ADR*

### On the Bench: Restrict Negotiations

Ethical canons governing judges, lawyers, and neutrals share the goal of fostering integrity in the public and private justice systems. Certainly, judges still active on the bench are subject to judicial conduct rules. Among these rules is the proviso that "[a] judge should neither lend the prestige of the judicial office to advance the private interests of the judge or others nor convey or permit others to convey the impression that they are in a special position to influence the judge."[103] Moreover, a judge is permitted to use official letterhead only "[i]f the judge indicates that the reference is personal and if there is no likelihood that the use of the letterhead would

---

Law Journal (April 5, 2006) (noting that in addition to California, at least four other states—Ohio, Indiana, Texas, and Colorado—in the last year have passed legislation or are considering new rules that broaden the authority of private judges to hear cases); Ann S. Kim, *Rent-a-Judge and The Cost of Selling Justice,* 44 DUKE L. J. 166, 190 (1994) (explaining California's "rent-a-judge process"); Jill S. Robbins, *The Private Judge: California Anomaly or Wave of the Future* (discussing the incorporation of private judging as an adjunct to public courts and authorized by the California Rules of Court), *available at* http://www.iaml.org/cms_media/files/the_private_judge_california_anomaly_or_wave_of_the_future.pdf?static=1.

99 Martin Kasindorf, *Rent-A-Judges Forced Out of California Courts*, USA TODAY (April 24, 2003), *available at* http://usatoday30.usatoday.com/news/nation/2003-04-24-rentajudge-usat_x.htm.

100 *Id.*

101 *Id.*

102 *Id.*

103 American Bar Association, MODEL CODE OF JUDICIAL CONDUCT, CANON 2B (2012), *available at* http://www.americanbar.org/groups/professional_responsibility/publications/model_code_of_judicial_conduct/model_code_of_judicial_conduct_canon_2.html. *See also* Id. at Rule 1.3 ("[a] judge shall not abuse the prestige of judicial office to advance the personal or economic interests of the judge or others, or allow others to do so").

reasonably be perceived as an attempt to exert pressure by reason of the judicial office."[104]

Although retired or former judges are not technically bound by such restrictions, where these former judges are using their judicial status to promote private employment, similar ethical principles should apply.[105] With this in mind, California's approach to limiting retired judges to either fill-in assignments or private judging, but not both, prevents a retired judge's personal activities from interfering with duties of the judicial office. Disqualification of judges on the bench who engage in discussions for prospective employment as a dispute resolution neutral is likewise justified.[106] A judge who negotiates for employment or uses the prestige of the judge's formal title on judicial letterhead in an effort to secure a position as a private neutral runs afoul of the spirit and even letter of this rule.

## Off the Bench: Restrict Use of Judicial Status in Private ADR Marketing

Judges who choose to leave the bench for private judging should not leverage the prestige of the judicial office to advance that interest. While a former judge may truthfully advertise his or her judicial experience, advertising that experience with a title like "The Honorable" tends to convey an aura of authority beyond a private professional.[107] The American Bar Association's (ABA) position is that a former judge who returns to the practice of law may not continue to use the titles "judge"

---

[104] American Bar Association, Model Code of Judicial Conduct, Canon 2, R. 1.3 cmt. 2 (2012), *available at* http://www.americanbar.org/content/dam/aba/administrative/professional_responsibility/2011_mcjc_rule1_3.authcheckdam.pdf.

[105] "A judge shall not act as an arbitrator or a mediator or perform other judicial functions apart from the judge's official duties unless expressly authorized by law." American Bar Association, Model Code of Judicial Conduct, Canon 3, R. 3.9 (2012), *available at* http://www.americanbar.org/content/dam/aba/administrative/professional_responsibility/2011_mcjc_rule3_9.authcheckdam.pdf.

[106] *See* Cal. Civ. Proc. Code § 170.1(a)(8) (West) (requiring disqualification where "(A) The judge has a current arrangement concerning prospective employment or other compensated service as a dispute resolution neutral or is participating in, or, within the last two years has participated in, discussions regarding prospective employment or service as a dispute resolution neutral, or has been engaged in that employment or service, and any of the following applies: (i) The arrangement is, or the prior employment or discussion was, with a party to the proceeding; (ii) The matter before the judge includes issues relating to the enforcement of either an agreement to submit a dispute to an [ADR] process or an award or other final decision by a dispute resolution neutral; (iii) The judge directs the parties to participate in an [ADR] process in which the dispute resolution neutral will be an individual or entity with whom the judge has the arrangement, has previously been employed or served, or is discussing or has discussed the employment or service; [or] (iv) The judge will select a dispute resolution neutral or entity to conduct an [ADR] process in the matter before the judge, and among those available for selection is an individual or entity with whom the judge has the arrangement, with whom the judge has previously been employed or served, or with whom the judge is discussing or has discussed the employment or service").

[107] Joanne Pelton Pitulla, *Trading on Titles,* 6 No. 4 Prof. Law. 14 (Aug. 1995).

or "honorable" because the use of such titles is "misleading" and "may be misunderstood by the public as suggesting some type of special influence."[108]

Despite the ABA's ethical opinion, ADR provider institutions continue to widely advertise their services, members and expertise, in legal newspapers, brochures, and on websites. For example, JAMS lists the honorific names and pictures of 43 former federal judges and provides the following announcement:

> These former and retired federal judges are exclusively associated with JAMS for the professional practice of ADR. They are all experts or experienced in federal law issues, such as securities, intellectual property, and employment, and in some cases have expertise or experience in such fields as bankruptcy, admiralty, and environmental law. [109]

The Florida Supreme Court Committee on ADR addressed the use and marketing of prior adjudicative experience in 2010. Florida Supreme Court Rule 10.610, governing mediator advertising and marketing practices, precludes former judges from using the title "judge" in marketing materials in connection with their mediation services, restricts a former judge serving as a mediator from using the prestige of the judicial office to advance his or her private interests, or from appearing in judicial robes in advertisements. The title "judge" may not be used with or without modifiers to the mediator's name in any advertisement.[110]

Unlike most other professional titles, judicial titles are not portable. They travel with the position, not the person. As such, judges must be prepared to gracefully relinquish the prestige of judicial office upon retirement.[111]

## Disclose and Abide by ADR Ethical Canons

As private neutrals, former judges are subject to the ethical canons of conduct for neutrals and are governed by state law.[112] The AAA/ABA *Code of Ethics for Arbitrators in Commercial Disputes* prescribes "Canons" for arbitrators similar to the Judicial Code of Conduct in imposing obligations for arbitrators to uphold the fairness of the arbitration process, to disclose conflicts of interest, adhere to standards of integrity and fairness.[113] Canon VII of the Code addresses arbitrator advertising,

---

[108] ABA Standing Committee on Ethics and Professional Responsibility, Op. 95–391 (Apr. 24, 1995).

[109] JAMS, *JAMS Federal Judges List*, http://www.jamsadr.com/files/Uploads/Documents/federal_Judges.pdf (dated Oct. 9, 2001 and updated Nov. 2012).

[110] Florida Supreme Court Rules, SC09-1384, Rule 10.610 (adopted Apr. 2012). *See* Mark D. Killian, *Court Sets Rules for Mediator Marketing Retired Judges Practicing as Mediators Can't be Pictured in Robes,* Florida Bar News, Vol. 37, No. 9 (May 1, 2010).

[111] Joanne Pelton Pitulla, *Trading on Titles,* 6 No. 4 Prof. Law. 14 (Aug. 1995).

[112] *See e.g.,* Am. Arb. Ass'n, Code of Ethics for Commercial Arbitrators (Oct. 2011), *available at* http://www.adr.org/aaa/faces/arbitratorsmediators/aboutarbitratorsmediators/codeofethics?_afrLoop=1472893722402940&_afrWindowMode=0&_afrWindowld=pzu6qy9u1_10#%40%3F_afrWindowId%3Dpzu6qy9u1_10%26_afrLoop%3D1472893722402940%26_afrWindowMode%3D0%26_adf.ctrl-state%3D6dyhj5pju_4.

[113] AAA/ABA, Code of Ethics for Arbitrators in Commercial Disputes (2004). http://www.americanbar.org/content/dam/aba/migrated/dispute/commercial_disputes.authcheckdam.pdf

permitting an arbitrator to engage in advertising or promotion of arbitral services which are truthful, accurate, and unlikely to mislead.[114] California requires private arbitrators to comply with a set of disclosure rules designed to ensure impartiality. While the ethical canons do not have the force of law, these best practices reflect a commitment to uphold integrity and fairness in the private dispute resolution context as well.[115]

## *The Judicial Conference Should Adopt an Explicit Ethical Canon Restricting Use of Honorifics in Private Neutral Advertising*

"The Honorable" and "Esquire" are honorifics, which are titles traditionally used to convey honor and respect. Derived from the Latin word *scutarius* ("shield bearer"), "Esquire" came to be a title of respect traditionally meant as having a social status higher than Gentleman, but lower than Knight.[116] Similarly, "The Honorable" traditionally applied to sons and daughters of men in social title, such as Barons. Use of the title "Esquire" by unlicensed and retired lawyers not current with their State Bar Associations constitutes the unauthorized practice of law in violation of state law and lawyer professional conduct rules.[117]

The ABA Committee on Ethics and Professional Responsibility has opined that "it is improper for a former judge who returns to the practice of law to refer to himself, or encourage others to refer to him, by any title that refers to his former judicial status."[118] Model Rule 7.1 prohibits "false or misleading communication about the lawyer's services." A communication is false or misleading if it "is likely to create an unjustified expectation about results a lawyer can achieve, or states or implied that a lawyer can achieve results by means that violate the rules of professional conduct or other law." Accordingly, the use of judicial titles in the practice of law is "misleading insofar as it is likely to create an unjustified expectation about the results a lawyer can achieve and to exaggerate the influence the lawyer may be able to

[114] *Id.* (Canon VIII). *See also* Bruce Meyerson & John M. Townsend, *Revised Code of Ethics for Commercial Arbitrators Explained*, 59 DISP. RESOL. J. 10 (2004).

[115] *See e.g.*, CAL. CODE CIV. PRO. § 1281.9. Ethics Standards for Neutral Arbitrators in Contractual Arbitrations, Division VI, California Rules of Court Appendix A (rev. 2003) ("(a) In any arbitration pursuant to an arbitration agreement, when a person is to serve as a neutral arbitrator, the proposed neutral arbitrator shall disclose all matters that could cause a person aware of the facts to reasonably entertain a doubt that the proposed neutral arbitrator would be able to be impartial, including… [1–8]."

[116] Gertrude Block, *Language Tips*, N.Y. ST. B. J., September 2007, at 54.

[117] http://minnlawyer.com/jdr/2010/10/22/the-honorable-esquires-what's-right-to-write/.

[118] Elizabeth K. Thorp & Kimberly A. Weber, *Recent Opinions from the American Bar Association Standing Committee on Ethics and Professional Responsibility*, 9 GEO. J. LEGAL ETHICS 1009, 1012 (1996).

wield."[119] The Committee was also concerned that the use of an honorific title might constitute professional misconduct under Model Rule 8.4(e), which states that "it is professional misconduct for a lawyer to… state or imply an ability to influence improperly a government agency or official."

Canon 2B of the Code of Conduct for US Judges instructs that, "a judge [shall not] convey or permit to convey the impression that they are in a special position to influence the judge." Advisory Opinion No. 72 further outlines that,

> A litigant whose lawyer is called "Mr.," and whose adversary's lawyer is called "Judge," may reasonably lose a degree of confidence in the integrity and impartiality of the judiciary. In addition, application of the same title to advocates and to the presiding judicial officer can tend to demean the court as an institution. Judge should insure that the title "judge" is not used in the courtroom or in papers involved in litigation before them to designate a former judge, unless the designation is necessary to accurately describe a person's status at a time pertinent to the lawsuit.[120]

While the Advisory Opinion provides this guidance with respect to prohibiting the use of honorific titles in courtroom litigation, the same rationale applies to former judges participating in private neutral work. To clarify the intended reaches of Canon 2B of the Model Code of Judicial Conduct, the Judicial Conference and ADR providers should adopt an explicit ethical canon restricting the use of honorifics in private neutral advertising.[121]

It could be argued that the title of "Judge" or "The Honorable" supplants the title of "Mister" and that stripping a retired judge of a title that he or she has earned would be discourteous. However, addressing a practicing attorney or private neutral as "Judge" or "The Honorable" may cause confusion and unwarranted deference. For example, decisions made by a private arbitrator who chooses to retain their honorific titles after retirement could cause a judge conducting appellate review to give excess weight to the arbitrator's decision, thereby unfairly bolstering the prevailing party's decision to stand on appeal.

Retired judges who have resumed the practice of law do not need to make their previous employment secret. They just should not be permitted to or allow others to flaunt their honorific title in a way that influences the judiciary or parties in an ADR process. While a former judge may advertise his or her experience, a former judge should not be allowed to market him or herself as "Judge Smith (former)" or "Honorable John Smith (Ret.)" for these purposes.

---

[119] Opinion 95–391.

[120] *Id.*

[121] For example, in Canada "Honourable" is only a lifetime title for certain public service holders, including the Prime Minister, the Chief Justice, and Senators. The Speaker of the House of Commons, Supreme Court of Canada judges, Federal Court judges, Tax Court judges, and judges of Provincial and Territorial Courts, by contrast, lose their honorific titles after they leave office. http://www.pch.gc.ca/pgm/ceem-cced/prtcl/titre-eng.cfm.

## Conclusion

Judges are trusted, revered for their wisdom, impartiality, and allegiance to justice and the rule of law. As their core roles, "[j]udges should imagine themselves as moral guardians, imposing from above their own notions of what is right and wrong."[122] Indeed, "[a]n independent and honorable judiciary is indispensable to justice in our society. A judge should participate in establishing, maintaining and enforcing high standards of conduct, and shall personally observe those standards so that the integrity and independence of the judiciary will be preserved…."[123]

Public perception of judges—public or private—has a significant effect on the public confidence in the justice system. A judge's respect for the judicial office must, and in most cases, likely is carried into their subsequent private career. The principles underlying the ethical and professional standards governing judicial conduct apply with equal force to private judges.

The public courts are clearly overburdened and underfunded, and the ADR movement is valuable for advancing effective alternatives to litigation. The legitimate concerns posed by judges leaving the bench earlier than they otherwise would have to pursue employment as private neutrals, and the risk of second class justice, compel attention to invest not only in the public justice system and to renew the calling and lure of public service, but also to attend to similar risks in the private justice arena.

[122] Diarmuid F. O'Scannlain, *The Role of the Federal Judge Under the Constitution: Some Perspectives from the Ninth Circuit*, 33 Harv. J. L & Pub. Pol'y 963, 969 (2010) (citing Seventh Circuit Judge Richard Posner).

[123] *See* Model Code of Judicial Conduct, Canon, *supra* note 44.

# Part VI
# Bringing Well-being to Children in Conflict

# Chapter 12
# Recess in Primary School: The Disjuncture Between Educational Policy and Scientific Research

**Catherine M. Bohn-Gettler and Anthony D. Pellegrini**

During a typical school day, children engage in a variety of activities. Some of these activities may be considered more academic in nature, such as formal phonics, science, or math lessons. However, other parts of the day may be less structured and considered to be more "playful." Recess is a time during which children can engage in unstructured social interaction. It constitutes a break in the school day from intellectual and academic lessons, and often occurs in tandem with lunch. It typically lasts approximately 10–15 min or longer (Centers for Disease Control and Prevention, CDCP, 2010). Recess usually occurs outdoors, often on playgrounds, although depending upon weather and facilities indoor recess is also practiced (Pellegrini and Holmes 2006). It is important to note, however, that much variation exists between schools and classrooms in the duration and implementation of recess (Pellegrini and Bohn 2005).

Importantly, recess is a time that is unstructured and undirected by adults. Adults primarily supervise children's behavior, ensure children's safety, and intervene when there is conflict or aggression. Otherwise, children choose their own activities, physical activity levels, and social interaction styles and levels. They are not restrained by adults and will often develop their own games and engage in free play. Free play represents a class of behaviors that are means-oriented rather than ends-oriented (Burghardt 1988; Pellegrini and Holmes 2006; Pellegrini and Smith 1993; Waite-Stupiansky and Findlay 2001).

Recess has been a normal practice in schools for decades, perhaps centuries. The primary rationale for providing breaks to students and employees is to increase productivity (Russell 1932/1972). Receiving breaks, such as a break during the office day or from factory assembly lines, has been a standard practice in the workforce. As another example, when drivers embark upon long road trips, it is considered

C. M. Bohn-Gettler (✉)
Education Department, College of Saint Benedict - Saint John's University, 37 South College Avenue, St. Joseph, MN 56374, USA
e-mail: cbohngettler@csbsju.edu

A. D. Pellegrini
Department of Educational Psychology, University of Minnesota, 56 East River Road, Minneapolis, MN 55455-0364, USA

B. H. Bornstein, R. L. Wiener (eds.), *Justice, Conflict and Wellbeing*,
DOI 10.1007/978-1-4939-0623-9_12, 

healthy and safe to take frequent breaks, because attention diminishes as time between breaks increases. In fact, because of attention-related issues, a variety of laws require that workplaces provide breaks to employees, and laws govern the length of time that individuals such as truckers or airline pilots can drive or fly without a break. The US Department of Labor (2007) specifies regulations for rest periods for adults in the workplace. It is recommended that employees receive periodic breaks of approximately 5–20 min, depending on the length of time they work (Howard 1994; US Department of Labor 2007).

Just as in the workforce, breaks in the day are normal practice in educational settings. In schools, breaks often take the form of recess. However, in recent decades, the nation has turned its attention to improving achievement and standardized test scores. This has led to calls for increased instructional time, and, as a result, reduced recess time. There is also a national emphasis on utilizing research to make evidence-based decisions regarding best practices in school policy and instruction (Jarrett and Maxwell 2000). This chapter aims to address the critical issue of whether recess adds value to education by describing research which examines the effects of recess on development and achievement.

## Overview of the Debate

In the early 1990s, the debate over the role of recess emerged in the state of Georgia. During this time, standardized test scores were the sole criterion for children's promotion from kindergarten to first grade. As a result of this environment, many legislators, school officials, and teachers began to seek ways to improve assessment scores. Considering the limited number of school hours during the day, it seemed only logical that minimizing or eliminating a seemingly trivial practice like recess would improve achievement. This may be why children's recess continues to be threatened in many schools across North America and the UK (Pellegrini 2005). From outside appearances, it would seem that recess activities are not very serious, and some argue that it may interfere with the educational mission of schools (for more information, see Jarrett and Waite-Stupiansky 2009; Johnson 1998; "No Time for Play" 2001).

The controversy over whether it is appropriate to reduce or eliminate recess continued to gain steam in the decades following the 1990s. Glickman and Pellegrini wrote articles in the *Atlanta Journal Constitution* and *Principal* (Pellegrini 1991; Pellegrini and Glickman 1989) in an effort to publicize research findings for the general public regarding standardized testing and the positive effects of recess. These articles were geared toward the community of primary school principals and teachers and the parents of young children. Despite these efforts, the anti-recess movement continued to grow and the debate became a hot topic for schools across the country.

Policy makers, teachers, parents, and reporters in the USA and the UK began researching and contacting experts about recess. This became such a hot topic that both authors of this chapter have been asked for interviews by journalists in several jurisdictions. One of this chapter's authors (Anthony Pellegrini) was even sought for an interview while travelling abroad (see the Pittsburgh Press, 27 October 1991).

The urgency of the debate over whether or not to reduce or eliminate recess has only increased over time. This topic is of critical importance when making policy decisions regarding education for children. The purpose of this chapter is to advocate for children so that decisions about recess are based on empirical data and theory. In an era of advocating for best practices, any drastic changes should be directed by scientific research. There is overwhelming evidence that the benefits of recess clearly outweigh its costs. To ignore this evidence is a tremendous waste of resources (e.g., kids' and teachers' time and effort and taxpayers' money). Stakeholders in the educational enterprise should demand accountability from their school boards, principals, and teachers when considering the elimination of recess in schools, just as they would when considering other major curricular changes.

## Overview of Chapter

This chapter presents an overview of issues central to the debate surrounding the role of recess in school, addressed in greater detail in other books and articles on the topic (e.g., Pellegrini 2005; Pellegrini and Bohn 2005). Specifically, we attempt to broach two views of recess: the movement to eliminate or reduce the school recess period from the primary school day and the perceived value of recess. We begin with a description of how recess has changed over history, highlighting the erosion of recess time. Next, we explain the arguments for reducing or eliminating recess time, such as the perceived increases in achievement, decreases in bullying, and the potential benefits of replacing recess with physical education. Following this, we describe the arguments in support of the inclusion of recess. We begin by describing the theories of classic scholars. Then, we examine scientific research investigating how recess and play benefits children by helping prepare them for adulthood, increasing well-being (e.g., physical fitness), improving classroom behavior, and enhancing social competence. We end this section by describing research linking recess and play to cognition and academic success, which is supported by research on massed versus distributed practice. We conclude with developmental research, which suggests that younger children demonstrate a greater benefit from recess and are less reliable test takers, considerations that should be taken into account when making policy decisions.

In addition, the chapter proffers the argument that theories are needed to guide our quests to understand the phenomenon of recess. Theories provide road maps to the questions we ask in the scientific enterprise. That is, theories offer us a frame around which we understand the data generated in empirical research. The quip, "There is nothing as practical as a good theory" holds merit: Without theory we cannot ask informed scientific questions, make sense of our data, or progress toward a deep understanding of our areas of study. Thus, any decisions regarding recess time should be based on theories and empirical research.

## The Eroding State of Recess

Breaks in the school day have been considered a normal practice for decades, and possibly centuries. Nineteenth- and twentieth-century primary school buildings in the USA and the UK had separate areas of school grounds designated for play. Some schools even had separate entrances and play areas for boys and girls to utilize during their breaks (this is not a common practice now). However, recess time has been eroding over the last 25 years, which provides a barometer of how recess is perceived as less important to the school day.

There is evidence that some schools began cutting recess to allow for more instructional time in the late 1980s (Jarrett and Waite-Stupiansky 2009). To our knowledge, one of the first surveys of recess conducted in the USA asked school superintendents in all 50 states and Washington, DC to specify how much time was dedicated to recess during the school day (National Association of Elementary School Principles, NAESP, 1989, as cited in Pellegrini 1995). Responses were received from 47 states, and the results indicated that recess existed in some form in approximately 90 % of the responding school districts. The amount of time allocated to recess was determined by individual schools, which resulted in variation within districts and states. For example, although 90 % of respondents indicated that recess existed in some form in their districts, 87 % of schools reported offering recess. In 96 % of these cases, recess occurred once or twice per day. In 75 % of the cases, the recess period lasted 15–20 min. From these data, however, we do not know the form of the recess period. For example, we do not know if organized physical education was counted as recess. Indeed, about one-half of those districts had "structured" rather than unstructured recess times.

The push to decrease recess time continued to gain steam in the 1990s. Some school districts began implementing no-recess policies on the basis that recess wasted time better spent on academics (Jarrett and Waite-Stupiansky 2009; Johnson 1998). In addition, some large school districts, such as Atlanta, built new elementary schools without playgrounds ("Schools becoming all work and no play," 2001). This led to a general trend such that, 5–10 years ago, 40 % of US school districts reduced or eliminated recess to devote more time to teaching and learning (Zygmunt-Fillwalk and Bilello 2005). Many school systems have abolished recess since 1989 (American Association for the Child's Right to Play, as cited in Pellegrini 1995).

Also in the 1990s, the US Department of Education[1] found that only 71 % percent of all American kindergarten classes surveyed reported having a daily recess period; 14.6 % had recess three to four times per week; 6.7 % had recess one to two times per week; and 7.7 % did not have recess at all. In terms of the duration of the recess period, 27 % had 30 min of recess, 67.4 % had 16–30 min, and 6 % had less than 15 min. Children attending private kindergartens were twice as likely to have recess as children attending public schools (48.3 % versus 22.2 %).

Likewise, in England, a national survey of recess, called "breaktime," was conducted by randomly sampling 10 % of all primary and secondary schools. There

[1] We acknowledge Ithel Jones for providing these data.

was a 60 % return rate such that 1,500 schools responded (Blatchford and Sumpner 1998). Recess in the UK is enacted in a more uniform manner when compared to the USA. Schools provide students with breaks in the morning, at lunch time, and in the afternoon. Although students across all grades received breaks, the duration of the break periods decreased with age: 93 min for children in infant school (5–7 years of age), 83 min for junior school (7–11 years of age), and 77 min for secondary school students (11–16 years of age). Nevertheless, there is also a reduction in recess time in the UK. Blatchford and Sumpner (1998) found reductions in lunch breaks in 26 % of infant schools, 38 % of junior schools, and 35 % of secondary schools between 1990 and 1996. Afternoon breaks were eliminated in 12 % of infant schools, 27 % of junior schools, and 14 % of secondary schools. These data speak to the trend of decreasing break times across a variety of age ranges.

The trend for reducing or eliminating recess time accelerated in the US when No Child Left Behind passed in 2001, and it still continues. Although 83–88 % of public schools report that they offer recess (National Center for Education Statistics, 2006), it usually lasts only 10–15 min at most (Jarrett and Waite-Stupiansky 2009). Legislative pressures continue to increase instructional time and minimize unstructured play time (Fedewa and Ahn 2011), and thus 40 % of public schools either eliminated or are planning to eliminate at least one recess period from the school day (Bland 2005; G. Klein 2006). Furthermore, only 18 % of states require elementary schools to provide daily recess, and there are exemptions in half of these states (National Association for Sport and Physical Education and American Heart Association 2010).

The data point to a general trend of reductions in recess. However, these studies are hard to compare to one another for multiple reasons. First, having a policy for recess does not necessarily mean that recess will be implemented in practice (Jarrett and Waite-Stupiansky 2009). Second, there is a wide degree of variation among schools with regard to recess. Although recess is present in most elementary schools, what is considered recess varies from school to school. The number and duration of recess periods per day or per week differs. In addition, the supervision and adult-directed behavior during these periods may be different, such that what is reported as recess time may not constitute unstructured free time. Finally, some schools report that children have recess when it is provided only once per week or when it lasts less than 15 min (Dills et al. 2011; National Center for Education Statistics 2006; Pellegrini 2005). Despite the challenges in interpreting this data, a clear trend still emerges: Recess time is being reduced. Since the late 1970s, children have lost 12 h/week in free time, including a 25 % decrease in play and a 50 % decrease in unstructured outdoor activities (Juster et al. 2004; Wingert 2000).

The data also lead us to consider a few interesting points. First, only 70 % of kindergarten-aged children receive daily recess. This is surprising considering that free play during the kindergarten years is important for learning and development (Bateson 2005; Bergen 1998). Second, private schools were more likely to provide recess than public schools. In fact, public schools with students from low socioeconomic backgrounds and with larger populations of minority students are the most likely to cut recess (Barros et al. 2009). We will examine this point further later on.

Finally, another point to consider is that British children have much more recess than their American counterparts, and the duration of their break periods seems more sensitive to the maturity of the students. However, like in the US, recess time in England is also decreasing. This is not simply a national issue, but is an international issue as well.

## Arguments Against Recess

The history of the erosion of recess can likely be explained by the political push to increase achievement by maximizing academic time in classrooms. Recess is an easy target for reduction, because it is a break from what is typically considered the most serious work of the day: reading, writing, and arithmetic. In addition, many children voice that recess is their favorite part of the day, and there is even a cartoon TV show for kids called *Recess!* This reinforces the popular notion that recess is trivial and not worthy of serious academic and scientific attention. This perception has led many schools to question the role of recess in the school day. Next, we outline some of the arguments against including and increasing recess time.

### *Maximizing Instructional Time Increases Achievement*

One of the most powerful forces driving school policy today is to increase achievement. In line with this, many politicians, superintendents, and school principals often argue that recess is a waste of valuable time that could be more profitably spent on instruction. It is often argued that recess can disrupt sustained concentration, work, and classroom patterns (see Blatchford and Sumpner 1998; Pellegrini 1995). The increased instructional time should, commonsensically, have a positive effect on achievement ("No Time for Play," 2001). Furthermore, if recess takes time away from learning and has a negative effect on achievement, states can reduce its time or funding (Schacter 2005).

Such an argument demonstrates that politicians and school officials are taking active measures to promote achievement. Questioning the role of recess in primary school education is similar to how the role of children's play has been questioned by some early childhood educators. Work is often perceived as being positive because it is productive, whereas play and leisure (and as an extension, recess) are more negatively perceived. This perception is partially rooted in the Puritan/Calvinist ethic of America and much of the Anglo-Saxon world (e.g., Sutton-Smith et al. 1999; Tawney 1969).

There are also origins of this perception that stem from a variety of different cultures. The positive role of labor and work was stressed by Karl Marx (1906), who argued that one's labor defined and formed one's consciousness and worth. Marx's notion of "unearned increment" argued that benefits could not be accrued without engagement in labor. China's Mao Tse-Tung also stressed the benefits of manual labor over intellectual activity during the Cultural Revolution ("Great cultural revolution in progress: Workers' Mao Tse-Tung's thought propaganda teams in colleges and schools," 1968). Those in Mao's China who engaged in activities of the mind were "re-educated." Thus, a long history in a variety of cultures documents the appeal of valuing work over less visibly "productive" activities. Bertrand Russell (1932/1972) referred to this bias as the "cult of efficiency."

Based on this general leaning toward work being preferable over play and leisure time, it seems a logical extension to argue that reducing recess and break times should increase achievement. Arguing for reduced recess time can send a message of "tough love" and concrete plans to increase assessment scores. Although it seems intuitively correct, the scientific evidence does not support the notion that eliminating recess increases achievement (in fact, scientific evidence documents the opposite, as described below). Children are a vulnerable population, and it rests with research experts, parents, guardians, taxpayers, and other concerned citizens to exert pressure against policies that are not based on empirical data. Just as accountability and evidence-based instruction are required in academic areas (Jarrett and Maxwell 2000), decisions regarding the educational policies of recess should likewise be evidence-based to ensure tax and tuition dollars and student and teacher time are spent on effective, research-based practices.

## *Bullying Occurs During Recess*

Another reason that some individuals and organizations advocate for reducing or eliminating recess, especially playground recess, is the perception that this is where peer conflict and bullying takes place. Although it is certainly the case that bullying occurs on playgrounds, it is also the case that bullying occurs in a wide variety of settings, such as cafeterias, hallways, bathrooms, and locker rooms. The commonality among all of these locations is that there is often little to no adult supervision (Pellegrini 2005).

Despite the limited supervision, the base rate of aggression on playgrounds is low (Pellegrini 1992; Pellegrini and Glickman 1989). On preschool and primary school playgrounds in many countries, such as Canada, the USA, and the UK, physical and verbal aggression account for less than 2% of all behavior observed (Pellegrini 1995; Smith and Connolly 1980). Thus, aggression tends to be the exception rather than the norm. These statistics are not intended to diminish the importance of bullying prevention. There are many cases of bullying that can have damaging effects on children and adolescents because, although overall aggression rates may be low, the aggression can have a high intensity level and result in grave consequences. Like other forms of school violence, such as the frequently observed school shootings and suicides, extreme violence does not happen often but can still result in people getting hurt.

It is clear that bullying is an important issue that should receive serious consideration and action, but reducing recess will not eliminate the problem of bullying. Instead, more adult supervision of recess periods, like adult supervision of the cafeteria and hallways, can have a potent effect on dampening aggression. When examining supervision during recess (when supervision exists), teachers assumed responsibility in 50 % of the cases, and in 36 % of the cases teachers' aides supervised. Of these aides, 86 % had no formal training for supervision (NAESP 1989, as cited in Pellegrini 1995). Training is not a trivial issue: A well-trained supervisor can support children's positive social interactions and guard against aggression and bullying.

Although aggression and bullying are serious issues that can occur in playground environments, we argue that recess is still important because it is one of the few times during the school day when children have the opportunity to interact with their peers on their own terms. As we will describe, such opportunities allow children to learn and practice social skills, such as cooperation, compromise, dispute resolution, and inhibiting aggression. Although these skills can be taught in lectures and lessons, recess provides opportunities for children to practice in real-life settings.

## *Replacing Recess with Physical Education*

Another argument for decreasing recess time is that recess can be replaced by physical education classes. Although it may make sense that physical education would provide a structured environment during which children can engage in physical activity to provide a break from academic demands and "blow off steam," it is not a true "break." Physical education, like other instructional disciplines, is a curricular area. It is a class in which students receive instruction on physical activity, fitness, and health; develop physical competence; and develop cognitive understandings about physical activity. These skills help students adopt healthy and active lifestyles. Physical education rightfully imposes rigorous demands on children and adolescents to build and stretch their skills, and physical education teachers adhere to specific standards (CDCP 2010; Council on Physical Education and Children, CPEC, 2001).

Physical education is different from recess. Physical education classes do not necessarily provide a break from stringent instructional regimens. Physical education provides sequenced curricular lessons where the activities and games are structured and adult-directed. Recess does provide a break because children have the option of choosing their preferred activities. Recess provides unstructured play time in which children develop their own fair rules for play, practice and use skills, and make their own choices. Thus, physical education and recess offer differential benefits (CPEC 2001; Jarrett and Maxwell 2005). In fact, both physical education and recess are recommended as regular parts of the elementary school curriculum, and one cannot be substituted for the other (Dills et al. 2011).

Another argument for replacing recess with physical education is that children need to release energy through physical exercise. As an anecdotal example, one of us (Pellegrini) and Benjamin Canada (then superintendent of the Atlanta Public Schools) discussed the role of recess in schools on the Good Morning America television show. Mr. Canada made national news for his policy of eliminating recess in Atlanta schools and replacing it with physical education. He claimed this move raised achievement scores because children did not waste time by "hanging on monkey bars," and that they could "blow off steam" in physical education. However, no real statistics of achievement data were provided. To our knowledge, there are no hard data to support such a claim. Arguments that physical education helps children to release energy also do not have strong empirical and scientific credibility (Evans and Pellegrini 1997). Again, policy decisions should be based on practices that have scientific merit, and utilizing arguments without such evidence does not fit within the theme of evidence-based practice.

## Research Supporting the Inclusion of Recess

Even with the arguments against the inclusion of recess, a strong body of research documents how breaks in the day, as provided by recess, are actually helpful for student learning and achievement. This has been demonstrated in numerous controlled experiments in which children's attention to academic tasks decreases as a function of the length of time they are deprived of a break. Correspondingly, children are more attentive after recess than before. In this section, we outline the theory and data that support the inclusion of recess.

### *Classic Scholars*

Despite the aforementioned view that individuals are more efficient with longer and more intense work periods (in line with Russell's "cult of efficiency"), classic scholars support the notion that there is real value in leisure and play. Bertrand Russell, arguably one of the most productive and original scholars of the twentieth century, was an empiricist who emphasized generating and testing hypotheses using rigorous scientific methods (Russell 1931/1959). In his essay *In Praise of Idleness,* Russell argues for the importance of break times (Russell 1932/1972, pp. 9–10):

> I think there is far too much work done in the world, that immense harm is caused by the belief that work is virtuous, and that what needs to be preached in modern industrial countries is quite different from what has been preached...I hope that after reading the following pages, the leaders of the YMCA will start a campaign to induce young men to do nothing. If so, I shall not have lived in vain.

Although Russell's argument can be applied to school settings, it is aimed at the role of work and leisure for modern society. Russell's use of the term "idleness" mirrors our definition of play: "a capacity for light-heartedness and play" (p. 24). Such behavior is what occurs during recess. Russell's larger point is that there are benefits in leisure to society's economic well-being. Specifically, he suggested that the work day be reduced to 4 h (although, note that this was written in 1932) to enable people to have time for leisure activities, such as playing games, dancing, listening to music, and going to the movies. For Russell, having increased leisure time would also produce benefits because people might choose to spend their time learning more about their careers and professions, continuing their education in related fields, or volunteering for public causes. Therefore, increased leisure time would result in society becoming a better, more productive place (Russell 1932/1972). Historians, such as Johan Huizinga (Huizinga 1939), also made the connection between play and leisure and the flourishing of arts and civilization.

Another valuable point about Russell's quote is that it forces us to reconcile an important educational conundrum. On the one hand, we have calls for more play and leisure time in school, but on the other, we have the very real problem of declining levels of achievement. This apparent contradiction begs serious attention, given the stature of the person advocating more leisure time. Russell's solution to the problem as it might relate to schools and recess (his solutions dealt mostly with the economics of the duration of the work day) proposed that leisure time results in "happy lives" instead of the "frayed nerves" associated with being overworked. Happy people live better, and indeed more productive, lives.

Before Russell's time, others also emphasized the importance of play and games. Thomas Hughes (1895) famously praised the moral instruction afforded by games in childhood. In his book, *Tom Brown's School Days,* Hughes discussed how youngsters learned moral and social lessons when playing games at Rugby School. His views are encapsulated in this often cited quotation:

> You say you don't see much in it all; nothing but a struggling mass of boys, and a leather ball, which seems to excite them to a great furry, as a red rag does a bull. My dear sir, a battle would look much the same to see, except that the boys would be men, and the balls iron; but a battle would be worth your looking at for all that, and so is a football match. You can't be expected to appreciate the delicate strokes of play, the turns by which the game is lost and won,–it takes an old player to do that, but the broad philosophy of football, you can understand if you will. (p. 99)

According to Hughes, the character and social skills that children develop when playing rugby can be compared to those required when leading men in battle. The lessons learned on the playing fields at Rugby generalize to Waterloo. Interestingly, Hughes' view of games and play is much more behavioral than that of Russell. For Hughes, there are specific skills and attitudes associated with games. This perspective is very similar to the views espoused by ethologists who study the play of nonhuman and human animals and make inferences about the value of play fighting, for example, in males' later fighting and hunting ability (Smith 1988).

## The Benefits of Play

A primary reason for why recess is beneficial is that it allows time for children to engage in unstructured, self-directed play that enables them to explore different roles and skills (Waite-Stupiansky and Findlay 2001). A variety of studies document the importance of play for development and for children's school performance (Bateson 2005). Traditionally, the deferred benefits of play are gauged in terms of a cost-to-benefit ratio. This means that play is considered beneficial if the deferred benefits outweigh the immediate costs.

There is an assumption that play is "costly" for children. This cost is often measured by the amount of time spent in play (Smith and Dodsworth 1978), energy expended in play (Pellegrini et al. 1998), or in the dangers inherent in play, such as injury (Fagen 1981). The few studies examining the costs of play have found that play is moderately costly in that children spend a substantial portion of their free time in play (Smith and Dodsworth 1978). Children expend substantial amounts of stored energy during play: Energy expenditure during outdoor recess exceeds basal levels by a factor of 7.5 (Pellegrini et al. 1998; Pellegrini and Smith 1998). Finally, childhood injuries can be incurred during play (Fagen 1981).

Despite these costs, there are beneficial outcomes of play. Evolutionary theorists propose that if a behavior is not beneficial despite its costs, it would not have been naturally selected for in human evolution (Fagen 1981). Many child development theories have evidence to support the benefits of play in terms of learning and practicing the skills necessary for adulthood. For example, playing with dolls may help prepare a child for parenting roles, and playing with a toy computer may help prepare a child for learning how to use a real computer (Pellegrini 2009).

Another benefit of recess is that it enhances physical fitness. Play behaviors exhibited during school recess periods are often physically vigorous social play (Pellegrini 2009). Although few studies have examined the long-term effects of vigorous physical activity in childhood through adulthood, brief experimental studies have shown a positive and immediate effect of vigorous physical activity on cardiovascular fitness (e.g., Simons-Morton et al. 1987). Physical play also stimulates children's senses as they learn about movement and develop their perceptual abilities. Play enables children to learn about their bodies, space, and the physical environment. These experiences go beyond what children can learn from television, computers, or books (Bergen 1998).

Play helps develop children's social and emotional skills (Rogers and Sawyers 1988). During social play, children must produce and understand social signals and learn about peers. Play helps children to manage stress, inhibit aggression, and increase resilience. Social-cognitive skills are enhanced as children enact roles and behaviors, take perspectives, and utilize imagination, reasoning, and manipulative skills (Bateson 2005; Bergen 1998; Fein 1979). In short, free play is linked to a variety of physical, social, emotional, and cognitive developmental milestones (Ginsburg 2007).

During recess, children can engage in free, unstructured play, enabling children to reap its benefits. Recess has also been associated with a variety of other benefits for children's health and development. In the following sections, we describe research that implicates recess in physical health, behavior, social competence, cognition, and achievement.

## *Recess and Physical Health*

During recess, many children will engage in some sort of physically active play that enables them to develop health and fitness. In fact, 60% of children will engage in some type of active play during recess (Pellegrini and Smith 1993). Some studies have found elementary-aged students to be even more active during recess than in physical education classes (Kraft 1989). In recess, physical activity tends to be highest during the first 6–7 min on the playground, and then activity levels start to decline. However, the duration and intensity of physical activity will increase if recess is delayed (Pellegrini and Davis 1993; Smith and Hagan 1980). These studies indicate that recess, especially outdoor recess, is a setting in which children are physically active.

Physical activity during recess brings a variety of health benefits such as aerobic endurance, muscular strength, coordination, and weight control (CDCP 2010; Dale et al. 2000). When considering that obesity rates in the USA have tripled since 1970 and that childhood obesity, in particular, is on the rise, providing children opportunities to be active would help offset this epidemic. This would also reduce the health problems associated with obesity, which include hypertension, diabetes, and high cholesterol (Waite-Stupiansky and Findlay 2001).

Some researchers have examined whether children would compensate for low levels of physical activity during the school day by engaging in more physical activity after school. However, children do not compensate. On days that children are less physically active at school, they are less physically active at home in the afternoon and evening. On days that children are more physically active during the school day, they also tend to be more physically active at home (Dale et al. 2000). Thus, providing opportunities for physical activity during the school day, such as what occurs during recess, can help to improve children's overall well-being in terms of health and fitness.

## *Recess and Classroom Behavior*

Recess has been implicated in improved classroom behavior. A variety of intervention and non-intervention studies document that children's fidgeting increases prior to recess, and decreases after recess. When recess is delayed (meaning that the instructional time preceding recess is longer), fidgeting increases as a function of the length of the delay. In addition, when children engage in moderately vigorous play during recess, it is associated with less fidgeting after recess (Jarrett et al. 1998; Pellegrini and Davis 1993; Pellegrini et al. 1995).

Students who have recess are more likely to be on-task in the classroom compared to students who do not receive recess (Pellegrini et al. 1995). Furthermore, when recess breaks are scheduled so that they occur directly before or after an academic lesson, children are more on-task for those lessons (Fagerstrom and Mahoney 2006). This indicates that overall classroom behavior is improved with recess. Even as little as 15 min of daily recess is linked with improved overall classroom behavior (Barros et al. 2009).

## *Recess and Social Competence*

Another critical benefit to recess is that it can increase children's social development and social competence (CDCP 2010). Social competence refers to a set of social skills, such as interacting cooperatively with peers, inhibiting antisocial and aggressive behavior, and having the skills and abilities necessary to form close relationships (Waters and Sroufe 1983). Recess is important for socialization because it is one of the few places where children can freely interact, and thus must interpret and learn from social experiences, as well as confront social conflict (Jambor 1994; Sutton-Smith 1990). This usually occurs in the context of social games: During recess, children will organize their own games in which they must negotiate with other children to set rules, such as which team will go first. These negotiations help children to respect rules, learn and practice self-discipline, control aggression, resolve conflicts, and practice leadership skills (Bishop and Curtis 2001; Jarrett and Maxwell 2000). As this demonstrates, children's behavior on playgrounds requires relatively high levels of social competence.

**Friendship and Adjustment** Children utilize social competence skills to build healthy peer relationships (Waters and Sroufe 1983). This happens in the context of social games, during which children interact with peers in a manner that does not occur in structured settings (Jarrett and Duckett-Hedgebeth 2003). Building peer relationships is important because friendships facilitate classroom learning, school success, and overall adjustment (Coie et al. 1998; Pellegrini 1992). In fact, when making the transition from preschool to primary school, children experience better outcomes when they make this transition with a friend (Ladd et al. 1996). Positive social competence and friendships are also critical for adjustment to school, especially for boys (Barros et al. 2009; Pellegrini and Bohn 2005). Relationships play such a critical role because they provide children with positive associations with school and social-emotional support to relieve stresses associated with school (Jambor 1994; Ladd et al. 1996; Ladd et al. 1988). Recess may be one of the only opportunities children have to interact freely with peers to build friendships.

**Cooperation and Conflict Resolution** As mentioned, recess presents children with situations in which they must cooperate, avoid conflict, and engage in conflict resolution, especially when setting rules for games (Rogers and Sawyers 1988). Children are more likely to develop conflict resolution skills with peers compared to adults: Children's interactions with adults tend to be more unilateral, whereas children are more likely to disagree with their peers. Children are also motivated to resolve such conflicts: If the conflict is not resolved in a free play situation, children are at liberty to leave the situation and engage in another activity. Thus, conflict resolution is necessary for the game or play interaction to continue (Hartup and Laursen 1993). Such conflict resolution and cooperation also helps to develop perspective-taking skills as children learn to accommodate others' viewpoints (Rogers and Sawyers 1988).

**School Success** Social competence skills, built during recess, are related to overall success in school. When children are in charge of directing their own behavior and activities, it is a form of self-determination that leads them to feel control, develop self-esteem, and develop problem-solving abilities. As another example, children will often engage in reciprocal social and pretend play during recess, such as rough-and-tumble play, which predicts social competence, perspective-taking skills, and hypothetical problem-solving. All of these form the foundation for success in school (Pellegrini and Smith 1998; Waters and Sroufe 1983).

## *Recess, Cognition, and Achievement*

Aside from building social competence, recess is related to a variety of cognitive skills. It can aid cognitive performance, learning, and academic behaviors (Jarrett 2002; Pellegrini and Bohn 2005). One of the primary explanations for this comes from the cognitive principle of massed versus distributed practice.

**Massed Versus Distributed Practice** One of the arguments for reducing recess is that its reduction can increase instructional time. Children certainly benefit from receiving quality instruction, and increasing the number of hours of instruction a child receives per year may increase learning under many circumstances. The time-on-task literature in American educational research (see Brophy and Good 1974, for a summary) communicates that educational attainment is directly and positively related to the amount of time spent working on tasks. Calls for longer school days and school years and the elimination of recess are logical extensions of this position. However, this is different from the claim that more intense, break-free hours of instruction will enhance learning. One solution might be a longer school day with frequent breaks and an extended school year. Such a practice would likely improve achievement and provide a safe and enriching place for children.

In support of this, a well-known principle of learning is that children (and adults) learn more quickly and retain information better when their efforts on a task are distributed, and not massed. What this means is that, when a person is given breaks during a task rather than having his/her efforts be concentrated and uninterrupted for a long period of time, productivity and learning increase (Ebbinghaus 1885/1964; James 1901). Spacing tasks out over time can help make academic work seem less boring, which improves students' attention (Dempster 1988). Recess may be beneficial for children in schools because it provides a break from sustained work periods.

Neuroscience research also supports the idea that distributed practice facilitates attention. The brain operates in cycles, during which the efficiency with which it can process verbal or spatial information decreases. Between cycles, which last approximately 90–110 min, novelty and rest time are required in order for the brain to recycle chemicals necessary to form long term memories (Jensen 1998; R. Klein and Armitage 1979). When an individual is asked to perform a task that requires a lot of attention, and to do so continuously for a long period of time, the brain becomes less and less efficient until it receives a break (Waite-Stupiansky and Findlay 2001). As academic tasks require this type of concentration, it makes sense that students require breaks to facilitate learning.

The advantage of distributed practice has been specifically addressed by examining the ways in which children learn numerous school-related tasks, such as learning native and foreign language vocabulary, recalling a text, and recalling math facts (see Dempster 1988, for a review). Distributed practice also helps to improve memory, alertness, achievement, and productivity (Kausler et al. 1990; Toppino et al. 1991). These laboratory studies yielded reliable and robust effects, documenting the efficacy of task spacing on learning. Indeed, the theory has been supported with humans across the life span, as well as with a variety of other animals.

Whenever a study is conducted, the results tend to be more robust in laboratory compared to field settings (Dempster 1988). Classroom studies examining massed versus distributed practice are no exception: These studies are less frequently undertaken, and they generally produce less impressive results. However, this might occur because a number of external factors affect classroom learning, such as whether the task is simple as opposed to complex. Rather than looking only at material learned, the results of classroom research become more powerful and match those of the laboratory when examining children's attention to the task at hand. Attention increases when tasks are distributed and spaced. Such spacing may help children to find the tasks less boring. This increased attention may be important to subsequent learning (Dempster 1988).

Although it might make sense to think that simply changing from one academic task to another would constitute enough of a break, there is research documenting that breaks should be more drastic (although how drastic the break may be varies as a function of development). Simply changing to a different topic of academic instruction is not enough of a mental change or a physical release to reap the benefits of distributed practice (Ginsburg 2007; Toppino et al. 1991). The reason is that academic learning usually occurs in sedentary settings where free social interaction between students does not occur. Children habituate to this type of setting and require more of a physical and social change, as is afforded by free play. The key is that children require a change to an activity in which they can be self-directed (Bjorklund and Brown 1998; Pellegrini and Davis 1993).

Given the positive effects of distributed practice on children's attention, it should be more readily practiced in classrooms. However, this practice is not utilized as frequently in schools as would be beneficial for students. One possible explanation for this disconnect, as suggested by Dempster (1988), is that the complicated contingencies of running a school may not easily accommodate the added complexities of a distributed practice regimen. There is a simple solution to this conundrum, using a well-established school institution: recess. Recess provides a break between school tasks, thus distributing practice on academic work. As theoretical and empirical evidence document that attention and learning increase as a function of distributed practice, recess has an important place in the school day.

**Cognitive Skills** That distributed practice is linked to improved attention is important for academic learning. Not only is attention important for learning (Dempster 1988) but it can also be used as an index for engagement in academic tasks (e.g., Toppino et al. 1991), and it is related to cognitive performance and achievement (e.g., Rowe and Rowe 1992). Recess is important for attention, because students (particularly boys and those with attention deficit hyperactivity disorder, ADHD) are more attentive, productive, and efficient following recess compared to before, especially when they have a sustained period of outdoor free play. Furthermore, as the length of a break-free work period increases, students become decreasingly attentive, productive, and efficient, especially younger children (Holmes et al. 2006; Jarrett et al. 1998; Pellegrini and Bjorklund 1997; Pellegrini et al. 1995). These data indicate that breaks can rejuvenate children to help them attend to academic tasks.

As discussed, children are often physically active during recess. Physical activity has general cognitive benefits for children and is linked to improved learning and concentration (CDCP 2010; Etnier et al. 1997; Sibley and Etnier 2003). However, whereas moderately vigorous playground activity is likely to increase attention, highly vigorous activity may actually decrease attention. Considering that delaying recess can result in more physically vigorous activity, offering frequent, short breaks for recess and physical activity would be the best way to encourage moderately vigorous activity and maximize children's attention and learning (Pellegrini and Davis 1993; Pellegrini et al. 1995).

**Achievement** When children freely interact with their peers on the playground or even in other settings (such as playing with blocks), they utilize relatively sophisticated cognitive skills that can help increase academic achievement. For example, they must follow rules of play and games and use language to negotiate. In addition, the types of language that children use to negotiate conflicts are similar to the languages of school instruction (Heath 1983) and literacy (Pellegrini and Galda 1982). Preschoolers utilize more oral language and a wider array of vocabulary words when engaging in open-ended activities (Isbell and Raines 1991). Playgrounds enable multiple opportunities for oral expression, and children will utilize language from a variety of genres, set rules, and more (Waite-Stupiansky and Findlay 2001).

Other cognitive skills that children learn and practice during recess are problem-solving skills and creativity. In play, children assemble a skill; play is disassembled when the skill is completed (Bateson 2005). Through this, and through negotiations on how to organize and direct their own games, children learn and practice problem-solving skills (Jarrett and Maxwell 2000; Jensen 1998). In addition, imagination and creativity are fostered during free play (Bergen 1998; Waite-Stupiansky and Findlay 2001). Children utilize these cognitive resources during play in an effort to meet the demands of interaction, conflict, and compromise. They are motivated because children generally enjoy interacting with peers at recess, and will try their best to initiate and sustain play. For example, they may have to compromise (share a toy or a turn) to continue to play with their best friend.

In fact, studies demonstrate that the activities associated with recess predict academic achievement in general. First, physical activity and fitness, especially aerobic exercise, improve achievement in mathematics, general intelligence, and reading (CDCP 2010; Fedewa and Ahn 2011; Hillman et al. 2008). Considering that moderate levels of physical activity occur on the playground, this can help improve achievement. Second, as previously mentioned, interacting with peers requires utilizing language and perspective-taking skills, which are related to classroom achievement (Bjorklund and Pellegrini 2000). Third, kindergarteners' social behavior on the playground predicts academic achievement (as measured by a standardized test) in first grade, even after statistically controlling for children's academic achievement in kindergarten. During recess, children who interact more with adults have lower achievement scores compared to those who interact with peers. Thus, there is predictive academic value in what kindergarten children do at recess, beyond the information provided in kindergarteners' basic academic achievement (Pellegrini and Bjorklund 1997). All of this research supports the notion that recess does not negatively affect achievement, but may actually improve it.

## Developmental Considerations in Relation to Recess and Achievement

When considering the effects of recess on children's social development and achievement, it is critical to account for age-related factors. For example, it is uncontroversial that young children think differently than older children, who in turn think differently than adults. Regardless of the much-debated underlying reasons for these cognitive differences (see Bjorklund 2004), the result is that younger children learn most things at a slower rate than older children. Despite young children's limitations, research over the past several decades demonstrates that preschool and school-age children can be taught skills that are spontaneously acquired only by older children, providing the impression that more rigorous instruction during the early grades will result in enhanced cognition. It is from this perspective that recess is seen as a superfluous activity, perhaps necessary to some degree to combat boredom, but an essentially non-productive part of the school day.

An alternative developmental perspective holds that children's immature cognitions are well-suited to the particular demands of childhood. This means that immaturity is not something to overcome, but rather children's immature nervous systems may be adapted to deal effectively with the cognitive demands they face in their daily lives at particular developmental periods. This is consistent with the view that behaviors and cognitions within early childhood have a value or function inherent to that period and should not be considered "imperfect" variants of adult behavior (Bateson 1981; Bjorklund and Pellegrini 2002). Therefore, young children's cognitions are particularly well-suited to learn and practice skills in informal, free-play settings. For example, children will often overestimate their cognitive skills (Yussen and Levy 1975) and social status (Smith and Boulton 1990), but this overestimation helps children to persist at challenging tasks, leading to perceived success and thus competence (Bandura 1997).

This developmental perspective, based on Bjorklund's theory of "cognitive immaturity" (Bjorklund and Green 1992), supports the notion that the facilitative effects of breaks between periods of intense work should be greater for younger than for older children. From this position, young children do not process most information as effectively as older children (Pellegrini and Bjorklund 1997; Piaget 1983). This occurs because young children's nervous systems are not as developmentally mature, and they have not had as many experiences upon which to build their prior knowledge.

The immaturity of their nervous systems and lack of experiences render them unable to perform higher-level cognitive tasks with the same efficiency as older children and adults, which has a direct effect on their educability (Bjorklund 2004; Siegler 1991). Young children must devote greater amounts of cognitive effort to their studies, which makes it challenging for them to focus attention for a long period of time. As a result, young children are especially susceptible to cognitive interference and experience the greatest gains from breaks between focused intellectual activities, which recess provides (Pellegrini and Bjorklund 1997).

Evidence in support of this hypothesis is drawn from the literature on memory and cognitive inhibition. Research using a wide range of tasks has shown that, with age, children are increasingly able to inhibit task-irrelevant thoughts and resist interference from unrelated stimuli (e.g., Bjorklund and Harnishfeger 1990; Harnishfeger and Pope 1996; Lorsbach and Reimer 1997). Inhibition abilities permit children to focus on task-relevant information, which is of central importance to attention and working memory. Young children experience difficulty keeping extraneous information from entering their short-term memory stores. As a result, their working memories are often cluttered with irrelevant information, leaving less mental space for task-relevant information or for the execution of cognitive strategies (e.g., Bjorklund and Harnishfeger 1990).

From this perspective, there may be a general increase in interference when younger children perform a series of highly focused tasks, regardless of the nature of those tasks. Although one would predict that changing from one type of focused activity to another would yield some cognitive benefit, children (especially young children) may experience a continued buildup of interference with repeated performance of even different highly focused tasks. Thus, they would experience greater benefit from a drastic change in activity, which is afforded by recess. This assertion is consistent with the evidence that younger children may require a greater change in activity or stimulus materials before they experience a release from interference (e.g., see Pellegrini and Bjorklund 1997). Interference makes school learning particularly difficult for young elementary school children, and opportunities to engage in non-focused, nonintellectual activities should afford them the needed respite to "re-energize" their nervous systems. Consistent with this reasoning, the unstructured play that occurs during recess periods across the school day should minimize cognitive interference and maximize learning and achievement (Toppino et al. 1991). Thus, recess serves a critical role in the development of young children.

## *Developmental Considerations Regarding Standardized Testing*

An important developmental consideration is that utilizing standardized tests to make decisions regarding educational policy is more appropriate for some age groups than for others. There is a movement to administer standardized tests to children as early as kindergarten, but research demonstrates that young children are unreliable test takers, meaning that they tend not to perform consistently across time (Messick 1983). For example, preschoolers tend to demonstrate greater variability in test-retest reliability for standardized tests than older children. This is because young children fatigue more quickly, are more distractible, possess limited attention spans, and are less tolerant of frustration than older students (Bracken et al. 1991; Bracken and Walker 1997; Nagle 2000).

This exemplifies a larger point that, although standardized assessments are valuable, they are limited in their predictive and explanatory power, especially for young children (Wentzel 1991). Seemingly harmless environmental factors can lead to swings in motivation and performance in young children, supporting the notion that young children are unreliable test takers. And, reliability is necessary in order to have a valid assessment: If test scores change from day to day (i.e., are unreliable) they tell us nothing about the truthfulness of the scores (i.e., validity). That children, especially young ones, are unreliable test takers is an important reason for educators to use a number of different assessment strategies. That is, tests can and should be used, but in conjunction with other measures such as attendance, grades, teacher assessments, and behavioral observations of competence. When all of these measures are aggregated we get a more valid picture of children's performance and achievement (Cronbach 1971).

What this research means is that policy decisions regarding recess should not be made on standardized test results alone. Research supports the conclusion that recess and free play are related to well-being, achievement, and social competence (Pellegrini 2005). Importantly, researchers came to this conclusion by conducting a number of different studies that utilize a variety of methodologies. This is critical, because their results provide converging evidence that recess, especially for young children, is beneficial for development.

Recess also provides valuable time for teachers and other school personnel to observe children freely interacting with peers in an undirected environment other than the classroom. Teachers can learn about their students' propensities toward leadership, prosocial behaviors, social isolation, and aggression. This can help teachers understand their students better, facilitate learning, and offer more knowledge when intervening in certain situations (Hartle et al. 1994; Pellegrini and Bjorklund 1996). However, also recall that children's behavior on the playground is a powerful predictor of achievement (Pellegrini 1992; Pellegrini and Bjorklund 1997), just as social competence is a predictor of school performance and adjustment (Pellegrini et al. 1998; Waters and Sroufe 1983). Thus, not only does recess afford an opportunity for teachers to learn more about their students, it also enables them to gain valuable converging or diverging evidence for achievement scores.

## Conclusions

In this chapter, we mapped the basic territory in the recess debate. Recess, like play in young children, is debased because it is assumed to be a waste of time—time that could be more "efficiently" spent. However, the counter-argument, that recess is helpful for development and learning, is supported by a large body of theoretical and empirical research. The research documents the variety of cognitive, social-emotional, and physical benefits of recess (Jarrett and Waite-Stupiansky 2009; Pellegrini and Bohn 2005; Pellegrini and Smith 1993). It is critical that any educational policy decisions be based upon evidence-based research, as is being required for instructional practices. We urge those on both sides of the recess debate to provide sound theoretical and empirical support for their arguments to best serve our children and their learning in schools. Based on the theory and data, there is clear evidence that recess has beneficial effects on children's physical health, behavior, social competence, and academic performance.

## References


Bandura, A. (1997). *Self-efficacy: The excercise of control*. New York: W. H. Freeman.

Barros, R. M., Silver, E. J., & Stein, R. E. K. (2009). School recess and group classroom behavior. *Pediatrics, 123,* 431–436. doi:10.1542/peds.2007-2825.

Bateson, P. P. G. (1981). Discontinuities in development and changes in the organization of play in cats. In K. Immelmann, G. Barlow, L. Petrinovich & M. Main (Eds.), *Behavioral development* (pp. 281–295). New York: Cambridge University Press.

Bateson, P. P. G. (2005). The role of play in the evolution of great apes and humans. In A. D. Pellegrini & P. K. Smith (Eds.), *The nature of play: Great apes and humans* (pp. 13–26). New York: Guilford.

Bergen, D. (1998). *Play as a medium for learning and development: A handbook of theory and practice*. Portsmouth: Heinemann.

Bishop, J. C., & Curtis, M. (2001). *Play today in the primary playground*. Philadelphia: Open University Press.

Bjorklund, D. F. (2004). *Children's thinking: Developmental function and individual differences* (4th ed.). Belmont: Wadsworth.

Bjorklund, D. F., & Brown, R. D. (1998). Physical play and cognitive development: Integrating activity, cognition, and education. *Child Development, 69,* 604–606. doi:10.1111/j.1467-8624.1998.tb06229.x.

Bjorklund, D. F., & Green, B. L. (1992). The adaptive nature of cognitive immaturity. *American Psychologist, 47,* 46–54. doi: 10.1037/0003-066X.47.1.46.

Bjorklund, D. F., & Harnishfeger, K. K. (1990). The resources construct in cognitive development: Diverse sources of evidence and a theory of inefficient inhibition. *Developmental Review, 10,* 48–71. doi:10.1016/0273-2297(90)90004-N.

Bjorklund, D. F., & Pellegrini, A. D. (2000). Child development and evolutionary psychology. *Child Development, 71,* 1687–1708. doi:10.1111/1467-8624.00258.

Bjorklund, D. F., & Pellegrini, A. D. (2002). *Evolutionary developmental psychology*. Washington, DC: American Psychological Association.

Bland, K. (2005). Schools pressured to cut recess: Instructional needs mean less time for kids to play. *Arizona Republic*. Retrieved 1 June, 2013 from http://www.azcentral.com/families/education/articles/0512recess12.html.

Blatchford, P., & Sumpner, C. (1998). What do we know about breaktime? Results from a national survey of breaktime and lunchtime in primary and secondary schools. *British Educational Research Journal, 24,* 79–94.

Bracken, B. A., & Walker, K. C. (1997). The utility of intelligence tests for preschool children. In D. P. Flanagan, J. L. Genshaft & P. L. Harrison (Eds.), *Contemporary intellectual assessment: Theories, tests, and issues* (pp. 484–502). New York: Guilford.

Bracken, B. A., Howell, K. K., & Harrison, T. E. (1991). Ipsative subtest pattern stability of the Bracken basic concept scale and the Kaufman assessment battery for children in a preschool sample. *School Psychology Review, 20,* 315–330.

Brophy, J., & Good, T. (1974). *Teacher-student relationships: Causes and consequences*. New York: Holt, Rinehart, and Winston.

Burghardt, G. M. (1988). Precocity, play, and the ectotherm-endotherm transition. In E. Blass (Ed.), *Handbook of behavrioal neurobilogy*, (Vol. 9, pp. 107–148). New York: Plenum.

Centers for Disease Control and Prevention (CDCP). (2010). *The association between school-based physical activity, including physical education, and academic performance*. Atlanta: US Department of Health and Human Services.

Coie, J. D., Dodge, K. A., & Damon, W. (1998). Aggression and antisocial behavior. In Nieisenberg (Ed.), *Handbook of child psychology. Social, emotional, and personality development*, (5th ed., Vol. 3, pp. 779–862). New York: Wiley.

Council on Physical Education and Children (CPEC). (2001). *Recess in elementary schools: A position paper of the Council on Physical Education for Children and the National Association for Sport and Physical Education*. Reston: National Association for Sport and Physical Education.

Cronbach, L. J. (1971). Validity. In R. L. Thorndike (Ed.), *Educational measurement* (pp. 443–507). Washington, DC: American Council on Education.

Dale, D., Corbin, C. B., & Dale, K. (2000). Restricting opportunities to be active during school time: Do children compensate by increasing physical activity levels after school? *Research Quarterly for Exercise and Sport, 71*, 240–248.

Dempster, F. N. (1988). The spacing effect: A case study in the failure to apply the results of psychological research. *American Psychologist, 43*, 627–634. doi:10.1037/0003-066X.43.8.627.

Dills, A. K., Morgan, H. N., & Rotthoff, K. W. (2011). Recess, physical education, and elementary school student outcomes. *Economics of Education Review, 30*, 889–900. doi:10.1016/j.econedurev.2011.04.011. ISSN: 0272-7757.

Ebbinghaus, H. (1885/1964). *Memory*. New York: Teachers College Press.

Etnier, J. L., Salazar, W., Landers, D. M., Petruzzello, S. J., Han, M., & Nowell, P. (1997). The influence of physical fitness and exercise upon cognitive functioning: A meta-analysis. *Journal of Sport and Exercise Psychology, 19*, 249–277.

Evans, J., & Pellegrini, A. D. (1997). Surplus energy theory: An enduruing but inadequate justification for school breaktime. *Educational Review, 49*, 229–238.

Fagen, R. (1981). *Animal play behavior*. New York: Oxford University Press.

Fagerstrom, T., & Mahoney, K. (2006). Give me a break! Can strategic recess scheduling increase on-task behavior for first-graders? *Ontario Action Researcher, 9*, 6.

Fedewa, A. L., & Ahn, S. (2011). The effects of physical activity and physical fitness on children's achievement and cognitive outcomes: A meta-analysis. *Research Quarterly for Exercise and Sport, 82*, 521–535. doi:10.5641/027013611x13275191444107.

Fein, G. (1979). Echoes from the nursery: Piaget, Vygotsky, and the relationship between language and play. In E. Winner & H. Gardner (Eds.), *Fact, fiction, and fantasy in childhood* (pp. 1–17). San Francisco: Jossey-Bass.

Ginsburg, K. R. (2007). The importance of play in promoting healthy child development and maintaining strong parent-child bonds. *Pediatrics, 119*, 182–191. doi:10.1542/peds.2006-2697.

Great cultural revolution in progress: Workers' Mao Tse-Tung's thought propaganda teams in colleges and schools. (1968). *Peking Review, 11*, 13–16.

Harnishfeger, K. K., & Pope, R. (1996). Intending to forget: The development of cognitive inhibition in directed forgetting. *Journal of Experimental Child Psychology, 62*, 292–315.

Hartle, L., Campbell, J., becker, A., Harman, C., Kagel, S., & Tiballi, B. (1994). Outdoor play: A window on social-cognitive development. *Dimensions of Early Childhood, 23*, 27–31.

Hartup, W. W., & Laursen, B. (1993). Conflict and context in peer relations. In C. H. Hart (Ed.), *Children on playgrounds: Research perspectives and applications* (pp. 44–84). Albany: State Universtiy of New York Press.

Heath, S. B. (1983). *Ways with words*. New York: Cambridge University Press.

Hillman, C. H., Erickson, K. I., & Kramer, A. F. (2008). Be smart, exercise your heart: Exercise effects on brain and cognition. *Science and Society, 9*, 58–65. doi:10.1038/nrn2298.

Holmes, R. M., Pellegrini, A. D., & Schmidt, S. L. (2006). The effects of different recess timing regimens on preschoolers' classroom attention. *Early Child Development and Care, 176,* 735–743. doi:10.1080/03004430500207179.

Howard, P. (1994). *Owner's manual for the brain*. Austin: Leornian Press.

Hughes, T. (1895). *Tom Brown's school days*. Cambridge: The Riverside Press.

Huizinga, J. (1939). *Homo ludens*. Amsterdam: Pantheon.

Isbell, R., & Raines, S. (1991). An analysis of the oral language production of young children participating in three types of play centers. *Journal of Research in Childhood Education, 5,* 140–146. doi:10.1080/02568549109594811.

Jambor, T. (1994). School recess and social development. *Dimensions of Early Childhood, 23,* 17–20.

James, W. (1901). *Talks to teachers on psychology: And to students on some of life's ideals*. New York: Holt.

Jarrett, O. (2002). Recess in elementary school: What does the research say? Champaign: *ERIC Clearinghouse on Elementary and Early Childhood Education.*

Jarrett, O. S., & Duckett-Hedgebeth, M. (2003). Recess in middle school: What do the students do? In O. S. Jarrett & M. Duckett-Hedgebeth (Eds.), *Play and educational theory and practice* (pp. 227–241). Westport: Praeger.

Jarrett, O. S., & Maxwell, D. M. (2000). What research says about the need for recess. In R. Clements (Ed.), *Elementary school recess: Selected readings, games, and activities for teachers and parents* (pp. 12–23). Lake Charles: American Press.

Jarrett, O. S., & Maxwell, D. M. (2005). Physical education and recess: Are both necessary? Retrieved 15 May, 2013 from www.southfayette.org/bohn/recess.html.

Jarrett, O. S., Maxwell, D. M., Dickerson, C., Hoge, P., Davies, G., & Yetley, A. (1998). Impact of recess on classroom behavior: Group effects and individual differences. *The Journal of Educational Research, 92,* 121–126.

Jarrett, O. S., & Waite-Stupiansky. (2009). Recess—It's indespensible! *Young Children, 64,* 66–69.

Jensen, E. (1998). *Teaching with the brain in mind*. Alexandria: Association for Supervision and Curriculum Development.

Johnson, D. (1998). Many schools putting an end to child's play. *New York Times*, A1, A16.

Juster, T. F., Stafford, F., & Ono, H. (2004). *Major changes have taken pace in how children and teens spend their time: Child development supplement*. Ann Arbor: Institute for Social Research, University of Michigan.

Kausler, D., Wiley, J., & Phillips, L. (1990). Adult age differences in memory for massed and distributed actions. *Psychology and Aging, 5,* 530–534. doi:10.1037/0882-7974.5.4.530.

Klein, G. (2006). Recess in jeopardy? *Media General News Service*. Retrieved 15 May, 2013 from http://washdateline.magnetwork.com/index.cfm?SiteID=wsh&PackageID=46&fuseaction=article.main&ArticleID=8086&GroupID=214.

Klein, R., & Armitage, R. (1979). Rhythms in human performance: 1 1/2-hour oscillations in cognitive style. *Science, 204,* 1326–1327.

Kraft, R. E. (1989). Children at play: Behavior of children at recess. *Journal of Physical Education, Recreation, and Dance, 60,* 21–24.

Ladd, G. W., Kochenderfer, B. J., & Coleman, C. C. (1996). Friendship quality as a predictor of young children's early school adjustment. *Child Development, 67,* 1103–1118. doi:10.1111/j.1467-8624.1996.tb01785.x.

Ladd, G. W., Price, J., & Hart, L. (1988). Predicting preschoolers' peer status from their playground behavior. *Child Development, 59,* 986–992. doi:10.2307/1130265.

Lorsbach, T.C., & Reimer, J. F. (1997). Developmental changes in the inhibition of previously relevant information. *Journal of Experimental Child Psychology, 64,* 317–342.

Marx, K. (1906). *Capital: A critique of political economy*. New York: The Modern Libary, Random House.

Messick, S. (1983). Assessment of children. In W. Kessen (Ed.), *History, theories, and methods* (4th ed., pp. 477–526). New York: Wiley.

Nagle, R. J. (2000). Issues in preschool assessment. In B. A. Bracken (Ed.), *The psychoeducational assessment of preschool children* (3rd ed., pp. 19–32). Needham Heights: Allyn & Bacon.

National Association for Sport and Physical Education, & American Heart Association. (2010). *2010 shape of the nation report: Status of physical education in the USA*. Reston: National Association for Sport and Physical Education.

National Center for Education Statistics. (2006). *Calories in, calories out: Food and exercise in public elementary schools, 2005*. Washington, DC: US Department of Education.

No Time for Play. (2001). *The Economist, 35*. Retrieved 15 April, 2013 from http://www.ed.gov/programs/edresearch/applicant.html.

Pellegrini, A. D. (1991). Kindergarten children's social cognitive status as a predictor of first grade success. *Early Childhood Research Quarterly, 7*, 565–577. doi:10.1016/0885-2006(92)90099-K.

Pellegrini, A. D. (1992). Preference for outdoor play during early adolescence. *Journal of Adolescence, 15*, 241–254. doi:10.1016/0140-1971(92)90028-4.

Pellegrini, A. D. (1995). *School recess and playground behavior: Educational and developmental roles*. Albany: State University of New York Press.

Pellegrini, A. D. (2005). *Recess: Its role in education and development*. Mahwah: Erlbaum.

Pellegrini, A. D. (2009). Research and policy on children's play. *Child Development Perspectives, 3*, 131–136. doi:10.1111/j.1750-8606.2009.00092.x.

Pellegrini, A. D., & Bjorklund, D. F. (1996). The place of recess in school: Issues in the role of recess in children's education and development. *Journal of Research in Childhood Education, 11*, 5–13. doi:10.1080/02568549609594691.

Pellegrini, A. D., & Bjorklund, D. F. (1997). The role of recess in children's cognitive performance. *Educational Psychologist, 32*, 35–40. doi:10.1207/s15326985ep3201_3.

Pellegrini, A. D., & Bohn, C. M. (2005). The role of recess in children's cognitive performance and school adjustment. *Educational Researcher, 34*, 13–19. doi:10.3102/0013189x034001013.

Pellegrini, A. D., & Davis, P. D. (1993). Relations between children's playground and classroom behaviour. *British Journal of Educational Psychology, 63*, 88–95. doi:10.1111/j.2044-8279.1993.tb01043.x.

Pellegrini, A. D., & Galda, L. (1982). The effects of thematic fantasy play training on the development of children's story comprehension. *American Educational Research Journal, 19*, 443-452. doi:10.3102/00028312019003443.

Pellegrini, A. D., & Glickman, C. D. (1989). The educational role of recess. *Principal, 68*, 23–24.

Pellegrini, A. D., & Holmes, R. M. (2006). The role of recess in primary school. In A. D. Pellegrini & R. M. Holmes (Eds.), *Play = Learning: How play motivates and enhances children's cognitive and social-emotional growth* (pp. 36–53). New York: Oxford University Press.

Pellegrini, A. D., Horvat, M., & Huberty, P. D. (1998). The relative cost of children's physical activity play. *Animal Behaviour, 55*, 1053–1061. doi:10.1006/anbe.1997.0658.

Pellegrini, A. D., Huberty, P. D., & Jones, I. (1995). The effects of recess timing on children's playground and classroom behaviors. *American Educational Research Journal, 32*, 845–864. doi:10.3102/00028312032004845.

Pellegrini, A. D., & Smith, P. K. (1993). School Recess: Implications for education and development. *Review of Educational Research, 63*, 51–67. doi:10.3102/00346543063001051.

Pellegrini, A. D., & Smith, P. K. (1998). Physical activity play: The nature and function of a neglected aspect of play. *Child Development, 69*, 577-598. doi:10.1111/j.1467-8624.1998.tb06226.x.

Piaget, J. (1983). Piaget's theory. In W. Kessen (Ed.), *Handbook of child psychology: History, theories, and methods* (pp. 103–128). New York: Wiley.

Recess: An issue of academic needs vs. social and emotional values. (1991, October 27). Pittsburgh Press, p. A9.

Rogers, C. S., & Sawyers, J. K. (1988). *Play in the lives of children*. Washington, DC: National Association for the Education of Young Children.

Rowe, K. J., & Rowe, K. (1992). The relationship between inattentiveness in the classroom and reading achievement: Part B: An explanatory study. *Journal of the American Academy of Child & Adolescent Psychiatry, 31*, 357–368. doi:10.1097/00004583-199203000-00026.

Russell, B. (1931/1959). *The scientific outlook*. New York: Norton.
Russell, B. (1932/1972). *In praise of idleness and other essays*. New York: Simon and Schuster.
Schacter, R. (2005). The end of recess. *District Administration, 41,* 36–41.
Schools becoming all work and no play. (2001). *The Journal of Physical Education, Recreation, & Dance, 72,* 11.
Sibley, B. A., & Etnier, J. L. (2003). The relationship between physical activity and cognition in children: A meta-analysis. *Pediactric Exercise Science, 9,* 113–126.
Siegler, R. (1991). *Children's thinking* (2nd ed.). Englewood Cliffs: Prentice Hall.
Simons-Morton, B. G., O'Hara, N. M., Simons-Morton, D. G., & Parcel, G. (1987). Children and fitness: A public health perspective. *Research Quarterly for Exercise and Sport, 58,* 293–302.
Smith, P. K. (1988). Children's play and its role in early development: A re-evaluation of the 'play ethos'. In A. D. Pellegrini (Ed.), *Psychological bases for early education. Wiley series in developmental psychology and its applications*. (pp. 207–226). Oxford: Wiley.
Smith, P. K., & Boulton, M. (1990). Rough-and tumble play, aggression and dominance: Perception and behaviour in children's enocounters. *Human Development, 33,* 271–282. doi:10.1159/000276524.
Smith, P. K., & Connolly, K. J. (1980). *The ecology of preschool behaviour*. West Nyack: Cambridge University Press.
Smith, P. K., & Dodsworth, C. (1978). Social class differences in the fantasy play of preschool children. *Journal of Genetic Psychology, 133,* 183–190.
Smith, P. K., & Hagan, T. (1980). Effects of deprivation of exercise on nursery school children. *Animal Behaviour, 28,* 922–928. doi:10.1016/S.003-3472(80)80154-0.
Sutton-Smith, B. (1990). School playgrounds as festival. *Children's Environment Quarterly, 7,* 3–7.
Sutton-Smith, B., Mechling, J., Johnson, T. W., & McMahon, F. R. (Eds.). (1999). *Children's folklore: A source book*. Logan: Utah State University Press.
Tawney, J. W. (1969). Training letter discrimination in four-year-old children. *Dissertation abstracts international, 30,* 1030–1031.
Toppino, T. C., Kasserman, J. E., & Mracek, W. A. (1991). The effect of spacing repetitions on the recognition memory of young children and adults. *Journal of Experimental Child Psychology, 51,* 123–138. doi:10.1016/0022-0965(91)900798.
United States Department of Labor. (2007). *Work hours, breaks, and meal periods*. Retrieved June 1, 2013 from http://www.dol.gov/dol/topic/workhours/breaks.htm#lawregs.
Waite-Stupiansky, S., & Findlay, M. (2001). The fourth R: Recess and its link to learning. *The Educational Forum, 66,* 16–25. doi:10.1080/00131720108984795.
Waters, E., & Sroufe, L. A. (1983). Social competence as a developmental construct. *Developmental Review, 3,* 79–97. doi:10.1016/0273-2297(83)90010-2.
Wentzel, K. R. (1991). Social competence at school: Relations between social responsibility and academic achievement. *Review of Educational Research, 61,* 1–24. doi:10.3102/00346543061001001.
Wingert, P. (2000). Young and overweight. *Newsweek, 135*.
Yussen, S. R., & Levy, V. M. J. (1975). Developmental changes in predicting one's own span of short-term memory. *Journal of Experimental Child Psychology, 19,* 502–508. doi:10.1016/0022-0965(75)90079-X.
Zygmunt-Fillwalk, E., & Bilello, T. (2005). Parent's victory in reclaiming recess for their children. Childhood Education, 82, 19–23. doi:10.1080/00094056.2005.10521335.

# Chapter 13
# Playground Conflicts: Everyday Opportunities for Children to Manage Conflict

**Beth Doll and Susan Churchill Sarver**

## Playground Conflicts: Everyday Opportunities for Children to Master Conflict Management

The multiple chapters in this volume address issues of human conflict including relations between conflict and mental health, jurisprudence, and international atrocities. This chapter addresses the conflicts of children and, in particular, the interrelations between school playground practices and the peer conflicts that occur on these playgrounds. We view these as everyday opportunities for children to learn about conflict and its resolution. Because children's school playground experiences are less constrained by adult oversight than other school situations in which children commonly find themselves, children are more likely to encounter conflicts with peers on playgrounds and, when conflicts occur, have less adult coaching and assistance in resolving them. Simultaneously, school playgrounds are highly valued by children because they provide very enjoyable opportunities to make friends, be with friends, and engage in peer play. Consequently, children are very motivated to fix any peer conflicts that might interrupt their play or result in their disciplinary removal from the playground. Thus, children on playgrounds gain considerable practice in managing their own peer interactions, such that playgrounds become the places where the seeds are planted for adult skills in conflict management.

Fortunately, there is a substantial body of developmental research that examines children's playground behaviors including their social aggression and social affiliation, and the interactions between these. This research has been nicely summarized

B. Doll (✉)
Department of Educational Psychology, University of Nebraska-Lincoln,
Lincoln, NE 68588-0234, USA
e-mail: bdoll2@unl.edu

S. C. Sarver
Deptartment of Child, Youth and Family Studies, University of Nebraska-Lincoln,
Lincoln, NE 68583-0801, USA

B. H. Bornstein, R. L. Wiener (eds.), *Justice, Conflict and Wellbeing*, 
DOI 10.1007/978-1-4939-0623-9_13, © Springer Science+Business Media New York 2014

by Ladd (2005) and includes meticulous examinations of children's sociability, peer relationships, social competence, and the relation of all of these to children's developmental adjustment. Although considerable developmental research has been conducted on school playgrounds, less research has been conducted about recess and playground practices. For example, researchers often collect peer interaction data by observing children while they are outside on the playground, but rarely do they explore the actual recess and playground characteristics that influence the peer activities of children. Exceptions are the prominent playground research conducted by Anthony Pellegrini (1995, 2005), Thomas Power, and Steven Leff (Leff et al. 2004; Leff et al. 2001). An important summary of this work is provided by Bohn-Gettler and Pellegrini in this volume (Chap. 12). The present chapter raises a critical question that is often overlooked in existing playground research: "What can schools do to foster effective playgrounds?" Building on the research describing children's peer conflicts and the impact of various recess practices, schools can alter their playgrounds in ways that foster successful peer experiences, strengthen children's capacity for conflict management, contribute to the safety of the school, and model the societal values that are endorsed in the surrounding community. This chapter describes a framework for such translational research. We first discuss four important findings of developmental research related to peer conflict, then describe our conceptual model for applying this research to schools, and finally describe our own early efforts to translate playground research into practice.

## *Developmental Research Examining Playground Conflicts*

While the developmental research on children's peer conflicts is quite useful for understanding playgrounds, the studies' results are not always intuitive and their insights are not always reflected in the daily recess practices of schools. In particular, four counterintuitive findings related to peer conflict will be emphasized in this chapter's discussion of playground practices. First, despite the public perception, conflict and even aggression are relatively infrequent, occurring in fewer than 2% of peer interactions on playgrounds (Blatchford et al. 2003; Bohn-Gettler and Pellegrini this volume; Pellegrini 2005). Regardless, most school playground handbooks devote the majority of their space to describing clear rules against and consistent consequences for peer aggression in order to minimize and control peer conflict. This is a classic example of an availability heuristic (Tversky and Kahneman 1973): Because instances of conflict are more vivid and memorable when they occur, it is easy to erroneously assume that these are also more prevalent than instances of positive play and friendships.

Second, peer friendships are integral to, rather than separate from, peer conflicts. Indeed, most peer conflicts occur between children and their friends (Rizzo 1989), a reasonable finding considering that children spend most of their playground time interacting with friends. Peer conflicts can only occur when children are together (Doll and Brehm 2010). Of course, the same is true for adults; constructive conflict engagements have the potential to deepen adult friendships (Weinstock and Bond 2000). A second reason that friendships are relevant to conflicts is that friendships act as motivators prompting children to resolve conflicts because they want to repair the friendship. Still, school playground handbooks often underemphasize the promotion of peer friendships, failing to acknowledge the importance of friends for conflict prevention and management. Thus, adults slip too easily into polarizing categorical thinking (Epstein 1998) in which conflicts and friendships are presumed to be opposite to one another without considering the possibility that these could be co-occurring.

Third, adult researchers and educators find it difficult to discriminate between actual conflict and jostling when observing the rough and tumble play of children on playgrounds (Blatchford et al. 2003; Leff et al. 2004). In both jostling and actual conflict, children may hit, trip, taunt, or push one another, but during jostling, they do it for fun and both children enjoy the ritual. Children use and learn important social skills when they engage in jostling and their social competence can be predicted by their skill in engaging in this type of play (Pellegrini and Smith 1998). Thus, eliminating all rough play on school playgrounds could ultimately be detrimental to children's acquisition of key social skills. In conflict, unlike jostling, the roughness represents earnest peer aggression and its resolution requires that children step outside of their anger and compromise with one another. Such conflict is inevitable when children play together. It might occur because children have competing demands for the same resources or activities, because one child's actions have intentionally or unintentionally hurt or frustrated another child (emotionally or physically), or because one child seeks to dominate or control the other. Discerning the subtle differences in intention, emotional tone, and consequences that characterize jostling and actual conflict can be challenging for children and nearly impossible for adults who look in from outside the actual interaction. Without a deliberate effort to self-correct their egocentricity, adults may selectively perceive the children's play and conflict through adult preconceptions about the intent and meaning of social behaviors (Epley et al. 2004)

Fourth, the occurrence of authentic conflict is not necessarily destructive (Doll 1996; Doll and Brehm 2010). While the occurrence of peer conflicts is often unavoidable, children's behavior in the face of conflict is malleable. Playground experiences allow children opportunities to practice responding to peer conflicts so that they are better able to manage and understand peer aggression when it occurs. Thus, one characteristic of effective playgrounds is the students' successful resolution of conflicts.

## *Playground Practices that Influence Children's Conflicts*

This chapter's discussion of the playground characteristics that affect peer conflict draws heavily on Bronfenbrenner's (1979) ecological perspective of children's development. The classic diagram (see Fig. 13.1) represents this perspective as a set

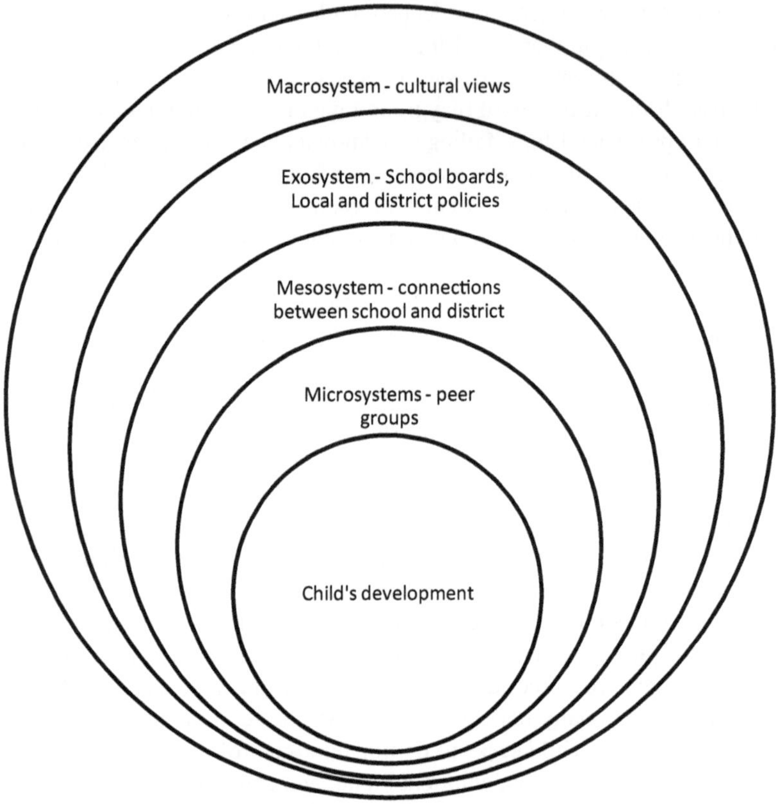


**Fig. 13.1** Classic representation of children's ecosystem

of concentric circles in which the child is surrounded by a microsystem (individual systems the child is involved in such as a peer group), mesosystems (connections and overlap between the microsystems), exosystems (systems in which the child does not have an active voice such as school board and school rules established by administrators), and macrosystems (cultural and societal guidelines). Typically, the child is located in the center (the bull's eye) of the concentric circles. Applying this perspective to peer conflict on the playground, the policies set by school staff and administration (typically with limited child input) comprise an exosystem in which rules, schedules, and disciplinary procedures shape children's playground experiences. One goal of our translational work has been to influence this exosystem to be more developmentally sensitive to the age-related shifts in children's social competence, peer experiences, and social perspectives. Additionally, the physical layout of the playground is another exosystem (typically planned by administrators within the school and district), and it too can directly affect children's peer interactions and conflict.

Many highly effective playground practices occur within the mesosystems and exosystems (at the rings of the concentric circles) rather than operating to change the child (the bull's eye of the circles). For example, adding more play equipment to the playground alters the physical system and the additional play opportunities it affords can pull children into more play and less conflict. Still, the traditional diagram is not entirely sufficient to understand the ecosystem of the playground. A typical elementary school playground has at least 100 children playing outside at any one time. While most of these children reside within a common school and community system, various children may have radically different family and friend systems. To truly acknowledge the complexity of these overlapping systems, imagine that a playground's ecosystem might be captured with 100 sets of concentric circles moving around a playground and intersecting one another in a dynamic fashion.

Bronfenbrenner emphasized the 2-way interaction of the systems within his ecological perspective and the school playground is an excellent example of this transactional phenomenon. Changes to the playground meso- or exosystems have the potential to alter children's conflicts on the playground and, in turn, children's changing conflicts might alter the entire ecosystem of the playground. The complexity of overlapping systems also means that the same change in routines might show different results on different playgrounds. Moreover, changes in routines will inevitably alter children's play which can, in turn, affect the ways in which routines are implemented. Thus, playground interventions must always include strategies to carefully track the actual positive or detrimental impact of changes since these can reverberate across the system in unanticipated ways. These tracking strategies are inherent to translational research.

## *Translating Research into Effective Conflict Management Practices*

A premise of this chapter is that altering school playgrounds and recess practices (the "rings" of the ecosystem) is an important strategy for strengthening peer experiences. This breaks precedence with earlier interventions that emphasized "change the child" strategies for solving peer difficulties. Two decades ago, the dominant paradigm for intervention with children's peer experiences was social skills training in which targeted students were taught specific behavioral scripts for acting in particular social situations (Cowan 2011). However, meta-analyses subsequently suggested that social skills training yielded disappointingly small changes in children's social successes (Gresham et al. 2001; Luellen 2003). Other efforts intervene within children's natural social settings so that there will be more immediate generalization to children's daily actions and so that the skills taught to the children will be authentic to the particular playground where they spend their recess. Examples include classwide programs to strengthen the social competence of all students in a class such as the Promoting Alternative Thinking Strategies Program (PATHS;

Greenberg et al. 1998) or lessons from the Strong Kids curriculum (Merrell et al. 2008) that address students' competent peer interactions. Evidence-based programs such as these provide a cohort of students with a common set of social scripts to guide their interactions in difficult situations. While these strategies still emphasize changing students, they are more ecosystemic because they advocate for change within all of the students who play together. Nevertheless, in our early work, it quickly became apparent that some playground weaknesses were vested in the setting rather than the children themselves (Doll and Brehm 2010). Thus, we argue that in some cases, interventions could target "fixing the playground" instead of, or in addition to, student change interventions.

The remainder of this chapter will describe critical steps towards the translation of research on peer interactions and playground practices into daily routines that schools can use to enhance the peer experiences and conflict management skills of children. Converting research findings into effective school playground practices requires careful attention to (1) assessment strategies that are brief, inexpensive, and technically sound while also yielding a comprehensive portrait of the existing playground experiences of children in school; (2) strategies to make sense of the assessment data given the experiences of adults and the perspective of children who populate the playground; (3) a conceptual framework for playground interventions with potential to strengthen the peer experiences of children and plant the seeds for their development of competent conflict management skills as adults; and (4) progress monitoring procedures that actively monitor the ongoing status of playground problems even while the setting-based interventions are designed and custom fit to a specific playground.

*Playground Assessment Strategies* As is true for most developmental research, strategies to strengthen school playgrounds begin with the collection of reliable data to describe the current status of peer interactions and playground practices. However, existing research-based protocols for collecting recess data are not easily adapted to school practice. Dominant strategies have used sociometric surveys and direct observations of playgrounds but school policies, time constraints, and conceptual frameworks limit the daily use of these research-based measures (Doll et al. 2013). Sociometric surveys are simple to collect. A typical sociometric survey will provide a young child with pictures of peers in their classroom and ask them about who they play with most often and least often. Older children may be asked to list the classmates they like to play with, or to select their preferred play partners from a class list. Mutual child preferences represent friendships while the total number of choices that a child receives represents that child's peer status. Still, child preferences are complex to collate and interpret and, more importantly, they violate many schools' values against negative evaluations of children's classmates (Bell-Dolan et al. 1989; Cook and Iverson 1993). Many schools now prohibit their use, because children are asked about negative feelings towards peers. Playground observations are very time intensive to collect, and they require comprehensive training to achieve inter-observer reliability (Leff and Lakin 2005). Also, there is good evidence that multiple observational samples need to be collected before observations are adequately representative of playground peer experiences (Hintze and Matthews 2004). Playground observations have shown that children's social success and social competence shift depending on the games and routines of the playground so that observations focusing only on children are insufficient to capture the full ecosystem of a playground's peer experiences. Thus, while these are rigorous research measures for assessing playgrounds, they are not practical for daily use in schools. In order for playground research to be applied to the daily practices of schools, it was critically important to find a time-efficient yet reliable way to describe the adequacy of a particular playground's peer experiences. And, if a school did work to improve these peer experiences, it was important that measures exist to determine whether their efforts had been successful.

To make the characteristics of effective playgrounds concrete, Doll et al. (2010a, 2010b) developed the ClassMaps Surveys (CMS) as anonymous student surveys, the results of which could be aggregated across all students in a class or grade to describe their collective peer experiences on the playground. CMS item content was drawn from developmental research related to three distinct aspects of peer relationships: the quality of children's friendships, their judgments about peer aggression, and their worries about peer aggression. Items describing peer friendship assess students' sense of a supportive peer community available to assist them in addressing conflicts with classmates and acting as an incentive to manage conflicts in ways that do not disrupt their friendships. Peer aggression items assess students' perceptions of the nature and extent of aggression among their classmates, while items describing worries about aggression describe the degree to which children are preoccupied with the possibility of aggression. In their current form, the surveys are computer-administered (requiring approximately 12 min of computer lab time per class) and schools can print out a profile of the results immediately. Across multiple studies and with elementary and middle school students, peer friendship items were rated most positively by students and the lowest ratings (signifying more problems) were evident on the peer aggression or aggression worry items (Doll et al. 2009; Doll et al. 2010a; Doll et al. 2010b). This is consistent with the children's ambivalence about recess: they very much appreciate opportunities for vigorous play with their friends, but they also worry about the peer aggression that they encounter.

The CMS peer relationship subscales were systematically refined to ensure that they were technically sound despite their brevity. First, factor studies of the CMS were conducted with both elementary (Doll et al. 2009; Doll et al. 2010b) and middle level students (Doll et al. 2010a). Results verified that the items clustered as predicted into the three subscales, reaffirming that it would be appropriate to use subscale means as indices in a playground assessment. For each of these studies, Alpha Coefficients were computed for the three subscales and ranged from 0.78 to 0.93, signifying adequate internal consistency and contributing to evidence that the subscale scores would provide reliable indices of students' experiences of peer friendships, peer aggression, and worries about aggression. Results of the three studies showed that gender effects were rarely evident in the subscale means while significant differences by grade were slightly more common. In one study (Doll et al. 2010b), third graders were more worried about peer aggression than fifth graders. In a second study (Doll et al. 2010a), seventh graders reported more peer aggression during their recess than sixth or eighth graders. In all cases, the effect sizes were quite small with partial eta$^2$ less than 0.02 (Cohen 1992).

A recent examination of three school playgrounds provided some preliminary evidence that the CMS is able to detect important differences between one playground and another (Doll et al. 2012). Compared to the other two schools in the study, one school was quite difficult to work with. That school's playground policies were top-down and imposed on classrooms from the principal's office and the policies were not always fully implemented. These weaknesses were also captured in observation data in which a partial-interval recording procedure showed that children were observed playing together less often than in the other two schools. Children's reports using the CMS also showed more frequent conflict in the difficult school and indicated that the children worried more about peer aggression. This has provided preliminary evidence that the CMS is able to detect differences between playgrounds, and to identify playground problems that merit intervention.

Computer-administered surveys are time efficient but may be developmentally inappropriate for younger children. Nevertheless, it is still quite possible to gather data about the playground from the children's perspective. For example, this chapter's second author consulted with an elementary school that was converting its traditional playground into an outdoor classroom. The administration of the school determined that in addition to the traditional use of the playground for recess, it would be used as an outdoor space supporting part of the school's curriculum. As is typical, original plans were to consult with teachers, administrators, and parents about the changes. Sarver convinced the school to also attend to the child perspective, convening focus groups in which children in the school were given large pieces of paper and asked to draw what they wanted on the playground. Subsequently, the children were asked open-ended questions about the playground changes they wanted. The children's suggestions were categorized into three general sets–physical activities (involving risk), interactive materials, and places to socialize. For example, children requested physically active equipment and areas such as swings, a sand box, a climbing structure, tire swings, slides, a bounce house, logs, and a miniature playhouse with a slide on the roof. They also asked for interactive materials for investigation and learning such as a pond or swimming pool and places to play with rocks, fish, frogs, snakes, and other flora and fauna. Finally, children requested places for peer interaction: benches and tables, places to rest, places to eat lunch outside in nice weather, a movie theater, walking paths, and grassy areas for sitting. Their suggestions varied quite dramatically from their existing playground that had traditional playground equipment and a very large gravel area. The children's requests also demonstrated a very different perspective from administrators. As would be expected, the principal was not as excited as the children about frogs, snakes and a slide on the playhouse roof. Still, other aspects of the children's suggestions did alter the adults' plans and, in particular, highlighted the importance of providing places for peer interaction. Thus, the children's focus groups provided adults with children's perspectives about the playground changes that were most important to them.

*Making Sense of Playground Data* Measures, in and of themselves, are not that exciting to schools. Ultimately, the work towards creating brief, practical, and technically sound measures is important only because these provide a data-based portrait of a specific playground in a specific school. When the measures are grounded in developmental research on effective playgrounds, they focus the school's attention on important features that are likely to affect the quality of children's peer experiences. We have worked to develop measures that incorporate positive peer experiences and children's strengths into a data-based portrait, so that schools remember to attend to positive as well as negative play. When such measures have appropriate reliability and validity, it is possible to use them as markers describing the amount or quality of the playground experiences. Using the markers, schools can define their goals for the playground change with clarity and specificity, and provide a baseline against which progress towards this data-based goal can be assessed. Thus, the data-based portrait provided by the measures make the developmentally relevant characteristics of a school's playground visible, available for inspection by adults in schools so that they can work to alter playground settings in ways that strengthen children's peer experiences.

Interpreting the data-based portrait of a school playground must occur within the school's very pragmatic and real-time frame of reference, and this is different from what occurs in traditional developmental research. In developmental research on school playgrounds, the research questions generally compare means and variance in key variables under different playground conditions, or develop norms to describe what is typical on a representative sample of playgrounds. Research questions might ask whether differences are significant when comparing two or more playground practices. When applying developmental research to a particular playground, the questions of interest shift. Schools compare the data-based portrait of their playground to school values representing what they believe ought to occur within children's peer experiences. They speculate about the playground practices that might be contributing to disturbances such as frequent playground accidents or peer conflict and arguments, and they want to know whether modified playground practices make a difference large enough to "solve the problem."

Above all, it is essential that the data-based portrait be easily understood by the principal stakeholders of school playgrounds: teachers and playground supervisors, administrators, the students themselves, and their parents. Fundamental to this understanding is that the data must be described with simplicity, so that even the youngest student immediately understands the meaning of the numbers or lists, and their attention can quickly turn towards forming opinions about the data that have been culled from the measures: Are the data accurate? What problems are described in the data? And how would the data look if the playground became more effective? Equally critical, the data must describe playground events and characteristics that are immediately recognized as compelling and worthy of attention. When the measures provide a clear description of playground characteristics that obviously matter, the adults' attention will turn towards understanding why the playground is this way and what to do about it. Thus, the face validity of the data is all-important in translational research.

Because school playgrounds are human systems, it is important to understand playground routines and practices through the perspectives of all of the various stakeholders that influence playground events. In particular, the children are often overlooked members of the playground who have important insight into playground events. To truly capitalize on data from the CMS, we typically show the data graphs to the students in a classroom meeting (Doll 2013). We ask the children's opinions about the data's accuracy and what they think is causing any problems. Their comments are often insightful. A fourth grader once explained, "I think that there should always be an odd number of teachers on the playground so that when two are talking, there is still one left to watch." The teachers had not noticed that their attention was wandering so badly. A second grader suggested that an easy way to reduce fighting at lunchtime recess was to "separate the brothers." Apparently, twin brothers often fought bitterly during recess even though they were separated into different classrooms for instruction. Students also describe innovative solutions for fixing their playground—identifying confusions over the rules of games, describing particular times or places or equipment that contribute to problems, or noticing when the biggest problem is boredom.

Insights of administrators and teachers in a school must also be captured, and they have distinctive needs. They need to have the data-based portrait in easily digestible forms, so they can attend to these during the too-brief planning times in between their teaching duties. Moreover, while they routinely discuss these results with colleagues, these are generally 15-min discussions. Thus, for the adults in the school, we have learned to collapse relevant findings of developmental playground research into five-to-seven key "talking points" that can help them make sense of their own data. Parents also have important insights. They may be a limited presence in a school, but they are frequently the children's primary "friendship coaches," so their indirect influence on playground experiences can be quite powerful. Schools can then combine the insights of the teachers, other adults, students and families with relevant ideas from the talking points and notes from the classroom meetings to plan strategies for change.

*Intervening* When intervening to alter playgrounds, we have emphasized three aspects of playground mesosystems and exosystems that strongly influence children's peer experiences (Doll and Brehm 2010): the physical context of playgrounds, the supervisory practices that occur on playgrounds, and the routines and traditions that characterize the peer culture of schools. Each of these holds important influence over children's peer experiences, is alterable in that these can be shifted and changed in deliberate efforts by the school, and has the potential, through change, to strengthen peer playground experiences.

The physical layout of playgrounds includes the grounds, locations, equipment, and games that characterize a playground and within which peer conflicts could occur. Sufficient playground space makes it possible for groups of children to play without encroaching on each other's space. Conflicts can occur when crowded conditions cause children from different games to bump into each other. For example, one school had been relocated to a temporary building during asbestos removal, and their temporary playground had a single concrete pad that was shared by children playing basketball, four square, jump rope, and tetherball. The frequent intrusions of children or balls into nearby games incited a large number of arguments and conflicts, requiring considerable negotiation of new playground practices. School and class meetings identified ways to adjust the games and establish temporary routines that fit the smaller playground.

Conflicts are more frequent when playgrounds have too few developmentally appropriate games for children to play. Often, the adequacy of the playground equipment can predict the availability of games, as long as these are evaluated with a developmentally sensitive eye. For example, one fairly affluent school had a large and attractive playground with colorful swings, slides, a climbing structure, and a sand box for younger children. However, thoughtful examination showed that there were very few games for fourth- and fifth-grade students to play. The tetherball poles had no balls, the four square court was painted on a hill, and the students were not allowed to climb above the first rung of the climbing equipment. As a result, over a hundred fourth- and fifth-grade students were crowded onto a poorly marked soccer field, and the resulting pandemonium contributed to frequent arguments and conflicts. An obvious solution was to resupply the playground so that students could play tetherball and four-square. Another effective solution was offering weekly "game clinics" in which students were taught new games that could be played as alternatives to soccer. The broader availability of games for the late elementary students was instrumental in reducing the number of students playing soccer, and greatly reducing the frequency of arguments on the playground.

Physical playground arrangements can also promote peer friendships. For example, a study of "greening" school grounds in Canada documented an increase in prosocial behavior after school grounds were naturalized (Bell and Dyment 2006). Naturalizing school playgrounds typically involves the inclusion of multiple smaller areas and structures for play, rather than a single large structure or ball court. These smaller areas facilitate peer interaction and help to minimize conflict. In Bell and Dyment's study, children's play became less hierarchical and was based less on children's athletic ability and more on their social competence and imagination once their playground was greened. Moreover, a greater proportion of children engaged in sustained moderate physical activity after greening compared to before.

The supervisory context describes what adults do to regulate the children's peer interactions. Control over playground regulations most often resides with the school administrators (typically a principal or vice principal) and they are advised by the US Consumer Product Safety Commission's (2010) recommendations for safeguarding the physical safety of the children. (These recommendations are disseminated online in the Public Playground Safety Handbook, http://www.cpsc.gov/PageFiles/116134/325.pdf.) For example, climbing, chasing, and running may be forbidden on playgrounds in an attempt to decrease children's physical injuries. It is now rare to see merry-go-rounds or open-platform slides on school playgrounds because these were frequent sites for falls. Climbing structures are engineered to prevent falls, scrapes, or punctures. Swings almost always have cloth seats that will not bruise or break bones if they crash into children's arms and legs. Relevant to children's conflicts, physical safety regulations principally prohibit physical aggression of any type.

Questions have been raised about whether this risk-reduction is uniformly positive since children need frequent opportunities to master ever-more-difficult challenges in order to foster their emerging sense of competence physically, socially, cognitively, and emotionally. When physically risky tasks are removed from playgrounds, opportunities are lost for children to experiment independently with risk. Similarly, when all occasions for peer conflict are controlled on playgrounds, children lose opportunities to manage their own peer interactions. Specifically, the prohibition of rough and tumble play (because of its apparent similarity to physical aggression) can dramatically limit children's peer interactions. Alternatively, the addition of noncompetitive games to a playground can create opportunities for vigorous and challenging play that is simultaneously non-aggressive (Fluegelman 1976). Developing protocols for conflict resolution (rather than a blanket policy of conflict prohibition) can provide students with direct instruction in managing conflicts with peers (Doll and Brehm 2010).

Playground supervisors always enforce rules against peer aggression. While these playground rules are typically stated in positive language (e.g., "Respect one another") the consequences that are imposed emphasize negative contingencies for rule-violating behaviors. The prototypic response to bad playground behavior is a call out or warning for a first or minor offense; sitting out (e.g., by a building wall or tree) for a second or more important offense; and loss of recess privileges for severe or repeated offenses. Of course, the loss of recess privileges, while seemingly a natural consequence for playground misbehavior, further limits a student's opportunities for successful peer interactions. Alternatively, more organized play and less aggression results when adults are "active supervisors" who circulate throughout the playground to facilitate games, praise positive behavior, and comment on students' play (Leff et al. 2004).

Finally, the peer context describes the "kidsociety" that populates playgrounds and within which children create social traditions, hierarchies, and conventions that are outside of the immediate control of adults because these are often unobserved, unnoticed, or not understood. For example, children on playgrounds may allocate certain games to particular spaces, teach each other new games, decide who can play with whom, and create new rules for games (Armitage 2005; Doll and Brehm 2010). This "playground culture" can cascade down from grade to grade. In almost every case, interventions to resolve playground disturbances involve reinterpreting the playground through the eyes of children. If these disturbances are misinterpreted, positive interactions could be mislabeled as negatives and the resulting interventions could interrupt budding friendships (Jones 2002). Song and Sogo (2010) explain how this same peer culture can be redirected towards reducing bullying on playgrounds. They note that peers are present when most bullying occurs on playgrounds and peers have the potential to intervene on behalf of bullied children. Consequently, within their framework, adults can intentionally create "protective peer groups" by increasing the number of friendships within the class and by prompting peers to interrupt bullying when it occurs and providing social and emotional support to the victims of bullying.

Decisions about whether and how to intervene with playground physical structures and games, supervisory practices, or peer contexts differ depending on the shared perspectives of the teachers, administrators, playground supervisors, and students. Some recommended changes are immediately evident while others may be less apparent upon initial examination of the data. As an example of an obviously needed change, some fourth graders explained that they spent most of their recess arguing over teams, and never had enough time left to play soccer. Their solution was to craft a simple and fair way to choose teams once a week. Less obvious, a group of fifth graders convinced their teacher that the reason for the frequent aggression on their playground was that new students were often left out of the classroom play and responded by being quite aggressive. The teacher had been blaming the excluded students for bullying. The eventual recommendation was a new student welcome program that pulled the excluded students more fully into the classroom's play. Both of these are examples of "micro changes" in which simple modifications in routines and practices hold promise for altering the peer ecosystem of the playground. There are also a growing number of evidence-based programs that schools can use to intervene with playgrounds (Doll and Brehm 2010). These manualized programs typically require substantial resources in staff time, program cost, and staff expertise. However, their impact may be stronger when simple changes in routines and practices are not sufficiently effective.

*Assessing impact* Ultimately, the success of playground interventions depends on whether or not students' peer experiences improve once the playground changes are implemented. Assessing impact is essential to the translation of playground research into daily playground practices. Optimally, schools need to know whether the playground changes that they have made are responsible for altered peer experiences. This is possible to assess using rigorous single-subject designs with continuous monitoring data and graphic analysis conventions (Kennedy 2005). For example, Murphy (2002) systematically introduced and withdrew classroom meetings in three different fourth grade classrooms and demonstrated that, in two of the classrooms, playground problems declined when the meetings were implemented and increased when the meetings were withdrawn. An alternative small-n design might introduce a changed routine into a classroom's morning recess for 1 month before introducing the routine into the afternoon recess, and then determine whether improvements in students' discipline reports co-occurred with the introduction of the routine. Still, these designs do not fit seamlessly into school practices. Schools' tendencies to make programmatic changes quickly and decisively conflict with the designs' need to defer intervention changes long enough to collect adequate baseline data. Schools are also reluctant to systematically implement and withdraw changes, or to systematically apply changes to each recess period in turn, as might be required to verify that the impact is attributable to the changes.

A less optimal but reasonable alternative is for schools to continuously collect simple playground data, graph the data, and use Response-to-Intervention principles (Brown-Chidsey and Steege 2005) to discern trends in graphed playground data. In applying these principles, a discernible difference is confirmed when there is a change in level between the pre-intervention and post-intervention recess data, a difference in trend (with improvements occurring more rapidly after intervention), and few non-overlapping data points. Even more convincing, schools can set a measurable goal describing how data should look for a satisfactory playground. Adding a goal line to the graph, it is possible to determine whether improvements in students' experiences are approaching the goals that the school holds for its recess. In either single-case designs or Response-to-Intervention assessments, it is essential that data-collection procedures are brief, simple, and have high face validity. Often existing data in the school (number of office referrals, number of students "on the wall" at recess) can be used as continuous monitoring data. In one case, students in the class were able to collect daily ratings of recess from their classmates, and the students maintained the database for the teachers. When continuous monitoring strategies are sufficiently convenient, many schools have been willing to use these to assess the impact of their playground changes.

A third, less satisfactory procedure requires that schools collect pre- and post-change measures and compare the two. For example, some classrooms re-administer the CMS to verify that the changes they made had an impact on students' perceptions of their peer experiences. This does provide a quick measure of the amount of improvement, but it does not definitively prove that the playground improvements were caused by the playground changes that were made. Still, many of the schools and classrooms comprising our case examples have used this third strategy to assess the impact of their playground changes. As long as the playground had improved, they did not need irrefutable evidence that their changed recess routines were responsible for the improvements.

## Next Steps

Based on the work that we have completed to date, we now understand that it may be possible to represent students' playground peer experiences through assessments of their friendships, perceptions of peer aggression, and personal worry about aggression. To the degree that these data operationalize a thoughtful, research-based conceptual framework, their application draws schools' attention to aspects of the peer relationships research that they had previously overlooked. Further, the collection of data describing the playgrounds within this framework can act as a catalyst for the schools' reflective decision-making about strategies and practices that they could implement to strengthen the playground. The use of classroom meetings is one strategy that has been valuable in securing student insights into the meaning of such playground data; the utility of student insights had been implied by peer relationships research that emphasized children's intentions and context when interpreting children's peer behaviors. Building on the insights of students and teachers, the case examples that we have collected—some of which we have described here—suggest that schools can change playground routines, sometimes in very simple ways, and these changes can affect students' social success on the playground.

There are clear limitations in our work to date. With the exception of the measure development studies, our playground initiatives have been a series of case examples that borrow liberally from procedures in applied behavioral consultation (Bergan and Kratochwill 1990) but differ in their emphasis on the system of the playground rather than individual behaviors of children. The vital next step in the CMS research is to move more fully into extended studies of data-based decision-making as a playground intervention. This is complicated because data collected from any single playground will be distinctive, and changes in routines and practices will need to be tailor fit to that playground's unique needs and contexts. Thus, this intervention strategy resists the uniformity that would be necessary to conduct a large-sample treatment-control study of its impact. One alternative might be to use small-n designs to examine the impact of school-specific playground changes because, with these designs, any playground could act as its own control (Kennedy 2005); aggregating results across multiple well-designed small-n studies could be a first step towards evaluating the effectiveness of the data-based decision-making process. As another alternative, changes in each playground's peer experiences could be assessed using goal attainment scaling (Kirusek and Sherman 1968); for example, teachers, administrators, or independent observers could rate the playground's change relative to the school's goal for change using a scale from −2 (things were much worse) to 0 (no change was evident) to +2 (the school's goal was achieved). Goal attainment ratings could then be summarized across a large sample of schools as an examination of the impact that the data-based decision-making procedures had on playgrounds.

One of the difficulties in using these data-based decision-making models is that schools are unaccustomed to conducting action research in which data inform planned changes to the playground which in turn are evaluated by data. Rather than being recognized as a common-sense practice, the use of data is often seen as an "expert" skill that depends upon outside consultants' assistance and that intrudes into the daily routines of a school. Thus, part of the solution may lie in making data-use a comfortable and familiar practice of the teachers themselves. Currently, Doll and her colleagues (Doll et al. 2014) are refining and piloting a curriculum (NU Data) that prepares teachers and other educators to use data routinely and well in making decisions about school-based interventions. NU Data includes a set of web-based resources, seminar materials, and coaching strategies that teach in-service teachers and other educators to choose measures for collecting data; organize, graph, and interpret their data; and use their data to solve problems and make decisions about school practices. Teachers who are familiar with data-based decision-making practices will be more prepared to use data to modify their school's playground practices.

This chapter describes a framework for translational research in which adults make decisions about playground practices using data gathered from children. Playgrounds provide natural everyday opportunities for children to resolve conflict and adults' decisions could strengthen or restrict children's experiences with peer conflict. Optimally, effective school playgrounds would provide fertile social experiences within which children would learn to respond adaptively to conflicts in ways that protect their friendships and enhance the social experiences of the entire peer group. Creating these social experiences can be a challenging task for adults who are predisposed to thinking about strategies for changing children instead of altering settings. Effective strategies require that they step outside of their adult perceptions and reimagine the playground as if they were one of the children. To the degree that they are successful, and that they embed healthy conflict management competencies into children's everyday interactions, they can plant the seeds for the children's subsequent capacities for interacting adaptively with conflict in their adult worlds.

## References


Armitage, M. (2005). The influence of school architecture and design on the outdoor play experience within the primary school. *Paedagogica Historica, 41,* 535–553. doi:10.1080/00309230500165734.

Bell, A. C., & Dyment, J. E. (2006). *Grounds for action: Promoting physical activity through school ground greening in Canada*. Toronto: Evergreen.

Bell-Dolan, D. J., Foster, S. L., & Sikora, D. M. (1989). Effects of sociometric testing on children's behavior and loneliness in school. *Developmental Psychology, 25,* 306–311. doi:10.1037/0012-1649.25.2.306.

Bergan, J. R., & Kratochwill, T. R. (1990). *Behavioral consultation and therapy*. New York: Plenum.

Blatchford, P., Baines, E., & Pellegrini, A. (2003). The social context of school playground games: Sex and ethnic differences and changes over time after entry to junior school. *British Journal of Developmental Psychology, 21*(4), 481–505. doi:10.1348/026151003322535183.

Bronfenbrenner, U. (1979). *The ecology of human development: Experiments by nature and design*. Cambridge: Harvard University Press. (Publication no. 325). http://www.cpsc.gov/cpscpub/pubs/325.pdf.

Brown-Chidsey, R., & Steege, M. W. (2005). *Response to intervention: Principles and strategies for effective practice*. New York: Guilford.

Cohen, J. (1992). Statistics a power primer. *Psychology Bulletin, 112,* 115–159.

Cook, G. R., & Iverson, A. M. (April 1993). An investigation of parental non-consent in sociometric research. A paper presented at the annual convention of the National Association of School Psychologists, Washington, D. C.

Cowan, R. (2011). Social skills assessment and intervention. In M. A. Bray & T. J. Kehle (Eds.), *Oxford handbook of school psychology* (pp. 442–455). New York: Oxford University Press.

Doll, B. (1996). Children without friends: Implications for practice and policy. *School Psychology Review, 25,* 165–183.

Doll, B. (2013). Enhancing resilience in classrooms. In S. Goldstein & R. Brooks (Eds.), *Handbook of resilience in children* (2nd ed.). New York: Springer.

Doll, B., & Brehm, K. (2010). *Resilient playgrounds*. New York: Routledge.

Doll, B., Kurien, S., LeClair, C., Spies, R., Champion, A., & Osborn, A. (2009). The ClassMaps survey: A framework for promoting positive classroom environments. In R. Gilman, S.

Huebner & M. Furlong (Eds.), *Handbook of positive psychology in the schools* (pp. 213–227). New York: Routledge.

Doll, B., Spies, R. A., Champion, A., Guerrero, C., Dooley, K., & Turner, A. (2010a). The ClassMaps survey: A measure of students' perceptions of classroom resilience. *Journal of Psychoeducational Assessment, 28,* 338–348.

Doll, B., Spies, R. A., LeClair, C., Kurien, S., & Foley, B. P. (2010b). Student perceptions of classroom learning environments: Development of the ClassMaps survey. *School Psychology Review, 39,* 203–218.

Doll, B., Chapla, B. A., Sikorski, J. D., Chadwell, M. B., & Dooley, K. (August 2012). Examination of the relation between playground characteristics and children's peer experiences. A poster presented at the 2012 Annual Convention of the American Psychological Association, Orlando, FL.

Doll, B., Haack, M. K., & Bieber, K. (2013). Population-based strategies for identifying schoolwide problems. In R. Brown-Chidsey & K. Andren (Eds.), *Assessment for intervention: A problem solving approach* (pp. 77–100). New York: Guilford.

Doll, B., Franta, E., Thomas, A. Chapla, B., & Sikorski, J. (April 2014). NU Data: Preparing educators to use data well. A paper presented at the Annual Meeting of the American Educational Research Association, Philadelphia, PA.

Epley, N., Morewedge, C. K., & Keysar, B. (2004). Perspective taking in children and adults: Equivalent egocentrism but differential correction. *Journal of Experimental Social Psychology, 40,* 760–768.

Epstein, S. (1998). *Constructive thinking: The key to emotional intelligence.* Westport: Praeger.

Fluegelman, A. (1976). *The new games book.* New York: Doubleday.

Greenberg, M. T., Kusche, C., & Mihalic, S. F. (1998). *Blueprints for violence prevention: Promoting alternative thinking strategies.* Boulder: University of Colorado, Institute of Behavioral Science, Center for the Study and Prevention of Violence.

Gresham, F. M., Sugai, C., & Horner, R. H. (2001). Interpreting outcomes of social skills training for students with high-incidence disabilities. *Exceptional Children, 67,* 331–344.

Hintze, J. M., & Matthews, W. J. (2004). The generalizability of systematic direct observations across time and setting: A preliminary investigation of the psychometrics of behavior observation. *School Psychology Review, 33,* 258–270.

Jones, T. S. (2002). An introduction to conflict resolution education. In T. Jones & R. Compton (Eds.), *Kids working it out: Stories and strategies for making peace in our schools* (pp. 17–43). San Francisco: Jossey-Bass.

Kennedy, C. H. (2005). *Single-case designs for educational research.* Boston: Allyn and Bacon.

Kiresuk, T., & Sherman, R. (1968). Goal attainment scaling: A general method of evaluating comprehensive mental health programs. *Journal of Community Mental Health, 4,* 443–453.

Ladd, G. W. (2005). *Children's peer relations and social competence: A century of progress.* New Haven: Yale University Press.

Leff, S. S., Power, T. J., Manz, P. H., Costigan, T. E., & Nabors, L. A. (2001). School-based aggression prevention programs for young children: Current status and implications for violence prevention. *School Psychology Review, 30,* 343–360.

Leff, S. S., Costigan, T. E., & Power, T. J. (2004). Using participatory-action research to develop a playground-based prevention program. *Journal of School Psychology, 42,* 3–21. doi:10.1016/j.jsp.2003.08.005.

Leff, S. S., & Lakin, R. (2005). Playground-based observational systems: A review and implications for practitioners and researchers. *School Psychology Review, 34 (4),* 475-489

Little, H., & Wyver, S. (2010). Individual differences in children's risk perception and appraisals in outdoor play environments. *International Journal of Early Years Education, 18,* 297–313. doi:10.1080/09669760.2010.531600.

Luellen, W. S. (2003). The effectiveness of social skills training for children with disturbed peer relationships: A review of meta-analyses. *NASP Communiqué Feb. 2003, 31,* #5 pp. 38–39.

Merrell, K. W., Gueldner, B. A., & Tran, O. K. (2008). Social and emotional learning: A schoolwide approach to intervention for socialization, friendship problems, and more. In B. Doll &

J. A. Cummings (Eds.), *Transforming school mental health services* (pp. 165–185). Thousand Oaks: Corwin Press, National Association of School Psychologists.
Murphy, P. (2002). *The effect of classroom meetings on the reduction of recess problems: A single case design*. Unpublished doctoral dissertation, University of Denver.
Pellegrini, A. D. (1995). *School recess and playground behavior: Educational and developmental roles*. Albany: State University of New York Press.
Pellegrini, A. D. (2005). *Recess: Its role in education and development*. Mahwah: Lawrence Erlbaum Associates.
Pellegrini, A. D., & Smith, P. K. (1998). Physical activity play: The nature and function of a neglected aspect of play. *Child Development, 69,* 577–598.
Rizzo, T. A. (1989). *Friendship development among children in school*. Norwood: Ablex.
Song, S., & Sogo, W. (2010). A hybrid framework for intervention development: Social justice for bullying in low resource schools. In B. Doll, W. Pfohl, & J. Yoon (Eds.), *Handbook of youth prevention science* (pp. 307–326). New York: Routledge.
Tversky, A., & Kahneman, D. (1973). Availability: A heuristic for judging frequency and probability. *Cognitive Psychology, 5,* 207–233. doi:10.1016/0010-0285(73)90033-9.
United States Consumer Product Safety Commission. (2010). *Public playground safety handbook*. Bethesda: United States Consumer Product Safety Commission.
Weinstock, J. S., & Bond, L. A. (2000). Conceptions of conflict in close freindships and ways of knowing among young college women: A developmental framework. *Journal of Social and Personal Relationships, 17,* 687–696. doi:10.1177/0265407500174012.

# Index



B. H. Bornstein, R. L. Wiener (eds.), *Justice, Conflict and Wellbeing,*
DOI 10.1007/978-1-4939-0623-9, © Springer Science+Business Media New York 2014

MIX
Papier aus verantwortungsvollen Quellen
Paper from responsible sources
FSC® C105338

If you have any concerns about our products,
you can contact us on
**ProductSafety@springernature.com**

In case Publisher is established outside the EU,
the EU authorized representative is:
**Springer Nature Customer Service Center GmbH**
**Europaplatz 3, 69115 Heidelberg, Germany**

Printed by Libri Plureos GmbH
in Hamburg, Germany